Classic
Love & Romance
Literature

Classic
Love & Romance
Literature

An Encyclopedia of Works,
Characters, Authors & Themes

Virginia Brackett

ABC-CLIO

Santa Barbara, California
Denver, Colorado
Oxford, England

Library of Congress Cataloging-in-Publication Data
Brackett, Virginia.
    Classic love and romance literature : an encyclopedia of works,
characters, authors, and themes / Virginia Brackett.
        p.   cm.
    Includes bibliographical references and index.
    ISBN 0-87436-955-X
    1. Love in literature Encyclopedias.   2. Love stories
Encyclopedias.   3. Romance Encyclopedias.   I. Title.
PN56.L6B73   1999
809'.933543—dc21

99-21350
CIP

05   04   03   02   01   00   10 9 8 7 6 5 4 3 2

ABC–CLIO, Inc.
130 Cremona Drive, P.O. Box 1911
Santa Barbara, California 93116–1911

This book is printed on acid-free paper ∞.

Manufactured in the United States of America

To my own romantics,
W. Wade, Shandra R., and Lisa P.

CONTENTS

Preface, xi
Introduction, xiii

Classic Love and Romance Literature: An Encyclopedia of Works, Characters, Authors, and Themes

PREFACE

Among the most ancient tales from Western tradition are stories featuring the deeds and accomplishments of the hero. They appealed to the desire for an earthly immortality in all humans, for through stories of their adventures, heroes survived forever in the imaginations of all who heard. Tales in the oral tradition, including versions of epics such as Homer's *Odyssey* and the Old English poem *Beowulf,* eventually would be committed to paper, preserving in writing what voices had long shared. Just as their form of delivery evolved, so did such stories themselves change over hundreds of years; one offshoot is the genre we now call "romance."

Originally a celebration of heroism, fealty to a lord or lady, and great deeds, romance evolved into the catch-all genre in which contemporary authors and their readers exult. Although the traditional romance plot did not necessarily incorporate love between a man and a woman, most contemporary romances, and literature containing romance and love themes, do. Most also incorporate elements of the original romance tradition. *Classic Love and Romance Literature* offers readers the opportunity to develop a familiarity with that tradition. This familiarity will lead to a better understanding and enjoyment of the novel-length works that represent the progeny of the romance tradition.

With a few exceptions, the encyclopedia includes discussion of novel-length works read in high school and college classrooms, as well as by general readers, and focuses on themes, issues, and characters with direct ties to traditional romance. Generally, this focus directly reflects the influence of the classical and medieval romance genre, either in its use of prototypical characters, themes, symbols, or plot elements or in its self-conscious subversion of those very elements. A discussion of important terms and concepts includes entries on

- the term *romance* itself, with a consideration of its Christian and pagan mythological roots. The discussion includes Italian writer Guillaume de Lorris's *The Romance of the Rose* (thirteenth century); Dante Alighieri's *Inferno* (early fourteenth century); *Sir Gawain and the Green Knight, Tristan und Isolde* by Gottfried von Strassburg, and Chrétien de Troyes's *Perceval;* Miguel de Cervantes's *Don Quixote* (1605), an antiromance narrative long considered the first novel; and English writer John Milton's *Paradise Lost* (1667)
- the *romantic quest,* focusing on Homer's *Odyssey* as the prototypical quest adventure
- the *bildungsroman,* or coming-of-age tale
- *forbidden love* and the change in its definition over the ages
- the *love triangle,* one of contemporary romance's most often used plot devices
- the *Byronic hero* and this prototypical character's enduring popularity
- *the black experience in the United States, 1600–1945,* an experience crucial in the consideration of African Americans as characters in modern literature
- *patriarchal marriage,* a tradition governing many of the relationships between men and women in romance
- the *Victorian Age,* a historical era that greatly influenced the development of the novel form
- *violence* and *war* as crucial elements used to frame romantic relationships
- *genre romance,* encompassing the various subgenres that compose the ubiquitous group of novels labeled popular, or formula, romance.

Authors discussed include the early masters of romance such as William Shakespeare, Henry Fielding, Sir Walter Scott, Mary Wollstonecraft Shelley, Jane Austen, James Fenimore Cooper, Alexandre Dumas, Gustave Flaubert, Charles Dickens, Emily and Charlotte Brontë, William Makepeace Thackeray, Nathaniel Hawthorne, Victor Hugo, Count Leo Tolstoy, Henry James, Edith Wharton, Thomas Hardy, and Kate Chopin. These authors set the stage for those who would follow, including Theodore Dreiser, D. H. Lawrence, W. Somerset Maugham, Willa Cather, Ernest Hemingway, F. Scott Fitzgerald, Pearl Buck, Margaret Mitchell, Evelyn Waugh, Zora Neale Hurston, Daphne du Maurier, and C. S. Forester. Readers will also find many mid- and late-twentieth-century authors among those considered, including William Styron, Toni Morrison, Pat Conroy, Anne Tyler, Margaret Atwood, Isaac Bashevis Singer, Ernest Gaines, Amy Tan, and Tabitha King. Authors outside the contemporary U.S. and British arenas include V. S. Naipaul, Amos Oz, Yukio Mishima, Jiro Osaragi, Festus Iyayi, Milan Kundera, Gabriel García Márquez, Isabel Allende, Laura Esquivel, Roy Heath, and Jean Giono. The encyclopedia covers a total of sixty authors and sixty-eight separate works.

I make no claim to inclusivity in this encyclopedia. Some readers will be disappointed not to find their favorite works discussed in this book. The vast number of works that qualify based on the romance tradition makes their consideration in a single volume impossible. The works chosen for consideration do effectively represent the traditional romance and contemporary romance and love literature enjoyed by contemporary students and other readers. Obviously, not all novels that feature the love between two humans qualify for inclusion within this book's definition of traditional romance as literature and "classic" works based on traditional romance. Those books include the previously mentioned formula romance; gay and lesbian literature; children's lit-erature; and some science fiction, fantasy, and other mainstream works widely enjoyed by readers today.

The encyclopedia's introduction provides a discussion of the elements important to an understanding of traditional romance as well as a brief historical overview of the development of the genre. Individual entries appear for each of the sixty-eight separate titles. In addition to novels, three dramas appear: William Shakespeare's *Romeo and Juliet* and *Much Ado about Nothing* and George Bernard Shaw's *Pygmalion*. These works are important for their development of character and element prototypes for romance works that followed them. Entries also appear for individual authors, major characters, and terms and concepts important for understanding the romance genre. All entries appear in alphabetical order, all refer for further study to secondary works listed in the bibliography, and all conclude with cross-references to related items within the encyclopedia itself.

With *Classic Love and Romance Literature,* the author and publisher attempt to make accessible a reference tool important to understanding a genre that continues to be wildly popular among readers. I hope that this attempt results in a celebration of the rich literary inheritance enjoyed by contemporary readers.

All works as ambitious as a single-volume encyclopedia depend on the efforts of many. Dr. Lynda Thompson of East Central University in Ada, Oklahoma, contributed all entries related to Willa Cather's *My Ántonia*. The fine research assistance of Lisa Meredith must be acknowl-edged, as must the editing, typing, and indexing efforts of Kayla Braddock Kelly and, most espe-cially, Kathy Tadlock. Discussions with Veda Boyd Jones regarding logistics and with Victoria Gaydosik regarding academic concerns proved most encouraging and helpful. Finally, without the continuing moral support of Edmund C. Brackett, this project would never have reached fruition.

INTRODUCTION

Romance has long fascinated readers. Focusing on human strengths and weaknesses that conflict and combine to ultimately produce a hero and heroine, fictional plots incorporating romance elements speak to the human desire for the triumph of good over evil. A nostalgia remains among many readers for an era in which chivalry reigned and damsels in distress found solace and rescue in white knights ready to face any threat. This longing makes itself known through the continued appearance of novels and movies based on the classic quest, the story of the hero or heroine who overcomes all odds to put lofty ideals into action. Although the genre labeled "romance" had disappeared in its pure form by the Renaissance, certain of its elements found a place in the literature that developed after medieval times. In more recent works, heroes and heroines have long outgrown the simple categorization of "good" or "evil," and they seldom embark on physical quests to win a legendary treasure or love. Instead, the protagonists and antagonists of contemporary romance and love literature may battle internal monsters of a psychological bent. Be that as it may, most figures of romance and love literature engage in conflicts and the development of relationships that still strike a chord among readers who, after all, are also embroiled in the day-to-day demands of the human condition. Our battles may have changed form, but heroes and heroines still emerge—sometimes the very figures who seem the least likely to merit such a label.

Contemporary literature is deeply indebted to the traditional romance genre. Literary scholars such as Canadian critic Northrup Frye and more recently the U.S. philosopher Joseph Campbell built upon psychoanalyst Carl Jung's theory of the collective unconscious to develop studies based on a model known as archetypal criticism. This approach to mythology reveals universal symbols and characters common to all romance tales. Among the conventional symbols of the romance genre, readers will recognize fire and water, both of which may represent baptism, cleansing, and birth or rebirth, and the rose, long a popular icon representing love and virginity. In addition, the term *hero* evokes a specific vision of an individual incorporating many characteristics, including an early resistance to the call to adventure; the eventual acceptance of that call; a journey, often across water; the search for identity in relation to a father or father figure; a series of adventures; the use of guides and weapons, often of a mystical nature; a fall from grace; an eventual triumph over evil to attain a specific goal; and a victorious return home. A brief overview of the history of the romance will provide insight into this rich, widely shared tradition on which contemporary writers still depend.

Early epics, from which romances would in time evolve, incorporated a blend of mythological and religious references. For instance, in *Beowulf* the hero confronts a mythological monster named Grendel, who is identified as a descendant of Cain, the world's first murderer according to Judeo-Christian tradition. Grendel also resembles a dragon, a fearsome creature in Western mythology directly related to that most reviled of reptiles, the snake. Many such references assumed particular literary significance over time as readers grew familiar with their presence. The dragon represents a threat; the serpent or snake, temptation; the lamb, innocence and purity; the cross, redemption; the tree and the river, wisdom; and bridges, hope. In addition, certain numbers such as three are significant due to their importance in Bible stories. The changing of clothing indicates the donning of a new identity, and the presence of darkness, shadows, or a downward climb represents a descent into a mythological Hades, or, to modern and postmodern readers, a psychological crisis.

Although written well before the romance proper had emerged as a genre, Homer's *Odyssey* was the prototype for the heroic quest, in which the mythological goddess Athena acts as guide. In Homer's tale, both Odysseus and his son Telemachus undergo "initiation" experiences involving a battle against evil that bring them to maturity. Dante's fourteenth-century work *Inferno* encompasses aspects of the quest while shifting its focus to a spiritual goal, that of redemption. Dante himself acts as his work's hero, a Christian pilgrim guided through various adventures in the circles of hell by the poet Virgil. John Milton also focuses on the ultimate quest for redemption and eternal life in *Paradise Lost* (1667), a work that imitates its predecessors in the incorporation of both Christian and mythological references. Many of the novels discussed in *Classic Love and Romance Literature* reflect the direct influence of the quest tale, incorporating a multitude of traditional symbols.

Just as symbols in storytelling became familiar, so did certain prototypical plots in addition to, or as variations on, the quest. Another classical example of the use of elements that have become part of the romance genre is a second- or early-third-century A.D. work titled *Daphnis and Chloe* by a writer named Longus. The story incorporates more than forty references considered to reflect Homer's work as well as other love stories of his age. On those traditional features, Longus built a story that would establish its own traditions for future novels.

Two elements in *Daphnis and Chloe* common to love stories of its time are a separation of devoted lovers by capricious incidents and an ultimate reunion brought about through coincidence. In such stories, the lovers' separation may stem from capture by pirates or other brigands, and the action turns on supernatural elements, visions, and prophesies by oracles of note. Near-rape and the threat of forced marriage affect the heroine, whereas the hero struggles to return to her side to effect her release. Instead of being organized around a more traditional quest, all of Daphnis's and Chloe's adventures directly relate

to their education in love. Longus also introduces pastoral devices such as the use of shepherds, fields, and piped music to frame his story. His characterization of Daphnis as a "foundling" whose discovery of his true identity sanctions his marriage to Chloe would be echoed in many works to follow, such as Henry Fielding's *Tom Jones* (1749), one novel featured in this encyclopedia. Yukio Mishima, also featured in the discussions to follow, developed a *Daphnis and Chloe* story about young, chaste Japanese lovers that incorporates pastoral imagery and multiple aspects of the romantic quest in his 1954 novel, *The Sound of Waves*.

Many of the first written medieval romances projected the knight as hero. They involved a knight's pursuit of honor, achieved through courageous acts and fealty to a master and the master's mistress, with whom the knight enjoyed a platonic relationship. Edmund Spenser's *The Faerie Queene* (1590), an epic poem written to honor Queen Elizabeth I, incorporated all those elements traditional to medieval romance, including knights, damsels in distress, disguise, magic, monsters, uncertain identities, and multiple confrontations between good and evil.

When Shakespeare wrote *Much Ado about Nothing* (1598), he used slander as a theme. He adapted as a framework for his comedy a time-honored plot in which a young lover or wife suffers through the false accusation of infidelity, which leads to her symbolic death. She triumphs later when the truth regarding her loyalty surfaces. To write *Romeo and Juliet* (1595), Shakespeare turned to a long tradition of tales regarding star-crossed lovers, doomed by the enmity of their parents.

For the most part, by the seventeenth century many of the traditional elements of romance no longer applied. When Miguel de Cervantes decided to write an antiromance, *Don Quixote* (1605), he intended to subvert those elements. He fashioned a medieval knight made to appear ridiculous by practicing the ideals of a previous age. Although Cervantes accomplished his goal of satirizing tradition, he simultaneously restructured the romance, offering new ways to adapt its elements. Not a true genre in itself, contemporary romance instead was characterized by a plot based on the development of love between members of a heterosexual couple. Thus, aspects of love and romance may be incorporated into any fictional genre, including science fiction, mystery, horror, children's literature, and others.

Much novel-length fiction termed "classic" for its enduring quality and its ability to, in the words of Sir Philip Sidney and others, "teach and delight," incorporates not only themes of love between heterosexual couples but also specific traditional romance aspects. Some works even incorporate the term *romance* in their titles, making their roots clear. Examples include Sir Walter Scott's *Ivanhoe: A Romance* (1819) and George Bernard Shaw's *Pygmalion: A Romance* (1913). Other authors sketch plots and heroes so firmly based on those of traditional romance that the term itself need not appear in the work's title to make clear its connection. Examples include James Fenimore Cooper's *The Last of the Mohicans* (1826); Alexandre Dumas's quest adventure, *The Count of Monte Cristo* (1844); two of Victor Hugo's novels, *The Hunchback of Notre Dame* (1831) and *Les Misérables* (1862); and more contemporary works such as Jean Giono's *The Horseman on the Roof* (1951) and Gabriel García Márquez's *Love in the Time of Cholera* (1985).

Traditional romance also produced the popular subgenre of Gothic romance, which incorporated ominous settings, ghosts and other metaphysical factors, a mysterious dark hero, and heroines under threat. Elements of the Gothic were seen as early as Tobias George Smollett's 1753 work, *Ferdinand Count Fathom*. However, Horace Walpole's 1764 work, *The Castle of Otranto,* generally lays claim to the label of first Gothic novel proper. Later examples included works by Clara Reeve, Ann Radcliffe, William Beckford, M. G. ("Monk") Lewis, and C. R. Maturin. The popularity of the Gothic romance decreased in the early decades of the nineteenth century, when, critics assert, the reading public tired of the Gothic's predictable plot and machinery. This change in attitude is evident in Jane Austen's *Northanger Abbey* (1817), a spoof of the Gothic in general and particularly of Radcliffe's *The Mysteries of Udolpho* (1794).

Mary Shelley helped renew interest in the Gothic with her 1818 novel, *Frankenstein*. By shifting emphasis from the Gothic's outward trappings to its characters' internal psychological landscape, Shelley contributed toward the genre's revitalization. Classic Gothic tales that followed, such as Charlotte Brontë's *Jane Eyre* (1847), Emily Brontë's *Wuthering Heights* (1847), and the more recent *Rebecca* (1938) by Daphne du Maurier, set the tone for a multitude of works in today's formula romance field.

As Cervantes did, many authors use romance elements in an ironic or subversive manner. William Makepeace Thackeray's *Vanity Fair* (1847–1848), discussed in the text, offers a good example in its subtitle, *A Novel without a Hero*. Two additional examples provided in the encyclopedia are two U.S. novels published in 1925, Theodore Dreiser's *An American Tragedy* and F. Scott Fitzgerald's *The Great Gatsby*. Possibly the best example of an ironic quest may be found in Evelyn Waugh's 1934 satire, *A Handful of Dust*. In all three of these novels, a young man's quest for wealth and happiness goes terribly awry. An ironic use of romance may also be found in many war novels. This is true of Ernest Hemingway's trio of works, *A Farewell to Arms* (1929), *The Sun Also Rises* (1926), and *For Whom the Bell Tolls* (1940). In Giuseppe Berto's *The Sky Is Red* (1948), Italian teenagers orphaned by the ravages of war must assume the terrible responsibilities of adulthood, with tragic results.

A major alteration in the romance over time, possibly with the rise of women writers and women's agency more generally, was the insertion of a female into the traditional male hero's role, seen in many of the works featured here. The Brontë sisters did this, as did Jane Austen in her many novels, including *Sense and Sensibility* (1811), *Pride and Prejudice* (1813), and *Emma* (1815). Kate Chopin would shape her own version of Gustave Flaubert's *Madame Bovary* (1857) in her 1899 U.S. novella, *The Awakening*. Like Flaubert, Henry James created many female protagonists, including those found in his 1879 novella, *Daisy Miller,* and his *Portrait of a Lady* (1881). More contemporary examples abound, including Margaret Mitchell's *Gone with the Wind* (1936), Zora Neale Hurston's *Their Eyes Were Watching God* (1937), Isabel Allende's *The House of the Spirits* (1982), Toni Morrison's *Beloved* (1987), Maureen McCullough's *The Thorn Birds* (1977), and Laura Esquivel's *Like Water for Chocolate* (1989). The most contemporary of novels, such as Amy Tan's *The Kitchen God's Wife* (1991) and Tabitha King's *One on One* (1993), framed in feminist themes, incorporate immediately recognizable aspects from the centuries-old romance tradition.

Even in a postmodern age, romantic elements retain their appeal. Perhaps people continue to crave imaginative tales that remove them, if only temporarily, from the realities of hourly news reports and the dreary future of humankind they project. Or perhaps the human spirit simply never outgrows a need for romance's emphasis on ideals. Whatever the reason, in the most modern societies, readers continue to find useful Homer's vision of the hero, Spenser's world of dragons to be defeated, damsels to be rescued, and knights, both male and female, who triumph through a dazzling display of ingenuity and physical prowess. For those living in what has been described as an unheroic age, reminders of heroes and heroines, past and present, and our inherent connections to them, cannot come around too often.

Classic
Love & Romance
Literature

THE ACCIDENTAL TOURIST

Anne Tyler's 1985 novel, *The Accidental Tourist,* provides a fine example of a modern realistic romance. The tragic death of young Ethan Leary, an innocent bystander gunned down during a robbery of a fast-food restaurant, creates an emotional and physical separation between his parents, Macon and Sarah. Because of the boy's death, Macon is left sadly alone yet also available for the romance on which the novel focuses.

The novel's title serves a double function. It offers both a literal and a figurative description of its protagonist, Macon Leary. He writes a series of books under the name *The Accidental Tourist,* but Macon also finds himself suddenly propelled on an emotional journey sparked by his son's accidental death. With his fitting surname, Macon is not only leery of but actually frightened by life in general. He distracts himself from harsh realities through his writing of travel pieces for those who search for reminders of home instead of enjoying new experiences abroad. The strain of Ethan's death causes Macon to appear emotionally closed to the outside world, although his thoughts about his son show his potential for emotional experiences, including love and sorrow. His silent suffering and compulsive neatness cause his wife, Sarah, who possesses a more open and social nature than Macon, to leave him because she fears she will become like her withdrawn and secretive husband.

Sarah's absence allows romance to enter Macon's life through the figure of an independent and spirited single mother, Muriel Pritchett. With a personality very different from Macon's, Muriel charges into his life, sharing her philosophy of always being on the lookout for a chance to better her future. Obviously a needy man, Macon Leary offers such a chance in the possibility of romance. Muriel sees promise for recovery and growth in Macon, whereas Sarah has given up on him.

Always organized to a fault, Macon operates under the misconception that he can stabilize his emotional as well as his physical life through time- and effort-saving activities. For instance, he places his dirty clothing in the tub while he showers in order to save water. Like his siblings, he apparently suffers from a confused sense of direction. Thus, he keeps dozens of neatly filed note cards bearing instructions that help him find his way even to long-familiar locations. Such ordering and sorting routines comfort Macon, who perceives threat rather than promise in change. For this reason, he refuses to cope with Ethan's death in a way that will allow him to move forward rather than dwelling in the past; he possesses no note card with instructions to guide him through his grief.

Muriel, by contrast, embraces change and new experiences for the spiritual and emotional growth they offer. She urges Macon to take risks, one being the development of a relationship with her. Although she finds him characteristically resistant to this idea of change as he waits for Sarah's return, Muriel will not admit defeat.

Muriel takes on the job of trainer for Ethan's dog, Edward, who has begun lashing out, snarling and biting in a display of frustration over the loss of his master. Macon's behavior is just the opposite of Edward's as he quietly struggles to restrain his frustration and give no outward sign of sorrow. Muriel shapes Edward's training into an opportunity to retrain Macon as well. Although in Muriel's animated presence Macon feels that he is losing a grip on the sense of order to which he desperately clings, he slowly discovers through his growing relationship with Muriel and her sickly son that the idea of order remains an illusion. No matter how many ways he may find to save time and movement during daily chores, or how neat his sock drawer may be, he must face the fact that he cannot apply the same methods to his environment; life is just too unpredictable and too complicated to be controlled. When he finally relaxes emotional control for a time, he finds he can act as a father figure to Muriel's son. This discovery provides a first step toward recognition of his own need for emotional freedom within the surroundings of Muriel's chaotic life.

Just as Macon decides that Muriel and her attitude offer a new and better outlook on life, Sarah returns, anxious for a reconciliation. In several humorous yet poignant scenes, Macon must juggle the attentions and emotional needs of both women. Suddenly the man who could not care for himself attempts to care for three people, all needy in different ways. The novel offers a sensitive and warm refashioning of the traditional love triangle. What is missing is the third corner, the character whom readers love to hate, as Tyler shapes three confused characters, all of whom remain sympathetic. Macon's choice to trust in a future with Muriel means the sacrifice of his past with Sarah. Because that past involves experiences with their son, Ethan, giving it up is a decision not lightly made.

Healing takes place on several levels as Muriel calms and comforts Edward and Macon; both dog and master regain their proper place in society. The novel remains a satisfactory experience in twentieth-century romance, a story framed by the random violence and unstable family situations many readers will recognize as characteristic of modern society.

See also: Love Triangle; Tyler, Anne
References: Croft, 1995; Evans, 1993; Kelly, 1996; Kissel, 1996; Salwak, 1994; Sweeney, 1996

THE AFRICAN QUEEN

Named for the twenty-year-old steamboat occupied by its heroine and hero during their adventure, C. S. Forester's World War I romance adventure novel, *The African Queen* (1935), remains one of his most popular. Containing multiple themes and elements from the traditional romantic quest, Forester's novel develops a romance within a wartime setting. This popular novel enjoyed a second, wider printing in 1940 in which the final two chapters, omitted from the original edition, were restored. It was made into a movie in 1951.

Set in 1914 in Africa, the novel features as its unlikely heroes two displaced English citizens, Rose Sayer and Charlie Allnutt. Both are left homeless when the army of German Central Africa, led by Von Hanneken, removes all able bodies from the mission town established by Rose and her brother and the mining community where Charlie has lived with his black mistress. Left alone when her brother dies, Rose swears to avenge his death, which she believes is brought on by the Germans' destruction of their mission. When Charlie, whom she knows vaguely as a cockney engineer employed by the Belgian gold mining company 200 miles upriver, happens by, he tells her she must leave. Because she was taught to obey men, Rose follows him. Their romantic quest begins when Rose insists that the *African Queen* travel hundreds of miles downriver to attack the German gunboat, the *Louisa*. She will not be talked out of this crazy plan by Charlie. Forester employs a traditional pattern of romance in which the couple at first hate each other, but then, due to circumstance, their negative passion grows first into admiration and then love.

After traveling several days downriver, hoping that Rose will see the foolishness in her plan, Charlie finally declares he will not chase the *Louisa*. In the wilds and alone with Charlie on *The African Queen,* Rose protests in the only way she can; she maintains silence. Charlie cannot stand to be ignored; he eventually gives in to Rose's tactics, and they embark on a seemingly hopeless journey to torpedo a German gunboat.

The two characters' names provide clues about their personalities. Rose, whose flower name represents the most immediately recognizable symbol of love in the English language, is, at age 33, still a virgin. Charlie Allnutt is described as brown, small, and tough, traits that compliment the "nut" of his surname. Their actions in moving the steamboat downriver symbolize the effects they have on each other. Charlie stokes the ever-necessary fire; its death during their descent down the dangerous rapids would ensure their own. Simultaneously, his masculinity fans the flames of Rose's passion. As she controls the rudder, guiding *The African Queen* around treacherous rocks, she also keeps Charlie focused on their mutual attraction while motivating him to pursue her patriotic ideals. Charlie is described early on as a man needing guidance, one who actually prefers to be driven. When Rose empties Charlie's store of gin overboard, she replaces the control the alcohol exercised over him with her own.

Forester uses war as a leveling device to question class distinctions. Through Charlie's cockney accent and Rose's obviously superior English and position as daughter of an English merchant and sister to a minister, the author emphasizes the dif-

Humphrey Bogart and Katherine Hepburn played Charlie Allnutt and Rose Sayer in the 1951 film version of The African Queen, *C. S. Forester's World War I romance adventure novel named for the twenty-year-old steamboat occupied by its heroine and hero during their adventure. (The Kobal Collection)*

ference in his characters' social stations. But in the wilds of Africa, during a military mission in which the man and the woman must perform physical labor requiring the utmost skill on both their parts, class differences become markedly less important. The author also takes the opportunity to provide what contemporary critics would label a feminist statement through Rose's thoughts regarding men. Early on, as Rose ignores Charlie, she occupies herself with sewing, a traditional preoccupation for women. But instead of emphasizing needlework as a way to keep Rose in her female "place," the narrator comments that men such as Charlie are irritated when women pay attention to trifles rather than to men's "fascinating selves." After Rose begins to sew, Charlie shaves his beard, providing a balancing male activity. Forester allows Rose to blossom appropriately in the open air, where she experiences

freedom and responsibility for the first time in her life. The wilds force a gender equality that Rose has never before enjoyed. The reader learns that Rose accepted males as creatures needing females to "smooth" their way; thus she does not expect perfection in a man she loves. In fact, the contrast between her large body and Charlie's frailties is appealing to her, so that the unlikely pair become not only partners in a quest but also devoted lovers.

In addition to the heroes' journey across water in search of a prize, many other aspects of the quest may be seen in *The African Queen*. These include a personal loss in the death of Rose's beloved brother; the two heroes' use of one another as guides; "monsters" in the form of malaria-bearing mosquitoes and leeches; the "magic" they encounter in their love; evil powers represented by the Germans; a descent down rapids and a journey through semidarkness in thick mangroves as well as into malaria-induced fevers; a spiritual renewal for Rose; and a literal battle with the dark forces of the enemy. A change in garments is also important: Rose dons clean clothes and sheds the confining undergarments within which she has long chafed. This symbolizes her assumption of a new and liberated identity.

Forester perhaps follows his own agenda in reminding the world of the dangers of the Germans and the threat they had posed to parts of the world just a few decades before the first publication of his novel in 1935. The book's 1914 setting may have reminded many of his readers of their or others' anti-German sentiment. At the same time, the background of war sharply focuses Charlie's latent heroism and newfound courage as he considers a suicide mission to destroy the German boat for England and for Rose. The uncertainty of a future that could be framed in either triumph or disaster arouses a passion in Rose related to the impending battle as well as to her love for Charlie.

By the novel's conclusion, the success that Rose and Charlie find in their physical quest is matched by the success of their emotional quest. They are unable to destroy the German boat and instead are taken prisoners after *The African Queen* sinks. The Germans release the two. Subsequently, Rose and Charlie are rescued by an English crew, and their rescuers complete the adventurers' quest by rendering the *Louisa* helpless. More important, Rose and Charlie develop an eternal admiration for, and devotion to, one another that leads to marriage.

> *See also:* Allnutt, Charlie; Forester, C. S.; Quest; Sayer, Rose; War
> *References:* de Rougemont, 1983; Drabble, 1995; Frye, 1976; Gilbert and Gubar, 1996

THE AGE OF INNOCENCE

In *The Age of Innocence* (1920), her study of the New York high society world at the end of the nineteenth century, Edith Wharton examines a phenomenon common to several of her works, the tension between obligation and romantic desire. This popular novel was made into a movie in 1934 and 1993.

As the title of the novel suggests, the members of the New York social scene preferred to think of themselves as highly principled figures. They believe that they remain innocent of the decadence they see exhibited in the actions of their European counterparts. Newland Archer, whose first name emphasizes the emerging society in which he flourishes, is the novel's protagonist. A young New York lawyer from one of society's "best" families, Newland looks forward to a life modeled after that of his strict elders. Conservative in action and in emotional expression, Newland gains approval from his peers when he announces plans to marry May Welland, a proper young woman of promise and purity who hails from a high society background. As May's name symbolizes the promise of spring, so does her character embody Newland's hopes for a future that will conform in every aspect to the high expectations of those pillars of society who surround him.

Newland adores and dotes on his new bride until he becomes inexplicably and almost uncontrollably attracted to May's cousin Ellen, the Countess Olenska. Estranged from her European

The 1993 version of The Age of Innocence, *Edith Wharton's 1920 study of New York high society at the end of the nineteenth century, starred Michelle Pfeiffer as the Countess Olenska and Daniel Day-Lewis as Newland Archer. (The Kobal Collection)*

husband, Ellen represents the perceived European debauchery that her New York family and acquaintances so abhor. Although suspicions are rarely spoken in this controlled Victorian atmosphere, Newland sees, or thinks he sees, signals of disapproval of Ellen all around him. Because the story is told from Newland's point of view, the reader must decide whether he is trustworthy. With the perspective allowed by the passing of time, Newland's actions during the early months of his marriage are analyzed.

Newland's narrow-minded vision of the world remains an important aspect of his character. He cannot see beyond his own milieu; New York and its boundaries constitute his points of reference. Newland's provincial character contrasts with that of the widely traveled Ellen, recently disillusioned by the breakdown of marital bliss. Ellen possesses a sophistication that allows her to understand and act on the weaknesses inherent in the members of Newland's and May's circle. She allows herself to be drawn dangerously close to having an affair with Newland. She underestimates, however, the tenacity of the group's devotion to its self-enforced rules of behavior. Their joint acquaintances close ranks, shutting her out and not permitting her to threaten the future of Newland and May.

May herself provides a surprisingly strong female figure. Her gender makes her even more convention-bound than her husband, but she well understands how to interpret the undercurrents of her social scene and the importance of rumor and innuendo. Having identified the danger to her marriage posed by Ellen, May launches a gentle and unerringly subtle campaign of hint and verbal parry to make her pregnancy known to Ellen. Thus May's actions, more than those of Ellen and Newland, help end the developing romance before it can seriously threaten the Archers' marriage. Guessing that Newland plans to divulge his love for Ellen and his intention to leave her, May informs him of her pregnancy and Ellen's planned departure. Her expert timing parallels the almost choreographed moves made by various members of their social scene to keep that scene intact.

In an interesting subplot, Wharton introduces Julius Beaufort. His partial surname, "beau," symbolizes his role as a man who occupies himself with extramarital sexual indiscretions that society chooses to ignore as long as he retains his wealth.

But society does recognize one unforgivable sin, that of poverty, and that sin Beaufort eventually commits when his financial empire crumbles.

The forbidden love between Newland and Ellen does not form a love triangle with May in the traditional manner because their relationship remains undiscussed. They communicate in pairs—Newland with May; Newland with Ellen; and May with Ellen—but never does the subject of love between Newland and Ellen surface directly in conversation. May seems at first a passive character, but she proves herself stronger than her husband when she sizes up the threatening situation and acts to remedy it. Ellen remains mysterious; the reader knows only the hints about her background that Newland supplies. In this realistic turn, readers may access only the limited knowledge of Newland as the novel's point-of-view character. In many instances, Newland presents imaginary conversations that he would like to have with his wife or would-be lover. He employs the same technique in discerning his wife's thoughts, never committing the indiscretion of asking her openly, but rather imagining what might be in her head.

See also: Archer, Newland; Love Triangle; Victorian Age; Wharton, Edith

References: Comfort, 1974; Davidson et al., 1995; Geist 1996; Gilbert and Gubar 1996b; Price, 1996

ALLENDE, ISABEL

Isabel Allende's use of magic realism has often been compared to that of Gabriel García Márquez. She draws on her own family's sometimes bizarre but rich history in her internationally celebrated books *The House of the Spirits* (*La Casa de los espíritus,* 1982), *Of Love and Shadows* (*De amor y de sombra,* 1983), *Eva Luna* (1987), and *The Stories of Eva Luna* (*Cuentos de Eva Luna,* 1988) and her first work of nonfiction, *Paula* (1994). Called one of the finest of the Latin American female writers, she received the prestigious Harold Washington Literary Award, presented in 1996 by the Printers Row Book Fair and the Chicago Public Library.

Allende was born in Lima, Peru, in 1944. Following her father's departure from the family, she moved with her mother to her grandparents' Chilean home at a young age. Allende later lived in Bolivia, Europe, and the Middle East after her mother's remarriage to a diplomat. She returned to Chile and worked as a journalist until a 1973

South American writer Isabel Allende, photographed in May 1987, draws on her own family's sometimes bizarre but rich history in her internationally celebrated books. (AP/Wide World Photos)

military coup resulted in the violent death of her uncle, President Salvador Allende. After receiving death threats herself, Allende left Chile for Venezuela, where she could not find a journalist position. Supporting her family by doing odd jobs, she thought about the stories she wanted to write, and in 1981, while working as a school administrator, she began her first novel, *The House of the Spirits*. Laced with magic realism, this story grew from a letter she wrote to her grandfather after receiving the news of his imminent death.

She later moved to northern California to live with William Gordon, also a storyteller. An admirer of the ability of women in the United States to pursue their own spiritual quests, Allende has commented on the difference between her new culture and her old. Although in North America people always seem able to change their lives, in developing countries there are too many connections to family and to what Allende calls a tribe or clan for people just to walk away. These connections provide the frame-

work for her novels. She writes of the ways in which people overcome their prejudices and fears to shape their identity.

Like *The House of the Spirits,* Allende's nonfiction work, *Paula,* also began as a letter. Allende claims letter writing became important to her at age fifteen after her mother and stepfather left her with her grandparents while they traveled to Turkey. She wrote daily letters to her mother and continues that habit, feeling the private world of the letter allows room for expressions of emotions and passions that impersonal electronic technology, such as the fax machine, does not. *Paula* deals with the loss of Allende's daughter following a lengthy coma, caused by a condition called porphyria. Allende's own search for spirituality and what she terms "the goddess religions" and family connections are themes in *Paula* as well as in her fiction.

Allende often emphasizes political issues, having been constantly embroiled in politics in Chile, where the topic is so important that, according to her, 97 percent of the population votes in each election. Because she moved around so much as a child, Allende claims her roots are in her memories; they offer her a strong sense of family not tied to geography. Although she considers herself an idealist rather than a romantic, romance and sensuality remain vital aspects of her writing. Her belief that love can alter reality is reflected in her use of magic realism. She enjoys writing about women and projects through her writings the hope for a world in which feminine values receive more credence.

See also: The House of the Spirits; del Valle, Clara; Esquivel, Laura; *Like Water for Chocolate; Love in the Time of Cholera;* Magic Realism; García Márquez, Gabriel

References: Baldock and Bernstein, 1994; "Isabel Allende," 1997; Jenkins, 1994; Tawse, 1997; Zamora and Faris, 1995

ALLNUTT, CHARLIE

For the hero of his World War I adventure novel, *The African Queen* (1935), C. S. Forester could not have created a less imposing man than Charlie Allnutt. Small, hardened, and browned by the African sun, Charlie resembles nothing so much as the nut suggested by his name. But if his physique does little to recommend him as a romantic partner to Rose Sayer, the novel's heroine, his spirit and his devotion to Rose do. The two join forces after German troops clear the missionary station where Rose and her brother have lived for ten years. Charlie and Rose at first seem an unlikely pair. He wants nothing more than to leave the jungle because the mine where he lived with his black African mistress has also been cleaned out by the Germans, who claimed its black workers for their war effort. Knowing of the existence of the missionary station, Charlie hopes to find company there in Rose and her brother. But Rose's brother dies, of a broken heart according to Rose, the day after the Germans invade the mission, and Rose wants revenge on the army of German Central Africa and its leader, Von Hanneken. Her sense of patriotism puzzles Charlie, who has never been an idealist.

He convinces Rose to leave with him on his boat, *The African Queen,* to escape up the Ulanga River. Although she agrees to accompany him, Rose desires not to escape but to travel downriver in hopes of torpedoing the German boat, the *Louisa.* Charlie exhausts himself explaining to Rose that they would have first to navigate 200 miles of river, pass an occupied and armed German outpost, plunge through rapids only previously navigated by canoes, and then pass through unprotected waters to approach the *Louisa.* These realities, coupled with the fact that all they have on board to make bombs are cylinders of oxygen and hydrogen and some gel explosives, seem not to dampen Rose's enthusiasm in the least. Charlie's struggles to understand the motivations of his new traveling companion challenge him almost as much as the river challenges his navigation skills.

Their trip mirrors a romantic quest in many aspects. The two adventurers/lovers journey across water seeking to defeat an enemy; they must make a descent down waterfalls and rapids; and Charlie acts as a guide for Rose, not only in matters of geography but also in physical love. Instead of a single hero, the novel presents two equally heroic persons. Charlie much admires Rose's ability to steer the steamboat while he stokes its engine; her skill at navigating through the rapids symbolizes her skill in guiding Charlie along the path she desires. Whereas Rose's hatred for the Germans, desire for revenge for her brother's death, and patriotism for her homeland of England pull her forward, Charlie's love for Rose provides his motivation. In English society, the

two would occupy slightly different social levels, as indicated by Charlie's cockney accent and Rose's correct English. Rose's merchant and ministry background would also rank her above Charlie's working-class heritage, but on the river, facing death together in the wilds, the two yield to a mutual attraction that seems quite natural. Charlie introduces the virginal Rose to physical love, and she provides a female nurturing he has never known; thus Charlie becomes a well-rounded, dynamic character, although he does not change as much as Rose does. Their partnership as lovers proves just as successful as their mission, and the two end the novel discussing their future marriage.

See also: The African Queen; Forester, C. S.; Quest; Sayer, Rose; War

References: de Rougemont, 1983; Frye, 1976

AN AMERICAN TRAGEDY

In his 1925 novel, *An American Tragedy,* Theodore Dreiser employs the basic plot that surfaces again and again in his novels, short stories, and dramas; a man falls victim to the chaos of human existence. In the novel's main character, Clyde Griffiths, Dreiser presents a solitary figure who chases an impossible goal and is left, in the end, standing alone and bewildered. Like many of Dreiser's tragic figures, Griffiths has a craving that he feels can be satisfied by material goods and a measure of worldly success, yet he tortures himself in his doomed attempts and never achieves any state akin to grace. These characters yearn for something unattainable and unidentifiable, and their subsequent striving after that ethereal goal affords them just enough self-awareness to realize they are failures. Declared by some to be Dreiser's crowning achievement, *An American Tragedy* contains prose modern readers might find a bit pretentious, but the style remains appropriate to this study of a middle-class American antihero trapped by his own ambition and inflated desires. The novel was made into a movie in 1931.

Griffiths is a lonely man set in the midst of a capitalist jungle who lacks the weapons necessary for survival. He begins life as the eldest child of a missionary, Asa Griffiths. None of the four Griffiths children cares for or understands the missionary life. Their attitudes may reflect Dreiser's own rejection of organized religion in the face of a social order altered by the theories of figures like Charles Darwin and Herbert Spencer.

The older Griffiths daughter, Esta, seeks her escape with an actor but returns later, abandoned and pregnant. Rather than acting with the forgiveness he preaches, Asa Griffiths rejects his sinful daughter, although his wife has more compassion and finds a room for Esta as she awaits the baby's birth. Clyde, who has worked as a bellboy since the age of fifteen, is less concerned with Esta's physical and emotional condition than with the possibility that her pregnancy might reflect unfavorably on the family. Clyde's attitude helps Dreiser emphasize his character's acute awareness of cultural attitudes and their importance for an individual seeking success. Clyde fears the social stigma that his sister may inflict on the family and worries that he may have to sacrifice his own savings to help Esta.

When Clyde joins a group of friends for an afternoon of drinking and partying, the car in which he is riding becomes involved in a hit-and-run accident. He escapes from the car, which wrecks again following the hit-and-run, and he leaves the scene. His fear of being connected to the accident and its implications drives him to escape from Kansas City in a boxcar; these panicked movements in reaction to threat begin a pattern of behavior that Clyde will evidence throughout the novel.

Working again as a bellboy, this time in Chicago, Clyde notices a wealthy New York City clothes manufacturer named Samuel Griffiths, recognizing the name as that of his father's brother. Seeing this as a chance to elevate himself in society, Clyde meets Samuel Griffiths and is offered an opportunity to work in Griffiths's shirt factory in New York. Clyde's move from Kansas City to Chicago, then from Chicago to New York, allows Dreiser to emphasize another favorite theme, that of the newfound mobility of the U.S. public in the early nineteenth century.

Clyde feels confident that he will work his way up the factory's corporate ladder, even though he begins in a very lowly position. His dreams are bolstered by exposure to the luxurious lifestyle of his relatives. In the factory Clyde finds his peers to be socially and intellectually inferior. His simultaneously real and imagined connections to wealth through a family hesitant to recognize him promote his feelings of false superiority. Although Clyde shares dinner with his relatives and meets a local society girl named Sondra Finchley who attracts his interest, his aunt, uncle, and cousins would never consider Clyde a peer.

With an increase in salary and a move to a supervisory position, Clyde imagines himself again on the way to success. He acts on a physical attraction he feels toward a factory worker, a farmer's daughter named Roberta Alden, even though relationships between supervisors and workers are discouraged. Roberta believes herself successful in having found an upwardly mobile husband-prospect, and she allows Clyde to seduce her. Although Roberta idolizes Clyde, most of his interest in her is sexual; he realizes there will be no place for Roberta in his future world of social success. While pursued by Roberta, Clyde meets Sondra Finchley again and is duped into believing she cares for him when Sondra pays him a measure of attention meant to arouse the jealousy of his cousin. Slowly Clyde begins to interact with members of an elite social circle. Harboring the mistaken belief that he fits into this unattainable social strata, Clyde feels success may be within his grasp. He sets out on a doomed quest to court and marry Sondra Finchley.

When Roberta becomes pregnant and insists on marriage, Clyde first tries to obtain medication that will cause an abortion but is unsuccessful. Then he takes Roberta to a doctor who refuses, on both moral and legal grounds, to perform an abortion. Instead he delivers a sermon of sorts on forbidden love to Roberta, instructing her to seek the help of her parents. Esta's earlier identical situation set the pattern for Clyde's reaction to women who get pregnant out of wedlock, and he has no desire to sully himself with Roberta. When Roberta realizes that Clyde has been moving and dating in another social circle while he was seeing her, she presses hard for marriage, hoping to force Clyde out of the love triangle he has established.

Sondra invites Clyde to join her and her friends on a visit to the lake district of the Adirondacks during the summer season. When Clyde receives a desperate letter from Roberta, who is visiting her parents, he decides he must take action. Having read of a recent double murder, Clyde believes he can duplicate the killing by drowning Roberta and their unborn baby. He lures Roberta to a deserted lake, characterizing the visit to a local lodge as a type of honeymoon. Once in the middle of the lake in a rowboat, Clyde suffers conflict regarding his chosen course of action. He wants to proceed with the murder but is contained by a natural revulsion over the thought of destroying a human life. Clyde's choice at this important crossroads will determine his entire future.

Roberta stands, causing the boat to rock and pitch her into the water; her head strikes the boat. Ironically, Clyde does not have to actually murder Roberta. He simply allows her to drown, then vacates the area in a panic. In his normal illogical fashion, Clyde flees the scene, leaving a trail of unmistakable clues for police to follow once Roberta's body is discovered.

Following Clyde's arrest, the fantasy world he had so carefully constructed evaporates as an order based on pretense dissolves into chaos. Sondra's parents take her from the scene, fearing social scandal, and use their influence to convince local papers never to print her name as journalists cover the sensational trial. Although Samuel Griffiths pays for Clyde's legal expenses, the young man stands no chance against the mountain of evidence presented against him. After being declared guilty, Clyde contacts his mother, who reconciles with her son and then leads attempts to save him from execution. Her attempts fail, and Clyde goes to the electric chair. He dies confused over the degree of his guilt in Roberta's death, never recognizing that futile pursuit of a social level beyond his grasp was his downfall.

See also: Bildungsroman; Dreiser, Theodore; Forbidden Love; Griffiths, Clyde; Love Triangle; Quest; Violence
References: Gerber, 1977; Howe, 1964; Pizer, 1995

ANDREWS, ROZ

Roz Andrews qualifies as the most "traditional" female figure in Margaret Atwood's ironic romance, *The Robber Bride* (1993). Married with three children, she has not only her husband Mitch to lose to Zenia, the novel's mysterious interloper, but also a family unit. As the story's villainess, Zenia is adept at discerning her victims' weaknesses and preying upon those vulnerabilities. Roz's particular vulnerabilities develop from her lack of self-confidence.

Because she lacks an attractive face and figure and because her father never expressed much confidence in her, Roz suffers from a diminished sense of self-worth. Despite her wealth, her position as the owner of a thriving publication, and her attractive husband, Roz feels less than successful. Unlike another Zenia victim, her friend Tony Fremont, who teaches history at a local college, Roz has no confidence in her own intellectual capacities. Possessing a Jewish heritage that her family tried to conceal for decades, she also lacks the spiritual strength of Zenia's third victim, Charis, a friend to both Roz and Tony. Her insecurities make Roz a perfect target for Zenia's attack.

Roz differs from Tony and Charis in that she already knows of Zenia's vicious capabilities when the villainess appears in her life. The three women all know Zenia simply as an acquaintance in college. Over the following years, Zenia will interact with each on a much closer and more personal level. By the time Roz and Mitch encounter Zenia, who claims to be a journalist posing as a waitress as part of a writing assignment, Roz has heard both Tony's and Charis's war stories about the loss of their loves to Zenia. Roz naturally regards Zenia with suspicion, but when Zenia mentions a connection with Roz's father, Roz is immediately drawn into a relationship with Zenia.

Atwood alerts the reader through flashbacks to Roz's troubled relationship with her father, much of which focuses on Roz's romance with Mitch. The question arises as to whether Mitch might be courting Roz simply for her wealth and her connections, a suggestion Roz feels is valid. Mitch is classically handsome, a charming and intelligent man, and Roz wonders why he feels an attraction to her. The lack of positive attention from her father causes a hunger in Roz for affection from a strong male figure such as Mitch.

Mitch later proves to have weak morals. While Roz exults in their twin daughters and their son, Mitch engages in nefarious activities in his law practice and has multiple sexual affairs. Roz's poor self-image prevents her breaking off their marriage until Zenia becomes Mitch's latest and final love interest. Simultaneously, Zenia worms her way into Roz's magazine business and very nearly steals the company. Zenia ultimately fails to break Roz, although she does escape with $50,000 of Roz's funds and with Mitch. Through the confrontation, Roz gains the strength to separate from Mitch, not allowing him to return to the family when Zenia casts him off. She defeats Zenia's bid to claim her business, developing a long overdue sense of confidence in her own abilities. And even though the tragedy of Mitch's drowning greatly affects Roz, it does not end her life as that loss once might have. She retains the love of her children, the friendship of Tony and Charis, and her business, all of which attest to her worth as an individual.

Along with her two friends, Roz believes Zenia dead for some years. When Zenia suddenly reappears, it is Roz she immediately threatens through her attempt to develop a relationship with Roz's son. This time, before Zenia can again attempt to ruin their lives, the three women unite to confront her. Like Tony, Roz wants to kill her nemesis, but Charis prevents this. The three survive another highly emotional incident with Zenia and then share in the disposition of her ashes following her later demise. Roz helps confirm Zenia's mysterious control, even in death, over the three women by fumbling as she says the final words at the ironic ceremony they hold for their torturer.

Like Tony and Charis, Roz ultimately gains strength and discovers a new, more orderly life following the chaos Zenia brings to them all. Roz's new life comes at a high cost, that of the sacrifice of her husband to Zenia's voracious appetite. Because Mitch himself made the choice to become Zenia's latest victim, Roz can embrace her future free from guilt. In the community of women she establishes with Tony and Charis and in her own family community with her children, Roz at last gains the independence fostered by a true awareness of self.

See also: Atwood, Margaret; Charis; Fremont, Tony; *The Robber Bride*
References: Morey, 1997; Wilson, Friedman, and Hengen, 1996

ANNA KARENINA

Leo Tolstoy's *Anna Karenina* (1875–1877) stands as a pillar of Russian novel writing and offers one of the great all-time stories of tragic romance. But true to its author's predilections, the novel remains as much a statement on philosophy and politics as a story of the loves of three couples that embodies multiple aspects of the conventional romance. Regardless of their major themes, Russian novels written in the late nineteenth century were often used as weapons against cen-

sorship and as the basis for expressions of ethical ideology.

Unlike many other novelists, Tolstoy did not choose symbolic names for his characters; instead he often supplied barely altered names of well-known contemporary personalities, thinly veiling the objects of his social criticism. The political overtones of *Anna Karenina* prevented its complete publication as a serial in the monthly magazine, *Russky Vestnik*. The magazine editor, M. N. Katkov, approved publication of part of Tolstoy's novel at the beginning of 1875 and again in 1876, to be followed by another installment in the summer of 1877. However, because Katkov favored the war with Turkey, the need for which Tolstoy questions in the epilogue, the eighth part of his novel, the editor refused to publish that portion. He chose, instead, to have another writer summarize the epilogue material, and that version was published separately. Following a few stylistic changes, the novel appeared in three volumes in January 1878, complete with Tolstoy's original epilogue. It would be filmed four times from 1935 to 1997.

Greta Garbo played the title character and Frederic March played her lover, Count Alexey Vronsky, in the 1935 film version of Leo Tolstoy's Anna Karenina *(1875–1877), one of the all-time great stories of tragic romance. (Photofest)*

The stories of love in the novel vary according to the characters that each plot and subplot address. Overlapping love triangles of sorts exist. Anna Karenina, married to the government official Alexey Karenin, eventually leaves Karenin for her lover, Count Alexey Vronsky. Konstantin Levin, a farmer from an aristocratic family and a supporter of workers' rights, loves Princess Catherine Alexandrovna "Kitty" Shtcherbatskaya, who at first loves Count Vronsky. Finally, Anna's brother, Prince Stepan Arkadyevitch "Stiva" Oblonsky, a spendthrift government official who engages in multiple extramarital affairs, is married to Kitty's older sister, Princess Darya Alexandrovna, called "Dolly." Although Anna remains the novel's tragic character and its namesake, much of the novel is reported from Levin's point of view. Tolstoy, however, remains an expert in capturing the feminine viewpoint and depicts concerns of his female characters with compelling understanding and empathy.

The book opens in the aftermath of Stiva Oblonsky's most recent love affair with a French governess. Because his wife Dolly insists that the affair has ended their marriage, Stiva calls upon his sister, Anna, to reason with his wife in hopes of convincing Dolly to keep the marriage intact. Anna travels to Moscow to speak with Dolly, pleading with her to forgive Stiva and resume their marital relationship.

The reader is introduced to Anna at the railroad station. She has traveled to Moscow in the same compartment as Vronsky's mother, who is totally charmed by the elegant younger woman. Vronsky and Stiva arrive simultaneously at the station to meet the two women and shortly thereafter learn that a railroad worker has accidentally fallen to his death beneath the wheels of a train. Anna is impressed with Vronsky's kindness in donating money to the worker's widow.

In the midst of his domestic commotion, Stiva meets with Levin, an old friend of the Shtcherbatskys, who plans to ask for Kitty's hand in marriage. Levin does not realize until he is told that Kitty has a fixation on the dashing Count Vronsky, a handsome socialite whom her mother, the Princess, favors, but whom her father, the Prince, does not. The Prince recognizes Levin as far superior in character to Vronsky, but Kitty sees him only as an older friend and a rather unromantic figure. Levin departs following the rejection of his marriage proposal by Kitty, who feels

confident that Vronsky will soon propose. The Count shows signs of having at one time considered making such a proposal, but with the arrival of Anna Karenina, his loyalties immediately transfer to this beautiful married stranger whom he finds so appealing. Kitty eventually recovers from what she discovers to have been a foolish fixation on the Count, and the short-lived love triangle is converted to Vronsky's forbidden love for a married woman.

At first, Anna attempts to resist Vronsky's attentions, looking upon them as a type of courtly love. He ignores her protests that she is married, that she will lose her social position if the two are discovered, and that she must protect her son. Vronsky's devotion stands in such contrast to the cold, unemotional approach of her husband that Anna finds Vronsky's passion impossible to resist. Alexey Karenin cannot ignore Vronsky's attention to Anna or her encouragement of it, and he becomes aware that society has also taken note. Although he warns Anna to use caution and diplomacy in her relationship with Vronsky, she at last acts on her own awakened passion, and the two consummate their love. The members of Anna's aristocratic circle immediately establish her as an object of ridicule and disdain, her previous state of seeming perfection causing their heightened delight over her present transgression.

Some critics find Anna's uncontrollable passion for Vronsky difficult to accept. That she should be so caught up in the throes of love as to allow it to completely destroy her social and familial position seems inconsistent with her aristocratic training and ideals. But Tolstoy makes no excuses for his heroine, and her actions seem absolutely consistent with her individual personality as shaped in the novel. Her egocentrism remains obvious, but it seems a naive self-centeredness in its honesty and charm. Tolstoy's great contemporary, Fyodor Mikhaylovich Dostoyevsky, upon remarking that *Anna Karenina* had no equal in the European writing tradition, noted especially Anna's tremendous appeal as a character. He points specifically to a scene in which, while on her supposed deathbed following childbirth, she accomplishes the impossible by convincing her husband and lover to forgive and accept one another.

But like all great tragic heroines, Anna has her flaw, or *hamartia,* and hers happens to be jealousy. After she recovers, she resumes her affair with

Vronsky, much to her husband's chagrin. She and Vronsky struggle successfully to remain together against the greatest of odds, but Anna allows jealousy to overcome her. While she remains in cruel isolation at home due to her "fallen" status in society, Vronsky is allowed to enjoy his social rounds. Rejected by society because the husband she detests will not grant her a divorce, separated from her beloved son, and forced to raise a daughter for whom she has little feeling, Anna then loses her one remaining possession, the love and respect of Vronsky. In a chilling replay of Tolstoy's earlier scene of death at the railway station, Anna throws herself beneath the wheels of a train, committing suicide close to the Vronsky estate.

While Anna loses her love due to blind self-absorption, Kitty is discovering love as she struggles to overcome her wounded sensibilities following Count Vronsky's dalliance with her. Both she and Levin must swallow their pride; he in order to overcome her rejection and offer her a second chance to accept his hand; she in order to communicate to the man she previously denied her regret over her actions. Theirs becomes a love match as strong as those of the other couples are weak, based on a mutual respect missing from the Oblonskys' union and from the relationships that Anna has shared with both of the men in her life.

Levin is a fascinating character, acting as a touchstone for the themes of revolution and religion that permeate the novel. He remains the key to Tolstoy's own attempt to understand the changes in Russia's socioeconomic conditions and national ideology resulting from the reforms that followed emancipation of the serfs in 1861. Although the other major male characters turn to various means of escape from the reality of crumbling tradition—Vronsky to military and social escapades, Oblonsky to alcohol and materialism, and Karenin to a false spirituality through mysticism—Levin experiments with and then rejects these approaches in recognition of his need for a greater inner strength and illumination.

Through his male characters, Tolstoy takes to task his countrymen who espoused social ideals and liberal views. Their hypocritical lifestyles in no way relate to the masses they profess to support; they offer lip service to liberalism, but their own lives lack any moral basis. Tolstoy treasured his aristocratic background; like Levin, he desired social justice but rejected capitalism and the bourgeois system. Thus, *Anna Karenina* reflects its author's desire to cling to aristocratic traditions. But Tolstoy never hesitates to reveal the moral and spiritual destruction of the nobility, in this way condemning the corruption caused by private ownership and the hypocrisy of the upper class as he attacks the state political machinery and characterizes many high state officials as thieves and embezzlers.

Anna Karenina's male characters approach their relationships with women as they do their everyday lives. Karenin's inability to express emotion or passion toward Anna directly parallels his cool, conservative actions at his czarist bureaucratic position. The only passion he manifests is his ambition for success in his career. Vronsky represents a product of aristocratic Russia; his selfishness manifests itself in his unadulterated desire for pleasures both physical and emotional. Although Tolstoy portrays the Count as a person capable of some good, a personality aspect necessary for Anna to fall in love with him, Vronsky remains a negative character. Likewise, Oblonsky's use of Kitty's fortune and goodwill is balanced by parasitism on his country as he blatantly seeks comfortable government positions that require little in the way of service but provide financial support.

Anna's honest approach to life, resulting in her embrace of passion outside an acceptable social structure, conflicts with the ideology of her hypocritical culture. Having committed the crime of falling in love outside marriage, she encounters hate and hostility from those who once claimed to be her friends and total rejection by a system intent only on money making and power brokering. Many of these same acquaintances engage in the very actions for which they condemn Anna, but they do it secretly. Anna asks not for approval but merely that others recognize her humanity and allow her to live in happiness while retaining her dignity. Their denial of her right to do so represents the true tragedy of the novel.

See also: Karenina, Anna Arkadyevna; Levin, Konstantin Dmitrievitch; Love Triangle; Nihilism; Tolstoy, Count Leo; *The Unbearable Lightness of Being;* Violence; War
References: Bayley, 1968; Bychkov, 1970; McMillin, 1990

ARCHER, ISABEL

In Isabel Archer, heroine of *The Portrait of a Lady* (1881), Henry James creates a character representing a blend of Emma Woodhouse, Jane Austen's spirited character, and the more psychologically dark romantic heroine, Nathaniel Hawthorne's Hester Prynne. Isabel leaves America for a visit with her aunt and uncle at their estate at Gardencourt to emerge into English society an optimist who believes in the individual's capacity for self-discovery. She possesses a desire for a freedom that will only be realized after she attains self-knowledge. Like other Jamesian characters such as Daisy Miller, Isabel projects an American self-reliance that both appeals to and repulses Europeans. It is her boundless enthusiasm for the new and the ever-changing and her excessive self-esteem that allow Isabel to make exactly the wrong choice in love. As she suffers the decidedly unpleasant fate of a disillusioned romantic, she learns that the intellectual and emotional independence she values are not necessarily shared by all.

In the first part of the novel, Isabel receives three marriage proposals. The first is from the aristocratic Lord Warburton, a seemingly perfect suitor. Isabel shocks all of those around her, except her cousin Ralph Touchett, by refusing Warburton's offer. Feeling her fate dictates that she should enjoy a bit more independence before marrying and a bit less security after, Isabel proceeds on her quest for love. She rejects the physical passion of a second suitor, Caspar Goodwood, an American who first fell in love with her at her home in Albany, New York. Although she appreciates the effort involved in Caspar's journey to Europe to claim her, she does not recognize him as part of the design of her future. Ralph convinces his dying father, Isabel's wealthy uncle, to leave half of his own inheritance to Isabel, giving her the financial freedom that will allow her to continue her search for love. Ralph represents the guide figure found in the traditional Quest; his fascination with Isabel and her behavior leads to his emotional and physical support of her actions.

Madame Merle represents the figure of doom for Isabel, who falls prey to Merle's sophistication. Isabel is fascinated by this woman and blind to her less-than-savory character, which readers easily recognize through scenes and comments to which Isabel is not privy. Merle introduces Isabel to Gilbert Osmond, whom she characterizes to Isabel as a fellow American of independent means and mind, a clever and eligible widower. Isabel is

seduced by Osmond's false demeanor. He simply plays the role of a disillusioned aesthete in order to rob Isabel, by inducing her to marry, of her most precious possession—her independence. Isabel accepts his proposal, much to Ralph's consternation, and she is immediately transported into an underworld of Osmond's villainous design, highlighted in the novel through multiple instances of dark imagery.

When Isabel realizes Osmond's true character, her pride will not allow her to abandon the responsibilities she incurred by marrying. She can, however, redeem the future of her step-daughter, Pansy. Isabel discovers that Pansy is actually the product of an affair between Osmond and Merle, added proof of Osmond's callous nature and Merle's moral weakness. Although he refused to marry Merle, Osmond kept her on hand, and he uses her to make the match with the wealthy and beautiful Isabel. When Lord Warburton returns to the scene, Osmond schemes to make a marriage match between Pansy and the older aristocrat. Isabel knows that Pansy's happiness remains far from Osmond's mind; cognizant of Warburton's previous attraction to his wife, Osmond wants only to "capture" Warburton for the twisted self-satisfaction such an act offers him. He sends Pansy to a convent when she refuses to marry Warburton out of love for her suitor, Ned Rosier.

When Ralph becomes terminally ill and Osmond forbids Isabel to visit her beloved cousin, she at last physically revolts against his oppression. She is at Ralph's side when he dies, and she lets Merle know that she has learned the truth about Pansy's heritage. Merle's election to ignore the needs of her own daughter, while Isabel swears to take up Pansy's defense, causes Merle the ultimate humiliation and allows Isabel to partially redeem her earlier romantic vision of life by facing its realities. Isabel experiences an additional moral victory when she resists the temptation to run away with Caspar Goodwood, who again appears to offer her his love. Instead, she returns to Italy to a miserable future simply because it was of her own making, and her honor forces her to uphold her decisions.

In this novel, James constructs a living portrait that shows the many aspects of Isabel's character. Three scenes in the novel best define her stages of development in this initiation story. In all three scenes, James dresses Isabel in black and frames her in backgrounds representative of her current situation. The first time, she appears youthful and innocent, stepping onto the lawns of Gardencourt, enthusiastically embarking on a spiritual quest for self-fulfillment. In a later scene, she has matured into a lady during her disastrous marriage and is viewed, at first, by Ned Rosier as the perfect married woman. Her disappointment in love and life is hidden by the decorum that has accompanied Isabel's "maturation" into a mere possession of Gilbert Osmond. Finally, following her refusal of Goodwood's offer at the novel's conclusion, Isabel again appears at Gardencourt in mourning for her cousin. Now she has come full circle, returning to the scene of her youth and naïveté but unable to return to her original state of innocence and expectation. She realizes her spiritual quest for romantic happiness has failed; the death of her guide, Ralph, symbolizes the death of her own quest. But Isabel's new knowledge enables her to assume a guiding role for Pansy so that another young girl does not repeat Isabel's mistake.

See also: Bildungsroman; James, Henry; Osmond, Gilbert; Patriarchal Marriage; *The Portrait of a Lady;* Quest

References: Bevilacqua, 1996; Budick, 1996; Feidelson, 1975; Hart, 1995; Pizer, 1995; Putt, 1966

ARCHER, NEWLAND

Newland Archer remains one of Edith Wharton's more interesting characters. Although his is the narrative viewpoint of *The Age of Innocence,* Newland does not elicit a strongly sympathetic reaction from the reader. Wharton restricts the reader's knowledge to what he himself knows and sees. That is not an unusual practice in itself, but the reader discovers that Newland remains truly limited by his refusal to recognize any truth beyond that accepted in his New York high society circle. His first name indicates his "new" position as a young explorer in the land of exalted society, and he suffers from a marked tunnel vision, brought on by his own inflated sense of self-importance. Ironically, his surname calls to mind Cupid, god of love, who intoxicated humans with the sting of an arrow shot from his bow. But Newland will neither publicly acknowledge nor act on the forbidden passion he develops.

A young New York lawyer in the 1870s, Newland feels his life has already been laid out for him. His marriage to the lovely and socially acceptable May Welland is an early step in the choreography that he must follow. Then May's cousin Ellen, the Countess Olenska, enters his life, destroying his security. At this point in the novel, the narrow-minded Newland begins to realize that he is a member of an elite group that is just as adamant about not letting its members stray as it is about not admitting new members.

Newland dreams not just of having an affair with Ellen, but of running away with her. Ellen has separated from her titled husband and left him behind in Europe, a place viewed by New York society as decadent and sinful. She provides the third point in a love triangle marked mainly by its secretive nature, for members of Newland's group are trained to repress their passions, and even deep feelings and thoughts go unrevealed.

As Newland's attraction to Ellen escalates, he senses that his peers have discerned his feelings. Wharton's emphasis on the secretiveness of the late-nineteenth-century set who speak in a type of decorous code helps the reader at once understand and disapprove of Newland's reactions. Although he desires escape from the stifling rigidity of the puritanical behavior forced on him, he lacks the courage to act or even to express his sentiments verbally.

His plans are foiled by May who, seemingly a meek and obedient wife, exhibits surprising strength in a behind-the-scenes battle to save her marriage. In an admirable tour de force, May releases her strongest weapon by discreetly announcing her pregnancy. This act squelches the developing relationship, and Ellen departs for Europe, suddenly receiving the financial support to do so from a wealthy aunt who loves May. Newland's anger and frustration cause a temporary disorientation, but he never verbalizes his feelings. He returns to his world of unspoken emotion and participates as society directs for the remainder of his life. In their predictable lives, Newland and May have several children, all of whom become successful and fulfill established roles. At the book's conclusion, Newland travels with his son to Europe but passes up an opportunity to meet with Ellen. Years after his attraction to her began, he remains so ensconced in his narrow vision of the world that he rejects any chance to see beyond it.

See also: Love Triangle; Victorian Age; Wharton, Edith

References: Bell, 1995; Comfort, 1974; Geist 1996; Gilbert and Gubar 1996b; Price, 1996

ARIZA, FLORENTINO

Florentino Ariza is described by Colombian author Gabriel García Márquez in his magic realist novel *Love in the Time of Cholera* (1985) as a serious, bony, dark, clean-shaven, seventy-six-year-old man. He seems an unlikely romantic figure, yet he stalwartly loves an unattainable married woman, Fermina Daza, for more than fifty years following an unsuccessful bid for her hand in marriage. The novel opens shortly before the death of Fermina Daza's famous physician husband, Dr. Juvenal Urbino. At Urbino's funeral, Fermina Daza feels happy to see Florentino Ariza again after so many years. She opens her mouth to thank him for coming, but with his hat placed over his heart, Florentino Ariza proclaims his everlasting devotion and love. Scandalized at the timing of this shameless pronouncement, Fermina Daza orders him from her home. Thus begins one of the most memorable of love stories.

Florentino Ariza remains a remarkable character, carrying the torch of unrequited love for fifty-one years, nine months, and four days before the incident at the funeral. The novel tells the story of a love forbidden because of the social gap between Fermina Daza and Florentino Ariza, who became aware of one another as teens. Florentino Ariza, the illegitimate child of a ship owner who will not claim him, must assume his mother's name. A mere apprentice in the local post office, his aspirations of love for a thirteen-year-old girl firmly ensconced in a social strata several levels above his own are not to be realized. Although Florentino Ariza is hardly a striking figure, Fermina Daza finds herself attracted to his vulnerability, and she feels there is something magical about the telegraph. This early suggestion of metaphysical powers within Florentino Ariza continues throughout the story.

García Márquez compares Florentino Ariza's passion to the symptoms of cholera, another common "disease" in the South American community that provides the novel's setting. So enthralled is the young Florentino Ariza with Fermina Daza that even his hair is uproarious in love. After two devoted years of much correspondence and little actual dialogue, Florentino Ariza receives Fermina Daza's acceptance of his marriage proposal. Unfortunately, when a nun at Fermina Daza's school discovers the letter and turns it over to her father, he takes steps to dissolve the romance by separating the young lovers.

What follows for Florentino Ariza are multiple sexual adventures, but he never really loves anyone except Fermina Daza. He even plays go-between for other lovers by composing love letters filled with the poetry for which he is famous. With his writing and musical talents (he plays the violin) and his unquenchable desire for Fermina Daza, Florentino Ariza symbolizes passion and creativity. But his rival, Dr. Urbino, a physician who offers a suitable social match for Fermina Daza, represents science or rationality. Thus García Márquez develops a love triangle based on an age-old tradition in which a woman must choose as her mate a man symbolizing either the rational world or the imaginative world.

At first crushed over the news that Fermina Daza will marry and then travel to Europe, Florentino Ariza eventually recovers after moving to another town. He doggedly pursues success in his chosen field, moving steadily up through the social ranks. García Márquez continually stresses the theme of imagination and creativity through Florentino Ariza's writing; at one point a character expresses the thought that no person could be more dangerous or lucid than a poet. Ariza enters a poetry contest in which Fermina Daza awards him the first prize. His victory over all other entrants, by which he recaptures her attention, remains reminiscent of a knight winning a joust for his fair lady. A true romantic, Florentino Ariza cannot imagine dying for any reason other than love.

Florentino Ariza barely escapes the wrath of various jealous husbands and lovers as he cuts a wide swath through the women of his community; he even beds a very young girl. The fact that he cares well for her for many years, long after their relationship as lovers ends, hardly seems to excuse his actions. But his extraordinarily compassionate attitude toward women and the magic of love seems to help to balance the immorality of his exploits. He experiences several epiphanies over the years, including a stunning realization following a conversation with Fermina Daza's husband, who has no inkling that Florentino Ariza once courted his wife. Twenty-seven years into his experience of unreturned devotion, Florentino Ariza discovers that Dr. Urbino shares his passion, its pain and intensity as well as its pleasure, for Fermina Daza.

After nearly a half-century of waiting, Florentino Ariza finally makes contact with Fermina Daza following Dr. Urbino's death. Their contact begins, as it had in their youth, through letters, but soon they meet and talk. Florentino Ariza ignores his various problems of emotion and age, including the curse of near-fatal constipation, allowing nothing to halt this slowly redeveloping relationship. Although acquaintances and family members inform both Florentino Ariza and Fermina Daza of the futility of passion at their age, they finally fulfill what Florentino Ariza knew to be his destiny. They become lovers on a cruise ship that has ejected all of its passengers and that flies a phony yellow flag warning of cholera, keeping all human contact away from the boat. They need no one else, for Florentino Ariza finally has Fermina Daza as his own.

See also: Daza, Fermina; *Love in the Time of Cholera*; Forbidden Love; Love Triangle; Magic Realism
References: de Rougemont, 1983; Zamora and Faris, 1995

ATA, SUTEKICHI

In his romantic novel *The Journey* (1960), Jiro Osaragi shapes a sad love triangle of which the idealistic teacher and scholar, Sutekichi Ata, is a part. In its title, this story makes the connection to the romantic quest, which always involves a journey on the part of its hero or heroine. Romance remains an important part of Sutekichi's psychological journey, but it is not the thing most crucial to his maturity. Although he eventually meets Taeko Okamoto and falls in love with her, he remains devoted to his studies and research and a traditional way of life that threatens to disappear from Japan altogether. With his willingness to sacrifice for the sake of those he loves, Sutekichi stands in stark contrast to the third element of the love triangle, a man he never meets, the self-centered Ryosuke Tsugawa. In a novel stressing the loss of faith in human nature that occurs from a war generation to the generation that follows, Sutekichi represents the link that offers hope for a future in which honor still enjoys a prominent role. His journey will ultimately succeed due to his fine nature and his respect for tradition in a postwar Japan that craves the newness that all things American seem to promise.

Sutekichi is a college graduate who continues his studies in two different ways. He pursues his own private research interests, and he also spends time with Seki, the ebullient professor whose philosophy on life and ideals Sutekichi values highly. Thus Sutekichi learns life lessons as well as those that books have to offer. His love for tradition is represented not only by his friendship with the old professor but also by his lifelong desire to trace the historic path followed by Alexander the Great as he moved across the lands he conquered. Although Sutekichi is not likely to complete that desired physical journey, mainly due to his poverty as a schoolteacher, his journey toward emotional and psychological maturity will be realized.

Sutekichi's character, as one might expect, greatly contrasts with that of Ryosuke, his rival for Taeko's attentions. Sutekichi follows a sedentary intellectual approach to life, whereas Ryosuke is an athlete who exults in life's sensual pleasures. Sutekichi carefully measures his actions, making sure they do not affect others in a negative way, but Ryosuke remains totally self-absorbed and turns to gambling to satisfy the unsettled issues in his life. Both men are college graduates, yet they could not face life in a more different fashion. Sutekichi unconsciously adopts the professor's approach to everyday matters, taking his lead from the idealism represented in the poetry the professor constantly quotes. The novel begins with the professor and his student on a short journey together by boat, during which they first encounter Taeko's uncle, who attempts suicide by drowning. This fateful meeting with Soroku Okamoto forever alters Sutekichi's life, for this connection causes him to eventually meet Taeko. On this one of many journeys featured by the novel, the professor quotes a line of poetry that will come to represent Sutekichi's attitude toward himself and others: "In our journeys, a companion; in life, sympathy."

When Sutekichi is disappointed that Taeko does not return his love, rather than feeling bitter about her decision to love Ryosuke, he instead offers her his wish for her smooth and happy journey through life. When Taeko expresses her gratitude and then questions his reason for speaking that wish, he explains his action was for the sake of human honor and dignity. He tells Taeko that he attaches little value to love and asks little of it in return, stressing that his main concern lies in pursuing his own path and in making that journey clean and honest. He later proves the veracity of his words when he places his own reputation for honesty in jeopardy for the sake of Taeko, thus passing a test of his ideals.

Although Sutekichi remains the better man, he is not Taeko's choice for love. He accepts her choice, believing that they would be unhappy in marriage, but he also acknowledges that this realization does not stop him from loving Taeko. He remains a most admirable character, carrying the hopes for a future Japan in which tradition will still receive its due reverence, even in the face of the rapid changes caused by the postwar climate.

See also: The Journey; Okamoto, Taeko; Tsugawa, Ryosuke; War

References: Hoffman and Murphy, 1996; Frye, 1976

ATWOOD, MARGARET

Margaret Atwood, author of multiple novels and poetry collections, was born in Canada in 1939 and raised in Ottawa, Ontario. Her schooling was interrupted by frequent trips north in order for her entomologist father to perform research. Her first book of poetry, *Double Persephone,* appeared in 1962 following her graduation from the University of Toronto. Advanced study at Radcliffe for a master's degree, followed by further graduate study at Harvard, launched Atwood into teaching positions in various Canadian institutions.

Between 1966 and 1974 she published six more volumes of poetry, most of which evidence her concern with the division of self caused by love affairs. Her identification with her country as a victim of the imperialism of England and the United States also led her to write of people, especially women, overshadowed and oppressed by others. She investigates how to revise traditional patriarchal mythology to incorporate issues important to women. Many of her characters find themselves involved with an "other" world, sometimes metaphorically, sometimes literally, as in her popular dystopia, *The Handmaid's Tale* (1986). This futuristic novel made her suddenly known to an international public as an important late-twentieth-century feminist writer. *The Handmaid's Tale* focuses on women used only for reproductive purposes as well as on those childless wives who must accept sex between their husbands and handmaidens as merely a "procedure" necessary to conception, from which love and romance are decidedly missing.

The Handmaid's Tale was followed by *Cat's Eye* (1989) and *The Robber Bride* (1993), in which Atwood features three females challenged by a fourth woman, Zenia, the temptress who steals their lovers. Atwood questions many assumptions about heterosexual love as well as stereotypical romantic ideas about both genders. In the Acknowledgments for *The Robber Bride,* Atwood reveals that she based several of the stories in the novel on the tales of friends, thus emphasizing the importance of the oral tradition to her storytelling.

See also: The Robber Bride
References: Blain, Clements, and Grundy, 1990; Gilbert and Gubar, 1996e; Ousby, 1988; Snodgrass, 1995

AUSTEN, JANE

Jane Austen was born in England on December 16, 1775, to George Austen, rector of the Hampshire village of Steventon, and his wife Cassandra, a woman known for her talent at impromptu verse making and storytelling. As a member of a large family with eight children, most of whom delighted in play acting, Austen chose as her closest companion her sister Cassandra, named for their mother. Both girls

An 1873 steel-engraving portrait of Jane Austen, the early-nineteenth-century novelist who is credited with creating the English novel of manners. (Library of Congress)

attended school off and on at an early age but were mostly educated at home by their father. Austen is known to have read widely, enjoying romantic classics by Samuel Richardson and Henry Fielding, as well as writings by Alexander Pope, Oliver Goldsmith, David Hume, Samuel Johnson, Sir Walter Scott, William Cowper, Lord Byron and her female contemporaries Fanny Burney, Mary Brunton, Ann Radcliffe, and Maria Edgeworth. Although neither Jane nor Cassandra, who was a painter, would ever marry, their visits to Bath and London and contacts with outside and extended family members (five of their six brothers married and had families) and friends gave Jane the stories and characters that would later fill her novels. Her characters were notable in being from her own class, the country gentry, as distinguished from the growing commercial class and the ever-present aristocracy.

Between 1787 and 1793, Austen wrote a number of plays, verses, prose works, and short novels, collected into three notebooks labeled Volumes I, II, and III. These early works, or juvenilia, demonstrate her developing talent for mild satire as she parodied literary forms such as sentimental fiction by female writers of her time. She clearly demonstrated an antipathy toward stereotypes of women and humorously attacked subjects such as the lack of education for women, an overidealized vision of love, the supposed weakness and passivity of women, and the exaggerated rivalry between women for the attentions of men. Although not published until 1871, her first manuscript, an epistolary novel called *Lady Susan,* was written in 1793–1794. In this brief book, Austen began to develop the frustrated, independent-minded female characters for which she would later earn fame.

Apparently Austen refused to marry a suitor in about 1802; most critics believe that she also experienced a great love that perhaps ended in tragedy. Ever protective of her beloved sister's privacy, Cassandra destroyed many letters and documents following Jane's death that might have shed light on her relationships and experiences. Her novels suggest Austen's comprehension of the female experience of grief and joy, offering a gentle but sharply correct portrayal of contemporary female values that were stymied by a social edict against personal expression.

Austen began her second novel, which eventually became *Sense and Sensibility,* in 1795 as another novel-in-letters called *Marianne and Elinor,* after the two main characters. Within the next five years she wrote *Pride and Prejudice,* originally named *First Impressions,* and *Northanger Abbey,* first sold under the name *Susan.* Austen's father was unsuccessful in attempts to sell *Pride and Prejudice,* and although *Susan* was sold to publisher Richard Crosby, who advertised the novel, for some reason it did not reach publication.

Austen's peaceful lifestyle ended in 1801 when her father retired to Bath at age seventy with his wife and two daughters. The subsequent eight years brought a number of moves for the family to temporary residences and the homes of various relatives. Austen tried to write again, beginning a novel called *The Watsons* in 1804, but she was unsuccessful. Her best friend, Anne Lefroy, died in 1804, and her father died a year later. From 1805 to 1809, Austen lived with her mother and Cassandra in Bath, Clifton, and Southampton.

In 1809, one of Austen's brothers, Edward, provided the women with a large cottage in a village called Chawton, close to his estate. Two years later, Austen approached Thomas Egerton about publishing her two early novels, and *Sense and Sensibility* appeared anonymously in November 1811, when Austen was thirty-six years old. Two major reviews appeared in the *Critical Review* and the *Quarterly Review,* both praising the novel's blend of instruction and entertainment. Egerton published *Pride and Prejudice* in 1813 and *Mansfield Park,* begun in 1811, in 1814. *Emma* would be published in 1815 by Lord Byron's publisher, John Murray, who also published a second edition of *Mansfield Park.* Although at first Austen remained anonymous, she became so popular that later books were published under her name; the Prince Regent, later King George IV, was said to have a complete set of her writings in all of his residences. At his request, Austen dedicated *Emma* to him. All of her novels were well received as welcome variants from the then-popular genre of romantic melodrama; nowhere in her writing is there evidence of the vulgarisms common to the romantically influenced Byronic hero. Her works were often described as moral and entertaining, with fine character development and a pleasurable, homey realism.

Until her death in 1817, Austen wrote constantly. *Northanger Abbey (Susan)* was revised, and she wrote *Persuasion;* both novels would be published posthumously. *Northanger Abbey* called attention to the Gothic romance, a subgenre long out of favor with reading audiences, both celebrating and mocking that romance type. At the time of her death, probably caused by Addison's disease, she was at work on *Sanditon,* a satire on invalidism and health resorts in which she engaged in a bit of self-mockery.

Her brother Henry made certain the world knew of his sister's identity as he supervised the publication of her additional novels. Although her work was generally enjoyed, and Sir Walter Scott positively reviewed *Emma,* declaring its unknown author to be important to the new realist tradition, the full importance of Austen's contribution as a novelist would not be determined until later. Together with Scott's essay, a posthumous review of *Northanger Abbey* and *Persuasion* in the January 1821 edition of the *Quarterly* by Richard Whaley form the basis for most modern criticism of Austen and her works.

Her novels gained lasting importance as domestic literature, highlighting the quest of various women for self-knowledge and a noncontrolling love partner. Austen is credited with creating the English novel of manners, and she began a great tradition in novel writing that helped prepare the way for nineteenth-century writers Mary Shelley, the Brontë sisters, George Eliot, and even Virginia Woolf. A skillful storyteller, Austen delights readers with a wit ready to take on foolish social convention as well as those who embody society's irrational demand for decorum and "proper" demeanor. Her comedies of manners continue to be enjoyed in their original form as well as onscreen.

See also: *Emma; Pride and Prejudice; Sense and Sensibility*

References: *Britannica,* 1997; Clayton 1987a; Copeland and McMaster, 1997; de Rougemont, 1983; Fraiman, 1993; Gard, 1992; Gilbert and Gubar, 1985c; McMaster and Stovel, 1996; Ousby, 1988; Praz, 1974; Watt, 1963

THE AWAKENING

As suggested by its title, Kate Chopin's romantic tragedy *The Awakening* (1899) deals with the development of self-awareness on the part of its main character, Edna Pontellier. Themes of the importance to women of sexual, spiritual, and emotional independence, developed through a character who transgressed against patriarchal dictates, shocked Chopin's contemporaries. Until

its "rediscovery" in 1960 by a scholar who brought the work to the attention of the reading public, Chopin's novel had received only negative reviews. After its revival during a period in which women's self-awareness was an acceptable topic for fiction, *The Awakening* became a regular feature of most U.S. and women's literature anthologies.

Edna Pontellier's marriage into what was, for her, the somewhat foreign culture of the Louisiana Creoles causes her internal as well as external conflict. The Creole custom in which a young man "courted" an older married woman remains reminiscent of courtly love, in which a young man could dedicate himself to an attached woman who remained untouchable. Although a spiritual devotion was allowed, physical love was forbidden. Creoles understood this tradition, but Edna did not. She finds the attentions of the young Robert Lebrun exhilarating and sustaining in her husband's frequent absences. Edna experiences a desire for sexual independence and also for the freedom of self-expression disallowed women trapped within patriarchal marriages.

Her frustrations surface early when her husband, Léonce, scolds Edna for not being a good mother. Although at first she can't identify the source of her conflict, Edna eventually desires to be known for something other than her roles as wife and mother. The reader first observes a change in Edna when she learns to swim. Having dreaded the water, Edna feels a particular exuberance when she completes her first swim alone; Chopin describes her as resembling a toddler who, taking its first steps, suddenly realizes its power. In a later scene, frustrated over having to fulfill societal conventions she neither believes in nor enjoys, Edna throws her wedding ring across a room in a symbolic rejection of marriage. Eventually she sees herself as part of a forbidden love with a younger man as she suffers under the illusion that she is caught up in the traditional love triangle. Ironically, neither Edna's husband nor Robert Lebrun share Edna's passion for the ideal of love represented by Robert's attentions. Ultimately, the conflict Edna experiences in trying to resolve her impossible desires within the constraints of society leads her to commit suicide by drowning herself in the very water that had at first represented new life.

Chopin creates two female figures who stand in contrast to Edna. The first, Adèle Ratignolle, represents the traditional mother figure found in literature and serves unwittingly as an ever-present reminder to Edna of goals to which she should, by society's standards, aspire. Adèle embodies the patriarchal ideal of womanhood, a perfect wife who has produced perfect children. She is the quintessential "angel of the house," so familiar to readers of Victorian literature, right down to her beautifully flowing spun-gold hair, sapphire eyes, and pouting lips, "so red one could only think of cherries" (Chopin, 1899: 10) in their presence. Adele also represents another female prototype from literature, the invalid. She suffers from what she calls her "condition," brought on by bearing three children over a seven-year period; such frequent childbearing is approved of in the patriarchal structure of Creole society. The second contrasting character, Mademoiselle Reisz, represents in some ways the "bad woman" of literature, and many members of the Creole community will not socialize with her. Edna, however, is drawn to her wit, strength, and revolutionary lifestyle.

Mademoiselle Reisz, herself a pianist, encourages Edna's creative aspirations. Edna establishes an art studio for herself within the confines of her home, much to the dismay of her husband, who refers to Edna's action as "the utmost folly" when, in his view, painting causes her to neglect her family. Mr. Pontellier begins to suspect his wife is losing her mental balance. Here Chopin makes use of another prototypical literary female, the madwoman. Ironically, in patriarchal society madness in a female is preferable to independence.

In Robert's absence, Edna allows herself to be seduced by another young man, Alcée Arobin. When Robert returns and she expresses her love to him, he reacts in surprise, reminding her that she is someone else's wife. Her reply that no one can own her frightens Robert, who writes a note telling Edna goodbye; ostensibly, he leaves because he loves her. Robert's departure represents the loss of freedom to Edna, and she chooses not to live in his (its) absence.

The aspect of *The Awakening* to which her contemporaries reacted so negatively was Chopin's suggestions through the character of Edna that female sexuality may be intimately connected to female creativity. This same suggestion had enraged readers earlier in the century when made by Gustave Flaubert in *Madame Bovary* (1857), a work said to have been a great influence on Chopin's novel. Filled with explicit themes all supporting the female desire for independence from a patriarchal society's constraints, *The Awakening,* like *Madame Bovary,* was summarily rejected at its time of publication and barred from many libraries.

See also: Bildungsroman; Chopin, Kate; Forbidden Love; Love Triangle; *Madame Bovary;* Patriarchal Marriage; Pontellier, Edna; Victorian Age
References: Budick, 1996; Comfort, 1974; Davidson, 1995; Hart, 1995; Praz, 1974; Williams, 1974

BAKSH, FOAM

Although not a romantic hero in the traditional sense, Foam Baksh from V. S. Naipaul's novel *The Suffrage of Elvira* (1958) may qualify as a postmodern hero. Postmodern philosophy sees traditional beliefs and ideas, such as those found in any religion or in science, or even in traditional literature, as a threat to the human search for knowledge. Many postmodernists believe that a focus on any one tradition, or metanarrative, that purports to offer the ultimate Truth cannot lead to complete knowledge. Through the young characters in his novel featuring religious tension and superstition, Naipaul seems to advocate this last idea. The clash between Muslim and Hindu ideas has held back progress in Trinidad, the setting for *The Suffrage of Elvira* and also Naipaul's home. This novel emphasizes the importance of change, and Foam and a young Hindu girl, Nellie Chittaranjan, play a great part in various changes that take place in Elvira.

This novel focuses on the romantic ideal of personal freedom, as Foam and Nellie battle old customs that threaten to suppress their individualism. A young Muslim campaigning for the election of the Hindu politician Surujpat Harbans, Foam is a visionary. Not only does he feel democracy and the vote is important for the progress and advancement of his Trinidadian village, Elvira, but he has an eye on his own future development. He represents a new breed of Muslim who, in contrast to his superstitious elders, pays little attention to what they term "signs." Such a "sign," in the form of a little black puppy named Tiger, causes Foam to interact with Nellie when he asks if she will care for the stray that his younger brother has taken in. Nellie agrees to meet Foam to pick up Tiger.

An observer who sees the two young people meeting begins a rumor that they are romantically involved. This represents forbidden love, or at least discouraged love, between young people of two different religions. Although Foam and Nellie never interact romantically, the rumor that they do eventually allows Nellie her freedom. When Harbans hears the rumor, he refuses to allow his good Hindu son to marry a Hindu girl who keeps company with Muslim boys.

The aid Foam gives Nellie is unplanned, but he proves himself quite clever in his campaign activities. He uses to his benefit the religious superstition that so controls his father's thinking to turn the campaign in the favor of his candidate. His candidate's victory allows a victory for Foam as well, for he ends up earning the job he has always desired: announcing cinemas from a mobile van in the nearby town of Caroni.

Foam Baksh embodies two characteristics of the true medieval romance hero: he fulfills a quest and helps a damsel in distress, although he does not love her. But cloaked as he is in the guise of a postmodern hero, his actions must be viewed as symbolically, rather than literally, "romantic."

See also: Chittaranjan, Nellie; Forbidden Love; Naipaul, V. S.; Romance; *The Suffrage of Elvira*
References: Baker 1994; Birbalsingh, 1996; Hussein, 1994

BARNES, JAKE

Although the American Jake Barnes acts as the male protagonist in Ernest Hemingway's 1926 realistic novel, *The Sun Also Rises,* he cannot be labeled a classic romantic hero. This character shaping is purposeful on the part of Hemingway who, like others of his "lost generation," suffered disillusionment due to World War I. As a believer in nihilism who abandoned what he saw as the false ideology presented by religion and patriotism, Hemingway wanted a character who symbolized his own loss. For this reason, Jake suffers a war injury that leaves him emasculated, causing his love for Lady Brett Ashley to become only a burden and frustration.

Whenever the reality of his physical and emotional impotence overwhelms him, Jake escapes through alcohol and also by enjoying sports outings, such as fishing and camping with male friends. When he plans a fishing trip from his temporary home of Paris to Spain, where he will view bullfights with a friend, he does not anticipate that a number of his acquaintances will want to join him. Although the situation will be awkward, as the group will include Brett's most recent sexual fling, Robert Cohn, along with her supposed fiancé, Mike Campbell, the trip proceeds.

Throughout the vacation to Pamplona, Jake must face his loss repeatedly. Observing Brett's constant flirtation with various men, including a promising young bullfighter, is torturous, but he enjoys the suffering as evidence of his loss. Jake has a perverse need to sustain his feelings of hopelessness. He even promotes his own misery by introducing Brett to the bullfighter, Pedro Romero, although he knows she is likely to have a negative affect on the young man. This causes him to lose the respect and confidence of a longtime friend and hotel owner, Montoya, who had previously honored Jake by accepting him as a true fan of the bullfight. Rather than finding a way out of his predicament, Jake only becomes further mired in his hopelessness.

Later, he undergoes an epiphany as he confronts Romero's heroism. The bullfighter represents Hemingway's ideal hero in that he faces life honestly and through that honesty vanquishes disillusionment. After suffering a beating at the hands of one of Brett's lovers, Romero still enters the bullring and performs magnificently, confronting his destiny, represented by the bull, and meeting the challenge with precision and grace. Jake seems to learn from Romero's example, and he can later let Brett go when she announces that she will release Romero for his own benefit and return to her fiancé, a much more suitable match for her.

Jake benefits by learning from both Brett's and Romero's actions. Because he is too disillusioned to return to a traditional spirituality, Jake can find meaning in life only by responding to his fellow human beings in the most honorable way possible. The novel ends, if not on an uplifting note, at least with the possibility that Jake will overcome his emotional emasculation to seek some satisfaction from honorable behavior during his remaining years.

See also: A Farewell to Arms; For Whom the Bell Tolls; Hemingway, Ernest; Nihilism; Romance; *The Sun Also Rises;* Violence; War

References: Cowley, 1973; Defazio, 1996; Donaldson, 1996; Hen, 1996; Hily-Mane, 1995; Hotchner, 1966; Moreland, 1996; White, 1933, 1968

BEATRICE

Although relegated to the subplot of William Shakespeare's romantic comedy, *Much Ado about Nothing* (1598), Beatrice never takes a subservient position to the true romantic heroine, Hero. Her intelligent and challenging repartee with the eventual object of her affection, Benedick, makes her a favorite character for viewers from Shakespeare's day to the present. Prepared for her independent, witty personality by Shakespeare's Kate from previous performances of *The Taming of the Shrew* (1593–1594), Renaissance viewers welcomed a female who, unable to challenge men on the battlefield due to her gender, could take on the most self-confident male in a verbal clash. Modern feminist critics prize Beatrice for her linguistic accomplishments in a time when the English female lived under the patriarchal edicts of "silence, obedience and chastity." Of course, the fact that her character is Italian and supposedly unrestrained by more repressive English gender distinctions may be the key to her behavior. Yet even Beatrice must draw the line of combat between verbal and physical, a line that she obviously resents because on several occasions she rues the fact that she is female, unable to right wrongs that only men may, by custom, confront. "If only I were a man!" becomes her repeated cry of sincere frustration.

Beatrice remains her shy cousin Hero's opposite in every way. Her brash, direct approach to life contrasts with Hero's submissive shyness in a way intended to please her audience as much as it infuriates Benedick. When Benedick, a lord of Padua, arrives at the province of Messina in the company of Don Pedro, Prince of Arragon, and young Claudio, a lord of Florence, Beatrice and Hero, who is the daughter of the governor, both take notice. Hero loves the dashing Claudio in an unabashed way that Beatrice seems at times to envy, despite her protests against a romantic attachment for herself. Early in the drama she hints that she may have previously been involved romantically with Benedick when she says, "You always end with a jade's trick. I know you of old" (1.1.145). Whether her acerbic remarks to Benedick ground themselves in an unfulfilled previous romantic inclination or just in her witty personality remains unimportant; the couple's bantering provides much of the drama's entertainment.

Beatrice and Benedick supply much of the comedic aspect of this play when they are tricked by their friends into believing each loves the other. In actuality, the only trick is the way by which they are made to realize their love, for as the audience has easily guessed, these two are fated to be together. This misunderstanding provides a great deal of good-natured humor, although the situation turns serious when the innocent Hero is rejected by Claudio. He and Don Pedro believe they have seen Hero romancing another man, providing the aspect of mistaken identity that is crucial to the plot. Not only does this action allow Claudio and Hero to be temporarily at odds, but it gives Beatrice the chance to make Benedick shift his loyalty from his comrades to her. When Claudio's public humiliation of Hero leads to disastrous consequences, Beatrice wants revenge, something she cannot accomplish as a woman. Instead, she calls on Benedick to prove his devotion to her by challenging Claudio. Thus, Beatrice is allowed in a secondhand manner to take the offensive, protecting her cousin and, symbolically, the honor of the members of her sex.

As expected in a comedy, all misunderstandings are cleared up by the drama's conclusion, with Hero's innocence and purity proven. It is also revealed that Beatrice had never pined aloud for Benedick, nor had he ever declared to his fellow soldiers his love for Beatrice. At first the two engage in their regular insults but soon overcome their pride when their friends supply written confessions of their mutual affection. Caught in the act on paper, their defenses break down, and Beatrice and Benedick readily declare what all the other characters and the audience have long anticipated, their eternal devotion to one another.

See also: Benedick; Claudio; Hero; *Much Ado about Nothing;* Romance; Shakespeare, William
References: Barton, 1974; de Rougemont, 1983

BEAUTY AND THE BEAST

Plots for some novels with romantic themes, such as Mary Shelley's *Frankenstein* (1818) and Victor Hugo's *Hunchback of Notre Dame* (1831), find their basis in the oral storytelling tradition of fairy or folktales such as "Beauty and the Beast," first committed to paper by a French teacher of young children, Madame Le Prince de Beaumont (1711–1780). The popularity of her tale followed the earlier publication in 1697 of the collection of stories titled *Histoires ou contes du temps passé avec des moralités* (*Histories or Tales of Times Past with Morals*), also called *Contes de ma Mere l'Oye* (*Tales of Mother Goose*). The stories were likely collected by either Charles Perrault (1628–1703), a member of the French Academy, or by his eldest son, Pierre Perrault d'Armancour.

As did the editor of the collection of fairy tales, Madame de Beaumont used her imagination to embellish an existing fairy tale, a favorite pastime at the French court of Louis XIV. The tales were filled with traditional elements including magical objects, such as shoes or coins; fairies; witches, both good and evil; and talking beasts. In both de Beaumont's "Beauty and the Beast" and "The White Cat" by Comtesse d'Aulnoy, a human-turned-animal is featured. In a beastly condition caused by a curse or bewitchment, both creatures return to human form only when their spells are shattered by human love and constancy. In each of these stories, the bewitched individual is male and a member of the upper class or aristocracy. The human woman who breaks the spell is rewarded by the love and devotion of the now-handsome young man in a life to be lived happily ever after. The transformation depends on the woman discovering the beast's true nature, whereupon the hideous disguise vanishes.

In *Frankenstein,* Shelley incorporates an ironic use of the "Beauty and the Beast" themes. In an attempt to discover a way to cheat death, a scientist creates a man using body parts from dead humans, which, despite its hideous appearance, begins its life with an amiable and intelligent disposition. However, through mistreatment by humans, the creation becomes a monster in the truest sense, murdering innocent humans when his request for a mate with whom to spend his life is denied by his creator. In this tragedy, no positive transformation or result occurs from the monster, who eventually kills or causes the death of every member of his creator's family and of the creator himself. The monster remains alive, a testimony to the perils of man's attempts to imitate God.

Jean Marais and Josette Day appeared in a 1946 French film directed by Jean Cocteau, The Beauty and the Beast. *In this prototypical tale, a final transformation depends on the heroine discovering the beast's true nature, whereupon his hideous disguise vanishes. (Photofest)*

In *The Hunchback of Notre Dame,* Hugo uses as his monster a deformed man who is reviled because of his ugliness. Love for a Gypsy woman motivates him to kill a devilish priest who has long taken advantage of him and who wants also to possess her. Like *Frankenstein,* this novel ends tragically with the hunchback's death, but he saves the woman he loves from the dark intentions of the priest. Redemption lies in his finding peace through a death ennobled by love.

Emily Brontë's 1847 Gothic novel, *Wuthering Heights,* contains some elements from "Beauty and the Beast." The male protagonist reflects aspects of a beast; as a foundling he is filthy and animal-like, and he acts as an adult on what seem to be the animal instincts of the wild rather than on more cultured human emotions. Although he and an upper-class woman have shared a fierce devotion to each other since childhood, he commits several morally corrupt acts of revenge against members of her family when she marries another. After their deaths, the two lovers reunite, and their spirits are observed walking together. The Gothic elements of the story lend a dark kind of spirituality to the setting and the main characters' relationships that is reminiscent of fairy-tale magic.

An additional altered version of the tale may occur in romantic stories when a human is released only from an emotionally or psychologically monstrous existence, rather than from the actual physical resemblance to a monster, through the powers of love.

See also: Forbidden Love; *Frankenstein; The Hunchback of Notre Dame; Wuthering Heights* *References:* de Rougemont, 1983; Russell, 1991; Sutherland and Arbuthnot, 1991

BELOVED

Toni Morrison's experimental 1987 novel, *Beloved,* which captured first the American public's imagination and then the 1988 Pulitzer Prize, finds its place among traditional slave narratives, ghost stories, and romances. As a former slave, the novel's protagonist Sethe must find a way to leave her ghosts behind, in both a figurative and a literal sense. Her memories of slavery serve to keep her a captive to the past, and the ghost of the child she killed in order to avoid its enslavement haunts Sethe's present. Having lost her husband Halle, her first true love, Sethe must also learn to trust and love Paul D, a man she had known in the past as a fellow slave.

Morrison approaches her narrative in a nonlinear fashion, moving the reader in and out of Sethe's present through flashbacks and allowing various narrators to tell pieces of Sethe's history from their own points of view. The reader learns that Sethe escaped from Sweet Home farm while pregnant and accompanied by her children; Halle stayed behind on the farm with plans to join her later. She was to travel to Ohio and live with Halle's mother, Baby Suggs, in a town with a large black contingent. Baby Suggs's freedom was purchased by her son, who had contracted for extra work to buy her from their master, Mr. Garner.

Baby Suggs also supplies personal and racial history in the novel, using such memories as the loss of children sold as commodities to provide a more general history of the suffering of all blacks under slavery.

Although not the cruelest of slave owners, the Garners and their white employees still inflict emotional, physical, and sexual abuse on their slaves. Readers learn that one slave, Sixo, was burned at the stake for supposedly stealing a pig. Sethe herself recalls the horrifying degradation of having the milk for her baby stolen directly from her full breasts by the nephews of Schoolteacher, the white overseer. Morrison paints most of the novel's white characters in a negative light, but one exception is a young white woman who helps deliver Sethe's baby, Denver, during Sethe's journey. Sethe settles into her new Ohio home, where she manages to enjoy twenty-eight glorious days of freedom before Schoolteacher appears to claim her under the Fugitive Slave Act. Rather than allow her children to be taken into slavery, Sethe slits the throat of her toddler and would have killed her new baby and herself if no one had stopped her. The child she kills returns as the spirit, Beloved, after Sethe serves a jail sentence for her crime.

As horrific as Sethe's crime may be, she remains a sympathetic character. Morrison allows the reader to see the limited choices available to Sethe as a mother. After leaving jail, Sethe returns to Ohio to live in number 124 with her children and Baby Suggs. But before long, the haunting begins, and Sethe's sons run away as soon as they are able. Denver remains and grows up fearful for her own life should Sethe ever have to make such a terrible choice again. Halle is never able to join his family, Baby Suggs eventually dies, and Sethe and Denver live ostracized by the community of blacks who know of Sethe's past.

Then one day, Paul D arrives. At first, he has a healing influence on Sethe; by touching the scars of her physical wounds, he seems to help her emotional injuries as well. Bent and broken himself by a past he can barely stand to think of, Paul D also benefits from the relationship. Sethe avoids telling him about killing her child, however; she just explains that she went to jail rather than returning to Sweet Home. Paul D shares with Sethe that her husband, Halle, had to watch his wife's disgraceful treatment by Schoolteacher's nephews from a hidden vantage point. He was so humiliated at his own helplessness that he had smeared himself with clabbered milk and walked about the farm, a marked and broken-spirited man. The reader also learns of Paul D's near-death experience in an underground cell that almost became his tomb during a flood. His story of survival balances Beloved's later story of death, as she recalls the experience of literal burial. Morrison's use of her own term, *rememory,* best captures the theme of coming to terms with one's past, a task that all of the characters, even the ghost, must undertake.

Paul D is able to temporarily exorcise the spirit from 124, and he and Denver and Sethe become a family unit, although Denver remains unwilling to accept him as a substitute for her father. But before long, the spirit seemingly returns, this time in a very physical form, and Paul D and Sethe will become enmeshed in one of the stranger love triangles ever to appear in fiction. A teenage girl, about the age Beloved would be had she not died, suddenly appears, apparently alone and in need of a home. Whether the girl is a ghost or a material representation of the past that Sethe needs to rememory so she can embrace the future is never made completely clear. What is clear are the overwhelming consequences of Sethe's acceptance of the girl. Soon under the girl's spell, progressively distracted and disoriented, Sethe is able only to look to Beloved's needs and demands, as a captivated lover might care for her partner.

Denver recognizes Beloved early on as her dead sister, and she tries to protect Beloved from Sethe and Paul D, not realizing they are the ones who require protection. At one point, Beloved even tries to kill Sethe to exact payment for her own death. She takes over 124 as Sethe becomes increasingly enthralled with Beloved. Because she no longer goes to work, Sethe loses her job, and eventually she stops leaving the house altogether. Beloved's power even extends to Paul D, who moves downstairs where the spirit girl attempts to seduce him, demanding to enjoy the sexual experiences she was denied by death. Paul D moves out of the house, and only then does he learn from another character, Stamp Paid, the full extent of Sethe's past actions and her involvement in killing her child.

In 124, Denver must step forward to rescue the group of three women by going to work. She eventually galvanizes the community into help-

ing her and her mother, convincing the black women that her mother will starve to death if her spirit sister is not evicted. The women appear at 124, at last willing to interact with Sethe, and an exorcism is performed. Beloved is removed, and Sethe and Paul D may pick up their love affair again, but only, Paul D tells Sethe, if they can both look to the future. Although Paul D remains important to the novel's romantic aspect, at the end the story focuses more on the survival instincts of a community of women, united by a common past.

Storytelling remains at the heart of Morrison's novel, as each character is allowed the voice to tell his or her story within Morrison's larger all-encompassing plot. Sethe repeats her own story again and again in an effort to bring herself and Beloved to terms with the killing. In the middle of the book, Morrison injects chapters from the point of view of each woman, Sethe, Denver, and Beloved, organizing their random thoughts and memories. Beloved's stream-of-consciousness narrative allows her to move beyond her individual grief into a collective awareness, filled with emotions and memories shared by every member of the human race. In so doing, this ghost story takes its place among those tales basic to the understanding of every race and culture.

See also: Beloved; The Black Experience in America, 1600–1945; Morrison, Toni; Romance; Sethe; Violence

References: Atlas, 1996; Dougherty 1996; McKay, 1997; Morey, 1997; "Morrison, Toni," 1997

BELOVED

In Toni Morrison's novel *Beloved* (1987), the reader must decide whether the figure called Beloved is indeed a reincarnation of the main character Sethe's dead daughter, an imaginary being who represents Sethe's guilt personified, or some type of evil spirit or succubus who haunts Sethe's house. Although she eventually assumes human form, Beloved exercises otherworldly powers over her mother, her sister Denver, and her mother's love interest, Paul D. Morrison masterfully works Beloved's presence into her narrative, allowing the dead girl to become a voice for all those who suffered and died in American slavery, as well as for those who died while captives in Africa or as prisoners in the coffinlike holds of slave ships, referred to in the novel's dedication as "Sixty Million and more."

Beloved remains crucial not only to the plot of the story, but also to its narration. Morrison includes three chapters of dramatic monologue, one for each of the three women in 124. Through a complicated stream-of-consciousness technique, Beloved relates a gruesome and horrifying story of her own death and burial and the parallel deaths of slaves in the dark holds of ships. In this chapter, her character becomes more fully developed and even sympathetic, but Morrison's tone intimates a wickedness about Beloved and her motivations.

See also: Beloved; The Black Experience in
America, 1600–1945; Forbidden Love; Love
Triangle; Morrison, Toni; Sethe
References: Atlas, 1996; Dougherty, 1996; McKay,
1997; Morey, 1997; "Morrison, Toni," 1997

BENEDICK
As half of the sharp-tongued couple who give focus to the subplot of William Shakespeare's *Much Ado about Nothing* (1598), Benedick has proved a popular character. In an 1861 operatic version of the comedy, French composer Hector Berlioz revised the title to *Béatrice et Bénédict,* and Charles I followed suit in his copy of a collection of Shakespeare's plays. These actions echo the sentiment of viewers everywhere, who find the witty exchanges between Benedick and his enemy-love, Beatrice, the more satisfying component of Shakespeare's romance.

As a young Paduan lord, Benedick arrives at Messina in the company of Don Pedro, Prince of Arragon, and Claudio, a lord of Florence. At Messina dwells Hero, daughter of the province's governor, Leonato, with whom Claudio becomes enthralled. Benedick, by far the most outspoken member of the male troop, makes his views toward women and marriage known early on. He declares that he will never marry and heckles Claudio for preferring romance to battle. Claudio's pursuit of the gentle and passive Hero constitutes the drama's main plot. Beatrice, niece of Leonato, also lives at Messina, and from her first encounter with Benedick, viewers understand the two are apparently longtime acquaintances and verbal combatants. Their jibes and insults delight viewers who know, before the squabbling couple does, that the two will be romantically involved before the drama's end. Shakespeare allows the two to play with language in riddles and challenges that Renaissance and modern audiences alike judge enthralling.

As Claudio's courting of Hero advances, Benedick spars continually with Beatrice. Just as Hero's and Claudio's courtly manners make them seem a good match, so too are Benedick and Beatrice linked by their appreciation and application of the nuances of verbal language. At once infuriated by and attracted to Beatrice, Benedick is easily tricked by Claudio, Leonato, and Don Pedro into believing that Beatrice loves him. When Hero and Ursula collaborate to play the same trick on Beatrice, the trap for these two reluctant lovers is set, as is the major vehicle for the misunderstandings so necessary to comic drama. Shakespeare uses Beatrice and Benedick to comment on language, even placing in Benedick's mouth the emotions the writer himself must have felt when stymied by rhythms and rhymes.

Benedick's part is not all comedy, however. When Claudio accuses Hero of a sexual encounter with a servant and cancels their marriage, the enraged Beatrice, unable due to her gender to extract revenge herself, appeals to Benedick to redeem her cousin's honor. The audience understands Benedick's change of heart when he remains behind at the church to speak with Beatrice at the crucial moment of division between the sexes, rather than leaving with his friends. Now hopelessly in love with Beatrice and feeling uncertain regarding Hero's guilt, Benedick agrees to challenge Claudio to a duel, symbolically ending his duel with Beatrice. Of course, the two men never need to fight because first Hero's innocence is proven, then Claudio repents and publicly recants his accusation, and the two reunite. The importance of Benedick's challenge of Claudio lies in his reprioritization of his own emotions and affections so that newfound love takes precedence over former ties.

Following their display of righteous indignation at discovering they have been tricked into proclaiming their love for one another, Benedick and Beatrice agree to marry. But the verbal sparks that fly between them before each "discovers" the other's true feelings lets the audience know their relationship will be based on wit as well as affection.

See also: Beatrice; Claudio; Hero; *Much Ado about
Nothing;* Romance; Shakespeare, William
References: Barton, 1974; de Rougemont, 1983

BENNET, ELIZABETH (ELIZA/LIZZY)
Elizabeth Bennet is the main character in Jane Austen's novel *Pride and Prejudice* (1813).

Elizabeth, sometimes referred to as Eliza or Lizzy, represents the prejudice that appears in the novel's title. Her romantic partner, who embodies pride, is Fitzwilliam Darcy. On the surface, no two people could be less alike, but as the novel progresses, they find themselves more alike than they and the readers would have at first believed. The trait they share is a tendency to judge others based on first impressions and then to cling stubbornly to that early judgment.

Unlike her older sister Jane Bennet, Elizabeth Bennet has problems following the accepted social code of her day. Without any particular training for employment and with no promise of inheritance thanks to a family entailment that moves only through male relatives, Eliza should be frantic to find a husband. Yet she refuses the marriage offer of her foolish cousin, Mr. Collins, who will inherit her home, even though it would mean that she could go on living in the house where she matured and eventually replace her mother as its mistress. As an intelligent woman, one her father labels early in the novel as having "something more of quickness" than her four sisters, Elizabeth desires to marry her intellectual equal, a man sensible to her needs, both mental and emotional. With her eyes on that goal, she rejects the material security represented by the intellectually deficient Collins.

When she overhears a disparaging comment about her made by Darcy to his friend and Jane's love interest, Charles Bingley, Eliza forms a low opinion of the wealthy bachelor. The reader gains a fine bit of insight into Elizabeth's basic strength of character when she honestly confesses that she would not have minded Darcy's show of pride, had it not injured her own. More importantly, she holds Darcy responsible for problems between Bingley and Jane, feeling that Darcy is the reason Bingley has hesitated to propose to Jane. She also dislikes Darcy because, according to her friend George Wickham, Darcy harmed him for no reason other than jealousy when they were both young men. In Elizabeth's mind, Darcy has three counts against him, and all of these actions she blames on his pride.

When Darcy later revises his initial opinion of Eliza as just another woman seeking a husband, he asks her to marry him. Eliza again demonstrates her strong will in refusing what many, even those who agree that Darcy has too much pride, would consider a wonderful match. But when

Darcy later acts with utmost compassion during the Bennets' family problems, Eliza begins to reconsider her initial opinion. Much time must pass and many discussions occur between Darcy and Eliza before she at last admits to herself her error in having allowed her early prejudice to spur her refusal of Darcy's proposal.

Recognized as a writer whose novels focused on economic and social issues, Austen uses Eliza to voice her disgust at a world where many women could not even inherit property. Both the character and her creator searched constantly for diversion within their own worlds, finding that diversion in the study of the people who surrounded them. Just as Austen seemed to categorize people into those who were cognizant of the realities of life and those who were not, so does Elizabeth. Elizabeth Bennet could have easily developed into a stereotype, consumed just as much by social ritual through her condemning of it as are those who willingly complied with it. But Austen graces her character with an independence that allows her to escape such a fate. Her change takes place gradually, as it should; no overnight emotional eclipse is responsible for her new outlook on Darcy.

True to the mores of Austen's era, Eliza wonders in silence at Darcy's civility, rather than sharing her newfound feelings with him. When at last she contemplates Darcy's kind attentions to herself and her family, wondering, "Why is he so altered? From what can it proceed?" she must find her answer in his love for her. After all misunderstandings are settled and the two are a couple, when Darcy admits he was first attracted to Eliza by "the liveliness" of her mind, she playfully corrects his assessment. True to character, she bids him not mince words; she was not lively but rather downright impertinent. She adds that she believes Darcy was weary of the deference and civility others extended to him, disgusted with women who acted as if they thought only of him and not themselves. But Austen competently avoids the type of conclusion to be found in the overly sentimental novel, which she abhorred. Elizabeth does not gush and fawn but rather plainly informs Darcy that he must praise her exceedingly and that she will continue to tease and quarrel with him at will.

See also: Austen, Jane; Darcy, Fitzwilliam; Dashwood, Elinor; Dashwood, Marianne; *Emma; Pride and Prejudice; Sense and Sensibility*

References: Britannica, 1997; Clayton, 1987a; Copeland and McMaster, 1997; de Rougemont, 1983; Drabble, 1995; Fraiman, 1993; Gard, 1992; Gilbert and Gubar, 1985c; Praz, 1974; Watt, 1963

BERTO, GIUSEPPE

Italian novelist Giuseppe Berto was born in 1914 at Mogliano Veneto in Treviso province. After graduating from the University of Padua, he enlisted to fight in Africa in 1943. He began his writing career while a prisoner of war at a Hereford, Texas, camp. Works by American authors Ernest Hemingway and John Steinbeck influenced his early writings. Berto published nine novels, three plays, a science-fiction fantasy, and several short stories. He also developed screenplays from several of his novels, which became successful movies in his native country. Because Berto suffered psychological crises, his work was often interrupted. And although his work proved commercially successful, the mixed critical attention it drew has caused his omission from most surveys of contemporary Italian literature.

Berto would base his narrative *A Small Success* (*Un po' di successo*) and his 1948 romance, *The Works of God* (*Le opere di Dio*), on his World War II experiences. He later added an essay discussing his life and interpreting his work through the midpoint of his career to the 1965 edition of *The Works of God*. An antiromance focusing on social and economic inequities suffered by poverty-stricken Italians, *La perduta gente* (literally, "the lost people") was translated into English and also published in 1948 under the title *The Sky Is Red*. Berto's emphasis on topics of love, death, pain, and the quest for identity separated him from his contemporaries, who used an approach labeled *neorealism*. Berto criticized this approach as stereotypical, formulaic, moralistic, and unrelated to the needs of its readership. Much of his work emphasizes the perception of a deeper truth to be found in the internal world of characters caught in the conflict between competing ideas of self. Berto's characters generally struggle with their environments to construct, organize, and simplify their lives. They may exist in a world of fantasy.

Critics group Berto's writings with those of Luigi Pirandello, classifying both as literatures of introspection and neurosis. Berto himself wrote that he used irony as a means to cope with an absurd world, acknowledging the influence of Sigmund Freud and existentialist philosophy on his fiction. The use of irony and humor in much of his work allowed him some distance from the agony of his protagonists, characters who were often autobiographical creations. It also permits the reader to empathize with the protagonist while finding some positive result in the character's suffering.

Berto later based an additional romance/diary, *War of the Black Shirt* (*Guerra in camicia nera*), on his African experiences. In addition to romances written for young adults, he wrote dramas, including *The Man and His Death* (*L'uomo e la sua morte*) and a collection of short stories, *And Perhaps Love* (*E' forse l'amore*). As in his novels, his short stories make of Berto's own life a metaphor for the lives of all humans.

In what is perhaps Berto's most famous work, titled *An Obscure Man* (*Il male oscuro*), published in 1964, the novel's protagonist is also named Berto. The author becomes a part of his own text, refusing to be separated from the fiction he creates, an idea emphasized in the novel's opening reference to Flaubert and to the autobiographical aspects of his highly influential novel, *Madame Bovary* (1857). *An Obscure Man* offers a complicated tale that features Berto's conflicts with his father, his multiple illnesses, what he viewed as sexual inadequacy, and his private ambitions, both as a person and a writer.

Although Giuseppe Berto often utilized war and its effects as a backdrop to his writing, he did not focus on socioeconomic issues so much as on the existential concerns of the individual, including sickness, old age, death, conflict in relationships, and the disparity between what one desires and what one may achieve. No triumph remains available to his characters other than their reconciliation to the absurdities of life. When Berto died in Rome in 1978, he left behind a collection of writing offering his readers suggestions for dealing with the same afflictions suffered by his characters.

See also: The Sky Is Red
References: "Biografia," 1997; Frye, 1976; Striuli, 1986–1989

BILDUNGSROMAN

The bildungsroman features the development of a main character from youth to maturity (see *The House of the Spirits; Like Water for Chocolate; Love in the Time of Cholera; My Ántonia; Of Human*

Bondage; Sons and Lovers; The Thorn Birds; Tom Jones). In a related category, the *erziehungsroman* presents a story of "apprenticeship" or "education" (see *The Sound of Waves*). A similar plot classification is that of the *kunstleroman,* a story of maturation that traces the development of a writer (see *Doctor Zhivago; Sophie's Choice*). The terms derive from the nineteenth-century German body of literary criticism, but many novels with maturation themes have been written in all languages, both before and after these specific labels became popular. The classification tradition began with Johann Wolfgang von Goethe's *Wilhelm Meisters Lehrjahre* (four volumes, 1795–1796; *Wilhelm Meister's Apprenticeship,* 1824). Originally focusing on males as main characters, the bildungsroman began to include female protagonists as well in the late nineteenth century.

Closely related to the bildungsroman, the initiation story, also called the coming-of-age story, may be found in children's as well as adult literature, including literature of romance and love. As indicated by its name, the initiation plot involves some type of experience on the part of a protagonist that makes him or her aware of a new aspect of life. When a character experiences love for the first time, either emotionally or physically, that character undergoes an initiation of sorts into the world of adult romance. The change represents some type of maturation. Although most initiation or coming-of-age stories focus on young characters enjoying their first experience in romance, occasionally the label may apply to plots containing more mature characters. For instance, even though a character may have experienced the physical aspects of love through sex previous to his or her presentation in a novel, certain emotional effects that accompany "true love" may be new to that character within the time period covered by the plot (see *A Farewell to Arms*). This circumstance makes that plot fit into the category of an adult initiation story. The initiation/coming-of-age story generally contains an epiphany, or a moment of life-altering discovery on the part of the protagonist, allowing that character to become dynamic and well-rounded through the change that he or she experiences. All romantic quest plots contain initiation/coming-of-age aspects. Traditionally, these stories featured males as the main characters, but modern plots may focus on females as initiates as well.

See also: Quest; Romance
References: Campbell, 1949, 1968; Carr, 1987; de Rougemont, 1956; Fetterley, 1993; Fraiman, 1993; Frye, 1976; Fuderer, 1990; Hardin, 1991; Kontje, 1992, 1993; Labovitz, 1986; LeSeur, 1995; Nagel, 1995; Russell, 1991

THE BLACK EXPERIENCE IN AMERICA, 1600–1945

As the American novel emerged as an important genre in the eighteenth century, blacks were increasingly included in love stories centered around white characters. Many of those novels featured black characters as slaves, generally fashioned as either trusting, childlike figures or as devilish creatures. Not until the mid– and late twentieth century were novels featuring blacks as major characters involved in same-race romance published with much regularity. As is true for most literature, eighteenth- and nineteenth-century writings with themes of love reflected the environment surrounding their authors; thus, with few exceptions, the majority of "classic" romances contain examples of the racism inherent in American and British culture of the times. Some knowledge of their historical treatment by white Americans is thus helpful in understanding these early characterizations of blacks.

Twenty African slaves were first brought to the colonies in 1619 in order to cultivate Virginia tobacco. Although records reveal that multiple measures were adopted to prevent interracial marriage, by the time the colonies enjoyed statehood, sixty thousand mixed-blood inhabitants peopled the new country. A large number of the mixed alliances were between escaped slaves and American Indians; the Seminoles mingled freely with blacks in Florida, making that state a haven for runaways. Attempts by landowners to recover slaves and seize their half-Indian offspring contributed to the outbreak of the Second Seminole War in 1835. The wars concluded when a black leader, Chief Abraham, successfully negotiated the Treaty of Fort Dade, and black Seminoles were allowed to move west despite landholders' claims to them as property.

The severity of attitudes toward interracial relationships is reflected in the terminology and clearly judgmental tone used in colonial records concerning punishment of specific instances of miscegenation (cohabitation or marriage between a white person and someone of another race). The appearance in judicial narratives of words such as "dishonor" and "shame," even "defilement," indicate that whites felt skin color determined humanity. In 1662 Virginia enacted the first statute that prohibited interracial marriage; six additional colonies passed such laws by 1725. Because the more common racially mixed relationship involved a white man and a black woman, the laws broke the patristic convention set down by British law, thereby relegating children to the status of their mothers. This approach ensured that any offspring would remain slaves so that slaveowners would not suffer the loss of labor that legal intermarriage might promote. If mulatto children happened to be born to white women, they retained freedom but generally served long terms of indentured servitude. The laws supported racism and provided economic protection for whites while they helped prevent an alliance of slaves with other servants that might threaten the ruling class.

Penalties against intermarriage became more stringent with time. A free white woman bearing a mulatto child was required in some colonies to pay stiff fines within thirty days to avoid a five-year indenture for herself and thirty years of service for the child. In 1705, a Virginia law added a fine of 10,000 pounds of tobacco leveled against any minister who performed an interracial marriage. Records show the threat landowners felt was posed by miscegenation, a growing practice during the seventeenth and eighteenth centuries. Colonial leaders seldom married blacks, but white men frequently participated in liaisons with female slaves. In general, these relationships were tolerated by whites, but those between white women and black males were not.

In spite of strict laws, harsh punishment, and social and religious proclamations against the mixing of the races, it continued basically unchecked. Large numbers of white men and a scant supply of white women interacted with people of other races. For example, in 1864, when freed slaves could be married by federal officials, records from a Vicksburg, Mississippi, office note that more than one-third of the nine thousand slaves registered at that time in the lower South were of mixed heritage.

Following the American Revolution, many slaves were freed. Because a large number were mulattos, whites felt a need to develop a definition of the free white citizen. The mixing of

whites and blacks was termed *amalgamation,* the name for combining mercury with other metals to produce a mixed substance. Between the Revolution and the Civil War, changes in legal codes took place in a renewed attempt to control interracial marriage. Proslavery measures increased in the South following the Slave Act of 1807, which prohibited further importation of slaves, and with the extensive use of the cotton gin after 1830. Previously, white men had occasionally freed their mulatto children. But despite attempts by some through legal wills and manumission to ensure the freedom of children of mixed race, after 1850 an increasing number of mulatto children were deemed slaves. This in part accounts for the stereotypical "tragic mulatto" character that appeared in abolitionist fiction of the day. A typical melodramatic plot line might feature the plantation owner's mulatto daughter being sold into slavery at his death. James Fenimore Cooper confronted the topic of miscegenation and resultant mulatto children in his 1826 novel, *The Last of the Mohicans.* In this story, Cora Munro's secret racially mixed heritage becomes an object of dispute between her father, Colonel Munro, and Duncan Heyward, whom Munro mistakenly assumes is rejecting his daughter due to her "black" blood. Such literature reflected the growing social obsession over issues connected to amalgamation.

These conditions caused many freed blacks to flee the South. In Louisiana miscegenation remained common due to a shortage of white women, and mulattos could, under the French Napoleonic Code, assume the free status of their fathers. After the Louisiana Purchase, children of slave mothers could be seized following a move by the Louisiana courts in 1832.

Exploitation by white males of black females naturally caused other problems than the determination of the legal status of their offspring. According to some critics, slaves followed a "premodern" code allowing for premarital sex without shame or censure. However, blacks who held sacred the bonds of marriage disallowed extramarital sexual activity. Male and female slaves attempted to live in long-term, stable family relationships, but these were often fractured by the sale of one or the other member of the couple or their children. Violations of marital fidelity by whites frequently caused resistance by both black females and males. Records reveal many instances when black males attempted to stop the rapes of their wives, or the women themselves tried to refuse approaches on the part of their white masters or overseers, resulting in severe physical punishment or death for the slaves. The rape, murder, and incest inflicted on blacks by whites led to problems in white marriages as well. Multiple divorce petitions of the time indicate that a husband's unlawful and carnal intimacy with a black slave caused the fracturing of his own marriage.

Best-selling romances such as Margaret Mitchell's Civil War novel, *Gone with the Wind* (1936), served to romanticize the view of the "peaceful darky" who became a beloved member of a white plantation owner's family. The character type represented by Mammy would appear multiple times in cinema and novels. But early black writers such as Frederick Douglass revealed the true lot of the slave, condemned to servitude by law and kept ignorant by enforced illiteracy among blacks. Laws against teaching blacks to read and write inflicted heavy penalties upon anyone who schooled their slaves.

Only in the twentieth century did black fiction writers appear in abundance to realistically present the horrors inflicted upon black family relationships by slavery. An example is Nobel Prize–winner Toni Morrison's award-winning novel *Beloved* (1987), in which an escaped female slave murders her own toddler rather than allow the child to face slavery and abuse by whites.

The view that no southern white woman would have anything to do with a black male relates to conditions after 1830, when slavery became an economic necessity, violent antimiscegenation practices escalated, and those benefiting from slavery justified these actions by racism. Because of the fines and penalties suffered by white women who had relationships with black men, cries of "rape" sometimes became a ploy to avoid punishment on the part of a white woman who had agreed to sexual acts with a black male. Prior to the Civil War, such rape cases were handled by the judicial system, rather than through the lynchings that often settled them afterward. The late-nineteenth-century stereotype promoting a black/mulatto rapist likely grew from a southern complex in which the "pure" white woman symbolized the South; her rape thus insinuated a rape of everything southerners held dear.

By 1850, when the Industrial Revolution promoted the South's dependence on cotton, black

and mulatto slaves became essential to industry. But by 1915, blacks faced exclusion from employment made possible by industrialization. Social studies reveal that in 1850, members of the southern white elite enjoyed by necessity a link to blacks and a separation from the white masses. Slavery found defense in the racial prejudice, based on a nineteenth-century "scientific" approach that argued for the inferiority of blacks, whom God had created to serve whites. Mulattos posed a threat in their blurring of the distinctions between the races. Slavery gradually increased in whiteness, causing consternation for slave owners. Preceding the Civil War, a scornful attitude toward blacks in matters of sex was basically reserved for black females as an excuse for the white man's abuse of them. The white male attitude toward black males as a sexual threat increased following the war, when it served the purposes of segregationists.

At the turn of the century, "passing," when a light-skinned black successfully pretended to be a white person, caused increasing problems, including an obsession among southern whites with racial purity. In the name of preserving such purity, white women were by all means possible to be kept away from black men; however, it was widely accepted that racial purity would not suffer from the fathering of mulatto children by white men. The theme of conflict caused by interracial romance and the resultant children of mixed heritage appears in many romance novels, such as Ernest J. Gaines's *Of Love and Dust* (1967). This novel depicts a Louisiana Cajun overseer involved in a long-term affair with a black plantation worker, which produces two children. Although this relationship enjoys a grudging, silent acceptance, when the overseer's wife falls in love with a black male worker, violence results.

The eventual movement by blacks from rural to urban areas represented a tremendous alteration of demographics; prior to 1915, about 90 percent of all blacks lived in the rural South. The movement of blacks into southern and northern cities profoundly changed African-American culture. Black urban communities afforded greater freedoms and presented greater access to social institutions and opportunities for education. Those intellectuals receiving an education at black colleges such as Fisk, Howard, and Hampton found cities attractive. Although blacks having any postsecondary education remained rare (in 1915, only about 2,000 were enrolled in colleges), they were still able to provide articulate, forceful leadership in the areas of politics and culture. Some of these individuals, such as Ida B. Wells and W. E. B. Du Bois, joined social protest groups in the pursuit of equal rights. Organizations such as the interracial National Association for the Advancement of Colored People (NAACP), formed in 1909, joined all-black groups in seeking equal rights for all Americans.

Cultural and intellectual activity increased due to growth in the size and education of the black community. At the turn of the century, black artists began to garner prominence; examples include the composers Scott Joplin, W. C. Handy, and John Rosamond Johnson; the writer James Weldon Johnson (brother to John Rosamond); and the poet-novelist Paul Laurence Dunbar. A concern for employment promoted tension between growing numbers of migrants and those local urban blacks already secure in service positions to whites. But black communities grew quickly, soon providing a minority of black professionals and businesspeople of both genders. The early deference to things white eroded before an escalating sense of racial pride among blacks that promoted social cohesion.

Black urbanization and industrial development gained a boost from World War I as black migrants assumed the positions of absent white males. Middle-class blacks began to develop a cohesion with their black clientele, increasing the drive for racial pride. Although some black leaders opposed war, they agreed with its supporters that the war provided an opportunity for racial gains. Blacks returned to the United States seeking the respect they deserved.

But opposition to any racial equality remained fierce. By the 1920s, whites often aligned to exclude blacks, converting the nineteenth-century dichotomy of "free and slave" to "white and black." A new flurry of antimiscegenation laws joined with Jim Crow laws enforcing racial segregation to destroy opportunity for social contact between the races.

In 1916, Marcus Garvey, a native of Jamaica, established in New York the self-help group called the Universal Negro Improvement Association (UNIA). The group grew in power, establishing a steamship concern, Black Star Line, to trade with Africa. But Garvey suffered political attack by black civil rights leaders as well as by whites, and he came under government surveillance. As racial friction increased, riots claiming hundreds of victims broke out in a number of American communities. East Saint Louis, Illinois; Houston and Longview, Texas; Washington, D.C.; Chicago, Illinois; Knoxville, Tennessee; and Omaha, Nebraska, all suffered violence sparked by racial issues from 1917 to 1919. Although Marcus Garvey was eventually convicted of mail fraud and deported in 1927, his brief experience with economic and political power helped coalesce black workers and small business owners into groups actively seeking racial equality.

Simultaneously, a black cultural movement known as the Harlem Renaissance gained support from the black community. Literary figures of the 1920s included Claude McKay, a Jamaican poet and novelist, and Jean Toomer, whose book *Cane* (1923), a mixture of plays, poems, and stories, promoted the Renaissance theme of identification with poor blacks. The best-known black poet from the 1920s, Langston Hughes, wrote works reflecting an identification with working-class blacks. Patronage from supportive white patrons and from black editors, like Charles S. Johnson, of the Urban League's *Opportunity,* and Du Bois, editor of the NAACP publication, *Crisis,* helped the flowering of black culture to gain momentum. Figures such as the black Rhodes scholar and Harvard graduate Alain Locke and Zora Neale Hurston, black anthropologist and novelist, preserved and promoted black culture. In addition to collecting and publishing black folklore, Hurston wrote novels featuring blacks functioning within near all-black communities like the Florida town in which Hurston herself was raised. Her novel, *Their Eyes Were Watching God* (1937), focuses on the romance and adventures of a black woman who participates in three marriages. This work would be considered important by twentieth-century feminists because of its promotion of issues important to women, regardless of race.

Serious black actors Charles Gilpin and Paul Robeson performed in dramas by Eugene O'Neill, and African-American music, jazz and the blues, previously popular mainly in the South, began to spread to big cities such as Chicago and New York. Musicians Louis Armstrong and Jelly Roll Morton moved from the New Orleans music scene to Chicago, forging a path that big band leaders Duke Ellington and Fletcher Henderson would later follow.

Like other cultural movements, that of blacks suffered during the onset of the Great Depression in the 1930s, when attention switched to matters of economics. The high unemployment and poverty suffered among blacks before the stock market crash increased significantly following it. One positive result of the economic slump was the motivation for blacks to join whites in seeking social reform. Some turned to the Communist Party, which included a black vice-presidential candidate in the elections of 1932, 1936, and 1940. But the alliance was short-lived because blacks became disillusioned with the group, which, by emphasizing their minority status, seemed to promote racist ideas. The black novelist Ralph Ellison later featured such an experience in his highly popular novel, *Invisible Man* (1947).

Black involvement in labor unions proved important and gave black workers the collective voice needed for economic advancement. The National Negro Congress, headed by A. Philip Randolph, worked to promote African-American interests but eventually dissolved due to internal dissent. But the union alliance caused a crucial political shift by many blacks from the Republican Party to the Democratic Party; 1934 would see the largest black support ever for Democratic candidates. Although President Franklin Delano Roosevelt swept the black vote in 1936, the benefits for blacks of his New Deal politics were mixed. Federally sponsored relief programs for the poor included blacks, and they could join projects executed by the Works Progress Administration (WPA). Several blacks gained official positions in the federal administration, and supported by Eleanor Roosevelt's efforts, federal policy came under influence by black civic leaders, organized in an informal manner by educator Mary McLeod Bethune as a black cabinet. However, the New Deal ignored southern black farmers. These individuals were not only hurt by falling agricultural prices but were also barred from participation in the Agricultural Adjustment Administration. Due to his fear of losing white southern votes, Roosevelt also refused to support legislation on the federal level against lynching.

In the 1930s, black organizations such as the NAACP launched campaigns against racial discrimination, particularly in American schools. With World War II at last came a strong stimulus in promotion of racial equality. The increased need for black workers, along with the public's heightened awareness of racism because of Hitler's policies, propelled activists to fight vigorously against segregation. Roosevelt was forced by the threat of a black march on Washington, to be led by A. Philip Randolph, to prohibit through executive order discrimination in defense industries and federal bureaus. Between 1940 and 1950, the migration this act encouraged caused blacks looking for defense jobs in western states to triple those states' black population. Subsequent conflict over lack of housing and resources triggered race riots, including the 1943 outbreak of violence in Detroit, which resulted in thirty-four deaths. Military action on the part of blacks also caused an increased demand for more equal treatment, sparking an outbreak of camp protests against discrimination. The war ushered in an atmosphere ripe for the multitude of political and social changes in areas of gender and racial equality that would take place in the United States during the second half of the twentieth century.

References: Coombs, 1972; Davidson, 1995; Flora and Bain, 1987; Hart, 1995; Kinney, 1985; LeSeur, 1995; Munro, 1992; Pizer, 1995

BLANCHARD, GILLIAN

Gillian Blanchard is a white English character who for the sake of love suffers British prejudice against blacks in Edward Braithwaite's 1959 novel, *To Sir, with Love*. Like the author himself, the book's autobiographical main character whom Gillian loves, teacher Rick Braithwaite, is a black man from British Guiana. As the romance with Rick develops, Gillian is exposed to an aspect of her society, its pervasive racism, that she has not previously experienced.

The two young teachers first meet when Rick takes a job in a school in London's poor East End. When Rick encounters Gillian, he recognizes her not only as a fellow teacher but also as a lovely, bright woman whom he immediately likes. As the two come to know one another better, Gillian confesses that she lacks Rick's dedication to the profession, explaining that she is just trying out the position as teacher. When Rick explains that he did not train to be a teacher but is actually an engineer who cannot find employment in that field because of his skin color, Gillian accepts this explanation without much thought. Only after she confronts proof of the racism to which Rick has become unwillingly unaccustomed does she gain any understanding of the problem.

In a scene vital to the development of the conflict between cultures that Gillian and Rick experience, they go to a restaurant. Gillian has carefully planned the event to be a special evening for the two. Before long, the duo notice the exceptionally slow service and the inattentive waiters. Other diners take no pains to hide their curious and disapproving glances from the mixed couple. It is Gillian who storms from the restaurant, and she later vents her anger on Rick, challenging him as to why he did not defend himself. She explains that she has observed him suffer ill-concealed insults from their fellow workers and from rude members of the public when they have taken students on field trips, and her frustration with his passive attitude has mounted. It is a telling moment that tries Gillian's love and proves her ignorance, and it serves as an epiphany for her character. She has two choices: she can trust that her love for Rick will be enough to help them overcome society's unvoiced but highly apparent attitude toward what it considers a type of forbidden love, or she can end the romance at that point.

Gillian Blanchard chooses the hope of romance to combat the threat of societal racism. Her choice, along with the strides the members of Rick's class make toward coming to terms with their own prejudices, allows the novel to conclude on an upbeat note.

See also: Braithwaite, Rick; Forbidden Love; *To Sir, with Love*
References: Herdeck et al., 1979; Ousby, 1988

BONBON, LOUISE

Louise Bonbon serves as the white half of a racially mixed couple in Ernest J. Gaines's novel *Of Love and Dust* (1967). Frail, childlike, and pitiful in appearance, Louise first attracts a black worker, Marcus Payne, as a way to seek revenge on her husband, the Cajun overseer Sidney Bonbon. Brought to a Louisiana plantation to work off a charge of murder through hard labor, Marcus joins Louise as a victim of Sidney's cruel treatment. The three become members of a tragic love triangle.

Louise's most noticeable characteristic, repeatedly mentioned by the novel's first-person narra-

tor and by other characters, is her childlike quality. Not only does she resemble a child in her small stature, but her emotional immaturity and total dependence on someone she hates allows her to assume the role of an abused young girl. Married to Sidney as a teen, Louise remains virtually a prisoner in her house on the plantation belonging to a man her husband is blackmailing. She tries repeatedly to escape, but her husband always finds her. When she once returned to her disagreeable original family, her father and brothers returned her to Sidney, encouraging her husband to beat her should she run again. When Louise at last stops running, she begins to plot revenge against her cruel husband, who takes a black mistress but gives her no love. She never leaves her small plot of land unless Sidney accompanies her. Left with only her sickly toddler daughter, Judy, and an elderly black maid, Aunt Margaret, for companionship, she experiences a loneliness that she hopes Marcus can remedy.

Although Louise does not realize that Marcus seduces her simply to get back at Sidney for his harsh treatment, she probably would not care; a desire for revenge against Sidney is something the two share. As Marcus repeatedly visits her during Sidney's absences, they eventually fall in love. They plan their escape, even though Aunt Margaret warns Louise that they will never be allowed to leave. True to her childish nature, Louise chooses to ignore the realities of attitudes toward relationships between white women and black men in the South in 1948. Her husband's relationship with a black woman, accepted grudgingly by the other black workers and ignored by whites, makes Louise's situation and her own forbidden love all the more frustrating.

In their naïveté, neither Marcus nor Louise recognize that the plantation owner sets them up to fail in their escape in order to rid himself of Sidney. Both Louise and her lover remain destined to meet a sad end. Although she does not die with Marcus, Louise's final vestige of mental stability does. The only positive aspect of her fate is that, gripped by an insanity causing her to be removed to a mental institution, she likely will not miss her daughter.

See also: The Black Experience in America, 1600–1945; Gaines, Ernest J.; *Of Love and Dust;* Payne, Marcus; Violence
References: Coombs, 1972; "Gaines, Ernest J.," 1994; LeSeur, 1995; Papa 1993

BOVARY, EMMA

Gustave Flaubert's creation of Emma Bovary as the main character of his novel *Madame Bovary* (1857) remains one of the more important literary acts of the nineteenth century. As a woman who seeks release for her passions in what ultimately prove to be unsatisfying love affairs, Emma became a Western archetype for female characters who would thereafter appear in novels the world over. She especially caught the imagination of American writers, from Kate Chopin to John O'Hara.

Although modern readers are unlikely to be offended by indiscreet physical love as an aspect of plot, Flaubert's contemporaries found his Emma shocking. That young women just like Emma existed in reality had rarely been openly acknowledged on the printed page; her creation opened a floodgate of reaction from women who wrote to Flaubert declaring that they recognized themselves in his young French heroine. An uncomplicated figure, Emma is a young woman raised on the romance offered by writers such as Sir Walter Scott; she identifies with the great tragic historical heroines like Mary, Queen of Scots, Héloïse, and Joan of Arc. She adores sentimental love songs and ballads, thrills over romantic keepsake albums of her schoolmates as she imagines herself in the Gothic engravings she views, and enjoys to excess portraying the suffering induced by her mother's death. No one could have been less prepared for marriage to the dull, unimaginative, and decidedly unromantic Charles than Emma.

To be fair to the character of Charles Bovary, no male could live up to Emma's romantic expectations. She symbolizes that woman tricked by an androcentric society into dreaming of attaining an ideal existing only in romantic novels. She remains a victim of deception perpetrated

Jennifer Jones played Emma Bovary and Louis Jordan played Rodolphe Boulanger, the man who seduces Emma, in this 1949 film version of Madame Bovary, Gustave Flaubert's *1857 novel that deeply shocked readers of the time with its tale of a woman who seeks release for her passions in what ultimately prove to be unsatisfying love affairs. (Photofest)*

by males who demand that women be passive in public but sexually aggressive in private. Most telling is the scene in which Emma is described as becoming more and more bold in her behavior while in public with her lover; she even dresses *like a man*. This, then, is Emma's true transgression; she assumes the active role of the male in a society unprepared for gender equality.

Flaubert employs the time-honored tradition in romance writing of pitting the rational world, represented by Charles as a man of pseudo-science, against a world born from imagination, represented by Emma through her interest in literature, art, and music. She longs for a soulmate who can share her passion. When Leon Dupuis, a neighbor in the Bovary's eventual home of Yonville, falls in love with Emma, she secretly welcomes his attentions and the interest his presence adds to her life, but her behavior reflects the high moral standards her society requires. Leon, discouraged over his unrequited love, eventually departs, and Emma sinks into despair over the loss of a man who represented the courtly love for which she had spent a lifetime preparing.

Emma soon comes to understand that pent-up desires may overflow in response to steady affection, causing her to consummate her forbidden love with Leon several years after their first meeting. But this happens only following an earlier affair with Rodolphe Boulanger, a man far more experienced than Emma, who sets out to seduce her and then severs their contact, leaving her to suffer depression and physical prostration.

Never does Emma participate in her affairs without tremendous feelings of guilt. Although Charles and her daughter repel her, Emma constantly attempts to fulfill the stereotypical role of the perfect wife and mother forced on her by her culture. Her inability to separate herself from the early moral teachings of the church causes Emma continual conflict. Even while betraying a husband who idolizes her (albeit for reasons she cannot recognize), Emma remains a sympathetic character, retaining an air of naïveté toward the world and those men who seek to use her. Charles wants her as a possession, something he can display to others to enhance his own image. Rodolphe, an aristocrat and the veteran of many love affairs, indulges himself in using Emma as an exquisite sexual object. The younger Leon loves and desires Emma, but he tires of her increasingly melodramatic behavior, brought on by her mounting feelings of desperation. Leon eventually sees Emma as a burden, the stereotypical married woman who threatens his future career. Finally, Lheureux, the local merchant and moneylender, takes advantage of Emma's lack of financial experience to lure her into monumental debt, ruinous to her family, her marriage, and her reputation. These men figuratively and literally extract all Emma has to give, driving her to self-destruction after first convincing her that they are trustworthy allies and then deserting her.

Although a pitiable character, Emma must be seen as complicit in her destruction. She constructs her own tragic plot, indulging in extravagant material goods as well as in forbidden passion and establishing relationships doomed to failure. She labels men "treacherous," yet she excels in duplicity and fabrication. She reviles Charles for demolishing her spirit through his dull devotion, yet her own bright flames of emotion consume and destroy. Her final stage of near-madness is predictable but not unworthy of sympathy. The fatal arsenic that she ingests mimics in its slow, horrific physical destruction the emotional dismantling of the romantic soul of Emma Bovary.

See also: Flaubert, Gustave; *Madame Bovary;* Patriarchal Marriage
References: Charlton, 1984; Comfort, 1974; Praz, 1974; Williams, 1974

BRAITHWAITE, EDWARD R. (TED)

Edward R. Braithwaite, author of the popular novel *To Sir, with Love* (1959) was born in Georgetown, Guyana (then British Guiana), on June 27, 1912. His early schooling in Guyana was followed by extended upper-level education in the United States and England. He graduated with a bachelor of science degree from New York City College (1940), received a master of science in physics from Gains College (1949), and went on to study at the London University Institute of Education. After serving in World War II in the Royal Air Force, he returned to London, where he worked as a schoolteacher from 1950 to 1957 and as a London County Council welfare officer from 1958 to 1960. While living for a time in Paris, Braithwaite, described as charming and reserved, served as a human rights officer in the Veterans' Foundation for three years (1960–1963), after which he lectured and served as an education officer for the United Nations Educational, Scientific, and Cultural Organization. Additional public service included a position as Guyana's representative to the United Nations and later as ambassador from Guyana to Venezuela (1968–1969).

His novel *To Sir, with Love* a highly autobiographical work, has been criticized by some for its lack of imagination. This is not because the book lacks entertainment value, as its continued popularity with modern reading audiences attest. Rather, the criticism stems from the fact that by drawing on his own teaching experience as a black in English society (his main character is even named Rick Braithwaite), Braithwaite adds little information that does not come directly from his life. In spite of such negative evaluation of the author, the novel received the Ainsfield-Wolf Award in 1960, enjoyed several reprintings, and also appeared in film version in 1967. Braithwaite wrote a sequel, published as *Paid Servant* (1962), and an underappreciated tragic novel, *A Choice of Straws* (1967), which offered a foray into the racial psychology of the white working class. His 1962 travel book, *A Kind of Homecoming,* projects nostalgia for preslavery connections to Africa, and the novel *Reluctant Neighbours* (1972) contains further autobiographical information.

Braithwaite supposedly felt honored when Jamaica's minister of education, Edward Allen, banned *To Sir, with Love.* The banning seems to undermine criticism that his novel was not an ideological work. Accenting the themes of racism and forbidden love in touching on a white schoolgirl's crush on a black instructor and interracial romance, Braithwaite challenges his novel's readers to consider the importance of societal views in shaping attitudes toward personal relationships.

See also: *To Sir, with Love*
References: Herdeck et al., 1979; Ousby, 1988

BRAITHWAITE, RICK

Author Edward R. Braithwaite gives his own name to the autobiographical main character, Rick Braithwaite, in his 1959 novel, *To Sir, with Love.* Rick, a black engineer from British Guiana who cannot find work in his chosen occupation because of his race, ends up teaching in a high school in London's East End. His students are poor, coarse, and verbally abusive, and they have used their highly developed sense of the offensive to drive other instructors away. Rising above their jibes to demand that his students address him as "Sir" in order to instill in them the idea of respect for authority figures, Braithwaite sets out to challenge his students' imaginations as well as their intelligence. He also must decide the extent of his feelings toward a female instructor, Gillian Blanchard. Ultimately, Rick becomes a teacher in all his relationships, including his romantic relationship with Gillian. She must learn the harsh reality of racism with which Rick is already too familiar.

Most of the plot focuses on Rick's classroom technique and its ultimate application to life outside the classroom. Rather than using textbooks, Rick establishes reality as his lesson plan. Under his guidance, the students acquire the social skills their poverty-stricken life styles have not encouraged. He involves the students in activities that vary from learning to make a proper salad in the classroom to taking field trips to museums and other cultural centers. He recruits a female teacher to guide the girls in learning how to apply makeup, while he discusses with the boys the fact that women are beings deserving of respect. Patient, but not indulgent, Rick gradually begins to gain the students' undivided attention.

Rick shares his own experiences to reach his students. He lets them know that he struggled to escape from poverty much like their own and that he found his escape through education. By treating his students with respect, Rick earns their esteem, and true communication begins to take place. The new relationships are not without their challenges, however. Rick must deal with a high school crush on the part of one student, Pamela Dare, and he must ignore the racial slurs in which even this racially mixed population of students occasionally indulges. Some of his fellow teachers become jealous over Rick's progress with the difficult class, but he handles their interference with as much grace as he does that of his students.

The major threat to Rick's confidence is Gillian's attitude. In a scene best reflecting his fear of the effect of racism, he and Gillian at last confront each other regarding that looming specter. This scene offers an excellent example of external conflict—that of man/woman versus environment—leading to internal conflict for the protagonists. Because both feel their love is worthy of sacrifice and defense, Rick is able to channel Gillian's anger and frustration into a positive plan for their future together as a racially mixed couple living in a hostile culture.

As a character, Rick remains relatively flat, causing change in others rather than experiencing any alteration himself other than that broadening of emotional horizons brought on by his experience of romance. His characterization threatens to shape him into an unrealistic being, a symbolic figure who represents a moral ideology, but it also sharpens the contrast between Rick and his students. He possesses integrity and self-respect, whereas they possess few morals and little, if any, self-respect; he represents an escape from oppression, but his students feel such an escape is beyond their capabilities; he trusts in a system of education, whereas his students trust nothing. In the end, Rick, or "Sir," becomes a mythical figure, but this works well within the context of this story chronicling a quest for freedom through education.

See also: Blanchard, Gillian; Braithwaite, Edward R. (Ted); Dare, Pamela; *To Sir, with Love*
References: Herdeck et al., 1979; Ousby, 1988

BRANDON, COLONEL

Colonel Brandon, the sensible older male figure in Jane Austen's *Sense and Sensibility* (1811), represents the strong, silent male stereotype of literature. Ever-devoted to the novel's younger heroine, Marianne Dashwood, he must wait in the shadows for her to notice him. Along with Marianne and the younger, more dashing Willoughby, Brandon makes up one of the novel's two love triangles. Although Marianne comprehends Brandon's feelings of affection, she remains distracted by the more ostentatious Willoughby, feeling she could never be attracted to a man twenty years her senior. Willoughby's storybook rescue of the slightly injured Marianne and his appreciation for poetry and the "higher" sensibilities captivate this younger of the two Dashwood sisters. Brandon's maturity, aristocratic background, and genteel observance of decorum cause him to withhold an expression of love that he knows will not be gladly received. These character traits conflict with those of the more brash Marianne and Willoughby, while they complement those of the older and more sensible Dashwood sister, Elinor.

In addition to his age, Brandon's own early and tragic experience in unrequited love allows him to act as a voice of wisdom for the novel. Austen uses Brandon's experience with the societal edict against mixed-class marriages to call attention to its injustice. His suffering due to the labeling of his affection as forbidden love causes him to look with indulgence on what he sees as Marianne's unspoiled approach to life. In this manner, Brandon becomes a more interesting character, showing his human frailty in allowing his concern for Marianne's happiness to override his better judgment. In addition, Brandon's knowledge of details of Willoughby's past cause conflict. Although he feels he should warn the Dashwood sisters, he hesitates to share his knowledge in the hopes that Willoughby may be sincere. Though his hesitation may later be viewed as foolish in the light of Marianne's desertion by Willoughby, Brandon proves his genuine love for the young woman by placing her desires before his own.

When Marianne again requires aid, this time Brandon acts the hero. His actions are far more important than those of Willoughby in the early "rescue" of Marianne. Brandon symbolically rescues her from suffering for the mistake she made by placing her faith in Willoughby. Like the knights of old who served their mistresses without question, he places himself in Marianne's physical and emotional service with no promise of reward; his steady, reserved constancy more than proves his devotion. After Marianne's recovery, she recognizes Brandon for the prize he is, and the two finally marry.

The character of Colonel Brandon remains essential to solving the intricacies of plot in the novel. In addition to providing necessary background on Willoughby and serving as his foil, Brandon offers a position as rector to Elinor's love interest, thereby eventually providing the means for that couple to marry. Through him, Austen states that consistency is one measure of good character.

See also: Austen, Jane; Dashwood, Marianne; Ferrars, Edward; *Pride and Prejudice; Sense and Sensibility*
References: Britannica, 1997; Clayton, 1987a; Copeland and McMaster, 1997; de Rougemont, 1983; Gard, 1992; Gilbert and Gubar, 1985c; Praz, 1974; Watt, 1963

BRODER, HERMAN

Herman Broder, protagonist of Isaac Bashevis Singer's 1972 novel, *Enemies: A Love Story,* represents the typically tortured Singer character. An emotionally complex but not particularly sympathetic man, Broder symbolizes well the paradox presented in the novel's title. Although he becomes involved in three different romances, he lacks the stability of personality to benefit from any of the relationships with three very different women. Instead, each of the relationships spawns wrenching conflict for Herman, a lecherous character who indulges in the newfound hedonism represented by America. As a Polish Jew forced to hide in a hayloft for three years to escape death through Nazi persecution, Herman feels the occasional attraction to his racial and spiritual heritage, the effects of which he covets in others but can never himself obtain. Rather than spend his energy in pursuit of spiritual and emotional happiness, he instead seeks to regain the anonymity of the hayloft, apart from his commitment to and persecution by love.

Admittedly, Herman has had a difficult life. His two daughters and his Polish wife, Tamara Broder, a dull woman whom Herman had already decided to divorce, were taken away to prison camps and, as far as Herman knows, killed. If not for the love of his mother's former servant, Yadwiga, a Gentile who risks possible execution when she hides Herman in the hayloft, he would have died with his family. Because Yadwiga is a Gentile, she represents an emotional threat and an "otherness" to Herman, just as the Nazis represent a physical threat and "otherness." His feelings of repulsion toward Yadwiga are overcome by a guilty gratitude based on his forced dependence. Lacking the strength of character to override his guilt and revulsion, Herman enters into a second loveless marriage when he takes Yadwiga with him to America. The unexpected return of Tamara makes Herman a bigamist through no fault of his own. But Herman's suffering does nothing to ennoble him. He is a crass, misogynist isolationist who confines Yadwiga to their Brooklyn apartment while he ventures into the Bronx for an affair with the beautiful and seductive Masha Tortshiner. He also visits the forgiving Tamara in her Manhattan apartment in search of purely physical love.

Although any of the three women could likely satisfy at least a portion of Herman's needs, he rejects all three. Yadwiga had been a servant; therefore, the love and devotion for Herman that ennobles her appears to him demeaning and con-

fining. Tamara remains a mother figure, literally the mother of Herman's children but also nurturing in the manner of a mature woman who knows her place in a strongly matriarchal domestic Jewish subculture. Herman sees himself caught in an oedipal relationship with Tamara, who, like Yadwiga, represents a sacred family relationship that Herman needs to deny in order to feel sexual gratification. Tamara's having remained sexually faithful to Herman during their years of separation does little to endear her to him, for he finds her fidelity oppressive. Only when she lies, pretending to have had affairs during her imprisonment, does he find her sexually attractive. Finally, Masha offers a passion and allure missing from Herman's other relationships as well as a pleasing appearance. Herman enjoys the "dirty" verbal exchanges that generally follow their sexual encounters in which he can act on his need for perversity. His need for Masha is reminiscent of the need for an addictive drug. She is as inconsistent as Yadwiga and Tamara are consistent. She supplies the open conflict Herman craves, but Herman also craves the control afforded by order, and Masha represents chaos, just as the Nazis did. As a representative Diasporan, or wandering Jewish figure, Herman cannot settle with any of the women. Not only has he been displaced geographically from Poland to America, but he has undergone a displacement from any emotionally stable center to which he might turn for orientation.

Herman, although complicated psychologically, remains a one-dimensional romantic figure, capable only of the physical aspects of love. Women seem the bane, rather than the balm, of his existence. Masha's ex-husband compares women to all-consuming spiders during a conversation with Herman, as Singer provides traditional imagery of woman as monster to bolster Herman's negative opinion of females. Herman denies his traditional male duty as progenitor when Masha and Yadwiga both want babies, and when Yadwiga becomes pregnant, he simply disappears, fearing that if he stays, he will be devoured by his three "wives" like an insect caught in a sticky web.

Herman does have some positive feelings toward women, acknowledging that at least they have always displayed compassion toward him. But even this aspect of his relationship with females represents a threat because he seems to lack the capacity for compassion himself. Herman fails to recognize that he is the weaver of the complicated web of deceit that represents his life. In an ironic turn, he assumes the traditionally passive female role as he victimizes and silences himself through absence, while each of the three women refuses to assume the stance of victim.

See also: Enemies: A Love Story; Singer, Isaac Bashevis; War
References: Bilik, 1981; Farrell, 1994; Forrey, 1981; Halio, 1991; Studies, 1981

BRONTË, CHARLOTTE AND EMILY

English authors and sisters Charlotte and Emily Brontë electrified a world used to novels of manners and sentimentality with the 1847 publication of their Gothic romances, *Jane Eyre* and *Wuthering Heights.* Modern readers consider both novels as seminal Gothic romances that, along with Mary Shelley's *Frankenstein,* provided blueprints for many to follow in their use of a dark, brooding Byronic hero. They also shaped novels dependent less on plot and more on the psychological world of their protagonists. These approaches to novel writing appeared totally alien to the Brontës' contemporaries.

Some nineteenth-century critics declared Charlotte's daydream-filled novel difficult to read and lacking in form, analysis, and restraint. But Charlotte's voice, mimed through the diminutive but determined governess Jane, struck a chord with oppressed women everywhere who, caught up like Jane Eyre in a patriarchal culture, craved independence. Emily's *Wuthering Heights* did not enjoy such a positive popular reception, and because of her early death, she would never know of the eventual success of her novel. Contemporary readers did not enjoy the contrast between the homely and somehow familiar hearth at Thrushcross Grange and the wild Gothic extravagances of Wuthering Heights. Many failed to realize that the conflicting traits of the two homes symbolized the conflicting ideology and values of their respective inhabitants. Readers accepting of Charlotte's Jane questioned the vulgarities of Emily's Byronic hero, Heathcliff, who seemed simultaneously a gentleman and the devil himself.

Born in 1816 into the family of clergyman Patrick Brontë and his wife Maria Branwell, Charlotte was the third daughter, following Maria and Elizabeth. Charlotte's birth was rapid-

ly followed by that of three additional children, Emily (1818–1848), Anne (1820–1849), and the Brontës' only boy, Patrick Branwell (1817–1848). The Brontë children apparently had strong literary-minded models in their parents: their father wrote poetry, a novel, and, of course, sermons, and their mother wrote essays. The family moved from Thornton to Haworth, a village on the Yorkshire moors, in 1820. The death of their mother in 1821 from cancer was the first of many untimely deaths in the Brontë family. Although Mr. Brontë attempted to find a wife to act as mother to his large brood, he did not succeed. The children's strict Aunt Branwell moved in with the Brontës to care for the family until her death in 1842.

Initial attempts at educating the girls proved disastrous. After their mother's death, Charlotte and Emily joined the older sisters at a charitable institution, Cowan Bridge School. Charlotte would later memorialize the school in *Jane Eyre* as the infamous Lowood. Maria Brontë, recognizable in the novel as the suffering Helen Burns, and Elizabeth both returned home in 1825. Having fallen ill in the spartan and sometimes unsanitary school conditions, both girls later died from typhoid fever and consumption (tuberculosis). Charlotte and Emily were immediately removed from Cowan Bridge.

The four surviving Brontë children entertained themselves in the isolation on the moors, following various imaginary pursuits. The writing of tales became a major form of escape from the reality of the world outside the parsonage. When Mr. Brontë gave Branwell a dozen toy soldiers, all four children set to work to create the imaginary kingdoms of Gondal and Angria. Together, Charlotte and Branwell constructed the history of Angria, whereas Emily and Anne had control over Gondal. These enthrallments resulted in the production of dozens of tiny volumes, chronicling adventures that mirrored the popular writing styles of the day, such as those of Sir Walter Scott and Lord Byron. A well-known Romantic Age poet, infamous for his scandalous love affairs, Byron would greatly influence characterization in novels by Charlotte and Emily.

The children's fantasy writing continued over many years, even during Charlotte's experience at Roe Head school, first as a pupil from 1831 to 1832 and then as an instructor several years later. Charlotte's 1831 departure to Roe Head, a different and far better school than Cowan Bridge, left Emily and Anne to help their Aunt Branwell care for the house and their moody brother. The importance of a strong domestic scene reflected in *Wuthering Heights*' nurturing Thrushcross Grange hearth had its seeds in Emily's experience at the Brontës' isolated home.

The tales of Angria seemed to have offered Charlotte some release from a daily classroom routine that she found neither challenging nor pleasurable. The position as a teacher offered no enjoyment for Charlotte, but she realized it was one of the few available to women. Harboring precise ideas about what she desired in a husband, Charlotte rejected a handful of marriage proposals and left Roe Head. In the interim between 1832 and 1835, she took charge of tutoring Emily, Anne, and Branwell, and their bonds of affection further strengthened. Eventually Charlotte departed to serve in several governess positions.

In 1842, after Anne and Branwell had served for a time as tutors, Aunt Branwell unexpectedly offered the girls a small amount of money to open their own school. Emily and Charlotte decided to first study in Brussels for a time at a French school in order to improve their own education, a move that had disastrous but important consequences for Charlotte. Her romantic ideas about life led her to fall in love with Constantine Heger, a devout Catholic and married man who ran the school Emily and Charlotte attended. Although no evidence exists that suggests Heger ever encouraged Charlotte in any way, when the sisters moved home following their aunt's death later in 1842, Charlotte was soon drawn back to Brussels. No doubt her unrequited love and experiences in Brussels yielded the material for all her novels. *Villette* (1853), in particular, is notable for its characterization of the terrible loneliness experienced by Lucy Snow, a thinly transparent version of Charlotte herself.

Charlotte's absence served as a period of creativity for Emily. She lived alone with her father and began working to separate her poetry into notebooks. When Anne moved back home, Emily enjoyed their reunion, and the two young women enthusiastically kept up their fantasy chronicles.

Charlotte at last returned to England, hoping to curb her unreturned passion, and the Brontë sisters attempted to open the school for which

they had long planned. The flyers they circulated announcing the school elicited not a single expression of interest. Soon after, the Brontës abandoned their hopes for founding an educational institution. Charlotte wrote love letters to Heger, to which she apparently received no replies other than a curbed friendliness and later total silence. By 1845, when Charlotte realized she would reap neither romance nor monetary profits from the world, she turned seriously to writing. Branwell, unsuccessful at painting and a failure in a previous job at a train station, was fired from his tutoring post, supposedly for falling in love with his mistress and for alcohol and drug abuse.

An accidental discovery of Emily's Gondal verses helped Charlotte envision a way to escape from poverty by selling the Brontës' writings. The sisters' verses, published at their own expense in 1846, were issued as a commercially unsuccessful collection titled *Poems by Currer, Ellis and Acton Bell*. With this first publication, the sisters adopted the pseudonyms they would also use with their novels. The pseudonyms provided anonymity for the women with the public but especially with publishers, who generally did not look seriously upon writing by women. Uninhibited by the failure of their first writing project, all the Brontë women continued writing by composing novels. Charlotte's first novel, *The Professor*, would be published posthumously in 1857; in this work she adopted a male point of view and drew heavily on her experiences in Brussels for her fictional elements. Like her final two novels, *Shirley* (1849) and *Villette* (1853), the surface realism of *The Professor* was supported on a framework of dreams, visions, and romantic adventures, some Gothic in nature. But Charlotte's second novel, *Jane Eyre*, best reflects Charlotte's own life and her desire for an independence and strength seldom associated with young women of her day. The fate of the ranting Bertha Mason Rochester stood as a cautionary tale about a woman denied freedom of creativity and passion within a patriarchal marriage.

As Currer Bell, Charlotte became an overnight sensation after publishing *Jane Eyre*, despite critical voices clamoring about the Gothic rendering of a woman's fantasies mixed with the romanticized madness represented by the mysterious Mr. Rochester. Charlotte's success was followed by the appearance of Anne's *Agnes Grey* and Emily's *Wuthering Heights.* Also published in 1847, they were held by T. C. Newby to be released following the raised interest and curiosity in the "Bells" created by the appearance of *Jane Eyre.* All three women at last journeyed to London to meet their publisher and to be introduced to the public by their true identities.

The Brontë sisters were not to enjoy their elated state for long. After a history of substance abuse, their brother Branwell died in September 1848. Emily caught a severe cold at his funeral, leading to a lung inflammation that caused her death in December; Anne would follow her siblings in death in May 1849. The sad fact that *Wuthering Heights* did not merit popular acceptance before Emily's death caused Charlotte to later tell her biographer that she had not been able to properly enjoy her own success. In 1850, she composed a biographical note for the reissue of Emily's novel along with a few of her poems.

The importance of Emily Brontë's writing lies in its sheer power of inventiveness, eye for macabre detail, and mystical approach to life's harsh realities. Considered the best poet of the three Brontë sisters, she endows *Wuthering Heights* with the poet's appreciation for concise expression and the production of dense imagery. Although passionate in tone, her novel retains a certain order, akin to Emily's own personality. An isolated young girl who loved the moors and the intensity that days shaped by romantic fantasy produced, Emily Brontë wrote of her characters' passions as if she found herself completely at home with them.

In Charlotte's remaining years, she lived alone with her father, continuing with her writing and her attempts to make and retain outside friendships. William Makepeace Thackeray voiced great admiration for Charlotte's work, and in its third printing, *Jane Eyre* was compared to Thackeray's *Vanity Fair* (1847–1848). Charlotte also became acquainted with the hugely popular writer Elizabeth Gaskell, who would later write the biography *The Life of Charlotte Brontë* in 1857. In 1852, Charlotte married her father's curate, Arthur Bell Nicholls, although indications exist that she never loved her husband. Pregnant in 1855 with their first child, she succumbed to tuberculosis and died.

The admiration for the Brontës as a group became official with the founding of the Brontë Society in 1893. Their influence on women writers who followed cannot be overestimated. Virginia Woolf would write in *A Room of One's Own* (1929) of the "fiery imagination, the wild poetry, the brilliant wit," and "the brooding wisdom" that stands as the modern writer's inheritance from women such as the Brontës.

See also: Byronic Hero; Gothic Romance; *Jane Eyre;* Patriarchal Marriage; Violence; *Wuthering Heights*

References: Allen, 1993; Blain, Clements, and Grundy, 1990; Drabble, 1995; Ellis, 1989; Fraiman, 1993; Gilbert and Gubar, 1996a; Leavis, 1966; Pater, 1974; Winnifrith, 1996

BUCHANAN, DAISY

As the lovely but insecure heroine in F. Scott Fitzgerald's *The Great Gatsby* (1925), Daisy Buchanan and her existence of material indulgence represent the lifestyle that Fitzgerald himself both admired and pursued. Daisy is beautiful, attracting male admirers since her youth, attracted herself by the ideals of romance, but not a woman who would ever trade the sick security of wealth for the challenge of true love. Having formed a relationship as a young debutante with the decidedly middle-class Jay Gatsby, Daisy was unable to maintain the passion of their love in the face of their later separation. While Gatsby is in the military, Daisy finds herself much in demand by society's most eligible bachelors, and she agrees to marry the wealthy college football hero, Tom Buchanan. By the time she realizes that Tom never intends to be faithful to anyone other than himself, Daisy is too dependent on indolent wealth to take the opportunity to escape her passionless marriage.

When Gatsby years later buys a mansion on property across Long Island Sound from the Buchanans, Daisy sees him as her salvation. Flattered by Gatsby's attentions and dazzled by his mysterious, newfound wealth, Daisy responds to his desire to rekindle their romance. As the familiar stranger, Gatsby becomes part of a love triangle that Daisy encourages, or at least she leads him to believe she encourages it. She finds Gatsby at once appealing and repellent, with a recent history of sudden riches that no one understands. The source of his money remains unknown, and Daisy joins the local idle rich in gossip on the subject. She knows his ostentatious parties are gauche, but she has not been the focus for a man's attention for a long while. Vulgar or not, Daisy takes comfort in Gatsby and the change he brings to her existence with her philandering husband.

Although Daisy disappoints Gatsby by admitting to having loved Tom in the past, if not in the present, Gatsby's disillusionment cannot be totally blamed on Daisy. He expects to find the Daisy of his youth, unsullied and innocent. Instead he meets a mature woman long ago seduced by the lifestyle he himself desires to adopt. Tom accuses Gatsby of achieving his fortune outside of the law, and Daisy's temporary courage in confronting her husband with her love for Gatsby fades. When the men argue, it is her husband to whom she appeals for help. There is no room for Gatsby in Daisy's established routine, other than as a temporary distraction from her unhappy but necessary role as Tom's long-suffering and very rich wife. Tom even orders her to leave the scene, remarking that her presumptuous would-be lover will bother her no more.

When Gatsby insists on pursuing his romantic role and playing white knight by assuming the blame for Daisy's hit-and-run accident, she is more than happy to allow it. As the narrator, Nick Carraway, remarks, Gatsby had supplied a false sense of security for Daisy, giving her, if only temporarily, the one thing she lacked in life. But when her husband acts as an agent of reality, Daisy realizes Gatsby's promises of a stable future are based on lies, just like the fantasy life he has created for himself. His ardor remains real enough, but he cannot offer Daisy the trustworthy material security that she needs for survival.

Just as she takes no responsibility for the vehicular homicide she causes, Daisy assumes no responsibility for Gatsby's subsequent death. Her conspicuous absence at his funeral means that she has been fully restored to her careless world where, according to Nick, she and Tom safely retreat, leaving others to clean up whatever mess they might leave behind.

> *See also:* Buchanan, Tom; Carraway, Nick; Fitzgerald, F. Scott; Gatsby, Jay; *The Great Gatsby;* The Lost Generation; Love Triangle
> *References:* Hart, 1995; Piper, 1970; Washington, 1995

BUCHANAN, TOM

Tom Buchanan is a character given one of the least enviable positions in American literature. As the brutish wealthy husband of Daisy Buchanan in F. Scott Fitzgerald's *The Great Gatsby* (1925),

Tom stands as a physical impediment to the realization of Gatsby's romantic dream. Gatsby cherishes his memory of a Daisy from his youth who was his first true love. He indulges in a romance fantasy that Tom, a character representing reality, helps to dissolve. Daisy, Tom, and Gatsby form a love triangle in which both men remain pawns to Daisy's egocentrism. Because neither Tom nor Daisy are particularly likable characters, they serve to make Gatsby more appealing to readers.

Tom symbolizes the American Dream realized, just as Gatsby represents a perversion of that dream. He is a member of the social strata supported by "old money," a strata Gatsby's nouveau riche status will never allow him to reach. Following his stint as a star football player at college, Tom and Daisy live close to his home in Chicago. After marriage, they travel in France before ending up on the East Coast, on Long Island Sound. He clearly represents the vice of indulgence, and although others may envy Tom, his wealth cannot buy their respect.

The origin of Tom's family wealth is clear, whereas that of Gatsby's is not; Gatsby may even have engaged in criminal activity to gain his money. Tom understands this, just as he understands his wife's attraction to Gatsby, who can never shake off his humble origins. Of all the male characters in the novel, Tom knows Daisy best, and he understands that Gatsby provides an easy escape from the life she does not enjoy but must have. He indulges Daisy's desire to participate in what he most likely views as "slumming," a credible activity for the idle rich.

The reader learns early of Tom's multiple betrayals of Daisy. When the novel's narrator, Daisy's cousin Nick Carraway, dines for the first time with the Buchanans, everyone at the party understands that Tom has received a phone call from his mistress. One guest even comments to Nick on the brazen character of the mistress's actions. Daisy herself resists that topic but tells Nick of Tom's absence at the birth of their daughter, whom she hopes will grow up to be a fool, declaring that the best condition for a woman.

When Gatsby compels Daisy to face Tom with the fact that she now loves Gatsby, Tom forces from Daisy a confession that she had, at least, once loved her husband. Tom knows this will cause Gatsby to doubt Daisy, and he plays his cards well. His threat to expose illegal business dealings by Gatsby represents the hard malice with which he confronts life.

The tragedy that shatters the triangle is not of Tom's design, and he need assume no responsibility. When Daisy commits vehicular manslaughter, accidentally killing Tom's mistress, Gatsby shoulders the blame. Tom easily exerts his power over the confused and culpable Daisy, convincing her to abandon Gatsby to suffer the consequences of her crime alone.

The message of the novel seems to be that established wealth, no matter how crass and self-indulgent it makes its owners, will triumph over true love. Tom's materialism holds Daisy's heart prisoner, whereas Gatsby's heroic sacrifice means little to her. Through no effort of his own, Tom retains his wealth, his wife, and his reputation, while Gatsby's dreams die with him. A flat character, Tom Buchanan remains static in his cynical view of love, based on an egoism that allows no room for concern for others.

See also: Buchanan, Daisy; Carraway, Nick; Fitzgerald, F. Scott; Gatsby, Jay; *The Great Gatsby;* The Lost Generation; Love Triangle
References: Hart, 1995; Piper, 1970; Washington, 1995

BUCK, PEARL SYDENSTRICKER

The first American woman to win the Nobel Prize for literature, Pearl Comfort Sydenstricker was born in Hillsboro, West Virginia, to Southern Presbyterian missionaries on furlough from China, on June 26, 1892. Although she had six siblings, Pearl was one of only three who would survive to adulthood. At age three months, she traveled with her family to China when her parents, Caroline and Absalom, returned to the mission field in Chinkiang (Zhenjiang) in the province of Kiangsu (Jiangsu). While Absalom spent months in the field and away from home, Caroline operated a small dispensary for the benefit of the local Chinese women. Pearl would live in China, where she learned to speak both English and Chinese, for most of her first forty years. The family's ministering routine was briefly interrupted by the 1900 Boxer Uprising, when Caroline evacuated with the children to Shanghai. Several months passed before the family could be certain of Absalom's safety. The family returned to the United States on furlough for a time.

Pearl attended and graduated from Randolph-Macon Woman's College in Lynchburg, Virginia

(1910–1914). Her plans to remain in the states were interrupted by a return to China in 1915 to attend her mother during a grave illness. While in China she met her husband, John Lossing Buck, whom she married in 1917, beginning an unhappy relationship that would endure for seventeen years. A Cornell graduate, John Buck was an agricultural economist. The Bucks lived in a poor rural province of China, Nanhsuchour (Nanxuzhou), where Pearl's experiences would later provide material used to write her many stories of China.

Following the birth in 1921 of a severely retarded child, Carol, who suffered from phenylketonuria, Pearl underwent a hysterectomy. The couple later adopted a second daughter named Janice. Both Pearl and John received teaching appointments on the campus of Nanking University, where they made their home from 1920 to 1933. These were very eventful years for Pearl. She began to write and publish in magazines, including *The Nation* and *Atlantic Monthly,* in 1920. Shortly after they moved to Nanking (Nanjing), Pearl's mother died, and her father moved in with Pearl and John. In March 1927, several westerners died in a military conflict called the Nanking Incident that sent the Bucks into hiding for a day. After rescue by Americans, the Bucks moved to Unzen, Japan, for a year before returning to their home in China.

Pearl's first novel, *East Wind, West Wind,* appeared in 1930, published by John Day Company. Its publisher, Richard Walsh, fell in love with Pearl, who returned his affections. Pearl's second novel, *The Good Earth* (1931), was a best-selling book for two years and won both the Pulitzer Prize in 1932 and the Howells Medal in 1935. In 1934 Pearl had permanently relocated to the United States to live in a farmhouse in Bucks County, Pennsylvania, allowing her to be closer to Carol, institutionalized in New Jersey, and to Richard Walsh.

In 1934, Walsh and Pearl divorced their respective spouses to marry; over the following years they would adopt six children. She became active in American civil rights and women's rights, publishing in various activist magazines and journals. Pearl also served as a trustee for Howard University from the early 1940s through the 1960s. With Walsh she founded a group dedicated to better understanding between the western and the eastern worlds that they named the

Pearl S. Buck, the first American woman to win the Nobel Prize for literature, is shown in a February 1968 photograph. (AP/Wide World Photos)

East and West Association. In 1949, Pearl established Welcome House, the first international adoption agency that encouraged interracial adoptions. In a related move, she also founded the Pearl S. Buck Foundation in 1964 to help provide support for children of mixed heritage living with their parents.

After winning the Nobel Prize for literature in 1938, Pearl Buck continued a prolific publishing career that would include more than eighty-five books of fiction, biography, autobiography, drama, and translation. She said she derived her simple, direct writing style from her study of Chinese novels. All of her novels depict the Chinese and their culture favorably, and she constantly stresses a concern for what she saw as the fundamental values of life: faith and family. *The Good Earth* and *Dragon Seed* (1942) remain highly popular. Her last works included *The Kennedy Women* (1970) and *China As I See It* (1970). When

she died in March 1973, she was buried at Green Hills Farm. Her farm was eventually included on the Registry of Historic Buildings, and it continues to draw thousands of visitors each year.

See also: The Good Earth
References: Conn, 1996; Davidson, 1995; Lipscomb, Webb, and Conn, 1994; Ousby, 1988

BURDEN, JIM

As the protagonist and narrator of Willa Cather's 1918 novel, *My Ántonia,* Jim Burden experiences unrequited love. Cather uses Burden to present her own memories of the Nebraska area where she grew up. Cather inserted a line from Virgil as the epigraph for her novel later translated by Burden as "The best days are the first to flee." As a college student, Burden remembers his first love and an earthiness about her that conflicted with his own intellectual aspirations. Still, when the quiet, studious Burden also contemplates Virgil's statement, "for I shall be the first, if I live, to bring the Muse into my country," he recalls as his own best days those spent with the Bohemian neighbor girl named Ántonia Shimerda in the Nebraska country cornfields.

Jim Burden's love for Ántonia has many layers of meaning. They meet as new arrivals on the great plains, where they spend their childhood years together exploring and celebrating the wonders of rural Nebraska. Although several years younger than Ántonia, Jim tutors her in English so that she in turn may teach her immigrant family new language skills. Jim remains in awe of Ántonia's strength, audacity, and grace as he observes her do a man's work on the farm. Jim and Ántonia share a brother-sister relationship, but Jim desires a more mature intimacy while Ántonia prefers to adore him as a sibling. He develops a mild jealousy of her male admirers, and she tries to protect him from the advances of loose young women.

My Ántonia is not, however, the story of a thwarted youthful crush. Jim and Ántonia enjoy a permanent emotional bond for several reasons. They share the wonder of their mutually new environment and maintain that wonder throughout their lives. Also, their grief over the suicide of Ántonia's father unites them. Finally, both Jim and Ántonia experience an intense and sincere pride in each other's accomplishments. Although Jim experiences romantic desire for Ántonia, the love they both share in their daily lives is based in their personal histories and remains more complex and satisfying than a merely erotic love.

For both characters, those "best days" that flee so quickly were the days of their childhood spent in the all-important American landscape. The great plains of Nebraska would remain the backdrop for the dreams of Jim Burden, even as he spent his adulthood in the big cities of the world. Ántonia, an inextricable presence in those "best days," indeed symbolized both the landscape and the muse to Jim. He names her as muse because she provides inspiration for his words: his story is her biography.

The name Jim Burden suggests both the burden of memory and the disappointment of lost love. But it is Ántonia's body, altered by hard labor on the farm and the burden of childbirth, that signifies the beautiful struggle that carved out the face of the American plains. The possessive pronoun preceding her name is ironic; she was not Jim Burden's or any other's Ántonia. Like the land she symbolizes, Ántonia could be neither possessed nor controlled. She thrived, stormed, and labored of her own will—a will made from love and suffering. Despite his strong attraction to the sophistication of the city, Burden feels forever enriched and privileged to observe and admire Ántonia's heroic struggle and ultimate victory over life's conflicts in the land from which she draws her sustenance.

See also: My Ántonia; Shimerda, Ántonia

References: Armstrong, 1990; Daiches, 1971; Davidson, 1995; Hoffman and Murphy, 1996; O'Brien, 1996

BUTLER, RHETT

Possibly one of the most recognized of all characters from romantic stories in the English language is *Gone with the Wind's* Rhett Butler. Author Margaret Mitchell's Byronic hero holds a position in an equally famous love triangle that includes the impetuous Scarlett O'Hara and the epitome of the southern gentleman, Ashley Wilkes. Independent and resourceful, handsome and wealthy, this roguish hero has captured female imaginations since his creation by Mitchell for her novel, first published in 1936. In her triangle, Mitchell establishes an interesting paradox through Scarlett's attraction to two men who stand in stark contrast to one another, both in physical appearance and in their ideologies.

Rhett first appears on the scene during a barbecue at Ashley Wilkes's plantation, where he makes plain that, although a Yankee, he represents no one and nothing other than himself and his own needs. He is rude, abrupt, and painfully realistic, injecting discord into the southerners' idyllic but obviously flawed view of life. Mitchell's novel is more than anything else a story of love and passion, but its political backdrop of the Civil War and the conflict slavery brings into its characters' lives cannot be ignored. Unlike Scarlett's various southern beaus, Rhett can see her for what she is, an intelligent but spoiled woman, self-centered but with a will and craving for independence that could be admired only by one who possesses an identical sense of self.

The reader first sees Rhett through Scarlett's eyes. His description places him firmly within the arena of the classic Byronic hero—tall and almost "too" muscular to be counted a member of the "gentility," with a dark complexion that's compared to that of a swarthy pirate. His black eyes boldly challenge the virginity of every "maiden" he sees, and although his outward demeanor remains cool, his personality exudes a passion hidden beneath that calm surface. The fact that Rhett, at thirty-five years of age, looks "old" to the teenage Scarlett supports his air of maturity and experience. According to rumor, that experience includes an overnight buggy ride with a Charleston girl, during which the girl remained pure, but Rhett was nevertheless told by her family that he must marry her or answer to her brother's dueling pistol. Declaring he'd rather be shot than marry a fool, he kills the brother in a duel and thus is no longer "received" by polite society, a fact that greatly heightens Scarlett's curiosity. When she responds to the story by respecting Rhett for refusing to marry a fool, the reader knows that these two will find reason to be together.

But that togetherness is long delayed, because Rhett at first offends Scarlett when he overhears her profession of undying love to Ashley Wilkes. Although Rhett declares Scarlett to be of a rare breed with admirable spirit, she considers him a boor. He will have to wait as Scarlett wades through two marriages before he can claim her as his own. He comes into contact with her on several important occasions over the years, embarrassing and frustrating her. Following the death of Scarlett's first husband, Charles Hamilton, Rhett dares to ask Scarlett for a dance while she remains in mourning, a social faux pas that scandalizes onlookers. They are even more scandalized when Scarlett accepts the invitation, and the two shock polite society for the first of what will be many times. Rhett later rescues Scarlett, Ashley's wife Melanie, and Melanie's baby from the Union Army's burning of Atlanta, earning the hero status he richly deserves.

In addition to his dashing physical presence, Rhett also evokes admiration for his own independent but scrupulously fair and generous spirit. After working throughout the Civil War in what appears to those around him to be a mercenary capacity, Rhett enlists to fight on the Rebel side just as they face defeat. Finding the role of the rebel irresistible, Rhett reinforces his reputation as a man who ignores odds that might cow other men.

He suffers from Scarlett's actions, but recognizes them as based on pure animal survival instinct. Thus, he understands her marriage to her sister's fiancé, as she moves to save her plantation

and support the many members of her family dependent on her. When Scarlett loses her second husband, Rhett at last proposes, promising the acquisitive Scarlett all the money she will ever need, and she accepts.

Left alone, the pair might have found happiness, but Scarlett's ever-present love and desire for Ashley Wilkes interferes. Rhett proves a fine stepfather to Scarlett's two children and dotes on his daughter, Bonnie, the couple's only child. In response, Scarlett locks Rhett out of her bedroom in misplaced loyalty to a nonexistent love that she imagines between herself and Ashley, even though he remains staunchly loyal to and in love with his wife, Melanie. In one of the novel's most famous scenes, Rhett scoops up his wife and carries her to her bed, then regrets his actions and departs on a trip with Bonnie. When he returns home, Scarlett is pregnant and, unbeknown to Rhett, would like for their relationship to improve. But in a fall, she loses the baby, and Rhett blames himself. This seems to give both a chance to work through their problems, at last settling the unrequited love each has felt for the other at various points in time.

When Scarlett throws away the chance for happiness with both hands, as Rhett says, readers can only wonder at her incapacity to recognize true love when it stands before her. Bonnie's death, followed closely by that of Melanie, brings the marriage to a crisis point from which it never recovers.

In the book's final scene between the two lovers, Rhett reveals his exhaustion. In a confession supremely ironic in its echoes of Ashley's ideals, he tells Scarlett of his need for tradition and an assurance that life was better at some time in the past. By the time Scarlett at last realizes that Rhett is the true object of her love, he has suffered too much, and he departs, leaving her at her door with the now-famous line, "Frankly, my dear, I don't give a damn."

See also: The Black Experience in America, 1600–1945; Byronic Hero; *Gone with the Wind;* Love Triangle; Mitchell, Margaret; O'Hara, Scarlett; Violence; War; Wilkes, Ashley; Wilkes, Melanie
References: Armstrong, 1990; Davidson, 1995; Flora and Bain, 1987; Frye, 1976; Hoffman and Murphy, 1996

BYRONIC HERO

Named for the English romantic poet George Gordon, Lord Byron (1788–1824), who popular-

John Barrymore and Mary Astor appeared in this 1926 film version of Don Juan, *based on Lord Byron's tale of a hero who combines seeming moral weakness with strength of character developed through a series of adventures. (Photofest)*

ized the dark, brooding male figure in his early-nineteenth-century poetry, the Byronic hero remains a type that appears often in romantic literature. Not surprisingly, Byron shaped his hero during a gloomy period in history, when all of Europe remained embroiled in the Napoleonic wars.

A man who fancied himself an aristocratic rake, Byron used his poetry to reflect upon his own notorious character. His reputation as a womanizer and adventurer was well deserved, and Byron's life remains as highly romantic and fascinating as that of his heroes. Driven from England due to his sexual antics, Byron was, according to legend, on retreat with Percy and Mary Wollstonecraft Shelley in Switzerland when Mary Shelley wrote her romantic classic, *Frankenstein.* He would later die while waiting to participate in the Greek struggle for independence.

In his novel-length poem, *Don Juan,* an epic work published between 1819 and 1824 in seventeen cantos composed of 1,973 eight-line verses, he presented a new elevated style of poetry based on the changing worldview of his age. In what seems a contradictory approach for a romantic, Byron stressed the importance of reality in the shaping of heroes. The poem emphasizes the fact that institutions supposedly founded to promote human happiness actually compromise human life by stressing ideal situations that can never be achieved, thereby offering a false sense of reality. This disparity compels humans to deny their own natures and allow material realities to undercut spiritual, emotional ones. Byron offers an introduction to *Don Juan* that, through references to many classical and contemporary poets, mocks the idea of the traditional epic hero. He makes clear his desire to alter these traditional notions yet becomes a participant in the very traditions he eschews by joining a distinguished group of hero-shaping writers. Byron begins Canto I by compelling his readers to examine and question the values of their age as he searches for an adequate hero for his times: "I want a hero: an uncommon want, / When every year and month sends forth a new one, / Till, after cloying the gazettes with cant, / The age discovers he is not the true one."

Like Byron himself, the character of Don Juan does not believe in or practice the morals society preaches. He engages in seduction and delights in deflowering women. He believes that revenge is sweet, even to be desired, and that winning one's prize, no matter what the cost to others, remains the ultimate heroic goal: "'Tis sweet to win, no matter how, one's laurels / By blood or ink; 'tis sweet to put an end/ To strife: 'tis sometimes sweet to have our quarrels, / Particularly with a tiresome friend" (Canto I, 126). But the reader is most struck, not by the hero's seeming moral weakness, but rather by the strength of character he develops through adventures that include everything from war to ghosts to cannibalism. This character's enigmatic bent at once repels and fascinates those with whom he associates.

On this model, famous figures of romance were created, many of them shaped in the Gothic tradition, such as Charlotte Brontë's Mr. Rochester from *Jane Eyre* (1847) and Emily Brontë's Heathcliff from *Wuthering Heights* (1847), along with countless other highly emotional and intelligent heroes; even Margaret Mitchell's Rhett Butler and Daphne du Maurier's Maxim De Winter qualify. In Mr. Rochester, one clearly notes Byron's themes of brute physicality, which Charlotte Brontë tempers through Jane's sensible approach to life, and also by the idea that one pays for one's sins. *Jane Eyre* presents an excellent example of a meshing of two traditional but slightly altered characterizations, that of the Byronic hero and of the beast from the "Beauty and the Beast" fables. In Heathcliff, the reader recognizes the moodiness of the Byronic hero, his fixation on revenge at any price, and his spirituality. Rhett Butler, although not quite as moody as the Brontës' nineteenth-century characters, was a scoundrel at heart and ultimately a realist when it came to romance. Maxim De Winter's crime of passion haunts him and his Gothic heroine, further darkening an already brooding personality. As such heroes fight to control their passions, readers hope they will lose the fight, for in their passion lies their attraction.

Byron's *Don Juan* forever put to rest the idea that only a highly moral, fair-haired golden boy can play the champion. This work offered a pattern that was realistic and terrifying in its concept precisely because readers recognize their own humanity in the Byronic hero.

See also: Butler, Rhett; De Winter, Maxim; Heathcliff; Rochester, Edward; Shelley, Mary Wollstonecraft Godwin
References: de Rougemont, 1983; Ellis, 1989; McGann, 1986; Radway, 1991; Williams, 1974

CAREY, PHILIP

As the main character of Somerset Maugham's novel *Of Human Bondage* (1915), Philip Carey represents the author himself in some respects. Many believe that Philip's club foot corresponds to Maugham's own physical defect, a severe stammer. Philip's status as an orphan, his guardian uncle, his medical degree, his wide travels, and the questions that Philip asks himself regarding his art and the meaning of life are all based on Maugham's life. Whether Philip's romantic trials and tribulations parallel those of the author can only be guessed, but certainly his practice of deep introspection and his complex emotions were shared by his creator.

Of interest in understanding Philip as a vital, well-rounded character are the plot's allusions to his various states of bondage suggested in the novel's title. After he is orphaned at age nine, Philip must endure an unhappy childhood and adolescence in emotional servitude to his hypocritical Uncle William, a minister who always serves his own interests first. In school, Philip is bound by his club foot to relative physical inactivity, and his self-consciousness over this causes emotional inhibitions as well. As a young adult, he seems bound by the intentions of adults, who dictate that, as a brilliant student, he will attend Oxford and enter the church. Finally, throughout his troubled romantic experiences, Philip seems destined never to break free from a low self-esteem that will not allow him to "deserve" a fitting mate.

His constant inner turmoil leads Philip to travel from place to place, never finding much comfort. A year spent in Germany after he leaves Oxford helps "finish" him as a gentleman but does little to give direction to his life; his sojourns in London and then in Paris are equally aimless. Even though he exercises his independence in going to Paris against the wishes of his guardian, Philip remains bound to Uncle William due to a promised inheritance that will be withdrawn if Philip does not attend school.

Rather than bringing him comfort, romance seems only to torture Philip. His first assignation with a governess leaves him feeling clumsy and inept. On his return to London, Philip feels inexplicably drawn to the immoral, nonintellectual, and frankly unimaginative Mildred Rogers. He cannot explain his attraction to a woman as vulgar as Mildred, yet he keeps returning to the tearoom where she works, hoping to gain her favor. His final victory in taking her to dinner is ruined by her announcement that she plans to marry. Although Philip seems to find more satisfaction in his next affair with Norah Nesbit, he is drawn away from this positive relationship when a pregnant and unmarried Mildred later reappears needing his help. This sets a pattern for Philip's constant return to the depressed and depressing Mildred, no matter how well his life might be proceeding. Mildred represents a blight on his happiness, much as his club foot has always represented a physical incompleteness.

Through his exposure to friendship and death, Philip does succeed in learning more about himself and the human condition. He watches a devoted would-be artist without talent drive herself to suicide while he resides in Paris attempting to be an artist himself. This experience likely makes more acceptable an accomplished artist's assessment of Philip's own artistic talents as mediocre. The tragedy of his friend's death and his disappointment in having to admit his lack of talent, ironically work to help Philip gain independence from a slavish devotion to an empty dream. His verbal interchanges with the poet Cronshaw also help Philip ascertain the futility of much of his struggle against fate. His newfound vision spurs his return to London and medical school, where illness and Mildred will once again interfere with his plans. Philip learns that all friends are not worthy of trust, when the very fellow student who nurses him back to health runs away with Mildred.

Before the novel's conclusion, Philip will see Cronshaw die an agonizing death from alcohol and tobacco abuse, his uncle meet a painfully lingering end, and Mildred and her child die. But if he can be sure of nothing else, Philip does learn to be confident regarding life's balance. The negative aspects of his experience are balanced by positive opportunities; he must only learn to recognize and accept their challenges. When a patient whom Philip helps later rescues him financially and Philip eventually completes his medical studies and marries the patient's daughter, he seems at last to have some chance at happiness.

Each of Philip's romances aid immeasurably in shaping his character. His constant preoccupation with the club foot affects all of his relationships, meaning he can never enjoy emotional peace long enough to form a close bond with a woman. His first round of sex with the governess, Miss Wilkinson, serves to free Philip from many of the romantic illusions he harbors about love, shaped by his voracious reading. He finds he can form a healthy platonic relationship with a woman named Fanny, the doomed Parisian artist. After listening to Fanny's philosophy regarding the efficacy of hard work and strenuous effort toward fulfilling one's dream, then observing her suicide when her ideology proves false, he learns that some dreams are meant to remain only fantasies. His continual haunting by Mildred is likely due to his childhood idea that he is undeserving, brought on by his painful awareness of a relatively minor physical deformity. Norah Nesbit represents his first bid for real love, and had Philip been further advanced in his intellectual and emotional development, he likely could have found happiness with Norah. But he still lacks the self-confidence necessary to cut the emotional chains that bind him to Mildred.

Philip remains capable of escape from his bondage due to his imagination. Although most scientific personalities represented in novels of romance symbolize logic and a decidedly narrow view of life, Philip's imagination helps him avoid this nearsighted approach. Although a physician-scientist, he remains a philosopher at heart, believing that the pursuit of answers through the constant asking of questions is every bit as important as attaining those answers.

Following Uncle William's death and the financial and emotional freedom it affords Philip,

he is at last ready to love and, more importantly, to be loved. Philip's affair with Sally Athelny, the daughter of his former patient, marks a watershed in his unsatisfactory love life. It is Sally's unconditional love for Philip that allows him to see himself as a person worthy of devotion. Her lack of any outward signs of guilt and her refusal to blame Philip following his seduction of her cause him to think more clearly about life's meaning. His quest for that meaning had taken him down the spiritual, emotional, and intellectual paths of both art and science as well as to many geographical locations. It had caused him to try to force Mildred into his own life pattern, a foolish and disastrous move. But finally, with simple acceptance by Sally and the offer of a place in a medical practice from a man he admires, Philip finds meaning in the commonsense side of life, in practicing the simply quotidian.

See also: Maugham, W. Somerset; *Of Human Bondage;* Quest; Rogers, Mildred
References: Drabble, 1995; Price, 1983; Frye, 1976

CARLA

In Giuseppe Berto's 1948 antiromance, *The Sky Is Red,* Carla's character represents those individuals who manage to survive any catastrophe. Although she loves Tullio, her devotion to survival overrides any passions she feels toward others. Her strength remains evident in her simple acceptance of her lot in life. With no one to depend on for support other than herself, Carla embarks on a career of prostitution in war-damaged Italy at the age of fourteen. Through Carla, Berto emphasizes the horrors of the effects of war and poverty on children.

Like the other children in the novel, Carla has no surname, a device employed by Berto to emphasize their positions as individuals rejected by the outside world. That world no longer exists after the bombing of the children's town, a community already economically ravaged by war. Carla bands together with the seventeen-year-old Tullio; her younger cousin Giulia; and a child, Maria, found wandering the streets after the bombing. While Carla contributes her earnings from prostitution toward support of their makeshift family, Tullio joins a gang of other orphans who engage in various nefarious activities made necessary by the war to ensure their survival.

From the novel's opening, Carla evinces a leadership and strength that might be admirable had her circumstances differed. But her limited outlet for expression of those characteristics, that of prostitution, denigrates her positive aspects through the introduction of the question of morality. Giulia's mother had been a prostitute, and both girls had been raised in a red-light district. With this way of life as her heritage, Carla can do little more than follow the role models around her. She contrasts with her cousin Giulia, who, although a bastard herself, remains a symbol of purity. Although she does not judge Carla for prostituting her body, Giulia chooses not to participate in that activity. But such morality has a price in the immoral atmosphere produced by war. With Giulia's eventual death comes Carla's understanding that goodness and weakness go hand in hand; if she is to survive, she must not indulge in an apparently destructive ideology.

The single factor causing Carla to momentarily waver in her cynical attitude is Daniele, an obviously upper-class boy who joins the orphaned group after discovering his parents died in the bombing. Fresh from the seminary, Daniele causes some brief discomfort among the gang of young people, who recognize that his social status is superior to their own. Although Daniele never negatively sanctions Carla for her actions that bring money and food to the group, he cannot hide his shock upon first discovering her profession. Carla's only defense is seduction, and she offers Daniele his first sexual experience. When she discerns his dissatisfaction with her kind of love, she does not allow his attitude to bother her. She cannot afford to indulge in self-pity or doubt; otherwise, she and those who depend upon her will die from starvation. She does later encourage Daniele's love for Giulia, never attempting to sleep with him again. This is the best Carla can offer in the way of bettering the lives of her more idealistic friends.

Carla's cynicism is the only type of wisdom allowed her in this grim initiation story. Only by retaining her suspicion and cold demeanor can she survive the loss of family and friends as one tragic death follows another. She represents a well-shaped antiheroine, one devoid of passion, whose only reward for her self-sacrifice is disappointment. This young woman's dreams will never be fulfilled as long as her fellow humans continue to insist on taking advantage of each other through the infliction of poverty by the greedy and war by the power-crazed. Berto's message that war delivers only loneliness and desolation is perfectly embodied in Carla. She may survive the hate of war and poverty, but, Berto asks his readers, to what end?

See also: Daniele; Giulia; Nihilism; *The Sky Is Red;* Tullio; Violence; War

References: Hoffman and Murphy, 1996; Price, 1983

CARRAWAY, NICK

In *The Great Gatsby* (1925), the character Nick Carraway serves as the narrator, describing and interacting with a lifestyle he finds attractive and yet cannot fully understand. F. Scott Fitzgerald inserts Nick, a midwesterner new to the eastern seaboard, into a foreign landscape, both geographically and emotionally, in order to provide the illusion of an objective narrator. Yet Nick is not objective, for one of the people he describes is his own cousin, the beautiful Daisy Buchanan, to whom he has an emotional attachment. Although a member of Daisy's extended family, Nick does not share in her wealth, nor would he normally move within her elite social strata. He does at first fill his role as objective commentator on the actions of the mysterious Jay Gatsby, a man inhabiting the mansion adjoining the Long Island Sound property where Nick is spending the summer. However, his objectivity departs as he quickly develops an attraction to and affection for Gatsby, and he experiences a great deal of conflict when his loyalties to Daisy and Gatsby are later tried.

Nick's presence helps to emphasize the theme of observation established by Fitzgerald, who seems to suggest that all humans are the objects of scrutiny by a silent, unforgiving society. The bigger presence that one might label fate is symbolized by the huge, staring eyes of the oculist advertisement on a local billboard that seems to hover over the characters. Gatsby observes Daisy, and Nick observes that observation, weaving into his story for the reader the information he gathers. Reminiscent of a Greek chorus, Nick comes close to serving as interpreter in this modern romantic tragedy, often musing in his narration about character motivations.

That Nick also becomes romantically involved with the socialite Jordan Baker helps focus reader attention on the theme of truth versus reality. Following Daisy's disillusionment with and abandonment of Gatsby and the revelation that Gatsby's wealth comes from crime, Nick himself realizes he was more enthralled with Jordan's milieu than with her person. He allows himself to be contaminated by an ideology apart from ethics, and the result is his return to his former, less glamorous, but more desirable, life. Unlike the antihero Gatsby, Nick is able to escape the trap represented by a lifestyle in which he does not belong.

At first, Nick romanticizes Daisy. He has always thought of her as beautiful and desirable, which she indeed remains, but he did not realize her unhealthy need for her husband Tom Buchanan's indolent and repulsive materialistic lifestyle. Nick's disappointment is great when he sees the truth about his cousin—that she belongs with her repulsive husband, that she could not survive apart from the crass lifestyle they have created. When Gatsby's dream world collapses, it is in great part due to the Buchanans' total disregard for anyone or anything outside of their own carefully constructed reality.

When Nick accidentally meets Tom following the events that lead up to Gatsby's murder, he refuses to talk with him. But he cannot resist listening to Tom's rationalization of his part in Gatsby's death. Nick is forced to realize that Tom believes he has committed no wrong. He concludes the novel with the observation that all humans look to the future for escape from their past. Just as Gatsby could not escape the humble beginnings that caused Daisy to reject him in both their youth and their maturity, Nick cannot escape the past that Gatsby's disillusionment and death created for him.

See also: Buchanan, Daisy; Buchanan, Tom; Gatsby, Jay; *The Great Gatsby*
References: Piper, 1970; Washington, 1995

CARTON, SYDNEY

Sydney Carton embodies that highly esteemed character from romance novels—the one who makes the ultimate sacrifice for his love. His position in Charles Dickens's 1859 historical romance, *A Tale of Two Cities,* begins as one of a ne'er-do-well. As a talented British writer, impeded by alcoholism and a lack of self-motivation, Carton first appears to be the most unlikely of heroes. Yet, his love for Lucie Manette will later ennoble the aimless Carton, affording him the courage he needs to die in place of Lucie's husband, Charles Darnay, in an execution demanded by those involved in the French Revolution.

Like all novels set in wartime, *A Tale of Two Cities* focuses on the effect of cultural conflict on the individuals who both willingly and unwillingly become caught up in wartime passions. The early scene introducing Carton is one of many in the book that feature trials and judgments. A French instructor of languages named Charles Darnay is on trial in England for treason. Lucie and her father Doctor Manette, a former prisoner in the French Bastille, are on hand to testify as to their acquaintance with Darnay, whom they met on their return from France after Doctor Manette's release from prison five years earlier. The scene is heavy with foreshadowing as Darnay's attorney, coincidentally the employer of the law clerk, Sydney Carton, gains an acquittal for Darnay based on his uncanny physical resemblance to Carton. This resemblance prevents an absolute legal identification of Darnay as the accused perpetrator.

Carton will bear an additional similarity to Darnay as the plot continues; both men fall in love with Lucie Manette. The love triangle is an intriguing one, for Lucie cares greatly for both characters. When she chooses Darnay's offer of marriage over Carton's, this allows Carton to take early steps along his path of moral redemption, a journey his love for Lucie has already allowed him to begin. He declares to Lucie that she should remember him as one willing to give his life for her or for any that she might love.

With his usual skill, Dickens completes Carton's metamorphosis into a character of depth and feeling. He wisely spreads his plot over many years, so that Carton's alteration through his love and esteem for the Darnays does not occur overnight, making it all the more realistic. Dickens's perpetuation of the theme of mistaken identity through the later confusion of Darnay with his French uncle, the Marquis St. Evrémonde, and through Doctor Manette's unintended participation as Darnay's later accuser, also makes Carton's ability to once again physically substitute for Darnay more believable.

Especially important to romance aficionados are Carton's reactions to Lucie's grief when Darnay is imprisoned in the Bastille and Carton's involvement in his friends' eventual escape to England. Before the menace to Lucie's happiness that arrives in the threat of her beloved husband's execution, Carton remains a relatively passive character. He behaves basically as he is told to behave, with the strongest voice of instruction being that of alcohol. But when he realizes that without action Darnay will be executed and Lucie will suffer for the loss, Carton sheds his passive demeanor and rallies the forces of his underutilized intellect. His clever plan serves as a double rescue. Not only is Darnay spirited away from the Bastille to spend the rest of his life with Lucie and their child, but Carton reaches the high point of his own life through his sacrifice. His execution in place of Darnay redeems what had seemed to be a fruitless, failed life.

Sydney Carton also allows what may be Dickens's only real political statement in a novel that seems to have been created as a protest yet offers no real suggestion of a solution for war and its evils. Carton is offered as an example of the possibility for ethical behavior in the midst of wartime's immorality. He represents the power of the everyday individual to better the life of others, not through grand political schemes but through the sacrifice of self for the only higher good in which humans may always retain confidence—the value of a single human life.

See also: Darnay, Charles, Marquis St. Evrémonde; Dickens, Charles John Huffam; Love Triangle; *A Tale of Two Cities;* Violence; War
References: Caeserio, 1979; Duncan, 1992; Furbank, 1986; Smith, 1996; Tambling, 1995

CATHER, WILLA SIEBERT

Although born in Virginia in 1873, Willa Siebert Cather used her many years in Nebraska as the rich source of much of her writing. The Cather family moved to Webster County, Nebraska, in 1883 and then to Red Cloud. The first of seven children born to a good-natured farmer, Charles Cather, and his domineering wife, Mary Virginia, Willa called herself Willie as a child and would later recall her mother with an ambivalence hinting at conflict. She was educated by her beloved grandmother, whom Cather later featured in her short story "Old Mrs. Harris" (1932). Cather gained much from her years in Nebraska and would later become known to many as a writer of the American frontier. Evidence of the courageous pioneer spirit appears in many of her characters, and Nebraska provided the setting for many of her finest works.

As a young student, Cather often dressed in boyish clothes and called herself William Cather,

M. D. In her early writing she imitated Henry James, and she equated artistry with masculinity. Her fascination with artists equaled that of her fascination with pioneers, and both interests provided themes for her many works. It was her friend and mentor Sarah Orne Jewett who encouraged her to make her own way and to find her own writing voice.

While attending the University of Nebraska until her graduation in 1895, Cather studied the classics and began her publishing career in the school's literary magazine. In addition, she reviewed cultural events for the Lincoln newspaper. After graduation, she left Nebraska to work for *Home Monthly* and the *Daily Leader* in Pittsburgh, Pennsylvania. During her ten-year stay in Pittsburgh, Cather also taught high school English and Latin for a time. In Pittsburgh Cather lived in the home of Judge Samuel A. McClung, sharing a room with his daughter Isabelle. Details of her personal life remain obscure because she destroyed most of her correspondence and forbade publication of any letters she did not burn, but most critics agree that the relationship with Isabelle remained of great importance to Cather, alleviating her loneliness. After leaving Pittsburgh, she moved

Novelist Willa Cather became widely known as a writer of the American frontier. (Corbis/Bettmann)

to New York to work for Samuel S. McClure as managing editor of *McClure's Magazine*.

Cather resigned from *McClure's* following the serialization of her novel *Alexander's Bridge* in the 1912 issues of the magazine. By 1913, she had moved in with Edith Lewis, with whom she would live until her death, and apparently reacted strongly against Isabelle's 1915 engagement to be married. Her writing career progressed steadily, and she became one of the most prominent women in America during the 1920s and 1930s. Cather's war novel, *One of Ours* (1922), garnered the 1923 Pulitzer Prize. In 1944 she received the Gold Medal of the National Institute of Arts and Letters, the highest award for creative achievement in the arts. The Gold Medal was awarded not for a single book but for an entire body of work, the sustained output of an entire career. In 1961 Cather became the first woman voted into the Nebraska Hall of Fame. Additional honors include induction into the Hall of Great Westerners in Oklahoma City, Oklahoma, in 1974 and into the National Women's Hall of Fame at Seneca, New York, in 1988. Cather' novels include *O Pioneers!* (1913), dedicated to Sarah Orne Jewett, and *The Song of the Lark* (1915), both written during visits to Isabelle McClung's house; *My Ántonia* (1918), considered to be autobiographical; *A Lost Lady* (1923); *The Professor's House* (1925); and *Death Comes for the Archbishop* (1927). Her short stories and novellas were collected in *The Troll Garden* (1905), *Obscure Destinies* (1932), *Youth and the Bright Medusa* (1920), and *The Old Beauty and Others* (1948). A 1936 collection of essays, *Not under Forty,* reveals Cather's fear caused by poor health.

Some questioned the authenticity of her frequent use of a male narrator, but she argued that her long, close friendships with Judge McClung and Samuel McClure provided insight into the male perspective. Characteristic of her work are the themes of conflict between the artist and society, human desire and necessity, the young and the old, and the city and the country. Also prevalent in Cather's work is her distaste for the increasingly indifferent and materialistic values of American society.

Cather died on April 24, 1947, and is buried in Jaffery, New Hampshire.

See also: My Ántonia

References: Blain, Clements, and Grundy, 1990; Daiches, 1971; Davidson, 1995; Fetterley, 1993;

O'Brien, 1996; Ousby, 1988; Robinson, 1983; Rosowski, 1989

CHARIS

Charis is one of the three antiheroines in Margaret Atwood's *The Robber Bride* (1993). The novel subverts tradition by presenting three women strengthened not through love for males but through respect and love for one another. Men do play a part in the plot because the women must deal with the problems in their romantic relationships caused by the femme fatale Zenia. Atwood establishes Zenia, the robber bride of her title, in the traditionally male role of the robber bridegroom and plays off the idea of the love triangle in presenting three characters of the same sex united, rather than divided, by romantic circumstance.

Although her friends Roz Andrews and Tony Fremont also suffer the consequences of Zenia's actions, Charis appears to be the most damaged by her experience, largely because she is the most physically and emotionally fragile member of the trio. At one time tempted by the idea of suicide, Charis draws strength from her relationship with Roz and Tony. A dynamic character in every sense of the term, Charis alters greatly from her first experience with Zenia to her last, but her inner strength becomes obvious only at the novel's conclusion.

A victim of physical, emotional, and sexual abuse as a child, and of forced separation from her beloved grandmother, Charis eventually adopts a new identity when she changes her name from Karen. Names remain important to her; thus she names her daughter August, for the month of her birth. Ironically, Charis is disturbed when her daughter follows, although for different reasons, the precedent set by her mother as she changes her name to Augusta. Charis's love interest and the father of her child is Billy, a U.S. citizen who takes up residence in Canada to escape service in the Vietnam War. Both Karen and Billy come of age in the 1960s, and each represents an opposite approach to that era. Karen-turned-Charis practices yoga for its emotional healing effects. She also retreats to the isolation of a small island plot off Toronto, where she can raise chickens as an escape from her deep emotional injury. Nonacquisitive and spiritual, she visualizes emotions as colors, recognizing auras that surround certain personalities. Her secluded house provides a perfect hiding place for Billy, whose exploitative personality and rejection of the spirituality in which Charis exults establishes him as her opposite. When Zenia appears and launches a carefully calculated plan to undermine their love, the reader almost applauds Billy's removal from Charis's life.

But whether the loss of Billy ultimately proves positive or negative for Charis, she suffers from it. Charis is betrayed by Zenia, who, under the guise of feigned illness, takes advantage of Charis's charitable personality to move into her home. As she so tenderly cares for her chickens and for Billy, Charis cares for Zenia, treating her supposed "cancer" with natural healing potions and working to support the parasitic Billy and Zenia. When she awakens to an empty house one day and drives to the island's ferry dock, Charis sees Zenia and Billy standing with men in suits; she wonders whether Zenia has turned Billy over to the authorities for draft dodging. Much of the conflict Charis feels following that episode is over Billy's unknown fate; he is, after all, the father of her unborn child.

Atwood unfolds the relationships among Charis, Roz, and Tony and that of each woman with Zenia through careful character developments that compliment one another. Despite their strength and contrasting personalities, all three fall victim to Zenia's amoral approach to life. Charis remains the character most closely associated with color and art, with an intuitive approach to life that the harsh realities of everyday existence cannot succeed in destroying. When Tony and Roz want to exact compensation for the pain Zenia caused them by killing her, Charis wants only to question her regarding Billy's fate. When she learns from Zenia that Billy was the one who killed her chickens before the two of them deserted her, not only killed the chickens but enjoyed it and laughed as he imagined Charis's reaction, Charis's greatest fear comes true. Karen, her old personality, that former self filled with rage and violence, emerges to push Zenia off the hotel balcony to her death. But Charis regains control, uses her inner light to take possession of her self and the situation, and realizes she has only imagined the murder. Karen is at last totally vanquished when Charis can tell Zenia that she is forgiven.

Charis remains an important part of Atwood's consideration of female identity and communication. Through Charis and her daughter Augusta, the author suggests that women may, indeed, take charge of their own identities by readjusting the "labels" given them as children. That Charis changes her name from Karen symbolizes her efforts to refashion a new, more healthy self as a rejection of her childhood abuse. She must later confront that former self in a moment of crisis, proving that more than just a name change may be required to truly escape one's past. In addition, the symbolic meaning of the name *Charis* also fits well with Atwood's emphasis on the importance of language and communication. From the term *Charis* the reader may easily visualize similar and related terms that serve to represent the character's personality, such as "charisma," "caring," "charity," "charm," and "Christian." Her lack of a surname is important as well, contrasting with the two married women who both assume, in a traditional manner, the last names of their husbands.

A pivotal scene in the novel centers on Charis and provides a tie to the world of the traditional fairy tale. Charis invites Tony and Roz to serve as godparents for the infant August, conducting her own ceremony in which she reads from her grandmother's Bible and also incorporates New Age spiritual symbols. She takes comfort in the fact that these women will provide the strength for August that Charis lacks. But Charis herself thinks of the dark shadow of Zenia, a presence bearing negative gifts, that falls over the ceremony. The scene recalls the christening of Sleeping Beauty and celebratory scenes surrounding other fairy-tale characters, upon whom both evil and good spirits act.

In the novel's conclusion, it is Charis who holds the vase with Zenia's ashes that will be scattered at sea. When the vase cracks into two pieces as Charis holds it at arm's length, Tony and Roz suppose Charis has struck it against the rail. But Charis understands that entities such as Zenia's spirit have strong powers. Her realization results partially from her recognition of the strength she herself has gained.

See also: Andrews, Roz; Fremont, Tony; *The Robber Bride;* Zenia
References: Morey, 1997; Wilson, Friedman, and Hengen, 1996

CHILLINGWORTH, ROGER

In Roger Chillingworth, Nathaniel Hawthorne created one of the finest examples of a character type common to the romance since Renaissance times, the rational man of science. His symbolic name fits this physician's chilling personality, which may be seen from the first moment Chillingworth appears in *The Scarlet Letter* (1850). In this, his first novel, Hawthorne produces a romance so pure that its characters are almost allegorical.

Chillingworth participates in a love triangle of sorts with his wife, Hester Prynne, and her lover and father of her illegitimate child, Arthur Dimmesdale. To his credit, Chillingworth does assume partial blame for Hester's sin; had he not been so much older than she, had he not sent her out on her own, she perhaps would not have made her error. He can rationalize her actions and tells her at one point that he does not seek revenge on her because having to wear the "A" is punishment enough. But he swears to discern the identity of the lover that Hester will not reveal, declaring his goal in life to make this man miserable. For all his education and erudition, Roger Chillingworth remains a man consumed by unhappiness and dissatisfaction. He cannot see that his sentence of a living death invoked upon Dimmesdale also represents his own sentence.

When he appears in the crowd to observe Hester's public shaming in the Puritan community of Salem, Chillingworth's face is described as growing dark with an unnamed emotion. What Chillingworth feels cannot be labeled love, and he spends the remainder of his life struggling with the emotions of fear and hatred. An acute desire for revenge against Dimmesdale gives the only meaning to his otherwise vacuous life.

When the book's narrator introduces Chillingworth, he is described as wearing a strange mixture of clothing that represents both the civilized and the savage world. As is true in many literary works, garb here remains important, and the mix of clothing describes Chillingworth's personality. On the one hand, he sees himself as a scientific and rational being, a member of the most civilized of societies, who turns to his intellect for the answer to life's problems. On the other, he battles a savage instinctual desire for vengeance. Ultimately, he assumes the role of the rational man of science to act as foil for Dimmesdale's instinctual man of passion, but from the beginning readers understand that Chillingworth's core smolders with anything but cool rationality. Just as he tries to hide the physical imbalance of his

uneven shoulders, Chillingworth attempts to conceal the imbalance in his soul.

In his first contact with Hester, Chillingworth offers comfort to her illegitimate child with medication, swearing that he would not harm a miserable innocent baby. He also treats Hester with medicinal herbs he has learned about while living as a captive among Indians for a year. His attitude toward her is made clear when he announces the medicine may not soothe in the way a sinless conscience would, but he promises it will calm her passion. As the rational physician, Chillingworth seeks to treat the soul with scientific medicines. Ironically, he desires to help Hester live so that she may suffer by wearing the mark of the "A" for all to see. He will use his skills to promote physical health for Hester and Dimmesdale in order to keep them both in psychological torment.

Unaware of Chillingworth's identity as Hester's husband, Dimmesdale accepts his physical treatment over the next several years. Chillingworth loses his cool composure in a scene when he stands on the ground, looking up at Dimmesdale, Hester, and Pearl standing atop a scaffold. Fraught with symbolism, the scene employs the light from fiery meteors in an extraordinary heavenly display, which the colonists superstitiously connect with many events, to expose Chillingworth's uncontrollable reaction to the sight of the lovers and their child. In this revealing scene, the narrator suggests that Chillingworth resembles the devil himself, so vivid is his expression of malevolence. Dimmesdale notices that the face seems to linger after the natural light has disappeared, glowing in the dark. But Dimmesdale's physical and psychological vision fails, and he does not recognize his own physician as the demon.

Chillingworth's constant psychological torment of Dimmesdale causes his physical deterioration over seven years' time. In the novel's climactic scene, Dimmesdale bares his chest to the crowd, where he claims to bear the same mark as Hester. The public report bears out the possibility that what was viewed by onlookers was the result of years of necromancing on Chillingworth's part, once his identity as Hester's true husband is revealed. When his victim falls prone on the scaffold, Chillingworth can only murmur, "Thou hast escaped me!"

In the end, Chillingworth will torment himself most. Like another seeker of vengeance in a nineteenth-century romance novel, the tragic police inspector Javert in Victor Hugo's *Les Misérables* (1862), Chillingworth's desire for revenge leads to his death. Following Dimmesdale's death, Chillingworth shrivels like a cast-off weed in the sun. However, Hawthorne allows his dark character a bit of grace in Chillingworth's final action, when he bequeaths a fortune in property to little Pearl. The narrator leaves the subject of Chillingworth by reminding the reader that both hatred and love share much in common, and that one may not be realized without the other.

See also: Dimmesdale, Arthur; Hawthorne, Nathaniel; Prynne, Hester; *The Scarlet Letter*
References: Abel, 1988; Budick, 1996; Charlton, 1984; Hart, 1995

CHITTARANJAN, NELLIE

In his novel *The Suffrage of Elvira* (1958), V. S. Naipaul presents a story of freedom for several individuals framed within a plot about a Trinidadian village gaining democracy through the public vote. One of those individuals is Nellie Chittaranjan, daughter of the village goldsmith. As daughter to a wealthy Hindu, Nellie must bow to her father's wishes for an arranged marriage to the son of the powerful Hindu politico, Surujpat Harbans. Because she desires to be released from this arrangement, she represents the traditional damsel in distress of medieval romance plots. But she greatly differs from her fictional sisters in the fact that she desires release from the arrangement, not in order to marry a true love, but to gain an education. Naipaul shapes Nellie as the postmodern heroine who believes in the importance of the individual.

Nellie does share, in a manner of speaking, the passivity of the damsels from western romance tradition. This is due to her religion's view of women as needing care and direction. The patriarchal system cares for its girls by directing their futures, placing them in patriarchal marriages, but in the process it hinders their independence. Nellie can do little to help alter her future, which totally depends on decisions made by her father and by Harbans on behalf of his son. She wants to depart from Elvira, a village that symbolizes tradition, and journey to London in order to attend school. Her desire to advance her education and improve her mind rather than immediately marry and begin a family sets her apart from the so-called traditional Hindu girl.

Ironically, the very religious beliefs that oppress her serve to set her free. When she is witnessed meeting clandestinely with a Muslim friend, Foam Baksh, the witness assumes the meeting has a romantic basis, and he circulates the rumor accusing the two of forbidden love. Although Nellie remains innocent of any wrongdoing, having met Foam only to be given a puppy by him, her father believes the rumor and orders Nellie to remain home. Just when she seems to have lost the freedom she enjoyed, Nellie is released from the arranged marriage by Harbans. He hears the rumor and declines to obligate his son to marry a Hindu who "runs around" with Muslim boys.

Nellie does little to gain her own release from an arranged marriage; circumstances simply work in her favor. This helps place Nellie in the tradition of the damsel aided by a white knight with whom she does not become romantically involved. But the fact that Nellie desires no romantic involvement at all aligns her with a new breed of heroines who gain release from an oppressive commitment to males in order to find fulfillment through self-improvement.

See also: Baksh, Foam; Forbidden Love; Naipaul, V. S.; *The Suffrage of Elvira*
References: Baker, 1994; Birbalsingh, 1996; Hussein, 1994

CHIVALRY

Originating in about twelfth-century Europe, chivalry became a name for an ethically based code of behavior on the part of heroic males encompassing virtues such as honesty, heroism, and fealty. Likely a derivation of the French term *chevalier,* meaning one who rides horses, chivalry connoted honor during a time when the European aristocracy practiced cavalry training for combat. Connected particularly with orders of knighthood, chivalry remained a desirable code of conduct that flourished into the thirteenth century and may be found in romantic literature focusing on the late Middle Ages and early Renaissance. As early as the seventh century, references in stories in several languages are found to the legendary Briton King Arthur and his knights, whose mythology would later be promoted by the English writer Geoffrey of Monmouth. The knight symbolized loyalty, skill, and generosity, and he used his sword not for self-aggrandizement but rather to protect church and home. The French developed the idea that a knight should serve an unattainable lady, often a woman married to his leader, in a chaste, idealized, romantic relationship known as courtly love. Such love was never intended to be sexually consummated. The young knight paid homage to his married mistress by honoring her through dedication of his heroic deeds and by serving as her personal protector.

In its later development, chivalry combined qualities of the aristocrat and virtues of Christianity with aspect of courtly love. A knight who had completed his apprenticeship or training dedicated his armor in church through prayer and fasting. Tournaments between knights became celebrations of their wartime skills, with the victor of the carefully staged pageant generally dedicating his win to an aristocratic lady. Popular as a theme of romantic literature, chivalry was celebrated in mythological fables and the Arthurian legend *Sir Gawain and the Green Knight,* among other stories. Works by the Italian poet Dante Alighieri, the Spanish writer Castiglione, and those produced by the English printer William Caxton emphasized chivalry, and it became a tool for the English aristocrat, Edmund Spenser, in his epic poetic work dedicated to Queen Elizabeth I, *The Faerie Queene* (1590). Spenser's Red Cross Knight symbolizes the highest attributes of chivalry in his heroic deeds. The Spanish writer Miguel de Cervantes satirized knighthood in his seventeenth-century novel, *Don Quixote,* but it enjoyed renewed popularity in nineteenth-century European romantic fiction, such as novels by Sir Walter Scott and Alexandre Dumas. Although twentieth-century sentiment, supported by the ideology of such movements as feminism, materialism, and socialism, finds the highly romanticized ideals of chivalry distasteful and even harmful to the development of identity and sexual mores, works of romance and love still often depend on chivalric precepts to shape their plots and male characters.

References: de Rougemont, 1983; Radway, 1991; Spenser, 1590, 1987

CHOPIN, KATE

Although late-nineteenth-century writer Kate Chopin gained a measurable amount of fame during her lifetime, since the 1960s her popularity as a writer known for her progressive ideas

regarding women has made her more widely read than ever before. Her novella *The Awakening* (1899) appears regularly in anthologies of American literature and of women's writing and has become a favorite tool for illustrating feminist thought in literature studies.

Born in 1851 in St. Louis, Katherine O'Flaherty was descended through her mother from French Creole aristocrats. Her father, a successful merchant who died when his daughter was only four years old, had emigrated from Ireland. With a Catholic education at school and training in proper Victorian manners at home, Kate made her debut at age seventeen and in 1870 married Oscar Chopin, a cotton trader of Creole heritage. They settled first in New Orleans, had six children, and then moved north to Natchitoches, Louisiana, where they lived on a plantation.

Oscar's death in 1882 from swamp fever caused Chopin great pain, but it most likely prompted her writing career. Although she had written informally in diaries and tried her hand at poetry and sketching, Chopin only settled down to serious writing in her early thirties. She gained some attention with her short stories based on her surroundings and containing characters fashioned after the Creoles she knew so well. A close friend and family doctor, Frederick Kolbenheyer, introduced Chopin to works by American author Sarah Orne Jewett and French writers Emile Zola, Gustave Flaubert, and Guy de Maupassant. Her later writings showed evidence of the influence of those writers, who often dealt with themes of personal liberation and nonconformity. Some critics suggested that the protagonist of *The Awakening,* Edna Pontellier, was an Americanized version of Flaubert's Madame Bovary.

The Awakening did not receive many positive reviews; nineteenth-century sensibilities were not yet ready to deal with a novel, especially one written by a woman, suggesting that women desired erotic freedom and release from the restrictions the Victorian age imposed on them. Critical reviews termed the work "sad and mad and bad," declaring it "an essentially vulgar story" with a married woman unacceptably assuming the active role in a love triangle. St. Louis libraries refused to stock the book, and some of Chopin's acquaintances no longer associated with her following its publication. The negative consequences of her publication of *The Awakening* included the later rejection of her third collection of short stories.

When Chopin fell ill and died in 1904, she had reaped little financial profit from the work that would make her famous decades later.

See also: *The Awakening;* Flaubert, Gustave; Forbidden Love; Love Triangle; *Madame Bovary;* Pontellier, Edna; Victorian Age

References: Comfort, 1974; Gilbert and Gubar, 1985d; Keesey, 1998; Ousby, 1988; Praz, 1974; Williams, 1974

CLARE, ANGEL

Angel Clare's character acts as balance for his nemesis, Alec d'Urberville, in Thomas Hardy's tragic romantic novel, *Tess of the d'Urbervilles* (1891). Both romance the "pure woman" of Hardy's subtitle, and each displays a character flaw where their passions for that woman are concerned. With the farm girl, Tess Durbeyfield, the two young men form a love triangle that demonstrates the ability of fate to make victims of the purest of humans. Whereas Alec represents the hypocritical, wealthy, religious Victorian Hardy so despised, Angel stands for a philosophy that rejected an all-knowing external God and searched instead for the divinity within all humans. But in his intellectual and spiritual myopia, Angel cannot recognize Tess as an innocent victim of the society whose mores he questioned. When facing a trial of his beliefs, Angel fails miserably by unconsciously regressing to support the very cultural ideals he had condemned.

The son of a minister, Angel bears the weight of his family's expectations that he also will enter the ministry. Far more interested in farming and the miracles of the land, Angel instead receives an education and then takes up employment on a dairy farm, where he can observe and learn the skills needed for successful farming. Here he meets Tess, nature's child, voluptuous and beautiful yet innocent. Angel associates Tess's earthiness with the nature he loves and soon develops romantic desires for the young milkmaid. When Tess resists his attentions, Angel believes her actions are based on her natural purity; he has no inkling of Tess's seduction several years earlier by Alec d'Urberville, a supposed landed "gentleman," or of the subsequent birth and death of her child.

Because the reader observes early on Alec's opportunistic behavior toward Tess, Angel's careful wooing of his love creates a fine contrast with the forced attentions of her previous suitor. In an early scene when Angel carries Tess across a swollen creek, he realizes the proximity of their faces, knowing he might kiss her, but instead decides he must not take advantage of the situation. He deals with the vulnerable Tess patiently, repeatedly urging her commitment to marriage over a period of time. In one of Hardy's most revealing passages regarding Angel, the narrator describes him as a man of conscience who envisions Tess as something more than a toy with which he may play and then dismiss upon a whim. The value of her peasant life remains equal to that of any member of the upper class in Angel's mind. At one point he even avoids Tess, acknowledging the importance of her feelings when he believes she lacks desire for him. His patience reaps the benefit of her shy attentions, and at last she openly returns his affection, although she will not agree to marriage. He continues to misinterpret Tess's reticence because he will not allow her to tell him of her past. At last unable to resist his attentions, Tess agrees to marry Angel.

Angel's silencing of Tess before marriage and his desertion of her following their marriage and the revelation of her secret constitute no less serious a crime against Tess than that perpetrated by Alec d'Urberville. For all of his education and supposed adherence to the new philosophy advocating freedom of will and individual worth, Angel cannot see that Tess remains pure; he blames the victim for her rape by Alec. His rejection of a woman consumed by love and devoted to his needs creates the pathos so important to Hardy's tale.

Angel's departure abroad exposes Tess to the undesired attentions of the hated Alec. Such actions unite him with the other characters in emphasizing the inevitability of fate that is a major theme of Hardy's novel. That Angel does not, in the end, fulfill the role of guardian that his name implies results from both his shortsightedness and the workings of forces no human can control. His final forgiveness and acceptance of Tess come too late to save her from execution but in time for both to enjoy a short idyllic period, during which they express their love with honesty and passion.

See also: Durbeyfield, Tess; d'Urberville, Alec; Love Triangle; *Tess of the d'Urbervilles*
References: Comfort, 1974; Goode, 1993; Pettit, 1994; Shires, 1992

CLAUDIO

In William Shakespeare's *Much Ado about Nothing* (1598), Count Claudio of Florence fills a part well known to English Renaissance audiences. Shakespeare used a popular romantic comic plot of misunderstanding, in which a virtuous maiden stands accused of lack of chastity and must have her name cleared before the drama closes. This type of comedy, with its subplots, secrets, innuendo, and clearly fashioned "good guys" and "bad guys" contributes to a formulaic story line that appears frequently in writing from all eras. In Shakespeare's version, Claudio plays the part of the accuser of his intended, Hero.

Of course, Hero remains innocent. Claudio and the prince he serves, Don Pedro, become the victims of trickery by the play's one evil figure, the prince's bastard brother, Don John. Don John plays havoc with the comedy's romance, but not because he rivals Claudio for Hero's love. He seeks to undermine the romance for no reason other than that he loves mischief and is likely jealous of Claudio's popularity with his brother. As a bastard who felt cheated of his inheritance of title and property, he remains a basic malcontent.

During a visit to the estate of Governor Leonato of Messina, Claudio proposes to the governor's daughter and heir, Hero, after her favor is won through a traditional third-party approach. Don Pedro, as the younger Claudio's representative, steps in during a night of revelry at a masked ball to woo Hero in his friend's stead. Shakespeare uses this moment in the play to allow the actions of Claudio to reflect on his immaturity. The young man at first believes the hint that Don John, in disguise, has planted, suggesting that Don Pedro seeks Hero's hand for himself. Along with the many other misunderstandings and mismatches in the comedy, this one clears itself, and marriage between Claudio and Hero is planned.

Don John plots with his serving man, Borachio, to woo Hero's lady-in-waiting, Margaret, at an open window on the night before the marriage. Don John brings Claudio and Don Pedro to witness Borachio's seduction of Margaret. As planned, Borachio calls out the name "Hero" while the couple are in the heat of passion, to make the observers believe that Hero is untrue to Claudio. At the wedding, Claudio accuses Hero of infidelity, rejecting her at the altar. But due to Hero's sincere pleas of innocence and because the local cleric and Hero's cousin, Beatrice, feel she remains pure, a plot is concocted whereby a false rumor that Hero died of grief will be circulated. The family hopes that Claudio will be so overcome with sorrow on learning this that he will retract the false accusation.

The perpetrators and the truth regarding Hero are quickly discovered, but Leonato carries out the concocted ruse, bringing the news of Hero's death and the subsequent affirmation of her innocence to Claudio. Reacting with appropriate repentance and sorrow, Claudio agrees to publicly retract his statement against Hero, balancing his previous public accusation, and to marry her cousin as penance. At the marriage ceremony, Claudio discovers that the veiled "cousin" is Hero in disguise. The young lovers marry, and the audience departs satisfied with the drama's congenial conclusion.

By the play's end, Claudio undergoes a change of heart toward Hero but no true change of character. Just as his violent reaction to what he believes is Hero's disloyalty would be expected by viewers, so is his repentance. Readers in later centuries would find unsettling the violence Claudio exhibits toward Hero, but his reaction satisfied Renaissance expectations of acceptable gender roles of the period. Claudio's importance lies in his usefulness in perpetuating a traditional comic plot that would be played out again and again in the pages of romance.

See also: Hero; *Much Ado about Nothing*
References: Barton, 1974

CLEARY, MEGHANN (MEGGIE)

Meghann (Meggie) Cleary, the heroine of Colleen McCullough's wildly popular novel, *The Thorn Birds* (1977), represents many young women born in the pre–World War I era. Resigned to a life of serving men and functioning within a man's world, she barely rates a second glance from her beautiful mother, Fiona, who dotes only on her sons. As Fiona thinks to herself early in the book, there is no mystery to Meggie; she knows only too well what her difficult lot in life will entail. But in Meggie's case, Fiona is wrong. With beauty, honesty, and an insight into herself that her mother lacks, Meggie will strike a blow for her own independence, thanks to her relationship with Father Ralph de Bricassart. The novel is not only a romance but also a coming-of-age story for Meggie Cleary.

Indications of Meggie's spirit emerge early during mistreatment by both her rowdy brothers and the nuns at the Catholic New Zealand school all the Cleary children attend. The little girl stands up bravely to the nun's regular administration of caning and to having her left arm tied down to eliminate her natural tendency toward left-handedness. The strong Cleary character supports her when, at age ten, she suffers through and survives a terrible ocean voyage as her family relocates to her aunt's Australian ranch, Drogheda.

Here Meggie first encounters Ralph, eighteen years her senior, and her beauty, vulnerability, and need for love capture his heart. Strikingly handsome and described as having a physique like that of a god, Ralph attracts the attention of all women, young and old, despite his priestly status. Meggie remains the only one to whom his heart belongs. She and Father Ralph, (eventually Bishop and then Cardinal Ralph) form two parts of the novel's love triangle. Upon their first meeting Meggie understands that in some way their destinies will remain intertwined. As she matures, she often turns to Ralph for help in dealing with the cruel wilds of Australia and her emotional neglect by her mother. In the rough patriarchal world Meggie occupies, only Ralph offers advice and comfort. The priest comforts Meggie when her cherished brother Frank leaves the family, and he also unwillingly explains the process of menstruation when Meggie believes her bleeding indicates cancer. The two seem to be able to share everything except for the forbidden love barred by Ralph's vows.

But Meggie's love for Ralph survive his ambitious plans for advancement in the church, which separate the two when Meggie is about eighteen. In Ralph's absence, she turns at last to the dashing Luke O'Neill, the third component in the story's triangle, for love and the children she has always wanted. But Meggie knows that the feelings she holds for her husband are only shadowy images of those reserved for Ralph.

It is Luke's physical similarity to Ralph that first attracts Meggie's attention. But Luke is "all man," lacking those feminine qualities that make Ralph so sympathetic and kind. Luke demands control of Meggie's generous savings and allowance, something she does not protest, being used to men controlling her world. But she cannot accept that the rough love-making Luke inflicts upon her is all the emotional attention he will provide. An ambitious man's man, Luke abandons Meggie for months at a time after relocating her to his native North Queensland. Luke's drive to save his own wages toward the purchase of acreage, even though Meggie has access to ample financial resources, causes him to work long, hard hours in the cane fields; he much prefers the company of his mates to that of Meggie.

She exercises her independence when she tricks Luke into making love to her without a condom. The thought of a baby is all that sustains Meggie in her isolation. But her pregnancy and delivery of little Justine are both torture, and their relationship lacks the warmth for which Meggie yearns from its beginning. She does not realize that she is reliving her mother's emotionally crippled relationship with her through her own relationship with her daughter.

That Ralph visits Meggie just as she delivers Justine is both positive and negative. He has successfully pursued his ambition and is steadily ascending the church hierarchy. Yet he still remains drawn to Meggie, his only love, a love that he admits to her but also declares futile. Although joyous over seeing him after so many years, for the first time Meggie lashes out at Ralph, releasing her long pent-up hostility, blaming him for her failed marriage to Luke. He departs knowing he has hurt Meggie but acknowledging they are both trapped in an impossible love.

Throughout Meggie's four years as a married woman often separated from her husband, her love for Ralph does not abate. When they finally make love, Meggie knows and accepts the futility of hoping for the conventional love relationship; all she desires is Ralph's baby. Having been surrounded by men and having survived in a world controlled by men her entire life, she understands that Ralph's ambition outweighs her own needs in importance; she vows never to tell him of his child. In a stark case of foreshadowing, a friend reminds her that, according to Greek legend, love beyond all reason can only cause tragedy because the gods will become jealous and steal away the object of such love. When Meggie replies that she will love her son with a purity like that of the Virgin Mary, she immediately recalls what happened to Mary's son.

She returns home to Drogheda and her mother to raise her son, Dane, keeping the identity of his true father secret as she endures and then finally ends her miserable marital relationship. In focusing all her love on Dane, Meggie again fails to realize that she cuts Justine from her attention just as her mother had done to her. Fate deems that she will follow in the footsteps of Fiona, who fathered her oldest brother Frank out of wedlock with the man she continued to love throughout her marriage to Paddy Cleary. But Meggie cannot help herself; Dane seems the only being that she may totally possess. Even Dane's sad fate seems sealed, however, when Meggie thinks that he will be the only male she has loved who has not deserted her.

The Thorn Birds remains a novel populated by men—Meggie's demanding family of multiple brothers; her adoring and adored priest, Father Ralph; and finally Luke and Dane. Yet Meggie shines as the novel's focus. Her strength and will alone survive as the men in her life fall away. In her sense of values, she contrasts vividly with the self-centered, scheming Luke, a fortune hunter who never loved her for herself but rather for her wealth. She displays her value system when she declines to sue for the $13 million in her aunt's estate that rightfully belongs to her family, labeling what she considers tainted money "pieces of silver." She also stands in contrast to Father Ralph, a weak slave to ambition, despite his true love for Meggie. His blindness to the importance of love, mimicked by his blindness to the fact that Meggie's son is his own, remains balanced by Meggie's clear vision for herself and her family. At last recognizing her own errors and refusing to pick up the life script her mother leaves her, she comes to terms with her own daughter and provides the strength their circle of surviving women demands.

In a romantic novel containing two male candidates who are potential heroes, Meggie Cleary stands above both. Assurance that she has evolved as a character may be gathered from her final thoughts. She compares herself to the thorn bird of the novel's title, a legendary creature who impales itself on the sharpest thorn it can find, rising above its death agony to sing briefly a song that outshines that of the nightingale and the lark. Meggie Cleary sings that same song through her many loves, realizing that the best in life is purchased only with much pain and sacrifice. That she realizes she has suffered willingly and knowingly as the result of her own choices is the epiphany that proves her forever changed.

See also: de Bricassart, Father Ralph; O'Neill, Luke; *The Thorn Birds*

References: Armstrong, 1990; Bridgwood, 1986; Kaplan, 1986; Price, 1983

CONROY, PAT

Pat Conroy, American writer of highly popular novels such as *The Prince of Tides* (1986) and *Beach Music* (1995), was born in 1945 into a military family as the first of seven children. Military assignments for Conroy's father, Colonel Donald Conroy, necessitated that the Conroys live in several different East Coast locations, all in the southern United States. Raised as a southern Catholic, Conroy's identity with the South is projected through his novels, which also emphasize religion as a theme. Much of his admittedly autobiographical work focuses on his family history of violence and abuse at the hands of Colonel Conroy. The author has admitted that his father's violence left an indelible impression that constantly surfaces in his fiction. In addition to religion, violence, and abuse, additional themes in his writing include prejudice, unresolved emotional schisms between close friends and family members, and psychological problems. Poetic imagery; abundant metaphor; and overbearing, often profane, language showcase his strong storytelling skills.

The Boo (1970), Conroy's earliest work, was written and published while he attended the Citadel in Beaufort, South Carolina. Although Conroy had been reluctant to attend the military school, preferring artistic endeavors to those of war, the experience afforded him much material for writing. Dedicated to Conroy's favorite teacher, his memoir *The Boo* was banned at the Citadel due to its critical approach to the institution's brutal training methods. Conroy's second work, also a memoir of sorts, *The Water Is Wide* (1972), chronicles his experience as a young teacher at an all-black southern school. Although his unconventional teaching techniques, including a rejection of the use of corporal punishment and the use of music to teach spelling and language, earned Conroy's dismissal from the job, the experience opened his eyes to his own racism and naïveté regarding the country that he loved. He married his first wife, a Vietnam war widow with two children, during this teaching year.

The Conroys relocated to Atlanta following the birth of their third child; here Conroy would write his first novel, *The Great Santini* (1976). This autobiographical work depicts the conflict Conroy felt as a child through his love and loyalty to a dangerously abusive father. Following publication of *Santini,* the Conroys as a group experienced a crisis causing not only Conroy's divorce but also that of his parents. His mother was reported as having introduced the novel as court evidence of Colonel Conroy's abuse.

In 1980 Conroy published *Lords of Discipline,* a novel featuring life within a military school. The book exposes the harsh military discipline, racism, and sexism of the Citadel. Following remarriage, Conroy lived in Rome and wrote his first highly romantic novel, *The Prince of Tides.* Aspects of Conroy's life and personality are immediately recognizable in the novel's plot and its main character, Tom Wingo. Conroy writes in the dedication to *The Prince of Tides* that his own father, now retired, is "still great, still Santini." After publication of *The Prince of Tides,* Conroy's mother succumbed to cancer and a younger brother committed suicide. His confessional work further damaged the novelist's relationship with family members and caused a loss of communication with the sister fictionalized in the novel as Savannah. The novel reportedly splintered the Conroy family, pitting brothers against sisters and leaving Colonel Conroy living alone in Atlanta.

After a nine-year publishing hiatus, Conroy produced *Beach Music* in 1995. Its protagonist, Jack McCall, remains yet another thinly veiled representation of Conroy himself. The American character moves to Rome to escape the trauma caused by a family suicide, fictionalized in the novel as that of the character's wife, who leaps to her death from a South Carolina bridge. Conroy's favorite themes are showcased here, as he blends Holocaust flashbacks with southern Gothic to help support his antiracist sentiment.

As a testimony to the popularity of Conroy's writings, all except for his first and final books have been made into successful films. Conroy garnered a humanitarian award from the National Education Association following the publication of *The Water Is Wide. The Prince of Tides* remains, with more than five million copies in print, his most successful novel, although *Beach Music* may one day surpass those sales figures. Conroy has been labeled a master storyteller, but some critics find his repetition of imagery and situations from one novel to another the technique of a less-than-classic writer.

See also: The Prince of Tides
References: Berendt, 1995; Frye, 1976; Shone, 1995; Toolan, 1991

COOPER, JAMES FENIMORE

Considered by many as the first great American fiction writer, James Fenimore Cooper did more than anyone else to contribute to Europe's romantic notion of the American West. A prolific writer, Cooper probably remains best known for the five popular novels comprising his Leather-stocking tales. These novels introduced one of American fiction's best-known characters, Natty Bumppo, a frontiersman who experienced the romance of the West through action-adventure stories.

Born in Burlington, New Jersey, on September 15, 1789, Cooper moved as an infant to Cooperstown, New York, a city founded by his father, a wealthy landowner. There on Ostego Lake

James Fenimore Cooper, shown here in a ca. 1830 engraving by James Thomson, remains best known for his five popular Leatherstocking tales about one of American fiction's best-known characters, Natty Bumppo, a frontiersman who experienced the romance of the West through action and adventure. (Library of Congress)

in the center of the state, the author would spend much of his life. From local members of the population as well as from books, he learned the information regarding American Indians and forest lore that he would later use in his books. He went to school in Albany in preparation to attend Yale, where he studied for two years during his teens. Expelled from Yale for his involvement in various escapades, Cooper developed a dislike for New England and departed the United States in 1806 to sail in the Merchant Marines. Two years later, he became a midshipman in the U.S. Navy and then departed the service at age twenty. After coming into an inheritance, Cooper married Susan De Lancey, a member of a landed family that had lost much of its wealth due to its British sympathies during the Revolution. Cooper acted as manager of his wife's estates in New York as they moved back and forth between Scarsdale and Ostego.

Cooper did not begin writing until age thirty. Legend has it that, while reading one of Sir Walter Scott's novels aloud to Susan, he declared that he could write as well. His wife challenged him to prove his claim, and the result was a conventional English novel of manners called *Precaution,* published in 1820 to a lukewarm reception. But when his second novel, *The Spy,* appeared one year later, it brought Cooper much success. This novel remained important as the first well-known historical romance that focused on the Revolution. Convinced that he had a promising career ahead, Cooper relocated to New York City to write full-time. His many subsequent works were marked by some unrealistic scenes and awkward dialogue, inconsistencies about which critics such as Mark Twain would remark. The importance of his work, however, lay not so much in any writing skill as in the fact that Cooper offered new American scenes and themes to writers and readers alike.

As the founder of a group called the Bread and Cheese Club, Cooper occupied the center of a literary and social coterie that included writers such as William Cullen Bryant as well as various notable artists and professionals. *The Pioneers* (1823) began the five-novel series featuring Natty Bumppo and secured Cooper's career. This was followed by *The Last of the Mohicans* (1826), *The Prairie* (1827), *The Pathfinder* (1840), and *The Deerslayer* (1841). Other of Cooper's prodigious achievements include the introduction of the sea novel with *The Pilot* (1823).

He departed America in 1826 to spend seven years abroad, and in Paris came to know Lafayette. There he wrote *Notions of the Americans* (1828), in which he defended his native country against the unfavorable reports that were issuing from European travelers. In another defensive move, he reacted against being known as an American version of Sir Walter Scott by producing a trilogy of realistic novels portraying medieval Europe, hoping to correct Scott's "glorification" of Europe's past. Poor reviews of his novels at home sensitized Cooper to the press, and after his return to the United States he filed several lawsuits, most not very important in themselves, designed to force journalists into truthful reporting. His publication of several pieces of social criticism, the most famous being *Letter to His Countrymen* (1834), demonstrated a conservative attitude toward democracy and met with antagonism, as did his attempts to prevent locals from using his lands for recreational purposes. Although legally credible, Cooper's moves protesting his negative portrayal in unsympathetic newspapers as a spoiled would-be aristocrat accomplished little in the way of transforming journalistic coverage.

While carrying out this private war, Cooper continued to write productively. In 1835 he produced a satire, *The Monikins,* and three years later *The American Democrat.* After completing the final two novels in his Leatherstocking tales series, he wrote the enormous *History of the Navy of the United States* (1839), a work that became a renewed focus for lawsuits against the press. From 1845 to 1846, Cooper completed a trilogy called the Littlepage manuscripts, including *Satanstoe* (1845), *The Chainbearer* (1845), and *The Redskins* (1846). This series dealt with several generations belonging to a New York family. The three novels defended the landed class of which Cooper remained a part against the nouveau riche whose wealth issued from industry and finance.

His novels lost favor for a time following Cooper's death on September 14, 1851. Whether deserved or not, Cooper had gained a reputation for pretentiousness and argumentativeness. Eventually his Leatherstocking tales were read only by children. By the 1920s, however, critics "rediscovered" his works for their importance as social criticism. Although weak in a literary vein, these American novels have been read and appreciated by an enormous audience that includes

Honoré de Balzac and Leo Tolstoy. Contemporary readers may appreciate Cooper's incorporation of themes such as the restriction of voting rights common in his time, the conflict between natural and legal rights, environmental destruction early in American history, and the continued conflict between change and order.

See also: The Last of the Mohicans; Scott, Sir Walter
References: Barker and Sabin, 1996; "Cooper, James Fenimore," 1986; Ousby, 1988

COSETTE

In Victor Hugo's novel *Les Misérables* (1862), Cosette acts as the female romantic interest of the young political revolutionary, Marius Pontmercy, but more importantly, she functions as the means of grace for the novel's protagonist, ex-convict Jean Valjean. The illegitimate daughter of a hapless young woman named Fantine, Cosette, a nickname for Euphrasie Fauchelevent, spends her early childhood in the care of the Thénardier family. Fantine pays the Thénardiers to care for Cosette while she works in a factory to earn a living, and they press the woman for more and more money to pay for support they do not actually provide. The family includes a daughter named Eponine, who is spoiled by her parents, in contrast to their abuse of Cosette, who is treated like a servant. However disagreeable Eponine's relationship with Cosette during childhood appears, she will later play an important part in uniting Cosette with Marius.

Following Fantine's death, Valjean keeps his promise to the woman and searches out Cosette, a child of only five. When he first encounters her, Cosette returns from one of her many difficult chores, this time fetching water in a bucket for the horse of one of the Thénardiers' customers. The skinny, unattractive child is rescued by Valjean as she stumbles beneath the weight of a load almost as big as herself. When Valjean grasps the load and lifts it from Cosette's hands, he symbolically removes her previous cares from her life, volunteering to shoulder them himself. Thus, Cosette's presence allows Valjean's performance of an act of kindness in the tradition taught to him by a kindly bishop, who once sheltered Valjean when others would not. When Valjean repaid the bishop's kindness by stealing his silver, the bishop allowed the ex-convict to keep not only that booty but also a pair of silver candlesticks. Cosette's later affection for Valjean will correlate

to the light from the candlesticks, both testaments to the redemptive power of love and mercy. Valjean wins the child's confidence when he supports a lie she tells her nasty foster mother in order to escape a beating. The child departs the home of the Thénardiers to live with Valjean, beginning a long series of adventures for the pair.

Cosette changes greatly during the twenty-year span of the novel. When she first catches the eye of Marius, about nine years later in Paris, she still appears plain and undernourished. But within six months, her appearance alters as she undergoes the transformation into womanhood that one would expect in a romance tale. Hugo comments on the transformation, calling it the most natural thing in the world as he compares Cosette's maturation to the age-old romantic symbol of the blooming rose. Her sudden, simple elegance the author labels dangerous, foreshadowing the future conflict her beauty will cause in attracting what at first appears to be a love that must remain unfulfilled.

Eponine causes an uncomfortable love triangle to form, as she interferes with an important correspondence between Marius and Cosette at the time when Paris's revolutionary fervor begins to escalate. Eponine becomes a strong romantic figure when she risks, and sacrifices, her life for Marius. As she dies, she makes an additional sacrifice in sharing with Marius a message from Cosette that might have remained hidden if not for Eponine's efforts.

Marius learns that Cosette will be taken from Paris by the protective Valjean, who also struggles to protect himself against the unrelenting pursuit of a police inspector named Javert. When Marius learns that he'll be separated from his love, he gives himself over to the cause of the war, not caring whether he lives or not. But through the good acts of Valjean, who at first seemed the instrument of destruction for their love, the two young lovers will unite.

In a memorable scene with Marius's grandfather, Hugo uses the future union of Cosette and Marius as an occasion for Gillenormand's commentary on the importance of love. The old man urges the two young people to be foolish in love, for love is the wisdom of God. Although Gillenormand expresses regret that they cannot inherit his fortune, Valjean presents his own ample savings to act as Cosette's dowry. Marius worries that the money represents ill-gotten gains, but its very connection with Cosette, a symbol of purity, disallows that possibility. Valjean later explains that it resulted from his years running a glassworks, following his theft from the bishop that set him on the track of justice and good works.

Cosette remains unaware of Valjean's true identity until the novel's conclusion, when Marius realizes that Valjean saved his own life at the barricades and also that of Cosette. He compares Valjean to a figure of darkness who helped elevate the star that is Cosette. She also acts as a means of enlightenment for Marius, who even labels her his light. Cosette's protection by Valjean proves to Marius that from the dark may come light, a highly biblical allusion indicating that Marius has matured as a character. Cosette, although important to the development of the novel's two major male protagonists, remains a rather flat character herself. The innocence and naïveté so important to her provision of light for the men confine her to a cocoon of goodness that smothers any true need for self-awareness.

Now married, the two young people seek out the old man on his deathbed, where Cosette will learn the truth regarding her mother and her adoption by Valjean. His presentation to Cosette of the candlesticks unites the two symbols of inspiration for his change in attitude toward his fellow humans. The fire from the candles symbolizes the light of knowledge that the bishop's act of kindness provided Valjean. Cosette, a figure also repeatedly represented by light imagery, has transformed Valjean through her unquestioning trust and devotion. Thanks to the girl, Valjean changes from a potentially lost soul to a man redeemed through love.

See also: Fantine; Hugo, Victor; *Les Misérables;*
Romance; Valjean, Jean; Violence; War
References: Grossman, 1994; Masters-Wicks, 1994

THE COUNT OF MONTE CRISTO

When the prolific French author Alexandre Dumas penned his nineteenth-century novel *The Count of Monte Cristo* (1844), he gave to humankind one of the most perfectly fashioned historical romances ever written. The novel also contributes several enduring devices, such as the secret message written in disappearing ink, to later adventure novels. Based on the true story of a young shoemaker betrayed by friends and imprisoned as a spy, the novel traces a tale of retribution and revenge. This popular story found its way to the screen in at least four versions between 1934 and 1975.

As a quest, *The Count of Monte Cristo* remains an excellent example of a novel based on traditional elements and themes, some of which can be traced as far back as *The Odyssey*. It features a sailor-hero, with much of its action and several journeys taking place on the sea. That hero, Edmond Dantes, later to be known as the Count of Monte Cristo, remains a paragon of virtue yet evinces the stern strength expected from a Byronic hero in his brooding administration of justice against those who betray him. Dantes's imprisonment represents a descent into Hades, where he will meet a guide, Abbé Faria. The abbé imparts knowledge in the form of book learning and wisdom through his philosophy that humans reap what they sow. The two form one of the several father-son relationships, whether based on blood or, more loosely, on friendship, presented throughout the novel. The death of this father-figure and also his real father, as well as the loss of his first love to a rival, represent for Dantes the personal losses quest heroes must suffer. Dantes answers a call to adventure when he seeks his freedom, employing the first of multiple disguises used in order to accomplish his purpose. Readers will recognize the parallels in these two elements to the Odysseus-Telemachus father-son relationship and Odysseus's many disguises granted to him by Athena. Naturally, Dantes receives a reward for the successful completion of his quest, both material, in the form of priceless jewels, and emotional, in the form of a new romantic love. But the quest does not end at this point.

The story remains plot-driven, with adventure piled upon adventure to hold reader attention. The novel opens in the year 1815 in Marseilles with the heroic feat of a nineteen-year-old Dantes, who skillfully guides a ship into port after the death of its captain. As a reward, he receives the rank of captain himself. The book moves quickly through a focus on his engagement to the beautiful Mercedes and his betrayal into prison by several individuals. The betrayal is based on a letter Dantes transports from the exiled Napoleon into France, allowing Dumas to introduce the political intrigue and historical factors that will run throughout his tale.

The many years Dantes spends in prison remain necessary to the novel's theme of revenge. Not only does Dantes want to identify and kill those who plotted his demise, but also he desires a long, slow, torturous decline for each. As he reaches this goal, he demands that the pain of the punishments equal the tremendous amount of suffering he endured during fourteen years of an imprisonment that would have killed most men. Thus the story remains one of revenge, and Dumas stresses this several times. Dantes speaks of vengeance in terms of heavenly retribution, aligning himself with God on various occasions as he acts as a tool of God's providence.

Dantes's identification with a higher power sent to purify the world is advanced by his making his escape from prison at the age of thirty-three, Christ's age when crucified. In addition, in ascending from the depths of the dungeon prison, he swims up through a sea, with the water representing baptism into new life. When Dantes sews himself into the sack that acts as a funeral shroud for the dead abbé, substituting himself to be "buried" at sea, he symbolically "dies" before resurrection. Dantes's miraculous rebirth might also be compared to that of the phoenix, a mythological bird that dies in flames every five hundred years, only to be reborn as a new creature. In *The Count of Monte Cristo,* Dantes emerges from the "skin" of the funeral bag carrying with him the spirit of the abbé, much like a phoenix arising in new form from certain destruction. This great bird also serves as a symbol for Christ.

In accordance with the romantic tradition, the novel includes much intrigue, misidentification, and a dependence upon coincidence to solve some of its problems. It also incorporates scenes of pageantry and carnival, celebrations often featured in romance and used in real life through the ages to relieve stress on the part of the lower classes. Often called celebrations of misrule, through costuming these pageants allowed the downtrodden to assume the guise of the powerful. Subsequent confusion of true identities permitted a release of tensions between various factions in the lower and middle classes. This "safe rebellion" was considered important by the ruling class as a factor in controlling the working classes and preventing true rebellion. Unfortunately, these pageants also allowed the disguise of evil, and crime sometimes resulted. Dumas's use of a Paris pageant as the scene of a staged kidnapping that aids Dantes in his quest for revenge resembles fellow French writer Victor Hugo's employment of such celebration in *The Hunchback of Notre Dame* (1831). The plot twists the two authors develop through carnival themes differ greatly, but their settings offer much similarity.

So "thick" becomes the plot in *The Count of Monte Cristo* that in-depth characterization does not occur. Each of the multitude of characters represents obvious "good" or "bad" elements in human nature, making the villains/villainesses and heroes/heroines easy to distinguish from one another. Madame Villefort, who delivers her illegitimate baby to his supposed death and later plots the murders of three family members out of a desire for wealth and power, represents one of the most wicked women in all of fiction. And Monsieur Danglars's actions in attempting to bury a baby alive stand as a chilling reminder of humanity's darkest side. Such behavior Dumas balances with that of Valentine, daughter of one of Dantes's enemies but a young woman of the purest heart, and by Albert de Morcerf, son of Mercedes and Dantes's hated rival, Ferdinand, whose honest intentions and behavior cause Dantes to spare his life.

For all of its general predictability, the plot provides unending entertainment and delights readers familiar with various romance formulas as they recognize even the best-cloaked plot elements. For instance, the fact that Dantes never marries his fiancée from his youth, Mercedes, an innocent who falls victim to the same trickery that trapped Dantes, may seem at first not true to the tenor of romance. But this disappointed love, along with Mercedes's decision after discovering the depths of her husband's wickedness to live her life in prayer, bears definite resemblance to the story of ruined love featuring King Arthur and Queen Guinevere. Like Arthur, who trusted Lancelot, Dantes believes the scheming Ferdinand Mondego to be his friend. When he entrusts the care of Mercedes to this so-called ally, he never dreams that Ferdinand covets Mercedes as his own. Mercedes's return to the small house that remains a pseudoshrine to Dantes's father echoes Guinevere's choice of a nunnery in which to spend her years following

the eruption of discord between Arthur and
Lancelot over her.

Although some readers may criticize the melodramatic presentation of one-dimensional characters in *The Count of Monte Cristo,* this work remains
crucial to the development of the romance novel.
It satisfactorily provides readers emotional release
as they vicariously identify with a wronged man
allowed to wreak vengeance on his enemies.

See also: Dantes, Edmond; Dumas, Alexandre;
Herrera, Mercedes; Mondego, Ferdinand; Quest;
Violence
References: Campbell, 1968; Campbell, 1988; de
Rougemont, 1983; Grierson, 1974; Hulme, 1974;
Spurr, 1972

COURTLY LOVE
See Chivalry

Golden Age," her connotation remains decidedly negative, a reflection on the reserved attitudes of the Victorian Age.

By the selection of symbolic names for his characters, James also hints to the reader that a romance between these two ill-matched young people will never occur. The wild flower that Daisy represents could never thrive in the cold social climate symbolized by Winterbourne's name and social class.

When the Millers move on to Rome, Mrs. Costello's judgmental voice is joined by that of Mrs. Walker. This good woman does her best to rescue Daisy from the imagined less-than-honorable attentions of a local man but is roundly rebuffed by the girl, who sees no harm in her actions. Daisy's mother is the only mature female who resists exerting much effort in discouraging in her daughter an independence that borders on stubbornness. Daisy and her brother, Randolph, are obviously more than Mrs. Miller can control or understand. The reader may get the idea that the absent Mr. Miller who, by report, remained in the United States to carry on business, purposely found something else to do for the summer other than be embarrassed by his children's exuberance.

The story is delivered by an unseen narrator, beginning in first person and then switching to third person from Winterbourne's point of view, an unusual approach to narration. Winterbourne remains exasperated yet enthralled by Daisy's lifestyle and penchant for pleasure. He admits being captivated by what he considers a rational approach to life on the part of a surprisingly intelligent young woman. Ironically, this very approach threatens others of his social group. When early in the story, Winterbourne announces to his aunt that he has made Daisy's acquaintance, she promptly categorizes the Millers as common. When Winterbourne later calls Daisy innocent, Mrs. Walker calls her reckless. Mrs. Costello keeps the Millers at arm's length, conjuring excuses not to meet "them," commenting that Daisy possesses the look "they" all have. When Winterbourne suggests that his aunt can't ignore the Millers, she responds that she can't not ignore them. Clearly, the Millers and Daisy in particular represent some threaten-

DAISY MILLER

In the preface to his 1879 novella, *Daisy Miller,* Henry James relates his inspiration for the story, which focuses on a type of heroine who would, two years later, be further developed in his novel *The Portrait of a Lady.* According to the author, in 1877 a friend told him a story about an American lady who had, during one winter in Rome, innocently and with great spirit acquired the company of a handsome Roman gentleman as an escort. The Italian had considered himself fortunate to find such a prize, not, apparently, for salacious reasons, but because he was so charmed by the American's naïveté. The social indiscretion was put right, however, and James admits that his friend heard no more of either the young woman or her paramour. The world, however, would hear of her later when James gave form to this unknown young lady as Annie P. Miller, nicknamed Daisy, an American hailing from Schenectady, New York.

Daisy acts as one of James's favorite character types, a displaced, young, beautiful American woman whose penchant for freedom of action and expression tends to scandalize the natives of whichever European country she might be visiting. Daisy begins in Switzerland, where she meets Frederick Forsythe Winterbourne, also an American traveling in the company of his dour aunt, Mrs. Costello. Mrs. Costello appears as the first cautionary voice in the novella, pointing out to Winterbourne, who is immediately charmed by Daisy, that the Millers are obviously undesirable because they address their courier, Eugenio, as an equal. This begins James's commentary on the social mores that governed the behavior of the wealthy socialites of his era. When Mrs. Costello later comments that Daisy's attitude, in living for the moment, resembles that of "the

ing "other" to the members of Winterbourne's circle.

When Winterbourne arrives in Rome, he visits Mrs. Walker and unexpectedly meets Daisy there. He has looked forward to and anticipated that moment, although he had hoped to plan it out, but Daisy's nonchalant welcome surprises him. She at once insists that he should have called on her first, while simultaneously warding off his attentions in favor of her new Roman companion, Giovanelli. Winterbourne's jealousy is mixed with the concern he shares with Mrs. Walker regarding Daisy's relationship to the attractive Italian. When he expresses this concern, Daisy makes clear that she feels it is unfounded. Clearly, for her, striking up a relationship with a pleasant, handsome, young Italian man who desires to share her company is the most natural thing in the world.

James provides additional social commentary as he traces Daisy's path of self-destruction. She commits one faux pas after another, first refusing to heed Mrs. Walker's warning about Giovanelli, then refusing the older woman's offer of a ride in the park. Mrs. Walker wishes to save Daisy the scandal of being seen walking unsupervised with the Italian, but Daisy sees no reason to bow to such misgivings. In exasperation, Mrs. Walker informs Daisy that she is of an age to conduct herself with more reason and to be "talked about," but Daisy does not understand the comment. When Mrs. Walker invites her again to enter her carriage so she can explain, Daisy replies that she does not *want* to understand.

Totally embarrassed by the scene, Winterbourne flinches when Daisy asks whether he feels her reputation to be at stake. He urges her to enter the carriage, but when she again refuses, he does so in order to end the scene. But Daisy will not be contained. She appears later at a social event with the uninvited Giovanelli in tow, even demanding that Mrs. Walker allow her friend to sing at the gathering. Daisy's conversation at that party with Winterbourne remains the most revealing interchange in the book. When Winterbourne attempts to explain that flirting is not considered innocent and naive in Rome as it is in America and that Giovanelli's attentions are likely "something else," her retort that at least her friend does not preach at her ends Winterbourne's hopes for a romantic relationship with Daisy. She delivers the ultimate blow when she informs Winterbourne that neither she nor Giovanelli are flirting because their friendship is more substantial than flirting would allow. When Winterbourne insists that he has delivered sound advice, Daisy replies that she would rather have weak tea.

Daisy will pay for standing her ground. When she approaches her hostess to thank her and take her leave, the imperious Mrs. Walker turns her back upon the girl. So fraught with meaning is this gesture that Daisy might just as well have been marked by Hester Prynne's infamous scarlet "A." When she flaunts convention to make a dangerous visit to the Colosseum at night, Daisy invites the Roman fever, or malaria, that will lead to her death.

Like others of James's characters, Daisy behaves like a totally independent being, when, in fact, she remains restrained by society's limitations. In her later reincarnation as *The Portrait of a Lady*'s Isabel Archer, this character will come to terms with these limitations, maturing into a disappointed but determined woman who pays throughout her life for practicing unflinching dedication to unreachable ideals. Daisy stands more as a tragic figure, literally killed by her desire to follow her instincts. She is, as James remarks, a work shaped in poetic rather than in critical terminology. According to James, such poetic rendering may have produced a flatness of character and a lack of stimulating scenes that both attracted and repelled readers. That poetry is supported by the rich Italian setting representative of the stunning staging that James, an expatriate American, always allowed his stories. In the novella's case, the Roman setting remains so beautiful and alluring that it must, indeed, be complicit in hiding the dangers that Mrs. Walker predicts. If Daisy's death is tragic, it is also poetically satisfying, for the perpetrator is not, as all of the Mrs. Walkers and Costellos predict, the manifestation of some social malfeasance but rather a perfectly natural cause. Daisy may have been nature's child, but that nature felt no more compunction to nourish and protect Daisy than did her fellow humans.

Daisy Miller represents James's favorite genre, that of the abbreviated prose narrative, one in which he excelled. The novella first appeared in 1878 in two issues of *Cornhill Magazine,* published by Virginia Woolf's father, Leslie Stephen. The work is marked by several Jamesian conven-

tions such as complicated syntax and verbal ambi-
guities. He deepens the effect of his narration by
handing it over to a specific, attentive fictional
character who adds drama to a plot marked by
psychological complexity on the part of its protagonist. In Daisy's case, this suggests a paradox,
for she supposedly chooses to live the simplest of
lives. That may, in the end, be the most complex
approach she could have taken, leaving her to run
a punishing gauntlet of public opinion and die
because of her inability to heed the warnings of
others. This excellent novella was made into a
movie in 1974.

See also: Archer, Isabel; Miller, Daisy; *The Portrait of
a Lady;* Winterbourne, Frederick Forsythe
References: Caeserio, 1979; Frye, 1976; McQuade et
al., 1987; Washington, 1995

DANIELE

Daniele is one of the antiheroes in Giuseppe
Berto's novel, *The Sky Is Red* (1948). Although
Daniele's love for Giulia ennobles him, it fails to
yield him the strength demanded for survival in
his war-ravaged environment. A young Italian
boy of almost sixteen years of age, given a seminary education by his wealthy parents, Daniele
should have been able to do anything he wanted
in life. But the interruption of his life by the evil
of war robs him of his future along with his self-
confidence. Vulnerable, sensitive, and idealistic,
Daniele does not possess the survival skills necessary to propel him through the horrors of postwar Italy.

When Daniele returns from school to his
home town, he discovers his parents have died in
the bombing that devastated an already economically depressed community. Because he does not
want to move to Rome to join relatives, he joins
a group composed of orphaned teens and children who have combined their meager resources
to live on their own with only marginal aid from
a shoe repairman in the neighborhood. In the
group, he develops relationships with seventeen-
year-old Tullio, the outspoken supporter of communism; Carla, Tullio's even younger lover who
turns to prostitution to help provide the physical
needs of the group; and Giulia, the youngest
teen, who symbolizes the innocence and idealism closest to Daniele's own. Although vastly different in upbringing from these young people
who have made due all their lives in less than
optimal social and economic conditions, Daniele

learns from each life lessons that at once repel
and impress him.

The sexual seduction of Daniele by Carla and
his later sexual relationship with Giulia remain,
for the age in which the novel was written,
morally shocking due to their tender ages. But no
less shocking should be the physical conditions
they are forced to survive. As the figure representing a privileged group, Daniele is censured
for his bourgeois ideology by Tullio, who uses
Communist political ideology to criticize the
inequities faced by the Italian working class.
Daniele's own belief structure is shaken by his
experiences with the young street people and the
discovery of his own lack of survival skills. The
idea of burglary repels him because he has been
taught that it is "wrong," yet starvation seems
even more a travesty. After facing the fact that
crime is relative, he cannot then return to his idealistic approach to life. He remains incapable of
recognizing the difference between human and
natural laws.

His match with Giulia creates a contrast to the
match between Carla and Tullio. Following
Tullio's death, Carla is able to proceed with her
life, no matter how seemingly barren of joy and
lacking in worth that life might be. But Daniele
views the continuation of his life as an exercise in
futility once he loses Giulia. For Daniele, the
strength he drew from love, first for his mother
and later for Giulia, was the only strength he had.
Desiring an understanding of his feelings of utter
desolation following Giulia's death from consumption, he seeks the solace of an elderly
teacher whom Tullio used to visit. The old man
attempts to explain to Daniele that war's gravest
infliction upon humans is the realization of loneliness, and that each person must stand on his or
her own with no support from fellow human
beings. Daniele finds this nihilistic attitude repugnant, yet he cannot deny its truth.

Daniele's decision to commit suicide remains
his only option. He watches Tullio, seemingly so
independent and self-sufficient, undergo a violent
end in trying to meet the physical needs of his
adopted family. He watches Giulia, an innocent
young daughter of a prostitute, die from a disease
that causes her undeserved pain and suffering. He
watches Carla cope with the horrors around her
simply by denying her emotions, remaining cold
and cynical in her approach to life. For these
young people, life simply equaled loss: a loss of

innocence, of love, of life. Unable to face an existence representing the betrayal of all he had ever been taught about humankind, he selects the only honorable substitute for that existence that he could imagine.

Daniele's character plays a large part in delivering Berto's message of futility and nihilism. A character with the potential to portray the hero in a more conventional romantic quest, Daniele instead remains caught up in a plot that subverts those conventions and leaves the reader with a barrenly realistic view of humankind's continuing strife through war and the tragic consequences inflicted upon the innocent by the greed of the powerful.

See also: Carla; Giulia; Nihilism; *The Sky Is Red;* Tullio; War

References: Hoffman and Murphy, 1996; Price, 1983

DANTES, EDMOND

Probably one of the best-known romantic characters of all time, Edmond Dantes, or the Count of Monte Cristo, represents the prototypical romantic quest hero. Connected to the sea through his vocation as a sailor from the novel's beginning, Dantes is the main character in Alexandre Dumas's historical romance, *The Count of Monte Cristo* (1844). This plot-driven story presents clear-cut heroes/heroines or villains/villainesses, shown to be in favor of or against Dantes in the novel's opening chapters. He will later assume several aliases throughout the novel, becoming both a guardian angel, rewarding those who offered him support, and an avenging angel, wreaking havoc in the lives of those who offered only betrayal.

Unfairly charged and illegally imprisoned for fourteen years, Dantes loses his promising future as a ship captain along with his fiancée, Mercedes Herrera. He then experiences all of the aspects of the quest. Like many quest heroes, he reacts reluctantly to a call to adventure represented by the promise of freedom because it arrives so late. The hope he at first experiences during imprisonment eventually dissolves through stages into doubt, dejection, anger, and finally surrender, as physical conditions that would kill many men threaten to break his spirit. When imprisoned, he also experiences the symbolic descent into Hades, in which the hero searches for a father figure to deliver advice early in his quest. After six years of struggling to retain his sanity, Dantes encounters the quintessential quest guide and adviser in the form of a fellow prisoner, Abbé Faria.

The abbé, or priest, assumes a symbolic significance as a "father" in a religious sense. He also substitutes for Dantes's own father during imprisonment. Over the next eight years, the abbé teaches Dantes all he knows of literature, mathematics, history, and languages. When the abbé collapses as the two tunnel toward freedom, he urges Dantes to go without him, but Dantes passes his first test of faith by refusing to leave the abbé. He also receives his first reward when the abbé tells him of a treasure buried on the island of Monte Cristo. The experience of loss for this hero continues when the abbé dies. But Dantes takes the abbé's place in his funeral "sack" that the prison employees throw out into a stormy sea, thereby offering Dantes a means of escape.

Dantes's close connection to the sea continues as he pursues his quest to the island of Monte Cristo. Here he procures the fortune in jewels and the companionship of Haidee, the island girl who eventually becomes the replacement for his first lost love, Mercedes. Both the jewels he finds and his future love represent prototypical rewards of the quest. But those material and emotional rewards are only the beginning, for revenge is the single reward that will satisfy Dantes.

He retains his identity only long enough to rescue his devoted patron Morrel and Morrel's family from financial destruction. Then he turns to the revenge that will occupy all his energies for years to come. Dantes's alteration into the vengeful count becomes apparent at a grisly scene of execution in Paris, when he tells his companions that he believes the suffering caused through punishment should match that caused by the perpetrator's crime. This statement warns readers that, rather than simply assassinating those responsible for his betrayal or hiring someone else to murder them for him, he will personally exact a lengthy repayment equal to his own exacerbated torture over fourteen years of imprisonment.

He uses the treasure to help discover the identity of his betrayers and to gain the necessary power to destroy them and their families. Throughout the novel, Dantes uses the skills learned from the abbé to seek revenge against each of the four main villains who caused his imprisonment and, by extension, his own elderly father's death. The swath of destruction wreaked

In this 1934 film version of The Count of Monte Cristo, *Robert Donat played Edmond Dantes, the prototypical romantic quest hero and one of the best-known romantic characters of all time. (The Kobal Collection)*

by Dantes evokes thoughts of Odysseus's own destruction of the usurpers in his house following his return home from his classic quest.

The physical changes Dantes undergoes during his imprisonment transform him into an individual fitting the mold of the Byronic hero; he becomes dark, brooding, and handsome, with eyes reflecting an inner turmoil and the loss of his initial naïveté. Some critics argue that these changes, symbolic of internal alterations also represented by his intellectual change as a result of the abbé's teachings, make Dantes into a dynamic, well-rounded character. Others argue he is too stereotypical and predictable in his role as a quest hero.

As Dantes continues his quest, he successfully ruins all those individuals for whom he bears much hatred. But he simultaneously discovers love, not only for the beautiful Haidee, but also for the son, Albert de Morcerf, of one of his declared enemies, the Count de Morcerf (alias

Ferdinand Mondego). Ferdinand had not only betrayed Dantes into prison but also succeeded in marrying Dantes's sweetheart, Mercedes; Albert is the product of that marriage. Dantes believes in the maxim that sons should suffer for the sins of their fathers, and he acts successfully on this idea in several instances. But his eventual love for Albert convinces him that he is in error. Their connection also allows for the continual emphasis on the importance of the father-son relationships that occur throughout the novel. Such relationships are traditionally all-important to the romantic quest plot structure, as younger men discover their identities under the influence of older role models.

In a similar vein, Dantes saves the life of Valentine, the daughter of one of his enemies, Monsieur Villefort, a prosecuting attorney who imprisoned Dantes in order to save his own future and reputation. Because Maximilien Morrel, son of Dantes's great friend and supporter, Monsieur Morrel, loves Valentine, Dantes intercedes to save her life and to reunite these lovers. But first he passes along wisdom to this younger man, just as the abbé years before had passed on wisdom to Dantes. He informs Maximilien that only a man who has truly suffered may experience happiness.

The hero explains to Valentine his hope that when passing future judgment upon Dantes's many acts of vengeance, God will also take into account these two lives saved. When Dantes and Haidee sail away, never to be seen again, the quest cycle is completed.

Edmond Dantes, the Count of Monte Cristo, represents in all aspects the ultimate romantic hero. His character proves what seems to be the novel's moral: true virtue will find reward.

See also: Byronic Hero; The Count of Monte Cristo; Dumas, Alexandre; Herrera, Mercedes; Mondego, Ferdinand; Quest; Romance; Violence
References: Campbell, 1968; Campbell, 1988; Charlton, 1984; de Rougemont, 1983; Frye, 1976; Grierson, 1974; Hulme, 1974; Spurr, 1972

DARCY, FITZWILLIAM

Fitzwilliam Darcy, of Jane Austen's *Pride and Prejudice* (1813), seems doomed from the novel's beginning to embody the character flaw of which he is accused by both the novel's title and by other characters, that of pride. But, due to Austen's genius for exquisite character shaping, the reader soon questions whether Darcy's pride is of the wicked or the wise school. Because Mrs. Bennet is revealed as a half-wit from the novel's first page, her estimation of Darcy as disagreeable and horrid, "fancying himself" and lacking the physical appeal to tempt a dance partner, remains open to doubt. Conversely, when Charles Bingley, a far more positive figure than Mrs. Bennet, holds Darcy's opinion in the highest regard and trusts his judgment over that of all others, the reader tends to accept Bingley's estimation. On the same page, Bingley describes Darcy as "clever," "haughty," "reserved," and "fastidious," with well-bred but not inviting manners. Because of the mixed reactions to Darcy, all of these adjectives are left open to scrutiny. The pride Darcy represents is not an unbending pride but more a product of self-assurance. The intelligence attributed to him by Bingley leaves the reader hoping that he will react well when that assurance is shaken.

His early declaration to Bingley that Elizabeth Bennet does not tempt him to dance is the thread used by others to weave a web of disagreeable rumor concerning Darcy's personality and demeanor. Elizabeth admits that she could forgive Darcy's pride, had he not offended her own. Interestingly enough, Austen then uses the voice of the younger Bennet sister, Mary, to reveal a certain truth about pride that particularly applies to Darcy, when she distinguishes between pride as the opinion we have of ourselves and vanity as what we desire others to think of us. Elizabeth fails to connect the comment regarding vanity to herself, and thus a misunderstanding that will last through a good part of the novel takes root.

Elizabeth Bennet finds Darcy deserving of attention, as she reveals in her early comment to Bingley that "intricate characters are the *most* amusing." Fitzwilliam Darcy certainly qualifies as intricate, and Austen's use of irony in shaping Darcy through the questionable opinions of others enables her to make a moral statement about class snobbery, but not at the ultimate expense of her character. Darcy is not a flat, undeveloped monolith, as is, for instance, the decidedly preposterous caricature, Mr. Collins. The novel's romantic hero will rise to the occasion when needed, revealing his humanity and employing his celebrated judgment not only to rescue Elizabeth's sister but to allow Elizabeth to make amends for her own misjudgment of him.

Although Darcy is declared by several characters as unfit to participate in social interaction, he redeems himself through Austen's polite but thoroughly ironic dialogue. After meeting Elizabeth Bennet, the jealous Miss Bingley declares to Darcy that Eliza Bennet is surely one of those ladies who "recommends" herself to men by "undervaluing" her own sex. When Miss Bingley declares Elizabeth's actions a practice of a mean art, Darcy responds that meanness exists in all of those arts employed by ladies for purposes of captivating men; anything of such a cunning nature is deplorable. Darcy is clearly identified as a person who is hard to fool and capable of assessing the motives of others. Neither would be possible for a person whose vision only turned inward.

The best clues to Darcy's character are revealed in his dialogue with Elizabeth Bennet. Their repartee remains reminiscent of Shakespeare's famous duo, Benedick and Beatrice from *Much Ado about Nothing*. Their exchanges are pointed and curt, but they also advance the relationship, as each methodically searches out the other's misgivings and misapprehensions. After reading Darcy's letter, which appears at almost the exact middle of the novel, Elizabeth will tell another character that one's estimation of Darcy improves upon further acquaintance, voicing the reader's thoughts exactly.

Darcy also knows when to remain silent. When Elizabeth receives the news that Lydia has eloped with Wickham, Darcy notes her considerable discomfort. After asking what he can do to help, he suffers as Elizabeth bursts into tears, observing her at length in a "compassionate silence." When Elizabeth declares herself to blame for not calling attention to Wickham's character, Darcy could have taken the opportunity to exercise the pride for which he had been condemned to agree with her and heap his condemnation on top of her own. Instead, he makes "no answer." In the end, he vows to keep the Bennets' secret, again willingly electing to observe silence, out of sorrow for Elizabeth's distress. Ironically, Elizabeth feels at that moment, when Darcy acts in the most devoted manner, that she will never see Darcy again. She still mistrusts him due to her prejudiced initial opinion.

When Darcy's true feelings are at last laid out in another letter, this time written to Elizabeth by her aunt, there can be no doubt that he has changed. He professes that pride had prevented his sharing the negative experience he had with Wickham; had he done so, Lydia might not have been caught up in near-disaster. As one who hides his knowledge of another, he resembles Austen's character Colonel Brandon from *Sense and Sensibility*.

When Darcy and Elizabeth finally admit their romantic feelings, he admits that, although her accusations of him during their early acquaintance may have been formed on mistaken premises, those premises were shaped by his own actions. As a strong character should, Darcy analyzes his shortcomings, admitting to having been taught what was right as a child but not how to follow such principles. When he tells Elizabeth that her humbling of him has revealed his pretense, he has finally taken shape as the complete character Austen intended.

See also: Austen, Jane; Bennet, Elizabeth; Brandon, Colonel; Ferrars, Edward; *Pride and Prejudice; Sense and Sensibility*

References: Armstrong, 1990; Britannica, 1997; Clayton, 1987a; Copeland and McMaster, 1997; de Rougemont, 1983; Gard, 1992; Gilbert and Gubar, 1985c; Praz, 1974; Watt, 1963

DARE, PAMELA

Pamela Dare, a character from Edward R. Braithwaite's *To Sir, with Love* (1959), represents a type known to many not only from novels containing themes of romance but also from real life. She is a high school student who falls in love with her teacher. Because her love can only be classified as a "crush," at first it does not seem to belong in the category of forbidden love. Rather, this feeling of attraction to her teacher is based more on admiration and a desire to please than on any hormonally motivated emotion. However, the interracial aspects of the relationship advance it into the category of forbidden love.

Pamela is one of the many rebellious slum students from London's poverty-stricken East End that British Guianan engineer Rick Braithwaite takes on in the classroom. Like her classmates, Pamela at first displays the vicious crudity toward the new teacher that she has to his predecessors. But "Sir," as the students learn to call their new instructor, quickly reveals a difference in management style that allows Pamela to relate positively to an adult authority figure for the first time in her life. Pamela adopts him as a father substitute, and she seems to experience the attraction to this father that most females experience as young girls. She finds the attention he bestows on the students flattering and appealing. Having never been treated with respect, she misinterprets the respect she receives as romantic affection. The fact that Braithwaite is a black man within Pamela's mostly white culture also adds an air of the exotic to this strange figure. Pamela is attracted to him not only for his maleness but also because he represents an "other" about which she knows little.

Because Braithwaite notices Pamela's crush, he is able, with the help of some advice from his fellow female instructors, to handle the situation gracefully. As is usually the case in real life with a girl inclined to fancy her teacher, Pamela undergoes disappointment and rejection when she discovers the attraction is not mutual. Her eventual acceptance and appreciation of him as a trusted adult role model shows that she has progressed as a character. She must experiment with her feelings for him before she can transfer these feelings to a more suitable subject and develop a satisfying relationship with a male peer.

Pamela becomes something of a rebel among rebels. She acts as a voice against the inherent racism among her peers, who automatically hurl racial slurs at their new teacher. Even though their comments are motivated by ignorance rather than hate, Pamela takes offense and is, for the first time, willing to separate herself from the pack when she takes a stand against her friends' racism. By the novel's conclusion, she has proven herself not only bright but promisingly ambitious having benefited by her education in life skills as well as in classroom topics.

See also: Braithwaite, Rick; To Sir, with Love
References: Herdeck et al., 1979; Ousby, 1988

DARNAY, CHARLES, MARQUIS ST. EVRÉMONDE

Although Charles Darnay acts as the main love interest for Lucie Manette in Charles Dickens's novel, A Tale of Two Cities (1859), his main purpose as a character is to help Sydney Carton in his metamorphosis from a passive to an active personality. Possessing the moral stamina and nobility of character necessary to the hero, Darnay remains worthy of admiration. In addition, he merits reader sympathy due to his conviction on false political accusations, to which his life may be forfeit. Although Darnay's positive traits remain inherent to his personality, the slacker Carton must exercise extreme effort to locate any heroic traits in the depths of a tortured psyche. Carton's engagement in struggle against his natural tendencies contrasts greatly with Darnay's effortless attainment of the heroic state.

Charles Darnay represents Sydney Carton's opposite in every way. Their physical similarity, emphasized early during Darnay's first trial for treason in England, appears to be the only thing the two share. As a Frenchman, Darnay suffers threat from a hostile English society as well as from his own society, which projects blame for actions committed by Darnay's aristocratic uncle onto him. Carton, however, is a drunk representing a threat only to himself. But their lives become more parallel over the course of years, mainly due to Lucie Manette. With Lucie the two men form a love triangle. Rather than leading to conflict among the characters, Lucie's acceptance of Darnay's marriage proposal over that of Carton results in the formation of an unbreakable three-way friendship. With Darnay in position as Lucie's husband, Carton may act on his love for Lucie to later rescue, at the cost of his own life, the man Lucie holds most dear.

Darnay's political and ethical views show him to be a man intent on gaining justice, not only for himself but for any group or individual that has been mistreated. This causes conflict with his uncle, who has long taken advantage of members of the French lower class. On a visit to France, Darnay pleads with his uncle to make amends to those against whom he has committed injustices, but his uncle refuses. When his uncle is murdered, Darnay inherits his aristocratic title and also the animosity of the French common people. Returning to France years later after the storming of the Bastille to help free an old family servant, Darnay's actions in the name of justice result in his imprisonment. These same actions will allow Sydney Carton to at last gain freedom from the mental and emotional prison that he has occupied for years.

By depriving Carton of the possibility of marrying Lucie Manette, Darnay causes Carton to seek another means of demonstrating his love for Lucie and his friendship for the Darnay family. Ironically, Darnay's heroic actions in support of his political views place him in the passive position of prisoner. This passivity then spurs the normally inert Carton into uncharacteristic action.

The novel serves as a fine example of an author's ability to successfully demonstrate a less common approach to traditional plot and characterization. In A Tale of Two Cities, the male love interest may "get the girl," but he is not the novel's protagonist. Instead, he serves as a foil to better illuminate the important changes undergone by the losing party in a love triangle that ultimately proves beneficial to all.

See also: Carton, Sydney; A Tale of Two Cities; Violence; War
References: Bullen, 1997; Caeserio, 1979; Duncan, 1992; Furbank, 1986; Smith, 1996; Tambling, 1995

DASHWOOD, ELINOR

Elinor Dashwood is the older of the two heroines featured in Jane Austen's romantic novel Sense and Sensibility (1811). More mature in behavior as well as age than her sister Marianne Dashwood, Elinor represents "sense" in the pair of young women. Having assumed the financial management of the Dashwoods' small income following her father's death, Elinor, who champions decorum and discretion, feels an obligation to manage Marianne as well. This proves a challenge after Marianne meets her first love, John Willoughby. The two young lovers engage in wild play that scandalizes some of the Dashwood's new neighbors. While Elinor attempts to guide Marianne toward an understanding of prudence in hopes that it will lead to proper behavior, she deals with her own developing love for Edward Ferrars, brother of Fanny, who is married to Elinor's half-brother, John. The two meet following Mr. Dashwood's death when Edward visits the Dashwood home that has passed through entailment to John. A relationship sparks between Edward, also a prudent and sensible personality, and Elinor. He offers her sympathy and affection as she searches for new lodgings for herself and her family.

Social mores intervene to separate Elinor and Edward because Fanny believes Edward should marry within his own wealthy class. He seems to be trying to explain something about his past to Elinor when he is called away to visit his mother in London. Elinor's later disillusionment and heartbreak, a result of her discovery that Edward has been "engaged" to the daughter of his former teacher for years, she hides from everyone, including Marianne.

Although the novel serves its purpose as a satisfying tale of romance, Austen reveals an additional agenda, that of social commentary. Through Elinor's character, the novelist stresses the difficulties faced by many women of her time. Although the eldest of her father's "second" family, as a woman Elinor will not directly inherit any of the family fortune. She must depend on the charity of the estate's heir, in this case, her half-brother. This matter of property entailment through the nearest male blood relative is a favorite theme for Austen, who emphasizes it in other novels such as *Pride and Prejudice*. Not having been trained in any field but rather educated in the social graces, Elinor cannot work outside the home to strengthen the family's financial position, yet she is responsible for meeting their financial obligations. In addition, society's expectation that one would not express one's feelings falls heavily on Elinor, who cannot tell Edward of her love. Reminiscent of Shakespeare's Hero in his romantic comedy *Much Ado about Nothing*,

Elinor has no choice but to have patience and endure.

Her patience eventually rewards her with true love because Edward does not have to marry his childhood sweetheart. When he asks for Elinor's hand, she willingly and gratefully bestows it. Unlike her sister, who eventually marries wealth and power in the person of Colonel Brandon, Elinor willingly chooses a life of relative poverty with Edward, who has revolted against his own family's wealth as a matter of honor and faith. He takes a clerical living given to him by Brandon— affording the sisters continued close proximity and broadening the family support the two sisters have always enjoyed.

Austen shapes a touching relationship based on love and respect between Elinor and Marianne, who remain completely devoted to one another. As Austen's lifelong devotion to her own sister seemed to indicate, the author apparently felt that two women could share bonds that the cruelest outside force might threaten but not sever.

See also: Austen, Jane; Bennet, Elizabeth (Eliza/Lizzy); Brandon, Colonel; Dashwood, Marianne; Ferrars, Edward; *Pride and Prejudice; Sense and Sensibility*
References: Britannica, 1997; Clayton, 1987a; Copeland and McMaster, 1997; de Rougemont, 1983; Drabble, 1995; Fraiman, 1993; Gard, 1992; Gilbert and Gubar, 1985c; Praz, 1974; Watt, 1963

DASHWOOD, MARIANNE

One of two heroines at the center of Jane Austen's plot in her novel of manners *Sense and Sensibility* (1811), Marianne Dashwood represents "sensibility." Her joie de vivre and enthusiastic embrace of romance lead her into an infatuation with a wealthy neighbor, John Willoughby. From their first meeting, when Willoughby, like a white knight, rescues Marianne after she turns her ankle in a rainstorm, the two seem a perfect match. They share a passion for Shakespeare and adventure. Although her more sensible sister, Elinor, feels that Willoughby may not be the proper mate, Marianne exults in her first true love, engaging in behavior that violates proper decorum. She disregards her family's concern for her reputation and openly pursues Willoughby's attentions. Marianne's romance helps soothes the distress she has felt since the loss of her father and the subsequent curtailment of their income that has forced the family to relocate to a smaller house.

Colonel Brandon, a suitor two decades Marianne's senior, completes the novel's love triangle. His traumatic experience with a youthful romance that his father shattered because of the lower social status of the woman Brandon loved makes him feel a special affinity with Marianne and Willoughby. Although Brandon knows of sexual peccadilloes on Willoughby's part, he does not share his knowledge with the Dashwoods. He hopes to save Marianne the pain he experienced. Brandon represents reason and maturity, two factors that hold little appeal for a young woman immersed in her first wildly romantic love. By acting in a reckless though innocent manner, Marianne serves Austen's purpose as a cautionary figure to romantic female readers. Marianne is never threatened by disgrace, because she discovers Willoughby's true intent as a fortune hunter before he takes physical advantage of her; instead he merely shatters her naïveté and belief in the joys promised by romance. As a character, Marianne is balanced by Brandon's luckless early love, who, heartbroken by what she saw as Brandon's abandonment, gave herself over to a wanton life. She died after delivering an illegitimate child.

One of Austen's themes, that of the importance of family, is emphasized by contrasting Marianne and her family support system with Brandon's first love, who lacked support. The love and respect shared by Marianne and Elinor give each a strength that helps counter the vicissitudes they suffer as they confront romance and shifting social status. Austen also emphasizes the cruelty of social convention, when Willoughby chooses a wealthy mate who can finance his profligate lifestyle, over Marianne, a woman of modest means.

In the end, Marianne gains the "sense" that balances her sensibility, following an illness from which she recovers through the devotion of Elinor. She recognizes the folly of her unseemly behavior with Willoughby and of taking for granted that her future would be spent with her first love. She trades empty dreams of wild romance for the more secure love Brandon willingly offers.

See also: Bennet, Elizabeth (Eliza/Lizzy); Brandon, Colonel; Dashwood, Elinor; Ferrars, Edward; *Pride and Prejudice; Sense and Sensibility*

References: Copeland and McMaster, 1996; de Rougemont, 1983; Drabble, 1995; Fraiman, 1993; Gard, 1992; Praz, 1974; Watt, 1963

DAZA, FERMINA

Author Gabriel García Márquez chose a rather unusual romantic heroine for his magic realist novel, *Love in the Time of Cholera* (1985). Fermina Daza is seventy years of age when she is romanced, for the second time, by Florentino Ariza. Described as stylish, long-boned, with straight posture and a slender body, Fermina Daza retains from her youth only her almond eyes and the haughty expression they reflect. Yet this face, still filled with character, is enough to summon Florentino Ariza back to her side at the death of her husband of more than fifty years, Dr. Juvenal Urbino. Uninvited, yet determined, Florentino Ariza visits the Urbino home within hours of the doctor's funeral to declare his undying affection for the new widow. Fermina Daza unceremoniously orders Florentino Ariza out of her sight, furious that he would insult her in her time of mourning. Yet she cannot rest for thinking of the small odd man who once captured her heart.

As teenagers, they had struck up a correspondence and had promised one another to marry. But when Fermina Daza's father discovered that his daughter intended to spend her life with a bastard who lacked any evident attributes other than that he was a poet and a musician, he quickly separated the two lovers. Fermina Daza suffered for a time but had a change of heart upon her return.

Although Fermina Daza did not marry Dr. Juvenal Urbino for love, she came to love him. He gave her the social status she deserved as he became one of the most famous doctors of his time. His reputation was earned from his battle against cholera, the deadly disease allowed to run rampant in the South American unsanitary conditions. Interestingly, García Márquez compares Florentino Ariza's love to the disease, drawing a parallel between the ravaging effect of both conditions. Although the couple had two children, Fermina Daza and Dr. Urbino served as the focus of one another's lives, even when engaged in the battles marriage always yields. His final declaration before dying after an accidental fall is one of immeasurable love for his wife.

Yet Fermina Daza's passion had been revealed first to Florentino Ariza. In their early distracted correspondence, she hid her passionate nature, avoiding her emotions by writing of the mundane. In this way she hoped to gently fan the coals of her own love while remaining in control, but her actions caused the unabashedly passionate Florentino Ariza to burn with desire.

Possibly one of the passages most revealing of Fermina Daza's character comes soon after her return as she strolls through the familiar South American market. The sights, sounds, and scents there remind her of her girlhood, and she samples all of the delectables available. She suddenly recognizes her own power and maturity, and when confronted by the lovestruck Florentino Ariza who has followed her through the market, she announces to him that what she had previously believed to be love was just an illusion. She does not speak with Florentino Ariza until fifty-one years, nine months, and four days later, when she hears him tell her again of his eternal devotion.

Although much of the book traces the actions of Florentino Ariza during the duration of Fermina Daza's marriage to Dr. Urbino, she constantly reappears, both in Florentino Ariza's thoughts and in reality, allowing García Márquez to reinforce his devotion to her. The last portion of the novel traces the rekindling of their romance as Fermina Daza recovers passions that she felt she had forever lost. Part of the rekindled love involves more correspondence and an emphasis on the diction and tone of the lovers' letters. Thus García Márquez reemphasizes the importance of the written word as a means of permanently recording fleeting emotion.

Although her children and acquaintances discourage her attempt to begin a relationship at her late age, Fermina Daza acts, for once, on her passion rather than her intellect. In a satisfying conclusion, she and Florentino Ariza finally consummate a forbidden love too long unrequited, but now realized in the ripe passion of age and appreciation.

See also: Ariza, Florentino; *Love in the Time of Cholera*
References: de Rougemont, 1983; Zamora and Faris, 1995

DE BRICASSART, FATHER RALPH

Father Ralph de Bricassart's status as a priest makes him an unlikely member of Colleen McCullough's famous love triangle in her novel *The Thorn Birds* (1977). Herein lies the conflict that will haunt Ralph and his love, Meghann (Meggie) Cleary throughout the novel. For Ralph, duty to the Catholic Church remains all-important, and in the direction of movement up through its ranks he focuses all his attention. But he cannot deny his love for Meggie, whom he meets as a child, a fondness that develops into full-blown romantic love despite their eighteen-year age difference. Ralph's ambition remains his weakness, for it blinds him to the truth about his feelings for Meggie and later causes him not to recognize the obvious—that Meggie's son is also his own.

An interesting and attractive character, Ralph charms all the females within his acquaintance, particularly his elderly patroness, Mary Carson, sister to Meggie's father Paddy. The powerful and wealthy owner of the Australian ranch Drogheda, Mary remains enthralled by Ralph's handsome features and his perfect body, regretting that her age renders her incapable of acting upon her desires. Ralph tolerates her jealousy of his relationship to Meggie, her own niece, and the two conduct a battle of wills over Ralph's future. An indiscretion has placed Ralph in the outback of Australia, but he does not intend to remain there forever. His sights are set on Rome, and he hopes that Mary's wealth and influence may help propel him there.

As Meggie matures, Ralph remains consumed by his feelings for the young woman. He wonders at times exactly why he does love Meggie, remembering her arrival in Australia and his attraction to her beauty and her sweetness. He sees her as the perfect female, passive yet strong, not rebellious and fated to obey others all her life. The fact that no one else deemed her important he found the most attractive feature of all; this left a wide space in her life that he could occupy fully and without question. The recognition of her need for attention helps him later discern that the reason for her unhappiness in marriage is not based on any material hardship but rather on the indifference of her husband. Although Ralph never questions his own loyalty to the church and his vows, he feels badly for Meggie herself, in love with a man she will never marry and eventually married to a man she will never love.

The best solution would be Ralph's absence and a totally severing of ties to the Cleary family, but Mary Carson's will precludes at least part of that plan. She does, indeed, enable Ralph to control her wealth and thus become important to the authorities of the Catholic Church, but she accomplishes this by withholding Paddy's just inheritance. Ralph's position as executor of Mary's estate necessitates continuing contact with the Clearys; worse yet, his own success comes at a great cost to the family of the woman he loves.

Ralph's future moves remain calculated as he advances to the office of cardinal, which his peers agree he merits. His honesty and openness in his confessions to his superior about his love for Meggie, even about the fact of their eventual consummation of that love, make him a sympathetic character. But his peculiar inability to recognize himself in Meggie's son, Dane, renders him weak and shows his lack of insight. His nurturing of Dane toward the priesthood reflects the immense feelings of a father for a son, but Ralph never recognizes this as more than a spiritual relationship. When, following Dane's death, Meggie reveals the truth about Ralph's fatherhood, he refuses at first to believe her.

Ralph de Bricassart follows a plan practically from his birth. Like many other plans in the novel, it remains patriarchal, as he embraces a way of life that excludes romantic involvement with women. His single mistake in the climb to success remains his invitation to Meggie to enter his heart. That caused him to, as Meggie puts it, steal from what he had vowed to God, and for that act, they all had to pay. In mourning Dane's death, Ralph finally realizes that of all his sins—pride, ambition, carnal knowledge of Meggie—his blindness to his own blood kin remains by far the worst. He acknowledges that his blindness was by his own design, so as not to interfere with his ambitions, and in this moment, Ralph faces his own mortality.

See also: Cleary, Meghann (Meggie); The Thorn Birds
References: Armstrong, 1990; Bridgwood, 1986; Kaplan, 1986; Price, 1983

DE LA GARZA, TITA

A beautiful, mystical woman, Tita de la Garza is the protagonist of Laura Esquivel's magic realist novel, Like Water for Chocolate (1989). Tita's birth, brought on by her own flood of tears in reaction to her pregnant mother's peeling of onions, marks the first of her many mystical experiences. A family tradition dictates that, as the youngest daughter, Tita must remain single in order to care for

her mother. This prevents her marriage to Pedro Muzquiz, who decides instead to marry Rosaura, Tita's oldest sister, in order to be close to Tita. Raised in the kitchen by the cook, Tita eventually assumes all the family's cooking duties. Her strong passions may be transferred to others through the food she prepares; such an incident occurs when her tears fall into her sister's wedding cake, causing a mysterious community vomiting among the guests.

Tita and Pedro secretly consummate their love and later nurture their passion, though they are separated. Throughout her life, Tita remains enveloped in a magical world where her internal passions produce external results. Mentally and emotionally slipping in and out of "reality," Tita, aided by the good spirits of deceased women such as her childhood nurse and cooking teacher, Nacha, confronts the wicked spirit of her deceased mother. Although she agrees to marry another man, John Brown, Tita never stops loving Pedro. She helps raise Rosaura's and Pedro's daughter following their return to Mexico from America. After Rosaura's death, Pedro and Tita join in a final passionate encounter. Their burning love literally consumes them, leaving behind only Tita's cookbook, which is passed on to her grandniece, the narrator of the novel.

Tita may be viewed as an important figure to feminist and also psychoanalytic critics of literature as well as to those interested in folktales and local mythology. Although relegated to the feminine domain of the kitchen, she uses her cooking as an art for self-expression. She is also pictured crocheting in the night when she cannot sleep, offering an inversion of that famous weaving woman of quest literature, Penelope, who tears apart her weaving at night in order to stave off would-be suitors as she awaits Odysseus's return. Tita crochets a blanket to cover the bed she and Pedro are prevented from sharing; thus the bed "dies" as a symbol of life and fertility and acts rather as a funeral pyre with the blanket as funeral shroud. This even more closely unites her with Penelope, who purportedly wove a shroud for her father-in-law's casket. When at last pushed too far by her mother, Tita adopts silence as a weapon, refusing to communicate with Mama Elena and so adapting a traditionally passive stance into a rebellious, active one. The novel offers several interiors or enclosures as important feminine areas; the kitchen, the dark room, and the pigeon coop. Tita symbolizes motherhood, as she works within the womblike kitchen, nurturing all those who enter. Mama Elena usurps the male position in the household, having symbolically killed her husband, using the phallus of her lover as weapon, and then demanding that the nubile Tita become her slave. When Tita revolts against her mother, she moves against the patriarchal-turned-matriarchal false hierarchy established by Mama Elena. Mythological elements are present in Tita's quest for true love, with her descent into the darkness of madness, the guiding presence of Nacha and of John, the monstrous presence of the evil spirit of Mama Elena to combat, and, of course, abundant evidence of magic and the power of spells.

See also: Esquivel, Laura; Fantasy; Forbidden Love; Like Water for Chocolate; Love Triangle; Magic Realism; Quest

References: de Rougemont, 1983; Frye, 1976; Zamora and Faris, 1995

DE THEUS, PAULINE

When, in the twentieth century, Jean Giono set out to write an early-nineteenth-century romantic novel, he shaped a heroine in Pauline de Theus to meet the classic demands of the romance tradition. The Horseman on the Roof (1951) represents a fine reshaping of a medieval romance, complete with much evidence of chivalry. As the damsel in need of aid, Pauline plays an important part in the tale.

Pauline's character bears great resemblance to the medieval lady of the manor toward whom knights owed fealty. The chivalric code demanded that a knight protect the lady with no thought of repayment, either material or through the development of a romantic relationship. Married to a French marquis, Laurent de Theus, Pauline is trapped within the cholera-plagued city of Manosque when the novel's hero, the Italian patriot Angelo Pardi, comes to her rescue. Just as medieval chivalric tales pitted knights against dragons and other fanciful figures, Angelo must rescue Pauline from the threats of cholera and the military rule that results from the plague. They combine their quests, his to return to his native Italy, and hers to travel to her estate in southern France to reunite with her husband.

In contrast to many of the damsels of classical romance, Pauline, although in need of aid, remains anything but helpless. She assists Angelo when, after escaping from crazed townspeople, he descends from hiding on a Manosque rooftop into an attic. Angelo explains to Pauline that the populace have invented the myth that someone is poisoning their water to account for the cholera; he succeeded in escaping execution by concealing himself on the tile roof. Without fear, Pauline offers what little food and drink she has to Angelo, recognizing that he is a gentleman and not the ruffian his unkempt appearance makes him seem. Her sympathy for Angelo's revolutionary stance reveals an understanding for the passion that led to his exile from Italy, when he dared to challenge the Austrian empire following Napoleon's defeat. When their paths again cross outside the city, Pauline accepts Angelo's invitation to travel with him because he will help her avoid the soldiers waiting to quarantine those who attempt to escape plague-infected cities.

Throughout their adventures, Pauline reveals little about herself, except that she longs to reunite with her husband, who was unable to meet her in Manosque. When she finally tells Angelo her story, the reader learns that Pauline was the poor daughter of a country doctor. Together they saved the marquis's life when, at sixteen years of age, she discovered him wounded and near death. She nursed him, a man forty years her senior, to health over several months, never knowing his identity and assuming she would not see him again when he departed. Upon his return and bid for her hand six months later, she agreed to the marriage, not having previously known of his immense wealth and power. This explains her own courage, resiliency, and spirit, because she is not a woman raised in a pampered and indulgent atmosphere. As Angelo himself observes, Pauline resembles more the figure of a fellow knight, with her talents at arms and on horseback, than that of a vulnerable female. She evinces cunning and wit, invoking memories for Angelo of his highly esteemed mother, further boosting his positive attitude toward Pauline.

Pauline manages, with Angelo's help, to evade soldiers, use a con man to gather information about her husband, and escape a military quarantine. But the knight offers his greatest service to the lady in rescuing her from the certain death of cholera. When Pauline experiences the vomiting and cold rigors associated with the disease, Angelo puts into practice the technique he learned from a Frenchman, of ripping off the victim's clothing to massage the freezing limbs.

Misinterpreting his intentions in removing her clothing, Pauline raises her head in the midst of her tortures to tell him, as an honorable woman should, that she would rather die than be taken advantage of. In this way, Pauline reveals that her code of honor remains equal to that of her knight and guardian angel.

Pauline recovers, due to Angelo's attentions, and they travel to the castle in Theus, only to find the marquis not in residence. In his absence, his elderly mother, the marquise, entertains Angelo as Pauline recovers. Once assured that danger no longer threatens his charge, Angelo departs, anxious to return to the revolution in Italy. True to the medieval tale, the knight delivers the damsel to the lord's manor, never having so much as kissed her.

See also: The Horseman on the Roof; Pardi, Angelo
References: Campbell, 1974; Campbell, 1988

DE WINTER, MAXIM

Daphne du Maurier shapes Maxim de Winter into a modernized version of the Byronic hero for her 1938 Gothic romance novel, Rebecca. He is a curious combination of hero and villain. As half of the novel's romantic couple, he should be heroic, yet the terrible crime he committed against his first wife should also classify him as a villain. Love, along with a sense of justice on the part of the reader, allows Maxim to be rescued from his villainous state.

Moody, dark, and mysterious, Maxim's personality constitutes that of the easily recognized Gothic hero. Even Maxim's surname suggests his cold personality and a connection with the death that winter brings. The at-first-unidentified narrator of the novel, Maxim's new young wife, describes him as a man unlucky and unhappy in love. He bears a terrible emotional burden from his first marriage that prevents happiness in his present marital state as well. Rebecca's ghostly presence is just as real to him as his new wife. Both need to rid themselves of Rebecca's memory in order to find happiness together.

At times, the reader may distrust Maxim's supposed love for Mrs. de Winter. He seems to have chosen her just for her youth, as a complement to his manhood, rather than for the affection she so desires. His cosmic punishment for his previous crimes by the loss of a portion of his ancestral home and of some of his physical function fits the traditional pattern for a Gothic protagonist. Only

through his physical loss and his resulting vulnerability can Maxim be open to the emotional gain and the strength that Mrs. de Winter's devotion can supply.

Maxim's major purpose is to allow the shaping of the protagonist, Mrs. de Winter. His supporting characterization remains important in helping du Maurier insert some surprising twists into the traditional Gothic plot. If not for Maxim's crime, Mrs. de Winter would not be able to exhibit the unusual sudden maturation that allows her to conquer the threat to her fulfillment through love. Generally, this overcoming of threat occurs only at the end of a Gothic plot, when forces beyond her control at last allow the heroine security. Mrs. de Winter's support, more than any other factor in the story, allows the eventual dismissal of suspicions against Maxim in regard to Rebecca's death. Although readers might expect Mrs. de Winter to pull away from Maxim in concern for her own safety, the revelation of his crime instead strengthens her resolve to make their love a success.

Other aspects of Maxim and his fate as a Gothic hero remain quite traditional. His tremendous internal conflict is accompanied not only by the external conflict with the object of his love but also by threat from other characters, such as Rebecca's cousin and apparent love interest, Favell, and by Rebecca's devoted servant, Mrs. Danvers. A man with a strong sense of ethics, his rejection of Rebecca's immoral behavior enables her to manipulate him into committing a crime against humanity and his own morals. Where the plot begins with the establishment of Maxim as the strong character and Mrs. de Winter as the weak, traditional male versus female characterizations of members within a patriarchal marriage, these aspects reverse themselves in the novel's climax.

Although du Maurier may afford more power and strength to Mrs. de Winter than previous novelists did to their heroines, Maxim's position easily parallels that of his fictional predecessors, particularly that of Mr. Rochester in Charlotte Brontë's Jane Eyre (1847). Du Maurier finds herself at home writing in this tradition, but she adds some contemporary twists that make the novel a fascinating example of its genre.

See also: de Winter, Mrs.; Gothic Romance;
Rebecca; Violence
References: de Rougemont, 1983; Ellis, 1989; Leng, 1994

DE WINTER, MRS.

In Daphne du Maurier's 1938 novel, *Rebecca,* Mrs. de Winter represents the typical Gothic romance heroine. For a good portion of the story, Maxim de Winter's new bride remains under threat from an unidentified evil force in the de Winter ancestral home of Manderley. That evil is quickly identified as the haunting memory of Maxim's first wife, Rebecca de Winter, who was ostensibly killed in a boating accident. The reader comes to know the mousy, youthful Mrs. de Winter mainly as Rebecca's replacement. Hence, this character assumes an unusual burden in having to compete with a ghost whose forceful memory lives on in the minds of others. Observant readers, however, will pick up on the foreshadowing of Mrs. de Winter's eventual development into a strong character when they identify her as the novel's narrator and one who has survived a fire that destroyed the de Winters' home but not their relationship.

The character of Rebecca, although only a memory when the plot begins, acts as a foil for Mrs. de Winter. Rebecca's much younger successor, never even identified by first name, is far less experienced in the wiles of love and society than her predecessor. This naïveté makes Mrs. de Winter a prime target for the ire of Mrs. Danvers, Rebecca's servant. Wildly jealous on behalf of her dead mistress of Maxim's attentions to the new Mrs. de Winter, Mrs. Danvers stubbornly protects Rebecca's memory as she attempts to destroy Maxim's bride emotionally and physically. This causes Mrs. de Winter to become a part of two of the most unusual love triangles within romance literature. The first she shares with a dead woman and that woman's widower, who also happens to be her husband. The second she shares with Mrs. Danvers, who acts as a "stand-in" for Rebecca, and Maxim.

Mrs. de Winter symbolizes, through her youth and innocence, the fresh start in love and romance that Maxim de Winter desires following a bitterly disappointing first marriage. Her lack of guile contrasts greatly with Rebecca's shrewd personality. For a brief time, her very innocence is a bane to her relationship with Maxim. Because she knows so little about Rebecca, she falls prey to Mrs. Danvers's plot to horrify Maxim when she allows herself to be dressed for a party in ancestral garb identical to that previously worn by Rebecca. Not only the outraged Maxim, but also his party guests, recognize the dress as one that had fit Mrs. de Winter's stunning predecessor so beautifully.

Du Maurier executes a neat ironic reversal when she uses a white dress, the traditional symbol of purity and marriage, as a dual representation for both the evil Rebecca and her more virtuous replacement. In addition, the loose white dress also resembles the figure of a ghost, suggestive of the memory of Rebecca that continues to haunt Mrs. de Winter's marriage. This scene recalls the masquerade tradition of comic romance, in which mistaken identity caused by disguise of appearance or voice or both may lead to a brief flirtation with disaster. Mrs. Danvers hopes to use the occasion of her designed "disguise" to shock Maxim into some admission of guilt in connection with Rebecca's death or, at the least, to cause him to reject Mrs. de Winter in the belief that she purposely mocks him. On a separate occasion, Mrs. de Winter's impressionable mind allows her to fall into a trancelike state under Mrs. Danvers's "spell," which almost leads to her death.

In an unusual plot shift for the Gothic novel, Mrs. de Winter sheds her vulnerable state and dismisses the threat to her personal safety when the truth about Rebecca's death is revealed. Deeply in love with Maxim, she willingly supports him even when faced with the terrible facts of her husband's complicity in the crime of murder. In her dealings with the ensuing accusations made against her husband, Mrs. de Winter matures and displays her own inner strength, gained through faith in Maxim and in their devotion to one another. This maturity allows her to step into the space left vacant by Maxim's first wife.

In the end, both members of the couple survive a test to their love. For all the reader knows, they live happily ever after once the mystery regarding Rebecca is solved and Mrs. Danvers is removed from the scene. The purifying Gothic fire, an image that began the novel, permits the de Winter's relationship to bloom in an environment cleansed of evil.

See also: de Winter, Maxim; Gothic Romance; *Rebecca;* Violence

References: de Rougemont, 1983; Ellis, 1989; Leng, 1995

DEL VALLE, CLARA

Clara del Valle is the matriarch of the group of women whose stories comprise Isabel Allende's magic realist novel *The House of the Spirits* (1982, trans. 1985). Possessed of a clarity of spirit allowing her to communicate with the otherworldly, Clara's name perfectly describes her: Clara, the clairvoyant. Her powers allow her to speak the identity of her future husband before he ever romances her, to predict a powerful earthquake that almost kills that husband, to levitate furniture, and to perform other feats that enthrall and frighten those around her. Her strongest seemingly magical effect is upon her husband, Esteban Trueba, a cantankerous, perpetually lonely man assured of his own importance as patron of his ranch peasants and his home. Only the overwhelming passion Clara evokes in Esteban can reduce him to a helplessness that mimics the physical impotence inflicted upon the lower classes, who are trapped within the patriarchal society Esteban so perfectly represents. Most important to her family will be Clara's ability to appear after death to her granddaughter Alba, when she will urge the girl to cling to life during torture at the hands of a revolutionary.

Clara first meets Esteban due to his engagement to her oldest sister, the Beautiful Rosa. The clairvoyant girl predicts a death in the family, and Rosa later dies from poison intended for her father, also a political candidate. During Esteban's subsequent nine-year absence from the city, Clara speaks not a single word. Her silence results from a combination of guilt over having predicted Rosa's demise and shock resulting from her having secretly viewed her sister's autopsy. The first words she speaks following nine years of silence express the identity of her future husband. Only when Esteban appears a short time later to romance Clara does everyone realize the significance of her words and her power.

As the center of a novel with sociopolitical themes stressing gender and economic injustice, Clara's character promotes those themes through her stance in favor of women's liberation. In her never-identified South American country, Clara urges peasant women to demand their rights in spite of the fact that she herself exists in a strictly patriarchal marriage with their patron, Esteban Trueba. Clara carries on the causes in which her own mother had held interest, passing along this fervor to a third generation in her children. She argues with the authorities that native children be taught Spanish and Esperanto, the universal language, rather than English, and encourages her children's involvement in social causes in spite of Esteban's hearty protests. Clara remains a figure strongly representative of feminist and humanist issues, removed from the power her husband's wealth and political office represent. She is, instead, aligned with the emotion her spiritual connections promote.

In this manner, Allende shapes Clara as the prototypical intuitive, warm, spiritual, emotional female to contrast with her highly scientific, organized, and (supposedly) objective husband. This pair becomes the first in the novel to symbolize the political forces at odds in their country. Throughout the story, Esteban fights those individuals and groups promoting equality among the classes, eventually becoming a senator in the long-ruling corrupt republican party that protects the property and rights of the wealthy. Beginning with Clara's mother, Nivea, each succeeding daughter symbolizes the opposite political party, either actively campaigning themselves for equal rights or supporting lovers who do. Thus, Clara and Esteban seem an odd match, remaining aloof or even hostile toward one another from time to time.

Readers will notice that several feminist symbols and examples of feminist ideology are connected with Clara throughout the novel. For instance, the birds in cages, an imagery abundant in feminist writings representing the oppressed female spirit, Clara herself liberates preceding her death; this act foreshadows the liberation of Clara's spirit. The notebooks/journals that Clara arranges, not in the chronological order associated with the scientific approach of males but rather in order by events or themes, symbolizes a woman's nonlinear style of writing.

In Clara's occasional silences rests another important feminine issue. Silence forced upon women by men in a patriarchal society has long been recognized as an encroachment on women's rights and viewed as a type of violence by some. But because Clara chooses her silence, she inverts the normal patriarchal weapon into a weapon of her own, which she uses to protect herself when she feels threatened. Although a woman who moves about often unaware of other humans as she navigates within a spiritual world, Clara del Valle Trueba is not a weak person. She possesses the capacity, through her strategies of silence and scorn, to bring the passionate, ill-tempered

Esteban to his knees emotionally, so great are his love and respect for her.

Clara's character remains all-important to this novel that traces three generations of women and their children as they cope with brutal, harsh government overthrows, the prejudice and racism of Esteban Trueba and the culture he symbolizes, and their uncertain relationships with one another. In the midst of their passions and conflicts, Clara, clarity incarnate, serves as a beacon that not even the darkness of death can extinguish.

See also: The House of the Spirits; Magic Realism; Trueba, Esteban

References: Zamora and Faris, 1995

DICKENS, CHARLES JOHN HUFFAM

A nineteenth-century English novelist and one of the most popular writers ever, Charles Dickens gained fame from his novels featuring social concerns and political issues, emphasized through the plights of hundreds of lower-class characters. His combination of irony, romance, humor, and, ulti-

mately, pathos attracted a huge contemporary audience that continues to expand. His own experiences with poverty and unfair treatment by the legal and social systems of his day form the background for many of his plots.

Born at Portsmouth on February 7, 1812, the second of eight children, he spent the majority of his childhood in Portsmouth, London, and Chatham, later adopting these areas as the setting for much of his fiction. His father, John Dickens, clerked in the Naval Pay Office and by all reports worked hard but could not manage to live within his income. This caused his family to dwell, for the most part, under the threat of financial insecurity and disaster. Charles was happy at a school in Chatham, where his abilities were recognized by a Baptist minister who supplied the attention needed to nourish those talents. But the Dickens's family poverty interrupted Charles's education, prompting a move to London where a relative gave Charles a job in a blacking business. He labeled bottles there at a job that began just prior to his twelfth birthday.

Nineteenth-century novelist Charles Dickens is shown in his study at Gad's Hill Place in this portrait painted and engraved by S. Hollyer, 1875. Dickens's combination of irony, romance, humor, and, ultimately, pathos made him one of the most popular writers of his day. (Library of Congress)

In 1824, the imprisonment of his amiable father for debt made a profound impression on Charles, the only member of the family who did not live in debtor's prison with the elder Dickens. The boy was changed forever by his family's shame and his having to work at a menial job, and, as an adult, he divulged information about this stage of his life only to his wife and best friend, John Forster. His feelings of abandonment and isolation stayed with Charles, who later described this very experience in his novel *David Copperfield* (1849–1850).

John Dickens left prison after three months, leaving Charles at work for several more weeks before allowing his return to school. From 1824 to 1826 Charles performed well in classes, and in 1827, at age fifteen, he gained worked with a group of Gray's Inn attorneys. He supplemented his education with much reading, especially enjoying eighteenth-century novelists such as Henry Fielding and Tobias Sollett. He taught himself shorthand and about eighteen months later left his job to become a reporter in the Parliament and various courts. He suffered through a nonproductive romance with the daughter of a banker, Maria Beadnell, meanwhile gaining a reputation for high speed and accuracy in reporting parliamentary debates. Just prior to his twenty-first birthday, Dickens published his first pieces, *Sketches by Boz,* in a London magazine.

This success sparked a London publisher, Chapman and Hall, to commission additional sketches by Dickens, and his achievements allowed him in 1836 to marry Catherine Hogarth, daughter of a journalist acquaintance. His characters from *Pickwick Papers* (1836–1837) eventually captured the imagination of the reading audience, and the characters became near-cult figures. The issue of this book in inexpensive monthly installments influenced publication in Great Britain as this method quickly achieved popularity. Described as ebullient and jolly, Dickens enjoyed taking long walks and dressing flamboyantly in a joyful style judged vulgar by some. His high level of energy and charm masked what friends described as a restless insecurity.

Over the next twenty years, Dickens produced a multitude of popular novels, including *Oliver Twist* (1837–1839); *Nicholas Nickleby* (1838–1839); a series of Christmas books, including *A Christmas Carol* (1843); *David Copperfield; Bleak House* (1852–1853); and *Little Dorrit* (1855–1857). Most of his novels denounced the organization of a government that withheld promised social and civil support from its citizens.

After producing ten children, the Dickenses' marriage ended in 1858 with the separation of Charles and Catherine. A young actress whom Charles later befriended, Ellen Ternan, is rumored to have become his mistress. While living mainly in Kent near Chatham, the home of his youth, Dickens wrote *A Tale of Two Cities* (1859), *Great Expectations* (1860–1861), and *Our Mutual Friend* (1864–1865). At this point his novel-writing career spanned fourteen well-received volumes, and he became famous for his popular public readings.

Although he attempted to continue the readings over several years, Dickens's health began to fail by the mid-1860s. A series of such readings in America between 1867 and 1868 renewed Dickens's overwhelming popularity but proved disastrous to his weakened physical condition. Undertaking additional public appearances upon returning to England, Dickens collapsed beneath the demanding schedule. In the midst of his exhaustion and weakness, he began work on his final novel, *Mystery of Edwin Drood* (1870), putting in full days of writing before suffering a stroke on June 8, 1870. He died the following day and was buried with much mourning and honor on the part of his public in the Poet's Corner of Westminster Abbey.

In his multitude of characters, Dickens's own insecurity and emotional turmoil is reflected. Ever a fan of the underdog, he wrote with great understanding of the suffering of the lower classes. He has been criticized, however, for presenting the social inequities caused by the practice of unethical politics without detailing plans for resolving those inequities. Some of his staunch supporters believe that his solution to general ills remained an encouragement of strong individual relationships that allowed the human spirit to blossom.

See also: A Tale of Two Cities

References: Bullen, 1997; Caeserio, 1979; David, 1995; Duncan, 1992; Furbank, 1986; Horsman, 1990; Ousby, 1988; Reed, 1995; Smith, 1996; Tambling, 1995

DIMMESDALE, ARTHUR

As the hero of Nathaniel Hawthorne's first major novel, *The Scarlet Letter* (1850), Arthur Dimmesdale's name has a double significance. That he remains shortsighted, unable to see the truth about his own blind ambition and the dimming of his spiritual talents, seems obvious to most readers. The significance of his first name, a most unusual name for a male in seventeenth-century Puritan New England, may not appear quite as obvious. Of course, the name Arthur might hearken back to the fabled knight of England, suggesting Dimmesdale's failed mission as a knight intended to rescue his damsel, not place her in a threatened position as Dimmesdale does to Hester Prynne. But the name also contains the word "art," and Dimmesdale is an artist. His creativity appears evident with each sermon he writes. In addition, Dimmesdale's sensitive and creative temperament, as well as his philosophical fascination with death and all things metaphysical, makes him a perfect candidate for the nineteenth-century romantic. He would be at home among Hawthorne and many of his contemporaries, except for one problem: Dimmesdale's promise as an artist remains unfulfilled.

Arthur Dimmesdale is a liar and a fraud. These are his important sins, not his act of adultery with Hester Prynne. That he should continue his public preaching to great acclaim, postulating ideas he himself cannot validate, makes him the worst kind of fraud. He merely plays at privately confessing to the sin and sharing in the guilt Hester must publicly bear alone. His art can never reach fruition, for it is all based on a lie. Thus Dimmesdale represents a man of great contradiction. His black clothing suggests death, but it also suggests the condition of priesthood, as does his unmarried and celibate condition. The young Puritan minister also engages in self-punishment and flagellation, as did members of Catholic sects. Hawthorne suggests that Dimmesdale, like a priest, should be consumed by dedication to his faith. His preaching of that belief should be secondary to his practice of it. In this, Dimmesdale fails. He avidly seeks the adulation brought to him by the crowds who listen to his performance art, and he instructs others to act in ways that he has proven himself incapable of acting.

Dimmesdale has the voice of an actor; it is described as sweet, rich, and deep. He attracts crowds wherever he goes. It is the chance to deliver a final speech before the governor that causes Dimmesdale to reveal his true character. Although he has agreed to leave Massachusetts,

at last admitting to his responsibilities and planning to set sail with Hester and Pearl, he is much relieved when he finds the departure date is delayed. This provides him the opportunity for one final great audience. That he does at last confess before those who have gathered to listen should be to Dimmesdale's credit. However, the confession, coming seven years after the day of Hester's public shaming, loses some of its importance.

Arthur Dimmesdale is a man tortured by the knowledge of his complicity in shaming Hester and God by his sin, but this alone does not force him to face up to this shame publicly. That requires the slow persistent application of revenge by Hester's husband, Roger Chillingworth. From almost the moment he appears in town, Chillingworth swears to discover the identity of Hester's lover and punish him in his own way. The doctor's identity remains a secret to all except Hester, who promises not to reveal to the townspeople that the physician is her long-awaited husband, believed to have been lost at sea. Dimmesdale believes Chillingworth to be his friend and personal physician because his dimmed insight prevents his discovering that the doctor's goal in life is to cause him nothing but misery. The same dim vision that allows Dimmesdale to deny his involvement with Hester allows Chillingworth to become his confidant, an intimate position that leads to Dimmesdale's death.

The survival of Hester Prynne proves that sin itself need not kill one's soul. It is Dimmesdale who stands as the example that fraud against part of one's nature, the creative and godly aspects, is the killing sin.

See also: Chillingworth, Roger; Prynne, Hester; *The Scarlet Letter*

References: Abel, 1988; Budick, 1996; Charlton, 1984; de Rougemont, 1983; Gilbert and Gubar, 1996g; Hart, 1995; Nissenbaum, 1984: xxvii–xxxvi

DOCTOR ZHIVAGO

When Boris Pasternak's novel *Doctor Zhivago* appeared in print in 1957, it enjoyed immediate acclaim as a political novel, important for its criticism of Communist Russia at a time when the Cold War enjoyed much publicity. Ironically, when closely read, the novel not only indicts the Russian political system for a seeming dismissal of the right of all humans to dignity, to highly moral

Omar Sharif played Yurii Andreievich Zhivago and Julie Christie appeared as Larisa Fedorovna Guishar (Lara) in the 1965 film version of Doctor Zhivago, *Boris Pasternak's 1957 novel of romance, separation, and heartbreak. (Archive Photos)*

treatment by others, and to love, but also criticizes members of any other political system, such as democracy, who do nothing to prevent such mistreatment of their fellow humans. Although the book received acceptance by many as a polemic work, this was not Pasternak's intention for his wartime novel. *Doctor Zhivago* remains primarily a story of romance, separation, and heartbreak, told through the use of symbols and imagery in a manner common to poets such as Pasternak.

To begin his tale of morality and human conduct, Pasternak introduces several young characters whose stories eventually intertwine as they all mature and occupy quite different roles in the unrest of pre–World War I Russia, through the war, and up until World War II. The novel's protagonist, Yurii Andreievich Zhivago, becomes an orphan when his mother dies following the

desertion of the family by his wealthy father. The bleak funeral setting is framed by snow and ice, offering a sterile, chilling imagery that foreshadows Yurii's eventual mistreatment by an uncaring political system. Yurii's friend, Misha Gordon, witnesses the suicide of Yurii's missing father, who throws himself from a train. A third boy, Nika Dudorov, lives a quite different existence from that of the first two boys. The son of a terrorist and a princess from the province of Georgia, Nika matures in the household of a philanthropist named Kilogrigov, who makes his money in industry. Pasha Antipov, also a son of a revolutionary who works on the railroad, is raised by the revolutionary Tiverzins following his father's exile to Siberia.

This group of displaced boys is enlarged by one female figure vitally important to the novel,

Larisa Fedorovna Guishar, known as Lara. Lara later becomes mistress to Yurii and mother to his illegitimate daughter, Tania. Although not an orphan like her male counterparts, Lara has no father, as he has died. Her mother, Amalia Guishar, the French widow of a Russian engineer, begins a dressmaking business in order to support herself and Lara. The business requires that Amalia depend on the financial support of her patron, a wicked attorney named Victor Komarovsky, who eventually seduces the innocent young Lara. The girl feels betrayed not only by Victor, whom she trusted, but also by her mother, who seems incapable of helping. Although serving as mistress to a wealthy patron was not uncommon for a young working girl, Lara's animosity toward Victor begins to build when she realizes he has no intention of marrying her.

Yurii and Misha live as children with a chemistry professor, Alexander Gromeko, and his family that includes his daughter, Antonina Alexandrovna Gromeka, called Tonia, and his ill wife Anna Ivanovna. Yurii later marries Tonia, and along with Lara the three form a love triangle that will produce lasting happiness for none of its members. As the novel follows the maturity of the boys, Pasha and Nika become involved in political student riots, whereas Yurii and Misha are indulged and trained as part of the aristocratic class. Yurii, in training as a physician, happens to meet Lara when he accompanies a doctor called to attend Lara's mother following a suicide attempt. Victor is also present, and Yurii notices a great tension between him and Lara.

Lara's animosity mounts, and she later attempts to murder Victor by shooting him in public surroundings. She succeeds only in wounding him, and he declines to bring charges against her. Supported by the opinion of his social group, he deems Lara one more unimportant working-class girl. She subsequently takes a position as a governess, emphasizing the fact that she is educated, in the Kilogrigov household where Nika lives. She meets Pasha and becomes emotionally involved with the young dissident, later marrying him. They depart Moscow to live beyond the Ural mountains. Her move to a natural environment apart from the institutionalized setting represented by the city emphasizes Lara's identification with the order and wonder of nature and passion. In contrast, Tonia remains closely connected to man's futile attempts at order in the ultimately cold, chaotic world of the city. Thus Yurii loves two women representing opposite value systems.

In the meantime, Yurii discovers a passion for poetry but rejects the practice of art for the more sensible vocation of medicine. Pasternak may depict his own struggle with the call to poetry; although he published a book of poetry at the young age of twenty-three, the suicides of other members of his circle may have brought on the long silence that preceded his writing of *Doctor Zhivago*. Yurii will deal with his dual inclinations throughout the novel, emphasizing the traditional romantic conflict between art and science. However, he handles the choice pragmatically, as is his manner, retaining an innocence toward others that allows him to be taken advantage of by an increasingly harsh government. Although shaken by scenes of slaughter and rebellion that occur literally in his own neighborhood, he continues to hope for eventual enlightenment on the part of his culture's leaders. An important symbol in the novel is a single candle, the light from which Yurii sees during one Christmas season, traditionally a time offering hope to humankind. The poem he writes about that small glimmer represents the efforts of art to preserve the smallest inkling of good will on the part of humans toward one another. The house itself is important as the scene of Yurii's eventual death.

Tonia and Yurii marry, meeting societal and familial expectations, prior to World War I, and they begin a family. But with the outbreak of fighting, Yurii must leave his family to serve in a hospital at the scene of battle, suffering the first of many separations that doom his relationship with Tonia. When he is wounded, Lara appears as a nurse to help in his care, and their lifelong unshakable love blossoms even in the environment made harsh and inhospitable not only by the endless cold but also by the killing and fear that war perpetuates. Ever loyal, Yurii retains his respect for Tonia, but Lara will remain his passion. Again, Yurii represents a dichotomy that cannot harmoniously reach resolution.

When Yurii returns to Moscow, he finds it ravaged by the October Revolution and subsequent disease, spurring him to escape the city with his family. They travel to a family estate in the Urals, a few individuals lost among a sea of migrants who seek to leave war and unrest behind. In the mountains, traditionally symbols of purity and elevation of the human spirit above the mundane business of life, Yurii reunites briefly with Lara. His capture by the group of politicos who label themselves the Reds causes another separation for Yurii, who must serve as the group's physician. Forced to accompany the band as they battle the White faction, Yurii eventually escapes, only to find that Tonia has returned to Moscow. Rather than chasing his family to the city, Yurii enjoys with Lara a brief respite from conflict. This idyllic time is the only one during which they will have each other's complete attention. When threatened by arrest, in an ironic choice Yurii sends Lara to stay with Komarovsky, her old lover and enemy; he now serves as a political official. Lara's husband Pasha, known as "the Shooter," commits suicide while in flight from Red authorities.

Yurii returns to Moscow but to a meaningless life. Tonia has moved the family to Paris, and Yurii marries a younger woman whom he does not really love. He practices medicine and works at writing scientific papers, but in a life without passion, he finds little fulfillment. In a strange coincidence, as is common to romance novels, Yurii's half-brother Evgraf turns up, and the two become friends. Even toward the end, Yurii proclaims the life force as triumphing over human attempts at control of fellow humans through various institutions. In this manner, the theme of imagination that accompanies the act of writing poetry as well as the practice of science for the good of humankind is privileged over that of institutional control. Evgraf is a thinly delineated character, placed in the novel ostensibly to neaten the many fragments of plot and subplot left dangling. When Yurii dies of a heart attack, it is Evgraf who publishes some of his poetry and during World War II discovers Yurii's daughter by Lara, for whom he provides.

Pasternak situates Yurii's twenty-four poems as the novel's concluding chapter. Through the poetry, his own natural medium, Pasternak continues his interrogation of love, death, life, and resurrection, emphasizing and repeating the rich nature imagery that appeared throughout the novel. Both science and art remain based in spirituality according to Yurii's poetry, which declares history a mere attempt to solve the eternal riddle of death.

Although Yurii dies with neither Lara nor Tonia at his side, his love and respect for the women that he knew argues for the value of that life. *Doctor Zhivago* remains a love story that suggests that such passion, not simply between a man and a woman but for a quality of life elevated by mutual respect and love, should be extended to all members of the human race.

See also: Guishar, Larisa (Lara) Fedorovna; Love Triangle; Violence; War; Zhivago, Yurii Andreievich
References: Brunsdale, 1996; Clowes, 1995; Frye, 1974; McMillin, 1990; Williams, 1974

DOOLITTLE, ELIZA

A character in a drama written by George Bernard Shaw, Eliza Doolittle represents a classical figure that has appeared many times in romantic fiction and novels. Shaw based Eliza's character in *Pygmalion* (1913) upon that of Galatea, a mythical woman created at first as a statue by the sculptor-king Pygmalion. When Pygmalion falls in love with his creation, Aphrodite pities his love and brings Galatea to life. This plot falls in line with what might be termed Svengali literature, in which a male takes credit for the success of a female over whom he exercises control. Due to the resounding popularity of the musical version of Shaw's play, *My Fair Lady,* both on stage and in a 1964 film presentation, Eliza Doolittle is probably the most famous of these Galatea-like characters.

Supposedly Shaw wrote his play in hopes of emphasizing the importance of proper English grammar and speech, with the poor cockney girl Eliza representing the successful result of training in these areas. Eliza offers to pay British phonetician Henry Higgins, Shaw's Pygmalion, to teach her proper elocution after hearing his bet with a cohort, Colonel Pickering, that he could pass her off as a duchess following three months of speech training. This act characterizes Eliza as proud and independent, hoping to gain more of an education than that supplied to her by poverty and the street. Eliza sets her sights a bit lower than Higgins, hoping only to be able to assume a sales position in a flower shop rather than having to peddle flowers on the street. What ensues remains a comic delight, as Higgins works his magic on Eliza's corrupt rendering of the English language. But it also has its serious side, when the transformed Eliza finds herself fit neither for her former position nor her fantasy role in life.

Higgins does not anticipate the emotion he develops for Eliza, mainly because for all of his education, he remains rather void of knowledge regarding humanity. Eliza expresses doubt over her future, wondering whether this transformation will achieve her goal or render her unsuitable for that job. Although Pickering understands her doubts, Higgins ignores them in the frenzy to win his bet. Eliza basically serves as a mirror for Higgins's flawed personality, revealing his overblown and unfounded attitude of superiority that prevents him from learning proper and polite behavior. Eliza purportedly remains the student, but in actuality she assumes the position of teacher for Higgins. Only her absence following the great success of the experiment causes him to recognize his need for others, shallow though it may be. Eliza makes Higgins dependent upon her company, threatening his highly touted claim to self-sufficiency.

Eliza's character is not a complicated one, with her reaction to her transformation remaining predictable. She does continually evince her spirited intelligence and independence, however, finally abandoning the insufferable Higgins. She refuses his offer that she remain with him and Pickering, not in a romantic alliance, but simply to live with them like three bachelors enjoying life together. She is arguably the only dynamic character in the story, having learned the dangers of humans tinkering with the fate of others. Shaw argues in a lengthy prose sequel to *Pygmalion* that Eliza's transformation qualifies her for the perfect romantic heroine, despite the fact that she and Higgins do not end up together in the expected happy ending. She remains, after all, a mortal while Higgins represents a god, and the two cannot unite as one.

See also: Higgins, Henry; *Pygmalion*
References: Campbell, 1988; *The Norton Anthology of English Literature*

DREISER, THEODORE

Theodore Dreiser was born in Terre Haute, Indiana, on August 27, 1871, the ninth of ten children. The family's poverty necessitated their constant relocation as Dreiser's father eked out a subsistence lifestyle similar to that of many of Dreiser's fictional characters. One of the novelist's favorite themes, the effect of a desire for wealth on ethical behavior, he derived from his early life in poverty. This topic would act as the focus for what have been called his best works: *Sister Carrie* (1900), *Jennie Gerhardt* (1911), and *An American*

Tragedy (1925). Dreiser's acute interest in the middle-class worker in pursuit of the American dream surfaces repeatedly in his writings. His novels reveal a fascination for the ordinary citizen who occupies the pages of his books in enormous numbers. Their foreign-sounding names reflect Dreiser's position as the first major non-Anglo-Saxon American novelist.

Beginning his career as a journalist on the *Chicago Globe* in 1890, Dreiser moved that same year to St. Louis to work at the *Globe-Democrat,* and he would later contribute to the *Republic.* He met his wife, Sara White, called "Jug," at the Chicago World's Fair while acting as escort to *Republic* contest winners. Subsequent relocation to New York took him through Toledo, Cleveland, Buffalo, and Pittsburgh; he worked as a reporter for the *Pittsburgh Dispatch.* During this time he was greatly affected by the novels of Honoré de Balzac and by Herbert Spencer's writing regarding evolution. In 1895 in New York, Dreiser worked for Joseph Pulitzer's *World*

Novelist Theodore Dreiser, photographed by Pirie MacDonald, derived one of his favorite themes, the effect of a desire for wealth on ethical behavior, from his early life in poverty. (Library of Congress)

and edited a magazine established with the help of his brother, Paul. He continued contributing to various publications, and in 1900, *Sister Carrie* was received in America with mixed reviews. Published the next year in Europe, the novel found greater success.

Dreiser continued publishing, but between 1901 and 1903 he suffered a nervous collapse. After regaining his health in 1904, he returned to work in the publishing industry and ended up editor of *Smith's Magazine* in 1905 and of *Broadway Magazine* in 1906. A famous murder, that of Grace Brown, and the subsequent Chester Gillette trial, would later yield the plot pattern for Dreiser's *An American Tragedy*. With the re-release of *Sister Carrie* in 1912, Dreiser's career revived, and in 1907–1909 he reached great editing success and began a friendship with the nonfiction writer H. L. Mencken. In 1910, Dreiser's affair with an eighteen-year-old caused him to lose his position with the Butterick Corporation and to separate from his wife.

His novel based on his sisters' lives, *Jennie Gerhardt,* appeared in 1911, after which Dreiser traveled to Europe, ostensibly to perform research for his novel *The Financier.* In 1912, he returned to America and agreed with Harper Publishing to produce the three-volume *Trilogy of Desire;* part 1, *The Financier,* appeared in 1912. Harper rejected the second part of the trilogy, *The Titan,* following a small printing (1914), but it was picked up by Lane publishing house. The outbreak of war further cemented Dreiser's friendship with Mencken as both suffered suspicion of German sympathies. A subsequent novel, *The "Genius"* (1915) was withdrawn from the market following accusations against Dreiser of immorality. He published six one-act plays in 1916 along with the book *A Hoosier Holiday.* His attempts to re-release *The "Genius"* in 1917 proved unsuccessful, but Dreiser would yet produce additional novels along with many essays, plays, and short stories.

In 1919, Dreiser met Helen Richardson. She became a longtime close friend whom he eventually married. In 1920 he published a collection of philosophical essays, *Hey Rub-A-Dub-Dub* and, in 1922, an autobiography titled *A Book about Myself.* Burton Rascoe wrote the first book-length study of the author, titled *Theodore Dreiser,* in 1925. Later that year, Dreiser published *An American Tragedy.* He continued writing as he traveled to Europe with Richardson, and in

1926, *Tragedy* appeared as a successful Broadway stage play. Influenced by a later visit to Russia, Dreiser voted Communist in the 1932 national election and began working as a representative for labor and antiwar movements. While attempting to at last complete the third volume in his trilogy, he published additional essays and several stories as well as a work of nonfiction, *America Is Worth Saving* (1941). In 1944 Dreiser received the Award of Merit medal from the American Academy of Arts and Letters, and he married Richardson. During his final year, he finished a novel based on Quaker life, *The Bulwark,* which would be published posthumously by Doubleday in 1946. Before his death on December 28, 1945, Dreiser finished most of *The Stoic.* It would also appear posthumously, issued by Doubleday in 1947.

Dreiser's realization in his teens that the city held the future for late-nineteenth- and early-twentieth-century America remains reflected in writings that celebrate both the importance and cold indifference of the urban setting. America's rapid move away from an agricultural economy and toward industrialized capitalism offered the pivotal point on which his characters' dreams and desires turn. Economics became America's new religion as it left behind old ideals and turned to science and evolution as the new authority. Dreiser's personal search for something to replace his lost religious faith also became a theme for most of his main characters. Like Dreiser in his formative years, his protagonists are without roots, either physical or spiritual. They spend their lives on his pages in an eternal search for satisfaction and contentment, but because they never recognize that for which they search, they are doomed to tragic failure. Forced to constantly adapt to new environments due to the mobility required of one seeking success, Dreiser's characters remain in a constant state of flux. Discontented with their social positions, they launch into courses of action that promise fulfillment but end in disillusionment and often in death.

Dreiser shaped his novels by stressing through his emotionally isolated characters the sense of estrangement many Americans actually experienced and with which they easily identified. Although his books portrayed life as a jungle in which a person with the right qualities might succeed, his characters lacked those qualities.

Most successful at novel writing, Dreiser also produced essays, dramas, poetry, and short stories. Because in his opinion and that of others he failed to produce a significant amount of well-written short fiction, Dreiser gave up writing short stories; many he left incomplete or destroyed. However, his short stories were collected and edited posthumously by Howard Fast.

See also: An American Tragedy; Griffiths, Clyde
References: Gerber, 1977; Pizer, 1995; "Theodore Dreiser," 1987

DU MAURIER, DAPHNE

Best known for her Gothic romance *Rebecca* (1938), Daphne du Maurier wrote, in addition to novels, short stories, poetry, drama, and nonfiction. With strengths in both plotting and the shaping of atmosphere, several of her stories have adapted well to cinema, a fact that led Alfred Hitchcock to convert her short story, "The Birds," to a highly successful film. Her melodramatic approach limits the appeal to contemporary audiences of some of her work, but few argue that du Maurier remained a master story teller.

Born in 1907 in England, Daphne du Maurier came from an artistic family. Her grandfather, George du Maurier, produced the novel *Trilby* (1894), a story incorporating Svengali, the famous conjurer, as a main character. Her parents, Gerald and Muriel du Maurier, found employment on the English stage. Their penchant for drama du Maurier adopted as her own as she fulfilled the legacy of her novelist grandfather. Supposedly Gerald, an alcoholic and a sufferer of depression, became quite dependent upon young Daphne, and she came to envy boys their strength and independence. Some say this early influence caused her later to prefer her son, Christopher, over her two daughters, Glavia and Tessa.

When she traveled to Cornwall in England as a young child, du Maurier became enthralled with an estate called Menabilly. She used Menabilly as a model for Maxim de Winter's palatial estate, Manderley, in *Rebecca*. Although Menabilly could never be purchased because of an entailment to a particular family, du Maurier did succeed in renting the estate and living there from 1943 to 1969. Du Maurier's writing so enthralled Frederick "Tommy" Browning that he traced her whereabouts and eventually married her. At one point a legal suit was brought against du Maurier, accusing her of stealing the plot for *Rebecca,* but it was eventually dropped.

Rebecca won the National Book Award in the United States in 1938 and secured du Maurier's fame. In 1951, du Maurier again approached the success achieved with *Rebecca* with the publication of *My Cousin Rachel,* but none of her thirteen additional novels attained such fame. She also wrote biographies featuring her family members, including *Gerald* (1934), *The du Mauriers* (1937), and *The Young George du Maurier* (1951), as well as one featuring the tragic life of the brother to the Brontë sisters, *The Infernal World of Branwell Brontë* (1960). A few of her many short stories were published on their own and then were later gathered into a group of five short story collections, such as *The Apple Tree* (1952), later published as *The Birds and Other Stories.* Her two dramas, *The Years Between* (1946) and *September Tide* (1949), reflect the influence of her parents' dramatic careers. In 1969 she was honored with the title Dame Commander, Order of the British Empire, to celebrate her literary achievements. Du Maurier died in 1989.

A producer of entertaining and often thrilling plots, du Maurier's narrative remains at times plodding, and some critics feel her characters are too one-dimensional. This, coupled with her traditional attitude toward women, has drawn criticism from several quarters. Feminists feel that her depiction of what they term an essentialist view of women, based on the female's supposed biologically determined suitability for domestic and child keeping chores, remains a grave flaw. But given the period in which du Maurier wrote, this point of view becomes understandable.

Daphne du Maurier's *Rebecca* stands as one of the best late modern examples of Gothic romance. Its odd love triangle, one that includes the ghost of the dead title character, continues to fascinate readers, regardless of its lack of political correctness in its depiction of women.

See also: Brontë, Charlotte and Emily; Gothic Romance; *Rebecca*
References: Armstrong, 1990; Blain, Clements, and Grundy, 1990; Drabble, 1995; Ellis; 1989; Graham, 1996; Hawes, 1994

DUMAS, ALEXANDRE

The contribution to romance writing of nineteenth-century French novelist and playwright Alexandre Dumas has been judged immense.

Writing under the influence of the Romantic period, commonly defined as 1785–1830, the prolific Dumas produced, with the aid of various collaborators, a collection of volumes estimated as high as twelve hundred in number. These include his two most famous historical romances, *The Three Musketeers* (1844) and *The Count of Monte Cristo* (1844). By the late twentieth century, Dumas's work had been translated into almost one hundred languages, and its continued popularity may be demonstrated by the fact that his works sold 140 million copies in 1993 in the former Soviet Union. The following year, French publishers printed seventeen new editions of Dumas's works, and his books have inspired a multitude of cinematic versions, fifty of *The Count of Monte Cristo* alone.

Dumas was born in Villers-Cotterets, Aisne, on July 24, 1802, the son of a mulatto father who achieved the rank of general. Once a fierce fighter for Napoleon, General Dumas was said to have halted the advance of the enemy by sustaining multiple bullet wounds, earning him the nickname "the black devil." Eventually, he and Napoleon parted ways due to General Dumas's devotion to republican sympathies. This led to the poverty suffered by the Dumas family on the occasion of the general's death in 1806, when Alexandre was only four. A generous priest supplied the boy's formal education, an education supported by Dumas's voracious reading, particularly of adventure stories from the preceding centuries. When of a proper age, Alexandre entered the employ of a lawyer and eventually formed a close friendship with Auguste Lafarge, whose published epigram that quickly gained popularity until it became cited by the entire country sparked jealousy and ambition in Dumas. He later wrote that he dreamed of the marvel of having people talk about him when he was not even present.

In time, Dumas took a position as clerk to the Duc d'Orleans, the man who would soon become king, securing for himself a promising future. After making the acquaintance of literary luminaries such as Victor Hugo and George Sand, he began his prolific writing career, enjoying many adventures that he would later compile in his wonderful *Memoir.*

Dumas produced various melodramas in Paris. At the age of twenty-two, he also produced an illegitimate son by a dressmaker. Dumas later took custody of the boy, also named Alexandre Dumas, who would become a writer himself, most famous for his novel *The Lady of the Camellias.* This work inspired a libretto of Giuseppe Verdi's opera *La Traviata,* and its plot was employed in the famous American film *Camille* (1937). During these early years of adulthood, Dumas is said to have witnessed a Shakespearean production that inspired him to try his hand at drama. The result was his *Henri III et sa cour* (Henry III and his court) and a romantic drama, *Christine,* produced by the Comédie Française in 1829 and 1830, respectively. His plays likely paved the way for a new type of drama on the bourgeois level and were said to have set off a revolution. His rousing plays caused crowds to almost destroy the marble busts of the theater's classical authors as the audience rejected the confining, restrained verses of playwrights such as Jean Racine and Voltaire to embrace Dumas's hearty scenes instead.

Although Dumas gained an appointment from the duc as the Palais Royal librarian, he still suffered the indignities of racism. The leading lady of the theater was said to have cried for the windows to be opened as the playwright departed to release the "smell of Negro." Such attitudes did not hamper Dumas in enjoying affairs of the heart. He was said to have had twenty-eight mistresses over his lifetime, and he produced two daughters in addition to the young Alexandre. His single marriage to a nonprominent actress was short-lived.

When his playwriting career suffered an interruption by a protest against the reign of the Bourbon king, Charles X, in 1830, Dumas continued to engage in high adventures, recorded in his *Memoir.* Ensuing years produced more peccadilloes, one in which he supposedly conspired in the "irregularities" reported at the funeral of an aristocrat. His subsequent prudent travel abroad led him to compose additional memoirs in the form of the popular travel narrative. Inexpensive newspapers allowed Dumas to introduce the newspaper serial story with his *Countess of Salisbury,* published as a serial novel in 1836. Collaborating to generate a series of historical novels with Auguste Maquet beginning in about 1837, Dumas achieved his purpose of reconstructing in his fiction major political events of French history. His *Three Musketeers* gained such popularity that he wrote two sequels in addition to *The Count of Monte Cristo.* Modern readers may learn much about the intrigues of the historical French aristocracy from these romances. Dumas's own political adventures included the looting of a ton and a half of explosives as he participated in a political protest, and in 1860 his own schooner ran guns for the Italian patriot Giuseppe Garibaldi.

Dumas enjoyed enormous wealth, but he failed to accumulate any financial security. He chose instead to spend his ample funds supporting a number of his mistresses, in addition to the mother of his son, at his uniquely designed estate that reflected the influence of both the French Gothic and the English Renaissance styles. This estate outside of Paris, dubbed Monte-Cristo, required eighteen months for construction and cost more than 200,000 francs. Its Gothic pavilion bears Dumas's own initials and sculpted medallions representing portraits of his favorite authors, including Homer and Sir Walter Scott. Along with his property, he maintained a theater, the Theatre Historique, built specifically to feature his plays. In order to escape creditors, he eventually moved to Brussels in 1851, where his relationship with a young American circus performer caused a scandal. Despite his tremendous popular and financial success as a writer, at the time of his death on December 5, 1870, Dumas was virtually bankrupt.

In addition to his well-known novels and his *Memoirs,* Dumas wrote the plays *Antony* (1831), *La tour de Nesle* (The tower of Nesle, 1832), *Catherine Howard* (1834), and *L'Alchemiste* (The Alchemist, 1839). Like his novels, Dumas's dramas reflect many popular ideas of romanticism, involving clearly fashioned heroes, heroines, and villains and a penchant for adventure. These aspects cause his writings, although not receiving the highest critical praise, to remain popular more than a century after his death.

See also: *The Count of Monte Cristo*
References: Charlton, 1984; de Rougemont, 1983; Foote-Greenwell, 1996; McDermott, 1988; McMillin, 1990; Williams, 1974

D'URBERVILLE, ALEC

Alec d'Urberville, the villain of Thomas Hardy's 1891 tragic romance novel, *Tess of the d'Urbervilles,* focuses the author's emphasis on two important themes. First, Alec's betrayal of the beautiful but innocent Tess Durbeyfield stands as a testimony to a fate influenced by forces beyond the individual's control. Second, Alec's social and religious standing allows examination of the false piety of hypocritical Victorian ideas toward social justice. Tess bears little responsibility for Alec's seduction that impregnates her, but as a "ruined woman," she is condemned by society. Alec, however, as a male bearing no physical sign of his sin, suffers no consequence for his actions.

Alec occupies the position of son and heir in a landed family who assumes the d'Urberville title and to whom Tess's father believes he is related. A classic scoundrel, Alec first makes improper overtures to Tess and then tricks her into performing the menial work of a poultry maid. Her naïveté makes her easy prey for Alec's seduction. When Tess departs the d'Urberville poultry farm to return home, she carries Alec's baby and a great load of shame.

The reader learns later, along with Tess, that Alec supposedly underwent a religious conversion, even taking up ministering to the misguided. In the meantime, Tess delivers her baby, who dies, and then travels 40 miles from home to work for several years as a milkmaid. She finds herself reluctantly drawn into a romantic relationship with Angel Clare, a minister's son and an intellectual.

Alec stands in stark contrast to Angel, the other male member of this tragic love triangle. Whereas Alec remains an opportunist, even under the guise of his newly donned religious mantle, Angel searches for the truth through philosophy, rejecting a religion that allows the hypocrisy evident in local beliefs and practices. Only Tess's terrible secret past, inflicted upon her by Alec, prevents her from agreeing to marry Angel. Several attempts to explain her previous affair with Alec to Angel fail, and Tess at last submits to the temptation for what seems a perfect lifetime relationship with Angel.

But Alec's presence lingers. When Tess at last confesses her past to her new husband, Angel rejects her. Again, fate summons Alec d'Urberville, supposed Christian convert, to Tess's side during this vulnerable time. Alec convinces Tess of her responsibility in providing the temptation that causes him to throw aside his faith. In his character's defense, Alec does express shock when he learns of Tess's pregnancy and their dead child; he claims he would have behaved honorably toward her, had he known. He also asks Tess to marry him, at first ostensibly to travel to the mission field. After his rejection of his ministerial aspirations, he later pursues Tess in order to find an outlet for his sexual appetite.

Alec's most hateful and opportunistic act consists of convincing Tess that her husband will never return to her. Angel has gone abroad to South America and does not receive Tess's letters pleading for his return, in which she expresses her fear regarding the temptation she faces. Persuaded by Angel's lack of response that Alec is correct in saying he will never return, she at last agrees to cohabitate with Alec. Fate could not act more cruelly, for Angel responds belatedly to her pleas and arrives just as Tess has slept with Alec.

Most readers agree that Alec's murder at Tess's hands remains understandable in light of the circumstances. But a civil code every bit as strict as the social code that condemned Tess must find her guilty of a heinous crime. Alec's part in her eventual execution remains undeniable, but as with his other characters, Hardy stresses this villain's position as a mere tool of fate.

See also: Clare, Angel; Durbeyfield, Tess; Forbidden Love; Hardy, Thomas; Love Triangle; *Tess of the d'Urbervilles*

References: Comfort, 1974; Goode, 1993: Pettit, 1994; Shires, 1992; Weber, 1951

DURBEYFIELD, TESS

Thomas Hardy's tragic romantic novel *Tess of the d'Urbervilles* (1891) presents a heroine at once pathetic and sympathetic. The operation of fate, which intrigued Hardy, allows Tess Durbeyfield no chance to realize her full potential as a human being or as a loving wife. However, that same fate allows her, if even for a brief time, to experience a glimpse of true love, something many humans never enjoy. Trapped in a classic love triangle with the opportunistic Alec d'Urberville and the idealistic Angel Clare, the young country woman finds that neither man is cognizant of her true character and needs. Tess's naïveté leads her into an unwanted sexual liaison with Alec, whose lack of morals and any feelings of responsibility toward his fellow humans renders him incapable of true love. Ironically, it is the expression of her morality in a desire for honesty that later ruins her chances at lifelong romance with Angel, whose own moral code blinds him to her innocence.

That readers recognize that innocence and Tess's position as a victim remain crucial to understanding Hardy's story. Readers who analyze Tess as a character should keep in mind Hardy's subtitle, "A Pure Woman." Hardy is referring to spiritual, rather than physical, purity.

Her victimization begins when her father, Jack Durbeyfield, discovers he may be related to the wealthy d'Urberville family line. His immediate assumption of the "airs" accompanying aristocracy would be laughable if they did not generate such horror for his daughter. Because he envisions himself as too good to work, Durbeyfield insists that Tess support their large family. Tess's mother agrees with her husband, and she persuades their daughter to approach the d'Urberville family. The Durbeyfields' expectations of the family's wealth and high standing are unfounded, for they had assumed the title simply because no one else living in Stoke-d'Urberville claimed it. Mrs. Durbeyfield hopes her daughter will develop a relationship with a wealthy "relative" that will lead to marriage. When Alec d'Urberville, the only such "relative" available at the family's poultry farm, makes advances toward Tess, she tries to restrain her distaste, out of respect for their class difference. She finds his overtures vulgar and resists his attentions to the best of her ability and, in this resistance, shows her own nobility to be superior to one of her social "betters." Only once had she felt an attraction to a young man and that only for an instant during a May Day festivity. While dancing with the other country girls, she saw a local scholar, Angel Clare, watching her. He would not dance with her, but Angel did make a permanent impression on the beautiful Tess, foreshadowing their future relationship.

The only other member of the d'Urberville family, Alec's blind mother, remains unaware that Tess might be a relation; she employs Tess to work on the farm. In this position, Tess relates to Alec as a servant to a master. Consequently, he treats her in the seductive way young aristocrats were allowed by the hypocritical Victorian Age society, which felt that title and wealth gave one the power to act with impunity. Eventually Tess's resistance breaks down, and Alec seduces her. Tess's conscience prevents her from telling Alec about her subsequent pregnancy or the birth of their baby, and she decides to love and raise the child alone. Fate steps in once again, this time through the baby's death. Suffering greatly over his loss, Tess leaves again to find work on a dairy farm 40 miles from her home.

In one of the coincidental situations typical of nineteenth-century romance, Angel Clare also works at the dairy farm. Although highly educated, he takes on the menial farm tasks to help prepare him for his later career in agriculture. With this exposure to Tess, Angel becomes smitten with her ample charms and begins a courtship that greatly contrasts with Alec's former pursuit. A highly moral person, Tess feels she cannot encourage Angel due to her previous seduction and pregnancy. After rejecting multiple requests for marriage from Angel, Tess admits her great love for him and tries to discuss her past on several occasions. Angel always stops her explanation, and they marry before he discovers the truth about her past.

Angel's negative reaction to Tess's later confession reinforces Hardy's themes of the importance of social and moral responsibility. Angel speaks of a philosophy he chooses over organized religion, in which each individual human remains as valuable as the next. Yet when faced with the truth about Tess, he lapses back into that Victorian judgmental mindset he so detests. His subsequent abandonment of Tess leaves her vulnerable to renewed attentions by Alec, who also heaps guilt upon Tess for separating him from his newfound religious lifestyle.

As the reader might expect, Tess's pleas to Angel for help never reach him, for he has left the country to work in South America. She knows her own nature, and although a moral person, she cannot survive alone. When Alec convinces her that she will not hear from her husband, she again falls prey to him, participating in a forbidden love.

Angel and Tess seem destined to remain unrequited lovers. Upon Angel's return to England, he reads Tess's letters, realizes and acts upon his love, but arrives just as Alec's seduction enjoys a second success. His immediate passionate reaction is again to abandon Tess, leaving her to stab Alec to death in a desperate reaction to a second loss of her husband.

When Angel returns to Tess, finally forgiving her and accepting her innocence in the affair with Alec, she has been condemned to die. But the few hours they enjoy together at last in wedded bliss are enough for her. She even asks Angel to consider marrying her sister, who possesses all of Tess's goodness and none of her "evil."

Tess Durbeyfield remains one of Hardy's most clearly drawn realistic characters. Through Tess, Hardy appeals to reader sympathy for all "poor wounded names."

See also: Clare, Angel; d'Urberville, Alec; Forbidden Love; Hardy, Thomas; *Tess of the d'Urbervilles;* Victorian Age

References: Bullen, 1997; Comfort, 1974; Goode, 1993; Pettit, 1994; Shires, 1992; Weber, 1951

EARNSHAW, CATHERINE

Even though she is the heroine of Emily Brontë's 1847 Gothic romance, *Wuthering Heights,* Catherine Earnshaw dies in the middle of the story. This technique may seem questionable until one understands that Catherine's death does not mean she vanishes from the story. Like her sister ghosts in other Gothic novels, such as Daphne du Maurier's *Rebecca,* Catherine remains a strong presence throughout the book, determining the actions of the still living characters.

Born on the Yorkshire moors to the well-heeled Earnshaw family, Catherine becomes inseparable at an early age from Heathcliff, the foundling her father brings home to live with the Earnshaws. Although their difference in social status makes their later affection a forbidden love, the moody Heathcliff believes that he and Catherine should be together forever. She is the only one who treats Heathcliff with any respect. But their pleasure in one another is shattered when Catherine injures herself at the neighboring Linton estate, necessitating several weeks of convalescence there. Heathcliff can hardly bear Catherine's absence, but she enjoys the company of Edgar Linton and his younger sister, Isabella. Catherine becomes caught up in a love triangle with Edgar, who wants to marry her, and Heathcliff, who wants to possess her.

Catherine struggles with her decision to marry Edgar. She considers him an eligible and desirable future husband, yet, as she explains to her nurse, Nelly, she cannot fathom the idea of separation from Heathcliff, who seems more herself that she does. Brontë foreshadows Catherine's early death in that scene, when Catherine explains to Nelly that she has dreamed of dying. Although heaven seemed marvelous, in her dream Catherine demanded to be returned to earth, where she exults in the presence of those she loves, namely Heathcliff. Unfortunately, Heathcliff overhears only the part of the conversation in which Catherine states that she plans to marry Edgar, and he understands only that she views him as being beneath her social status. He disappears without explanation, and Catherine marries Edgar. She never gives up longing for Heathcliff, her true soulmate, however.

When Heathcliff returns, he has matured into a dark, powerful man, every inch the Byronic hero of the Gothic genre. He loves Catherine still, but it is a ferocious and destructive love, one that spurs him to desire revenge against the Lintons and the Earnshaws, who worked together to separate him from Catherine. At this point in the novel, his personality greatly overpowers that of Catherine, who begins to dissemble in his presence. She can no longer pretend devotion to Edgar and rejection of Heathcliff. His nearness acts as both torture and sustenance for her, but she knows she cannot survive long in her role as another's wife.

Catherine suffers a fatal illness as a result of pregnancy with Edgar's child. She and Heathcliff resolve their hate-love relationship only on her deathbed. They at last embrace, coming together with such ferocity that Nelly wonders whether Catherine can still be breathing when Heathcliff relaxes his crushing hold on her body. Catherine's presence acts to reduce Heathcliff to an animalistic state, emphasizing their unnatural relationship. When she dies in childbirth, Heathcliff places a curse on her that she may never enjoy peace in the afterlife. He dares her spirit to haunt him for the remainder of his time on earth, and it meets that challenge. Thus, Catherine's prophetic dream is fulfilled: she is denied a journey to heaven as her earthbound spirit lingers, waiting for Heathcliff to join her.

The wait is a long one, as Heathcliff methodically brings personal and financial ruin to every member of the two families who so mistreated him, except for Catherine's daughter, Cathy, and her nephew, Hareton. Catherine lives through her daughter and in Heathcliff's constant awareness as his memory of her continues to make his life unbearable. After he partakes in all the revenge that his soul can stand, Heathcliff sees a vision of his dead love on the moors. He then begins his own journey toward death, answering her call. The two lovers unite as he dies and are seen walking the moors together after Heathcliff's burial. Although an essential character to Brontë's novel and the development of Heathcliff's character, Catherine remains secondary in importance to the portrayal of Heathcliff himself. His ferocity and faithfulness, his violent love, and his ghoul-like worship of the dead Catherine overpower her living presence.

Brontë offers little to admire in her descriptions of Catherine, a self-centered and indulgent girl given to fits of temper, who seals her own unpleasant fate, along with that of those around her, through her foolish actions. Yet she remains appealing for her awareness of the supernatural attachment she shares with Heathcliff. She honestly acknowledges her weaknesses, her undeserved happiness with Edgar, and finally her inability to survive without Heathcliff. In this acknowledgment lies her heroism.

See also: Forbidden Love; Gothic Romance; Heathcliff; Linton, Edgar; Love Triangle; *Rebecca;* Violence; *Wuthering Heights*
References: Allen, 1993; Ellis, 1989; Gilbert and Gubar, 1996a; Leavis, 1966; Pater, 1974; Winnifrith, 1996

EMMA

Of Jane Austen's six novels, her romantic comedy of manners *Emma* (1815) probably best represents her. Although not the most popular of her books, for *Pride and Prejudice* claims that distinction, *Emma* remains the title that all serious readers of English literature deem Austen's greatest work. With its complex heroine, Emma Woodhouse, Austen's novel challenges readers to come back to it again and again to gain a full understanding. Austen herself judged Emma to be a heroine only she could like, but time has proven that judgment decidedly incorrect.

The novel's attention remains squarely upon the beautiful Emma Woodhouse for its duration. It reveals immediately that her mother died when Emma was a young child, she lives alone with her respected father in Highbury, her sister Isabella married John Knightley prior to the novel's opening, and Emma is spoiled by everyone around her. Completely unsupervised following the marriage of her governess, Anne Taylor, to Emma's neighbor, Mr. Weston, the young woman indulges in any romantic whim she desires.

Emma gains a great deal of amusement in playing matchmaker. She takes credit for Anne's marriage to Mr. Weston and sets to work to find a proper match for Harriet Smith, a young girl of uncertain parentage whom Emma takes on as a kind of social project. Although Harriet is without income and feels an attraction to the good farmer Robert Martin, Emma manipulates Harriet into rejecting Robert's proposal of marriage. She convinces Harriet that her status is far above that of a simple farmer, and, desiring to keep Emma's friendship, Harriet places her future in the capable social hands of her wealthy acquaintance.

Naturally Emma's matchmaking causes much mischief, and she might escape censure for her meddling in the lives of others except for the friendship of George Knightley, her sister's brother-in-law and a great friend of the entire family. When Emma determines that the local vicar, Mr. Elton, would be a good match for Harriet, only George warns her against such attempts. His honesty and good humor provide a balance to Emma's flighty actions because George understands her and recognizes her weak points as well as her strong. Mr. Elton desires a woman of higher status than Harriet and dismays Emma by revealing his affection for her, rather than for her friend. His actions prove George Knightley's assessment correct, but Emma still ignores his advice to encourage Harriet to unite with Robert Martin. When she must break the news to the impressionable Harriet that Mr. Elton has no desire for her, Harriet is heartbroken. Emma's feelings of guilt only increase when Mr. Elton marries a wealthy snob. This is the first of many events that will prove George Knightley to be of sound judgment, and Austen uses it as foreshadowing that Emma's future efforts will prove no more successful.

Still, Emma stubbornly pursues a match for Harriet, having learned nothing through the debacle with Mr. Elton. Her stubbornness helps to identify her character as one that needs to change. When the handsome Frank Churchill, stepson of Emma's former governess, visits his father, Emma thinks he may make a match for Harriet. Unexpectedly, she finds herself attracted to the outspoken and sometimes vulgar Churchill. He indulges Emma's penchant for gossip, promoting rumors regarding the beautiful

Jane Fairfax, who is visiting her silly and talkative aunt, Miss Bates. Having always disliked Jane, Emma is delighted to join in Churchill's jests. Eventually she decides that she does not love Churchill after all, and she pursues her objective of uniting him with Harriet. Churchill acts as a cautionary tale for Emma, whose worst tendencies seem to appear in his presence—in short, he is a bad influence.

Knightley lives up to his name when he rescues Harriet from the embarrassment of being snubbed by Mr. Elton, who refuses to dance with her at a local ball. Ever concerned for her poor friend's feelings, Emma is charmed by George's act and begins to change her opinion of him as a cold, judgmental man. The novel supplies foreshadowing of the eventual romantic involvement of Emma and George when they agree to dance, settling the fact that they are not, after all, really brother and sister. In this manner, their relationship gradually gains a new importance as something outside that of family.

Harriet needs rescue again the following day, when she is attacked while in Emma's company by Gypsies. Frank Churchill arrives, saving the ladies and leaving them to arrive at more incorrect conclusions. When Emma asks Harriet whether she has feelings for a man who saved her, without mentioning a specific name, Harriet confesses that she does. Only later will Emma discover that while she had in mind Frank Churchill, Harriet was thinking of George Knightley. This explains why Harriet is not upset when Emma discovers and tells her that Churchill was secretly engaged to Jane Fairfax all along. This revelation shows Churchill's manipulative and ungentlemanly behavior in having led Emma briefly to believe he might be romantically interested in her.

In the midst of all the confusion, Austen inserts highly humorous scenes that help delineate her characters. One of the more classic is Harriet's burning of various "remembrances" of Mr. Elton. The high drama of Harriet's actions causes Emma amusement, helping readers see Emma's condescension in believing her friend silly, when her own actions have been just as foolish. Austen also uses the Victorian Age convention of innuendo to its maximum benefit. Because readers remain privy to a particular situation, they understand the real meaning behind veiled comments that certain characters do not grasp.

Harriet's revelation that she loves George Knightley makes Emma realize for the first time her own feelings of love toward George. Caught up in a conundrum of her own design, Emma fears that George also loves Harriet. She tells Harriet of her own love for George, sending Harriet into yet another depression. The girl departs for London to visit Emma's sister Isabella. There she will encounter Robert Martin, whose passion for Harriet has not lessened, and this time she agrees to marry the upstanding farmer. Meanwhile, George confesses his love for Emma, and the two plan marriage.

Emma at last realizes her folly in trying to plan the lives of others and George's wisdom in attempting to discourage such activity. George remains the voice of reason that helps Emma achieve her epiphany, which leads to a change in her self-conception. In a poignant scene, Emma insults poor Miss Bates at a picnic, leading George to sharply correct her at a later time. The fact that he offers to accompany Miss Bates away from the scene, allowing her an escape, proves him to be a true gentleman. Emma's childish remark returns to haunt her as she at last realizes the strong effect of her words. As Miss Bates's social better and possessing more wealth and its resultant power than almost everyone at the picnic, Emma lacks the social graces that should accompany her position. The respect she gains for George through this event, even though his words hurt her deeply, allows their relationship to reach its fulfillment and Emma to become a dynamic character.

See also: Austen, Jane; Knightley, George; *Pride and Prejudice; Sense and Sensibility*
References: Copeland and McMaster, 1997; Drabble, 1995; Fraiman, 1993; Gard, 1992; Trilling, 1957

ENEMIES: A LOVE STORY

In his novel *Enemies: A Love Story* (1972), Isaac Bashevis Singer presents a strange and ironically humorous romance tale that explains the contradiction suggested in its title. Its Jewish protagonist, Herman Broder, survives the Nazi regime only to suffer emotional defeat at the hands of three different women when he moves to America. By the novel's conclusion, the reader may remain uncertain as to whom the term "enemies" refers, for Herman's three women, supposedly competitors for his time and affection, seem

Anjelica Huston and Ron Silver played Tamara and Herman Broder in a 1989 film version of Isaac Bashevis Singer's 1972 novel, Enemies: A Love Story, *a strange and ironically humorous romance tale. (Photofest)*

far more reconciled to one another's existence than does Herman.

The novel introduces Herman in a nightmarish dream state, as he imagines that the Nazis have at last discovered his hiding place in the Polish hayloft where he existed for three years during World War II. This clandestine state remains symbolic of Herman's mental condition throughout the novel; he never recovers from his fear of being discovered. Yet he constantly tempts fate, as if daring life to recognize his hidden shame, born of his lack of self-worth and the guilt he feels over his survival when his wife and two children died in the Holocaust. Herman appeals to various women to help heal a wound that none possess the power to heal. Only Herman can rid himself of the horror of the Nazi threat, and he remains unequal to that task; he simply turns his life over to three strong female personalities in hopes of rescue. This move is ironic in that Herman supposedly mistrusts the female intellect, viewing women basically as objects for his physical pleasure.

Herman's wife, Yadwiga Broder, is the Polish farm woman, once a servant of the Broder fami-

ly, who risked her own life and that of her family to hide Herman during the war. He marries Yadwiga following the years of secretive existence, taking her to America where they may begin a new life together based on his gratitude for her. Curiously, Yadwiga remains more devoted to the Jewish religion than does Herman; she wants to adopt it as her own. She encourages Herman to observe proper Jewish behavior and ritual, but her pleas fail to motivate him. In contrast to Yadwiga, he does not hold his religious and genetic heritage in esteem. This is symbolized in his agreement to ghost-write papers for an unscrupulous rabbi who uses religion to take advantage of others. Herman cannot love Yadwiga because she continues to act the part of a servant, yet he keeps her in that very position. She gains none of the independence offered by America, instead cowering inside their Brooklyn apartment due to the scary stories of New York that Herman has told her. In an ironic reversal, he holds Yadwiga physical and emotional prisoner, when she had been instrumental in his own physical independence. He even denies her the child she desires. This denial cannot be blamed on his having lost his first two children to the Nazis, but rather on a simple selfishness on his part.

Because Herman finds no love at home, he takes a mistress, the beautiful and sensuous Masha Tortshiner, a Jewish survivor of the Nazi prison camp. Separated from her husband, Masha lives in the Bronx with her mother and welcomes Herman into her home as if he were her legal husband. Herman accomplishes his frequent clandestine overnight visits to Masha by convincing the naive Yadwiga that he must go on the road as a salesman. The two women could not be more different, not only in looks but in temperament. Masha's sexy demeanor stands in sharp contrast to Yadwiga's drab eagerness. Whereas Yadwiga caters to Herman, Masha enjoys taunting him. She challenges his dominance and sexual security by threatening to have sex with her estranged husband, thus being "unfaithful" to Herman. Herman also lies to Masha, pretending they will one day live together, even though he lacks the nerve to ever leave Yadwiga, to whom he owes his life but apparently not his loyalty.

A notice appearing in the paper one day greatly complicates Herman's already complicated life. It appeals to Herman to call his first wife's uncle, who lives on East Broadway in New York City. He places the call and discovers that his first wife, Tamara Broder, did not die in Poland after all; she survived a shooting that left her lame. Herman calmly pays a visit to Tamara and her aunt and uncle, wondering all the while what his future actions should be but unconsciously placing the responsibility for that action upon the three women in his life. When he tries to recall his married life with Tamara, he remembers her outspoken nature. This places her also in direct opposition to the retiring Yadwiga, but her pushiness differs from that of Masha. Tamara had been interested in the Jewish religion, in the political rumblings that eventually resulted in full-scale destruction, and in issues important to women. As the reader might expect after developing ideas regarding Herman's character, Herman had also never really loved Tamara. They speak pragmatically of his options, more like a brother and sister than a couple considering affairs of the heart. Herman ends up relating to Tamara in the only way he seems to be able to relate to women, through sex. He remains a misogynist, adopting a view of women that supports the view to which

Masha's husband also adheres. Tortshiner describes women as spiders, considering them all-consuming of a man's energies and intellect.

Herman barely escapes being caught in his ruse with three different women on more than one occasion. Although these escapades produce the humorous effect that all such instances of near-escape have promoted in romance fiction, they are at the same time pitiful. They reveal Herman as a spineless, egocentric character and occur at the emotional expense of the women he involves in his shame, particularly Masha.

Because Herman is typical of Singer's Diasporan characters and because he cannot deal with reality, the reader anticipates his disappearance. True to his irresponsible nature, he eventually disappears following Masha's suicide. In a profoundly sad scene, she asks Herman to agree to commit suicide with her, but he refuses. When she urges Herman to return to Yadwiga, who has become pregnant, he tells her simply that he will leave them all. Masha remains true to her independent but crushed spirit as she takes her own life following the death of her mother.

Honest regarding his own character if nothing else, Herman does depart, never answering the advertisements that Tamara places in the paper in hopes of discovering his whereabouts. Ironically, Tamara moves in with Yadwiga to raise the daughter they name Masha. Like Masha Tortshiner, these women also demonstrate the courage of their convictions and bear no ill will toward Herman. The rabbi for whom Herman had worked takes an interest in the women and looks after them. He even tells them that, because of the Holocaust, deserted wives may remarry. Tamara answers that she will wait until the next world, when she will seek Herman again.

Because all four of the novel's main characters survive the Holocaust, an example of ultimate chaos, they accept the preferable insanity of a peaceful world. Herman's wandering nature remains balanced by that of the three women who want nothing more than to settle in, producing a new generation that will have no first-hand memory of the unspeakable horrors inflicted by the Nazis. Although Herman remains a hopeless character, the birth of the baby Masha permits the novel to end on a positive note. Herman could offer little of himself to Yadwiga and Tamara, but he did present them with a new life, in a literal as well as a symbolic sense.

See also: Broder, Herman; Singer, Isaac Bashevis
References: Bilik, 1981; Farrell, 1994; Forrey, 1981;
Halio, 1991; *Studies,* 1981

ESMERALDA

In Victor Hugo's 1831 novel, *The Hunchback of Notre Dame,* Esmeralda remains the character most crucial to the novel, playing a major role in its main plot and all subplots. She also represents Hugo's theme of social inequity and acts as a symbol of virginal purity. Esmeralda is a member of multiple love triangles and is also the missing daughter of the pitiful madwoman, Paquette la Chantefleurie. The young Gypsy girl, famed for her exotic beauty and trained pet goat, loves only Captain Phoebus de Chateaupers, who, as one might expect in the complications common to romance plots, does not return her love. To the captain, Esmeralda represents only an additional opportunity for sexual seduction. Although her love for de Chateaupers remains unrequited, so do the loves for Esmeralda on the part of Quasimodo, the deformed cathedral bell ringer, and on the part of Claude Frollo, the evil priest. In a mock ceremony, Esmeralda "marries" the foolish poet, Gringoire, in order to rescue him from a Gypsy trial that almost leads to his execution. Their relationship remains platonic and forms her final connection to the novel's male characters.

Throughout the tale, in spite of her pursuit by several men with carnal intentions, Esmeralda retains her innocence. All of Paris seems to hold her in esteem as a kind of icon. They symbolically equate her with the Virgin Mary, an appropriate parallel suggested by Hugo to better integrate her into the plot of the sinful undoing of Claude Frollo and emphasize the importance to the novel of the cathedral. Eventually the reader learns that Esmeralda was likely abducted by the Gypsies from Paquette, now famous to Parisians as the recluse of Trou aux Rats, a woman driven to distraction and madness by the kidnapping of her toddler Agnes in about 1467. This story helps establish Esmeralda's age at about sixteen years. Raised in the Gypsy culture, Esmeralda dances for a living, accompanied by her trained goat, Djali. The two become a well-known duo in their Parisian quarter, causing Claude Frollo to develop an unholy lust for the young girl.

Quasimodo also is smitten by love for Esmeralda, which contrasts well in its purity to that of the lustful priest. When Quasimodo is placed on trial for keeping the company of Claude Frollo, believed by some to be a sorcerer, and of Esmeralda, presumably a witch, his sentence results in his public flogging in the pillory. The hunchback stoically endures his beating and disgrace but suffers a terrible thirst; Esmeralda is the only spectator who furnishes him a drink from her flask. This act gains Quasimodo's devotion and eventually causes the conflict that leads Quasimodo to turn away from the priest in loyalty to Esmeralda.

When Esmeralda first encounters the man she believes to be her true love, Phoebus de Chateaupers, he rescues her from a kidnapping attempt by Quasimodo, who is simply following the priest's orders. A romantic and uneducated person, the girl misinterprets the captain's protective action as an act of love. Early in the story, Esmeralda asks her poet/ "husband" Gringoire to explain to her the meaning of the name Phoebus. When she learns it means "the sun" and that Phoebus was a god, she murmurs the phrase, "a god," indicating that she believes Captain de Chateaupers to be far more than human. Hugo uses his character's falling in love with an unreachable man to emphasize his theme of fate and Esmeralda's total lack of control over her tragic future. When she later agrees to meet with the captain, Gringoire arranges to allow the evil priest to observe the meeting. When the two young people embrace, Claude Frollo springs on de Chateaupers from his hiding place, stabbing him several times.

Esmeralda is accused not only of murdering the captain but also of practicing witchcraft, supposedly manifested in the seemingly mystical powers of her goat. As an animal with a long biblical history of use in sacrifice, the goat symbolizes Esmeralda herself, who will be sacrificed to the evil blood-lust of the populace, invoking further imagery of the virgin sacrifices demanded by primitive tribes. Djali even resembles Esmeralda in his slender conformation and intelligent, loyal demeanor.

The girl's ill fortune in being accused of crimes she did not commit spurs Quasimodo's rescue of her. He sweeps her away to live in the cathedral of Notre Dame, where she may claim sanctuary. The fact that she rejoices upon learning that Phoebus did not suffer death from Claude Frollo's attack may lead readers to wonder about

Esmeralda's intelligence. Rather than questioning why the captain never appears in her defense, she desires to see him again in order to express her devotion. Such melodramatic elements cause some critics to question the literary value of the novel, but its romantic aspects remain true to traditional themes of romance literature, such as the unquestioned passion of one unrequited lover for the object of that love.

Despite Quasimodo's intervention, eventual execution is Esmeralda's fate. Like the other characters, she represents a type and simply acts her part until her fate can be fulfilled. Therefore, she experiences no epiphany and remains a flat character as she approaches her life's inevitable end. Previous to her death, she does enjoy a brief reunion with her loving mother, and she has experienced gentle and loving treatment at the hands of Quasimodo. A crucial element in Hugo's Gothic novel, Esmeralda plays the part of beauty to the hunchback's beast and allows the author to reflect on one of his own favorite themes, opposition to capital punishment.

See also: Beauty and the Beast; Frollo, Claude; Gothic Romance; *The Hunchback of Notre Dame;* Quasimodo; Violence
References: Brombert, 1986; Charlton, 1984; Dahl, 1947; Ellis, 1989

ESQUIVEL, LAURA

Laura Esquivel, a teacher and screenwriter, burst onto the novel-writing scene and into the public consciousness of the United States in 1992. In that year, the simultaneous release to foreign markets of her first book, *Like Water for Chocolate* (1989), along with its movie version, which the United States made one of the highest-grossing foreign films of all time, called attention to this Mexican writer. Esquivel's earlier work, *Chido One,* was nominated for the Ariel Award for best screenplay by the Mexican Academy of Motion Pictures before the film version of *Like Water for Chocolate* was nominated for the U.S. Golden Globe Award for Best Foreign Language Film in 1993.

A tale of forbidden love, *Like Water for Chocolate* remained a best-seller in Mexico for two years. Esquivel's romantically charged novel supplies readers not only with stories but also with recipes to tempt various of their senses while reading. Her inclusion of a traditional Mexican recipe to introduce each chapter demonstrates her unique approach to the telling of old stories. *The Law of Love* (1996), Esquivel's second novel, contains a similar approach that some call blatantly commercial. This plot-driven book includes illustrations by Miguelanxo Prado, and a compact disc containing traditional Mexican love songs and arias is provided for the reader to enjoy in between chapters.

The use of multimedia to get her message across to the public reflects Esquivel's background as a schoolteacher. Following the classical ideas of Horace, she believes in a dual purpose for literature—it should both delight and teach. This approach is evident in her development of new methods to apply to classic romance formulas. Her marketing "gimmicks," however, have led some critics to bar her from consideration as a major literary figure, relegating her instead to the category of a popular fiction writer.

Both of her novels have been structured with a movie in mind, an approach that befits former screenwriter Esquivel. Her heroines find ways to overcome what at first appears to be thwarted love. Like South American writers Gabriel García

Laura Esquivel's 1989 tale of forbidden love, Like Water for Chocolate, *supplies readers not only with stories but also with recipes to tempt their senses while reading. (AP/Wide World Photos)*

Márquez and Isabel Allende, Esquivel uses magic realism in presenting tales, thus creating a mythological quality.

Although her first novel was set in early twentieth-century Mexico and her second in futuristic twenty-third-century Mexico City, both focus on themes of the relationship between materiality and spirituality and the capability of emotion to overcome reality. The author applied this rule of love to her own life when her twelve-year marriage to the Mexican movie director Alfonso Arau dissolved. Following her lawsuit against Arau for profits due her from their movie, Esquivel married the dentist Javier Valdez, whom she calls her platonic soulmate. They moved to Mexico City, where she continues to write, hoping next to publish a children's book.

See also: Forbidden Love; García Márquez, Gabriel; *Like Water for Chocolate;* Magic Realism
References: Smith, 1997; Zamora and Faris, 1995

ETHAN FROME

In *Ethan Frome* (1911), a novel considered to be Edith Wharton's masterpiece, Wharton shapes a story of tragic romance. Named for its main character, the novel features a wrenching love triangle made up of three good but unfulfilled people: Ethan Frome, his wife, Zeena Frome, and Zeena's young cousin, Mattie Silver. Like most of Wharton's novels, this one she frames with themes of personal dissatisfaction, disappointment in love, and cultural alienation.

The three characters remain highly symbolic of Wharton's own life and times. Ethan embodies positive, noble nineteenth-century characteristics that the author cherished. Although trapped in a loveless marriage to Zenobia, or Zeena, he perseveres, attempting to lead a good life. As Mattie's last name, Silver, indicates, she represents the shine and promise of a better life for Ethan but remains a temptation he cannot enjoy. His marriage vows to a woman he does not love trap him in a situation his judgmental culture insists on preserving, even at the cost of individual happiness. Zeena, an unfortunate invalid and unloved wife, represents those repressive social conventions about which Wharton often wrote. Although not a basically evil person, Zeena erases the chance for true love on the part of two people for whom she feels a great jealousy.

Additional symbolism exists in the name of the town near the Frome's farm. Starkfield

describes the desolation in the fields of Ethan's nonproductive farm as well as in the Frome marriage. Neither love nor harvest is nurtured in Starkfield. The wintry setting also clues in readers to the fact that the tale will focus not on regeneration, but rather on the death of hope.

The reader knows of Ethan's bitter fate from the novel's opening and discovers the details leading up to his condition through flashbacks. His marriage to Zeena comes about through his loneliness and his feelings of gratitude toward Zeena for having nursed his ill mother before her death. No love exists between the two, and Zeena's own developing illness symbolizes the weakened and sick condition of her relationship to Ethan. As a man who had ambitions to become an engineer or scientist, Ethan watches his dreams die due to his poverty and his attachment to a woman who drains his physical and financial resources. His one bit of joy is Mattie, Zeena's cousin, who moves in with the Fromes to act as Zeena's companion.

Ethan tries to deny his developing love for Mattie, but he realizes its strength when he grows jealous over her interaction with local eligible males. When Zeena departs for an overnight visit to an out-of-town doctor, Ethan takes advantage of her absence to spend one wonderful evening with Mattie. The broken pickle dish, Zeena's favorite, foreshadows disaster for the two lovers as they immensely enjoy one another's company, discussing sledding and the outward affection displayed by local sweethearts. Their love remains chaste and unconsummated, but it allows Ethan to fantasize about a life with Mattie. He plans to repair the broken dish, representative of his marriage to Zeena, but she returns before he can do so.

Zeena announces that the doctor had ordered her to hire a stronger girl than Mattie to help with household chores. When she discovers the broken dish, she accuses Mattie and Ethan of romance and orders Mattie from the house. Ethan takes her on the sleigh ride they had discussed. Consumed with desire to simply depart with Mattie, his poor circumstances and feelings of responsibility toward Zeena prevent his acting on this impulse.

When the two narrowly miss a tree standing in the path of their sled, they elude fate momentarily. But in a moment of tragic irony, Mattie convinces Ethan to make a second run down the hill, suggesting that he guide their sled into the tree so they may die together. He agrees, and their plan emphasizes the age-old romantic idea of two lovers joining their souls forever in death, such as the fate that befalls Romeo and Juliet. But in Wharton's novel, her characters cannot achieve this relief. They hit the tree, but instead of resulting in their deaths, the crash leaves Ethan lame and Mattie paralyzed. In a sickening instance of situational irony, Zeena ends up nursing the two impotent lovers.

Ethan Frome is the story of romance gone awry, in which two devoted and innocent lovers are emotionally destroyed and sentenced to a living death by social edict. In their attempts to elude the roles foisted on them by society, they think to employ their love as a manner of escape. Instead, their actions entrap them, proving Wharton's message that society often kills those it seeks to control.

See also: Frome, Ethan; Wharton, Edith
References: Bell, 1995; Blain, Clements, and Grundy, 1990; Davidson, 1995; Geist 1996; Gilbert and Gubar, 1996b; Pizer, 1995; Price, 1996

FANTASY

Fantasy, simply defined, is a state in which the rules of reality do not apply, constituting a necessity for the suspension of disbelief. The use of fantasy may be found in all subject areas of fiction, and stories of romance and love are no exceptions. Fantasy stories are distinguished from reality-based stories by their mix of imaginary elements with those of reality. Although realistic plots may include the improbable, fantastic plots include the impossible. This allows fantasy to propel readers beyond real-life constraints, challenging their imaginations while naturally blending normally preposterous ideas, characters, settings, and actions with more realistic aspects to make the strange appear somehow familiar. The normal narrative elements of character, setting, plot, and theme remain crucial to fantasy. But those same elements may be released from the restraints of reality through a suspension of natural forces, such as the need by humans for a physical body in order to make their presence known, the action of gravity on objects, or a recognizable environment that complies with known physical laws. Incredible elements are used in such a way as to bring credibility to the plot.

Examples of literature of love and romance that emphasize fantasy elements include Mary Wollstonecraft Shelley's *Frankenstein* (1818), in which the force of death is overcome during the creation of a new being by a human; Emily Brontë's *Wuthering Heights* (1847), in which love transcends death in a Gothic plot that reunites two spirits; and Toni Morrison's *Beloved* (1987), in which a child who dies as a toddler ostensibly returns as a teenager to haunt her family. During the twentieth century, magic realist novels first produced by South American and Mexican writers gained popularity. Although the label applied to these novels contains the term "realism," they are in truth fantasies, dependent on fantastic elements in order for their plots to work well. Examples of magic realist novels include Gabriel García Márquez's *Love in the Time of Cholera* (1985) in which constraints of time and space are often transcended; Isabel Allende's *The House of the Spirits* (1970), in which ghosts play a major role in the plot; and Laura Esquivel's *Like Water for Chocolate* (1989) in which transcendent states are reached through the ingestion of foods containing the emotions of the protagonist.

See also: Magic Realism
References: Rothlein and Meinbach, 1991; Zamora and Faris, 1995

FANTINE

Fantine, the ill-fated prostitute in Victor Hugo's romance *Les Misérables* (1862) is used by Hugo to illuminate the crass values of early nineteenth-century France. Fantine attempts to make an honest living, working in a glass factory in order to support her secret illegitimate child, Cosette, born in 1817. The wicked Thénardiers, a couple in whose care Fantine places Cosette, demand more and more money for the child's upkeep, even though they mistreat her horribly. Out of cruelty, the Thénardiers let slip Fantine's secret that she has a child born out of wedlock. This causes her coworkers to demand her dismissal. Unbeknownst to the kindly factory owner, Monsieur Madeleine, an alias for the novel's main character, Jean Valjean, his foreman dismisses Fantine from employment.

Unemployment forces Fantine to live on the streets, where, after selling first her hair and then a bit of jewelry, she sells her body in a desperate attempt to collect enough money to support her child and pay for Cosette's medication. The degrading pursuit on the street takes a toll on her already fragile health, and she develops tuberculosis. She falls under further pressures from the Thénardiers to increase her payments for her child's care.

When Monsieur Madeleine, also the mayor of Montreuil-Sur-Mer, discovers that his own nemesis, police inspector Javert, is ready to take Fantine prisoner following an argument with one of her customers, he demands that she go to a hospital. Later when Javert discovers the mayor's true identity as Jean Valjean, he locates the convict at Fantine's bedside. Valjean has promised Fantine to care for Cosette. When Javert arrives, Fantine dies from fright.

Although Fantine is a short-lived character, she supports Hugo's focus on various themes. One of those themes is the vulnerability of humans to fate. Regardless of her efforts and her good character, Fantine becomes a pawn of socioeconomic forces that not only cause her moral downfall but also hasten her death. An additional interest on the part of Hugo is the religious idea of salvation, achieved through the performance of good works. The care of first Fantine and then her child Cosette both serve as good works to help liberate Valjean from his early guilt as a breaker of civil law. Finally, Fantine's "product of sin," Cosette, serves as an object of love for the aging Valjean, helping rescue him from cynicism and doubt. Hugo believed that love remained connected to acts of charity, and this belief is embodied by Cosette, a material result of those acts. Although Fantine dies without the love she craves, her child will live to attain not only the familial love provided by Valjean but also romantic love with the liberal-thinking young attorney, Marius Pontmercy. In typically poetic fashion, Fantine dies in order that her child may live.

See also: Cosette; *Les Misérables;* Valjean, Jean; Violence; War

References: de Rougemont, 1983; Grossman, 1994; Lovejoy, 1974; Masters-Wicks, 1994

A FAREWELL TO ARMS

In his tragic war romance *A Farewell to Arms* (1929), Ernest Hemingway offers a chillingly realistic consideration of the violence that the everyday business of life inflicts upon humans. The novel reflects Hemingway's belief in the inevitability of fate and people's inability to alter their destiny in a godless world. The story's protagonist, the American Frederic Henry, a semiautobiographical character, represents Hemingway's idea of the modern hero. Helpless to deflect or control the harm inflicted by his surroundings, the hero has only the choice to react with grace to the pressures of his environment. Frederic undergoes a test of his capacity for endurance with the tragic loss of his first and only true love, Catherine Barkley, an English nurse. Set against

the backdrop of a war during which Frederic loses his patriotic idealism, this romance proves a basic tenet of nihilism: in an uncaring world, the best humans can hope for is the company and comfort of another human.

Frederic meets Catherine as he drives an ambulance in Italy during World War I. Driving back and forth to the Italian front, he strikes up a casual romance with Catherine, who remains particularly vulnerable due to the loss to war of the man she loved. Frederic suffers a serious leg injury, followed by Catherine's total devotion to him as her patient, before he realizes his feelings go beyond those of the shallow romantic dalliance the situation of war often promotes. Never having experienced true love, Frederic undergoes a transformation when he realizes he loves Catherine. She represents a more mature and basically flat character, having already experienced the transformative effects of true love. Their period together in Milan following surgery on Frederic's knee allows time for his passion to solidify into a devotion to Catherine that distracts him from his enthusiasm for war.

The reader understands that Frederic has changed when his friend notes a difference in Frederic's demeanor upon his return to the front; he acts like a married man. Now Catherine and her pregnancy with Frederic's child occupy most of his imaginative energies. Thus, when the tide of battle turns and the Italians retreat, Frederic feels no sense of loss connected to the failure of the Italian troops to stave off the Austrians. His taking part in the retreat south symbolizes his own retreat from one interest, that of war, the world of the male, toward another, that of family and the happiness that the love of a woman offers.

During Frederic's protracted retreat, leading to capture and an ultimate bid for freedom by escape, water remains symbolic. Early in the story, Catherine reveals that she is frightened by rain; thus, whenever it rains in the book, the reader understands it foreshadows disaster. This proves true during the troops' retreat during rain. Frederic drives his ambulance off the regular road in an attempt to reach Uldine faster and becomes mired in mud, and the subsequent conflict between Frederic and his Italian sergeants causes Frederic to shoot both. One of his loyal troops is killed by an Italian sniper, and the whole Italian army seems to dissolve into chaos.

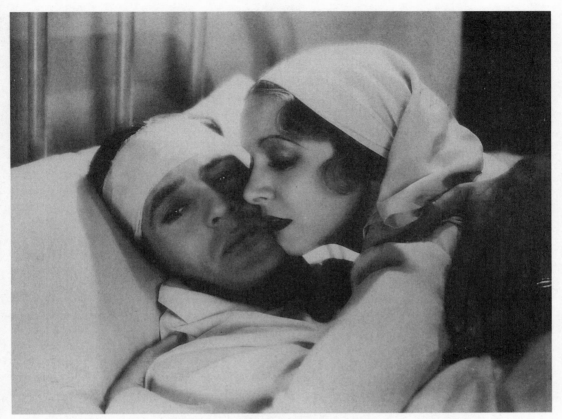

Gary Cooper as Frederic Henry and Helen Hayes as Catherine Barkley appeared in a 1932 film version of A Farewell to Arms, *Ernest Hemingway's 1929 war romance that proves a basic tenet of nihilism: in an uncaring world, the best humans can hope for is the company and comfort of another human. (Archive Photos)*

The confusion allows Hemingway's use of another important traditional symbol, that of clothing. Officers begin frantically cutting away the insignia from their uniforms, and Frederic eventually rejects his uniform for civilian clothing. This assumption of a new outfit symbolizes his new personal identity.

In addition to his use of rain, Hemingway employs water as a traditional symbol of purification and source of rebirth when Frederic swims across a river to freedom. Reminiscent of the journey involved in a traditional hero's quest, Frederic not only crosses water but also traverses the Venetian plain on foot and then jumps on a train to reach his destination in Milan, where he had recovered from his wound. In his particular quest, Catherine represents his treasure. When he learns she has moved on from Milan, he follows her to Stresa. This journey remains important to the novel's title as well. It represents Frederic's

bidding farewell to the arms that represent war and destruction as he seeks to embrace a new life with Catherine and their baby.

When he finds her again, he learns that he will be arrested for desertion if he remains in Italy. The two escape to Switzerland, again crossing water by boat, where they are arrested. Frederic, using passports and ample funds, convinces the authorities he is a sports enthusiast, and the couple gain admittance to Switzerland. The mountains and snow symbolize the purity of the elevated emotion of hope, and Frederic and Catherine settle in happily to their new life together. Although they discuss marriage during their stay outside Montreux, Catherine refuses the ceremony, saying she wishes to wait until after the baby's birth.

Frederic brings Catherine to a hospital at Lausanne, but she still suffers greatly during labor and delivers a dead child. The falling rain foreshadows Catherine's subsequent bleeding and death, which Frederic witnesses. The meaninglessness of her death allows Hemingway to emphasize the absurdity of life. Frederic can find no solace in religion, for neither he nor Catherine are believers. The presence of a priest as a fairly important minor character throughout the novel emphasizes for readers that although faith may comfort some, it does nothing for the lovers; early on, Catherine tells Frederic that he is her religion.

Frederic Henry must simply accept the tragic events as part of life's absurd pageant. Although he was fortunate enough to survive the war, Catherine and the baby were unlucky enough to become victims. To question why some die and others survive serves no purpose. To Hemingway, only the manner by which one accepts life's tragedies is of ultimate importance.

See also: For Whom the Bell Tolls; Hemingway, Ernest; Henry, Frederic; The Lost Generation; Nihilism; War

References: Cowley, 1973; Defazio, 1996; Donaldson, 1996; Hart, 1995; Hen, 1996; Hily-Mane, 1995; Hotchner, 1966; Moreland, 1996; White, 1933, 1968

FERRARS, EDWARD

Serving as Elinor Dashwood's romantic interest in Jane Austen's novel *Sense and Sensibility* (1811), the character of Edward Ferrars emphasizes the importance of virtues such as loyalty and personal commitment. Edward represents the wealthy level of society from which the Dashwoods are excluded once the family patriarch dies. Even though the Dashwood family retains wealth and land, the Dashwood daughters, as females, may not inherit due to an entailment of the property on the male heir.

Elinor meets Edward through her half-brother, John, who is married to Fanny, Edward's sister. When John and Fanny take charge of the Dashwood home, necessitating the relocation of Elinor, her mother, and her two sisters, Edward visits the home prior to their move. His great compassion toward the loss suffered by the Dashwood women contrasts with the attitude of his not-so-noble sister. Fanny reduces to a tiny sum the original yearly income John had thought to supply his stepmother and stepsisters and worries little about their suffering. Edward's gentle, sympathetic, and caring attitude shapes him as a fine match for Elinor, who shares many of these characteristics. Austen demonstrates through Edward that not all of those born to wealth are as self-centered and grasping as Fanny. However, because his personality remains set from the book's opening, Edward cannot be considered a dynamic character.

Naturally, the affection shared by Edward and Elinor must be put to the test that all good fictional couples suffer. The conflict begins through a misunderstanding, as is common in Austen's novels of manners. Edward attempts to reveal to Elinor a prior engagement, made in his youth to the daughter of his teacher, but he is interrupted before he can complete his explanation. Thus, when he separates from Elinor to return to London, she feels that they may have a future together. But when she later learns of his engagement and suffers the natural disappointment attached to her knowledge, she remains mindful in her disappointment of the fact that Edward never formally proposed to her. This lack of a spoken vow to underline the obvious unspoken emotions is a plot device often used in novels of manners. Elinor is careful to think of Edward as an honorable man who will naturally uphold any promise he has made. A gentleman representing the element of "sense" offered in the novel's title, Edward will not sever a contractual commitment to another on the basis of his later-formed emotional tie to Elinor.

By the novel's conclusion, Edward's problem finds a solution in his younger brother, who falls in love with the girl to whom he had been engaged. Because she felt no more love for Edward than he did her, he releases her from the engagement, and she becomes his sister-in-law instead of his wife. But not satisfied with this simple resolution to the problem she created, Austen causes Edward to lose favor in the eyes of his mother, who disinherits him and gives his fortune to his younger brother. Thus Edward is reduced to the same socioeconomic level as Elinor, which also creates a need for him to find a means of financial support. Unaware of Elinor's love for Edward, Colonel Brandon, lover of Elinor's sister Marianne, extends an offer to Edward to accept a clerical living that he has in his gift, a position in which Edward had previously expressed an interest.

When Edward is finally free to propose, to Elinor's ecstatic acceptance, his fortune obviously remains of small importance. This permits a better balance between these two who symbolize the value of sense over sensibility. It also allows the two devoted sisters to continue their lives closely connected by proximity and love.

See also: Austen, Jane; Darcy, Fitzwilliam; Dashwood, Elinor; Dashwood, Marianne; *Pride and Prejudice; Sense and Sensibility*
References: Britannica, 1997; Clayton, 1987a; Copeland and McMaster, 1997; de Rougemont, 1983; Gard, 1992; Gilbert and Gubar, 1996c; Praz, 1974; Watt, 1963

FIELDING, HENRY

British writer Henry Fielding had a profound effect on writing in the eighteenth century, particularly in the area of the novel. In addition to publishing such important novels as *Tom Jones* (1749), Fielding wrote comic dramas, satirical works of both fiction and nonfiction, and journalistic pieces. Regardless of the writing genre he chose, Fielding remained a tireless proponent of reform, concentrating on judicial, criminal, and social topics, and his work strongly reflected this approach.

Born in Somerset in 1707 as the eldest son of a lieutenant general and grandson of a judge, Fielding would eventually study law. During his youth, he received an education at Eton in the classics of Greek and Latin and supposedly knew Horace by memory when he graduated at the age of eighteen. For two years he studied law and literature at a university in Leyden, Holland. Having exhausted his financial holdings, he returned to London and spent most of his life living in the shadow of poverty.

The tall, handsome writer began writing for the stage at the age of twenty. His satirical plays, especially *Pasquin* (1736) and *The Historical Register for the Year 1736* (1737), so incensed the Walpole administration that a censoring act, called the Licensing Act of 1737, was passed. The act succeeded in closing most London theaters, leaving only two functioning. In his quest for social justice, Fielding temporarily destroyed his own career.

Unable to support himself through writing, Fielding returned to his legal studies and became a barrister, or attorney, in 1740. He also published a political periodical, *The Champion,* for two years and wrote most of its essays himself. His bent for satire found expression in several parodies of popular writings. When Samuel Richardson published *Pamela, or Virtue Rewarded* (1740), Fielding decided to parody this epistolary novel in his own work, *An Apology for the Life of Mrs. Shamela Andrews, by Mr. Conny Keyber.* The book appeared in 1741, and although Fielding never acknowledged himself as its author, he was attacked in print by Richardson and others for his work's "indecency." When he again chose to parody Richardson, a highly moralistic writer whose work he found disgusting, in his 1742 novel *Joseph Andrews,* Richardson labeled the book lewd and took offense at its blatant insult of his own works. Thus, Richardson was in large part responsible for launching Fielding's career as a novelist.

Much of Fielding's work appeared in the three-volume publication *Miscellanies* (1743). It included another ironic attack on the government administration of Walpole in *The Life of Jonathan Wild the Great.* After receiving an appointment as justice of the peace for Westminster in 1748, Fielding presided over a busy police court. His conscientious approach to the handling of dozens of cases involving all types of criminals may be seen in the tireless writing his experiences inspired.

But his masterpiece was, and still is considered to be, the enormous undertaking in novel form, *Tom Jones.* It first appeared in 1749 in six volumes and, unlike his earlier work, bore his name as author. Taking an innovative approach, Fielding has the narrative voice theorize in short essay form about various topics, including the genre of fiction, his theory regarding character shaping, and the necessary talents for novel writing, in which he again takes an editorial swipe at Richardson. Some critics found the novel coarse and vulgar, its hero a rascal, probably due to Fielding's carefree attitude toward sex as exemplified in Tom's various romantic conquests. But others expressed their delight over the romance's energy and insightful view of human interactions.

Fielding's personal favorite among his writings was his last novel, *Amelia* (1751), a narrative featuring a virtuous woman and her domestic trials in marriage. As his health failed, the author still gathered enough energy to publish *The Covent-Garden Journal* in 1752. He suffered emaciation due to gout, asthma, and dropsy, prompting him to set sail in 1754 for Portugal, where he hoped the warm weather would alleviate his problems;

he died that same year. A record of his travel experiences was published posthumously as *Journal of a Voyage to Lisbon* (1755).

Fielding remained a lover of the classics but is best known for his practical Christian morality. His writings emphasize the importance of good works over that of faith. Even in his most judgmental writing, critics observe that his sympathetic nature always surfaces.

See also: Tom Jones
References: Hawes, 1993; Hipchen, 1994; Mace, 1996; Richetti, 1996; Smallwood, 1989; Smith, 1993; Tillotson, Fussell, and Waingrow, 1969; Tumbleson, 1995

FITZGERALD, F. SCOTT

More than almost any other American writer of fiction, F. Scott Fitzgerald is said to have served as a mirror of his times. He was at once attracted to and betrayed by the glamorous environments of Prohibition in New York and post–World War I Europe, and his aspirations for wealth and power out of his reach are portrayed through many of his characters. His own private despair is reflected in the characterization of classic figures such as Jay Gatsby from what is arguably Fitzgerald's most widely read romantic novel, *The Great Gatsby* (1925).

Born in 1896 in St. Paul, Minnesota, Fitzgerald moved with his family to New York, where he lived during early childhood. In 1908, the family returned to St. Paul, where the future author attended first St. Paul Academy and then Newman and finally left for Princeton in 1913. He left school during his second year and scored his first sale of a poem to *Poet Lore* in 1917. Late that year, he entered the regular army as a second lieutenant and underwent officer training at Fort Leavenworth, Kansas. The year 1918 was propitious in Fitzgerald's life for two reasons; he finished a first draft of *The Romantic Egoist,* and he also met the love of his life, eighteen-year-old southern socialite Zelda Sayre. This relationship would prove both satisfying and devastating over Fitzgerald's lifetime, as Zelda sank progressively into insanity.

Following discharge from the army in 1919, Fitzgerald traveled to New York, where he assumed a position with the Barron Collier Advertising Agency. In June of that year, Zelda broke off their engagement, and in July, Fitzgerald returned to St. Paul to rewrite a novel. *This Side of Paradise* was accepted by Scribner's in 1919, and the first of many short stories, "Head and Shoulders," was sold to *The Saturday Evening Post.* By the conclusion of a year that had begun badly, Fitzgerald's future fame as an author was assured, and his engagement to Zelda had been reinstituted. In 1920, he published his novel and married Zelda, to whom he would formally dedicate much of his work.

Following a move to Westport, Connecticut, the Fitzgeralds embarked on their first European trip in 1921, after which they took up residence in St. Paul, where their daughter, Scottie, was born. In 1922, Fitzgerald's second novel, *The Beautiful and the Damned,* was published and received a favorable response. This was followed by the Fitzgeralds' move to Great Neck, Long Island. In 1923, his play *The Vegetable* proved a failure, and the Fitzgeralds departed again for Europe. The author regained his reputation with the publication of *The Great Gatsby* (1925), a novel that would not enjoy its strongest acclaim until later in the twentieth century.

Fitzgerald established his famous and sometimes rocky relationship with Ernest Hemingway in 1925. His attitude toward the gruff, blunt Hemingway, in every way Fitzgerald's own opposite in personality and demeanor, remained throughout his lifetime one of admiration mixed with jealousy over his contemporary's critical and financial success. His correspondence to Hemingway reveals a kind of self-contempt suggesting that he recognized a greater talent in his friend. Hemingway would later turn against Fitzgerald, whom he accused of wasting his talent.

The publication in 1926 of *All the Sad Young Men* preceded Fitzgerald's return to America and his first trip to Hollywood. Zelda's escalating mental problems and alcoholism proved of great concern, as did Fitzgerald's own propensity for alcohol and a profligate lifestyle. The two spent the summer of 1928 in Paris, and they moved permanently abroad the following year. But in 1930, Zelda suffered a complete mental breakdown, requiring her institutionalization in Prangins. Following her release a year later, the two returned to Zelda's hometown of Montgomery, Alabama, and Fitzgerald made a second trip to Hollywood. In his absence, Zelda suffered a decrease in mental stability and a second breakdown in 1932. They would move to Baltimore and endure Zelda's third breakdown in 1934, which required long-term institutionalization.

Fitzgerald's popular novel *Tender Is the Night* was published in 1934. Over the next few years, he moved often and, in 1937, entered into a six-month contract with the movie studio, MGM. A lonely and sometimes bitter man, Fitzgerald suffered greatly from Zelda's condition as a hopeless invalid. After moving to the Garden of Allah Hotel in Hollywood, Fitzgerald met Sheilah Graham, a woman who became his companion. His correspondence to Zelda during his final two years reflects the diminishing of a once all-consuming passion into more of a sense of responsibility for their past together and their relationship as parents of Scottie. Although his contract was renewed for an additional year, Fitzgerald's writing career began to suffer from inattention and his drinking, and he was informed of his release in 1938. He began work on *The Last Tycoon* in 1939, but in 1940 suffered a first heart attack in November, followed a month later by his death.

Late correspondence with his daughter and various publishers, editors, and friends reveals that each day held the promise of victory for Fitzgerald, regardless of the obstacles to success that lay in his path. His eternal optimism exceeded his capacity to pursue his dreams of a career that began brilliantly with publication of his first novel at age twenty-three but subsequently dissolved into alcoholic bouts of depression and night sweats. Although he died in 1940 virtually forgotten by the American public, Fitzgerald's works rebounded to great popularity decades later.

See also: The Great Gatsby; Hemingway, Ernest; The Lost Generation; War

References: Beach, 1959; Bruccoli and Duggan, 1980; Carpenter, 1988; Cowley, 1973; Hart, 1995; Massa and Stead, 1994; Moreland, 1996; Piper, 1970; Turnbull, 1971; Washington, 1995

FLAUBERT, GUSTAVE

Noted for his objective approach and perfection of style, Gustave Flaubert remains best known for his realistic romance, *Madame Bovary* (1857). Considered by some as the most influential nineteenth-century novel, Flaubert's work reflects his lifelong scorn for the conventions of society and for its rejection of intellect and lack of sensitivity to beauty.

Born in Rouen, Normandy, in 1821, Gustave Flaubert was the son of a doctor. Although he studied law briefly in Paris, he left his study to write full-time. With his friend, the famous daguerreotypist Maxime Du Camp, Flaubert participated in a photographic walking tour of Greece and Egypt from 1849 to 1851. Although he did not like daguerreotypes, Flaubert sat for Du Camp for one of the rare portraits available of the author. During their tour, each man had a government appointment that brought no income but caused them to be treated in foreign lands, as Flaubert expressed it, like royalty. In addition to remaining a lifelong personal friend of Flaubert, Du Camp was responsible for much of the famed author's sexual education. The two men indulged in various hetero- and homosexual relationships while abroad; these and other travel adventures later contributed much to Flaubert's novels. When he complained at the age of twenty-five to his mistress, Louise Colet, that he wished she had known him as a young man when he still had his hair, he probably did not realize the reason for his early hair loss. It may have been one of the many symptoms of syphilis, a common disease among young Frenchmen of the period. His visits to brothels, like those of his contemporaries, began very early, and he consequently suffered through many painful treatments of venereal disease with mercury, a potentially fatal poison. Afflicted by a nervous disorder, possibly also attributable to syphilis, Flaubert would spend most of his life living quietly in the country near Rouen.

In spite of his desire for a quiet lifestyle, Flaubert became the target of various scandals throughout his lifetime. His infamous relationship with Colet, who acted as a model for his well-known character, Emma Bovary, resembled the romance of his writings. Colet, eleven years Flaubert's senior and married with a child, was a minor poet known in her own right as an early feminist; she was the model for Jean Courbet's famous painting, *L'Amazone*. The author referred to her in the early days of their relationship as his muse and his Sappho, a woman who released his inhibitions. Following their meeting in James Pradier's Paris sculpting studio, they spent several days together. When Flaubert returned to Croisset to rejoin his mother, he began a round of quarrelsome letter writing with Colet. For all of his wild behavior, Flaubert could never give Colet the amount of attention she demanded. Their affair remained fraught with her jealousy of

Flaubert's relationship with his mother, prompting him at one time to remark on the "double reins" and "bit" the two women he loved employed to drive him. He declined to separate from his mother in order to fulfill Colet's demands; she even expressed jealousy over his relationship with Du Camp. Flaubert likely feared that his mother would learn of his affair if Colet acted indiscreetly. Such misgivings were well founded, for the adventuress remained well known to the French press. She once attempted to stab Alphonse Karr, himself a journalist, when he implied that the father of Colet's daughter was not Monsieur Colet but the celebrated philosopher, Victor Cousin.

Flaubert managed to convince Colet to utilize Du Camp as a go-between for their correspondence, thus shielding his mother from knowledge of his affair. But Colet may not have been Flaubert's only mistress. The author later served as patron to French novelist Guy de Maupassant, rumored to be his son by the sister, Laure, of Flaubert's good friend, Alfred de Poittevin.

The scandal that erupted with the publication of *Madame Bovary* almost ended Flaubert's career because he and his work were both declared immoral by the French government. Encouragement and aid from Colet and Flaubert's notable friends, including writers Victor Hugo, George Sand, Emile Zola, and Ivan Turgenev, made possible the survival of his work. Acquitted of charges of immorality, both Flaubert and his publisher achieved a legal victory, but the moral scandal diminished the novel's chance for success for some time. Eventually recognized as a literary masterpiece, *Madame Bovary* experienced frequent subsequent publication in translation, greatly influencing American writers Kate Chopin and Henry James.

Featuring the romance and adultery of a married woman in a French provincial town, the novel promoted a flurry of correspondence to Flaubert from female readers who recognized themselves in the oppressed and romantically starved figure of Emma Bovary. Feminist critics also find much to discuss in Emma's plight. The novel indicts the drab pretentiousness of bourgeois life, portraying seemingly dull characters with perception and detail that made the novel a hallmark of realistic romance, although Flaubert himself resisted the label applied to him of a master of realism.

In the 1870s, Flaubert underwent a financial crisis. He had invested much capital in the Rouen sawmill owned by the husband of his niece. When it dissolved, de Maupassant advised Flaubert to accept a government pension; more than six hundred writers at the time received such support. Too proud to accept a handout, Flaubert opted for less income with a sinecure as assistant librarian at the Bibliotheque Mazarine. A longtime friend of the novelist, de Maupassant writes of being present shortly before Flaubert's death almost a decade later and witnessing the destruction of many letters and relics, one of which was a silk slipper holding a faded rose, no doubt the last physical reminder of Louise Colet.

Other important works by Flaubert include *Salammbô* (1863) and *The Temptation of Saint Anthony* (1874). Both of these novels are considered more traditionally romantic than *Madame Bovary,* but all of Flaubert's writings reflect significant romantic and naturalistic themes. Flaubert was so obsessed with detail that he would read written sentences aloud repeatedly until he found them satisfactory. For Flaubert, writing involved painstaking labor and the exertion of elaborate physical and mental energies. Unlike some of his contemporary romantics, such as the American James Fenimore Cooper and English writer Sir Walter Scott, Flaubert produced works that do not diminish in readability or applicability to social issues with the passage of time. He died suddenly in Croisset in 1880, a recognized leader among French novelists.

See also: Bovary, Emma; Chopin, Kate; *Madame Bovary*
References: Charlton, 1984; Cowley, 1959; Gourgouris, 1995; Sturrock, 1994; Wood, 1994

FOR WHOM THE BELL TOLLS

Ernest Hemingway's 1940 novel, *For Whom the Bell Tolls,* occupies a position among the best of the twentieth-century war novels. Focusing on Robert Jordan, a Spanish instructor from Montana fighting in Spain for the Republican cause, the novel is highly autobiographical and is said to be Hemingway's personal favorite. The title, taken from English Renaissance poet John Donne's *Meditation XVII,* reminds readers: "Never send to know for whom the bell tolls; it tolls for thee." Through his adoption of Donne's idea, Hemingway emphasizes the great leveling

Gary Cooper as Robert Jordan and Ingrid Bergman as Maria appeared in a 1942 film version of For Whom the Bell Tolls, *Ernest Hemingway's 1940 novel that emphasizes the great leveling effect of death, as well as the necessity for humans to show concern for one another. (Photofest)*

effect of death, as well as the necessity for humans to show concern for one another.

Jordan carries dynamite and other explosive materials behind enemy lines into the Spanish mountains, where he is to blow up a bridge, contributing to the victory of the rebel General Golz. He travels with an older guide, Anselmo, and joins a group of guerrillas led nominally by the veteran of many rebel attacks, Pablo. Pablo, however, seems to be losing his nerve, and his wife Pilar increasingly shoulders leadership responsibilities. By supporting her home and her family, Pilar represents feminine strength and, in a universal sense, Spain and its people. In a more personal sense, she nourishes and protects the young and beautiful Maria, destined to become Jordan's love interest. Maria's insecurity bordering on insanity results from her mistreatment after she was captured by Fascists. The band of guerrillas is completed by several other minor characters, including Fernando; the Gypsy Rafael; two brothers named Andres and Augustin; and, finally, Eladio.

The novel spends much time developing the external conflict between fighting factions as well as the individual conflicts that develop within the small group of guerrillas. The romantic conflict for Jordan, who soon develops strong feelings for Maria, remains concern for her safety and a fear for their future together.

Through the power struggles experienced by the guerrillas, Pilar emerges as their true leader. Although Pablo displays a loyalty to the cause that wavers from time to time, he eventually joins with Jordan to complete the mission to blow up the bridge. Circumstances work against the small rebel band to leave them without enough help, until Pablo arrives with reinforcements, a group of local shepherds who agree to join their cause.

In the brief time span of the book, which covers only about four days, Jordan experiences love for the first time with Maria. Highly symbolic of all innocent victims of war, Maria allows Jordan to express his concern for all the Spanish who are oppressed by the Fascists as well as his love for the woman herself. A very physical person, Jordan finds several opportunities when he and Maria may make love, thereby consummating their doomed relationship.

This allows Jordan to succeed on the dual levels of war and love. He shows courage in proceeding against great odds with the plans to destroy the bridge. At the same time, his willingness to engage in love with Maria allows expression of his own vulnerability. When the guerrilla band to which Jordan has attached himself reaches its target, the members achieve success even though escape proves difficult.

Too badly wounded to continue his retreat, Jordan urges the remainder of the band, including Maria, to go on without him. In his promise to Maria that they will always be together, he fulfills one of the oldest of romance ideas, that of two souls joined for all time by love. Remaining behind with a machine gun, he plans to hold off as long as possible the Fascists who follow the escapees, buying the precious time needed for the rest of his band to leave the area.

As the story's hero, Jordan is called upon to make the ultimate sacrifice for his love and his political ideology, and he does not hesitate. He willingly gives his life, conceding its insignificance when compared to the promise of freedom for the Spanish people and especially for Maria.

> See also: A Farewell to Arms; Hemingway, Ernest; Jordan, Robert; Maria; Pilar; The Sun Also Rises; Violence; War
>
> References: Cowley, 1973; Defazio, 1996; Donaldson, 1996; Hart, 1995; Hen, 1996; Hily-Mane, 1995; Hotchner, 1966; Moreland, 1996; White, 1933, 1968

FORBIDDEN LOVE

Any form of love, whether physical or emotional, discouraged either through civil or social law within a community may be considered forbidden love. Because such "laws" erroneously imply that love can be controlled through an application of logic, they *will* be broken. Love remains the product of an emotional reaction, based on intuition rather than logic. Thus, human attempts to control who loves whom and how often fail. In various situations, forbidden love may be tacitly but not openly accepted or acknowledged by members of a culture. Attitudes toward forbidden love continue to alter over time, so that relationships that were forbidden in the past may be accepted in the present.

Those types of love labeled "forbidden" may vary widely among social, religious, and political communities within individual cultures, although some forbidden relationships remain fairly uniform. For example, the act of incest, or physical love with a member of one's immediate family, is forbidden in most cultures. Traditionally, the cultural edict against this act, which later caused the production of civil laws forbidding incest, likely grew from religious guidelines that established incest as unclean and nonspiritual behavior.

Many other types of forbidden love are based on moral or religious ideas alone, rather than on civil law. Although not necessarily an offense punishable in a court of law, the experience of physical love, or fornication, without the benefit of marriage or some other type of legal commitment between two individuals may be forbidden, traditionally because such an act might produce an illegitimate child. Used in a romantic plot, such a situation could force the marriage of a pregnant woman to a man she does not really love (see *My Ántonia* and *The Thorn Birds*). Because a woman, through pregnancy, outwardly bears the sign of her "transgression," men traditionally have been more easily excused for participating in sex out of wedlock than have women. The act of adultery, when at least one member of a couple who falls in love is already legally or culturally paired with another, also forms the basis of a multitude of romance plots (see *The Age of Innocence, An American Tragedy, Anna Karenina, The Awakening, The Kitchen God's Wife, Like Water for Chocolate, Madame Bovary, Of Human Bondage, Of Love and Dust, The Prince of Tides, The Robber Bride, The Scarlet Letter, The Sky Is Red, Sons and Lovers, The Unbearable Lightness of Being,* and *Vanity Fair*).

Closely associated with ideas about forbidden love is the concept of power. A group in power may behave in ways that would be unacceptable in a less powerful group. This has proven true in the consideration of sexual activity on the part of males versus that on the part of females. Even up to the present day, a double standard regarding men's and women's sexual activity has existed in many cultures. Although illicit sexual activity on the part of males was condoned or even expected, ostensibly due to hormonal "needs," the identical activity on the part of females was harshly regarded (see *The Awakening, Madame Bovary, Tess* of the d'Urbervilles, and The Portrait of a Lady). In part, this was based on the woman's ability to bear children. For instance, among members of the aristocracy, the retention of "pure" bloodlines was crucial. Often the inheritance of great amounts of power, either through property or political control or both, was available to the children of the wealthy. If a woman through adultery conceived a child that was not her husband's, that child might inherit wealth and title properly due the husband's genetic offspring. In some plots, this situation may appear in slightly altered form. For instance, a man whose wife has committed adultery and produced a child with another man is not allowed a divorce due to feelings of revenge or ideology on the part of her husband. This causes the child to belong to the husband, should something happen to the adulterous wife (see Anna Karenina). Because in many cultures a woman was not allowed to own or inherit property, the purity of the male line was of the utmost importance. Also, women were often viewed, both legally and culturally, as the property of males and thus were under the control of their fathers, husbands, and so on. Adultery on the part of women was thus viewed as a greater affront to their controlling males than adultery on the part of the males would be to the women. Over time, the stigma formerly attached to adultery has lessened for a number of reasons. Those reasons include an increased equity among actions acceptable on the part of men and women, changes in cultural mores, approved methods of birth control, and a decrease in the stress placed by some societies on the importance of religious ideals.

Not all cultures forbid love between a married person and an unmarried person, as long as the love lacks a physical dimension. The idea of courtly love, or a younger man's chaste "worship" of an older married woman through attention and gifts, may even be encouraged. This is particularly true in cultures that condone husbands' affairs but not wives'. Courtly love is believed by men to supply the wife with the romantic aspects of love she cherishes, allowing her husband to find sexual release with other women. This situation also allows the younger inexperienced man to develop his romantic technique in a "safe" manner (see The Awakening).

Marriage may interfere with romance in another way than adultery. In some plots, a previous marriage has been emotionally but not legally terminated, threatening the legitimacy of a future romance/marriage (see Jane Eyre). In other instances, a partner in a previous marriage may have been thought dead when, in fact, he or she has not died; that person's return makes his or her spouse an unwitting bigamist (see Enemies: A Love Story).

Because men have traditionally been allowed more sexual freedom than women, and because women have been viewed as the property of men, violence within a romantic or marriage relationship has only recently been viewed as unacceptable. This is another cultural area in which a double standard functions. Acts of violence on the part of a male toward a female that would be unacceptable outside marriage, such as beatings, rapes, and even murder, were at one time acceptable within a marriage. Thus, romantic plot conflict may revolve around the entrapment of and physical threat against one partner, usually a female, by the other. Acts that lack a physical aspect of violence but encompass an emotional or psychological one, such as the purposeful physical exposure of the faithful member of a romantic pair to the object of infidelity by the other member of the pair, may also be a part of plot conflict (see The Kitchen God's Wife and The Portrait of a Lady).

Another example of forbidden love could include love between individuals belonging to different racial or social groups. Interracial romance, more acceptable in modern times, was anathema in many cultures until the late twentieth century (see Of Love and Dust and To Sir, with Love). An exception would be the culturally accepted act of a slaveowner engaging in sexual acts with a slave of a different race (see Beloved). As with other types of forbidden love, physical and emotional interracial love has existed in all ages, despite civil and cultural edicts against it. Likewise, an individual lacking wealth was not seen in various cultures as an acceptable legal mate for one possessing the power and status that accompanies wealth or political position (see An American Tragedy, Love in the Time of Cholera, Of Human Bondage, and Wuthering Heights).

Such restrictions did not, however, preclude physical love between a wealthy male and a subservient female. Thus, romances between a male employer and his secretary, housekeeper, or simply a female of lower social status might be acceptable in societies that are androcentric (in which male interests are paramount) or patriarchal (in which men hold more power than women), as long as no legal ties joined the two. In a variation on this plot sequence, a wealthy man may truly love a woman from a lower social class, but he may be forbidden from making a "match" beneath his own level (see *Doctor Zhivago* and *Jane Eyre*). Because fiction imitates reality in most instances, only in a very few romances is the person in power a female. When that occurs, as in mythology or in a plot based on the activities of a queen, the female character may have unlimited power to exercise her right to romance as she pleases.

An additional type of forbidden love based on cultural rather than legal rules is that of love between partners whose age greatly differs, sometimes termed a "May-December romance" (see *Rebecca*). In this area a double standard based on gender has existed for some time. Although a mature man in his thirties may court and marry a girl of eighteen without prohibition, a mature woman may not do the same with a young man without attracting social sanction. Again, this viewpoint is one inherited from tradition. In centuries past, when many women died at a young age due to the physical demands of unregulated childbirth and labor, men remarried in order to produce more children to carry on their name or to manage and inherit property. Even if a man had daughters by an early marriage, sons were valued over daughters, who gave up their last names and most claims to property through marriage; this situation caused men to desire an additional marriage to a young strong female of childbearing age in the hopes of procuring a son. Although ideas have changed over time, even in the late twentieth century an older man may be praised for his sexual prowess when he produces a child with a younger woman. Another outdated idea viewed sex for the woman as necessary only for reproduction and not as an action in which she would engage for pleasure, an outlook particularly associated with the Victorian Age. Because women reproduced most often in their twenties and early thirties, romance and remarriage might be viewed as unnecessary for the mature woman who did not desperately need financial support.

Some romances also label young men who romance older wealthy women as fortune

hunters or even gigolos, another example of a double standard. Although young women might be encouraged to "catch" a wealthy older man to be literally rewarded at his death for having made him happy in his old age, a younger man who does the same for an older woman is viewed as an opportunist (see *Their Eyes Were Watching God*).

Some love between individuals may remain forbidden because their families have been in longtime disagreement with one another due to social or political differences or what one side perceives as an act of treachery on the part of another. William Shakespeare's *Romeo and Juliet* best reflects this common romance plot that focuses on "star-crossed lovers" forbidden from realizing their love. A similar situation may also occur when cultures, religions, or groups with differing political ideologies clash, resulting in prohibitions on unions between, for instance, an American and a German during World War II or a member of the Jewish faith and the Christian faith. These books often incorporate aspects of war or political upheaval (see *For Whom the Bell Tolls* and *The House of the Spirits*).

In an additional instance of forbidden love based on religion, members of certain religions must remain celibate. This is true for priests and nuns of the Catholic faith, who pledge chastity and devotion to their church. Any romance by that person is forbidden by rules of morality and generally open to social negative sanction. In plots based on romantic relationships in which one person has publicly taken an oath of celibacy, the production of a child by this union may then be kept secret or denied (see *The Hunchback of Notre Dame* and *The Thorn Birds*). In a similar situation, a person not required to be celibate but whose service is pledged to the church may be more harshly condemned for adultery than one who is not religion-bound, causing a romance to remain unrevealed (see *The Scarlet Letter*).

Finally, love may be forbidden because of a physical or mental defect on the part of one member of a couple. The "Beauty and the Beast" stories are built on this tradition. In these fables, the beast, generally a male, must alter his appearance in order to permanently join with his romantic interest. His deformity may be caused, in fantasy, by some evil magic or, in more realistic fiction, by a cruel blow of fate. When the deformity cannot be corrected, the majority of such pairings end in tragedy (see

Frankenstein and *The Hunchback of Notre Dame*). Sometimes the deformity may be unseen, caused by an injury of some kind that precludes the engagement in satisfactory physical love (see *The Sun Also Rises*). In other cases, the victim of the deformity may suffer an identity crisis, causing an additional emotional problem that prevents the formation of a satisfactory love relationship (see *Of Human Bondage*).

See also: Patriarchal Marriage; Victorian Age; Violence; War

References: de Rougemont, 1983; Ellis, 1964

FORSTER, C. S.

Although most famous for his series of eleven Horatio Hornblower novels, C. S. Forester wrote more than fourteen additional novels, including the 1935 war novel *The African Queen*. Born Cecil Louis Troughton Smith in 1899, Forester was the fifth child of an English schoolteacher. His early years were spent in Cairo, where his father, George Smith, taught in a British school established to offer upper-class Egyptian boys an English education. At the age of three, Cecil moved with his mother Sarah to England following the breakup of the Smith marriage. George continued to teach in Cairo and visited England for one month every year. George found supporting two households a staggering financial burden, and the Smiths remained quite poor. The Smith children felt themselves superior to their neighbors where they lived in Camberwell, close to London slums, and they did their best to lie about their mother's increased drinking.

The children enjoyed staging Napoleonic naval "battles" using cardboard ships, and naval combat was to remain a lifelong interest for Cecil, forming the focus of many of his novels. He made up stories early on in order to enhance his image to others and claimed the parents of school friends, George and Florence Belcher, as his own second set of parents. Although accepted at a medical school, Cecil wasted the money supplied him by his brother Geoffrey and rarely attended classes. From early maturity, he had engaged in sexual adventures with adult women, and his lifestyle was one of lazy self-indulgence. He lived on his parents' charity until he became a self-sufficient writer in his late twenties.

A Pawn among Kings (1924), his first novel, hearkens back to Cecil's childhood games, as it features a fictional woman responsible for Napoleon's historical errors. For this novel and all those that followed, Cecil adopted the pen name C. S. Forester. *Payment Deferred* (1926), with a plot featuring a murderer hanged for a murder he did not commit, yielded Forester his first success. Supported by the income from this novel, he secretly married Kathleen Belcher. Other novels with war themes followed, including *Brown on Resolution* (1929), *Death to the French* (1932), *The Gun* (1933), *The African Queen* (1935), and *The General* (1936), and Forester produced an early autobiography, *Long before Forty* (1967).

Prior to World War II, Forester traveled to Hollywood to write a film about pirates; there he worked with Arthur Hornblow, no doubt the inspiration for the name of his later hero. The release of *Captain Blood* staring Erroll Flynn before the completion of Forester and Hornblow's movie ended that project. Accused of being the father of an illegitimate child by an opera singer, Forester left the country and a short time later released the first of his Hornblower novels, *The Happy Return* (1937). With the advent of the war, he returned to the United States, ostensibly to write propaganda convincing the Americans to support the British government.

Forester remained in Berkeley, California, where he continued to write, even though he suffered crippling atherosclerosis of his legs in 1943. He divorced Kathleen two years later. They had two sons together, John, born in 1929, and George, born in 1933. In 1947, Forester remarried a woman he had known since his youth, Dorothy Foster. A stroke in 1964 left him disabled, and he died in 1966.

See also: The African Queen; Allnutt, Charlie; Sayer, Rose

References: Drabble, 1995; Forester, 1997; Sternlicht, 1981

FORSTER, E. M.

Born in London in 1879, Edward Morgan Forster would become one of England's most renowned early-twentieth-century novelists. Educated as a young man at Tonbridge School, he began study at King's College in Cambridge in 1897 and later received an honorary fellowship to King's in 1946. Known as a modest man, Forster had as friends several members of the Bloomsbury group, one of whom was the early feminist, Virginia Woolf. Forster, whom Woolf calls Morgan in her journal entries and letters, once insulted Woolf by refusing on her behalf the chance to sit on the board of directors of the London Library, telling the other members of the board that she would not be interested. Woolf was furious when she learned of his actions, for she would have been the first woman appointee. In addition to being friendly with Forster, Woolf also reviewed several of his novels for magazines such as *The Atlantic Monthly.*

Forster produced six novels. His first was titled *Where Angels Fear to Tread* (1905). This was followed in 1907 by *The Longest Journey,* in 1908 by *A Room with a View,* and in 1910 by *Howards End.* Fourteen years would pass before he wrote the novel considered his greatest work, *A Passage to India* (1924), which garnered the James Tait Black Memorial Prize and the Prix Femina Vie Heureuse. His final novel, *Maurice,* featuring a homosexual protagonist, was written in 1912 but appeared only posthumously in 1971. In addition to his novels, Forster published two volumes of short stories, two biographies, two collections of essays, and a critical work titled *Aspects of the Novel* (1927), as well as various other writings. He also collaborated with Eric Crozier in writing the libretto for Benjamin Britten's opera titled *Billy Budd* (1949).

Forster died in 1970, having contributed to the romance genre six popular period novels that generally featured characters confused about what they really wanted. They act confident in their places in life yet secretly realize how much their lives lack. He has been called an author who took chances, mixing lovers from various races, classes, and cultures and creating a web of connections that resulted sometimes in tragedy, sometimes in the proverbial happy ending. Woolf called Forster a man whose artistic gifts were both baffling and evasive, at times producing stronger writing than at others. She saw his writing as containing skill, beauty, and wisdom but lacking cohesion. Most of his popular romances translate well to the screen, however, their passion-riddled heroes and heroines perfectly demonstrating traditional romantic struggles within a changing world order. Imbued with a strong sense of place and time, Forster's works present reading adventures in culture as well as in romance.

See also: *A Room with a View*
References: Albright, 1997; Das and Beer, 1979; Drabble, 1995; Ellem, 1971; Lago, 1995; McDowell, 1977; Stone, 1966

FOWLES, JOHN

John Robert Fowles, born on March 31, 1926, in England, has contributed much to the modern and postmodern romance. His mother was Gladys Richards Fowles, and his father, Robert J. Fowles, imported tobacco for a living. During World War II, the Fowles family moved from their home in Leigh-on-Sea to South Devon. The countryside in this area of England would appear later in much of Fowles's fiction. After studying French and German at Bedford School, Fowles enrolled at the University of Edinburgh in 1944. He left school for a time to become a lieutenant in the Royal Marines, returning to university from 1947 to 1950. After graduating with a bachelor's degree, he began teaching first at the French University of Poitiers and later at Anargyrios College, located in Greece.

During this time, Fowles made his first serious attempt at writing, producing a book of poetry and a travelogue. His literary agent, Paul Scott, published the travelogue mainly because of the virtues of a small fictional section it contained. Encouraged by Scott to continue his writing, Fowles began a novel, and the college's surroundings at Spetsai became the setting for *The Magus,* although it would not see publication until 1966. Fowles met Elizabeth Whiton in Greece, then later returned to London. He began teaching French again and married Whiton in 1953.

As he continued work on *The Magus,* Fowles produced other novels, including *The Collector* (1963), which met with much success in England and the United States. At that point, Fowles terminated his teaching career and began to write full-time. After two more years of work, *The Magus* at last appeared and was followed by his tremendously popular postmodern romance, *The French Lieutenant's Woman* (1969). *The French Lieutenant's Woman* won the Silver Pen Award, presented by the International Association of Poets, Playwrights, Editors, Essayists, and Novelists, as well as the W. H. Smith and Son Literary Award, and it was the number-one bestseller in the United States in 1969. Those high sales became indicative of Fowles's future with the popular reading public in the United States, where he has long been better received than in England. Although British critics pigeonholed *The Collector* as a suspense tale in which demonic symbolism is used to teach morality, American critics categorized it as a social psychological study.

Fowles's fans see his characters as representative of existentialist thought. These characters suffer alienation from God, culture, and self. Like the nineteenth-century characters of Thomas Hardy and Charles Dickens, they struggle to learn that meaning must come from within. When Fowles added a fourth novel, *Daniel Martin,* to his writings in 1977, his reputation as a serious writer became secure. Additional major works include *Mantissa* (1983) and *A Maggot* (1985). Fowles has also written three autobiographical works, *The Aristos: A Self-Portrait in Ideas* (1964), Islands (1978), and *The Tree* (1980). In these books he explains his application of philosophy to life, discusses his fondness for the Isles of Scilly, shares some concerns regarding nature, and uses a meditation on trees to reflect upon his own life.

A lack of optimism for the world due to its mistreatment of nature occasionally surfaces as a theme in Fowles's writings. A proponent of Marxism, he believes England would benefit from a Marxist government. He unabashedly confesses that he writes in order to investigate himself, believing that his destiny and that of others remains controlled by their ancestry. Some critics believe all of Fowles's writings should be viewed as romances rather than in conventional terms usually applied to realism. Yet from within the very structure of Victorian Age romance, which he chooses for *The French Lieutenant's Woman,* Fowles presents a postmodern view, entering the narrative to comment on his characters' actions and offering alternate conclusions to his novel. Love and the nature of human freedom are two themes reflected in most of his writings, with each working to realize the other in stories that remain rooted in everyday human experience.

See also: The French Lieutenant's Woman; Victorian Age

References: Baker and Vipond, 1996; Foster, 1994; Friedman and Siegel, 1995; Hart, 1995; Neary, 1992

FRANKENSTEIN

Mary Shelley's *Frankenstein* (1818), a widely read example of the Gothic romance, is replete with more horror than most other contemporary members of its genre. Although the monster himself drew much attention in Shelley's times and in later movie depictions, the creature remains too sentimentally drawn to extract a reaction of terror from modern-day readers. The novel's appeal lies in its usefulness as a morality tale, as it assumes its place among those stories that warn against man's attempts to imitate God. Although the theme of love, centered on the relationship of the protagonist, Victor Frankenstein, and Elizabeth Frankenstein, exists in the novel, it is Victor's love/hate relationship with the monster of his own creation that occupies reader attention.

Shelley presents much of the story through flashback, as Victor relates his hellish tale of destruction to Robert Walton, an English explorer. When Walton's ship becomes trapped in polar ice, his company sees at a long distance a figure on a dogsled flying over the snow. Such a vision in what they believe to be a totally uninhabited area causes them much unrest. Another figure, Victor Frankenstein, appears later that night, floating on the ice with a single dog. The frozen landscape supporting Victor remains highly suggestive of his attitude toward the monster and also of his frozen heart and isolation fol-

Boris Karloff played Frankenstein's monster in the 1931 film Frankenstein, *based on Mary Shelley's 1818 novel, a widely read example of the Gothic romance replete with more horror than most other contemporary members of its genre. (Photofest)*

lowing the loss of everyone he loves. After rescuing Victor, Walton tells him of their earlier sighting, causing Victor to become upset. During the remainder of Victor's short time on earth, he relates his story to the curious explorer. Shelley uses Victor's narration, a story within a story, to heighten tension and better reveal her character through his own words to her readers.

Born to a wealthy family in Geneva, Victor grows up enjoying the loving attentions of a group that includes Elizabeth Lavenza, a young girl adopted by Victor's parents to serve as his playmate. Another son named William is born later. Victor and Elizabeth share a close brother-sister relationship, but when they are grown, the two realize they are in love and make plans to marry. Shelley shapes these characters to represent the conflict between science/rationality, symbolized by Victor, and poetry/imagination, symbolized by Elizabeth.

Victor departs Geneva in order to complete his education, emphasizing an area in which he had shown much aptitude, that of the natural sciences. Quickly outdistancing his professors, Victor begins experiments on his own because he desires to reproduce the life force. After discovering the necessary secret, he works alone in his laboratory at a frenzied pace, assembling a human form. The gruesome quality of his activity allows Shelley to emphasize the depravity of such ideas.

Even though Victor succeeds in bringing a creature to life, he fails in not considering the consequences of his actions for others, most notably the monster himself. Modern readers find the creature worthy of sympathy as he seeks love and approval for his internal qualities but receives only rejection by humans due to his hideous appearance. Overcome by horror at his accomplishment, Victor falls ill, and the creature flees. Nursed back to health by his best friend, Henry Clerval, Victor keeps his creation a secret.

When he receives shocking news regarding the kidnapping and death of his young brother William, Victor returns to Geneva. Justine, a trusted and innocent family servant, is blamed for the murder. Her name, suggesting the idea of justice, becomes particularly ironic when she is executed despite her innocence. The bit of evidence that damns her in the court's eyes is William's necklace, found in her pocket. Haunted by his past actions, all that Victor fears comes true when he meets the monster and discovers that his own creation killed his beloved brother. He also learns that the monster caused Justine's death by planting William's necklace on her as she slept.

Readers raised on Hollywood images of the monster may be startled to discover sympathetic reactions on their part to him when they read Shelley's novel. His crimes cannot be denied, but neither can the reasons supporting his motivation for violence. No more heartrending scene exists in literature than that of the monster's rejection by a family he has carefully nurtured unseen through a dangerous and bitter winter. Ironically, the blind elder member of the family accepts the creature when he reveals that he has hidden close by and furnished the family with necessary supplies, literally securing their survival. Only when those with sight return home to chase the monster away in revulsion does he suffer at their hands. A self-educated being, willing to attempt to fit into society, the monster is rejected because of his ugliness. He remains strongly representative of the romantic belief that people should be valued for their inner characteristics, not their outward appearance.

It is his rejection and isolation, forced upon him by Victor, that causes the monster to turn to violence. Thus, Victor himself remains responsible for the recent deaths. When the monster demands a mate of his own, promising to disappear if Victor will supply one, the young scientist feels he must do as bidden. Otherwise, the monster promises to commit further violent acts.

At this juncture in the story, Victor clearly has a choice. Should he create a female monster, he fears the two might reproduce and raise a race of monstrosities. But should he fail to fulfill his monster's desire, more deaths will occur. At first Victor chooses to make the female but later decides he cannot have on his conscience the creation of an entire group of such hideous beings. Thoroughly enraged when Victor destroys his promised mate, the monster kills again, this time claiming as his victims Victor's best friend, Henry, and his new wife, Elizabeth.

An important aspect of Shelley's novel may be seen in her granting the monster the final word. When Victor dies as a result of his pursuit of his creation through the bitterly cold snow and ice, the monster appears in the ship's cabin to claim Victor's body. Walton substitutes as an audience for readers who want to hear again from the monster, regardless of the havoc he has wreaked.

The monster argues convincingly that Victor's crime remains far worse than his own, for he irresponsibly created a human and then withheld love and companionship from his creation. He deserved the grim losses and death as punishment for not allowing the monster a soul. With that pronouncement, the monster leaves Walton and presumably disappears forever.

One measure of a well-written story is whether its characters' motivations remain understandable. Tales of mass murder seldom produce empathy in readers, but *Frankenstein* is an exception. The monster's loneliness compels him to commit terrible acts of retribution, but readers understand his reasons for doing so, even if they are not likely to approve. Also a believable character with clear motives, Victor nurtures an ambition of unholy evil. In acknowledging this ambition as detrimental, readers must question modern science in its continued desire not only to maintain but also to create life. That a romance novel like *Frankenstein* can cause an interrogation of a social system centuries after its production ensures its reputation as a classic.

See also: Beauty and the Beast; Fantasy; Frankenstein, Victor; Shelley, Mary Wollstonecraft Godwin; Violence

References: Drabble, 1995; Forster, 1956; Praz, 1974

FRANKENSTEIN, VICTOR

Victor Frankenstein, the protagonist of Mary Shelley's 1818 Gothic romance, *Frankenstein,* cannot properly be considered a hero. He behaves in a very unheroic manner, tempting a fate that brings death not only to himself but to all those he loves. Victor represents the possible consequences a human may incur when attempting to discover truths better left uninvestigated. Such an idea was common during the era of nineteenth-century romanticism, during which Victor's character was created. In contrast to the Romantic period's great concern for the worth of the individual, Victor represents a society that mistreated those who differed in any way from cultural expectations. By the novel's end, modern readers question who exactly is the monster in this tale of horror: Frankenstein's creation, or Victor Frankenstein himself.

As a young Swiss student, Victor possesses a genius for the natural sciences. When he attends a university at Ingolstadt, he absorbs all the information that science classes offer while also engaging in original research on his own. Isolated in his laboratory, he neglects his family, particularly the lovely Elizabeth, adopted by his parents as a playmate for Victor when he was a child. Victor discovers the secret to life by accident, and he uses it to create a living being, without considering the possible results of his action. He produces a monstrous being of prodigious strength that lives. Exhausted and weak from his efforts, Victor sleeps, his fitful dozing representing the loss of his own energies that now inhabit the monster. When Victor scares the monster away by screaming in horror at his appearance, he begins a cycle of rejection and mistreatment that leads the monster to violence.

The monster, whom some see as Victor's alter ego, remains a sympathetic character for the first portion of the story. Like humans, he seeks only acceptance and love. But judged by his physical appearance only, he becomes a pariah, lacking friends and family. Even those he aids treat him badly. Victor enjoys the opposite experience. Although he has isolated himself from others and keeps his terrible act a secret, his best friend, Henry Clerval, comes from Geneva to nurse Victor back to health. Elizabeth still loves him, regardless of his behavior, and the two plan to marry. This establishes a contrast between the behaviors of creator and created and the undeserved responses those behaviors elicit from others.

In this tragic story, Victor's creation will also be the cause of his death. But his egoistic act will bring untold misery on others first, resulting in the loss of everyone Victor holds dear. Following the murder by the monster of Victor's younger brother and the conviction and execution for the crime of an innocent servant long faithful to the Frankenstein family, Victor agrees to create a mate for his creature. Unable to complete the creation, for fear the two monsters will spawn a monster race, Victor destroys the female, robbing the monster of his only chance for some happiness in this world. In response to Victor's act, his creation continues on his own path of destruction, first murdering Henry. The loss of his best friend is blamed on Victor, but following his acquittal of that charge, he marries Elizabeth. Victor continues his descent into a hell of his own making when the monster kills Elizabeth on their wedding night.

Victor could be said to be a dynamic character because he experiences an epiphany when he realizes his folly in attempting to play God. However, contrary to most epiphanies, this one does not lead to a better life for the character. As *Frankenstein*'s tragic antihero, Victor at last falls prey to his dream, losing his own life to that life he created.

See also: Frankenstein; Gothic Romance; Shelley, Mary Wollstonecraft Godwin

References: Forster, 1956; Hunter, 1996; Praz, 1974; Williams, 1974

FREMONT, TONY

Tony Fremont is the most logical of the three female friends who act as the protagonists of Margaret Atwood's ironic romance *The Robber Bride* (1993). As a female historian fascinated by war, a traditionally male attribute, Tony represents an antistereotype. She approaches life as she does her study of historical battles, concocting logical strategies for determining her next move. Thus, her life resembles the war model she constructs at home in order to manipulate tiny figures that dot its battle scene. Such actions work against the stereotype of the female as intuitive and unintelligent; she also bears a man's name.

But even the logical Tony allows herself to be bested by the novel's villainess, Zenia. Zenia wins Tony's husband, West, in the biggest battle of Tony's life. Like her two friends, Charis and Roz Andrews, Tony suffers from Zenia's thirst for other women's lovers. When the three women, who had known each other before Zenia began to wreck their lives, come together to share their common experience, Tony's logic often clashes with Charis's New Age approach to life. The tension between Tony and Charis causes Roz to act as a buffer for her two friends. This conflict helps cement the relationships and emphasize Tony's personality.

Of the three women, only Tony redeems her lover. West returns to her, totally defeated after rejection by Zenia. For the logical Tony, the fact that her husband came home is enough to bolster her happiness. She spends little time dwelling on his desertion or ill treatment of her. Tony even protects West by keeping secret the memorial service held for Zenia when she supposedly dies. This fact allows Atwood to reflect on the various ways in which women handle desertion and betrayal.

Tony's character brings much to the novel by way of her vivid imagination. Like all historians,

she remains a creative being, understanding that history cannot be considered "factual" in the literal sense of the term. One's opinion always colors one's reporting of events, and Tony is no exception. From her point of view, Zenia is a warrior, a capable enemy deserving of some type of honor and recognition. Early in the novel, as Tony considers Zenia's memorial service, she reflects that flowers would not be a sufficient marking of the event; Zenia would demand instead a bowl of blood.

Tony remains a cynic, as Charis observes, bothered by the innocence and naïveté that Charis represents. This attitude appears ironic later when Tony herself suffers from naïveté concerning Zenia's surprise reappearance and her effect on West. When the group discovers that Zenia has not really died, that she has returned to once again wreak havoc in their lives, Tony divulges the fact of her presence to West. When West visits Zenia, Tony admits her fear of a repeat desertion but also exercises her cynicism when she thinks that men seem to confuse their desire to correct Zenia's unhappiness with their desire for her body.

Tony represents a new kind of active woman, possessing a strength that the novel's men lack. Although tiny in stature, she makes up for her lack of physical muscle with her appreciation of violence and her intelligence. When she finally faces Zenia, Tony brings along her father's Luger pistol. Her actions are reminiscent of those of a young male quest hero who seeks his own identity by investigating his relationship with his father.

Tony's imagination is emphasized in the word game she plays, as she envisions words backwards. She does this with her own name so that it becomes *Tnomerf Ynot,* a name allowing her to assume a new identity as a barbarian queen who will do things that Tony Fremont will not. Again, Atwood introduces the theme of identity and the importance of names, an importance stressed with regard to all her female characters.

Like her two friends, Tony evolves into a complex person who faces and quells her fear and loathing of Zenia to emerge positively altered by the experience. Her triumph is both private, in acknowledging that by coping with her conflict, she defeats Zenia, and public, as she shares her triumph with her friends. She is one of three female characters who, in Atwood's capable hands, subverts traditional ideas of romance, claiming the agency that feminists believe to be the right of all women.

See also: Andrews, Roz; Atwood, Margaret; Charis; *The Robber Bride*

References: Morey, 1997; Wilson, Friedman, and Hengen, 1996

THE FRENCH LIEUTENANT'S WOMAN

John Fowles's mock Victorian Age romance, *The French Lieutenant's Woman* (1969), represents a unique approach to storytelling. Its plot appears predictable at first, centering on an English aristocrat who must choose between two women, one symbolizing the safety and boredom of the traditional Victorian marriage and the other a lifestyle forbidden by nineteenth-century British mores. But Fowles's unusual technique of intruding into the narrative to cast a twentieth-century perspective on the tale succeeds in making it anything but predictable.

At age thirty-two, the novel's protagonist, Charles Smithson, is ready to marry. In Ernestina Freeman, Smithson has found a young woman who seems a perfect match. Her fortune, although based on new wealth, remains attractive, but that is not the only reason Smithson finds himself drawn to Ernestina. An aristocrat with title and status, he does not have to worry about money. Far more important remains the fact that, although a thoroughly modern young woman who chooses to don shocking new fashions and express her opinion at will, Ernestina still conforms to the social strictures regarding women put forth by her repressive Victorian culture. She plays the necessary role in Smithson's courting game; she can be obsequious in her attentions; and on the few occasions that she contradicts Smithson in public, she always apologizes later. Like the stone artifacts he studies as an anthropologist, Smithson remains in danger of hardening into a fossil and of never realizing his potential as an independent individual if he marries Ernestina.

When the novel opens in the village of Lyme Regis on Dorset's Lyme Bay, Smithson seems content with his future in his 1860s–1870s Victorian world. From the moment he encounters the enigmatic Sarah Woodruff, a dark figure gazing out to sea, Smithson finds himself attracted to her. The scandalous story regarding her shadowy past relationship with a French lieu-

tenant who deflowered her piques his interest. When he calls out to Sarah, and she turns her head, her gaze lancelike in its sorrowful effect upon Smithson, he cannot dismiss her countenance from his mind. The lance imagery in which Fowles frames Sarah's gaze acts as foreshadowing, alerting readers that, for all her silent posture, she remains an active agent, assuming the masculine role in her bid for independence. Now caught up in a conflict-laced love triangle, Smithson must choose between Ernestina, her very name describing her demeanor, and Sarah, a temptress who disregards Victorian sexual mores.

Ernestina represents the most modern of young Victorian women, but even this stance leaves her burdened with a stereotype she must fulfill. She clings to Charles, showing every sign of being impressed by his views, whether she is actually impressed or not. As a product of her times, she participates in the courting ritual as expected. Charles must follow her about to show his devotion to their rather bland relationship. Ernestina represents chastity incarnate, contrasting directly to Sarah as the fallen woman. Her surname is ironic in that, in contrast to Sarah, Ernestina is not at all free to do as she pleases, remaining instead trapped within a predetermined lifestyle. She also represents the power structure of Victorian society as daughter of a wealthy man (although admittedly her father is nouveau riche, whereas Charles is a member of the aristocratic class) whose approval Charles must capture in order for the match to be made. The reader attains a glimpse of what the future Ernestina will be like in a scene in which she echoes the statements of the odious Mrs. Poulteney, a pompous, hypocritical woman who mouths Christian ideals but practices cruelty against others. Although naïve and well-meaning, as evidenced by her first name, and a modern young woman who adores bright colors and high fashion and rejects some Victorian strictures, Ernestina will yet be shaped by her repressive culture. Thus, she represents one of the extremes, Sarah being the other, between which Charles must choose. If he settles into a lifetime with Ernestina, he will merely turn stagnant, giving in to his stuffy tendencies and finding a dull comfort in conventional behavior and beliefs.

Much has been made of Fowles's use of the twentieth-century existential approach to his characterization of the nineteenth-century Smithson.

In his struggle to choose his fate, Smithson suffers the reality of isolation and the knowledge that he must shape his own reality, a circumstance in which many nineteenth-century fictional characters, most notably those of Charles Dickens and Thomas Hardy, find themselves. The difference between those authors and Fowles is that Fowles has a different vocabulary in which to discuss such feelings, a vocabulary influenced by, among other things, a Great Depression and two world wars. In addition to social mores, Fowles reflects upon religion and politics, among other subjects, from his vantage point one hundred years into the future. As he focuses on the aspects of enforced conformity in the Victorian Age, Fowles forces twentieth-century readers to consider similarities between that era and their own. Formal institutions, such as organized religion, government, and politics, continue to force humans into a lockstep mentality, best and most horrifyingly evidenced by Nazi politics earlier in the century. But Fowles writes at a time in which the importance of self has never been more forcefully stressed in western society. In short, he seems to offer Smithson a choice. His hero may conform to societal expectations and wither away intellectually and emotionally, or he may seize upon the idea of rebellion symbolized by Sarah as a path to liberation. Sarah's gaze, which seems to see into the future—Smithson's future—beckons him to separate from the myopic Ernestina and join her instead.

Smithson easily surrenders to Sarah's sexual allure but suffers abrupt disillusionment upon discovering her to be a virgin. She had simply fabricated her history with the French lieutenant in order to weave her own identity, an identity that she may completely control. Her attitudes and actions contrast greatly with those of Ernestina; when she speaks her mind in disagreement with Smithson, she rarely apologizes later. Often she is abrupt with or rude to him. In Fowles's first conclusion, Sarah plays her part perfectly, rejecting Smithson when he locates her following her disappearance, claiming herself unworthy, showing him his child, and then refusing to create a family with him. This is the Victorian Age's romantic conclusion of choice.

But Fowles will not settle for that conclusion. Injecting himself into the story as a mysterious lone figure observing Smithson and Sarah in the house of the celebrated nineteenth-century Pre-Raphaelite painter, Dante Gabriel Rossetti, he kidnaps his own tale. Applying the twentieth-century technique of "replay," Fowles returns the reader to the previous scene, but this time different roles are assumed. Smithson walks willingly away from Sarah, deserting her in a most un-Victorian move as he refuses to be manipulated. When he leaves Sarah, it is because he has discovered a faith in himself. Sarah set him on the quest for this goal, but only Smithson may claim responsibility for his success.

In *The French Lieutenant's Woman,* John Fowles presents what appears to be a Victorian romance. In reality he follows all of the rules of that genre simply in order to counteract them with an experimental and memorable narrative.

See also: The Age of Innocence; Love Triangle; Smithson, Charles; Victorian Age; Woodruff, Sarah
References: Baker and Vipond, 1996; Foster, 1994; Friedman and Siegel, 1995; Hart, 1995; Neary, 1992

FROLLO, CLAUDE

As the priest of Victor Hugo's French Gothic romance, *The Hunchback of Notre Dame* (1831), Claude Frollo supplies the villainy expected in novels featuring strong conflict. One of several characters who loves the beautiful Gypsy girl, Esmeralda, Claude Frollo is the most evil. Although a priest, he is a character whose insatiable intellectual thirst has turned him to alchemy and the occult in an attempt to satisfy his obsession with knowledge. In his self-inflicted isolation, he communes with his books but cuts off contact with humans, permitting his animal nature to become more pronounced than the spiritual nature that modern Christianity claimed existed within man. This allows Hugo to develop a pronounced situational irony; although Quasimodo the hunchback outwardly resembles a monster due to his physical deformity, the priest's inner deformity, evident in his twisted nature, causes him to be the true animal. In a near-allegorical tale, Claude Frollo represents the degenerative effects of lust.

As a priest, Claude should symbolize the cathedral of Notre Dame, heaven's fortress, but instead resembles a figure from hell. Securely cloaked, with even his face hidden most of the time, Claude Frollo skulks about fourteenth-century Paris, where many people believe him to be a sorcerer. He has chances to redeem his dark soul by helping his ne'er-do-well scholar-brother,

Jehan, therefore supporting the idea of brotherhood metaphorically represented by his priestly calling. However, Claude does not act upon that opportunity. Similarly, his adoption and upbringing of the deaf and deformed Quasimodo could enrich the charitable aspects of his nature, but Claude instead takes advantage of the hunchback, using him miserably as a servant and church bell ringer. He also uses Quasimodo in his attempt to kidnap Esmeralda, an attempt foiled by the handsome army captain who captures the girl's heart. Later the priest ignores the hunchback during a public punishment in which Esmeralda is the sole individual to tend to Quasimodo's desperate need for drink.

Claude Frollo's fall to temptation emphasizes Hugo's stress on the importance of fate to the human condition. Although Frollo has several opportunities to conclude his nefarious activities, he rejects those chances, remaining powerless against his bestial nature. His lust for Esmeralda brings him into conflict with his vows of celibacy, his devotion to things spiritual, and the loyalty of his one devotee, Quasimodo.

See also: Esmeralda; Forbidden Love; Gothic Romance; *The Hunchback of Notre Dame;* Quasimodo; Violence
References: Brombert, 1986; Charlton, 1984

FROME, ETHAN

Edith Wharton's tragic romantic hero Ethan Frome remains one of her most well-crafted characters. As the protagonist of *Ethan Frome* (1911), Frome represents all that Wharton felt was good about the nineteenth-century man. He accepts responsibility for his own life and that of others whom his actions affect and then suffers stoically a fate that he helps shape for himself. These same noble characteristics also doom him to a life without love.

Frome's marriage to his wife Zenobia Frome occurs for all the wrong reasons, leaving him shackled to a woman he comes to detest. His gratitude toward Zeena, as he calls his wife, following her help with his ill mother only adds to his sense of loneliness and proves a shaky foundation for a lifelong relationship. Within a year of their marriage, Zeena becomes ill, and Frome is trapped in a loveless marriage on a worthless farm.

The only love in his life appears in the form of Mattie Silver, appropriately named for the sparkle and value she brings into Frome's life.

Mattie joins the Fromes in the aptly named community of Starkfield, ostensibly to provide companionship for Zeena, but ends up as a love object for Frome. The three form a depressing love triangle in which Frome valiantly attempts to be loyal to both women, a Herculean task that proves impossible. True to his heroic status, Frome never acts on his feelings to engage Mattie in a physical relationship. But they do express their love for one another, a love doomed before it ever reaches fruition.

Frome's sense of responsibility to Zeena combines with his poverty to inhibit his accompanying Mattie when Zeena orders her from the household. His marriage to Zeena has been shattered by his love for Mattie, symbolically depicted by their having broken Zeena's favorite pickle dish in her absence. Frome's procrastination in repairing the broken object reveals his reluctance even to attempt improvement of his relationship to Zeena. But because his culture demands that he remain faithful to his marriage vows, he cannot leave her.

When their only escape seems a shared death, Frome and Mattie agree to ram their sled into a tree. Hopeful that they may share eternity together in a bond of love that is forbidden during their lifetimes, they enact their plan. But the consequences serve as a bitter reminder that one may not escape one's fate. The cruelest irony in this most ironic tale is that Zeena ends up caring for both Frome and Mattie after their suicide attempt. She represents a society that prefers emotional cripples who follow its rules to independent and happy agents who transgress social law.

Ethan Frome combines characteristics of the typical late-nineteenth-century hero, such as quiet acceptance of his lot and perseverance in the face of cruel fate, with those of a Greek tragic hero. His strength also becomes his flaw, ultimately bringing upon him an even more miserable existence than that which he knew previous to enjoying true love.

See also: Ethan Frome; Victorian Age; Wharton, Edith
References: Bell, 1995; Comfort, 1974; Davidson, 1995; Geist, 1996; Gilbert and Gubar, 1996b; Pater, 1974; Pizer, 1995; Price, 1996

FU, WEN

In his role of villain in Amy Tan's *The Kitchen God's Wife* (1991), Wen Fu represents well the traditional Chinese patriarch. In his relationship with Winnie Louie, he controls her actions and makes all decisions involving her as well as himself. At first he charms his young wife-to-be and her cousin, Peanut. Winnie acts as go-between for Wen and Peanut but ends up being the target of Wen's supposed affection. Once married, Wen reveals his character as a bully. He presents his wife's dowry to other members of his family and often steals her money, acts which are permissible on the part of the male head of the household. He immediately exhibits his power by forcing Winnie to perform sexual acts she considers perverse. Wen's violence escalates as he emotionally and physically abuses Winnie, often publicly, and eventually abuses their children and other women, sometimes contributing to their deaths. He lies to and cheats fellow members of the armed forces, has sex with multiple women outside marriage, manipulates Winnie's father through threats of violence, and refuses to grant Winnie a divorce.

Wen hides behind pseudohero status based on his supposedly honorable participation in the Chinese air corps. In truth, Wen runs from battle against the Japanese. He participates in a love triangle with Winnie and her eventual second husband, Jimmy Louie, and is revealed to be the father of Winnie's Americanized daughter Pearl, the result of a final rape before Winnie escapes to America and Jimmy. Therefore, he functions as Jimmy's opposite, emphasizing the negative aspects of his own dreadful character.

See also: The Kitchen God's Wife; Louie, Jimmy; Louie, Winnie; Love Triangle; Patriarchal Marriage; Tan, Amy; Violence; War
References: Armstrong, 1990; Brown, 1996; Chan and Harris, 1991; Chen, 1995; Foster, 1996; Price, 1983

GAINES, ERNEST J.

Born in 1933 on River Lake plantation in Pointe Coupee Parish near New Roads, Louisiana, Ernest J. Gaines would use those locations, dubbed Bayonne and St. Raphael Parish, as the setting of much of his later fiction. His eight medium-length novels and a collection of short stories consistently depict the volatile subject of race relations in southern Louisiana. Although his plots offer much external conflict, as individuals remain pitted against their culture, he also offers readers an intimacy with the internal conflict his protagonists suffer.

The young Ernest picked cotton as a child, attending the black quarter's school during the five or six months each year it remained open. His parents left Louisiana during World War II, and Gaines joined them in California at the age of fifteen. After Gaines attended San Francisco State University, Stanford University awarded him a writing fellowship, and he has taught at the University of Southwestern Louisiana. For most of his life, more than forty years, he has been a resident of California, but he has never written successfully about that state or his experiences there. His southern roots and family always take him back to the same big plantation house where he matured.

His first published short story appeared in 1958. His 1993 novel, *A Lesson before Dying*, won the National Book Critics Circle Award for that year and later the 1994 National Book Award for fiction. Arguably his best known and most widely read book is *The Autobiography of Miss Jane Pittman* (1971), due to its frequent use in American classrooms. In *Catherine Carmier* (1964), Gaines features an affair between two black individuals whose complexions differ, and his novel *Of Love and Dust* (1967) presents the tragedy of an interracial romance in the 1940s on a Louisiana plantation. *Bloodline,* a 1968 collection of short stories, contains autobiographical elements, and the novel *In My Father's House* (1978) presents a profile of a minister and civil-rights leader haunted by his past sexual flings. Other works include *A Gathering of Old Men* (1983).

For his most recent work, *A Lesson before Dying* (1993), Gaines corresponded with the warden at Angola, the state prison in Louisiana, regarding the prison situation during the 1940s. To gain additional information, he corresponded with others who knew stories about Gruesome Gertie, the name of Angola's electric chair, and interviewed some witnesses of Louisiana executions by electrocution. When asked about his political affiliation, Gaines has said that any such involvement is indirect and that politics never acts as the main focus of his stories. Instead he chooses to emphasize the characters and the effect of politics upon them.

Gaines has said that he features as his audience not only southern African-American youths but

The eight medium-length novels and collection of short stories by Ernest Gaines, pictured ca. 1984, consistently depict the volatile subject of race relations in southern Louisiana. (Philip Gould/Corbis)

also the white youth of this country. He hopes that through his novels black youths may achieve better knowledge of self and pride in their history and that white readers may better know their black neighbors in order to fully grasp their own history. In composing his novels, Gaines follows the five points of advice that he has shared with would-be writers: "Read, Read, Read and Write, Write, Write." He adds to this basic but important instruction: deliver language naturally; write simply; practice an economy of words; remain with a single character's point of view; and begin each story by placing characters in the midst of conflict, following with action to resolve that story. Although his novels remain realistic regarding the often negative situation of blacks in America, they are also optimistic, featuring individuals experiencing a moment of clarity that frees them.

> See also: The Black Experience in America, 1600–1945; Of Love and Dust
> References: "About the Author," 1997; Coombs, 1972; "Gaines," 1994; Magnier, 1995; Summer, 1993; Upchurch, 1995

GARCÍA MÁRQUEZ, GABRIEL

The eldest of twelve siblings, Gabriel García Márquez was born in 1928 in a remote Colombian village called Aracataca. He matured listening to the stories of his grandparents, developing a love for the stories' mixture of myth, legend, and South American history. This love would later reveal itself in his dozens of short stories and novels. He experimented with fiction while a student at the University of Bogotá, publishing his first stories during that time. His education and his fiction-writing career were interrupted in 1948 by the outbreak of one of Colombia's many "unofficial" wars. The civil unrest labeled *la violencia* ravaged his country for a decade, and García Márquez's political writing career was born.

As a journalist with the *El Espectador,* a Bogotá newspaper, García Márquez gained fame beginning in 1954. His first novel, *Leaf Storm* (*La hojarasca*), appeared in 1955, but its appearance was overshadowed by his series of controversial articles. Because the articles embarrassed the administration of Gustavo Rojas Pinilla, Colombia's dictator, García Márquez left the country for fear of punishment. The government dismantled *El Espectador,* a move that left García Márquez living in Paris in abject poverty. He continued to write, completing the novels later

Colombian writer Gabriel García Márquez pioneered the style of writing that came to be known as magic realism with his 1967 novel, One Hundred Years of Solitude. *(AP/Wide World Photos)*

published as *In Evil Hour* (*La mala hora,* 1962) and *No One Writes to the Colonel and Other Stories* (*El coronel no tiene quien le escriba,* 1961). These stories, described as dark and eerie, reflect the influence of Franz Kafka. When García Márquez finally returned to South America in 1957, he again worked as a journalist in Caracas, then Venezuela, and later in Bogotá. He moved on to Havana and began a lifelong friendship with Fidel Castro, then traveled to New York City, finally settling in Mexico City.

During his years of moving about, García Márquez wrote short stories more than novels. Although those novels written in Paris were well received upon publication, García Márquez himself felt dissatisfied with his work and entered a period of unproductivity. After several years of frustration, he had a vision of his next novel, saying he saw the first chapter as clearly as if it already existed. He drew upon the style of his grandmother in telling the story of a number of generations of a Colombian family. His story incorporated the supernatural events and unrealistic occurrences his grandparents wove so naturally into their tales. Eighteen months of work produced his first landmark novel, *One Hundred Years of Solitude* (*Cien años de soledad,* 1967). Totally unique in its style, later to be labeled magic realism, the novel became an instant success following its release to an enthusiastic public. Its first edition sold out within one week, and it was later translated into thirty languages and achieved sales in excess of twelve million. García Márquez gained a reputation as South America's best-known author. His magic realist style continued in subsequent novels, and it was adopted by many other authors. García Márquez has said that stories of harsh political oppression work well within a framework of the magic represented by his characters' beliefs in things supernatural.

After the publication of one additional novel in 1975, *The Autumn of the Patriarch* (*El otoño del patriarca),* a novel not as well received as *One Hundred Years of Solitude,* García Márquez announced he would cease publishing. His moratorium protested the oppression of the regime of Augusto Pinochet, Chile's dictator. The author remained true to his word until 1981, when he published a novella titled *Chronicle of a Death Foretold* (*Crónica de una muerte anunciada).* In 1986 he issued a collection of his articles from *El Espectador* under the title *The Story of a Shipwrecked Sailor,* originally published in 1970 in Spain as *Relato de un náufrago.*

He entered the world of romance with a wildly popular 1985 work, *Love in the Time of Cholera* (*El amor en los tiempos del cólera),* a chronicle of love between two septuagenarians set against the backdrop of a politically and socially diseased South American culture. It remained on the *New York Times* best-seller list for thirty-four weeks. *The General in His Labyrinth* (*El general en su laberinto)* appeared in 1989 and was followed by *Strange Pilgrims: Twelve Stories* (*Doce cuentos peregrinos,* 1993) and *Of Love and Other Demons* (*Del amor y otros demonios,* 1994).

García Márquez has received many awards, including Italy's Premio Chiancian and France's Prix du Meilleur Livre Etranger, and is South America's most widely acclaimed author. In 1972 he claimed the Newstadt International Prize for Literature and garnered the Nobel Prize for literature in 1982. He has said his goal is not to feature political oppression in his work but rather to create a Latin American identity that will generate respect and appreciation from the rest of the world. He sets many of his stories in a fictional Colombian town called Macondo that resembles his true-life village of Aracataca. Some believe his setting to be inspired by William Faulkner's southern fictional geography of Yoknapatawpha County. Along with the brightness afforded by magic realism, García Márquez's works also transmit a distinct melancholy.

The author's creative involvements include the foundation of New Latin American Film in Havana in 1985, an outgrowth of his continued friendship with Castro. He also joined with one Spanish and five Latin American directors to develop a collaborative Latin American cinema that produced six films based on his stories. An individual with an abiding interest in fiction, he desires that stories be told, and told repeatedly. In this manner, the oral tradition so important to his grandparents may be preserved.

See also: Love in the Time of Cholera; Magic Realism
References: Serafin, 1996; Zamora and Faris, 1995

GATSBY, JAY

For his romantic tragedy *The Great Gatsby* (1925), F. Scott Fitzgerald created one of his most enduring characters. Jay Gatsby becomes a victim of the American Dream, allowing Fitzgerald to suggest through his character the devastation that may result when a "commoner" attempts to find a place among the aristocrats of America.

In this story of unrequited love, Gatsby's fate is to worship for a lifetime his first love interest, the wealthy Daisy Buchanan, who is married to Tom Buchanan when the novel opens. Readers learn through exposition that Daisy's love for Gatsby fades when he departs to go to war. She agrees to marry Tom, a nationally known football star and a member of one of the wealthiest and most powerful families in Chicago. Gatsby reappears years later, buying a mansion with his mysteriously found wealth close to that of the Buchanans, who have moved East. He forms with Daisy and Tom a love triangle that allows him, if only briefly, to live out the fantasy of love and riches he has nourished for so long.

Born Jimmy Gatz, Jay Gatsby earned several decorations in World War I but returned to the states as a major without prospects. An early "sponsor" of Gatsby describes him at that time as so poor that he had no clothes other than his uniform. The reader does not learn until the book's conclusion that Gatsby apparently began the path to his ill-gotten gains by working for Meyer Wolfsheim, owner of the Swastika Holding Company. This bit of information suggests confirmation of a rumor expressed early in the story that Gatsby's mysterious wealth was gained partly through illegal dealings with the Germans. When Gatsby finally locates Daisy, he carries with him all of the vulgar accoutrements of the nouveau riche, including the gaudy mansion that he fills with members of high society.

Gatsby's tragedy lies in his failure to realize Daisy's motivations. When she responds to his attentions, she never intends to make a life with her former love. Tom's well-known sexual affairs cause her to desire revenge against her husband, who lavishes attention on other women instead of her. Tom remains aware, however, that although Daisy professes to hate their lifestyle, in actuality she cannot live without it. When he learns of Daisy's affair with Gatsby, he does not interfere; he understands that his wife's dalliance will never amount to more than a brief fling. Even though Gatsby and Daisy announce plans to run away, Tom's convictions are realized; Gatsby cannot compete with Tom's power and the appeal of his socially approved old money in Daisy's eyes. When Daisy commits vehicular homicide, accidentally killing Tom's mistress, Gatsby volunteers to assume responsibility. Such an act remains foreign to the Buchanans, who, as the narrator explains, make messes and allow others to clean them up.

Gatsby's heroism in rescuing his heroine remains wasted. He represents the fantasy life imagination allows, whereas Tom Buchanan represents the reality that life demands. Gatsby's carefully constructed facade of wealth and happiness collapses like the proverbial house of cards when it undergoes a challenge from the real world. His ironic murder by the husband of the dead woman is tragic not only because he dies but because in its aftermath his "friends" desert him. Even Daisy does not attend his funeral. His father's presence at the service symbolizes the great Jay Gatsby's reduction to his true identity as Jimmy Gatz, a poor midwesterner destined, for the sake of love, to be trapped and destroyed by the lifestyle of the morally corrupt rich. Gatsby remains a flat character, undergoing no realization about himself or life in general that might cause him to change.

See also: Buchanan, Daisy; Buchanan, Tom; Love Triangle; *The Great Gatsby*
References: Piper, 1970; Price, 1983

GENRE ROMANCE

Sometimes termed traditional romance's "stepsister," popular romance developed a huge following from the moment it appeared. With a history that may be traced back to at least the seventeenth century, the romance offered a premiere opportunity for early modern women who desired a writing career. Often framed in sensationalism and provocation, the French *nouvelles* and romances by Madeleine de Scudéry also reflected a deep concern with politics and the importance of her nation's past to its present. Her works sparked a fury of imitations in nearby England. Only in the twentieth century did the importance of this early fiction writing by women become clear. Critics now believe that the strong presence in the marketplace of early women's fiction, and these writers' influence on the development of the early English novel, a form advanced by writers like Henry Fielding, made women's narratives the most important fiction produced between 1680 and 1740.

From the late seventeenth into the early eighteenth centuries, women such as Aphra Behn, Mary de la Rivière Manley, Eliza Haywood, Jane Barker, and Penelope Aubin became England's most popular writers. Their brief novels, with titles like Manley's *The Secret History of Queen Zarah and the Zarzarians* (1705) and Haywood's *Miss Betsy Thoughtless* (1751) and *The History of Jemmy and Jenny Jessamy* (1753), were labeled "amatory fiction." Amatory fiction generally involved the seduction of young virgins by wealthy, powerful men who then abandoned the women to the gutter. Such stories originally acted as cautionary tales for their young female readers. Popular romances also assumed the form known as the roman à clef, in which real-life figures, recognizable by the reading public, would be thinly disguised as fictional characters, generally marked by greed and debauchery. For instance, Aphra Behn's "trilogy," "Love Letters Between a Nobleman and His Sister" (1684–1687) was based on a contemporary sex scandal. It also featured a character based on the Duke of Monmouth, an illegitimate son of Charles II, executed in 1685 for his attempt to eject his uncle, King James II, from the throne. These early fictions served as precursors for the later writings collected under the heading of "formula," meaning that the plots followed a predictable pattern, or "mass market" fiction. By the twentieth century, the label "popular romance" referred most often to a narrative featuring idealized characters or environments.

Since its early days, the popular romance has enjoyed various elaborations. Representing over one-half of all paperback book sales in the United States, romances, the majority of which are still written by women, are framed in various plot structures. Publishers of formula romance generally require very specific elements for particular "lines." A brief description of some of the more abundant romance story types follows:

- *Christian.* Although not overtly didactic, the Christian romance must contain Christian themes that encourage moral behavior. Its female protagonists usually have never been married, and the male protagonists may be widowed. Rarely will either character be divorced. Very little inference to sex occurs; even kisses on first dates might be forbidden by certain publishers. Christian romance rose to popularity in the late twentieth century.

- *Contemporary.* This term refers to any romance set in present times. It may appear as a "contemporary/exotic," requiring an unusual setting, such as the desert or the Amazonian jungle. It may also contain fantasy or supernatural elements. The "contemporary/innocent," or naïve, contains little or no sex. Examples of innocents include Harlequin Romances and those romances published by Avalon Books. Also included in this category are "contemporary/Christian" romances, a subgenre growing in popularity (see above).

- *Gothic.* This subgenre of formula romance borrows heavily from the traditional Gothic romance made famous by Charlotte and Emily Brontë, among others. All Gothic romances include a plot emphasizing a mysterious atmosphere or setting. Supernatural and unexplained events, hidden family secrets, and a tone of doom dominate the popular Gothic plot. These romances most often have a past era as part of their setting, but some contemporary authors, such as Phyllis Whitney and Barbara Michaels, stage their Gothic novels in the twentieth century.

- *Historical.* The historical romance, as its name suggests, takes place in the past. This is its major qualification. Many variations on the historical popular romance appear, including "historical/wars," "historical/American West," "historical/Antebellum South," and "historical/American colonial." Some are tied to particular eras such as the Renaissance (widely defined, depending on the country serving as setting), the seventeenth century, and the reigns of Queen Victoria (1837–1901) and Edward VII (1901–1910). Historical romances incorporate factual political and socioeconomic factors from their time period.

- *Lesbian/Contemporary.* This type of romance occurs in the present and features a lesbian protagonist.

- *Lesbian/Historical.* This type of romance features a lesbian protagonist and may occur in any era other than the present.

- *Regency.* One of the most popular of the romances, the Regency features a light love story among members of the British upper class during the period 1811–1820. It takes its name from the fact that the Prince of Wales served as Prince Regent due to King George III's incapacity to reign. Many Regencies imitate the style of Jane Austen, emphasizing manners, wit, language, and style. Georgette Hyer represents the prototypical Regency author.

- *Saga.* Saga romances tell the story of several generations from the same family, emphasizing their trials as well as their joys.

- *Science Fiction.* The setting defines this subgenre, which may take place on another planet, in another galaxy, on spaceships, or in the far future on Earth.

- *Time Change.* In this plot type, characters move from one era to another through time travel.

- *Young Adult.* Aspects of this type of romance fit its younger reader. Plots may be sweet and innocent but also may involve serious conflict along with a strong romantic element.

See also: Austen, Jane; Brontë, Charlotte and Emily; Gothic Romance; Romance
References: Backsheider and Richetti, 1996; de Rougemont, 1983; Frye, 1976

GIONO, JEAN

In his romantic fiction, the French novelist Jean Giono used most often the theme of his characters' connection to their geographic roots. Born in 1895 in Manosque, Giono features his native province where he spent his entire life as the setting for much of his writing. His father was a cobbler of Italian ancestry, and his mother served as a laundry operator. Although the family had few funds, they recognized Giono's talents and attempted to surround him with music and literature to encourage his creativity. His literary influences included Herman Melville, Walt Whitman, Rudyard Kipling, Homer, Sophocles, and Virgil, and as a romance writer, Giono was strongly inspired by his compatriot, Gustave Flaubert. He would later refer to his family's sacrifices for his sake in his autobiographical novel, *Jean le bleu* (*Blue Boy,* 1931). His family's penchant for tale telling as entertainment supports Giono's habit of adding fantasy "facts" to his writing; he once fabricated a grandfather who had been a member of the Italian *carboneri* (civilian police). His first verse writings attracted little attention, and his first major work, *Naissance de l'odyssée* (1925), reflecting directly the influence of Homer's *Odyssey,* remains untranslated.

By nineteen, Giono underwent induction into the French army and fought in World War I. His four years of service as a private and his injury in battle converted him to pacifism. This ideology would cause him problems later and also would alter his writing style following World War II.

Giono first achieved acclaim as an author with his collection of three novels, the first of which, *Trilogie de Pan: Colline* (translated as *Hill of Destiny*), appeared in a Paris magazine in 1928. It appeared in book form in 1929 and became the first French novel awarded the American Bentano Prize. This work Giono followed with *Un de baumugnes* (*Lovers Are Never Losers,* 1929) and *Regain* (*Harvest,* 1930).

The author became a celebrity, and between the years 1935 and 1939, he entertained his devotees at his Contadour farm. He promoted himself as a sage or prophet of peace, emphasizing the importance of humankind's harmony with the natural elements, a posture in which his followers placed great faith. Although Giono privately mocked many of these disciples, he vastly enjoyed entertaining them with fabulous tales, at various times claiming to be a champion cyclist or snow skier. Impolite critics labeled him a liar; others preferred the term *imaginative.* He occasionally caused problems for himself and his publishers, committing a work to more than one publishing house at a time. Later critics found some of his work extraordinarily naïve, offering little more to readers than a mystical feel for nature, reminiscent of works from the Romantic period.

In the 1930s, Giono earnestly campaigned for peace, cofounding with a friend the paper *Cahiers du Contadour.* In various writings, he preached a kind of civil disobedience, even urging women no longer to give birth to children who would mature only to become cannon fodder. His rants and threats regarding Adolf Hitler seemed ridiculous when compared with his sedentary and parochial nature. Giono's 1931 novel, *Le grand troupeau* (*The Great Herd*), focused on the horrors of war as he had experienced them. His creed as a pacifist is reflected as a theme in various of his works, particularly in the 1937 *Refus d'obéissance* (*Refusal to Obey*). In 1939, after refusing military induction, he was sent to prison; later he would be accused of collaboration with the Nazis.

Giono's World War II contributions included the sheltering and financial support of several individuals, including Jews. At the storming of Normandy, he was low on funds and contacted his Paris agents with orders to sell certain of his beloved manuscripts in order to support his efforts toward peace. Although he had fallen out of favor with his followers, Giono continued to write. He suffered the stigma inflicted by France's postwar attitude toward some of those writers who participated with the collaborationist press. Never shy in his pronouncements, Giono remained hostile toward the possibility of a Communist takeover of France following the war and clung to his early ideas regarding the dichotomy between industrial workers and peasants. After 1930, many of his works reflect an apocalyptic quality, in which Giono seems to fantasize about wars to end all war.

Arguably his most widely read romance novel, *The Horseman on the Roof* (*Le Hussard sur le toit*), published in 1951, represents Giono's return to the legitimate ranks of literature. The novel features a youthful Italian army officer, exiled to France, who becomes involved in the adventures of the traditional medieval knight. It naturally includes Giono's attacks against the arrogance of the French bourgeoisie and their army pickets, a rhetorical strategy usually expected from French authors, regardless of their political commitment. By the time of this novel's publication, Giono was in his fifties, and the story helped promote his reputation as a gritty writer whose style borders upon the bitter. His style and his vivid sense of the visual are sometimes said to recall the English writer Thomas Hardy. Such characteristics have made the works of both authors especially suitable for conversion to film. Some critics feel that the novel, often cliché-ridden and evincing the naïveté associated with Giono, achieved such popularity due to the public's sense of shame over the humiliation it inflicted upon its once-favored author following the war.

Considered prone to exaggeration, the imaginative Giono swung from utopian fiction, filled with violence but also love, to writings presenting dystopic denunciations of anything blocking the individual pursuit of happiness. But in actuality, his works rarely evince a totally utopic presentation; all are liberally sprinkled with themes of greed and lust. They remain, however, devoid of any hint of the idea of original sin, in which Giono did not believe.

All of his mostly male characters adhere to an internal moral code of conduct. His diaries reveal a theme of a final male utopia, where weak women are nowhere to be seen. Fortunately, he failed to adhere to his own stated intention to fashion later writings after the less effusive style of William Faulkner, Miguel de Cervantes, and Niccolò Machiavelli. Although some have tried to categorize his writings into prewar optimism and postwar cynicism, such a relegation remains too simplistic.

At his death in 1970, Giono could claim one of the largest oeuvres by a French author. His voluminous diaries have since been published. Other important works include *Les vrais richesses* (translated as *True Riches*), published in 1936, and his series of adventure stories titled *Chroniques,* or *Histories,* the first of which, *Un Roi sans divertissement,* appeared in 1947.

See also: Chivalry; *The Horseman on the Roof;* War
References: "Jean Giono," 1996; Raphael, 1996; Redfern, 1995

GIULIA

In Giuseppe Berto's antiromance novel *The Sky Is Red* (1948), fourteen-year-old Giulia represents the innocence that all of the story's main charac-

ters lose in postwar Italy. Her tender years serve as no protection against a violence that continues after the guns have ceased firing. Like the flowers with which she is associated, Giulia remains easily bruised and extremely fragile. Her delicacy would make her a fine candidate for the heroine in a classical romantic novel, but in Berto's grim undercutting of romance elements, she stands as a helpless target of life's inequities. She enjoys a brief experience in romance through her love for Daniele, but its joy cannot substitute for the strength she needs to survive the devastation that represents her life.

Following the death of their grandmother in a bombing, Giulia and her near-fifteen-year-old cousin, Carla, join Carla's seventeen-year-old boyfriend, Tullio, and a young orphan girl in establishing a household so they may remain together. Even before the final bombing of the city, Carla has engaged in prostitution, an act Giulia discourages. Because her mother had to support her family through prostitution, Giulia never wants to engage in the selling of her body to men. Carla provides a fine contrast to the timid and vulnerable Giulia, in that she knows what is needed to survive. She cannot allow even her love for Tullio to threaten her survival instincts. Although the rest of the group never quite recovers from Tullio's eventual violent death, Carla learns to cope with such loss. Giulia, however, lacks this coping mechanism.

Giulia finds someone to love for herself upon the arrival of Daniele, an educated teen from an upper-class family who also ends up on the street as an orphan. Raised to believe in the basic goodness of humankind and in the promise of his future as a member of the elite, Daniele identifies with Giulia's own desire for a better life. Although their backgrounds starkly contrast, Daniele returns Giulia's love, and the two find brief respite with one another.

Giulia suffers in silence when Carla seduces Daniele, doggedly performing her cleaning and cooking tasks and attempting not to inflict moral judgment upon her companions. But her sensitive nature makes her emotional wounds all the more painful, and she resembles nothing more than the magnolia blooms she so loves that bruise when roughly handled. Her death by consumption symbolizes the slow death that society undergoes, and her constant references to her internal illness represent the attacks mankind inflicts upon itself through war and social inequities caused by greed. Giulia's death thus represents the death of all hope for things good in what Berto views as a hopeless society. Italy loses its innocence along with its children, who remain hapless pawns sacrificed to war.

See also: Berto, Giuseppe; Carla; Daniele; Nihilism; *The Sky Is Red;* Tullio; Violence; War

References: Hoffman and Murphy, 1996; Price, 1983

GONE WITH THE WIND

As one of America's best-known twentieth-century romances, Margaret Mitchell's *Gone with the Wind* (1936) contains many of the aspects of traditional romance. Included are a Byronic hero in the character of Rhett Butler, themes of unrequited love and forbidden love, an enduring love triangle, an example of true devotion in the relationship between characters Ashley Wilkes and Melanie Wilkes, the violence of the American Civil War, and the deaths of characters important to the hero and the heroine. In addition to these well-known romantic elements, Mitchell introduces in Scarlett O'Hara a heroine who is a curious blend of the active and passive, negating the image of an often stereotypically helpless female promoted by traditional romance. Scarlett remains an active agent, finding her own solutions without depending on men. At the same time, she must maintain an air of passivity, pretending to comply with southern customs that insist on the female's subservience to the male yet in reality behaving in an aggressive manner. It is her enduring spirit, her determination not only to survive the horrors of war and death but to triumph over personal conflict, that endears her to Rhett Butler.

At the novel's beginning, Scarlett represents the naïveté of the South, caught up in a way of life that cannot endure. Although naïve, many of the South's residents are not innocent; their cruelty is reflected in their often despicable treatment of slaves and women. But as a wealthy teenager of marriageable age, Scarlett ignores the obvious conflict around her, concentrating only on capturing as a husband Ashley Wilkes, the man she thinks she loves. As the only male who resists Scarlett's ample charms, Ashley represents the unconquerable. Scarlett's desire for Ashley is based not on love but rather on pride and a feeling of competition, two stereotypically male traits. Her passion finds birth not in feelings of respect for

Clark Gable played Rhett Butler and Vivien Leigh played Scarlett O'Hara in the famous 1939 film version of Margaret Mitchell's 1939 novel, Gone with the Wind, *one of America's best-known twentieth-century romances. (Archive Photos)*

Ashley but rather in a desire to possess him, reflecting her fickleness. His choice in marriage of a cousin, Melanie, whom Scarlett views as mealymouthed and weak, enrages her. She focuses so intently on capturing Ashley's heart that she marries Melanie's younger brother in order to provoke Ashley's jealousy.

Rhett Butler encounters Scarlett for the first time before Ashley's marriage, when the beautiful southern belle boldly declares her love to Ashley. Such an act is unheard of on the part of a well-bred southern woman. An unseen witness to Scarlett's claims of affection and to Ashley's rejection of her, Butler uncharacteristically falls in love with Scarlet in a passion that will endure for years. In this pivotal scene, Scarlett rejects Rhett for not being a "gentleman," in other words, for not being like Ashley. Her tendency to cling to this fantasy of the ideal man dooms Scarlett to a loveless life. With the Civil War raging around her, Scarlett suffers her own internal battles. Although blessed with a keen insight into life's challenges and an adeptness at handling its demands, she remains blind to the reality of love.

In addition to the war, Mitchell introduces a vast amount of internal conflict, as well as conflict between characters, to cause problems for her two pairs of lovers. Although Ashley and Melanie remain devoted to one another, Ashley is forced into close proximity to Scarlett, who constantly tempts him. Melanie, the one true innocent of the group, remains fiercely devoted to Scarlett, who saves her life and the life of her son when Yankees invade and burn Atlanta. Ironically, it is her loyalty to Scarlett that causes the Wilkeses to remain in the South following the war. Rhett, himself an opportunist, understands Scarlett and her motivations and endures the frustration of her unfounded devotion to Ashley. His desire for and devotion to Scarlett never lessens, even though he is forced to watch her go through two loveless marriages and bury both of her husbands before she is free to marry him. Scarlett's refusal to recognize and embrace Rhett's love for her reflects a lasting immaturity; for all the strength she shows through war and near-starvation, the loss of her beloved mother, and marriages to men she despises, she remains startlingly naïve in her romantic view of Ashley. Her confusion is reflected in her recurring dream, where she stumbles through a fog in search of something she never discovers.

Although Rhett and Scarlett marry and have a child, Scarlett never returns Rhett's affection. She remains fixated on Ashley Wilkes, who desperately loves Melanie and does little to encourage Scarlett. Only at Melanie's death, when she requests that Scarlett care for Ashley, does Scarlett realize the mistake she has made. This moment of epiphany, in which she sees at last that Rhett was what she searched for in her nightmare, confirms Scarlett's growth as a character. But her change comes too late. In a supreme moment of irony, Rhett rejects Scarlett's declaration of love as he leaves her. When he remarks that Scarlett is still a child, he sums up her attitudes and behavior perfectly.

Mitchell's novel supplies a satisfying and realistic view of romance. Her characters' lack of satisfaction in love, while somewhat frustrating to readers, involves those same readers with the story's plot and its hero and heroine. For all of the romanticism reflected in *Gone with the Wind,* Mitchell remains true to the novel's title and declines to supply the requisite happy ending. These factors, along with detailed scenes of war, death, and suffering heightened through wrenching imagery, combine to overcome what might have been a sentimentalized story, transforming it instead into an enduring romantic work.

See also: Butler, Rhett; Forbidden Love; O'Hara, Scarlett; Violence; War; Wilkes, Ashley; Wilkes, Melanie

References: Davidson, 1995; Flora, 1987; Hoffman and Murphy, 1996; Price, 1983

THE GOOD EARTH

Pearl Buck's 1931 novel, *The Good Earth,* is a social chronicle novel, meant to provide a literary snapshot of one culture at a particular moment in time. It includes some aspects of romance between the protagonist, Wang Lung, and his bride, O-lan, and also between Wang Lung and his concubine, Lotus Blossom. This represents a traditional arrangement for all three parties, and no love triangle develops. O-lan objects to Lotus Blossom's presence because it alters the domestic power structure, not because of jealousy over Wang Lung's affection. The book remains realistic, narrated in a near-pastoral tradition, faithfully describing the life cycle by featuring Wang Lung's close relationship to the land from which he earns his living. The novel does not represent a romance in the classic sense, although it does emphasize the relationships between the main character and the various women in his life.

When the novel opens in the early twentieth century, Wang Lung prepares to wed the wife his father has chosen for him. O-lan, a slave girl, will make an acceptable wife because she already knows all the necessary housekeeping and cooking skills, and due to her slave status, she will not spend her husband's income frivolously. When the couple burns incense at a temple to seal their lifelong pact in a simple marriage ceremony, Buck emphasizes one of many Chinese customs presented in her novels. Although O-lan continues her slave existence, gathering wood to save the money that would have been spent on fuel, repairing clothing for her husband and father-in-law, and tending to a myriad of additional domestic duties, she finds satisfaction in performing what she accepts as her duty. She also works in the fields with her husband and, in a famous scene, delivers their first baby there, then immediately returns to the strenuous activity of farm labor.

The healthy baby symbolizes a good first year for the couple, as does their healthy crop. The

Louise Rainier as O-lan and Paul Muni as Wang Lung appeared in the 1937 film version of Pearl S. Buck's 1931 novel, The Good Earth, *a social chronicle novel that provides a literary snapshot of one culture at a particular moment in time. (Photofest)*

theme of renewal through birth represents a major thrust of the novel, which seeks to present the challenges and joys of Chinese peasant life. With the silver earned from his crop of grain, Wang Lung purchases coats and clothing for the baby. The entire family travels to O-lan's previous slave home, that of the house of Hwang, where they respectfully revisit her past. The visit also allows Wang Lung to invest in some land the Hwang family sells to him. When a second healthy son arrives one year later, its birth is also accompanied by abundant crops. During these years O-lan and Wang Lung remain respectful of one another, but they express little passion.

However, Wang Lung sees the birth of his third child, a girl, as an ill omen. The presence of screeching crows portends future bad luck, and no one rejoices when the baby's gender is revealed. Everyone understands that girl children

are born only for servitude, and to make matters worse, this child apparently suffers from mental retardation.

The child indeed ushers in bad luck for her family, as her birth is followed by a drought and a resultant poor harvest. Their food supply exhausted, the family must travel to a southern province where there are more resources. Their possessions must be sold, and an additional tragedy occurs when Wang Lung views his fourth child. The infant lies dead, her neck bruised, and it is understood that O-lan has killed the baby. Thus, the various births and deaths of Wang Lung's offspring parallel exactly the natural cycles he experiences of life and death, harvest and famine.

The family does find work in a city following a train ride. Their home consists of mats propped against a wall, and Wang Lung begins his career as the puller of a rickshaw while the rest of the family begs for a living. Buck inserts commentary on social inequity through the revolutionary rumblings that spread through the city. Ironically, the family's hard work does not bring prosperity, but fate offers them a chance to benefit when the city's wealthy desert their homes due to the threat of military action. This allows the peasants to engage in looting and robbery that reaps for Wang Lung enough money, and for O-lan some valuable jewels, to return with their family to the farm. The looting represents an important step for Wang Lung, who has previously scolded his son for stealing. Having been raised a slave and a beggar, O-lan does not share her husband's moral ideology, and she participates freely in the looting. Their treasures allow them to refurbish the farm and begin a life working the land once again.

Wang Lung's purchase of additional acreage from the Hwangs again symbolizes the prosperity of life. He needs to hire labor, so Ching comes to work for Wang Lung and eventually oversees a group of six workers. O-lan, the proud owner of two pearls retained from her plunder that balance the twins to which she gives birth, need work the fields no longer. Her two older sons grow old enough to attend school, symbolizing a type of progress that will ironically work to separate them from the land their parents so highly value.

On repeated trips into town, Wang Lung encounters Lotus Blossom at a tea shop, and he brings her home to be his concubine. One of the more bittersweet scenes occurs when Wang Lung demands the pearls that O-lan has long treasured in order to present them to his mistress. The trustful and trustworthy O-lan sacrifices the only beauty in her life at her husband's command. Lotus Blossom must live apart from O-lan, who does not like the arrangement but remains powerless to alter it.

Conflict eventually arises when one of O-lan's sons is discovered visiting Lotus in his father's absence, with the suggestion of a type of forbidden love, that of the son for his father's sex object. Wang Lung settles this problem by first sending his son away and later recalling him for an arranged marriage to the daughter of a grain merchant. The wedding, traditionally a time for celebration of new beginnings, instead heralds tragedy as O-lan dies of a stomach illness. Her death is followed by that of Wang Lung's father. There is no hint from the author that Wang

Lung's bad luck or the deaths of family members relate in any way to his actions. Rather, the deaths allow Buck to emphasize repeatedly the unalterable cycle of the seasons of life and death. Although not a traditional hero, Wang Lung is heroic in his particular setting; his heroism lies in his faithful attention to and stewardship of God's natural blessings.

Always looking to the future, Wang Lung hires his remaining older son out as an apprentice to the grain merchant and offers his daughter as a wife for one of the merchant's sons. Once again, Wang Lung's fortunes take a turn for the worse. Family members move in and cause problems. Wang Lung's uncle, a local hoodlum, basically takes over his host's house in exchange for promising safety from his henchmen robbers. Always shrewd in terms of protecting his investments, Wang Lung convinces his uncle and aunt to smoke opium, and their subsequent addictions distract them from the household activities. This allows emphasis on the theme of labor as good and inactivity as evil. The troublemaking son, however, continues to bother Wang Lung's daughter-in-law, so he moves his family into town. The move represents a bitter irony: because he has reaped fine profits, Wang Lung must leave the very earth from which he came.

Ching, the overseer, also dies, returning to the earth that had demanded so much of his energy. No longer involved with the physical labor of the farm, Wang Lung rents his land, hoping that his son will take it over eventually. The second generation, however, has no interest in farming. Wang Lung's youngest son eventually deserts his father, who takes on a slave girl young enough to be his granddaughter, and in whom the boy himself had a romantic interest.

The new servant, Pear Blossom, reintroduces a strong male-female relationship, but it is not one of passion. Wang-Lung never relates to women in anything other than a master-to-servant mode. Along with his mentally handicapped first daughter, Wang Lung returns to his farm when he feels his death is imminent. The novel concludes with Wang Lung's discovery of his sons' plan to sell all his property when they inherit it. Although he protests, trying to convince them of the irreplaceable nature of land, they simply indulge him with no intention of changing their plans.

The Good Earth realistically chronicles one man's achievement and heroism through hard work and good stewardship of his gains. It also demonstrates the power of wealth to separate that same man from his beloved land, moving him into the very class of people he at first feared and envied. Plot assumes a secondary importance to characterization, as Buck shapes her figures with sound motives. Although none are stereotypical characters, the theme of absolute obedience on the part of the female to the male is emphasized. With the novel's major conflict reflecting Wang Lung's struggle to maintain his relationship with the earth, dramatic interest must be sustained through Buck's chronicling of the various twists and turns in that struggle. Her story's universal appeal likely emerges from her clear and realistic portrayal of a single individual's confrontation with life and his proven success.

See also: Buck, Pearl Sydenstricker; Lung, Wang; O-lan; Patriarchal Marriage
References: Conn, 1996; Forster, 1956

GOTHIC ROMANCE

Prose fraught with the elements of threatened or realized violence and the supernatural may be labeled "Gothic." Distinct emphases mark the Gothic work, including a mystery plot; dark, even depressing imagery; tinges of horror; ghosts or other metaphysical signs; haunted houses or ships that harbor secret passages, stairways, or storage areas; graveyard scenes; and suggestions of a monstrous past on the part of a character, usually the principal male. Its action always has an undercurrent of impending doom. The Gothic romance was introduced by English writers during the end of the eighteenth century and the first few decades of the nineteenth century and has been a mainstay genre, for the most part, ever since. The interest of novelists in human reactions to the pressures of a society that seemed to ignore their needs found expression in the Gothic. Generally the Gothic male protagonist fits into the category of the Byronic hero, which is unsurprising because the Gothic novel represented one phase of the Romantic movement in literature.

Horace Walpole's *The Castle of Otranto* (1764) and Ann Radcliffe's *The Mysteries of Udolpho* (1794) were among the first Gothic romances. Mary Wollstonecraft Shelley's horror story *Frankenstein* (1818) is a classic example of the Gothic in which a literal monster appears and the threat of death is realized. Victor Hugo, France's principal nineteenth-century romantic writer, offers a continental version of the Gothic in *The Hunchback of Notre Dame* (1831). In this novel the misshapen title character, Quasimodo, brings a sense of the physically hideous to the scene, as he plays beast to the beautiful Gypsy girl Esmeralda. But Hugo employs irony in his presentation of the story's villain, Claude Frollo, a priest whose normal exterior hides an evil nature; he is the true monster of Hugo's plot. The cathedral Notre Dame, with its noble spires and abundant dark corners, twists and turns, and gargoyle decorations, provides a strongly Gothic setting. Again Hugo incorporates irony by utilizing a supposedly spiritual setting to hide the macabre occultism of its perverted priest.

Later Gothic romances of enduring popularity included Charlotte Brontë's *Jane Eyre* (1847), which features a house "haunted" by the witch-like wife of the Byronic hero, Mr. Rochester. That same house is burned to the ground in the novel's conclusion, with the fire acting as purification, leaving Rochester disfigured but reborn into a new life. This work was one of the first to allow readers an inside view of a character's fears and concerns, making way for the psychological novel and stressing internal as well as external conflict. In the same year, Charlotte's sister Emily Brontë published one of the most famous Gothic romances of all time, *Wuthering Heights* (1847). In this novel, also featuring a Byronic hero in the form of Heathcliff, the wind-swept moors allow an emphasis on nature as monster. They provide an apt setting for a mystical tale of two lovers who remain unseparated even by death.

Daphne du Maurier's more recent novel *Rebecca* (1938) incorporates many aspects of the Gothic, but an inversion occurs in that the book's namesake, Rebecca de Winter, represents the ghost who haunts Manderley and her one-time husband, Maxim de Winter, along with his new bride. Thus, a silenced female character shares the dark past with the male protagonist. The ghoulish character of Mrs. Danvers, Rebecca's servant, lurks about the mansion and eventually burns it to the ground, wiping away all traces of her dead mistress. Like his Gothic ancestor Rochester, Maxim is injured in a fire that represents a new beginning for the romantic couple.

Gothic romance plots remain popular, particularly in commercial romances written for the popular market. All of the classic Gothic tales have enjoyed continual reprinting and have also been converted to film versions. The Gothic's combination of horror and romance make it particularly appropriate for big screen enjoyment.

See also: *Frankenstein; The Hunchback of Notre Dame; Jane Eyre; Rebecca; Wuthering Heights*
References: Duncan, 1992; Ellis, 1989; Richter, 1996

THE GREAT GATSBY

F. Scott Fitzgerald's romantic tragedy *The Great Gatsby* (1925), a study of a common man caught up in the ethically vacuous world of the ultrarich, is probably his best-known work. His story of the love triangle composed of the powerfully wealthy Daisy and Tom Buchanan and Daisy's love interest, the ill-fated Jay Gatsby, portrays several kinds of love and romance. Jay's enduring love for Daisy, although at first founded on true emotion, builds into an unrealistic fantasy that dooms him to fail in his later pursuit of a girl who no longer exists. Daisy suffers a corruption at Tom's hands, caused by her love of money and power rather than of Tom himself. Tom marries Daisy not for the kind of love Gatsby feels for her but more as a proof of his power; she becomes a possession that he easily controls through his wealth. Gatsby erroneously believes the early love he shared with Daisy will motivate her to abandon Tom and the high-society life she needs to survive. An additional love triangle consists of Tom, Daisy, and Tom's lover, Myrtle Wilson. It is partly due to Tom's affair that Daisy ventures into a relationship with Gatsby.

Much of Fitzgerald's depiction of the idle rich in *The Great Gatsby* was based on his real-life observations. Gatsby's character reflects the author's own longing for the power and advantages afforded by wealth. Fitzgerald's use of a narrator, Daisy's cousin Nick Carraway, allows him some perspective on the activities of the three main characters. Also a member of a privileged family, Nick comes East following World War I to enter the bond business, and he reacquaints himself with Daisy and Tom. He coincidentally moves into a small house next to the mansion recently occupied by the mysterious Jay Gatsby.

The reader learns Nick's qualification as narrator on the first page, when he comments that he has always been inclined to reserve judgment. This made him a target for all sorts of unwanted confidences in college; people trusted him not to criticize and to keep secrets. Nick does admit to feeling an unaffected scorn for the nouveau riche, but

he finds his outlook toward Gatsby as a representative of that group changing over the course of the story when he comes to know Gatsby personally. Gatsby's naïveté and unabashedly romantic nature cause Nick, in the end, to feel disgusted by the lifestyle that condemned Gatsby to death but not the man himself.

Gatsby arrives in West Egg, New York, amid rumor and gossip as to the origins of his wealth. Some believe him to have been involved in illegal dealings with the Germans, claiming he had even murdered a man. This claim ironically foreshadows Gatsby's later assumption of responsibility for a killing he does not commit. The mystery draws the curious locals to participate in his wild parties; a horde of thrill-seekers arrive to mill about the mansion. Nick soon ascertains that Gatsby's motive in moving to West Egg involves his romantic feelings toward Daisy, who lives across Long Island Sound in East Egg. In one of the novel's most memorable scenes, the narrator observes Gatsby stretching out his arms to the green light at the end of an East Egg dock. That tiny pinpoint in the darkness represents Gatsby's hope for a future that will allow his long-nourished passion for Daisy to be realized. When he then vanishes into the dark, readers should acknowledge the foreshadowing of Gatsby's eventual destruction by the darker forces represented in the morally corrupt world of the Buchanans.

Fitzgerald supplies additional foreboding symbolism through the omnipresent billboard advertising optometric services. It bears huge eyes peering from behind enormous glasses that observe the lovers as they flounder from one embarrassing scene to another. They play out their relationships beneath the figure on the billboard that seems to represent a higher power, one intent on meting out the judgment on Gatsby that the narrator avoids.

If Gatsby has a tragic flaw, it is his unrealistic approach to life. Not a pragmatist like Tom Buchanan, he cannot make decisions that work against his fantasy of spending a life with Daisy. Even when others can see that Daisy never intends to make permanent her romantic liaison with Gatsby, he continues to hope that she will sacrifice a lifestyle on which she has become totally dependent. The mature Daisy lacks resemblance to the young woman Gatsby loved, but his plans have been so long in the making that he cannot surrender them even when disaster impends.

Following his romantic code as closely as any knight of chivalry, Gatsby has no choice but to accept the blame for Daisy's accidental killing of Myrtle Wilson while Daisy was driving his car. Although he could not have foreseen that this action would lead directly to his own death, even had he known the consequence of his choice, he would have behaved no differently. Readers may be tempted to blame Gatsby's murder on Tom Buchanan, the man who encourages Mr. Wilson's intentions to do Gatsby harm, but the blame for his demise must be attributed to Gatsby himself. His attempt to bring to the life of the indolent rich his own romantic ideals is doomed to fail miserably.

A third romance exists as a subplot, involving Nick and Daisy's socialite friend, Jordan Baker. Nick is lured into the same social circle that so attracts Gatsby. But unlike Gatsby, Nick is able to reject a life that seems bereft of ethics and beauty before he suffers any permanent harm. With Gatsby die Nick's romantic notions about the life Jordan represents, and this may be the one positive effect of Gatsby's untimely death.

But Nick does not abandon Gatsby's fantasy of a life containing the perfect relationship. He concludes the novel by remarking upon the green light that drew Gatsby inexorably to his fate. He affirms that all humans pursue their futures with the hope of one day procuring their dream. He concedes, however, through his comparison of individual lives to boats fighting rough seas, that life's currents will push all of us backwards into a past we remain helpless to avoid. Gatsby bases his hope for a future with Daisy on a dream. He has so elaborated upon the reality of their early relationship that even Daisy could not live up to her image created in the mind of Jay Gatsby.

See also: Buchanan, Daisy; Buchanan, Tom; Carraway, Nick; Fitzgerald, F. Scott; The Lost Generation; Love Triangle
References: Beach, 1959; Carpenter, 1988; Cowley, 1973; Hart, 1995; Piper, 1970; Washington, 1995

GRIFFITHS, CLYDE

As the main character of Theodore Dreiser's 1925 novel, *An American Tragedy,* Clyde Griffiths aptly represents the character type for which Dreiser became so well known. As indicated by its title, the novel relates a tragic story of perversion of the American dream, with Clyde as its antihero. His innocence and naïveté in believing he can alter his social circumstances and thus his fate make him a sympathetic character, but his blindness to the impossibility of achieving his dream and refusal to recognize the futility of his foolish quest simultaneously cause Clyde to be unlikable. He remains a classic tragic figure, his death and that of others brought on by his own mistaken sense of self-importance.

Clyde rejects his poor, religious Kansas City missionary parents to pursue a desire for wealth and an increase in social status. When he ends up working for his rich uncle in New York, his contact with a member of the social elite, Sondra Finchley, increases his desire to be in her crowd of friends. He dates and impregnates Roberta Alden, a farm girl from the factory where he works but tries to ignore her situation in order to advance his standing with Sondra. Sondra unwittingly deceives Clyde into thinking she likes him by flirting with him in order to make his cousin jealous. Clyde misinterprets Sondra's obvious ploy as his fantasy grows to encompass a dream of one day marrying her. Eventually he plans Roberta's murder and that of her unborn child to remove her from the love triangle he has imagined. She ironically dies in an accident in the very setting Clyde had chosen for her murder.

The strength of character implied by Clyde's hesitation to destroy a life just before Roberta drowns immediately fades into a weakness marked by indecision. While Clyde probably could not have prevented the accident, he could have saved Roberta, but he hesitates too long. Still clinging to hopes of social advancement, Clyde panics and leaves the scene. The error he makes in not enacting the rescue is overshadowed only by his tragic flaw in refusing to accept his life for what it is, a common ordinary middle-class existence.

Clyde fights for order in a chaotic world where social lines are drawn, and he is relegated to a certain destiny by his birth. His refusal to recognize and adhere to social constraints leads to arrest for murder and his subsequent death by execution. As sad as his death may be, sadder still remains the fact that Clyde never recognizes or understands his own part in his demise. Like most of Dreiser's tragic characters, Clyde reaches no important self-realization. His tale undermines the usual initiation/coming-of-age story because no epiphany occurs to afford him even a spiritual satisfaction or sense of grace before his death.

See also: *An American Tragedy;* Bildungsroman; Dreiser, Theodore; Forbidden Love; Love Triangle; Quest

References: Gerber, 1977; Hart, 1995; Howe, 1964

GUERINE, PAULINE

In Ernest J. Gaines's realistic novel *Of Love and Dust* (1967), Pauline Guerine represents a host of black female slaves and servants who fell prey to southern white landowners and overseers. Gaines's novel takes place in 1940s Louisiana, where circumstances since the end of slavery have not improved much for blacks. When the overseer of the plantation Pauline inhabits approaches her for a sexual liaison, apparently she does not resist. As a single black female, her economic future in the South remains bleak. One way she can ensure her own livelihood is to make the most of the only chance offered to her, and so she becomes the longtime mistress of Cajun overseer Sidney Bonbon.

Pauline's position in a love triangle with Sidney and his wife, Louise Bonbon, though not approved of by her peers, is one they understand as a matter of survival. Whites also accept the relationship as meeting that peculiar southern code that approved love or sex between white men and black women but severely punished such forbidden love between white women and black men. Sidney fathers children by both his wife, Louise, and his mistress, Pauline, and adheres strictly to the approved treatment of all. His daughter by Louise he openly dotes upon, but he must keep secret his affection for Pauline's mulatto sons. However, his frequent visits and gifts to the boys allow him to make some connection with his offspring.

This situation might continue indefinitely except for the arrival of Marcus Payne, a young black man accused of murder. He comes to the Louisiana plantation to work off his charge through hard labor, and he quickly learns to hate Sidney Bonbon. Marcus at first attempts to seduce Pauline in order to injure and insult Sidney, but she remains faithful to the white man. She knows that vengeance will fall on all the plantation's blacks if she relinquishes her fidelity to Bonbon. Her rejection spurs Marcus to seduce Louise, also a victim of Sidney Bonbon's cruelty.

Pauline remains important to Gaines's portrayal of the injustice and racism that controlled the South long after slavery was declared illegal. The few choices blacks had to make a living remained closely controlled by unsympathetic whites, causing the socioeconomic chains to remain almost as binding as those of slavery. The tragic plot leaves some hope for Pauline, as she plans to join Sidney Bonbon when he leaves the plantation following Marcus's murder and Louise's commitment to an asylum for the insane. But their future offers little promise, and the mixed couple represent well countless pairs who found themselves in similar circumstances in an unforgiving post-Reconstruction South.

See also: The Black Experience in America, 1600–1945; Bonbon, Louise; Forbidden Love; *Of Love and Dust;* Payne, Marcus

References: Hoffman and Murphy, 1996; Price, 1983

GUISHAR, LARISA (LARA) FEDOROVNA

As the more passionate female member of Boris Pasternak's love triangle in his 1957 war romance, *Doctor Zhivago,* Lara remains closely identified with the novel's themes of art (imagination) and nature. Her union with Yurii Andreievich Zhivago, a physician-poet, although fated not to last, remains successful. This is evidenced through their parenting of Tania, an illegitimate daughter who symbolizes the fruit of their passionate union outside the boundaries of the approved institution of marriage. Although Yurii also produces a family with his legal wife, Tonia Gromeka, a childhood friend whom he respects and loves, that family exists within the legal and political institutions ultimately seen as controlling and stultifying to the human spirit.

Lara's story begins in a venue quite different from that of the aristocratic surroundings in which Yurii and Tonia mature. Although a child of tragedy, Yurii joins a wealthy family who adopts and cares for him. Lara, however, as the daughter of a working-class widow, remains the victim of class difference when she suffers seduction as a teenager by an unscrupulous attorney named Victor Komarovsky. Purportedly her mother's patron in establishing her Moscow sewing business, Komarovsky represents the wealthy taking advantage of the lower class. Lara meets Yurii early on when, as a physician trainee, he accompanies her family physician to care for her mother following a suicide attempt. The suicide attempt could foreshadow Lara's future, but she soon reveals herself a social rebel in the midst of the political rebellion that surrounds her. Unwilling to sacrifice herself for anyone, Lara makes her presence known by refusing to be taken for granted and then simply cast off by Komarovsky. She eventually shoots Komarovsky in an unsuccessful murder attempt.

Lara later marries a Russian dissident student named Pasha Antipov, and the two depart Moscow for a home in the Ural mountains. Her marriage to Pasha, a passionate disciple of freedom for the working class, and their station in the natural surroundings of the mountains, emphasize Lara's representation of a natural approach to a life in which all humans should enjoy equality. Her life both parallels and contrasts that of Yurii, who makes the pragmatic choice of medicine over poetry for his life's work and who marries Tonia, a woman for whom he feels fondness rather than passion. Lara and Yurii meet again when she ends up his nurse, caring for wounds he suffers while treating soldiers at the front. Lara awakens a passion in Yurii he did not know he possessed, but the two separate following the October Revolution, when he must return to Moscow. It is the first of several separations, this time caused by Yurii's devotion to the institutions of marriage and family.

As Yurii attempts to protect his family from the war-and-disease-torn city by escaping to a family estate in the Urals, he tempts fate by exposing himself again to Lara. They reunite in their forbidden love, only to be forced apart again by the continually raging war. Yurii is forced to care for the Bolshevik guerrilla contingent. When he eventually escapes, he returns to find his family gone to Moscow, allowing another reunion with Lara. She remains the symbol of all that he values in life, and her closeness to nature and removal from the cultural, social, and political institutions that control Yurii's life again align her with Pasternak's theme of freedom of the human spirit. She also represents the sacrifice the author considers necessary to a moral existence, but in a different way than the sacrifices made by Yurii. Lara's sacrifice, that of her relationship with Yurii, she makes voluntarily, knowing they can never marry. Yurii, however, is forced to sacrifice his love with Lara because it is considered illicit by society. The sacrifices on both parts remain heroic.

Although Lara and Yurii do not enjoy a life together, they do share peak moments of passion and regeneration. Lara represents the fecundity of life, whereas Yurii symbolizes the imagination that can celebrate the physical and spiritual reproductive capacities of humankind through poetry. Lara's character remains important to the novel not only as the love interest for its protagonist but as a symbol of Pasternak's spiritual feelings, unhampered by dogma or ritual.

See also: Doctor Zhivago; Forbidden Love; Love Triangle; Pasternak, Boris; Violence; War; Zhivago, Yurii Andreievich

References: Brunsdale, 1996; Clowes, 1995; Frye, 1974; McMillin, 1990; Williams, 1974

H

A HANDFUL OF DUST

In his 1934 novel of social satire, *A Handful of Dust,* Evelyn Waugh presents the perfect example of an ironic romance. His characters represent stereotypes from British high society, and through their supposed romantic relationships, Waugh reveals the arrogance and hypocrisy he believed this group espoused. An entire page is dedicated to Waugh's disclaimer that all characters, names, and incidents in the novel remain fictitious precisely because the author knew so many readers would recognize themselves in his satire of adultery and love triangles. The popular book appeared in a screen version in 1988.

The novel's aristocratic protagonist, Tony Last, possesses a symbolic surname, in that he will be the last of his bloodline. Tony represents the landed gentry, that proud group that often lacks the wealth that once supported their property in style. Described by one character as a prig, Tony adores the family estate of Hetton and remains firmly rooted in the world of tradition, even though others mock his preoccupation with his grounds and a home described as hideous by some.

The surname of Tony's wife, Brenda Last, also remains symbolic for a different reason; her affections are not meant to endure. She first deserts Tony out of boredom, striking up a romance with a young dandy, John Beaver, then at last marrying a third man, Jock Grant-Menzies. Beaver's surname also describes his busy efforts to break into a social strata where he does not belong by using supposedly wealthy women such as Brenda. Before marrying Brenda, Jock is involved in a romance with a wealthy, manipulative American who never loves him but uses him to vicariously fill her wish to be an English aristocrat. All the characters except Tony, who actually loves his wife in a naïve way, merely use one another in their climb toward some goal.

Waugh's inclusion of an "arranged" affair between Tony and a common girl hired to act the part of his mistress remains one of his most bitingly satiric scenes. He makes fun of the English aristocracy's hypocritical approach to divorce, for Tony must "stage" an unfaithful event in order for Brenda to be able to divorce him. Although Tony claims the final victory in romance against Brenda by not allowing her to inherit any of his small moneys or property, he loses his own life when he embarks on an ironic quest to South America. Again Waugh is in fine form, constructing a traditional journey by boat for his "hero" who seeks treasure. Unfortunately, the skills of Tony's guide leave much to be desired, and he lives out his years deep in the jungle, forced to read and reread Charles Dickens's romantic novels to the egomaniacal Mr. Todd, who has constructed his own kingdom far from civilization with the local natives as his slaves.

Waugh leaves no aspect of aristocratic life untouched by his sometimes painfully sharp wit. But he is especially hard on the characters in relation to their seemingly amoral approach to love. Even the tragedy of the death of little John Last is used to reflect the shallowness of his mother. Brenda at first believes that her lover, John Beaver, has been killed and shows relief when she learns the John about whom Jock brings bad news is "only" her son. The author uses traditional romantic aspects to turn that tradition upside down, resulting in a satisfying and entertaining novel.

See also: Last, Brenda; Last, Tony; Waugh, Evelyn
References: Drabble, 1995; Gaye, 1996; Hoffman and Murphy, 1996; Price, 1983; Read, 1974; Wolk, 1993

HARDY, THOMAS

With his realistic approach to storytelling, English Victorian Age writer Thomas Hardy brought to his novels containing romance an attention to detail and an emphasis on the everyday difficulties encountered in ordinary human lives. As a member of the working class himself, Hardy focused on the concerns of common men and women who are often trapped in a preordained social structure from which they cannot escape. Thus, much of his fiction contains themes of economic oppression and of the hypocrisy Hardy viewed as inherent in the gentry and aristocracy.

Hardy was born and matured in a cottage at Higher Bockhampton, near Dorchester, in 1840. The eldest son of Thomas and Jemima Hardy, he experienced a stable, working-class upbringing. A delicate child, he was at first tutored at home by his mother. His life would encompass three different careers in all, including that of an architect's assistant, a fiction writer, and a poet; he studied the classics and architecture in his early education. Although he desired the life of a clergyman when young, he became an agnostic as an adult, and at the age of twenty-one moved to London. He worked as an assistant architect for five years in an office overlooking the Thames River. Lined with wharves and warehouses, the river produced a stench from sewage-contaminated mud that Hardy would blame in part for his poor health.

After the five years spent in London, Hardy returned to Dorset, where he continued his work in architecture while studying poetry. A keeper of copious lists reflecting his fascination with words, Hardy would read extensively for hours every evening. He eventually designed a house for himself, Max Gate, constructed close to his original home, as well as Turnworth Church, which is located in central Dorset. A successful architect, Hardy eventually enjoyed a large income, although he basically lived as a member of the middle class.

From the age of thirty-two on, Hardy devoted his life to writing. His first novel had been rejected in 1867, causing him to burn the manuscript, but his next twenty years saw the production of fourteen novels and other prose. His first published novel, *Desperate Remedies,* appeared in 1871 and secured his reputation as one of the greatest of the Victorian writers. Hardy wrote prolifically, producing books of importance every one to two years. Other major works include *Far from the Madding Crowd* (1874), *The Return of the Native* (1878), *The Mayor of Casterbridge* (1886), *Tess of the d'Urbervilles* (1891), and *Jude the Obscure* (1895). After the outcry against what some saw as the unconventional subject matter of his last two novels, he swore he would never write fiction again. The remainder of his writing energies he spent in crafting almost one thousand poems.

His trademark tone of pessimism and gloom marks all of his novels. His voice remains one of skepticism because he lived in an era marked by its loss of innocence to a growing turbulence that would culminate in the world wars. His characters seem destined to failure and defeat; they struggle to exist in a society that rejects all who are not wealthy and powerful. His tragic story of ill-fated romance, *Tess of the d'Urbervilles,* depicts an innocent working-class woman seduced by an immoral man who supposedly represents a "better class" of people than Tess herself. Following the death of her illegitimate child, she is prevented from enjoying a fulfilling life and love, because her sexual experience marks her as an undesirable. Although a spiritual and emotional innocent, her inevitable descent into guilt and psychological suffering sparks an act of violence that ends her life through execution at the hands of an unjust society. This and other of Hardy's novels allowed him to showcase his cynicism regarding organized religion and the rigid class system of the British, along with his profound grasp of the elements of tragedy. Due to his frank dealing with details regarding sexual relationships outside marriage, some of his novels were deemed obscene by Victorian readers.

In both his novels and poetry, Hardy features the land in which he matured, shaping characters that emerge from his real-life experience. Like the landscape of old England, his work is filled with references to relics and structures that generally act as symbols of the age-old system that inflicts itself upon the natives. His writings also reflect the appearance, at the turn of the century, of new approaches to philosophy, science, and logic, all of which profoundly affected Hardy himself. Married first in 1874 and again in 1914 after his first wife's death, he enjoyed a close lifelong relationship with his extended family. He received multiple honors for his writing.

When Thomas Hardy died at the age of eighty-seven at Max Gate in 1928, he was buried in Poet's Corner in Westminster Abbey. This would have satisfied the writer, who wished to be remembered for his poetry, but contemporary critics judge Hardy's fiction as the more memorable of his contributions to English literature.

See also: Tess of the d'Urbervilles; Victorian Age

References: Bullen, 1997; Comfort, 1974; David, 1995; Drabble, 1995; Goode, 1993; Horsman, 1990; Pettit, 1994; Richardson, 1997; Shires, 1992; Weber, 1951

HATSUE

Many aspects of Yukio Mishima's 1956 romance, *The Sound of Waves,* including characterization, echo aspects of Longus's classical romance, *Daphnis and Chloe.* Mishima's virginal heroine, Hatsue, has much in common with Chloe and other classical romance heroines. Longus's work has, at various times, been considered obscene due to its sexual references, even though his hero and heroine remain chaste throughout his story. *Waves* also contains a number of explicit erotic images, mostly made up of references to women's breasts; however, modern readers would never consider such scenes to be even mildly pornographic.

Hatsue's love, Shinji, is about two years older than she is, just as Daphnis is two years older than Chloe. Both pairs of young lovers see one another naked and yet resist the urge to engage in sexual intercourse in these initiation/coming-of-age stories. In *Waves,* Hatsue convinces Shinji of the error in enjoying physical love outside marriage, and chastity becomes an important aspect of their pact of mutual fidelity. Like Daphnis and Chloe, Shinji and Hatsue fall in love, suffer a forced physical separation, and yet remain true to one another. When Shinji's rival for Hatsue attempts to rape her, she successfully resists. An aspect of romantic mysticism is represented by the convenient presence of a persistent wasp whose stings to the love rival make possible Hatsue's escape.

While Hatsue and Shinji become separated due to the mistaken assumption by Hatsue's father that they have had premarital sex, Shinji develops a plan by which the lovers can see one another. When their meeting is foiled, their physical separation increases as Shinji leaves their island for work at sea. Hatsue sneaks to Shinji a picture of herself and a written declaration of love, knowing that Shinji will return victorious from his quest to claim her as his prize.

One memorable scene in the novel focuses on the fishing village's diving women who seek abalone, among them Hatsue and Shinji's mother. When Hatsue wins a diving competition, besting Shinji's mother in the number of abalone she procures, she presents her prize to the older woman. This illustrates the importance of politically astute maneuvers between the young lovers' families. Hatsue remains a flat but vital character in Mishima's modern romance tale.

See also: Longus; Mishima, Yukio; Quest; Shinji; *The Sound of Waves*

References: Atkinson, 1989; Campbell, 1949, 1968; Hutton, 1993; Keene, 1995; Longus, 1989; Turner 1989; Wolfe, 1989

HAWKEYE

Although not romantic in the traditional sense of a man who enjoys the love of a woman, Hawkeye, the wilderness scout in James Fenimore Cooper's historical romance *The Last of the Mohicans* (1826) definitely qualifies as a romantic figure. He represents particular ideals that set him apart from the concerns of everyday people. Established by Cooper as a symbol of the adventurer caught in the civilization of the American wilderness, Hawkeye, a nickname for Natty Bumppo, would become one of the most popular characters in American fiction. Cooper originally intended to write this novel as a lone vehicle for Hawkeye, but its tremendous success led him to create an additional four novels featuring Bumppo at various stages of his life.

The setting for *The Last of the Mohicans* is 1759, during the French and Indian War (1754–1763). Hawkeye occupies a position between the sympathies represented in the conflict. Because he is white, he naturally sympathizes with the settlers and the soldiers who populate the novel. However, he remains highly sympathetic to the plight of the American Indian as well, although not necessarily that of the warring tribes spurred to action by the unscrupulous French. His best friend and ever-present sidekick, the tall and stately Chingachgook, is a Mohican Indian. Much of their interchange focuses upon Hawkeye's attempting to educate his friend in the ways of the white man while practicing much of the Mohican's approach to life.

The two become reluctant guides for a party of whites that includes the novel's two love interests. The main couple is that of Alice Munro and Major Duncan Heyward, but a secondary relationship between Alice's sister, Cora Munro, and Chingachgook's nephew, the Mohican brave Uncas, also occupies reader attention. Such forbidden interracial love introduces the theme of the difficulty of blending two cultures. This theme gains further import with the revelation that Cora herself is part black. As if to confirm Hawkeye's doubts that the two worlds of Indian and white can successfully blend, both Cora and Uncas will be killed before the novel's conclusion.

After engaging in a number of adventures and conflicts with both white and Indian men, Hawkeye joins others of his party in grieving for the loss of Cora and Uncas. But most of all, he grieves for the loss of innocence represented in the settling of the West. Cooper uses Hawkeye to mourn the development of a naturally beautiful land and the way of life its disappearance will destroy. For this reason, some critics see Hawkeye as an early voice for environmental concerns. Hawkeye remains the most romantic of characters, part of an idyllic and idealized life and time that can never be recaptured.

See also: The Black Experience in America, 1600–1945; Cooper, James Fenimore; Heyward, Major Duncan; The Last of the Mohicans; Munro, Alice; Munro, Cora; Violence; War

References: Barker, 1996; Campbell, 1949, 1968; "Cooper, James Fenimore," 1986; Frye, 1976; Price, 1983

HAWTHORNE, NATHANIEL

Nathaniel Hawthorne has been labeled one of the greatest influences on the American novel due to the style of narrative fictional romance he created. Born Nathaniel Hathorne, Jr., in Salem, Massachusetts, on July 4, 1804, Nathaniel would lose his father, a sea captain, at the age of four. With his sisters and his mother, Elizabeth Clarke Manning Hathorne, Nathaniel joined the Manning family in 1809. Recognizing Nathaniel's imaginative and intellectual potential, the Mannings made sure he was educated. He spent some of his formative years in Raymond, Maine, near Sebago Lake, but returned to Salem in 1819 to prepare for college by attending Samuel Archer's school. Here he enjoyed the tutelage of Benjamin Oliver, eventually attending Bowdoin College in Brunswick, Maine, along with classmates Henry Wadsworth Longfellow and future president Franklin Pierce. Hathorne's interest in literature caused him to adopt a rather solitary lifestyle, and he graduated at the middle of his class in 1825.

The future author returned to Salem, Massachusetts, following graduation to live again with his mother and sisters. He began his writing career by producing early works with romance plots focused on mystery and adventure. His first work, *Fanshawe* (1828), a book that featured Bowdoin College as its setting, was published anonymously. Eventually he attempted to recover and destroy all copies of his book, but it would be republished posthumously.

His Salem years were spent in solitude, allowing an introspection that deepened and made individual Hathorne's talent. Some critics feel the author's life may be viewed as a struggle between his desire to join the daytime world of society and his need for withdrawal into his own shadowy brooding. Although a secretive person, he wrote more about himself in the introductions to his later works than almost any other American writer of his period. These autobiographical notes allow readers great insight into the author's ideology and intentions. By 1830, his short works appeared in various publications, and Nathaniel added the "w" to his surname, changing it from Hathorne to Hawthorne. Purportedly, he hoped the alteration would distance him from ancestors who participated in persecution of the Quakers

Nineteenth-century novelist Nathaniel Hawthorne, shown here in an 1840 painting by Charles Osgood, is considered one of the greatest influences on the American novel because of the style of narrative fictional romance he created. (Library of Congress)

and from his great-great-grandfather, John Hathorne, a hanging judge at the Salem witch trials. Although not a churchgoer, he enjoyed watching people gather for services, and from his guilt and inner turmoil he developed a type of theology described as Christian and orthodox. Much of his later writing seemed to act as an apology for his ancestors' abominable actions as he focused on highly moral themes that reflected his belief in original sin and predestination. An excellent example is "Young Goodman Brown," first published in *New-England Magazine* in 1835 and today one of the most often-published short stories in classroom literature anthologies containing short fiction.

The best of Hawthorne's early publications, *Twice-Told Tales,* was published in 1837, the same year he became acquainted with the Peabody sisters. Although Elizabeth Peabody supported his writing efforts, Hawthorne became engaged to Sophia Peabody in 1839. While he spent six months at the utopian community, Brook Farm, he came away unsatisfied with the experience in 1841; his friend Thoreau declined the invitation to experience the transcendental lifestyle. He would later write of his experience at the commune in *The Blithedale Romance* (1852).

He married Sophia Peabody, a woman representing the propriety and social position Hawthorne revered, in 1842; they had a son and a daughter. His romantic and family experiences added new dimension to his writings, as Sophia respected his need for solitude and considered him the center of her world. Many feel that his contentment in marriage made possible his successful public career as a writer.

Hawthorne occupied Ralph Waldo Emerson's vacant home as he wrote during an age in which Edgar Allan Poe and Herman Melville also helped lay the foundation for the American short story and novel form. The ensuing four years were happy ones, allowing publication of *Mosses from an Old Manse* in 1846. His use of interactions among a few main characters formed a balanced series of action, causing him to be the first American writer to employ such an architectural approach to the novel. Like Gustave Flaubert in France, Hawthorne in America constructed novels as a bid for perfection that resulted in a mixture of realism with romance and an individuality in each novel that is clearly reflected in its organization and narrative tone. In 1849, Hawthorne began the American romance classic, *The Scarlet Letter,* published the following year. This story reflected Hawthorne's belief in Providence and a future life where sins would be punished. Self-knowledge, such as that experienced by the tormentor character of his novel, Roger Chillingworth, could also serve as a punishment on earth.

Unlike his contemporary Poe, who stated that he hated mirrors, Hawthorne used mirrors and reflective surfaces in abundance in his fiction. He once stated that he remained partly convinced that the reflection actually served as reality. His fiction overflows with oppositions such as that between sunlight and moonlight. Sunlight represents practicality and culture that often aids his protagonist's triumph over internal struggles, whereas moonlight and shadow symbolize the hidden evil of an individual's past or his or her innermost thoughts. Twilight may represent the separation of an artistic or imaginative temperament, such as that possessed by Arthur Dimmesdale, from the world of reality.

At once a shy and passionate man, Hawthorne wrote often of strongly passionate women. Of his four novels, two focus on adultery and one on a woman's attempt to escape from her undesirable mate, a man who has forced her sister into a kind of moral servitude. He considered his characters' inner worlds as he focused on the individual isolated by a society in which he or she struggles to regain a position. Like *The Scarlet Letter,* his novel *The House of the Seven Gables* (1851) reflects such themes.

Hawthorne wrote nonfiction as well, such as the campaign biography that helped propel his college friend Franklin Pierce into the office of president of the United States. Pierce's victory led to Hawthorne's appointment as consul at Liverpool, England, ensuring him an income after several unsatisfactory positions. Following the four years of consulship, he traveled in Europe, studying museums and galleries while living in Rome and Florence for one year. His novel *The Marble Faun* (1860) resulted from Hawthorne's European experiences. In 1863 he dedicated *Our Old Home,* a collection of English travel pieces, to Pierce, who suffered a wide unpopularity. Ironically, the author died in 1864 during a carriage tour with Pierce intended to restore Hawthorne's health.

Known for his examination of the tensions between the early American Dream and its resulting disenchantments, Nathaniel Hawthorne captured in romantic fiction studies of individuals who persevered against the challenges of their environments to enjoy spiritual and emotional victories. Those characters often remain so strongly symbolic that plot becomes secondary to his favorite theme; the ever-important effect of the past upon the present.

See also: Romance; *The Scarlet Letter*

References: Budick, 1996; Cowley, 1948; Hart, 1995; Stephenson and Stephenson, 1993; Stern, 1986

HEATH, A. K. ROY

Born in 1926 in British Guiana (later Guyana), Roy Heath would later utilize his homeland, particularly Georgetown, Guyana, in shaping his nine novels and the first edition of his memoir. His parents were both teachers, but his father died while Heath was a toddler, leaving his family in poverty. He managed to graduate from Central High School and attend Queen's College, and then he took a position working briefly as a civil service clerk. At the University of London, Heath received a bachelor of arts in French and then studied law, passing the bar in both England and Guyana but never practicing. Instead, he taught French in London secondary schools. He married and helped his wife Aemilia Oberli raise their three children, delaying his writing career until the age of forty-eight.

Heath manages to weave as naturally as does life themes of love and romance throughout his stories. Although a resident of London since 1951, Heath considers himself an immigrant there and has little interest in writing about his experiences. Instead, he writes of Guyana, a country he shapes in repeated natural renderings. Heath describes his ability to write of a country he left twenty years previously as a power to recall details that mesmerize. His detailed imagery features a stark demographic contrast between the opulence of the wealthy Guyanese neighborhoods and the degeneration of Georgetown's brothels and slums. Such settings are framed in stories at once realistic and simultaneously interlaced with the legends, myths, and religious customs and prejudices stemming from the Guyanese mix of aboriginal, African, and East Indian cultures. He delves beneath surface images to reveal ancestral influences on modern individuals. His interest in tradition is reflected in the romantic conflicts caused by interracial or interreligious marriages and the older generation's infliction of its beliefs upon the new.

Heath's characters resemble those on a traditional quest, but many become ironic quest characters as they investigate internal inconsistencies in their outlooks on life and love, outlooks generally influenced by the past. He experiments with a shifting point of view to offer narrations in which characters never clearly evaluate themselves. In a method that could be described as postmodern, Heath presents a narrative focused on complex characters that hides almost as much as it reveals.

In 1974 Heath's first novel, *A Man Come Home,* was well received for its realistic texture. His second book, *The Murderer* (1978), received the *Guardian* fiction prize as well as much praise. He followed this novel with what has become known as the Georgetown trilogy. *From the Heat of the Day* (1979) introduces the Armstrong family, and Heath's next books, *One Generation* (1981) and *Genetha* (1981), follow the lives of the Armstrong children. The trilogy, with some autobiographical basis, depicts Guyanese life, especially its racial and religious prejudices, from the 1920s through the 1950s. These were followed by *Kwaku: or, the Man Who Could Not Keep His Mouth Shut* (1982), *Orealla* (1984), and *The Shadow Bride* (1988), which won the Guyana Fiction Prize in 1989. In 1990, Heath published *Shadows Round the Moon,* which he calls the first volume of his autobiography. Although he has been labeled a prolific writer, having produced six novels between 1978 and 1984, he points out that not all of his novels were written just prior to publication. The trilogy was complete before the publication of his first novel; he simply could not find a publisher for it prior to his success.

Novels such as *The Shadow Bride* brim with detail regarding Indian philosophy, spiritual beliefs, music, clothing, and even food. Although such description and narrative would seem to demand much preparation, Heath has said that too much study and reflection can kill good writing. He believes the most important aspect of writing is an approach centered on genuine personal experience; otherwise, writing will not appear authentic. He addresses a Caribbean or Guyanese audience and incorporates many terms from his homeland, even though his largest reading audience is English. Although his writing greatly differs from that of earlier Caribbean authors, such as Edward R. Braithwaite and V. S. Naipaul, Heath gives such writers credit for making the market amenable to his own voice. Much of his writing incorporates themes of Marxism, natural to an author writing of what he terms a Third World illness caused by domination by other countries.

Roy Heath remains a novelist whose compassionate connections to his homeland are reflected through his obvious understanding of human nature and the suffering that shapes it. This makes the messages presented in his books accessible to readers of all cultures.

See also: The Shadow Bride
References: Birbalsingh, 1996; Munro, 1992

HEATHCLIFF

Heathcliff represents the quintessential Byronic hero in his position as the male protagonist in Emily Brontë's 1847 Gothic romance, *Wuthering Heights.* Like Mr. Rochester, the creation of Emily's sister Charlotte Brontë in *Jane Eyre,* also published in 1847, Heathcliff is not a likable figure. He has a tempestuous, willful, and vindictive nature, and his only positive feature is his devotion to Catherine Earnshaw, his childhood love. But even Heathcliff's love remains tainted by his fury, as he comes to think possessively of Catherine as his own. As suits a Gothic romance hero, Heathcliff deals in the black arts when he curses the dying Catherine to remain earthbound, even when a spirit, in order that the two may not be separated.

The wild moors that act as a setting for the Earnshaws' home, Wuthering Heights, effectively frame the uncontrollable passions of Heathcliff and Catherine. They pledge undying love as children, but when Catherine makes marriage plans with a neighbor, Edgar Linton, their fierce affection becomes part of a love triangle that will mean disaster for all parties involved. Because Heathcliff is a foundling, adopted by Catherine's father as a child without known parentage or property, his feelings for Cathy become a forbidden love when both mature. This means little to Heathcliff, but because he overhears a part of a conversation between Catherine and her nurse, Nelly, regarding their differing status, he departs Wuthering Heights. He leaves too soon to hear Catherine declare that Heathcliff is more a part of her than she herself can be.

When Heathcliff returns from America years later as a financially successful man, his riches bring him no joy. They act simply as a means to the end of destroying all those individuals who had a part in separating him from his beloved Catherine. The feeling he portrays for Catherine, now Mrs. Edgar Linton, seems closer to hate than love; he tortures her with his presence. To spite Edgar and Catherine, Heathcliff lures Edgar's sister Isabella Linton into a stormy marriage in which he emotionally abuses a woman who had really cared for him. They do have a son named Hindley, but the boy remains weak and sickly. Upon Isabella's death, Hindley comes to live with his overbearing father.

Catherine suffers an illness just before delivering her baby that briefly allows her to reunite with Heathcliff. In his tremendous hunger for their previous relationship, Heathcliff comes to the Linton home, embracing Catherine so fiercely that she seems to die in his arms. She does die later with Heathcliff standing vigil outside her bedroom. It is when he hears of her death that he places the curse on her spirit that will allow him one day to join her following his own death. The howl that Nelly hears from Heathcliff at that moment symbolically connects Heathcliff to the animals his nature seems closely to resemble. This is one of many ways in which Heathcliff shows that he may be considered, for the most part, inhuman.

Before his reunion with Catherine through his own death can take place, Heathcliff continues his revenge. He eventually financially ruins Catherine's older brother as well as Edgar Linton, taking Wuthering Heights for himself. He forces Catherine and Edgar's daughter Cathy to marry his son Hindley when both are still children, in a kind of self-torture as he watches the second generation complete a legal relationship that he and Catherine could not. But with Hindley's almost immediate death, Heathcliff must care for Cathy, a being he detests because she caused Catherine's death in childbirth. Eventually, only Heathcliff's own death can bring him peace. He and Catherine are seen walking together on the moors following his burial right next to her coffin.

Heathcliff remains one of the most memorable of the Byronic heroes. Although he cannot be considered a dynamic character in the true sense of that term, his disposition does alter toward the story's conclusion. That change comes not, however, from any realization on his part. Rather, he becomes seemingly complacent as he anticipates his impending death and enjoys the knowledge that, after years of separation, he will at last be reunited with his soulmate Catherine. Heathcliff's dark brooding nature, set upon revenge, fits well into Emily Brontë's Gothic tale of spirits and an immortal love that even death cannot kill.

See also: Earnshaw, Catherine; Forbidden Love; Gothic Romance; Linton, Edgar; Love Triangle; Violence; Wuthering Heights
References: Allen, 1993; Ellis, 1989; Gilbert and Gubar, 1996a; Leavis, 1966; Pater, 1974; Winnifrith, 1996

HEMINGWAY, ERNEST

Award-winning American writer Ernest Hemingway may be best known for his talent at understatement, especially his laconic dialogue. In his multiple novels and short stories, his "heroes" and "heroines" manage, at most, to function with grace in the face of life's pressures. Thus, in his romance plots, love is most often thwarted by unfavorable circumstances, leaving characters to cope in the best way they can with their resultant losses.

Hemingway grew up in his 1899 birth place of Oak Park, Illinois, son of Dr. Clarence Edmonds and Grace Hall Hemingway. While he remained close to his father, who taught him the outdoor skills involved in hunting and fishing, he disliked his mother, a fact made plain by later commentary. Following high school, where he distinguished himself in English and enjoyed swimming and boxing, he worked as a reporter for the Kansas City Star, an experience that many believe laid the foundation for his spare writing style. But unlike his fellow journalists and correspondents, Hemingway never wrote only for the moment. He remained first and foremost a creative writer, regardless of audience, using his journalistic material for imaginative purposes. His reporting reflected the ability to observe, evaluate, and record in a way that presented the whole picture to readers.

He left the newspaper job after a few months to volunteer as an ambulance driver in Italy during World War I. He became an honorary second lieutenant in the Red Cross but was unable to qualify for combat due to weak vision in his left eye, an inheritance from his mother for which he remained forever resentful. His duties included collecting body parts, mostly those of women, from an exploded munitions factory. When he transferred into the artillery, he suffered a serious wound; on this experience he later based details of his novel A Farewell to Arms (1929). He received the Italian Medal of Valor for courageous action in dragging a fellow soldier to safety, even though his leg had received damage from more than one hundred pieces of shrapnel and a machine gun bullet. In that novel he also reshaped his love for a thirty-year-old nurse, Agnes Hannah, who did not return his affections to the point of a fully developed love affair.

Following the war, Hemingway returned to Oak Park and lived for a time with his mother, who eventually asked him to leave when he refused to take employment. Convinced that he could write fiction, he supported himself as a correspondent for the Toronto Star. Living for a time in Chicago, he met Elizabeth Hadley

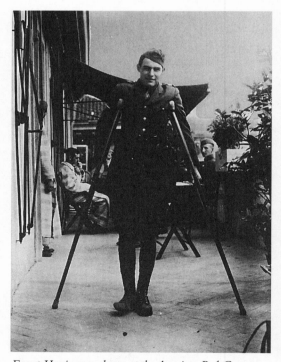

Ernest Hemingway, shown at the American Red Cross hospital in Milan in 1918, wrote romance plots in which love is most often thwarted by unfavorable circumstances, leaving characters to cope in the best way they can with their resultant losses. (Library of Congress)

Richardson, eight years his junior, and the two began a romance. They married and settled in Paris to become part of what Gertrude Stein referred to as "the lost generation," joining a group composed of notables such as James Joyce, F. Scott Fitzgerald, Ford Madox Ford, and John Dos Passos. Stein and Ezra Pound both encouraged Hemingway's writing. He and Hadley moved to Toronto for the birth of their son in 1923; shortly afterward, they returned to Paris. By 1927, Hemingway became involved in an affair with Pauline Pfeiffer, a fashion editor for *Vogue* magazine, and he divorced Hadley. His guilt over their breakup caused him to assign to her the royalties from *The Sun Also Rises* (1926).

Early work included a collection of short stories published in 1923, *Three Stories and Ten Poems,* and the volume including the short story of doom, "The Killers," titled *Men without Women* (1927). In 1928, he married Pauline Pfeiffer. They temporarily settled in Kansas City, where Hemingway's second son was born. Later they relocated to Key West, Florida, which would become his permanent home.

His reputation was established with the publication of *The Sun Also Rises,* a novel featuring American and British expatriates living in France and Spain. This irresponsible and restless group of young people symbolize that confused postwar generation termed "lost." Their loss is of a prewar ideology based upon trust that human beings would treat one another well simply as a matter of principle, a trust destroyed by the horror of the destructive forces of World War I. Left with no moral grounding, this once-hopeful group drifts from place to place seeking to regain that lost faith, a fruitless search that produces a nihilistic view of life. In his second important novel, the wrenching romance *A Farewell to Arms,* Hemingway promoted the nihilistic themes for which he would become well known through the tragic love story of an American fighting in Italy who falls in love with a British nurse. War would form the setting for a great deal of Hemingway's work as he focused on disillusioned individuals left with only cynicism toward others.

Throughout his life, Hemingway remained an avid sportsman who participated in hunting and fishing and who enjoyed watching bullfighting. His works reflecting these interests focus on men of primitive emotions and simplicity in thought,

a different type of protagonist from those of his war stories. An amateur boxer himself, the author wrote of prizefighters as well as characters reflecting his fascination with bullfighting. These fighters and matadors represent courage in the face of brutal physical circumstance. His famous nonfiction works include *Death in the Afternoon* (1932), featuring bullfighting, and *Green Hills of Africa* (1935), featuring big-game hunting. His writing about Africa was inspired by his family's move there following the birth of their second son. Hemingway hoped in Africa to redefine the traditional ideal represented by the term *courage* and in so doing create stability in his own tumultuous emotional life. He had earlier rejected his father, the man who had first interested him in sports, when Dr. Hemingway took his own life while struggling with crippling illness. The author made clear to his acquaintances that he considered such an act cowardice, a surrendering of life to death. Such statements made his own later suicide especially ironic.

His real-life adventures yielded much material for his writing. In addition to his experience in World War I, Hemingway gained further war experience as a newspaper correspondent in Spain during the Spanish civil war and as a reporter for the U.S. First Army during World War II. Enemy shells actually burst inside his hotel room in Spain, and he was struck by a taxicab during a blackout in World War II.

Social themes may be found throughout Hemingway's works, particularly those appearing after 1930. In the novel *To Have and Have Not* (1937), he condemns political and economic inequities, as he does in his play *The Fifth Column;* it appeared along with several famous short stories in *The Fifth Column and the First Forty-Nine Stories* (1938). These stories included "The Short Happy Life of Francis Macomber," featuring a big-game hunter betrayed by his wife, and "The Snows of Kilimanjaro," in which a dying man recalls details of his life. His novel *For Whom the Bell Tolls* (1940) focuses on the Spanish civil war and themes of the potential general threat to liberty that any localized military conflict imposes on the world. This would be his last well-known work until the appearance in 1952 of the powerful novella *The Old Man and the Sea;* this tale of a Cuban fisherman garnered the Pulitzer Prize. Hemingway received the Nobel Prize for literature in 1954.

The final work published before Hemingway's suicide in 1961 was *Collected Poems* (1960). Several works appeared posthumously, and thousands of pages of manuscript remain unpublished. No explanation for Hemingway's decision to kill himself has ever been formulated, but his attitude toward life in general was well known. When questioned once about the harshness Hemingway displayed in labeling F. Scott Fitzgerald a man of wasted talent, he stated that one would ultimately be judged not by the manner in which he died, but rather by the manner in which he lived. An adventurer, war correspondent, decorated war veteran, sportsman, and award-winning and highly influential American author, Ernest Hemingway must be judged to have lived a successful life.

See also: A Farewell to Arms; Fitzgerald, F. Scott; For Whom the Bell Tolls; The Lost Generation; Nihilism; The Sun Also Rises; Violence; War References: Beach, 1959; Carpenter, 1988; Cowley, 1973; Defazio, 1996; Donaldson, 1996; Hart, 1995; Hen, 1996; Hily-Mane, 1995; Hotchner, 1966; Moreland, 1996; White, 1933, 1968

HENRY, FREDERIC

As the antiromantic hero of Ernest Hemingway's novel *A Farewell to Arms* (1929), Frederic Henry represents the author's typical protagonist, one who suffers at the hands of an uncaring world, illustrating Hemingway's own nihilistic attitude. A highly autobiographical figure, Henry finds neither happiness nor satisfaction in life. He proves himself a hero in the only way deemed possible by his author-creator, by exhibiting grace under the pressure caused by his environment.

As Hemingway did, the American Henry voluntarily joins the Italian army during early World War I; he drives an ambulance and ultimately suffers a wound. Hemingway's characters often suffer physical wounds that symbolize the more serious emotional and psychological damage they suffer. Their mental stability is challenged when life tests and defeats their ideology. Through several interchanges with his fellow soldiers, Henry reveals his idealism regarding the political and moral motivations supporting the Italian rebels. This dialogue allows readers insight into Hemingway's own eventual disillusionment following a war that convinced many idealistic young people of their foolishness. They witnessed devastation formerly undreamed of, foisted by one group of humans upon another through technology.

Henry finds his only hope in his love for Catherine Barkley, an English nurse he meets early in the war who later cares for him following his wounding. Whereas Catherine has already enjoyed and lost her first love to the war, Henry's feelings of love are a new experience for him, and he changes because of them, making the story one of initiation, or coming-of-age. Believing at first that he will simply enjoy one more sexual fling with Catherine, Henry soon becomes convinced he wants to share his life with her. Thus, the comments of his comrades upon his return to the front after his wounding that he has changed and seems a conventional married man are correct. When he leaves Catherine behind she is pregnant, and his concerns about the Italian cause assume a secondary importance to his concerns for Catherine and the baby.

This concern helps him survive capture by the enemy and a subsequent escape. Henry decides to abandon altogether the public political cause for the more important personal commitment to love. Some might view this running from duty as cowardice that acts to negate any hero status Henry has, but others characterize it as an epiphany, the action bringing with it a realization necessary to the completion of Henry's ironic quest. His subsequent swim across a river to freedom symbolizes his "baptism" into a new life, as does the casting off of his uniform. When he trades his official clothing for that of a civilian, he assumes a new life role along with his change in garb.

Henry's escape with Catherine to Switzerland represents his attempt to escape his destiny. Naturally, this remains impossible, and the deaths of Catherine and their baby leave him feeling abandoned, with neither religious nor political ideology for comfort. He experiences the adventures of a hero but none of the hero's satisfaction when his emotional quest for lifelong love fails; thus, his quest becomes ironic. Henry's defeat echoes Hemingway's view of humanity as subject to ultimate ruin. The only redeeming factor in life remains one human's capacity to care for another and our power to accept defeat with aplomb.

See also: A Farewell to Arms; Bildungsroman; Hemingway, Ernest; Nihilism; Violence; War References: Cowley, 1973; Defazio, 1996; Donaldson, 1996; Hen, 1996; Hily-Mane, 1995;

Hotchner, 1966; Moreland, 1996; White, 1933, 1968

HERO

William Shakespeare chose the name Hero for the romantic heroine of his dramatic comedy *Much Ado about Nothing* (1598), a play based on a plot line that can be traced back to ancient Greek romance literature. Hero represents a stock character that audiences of the day would have easily recognized: a woman falsely accused of enjoying a sexual relationship with someone other than her intended husband. For a time, the accusation causes much consternation and concern for other characters and for members of the audience alike, but viewers remain confident that misunderstanding would be put right in the end. All live happily once the woman's purity is proven.

An Italian villa in Messina, owned by the provincial governor, Leonato, also Hero's father, provides the setting of the play. When several soldiers visit the villa accompanying their leader, Don Pedro, Hero's love for the dashing young Claudio becomes apparent. Claudio's friend Benedick remains a confirmed bachelor and disapproves of marriage, but Claudio proposes to Hero, who accepts. Because Don Pedro's bastard brother, Don John, craves mischief, he arranges for Claudio and Don Pedro to observe, at a distance, two people making love. The man calls out Hero's name, supposedly in the height of passion. Although Claudio believes himself betrayed, in reality Hero's serving woman stands in the arms of the other man.

When Hero suffers public accusation of infidelity at her wedding ceremony on the following morning by Claudio, even her father wants to kill her. Although harsh, his reaction was typical of the era about which Shakespeare wrote. A maiden's virginity was of great value to her future husband, not only as a sign of the obviously desirable practice of chastity but also as an assurance that any baby born would indeed be genetically his own and worthy to carry his name and inherit his fortune.

Hero receives moral support for her claim of innocence from a friar who serves as the voice of spirituality. Hero's devoted cousin, Beatrice, also supports her. As a woman, Beatrice cannot physically defend Hero but must instead remain passive. An intelligent and verbal creature, Beatrice finds Hero's false accusation impossible to bear, and she calls upon her love, Benedick, to challenge Claudio to a duel. Hero must follow her father's advice to suffer in silence until the situation reaches resolution.

Although Hero remains necessary to the main plot of the drama, many viewers find her an unimaginative and unsatisfying character. Hero serves as a stock aristocratic figure whose elevated social status in life requires that she play out all of her love scenes with Claudio in public. Thus, viewers catch no private view of Hero. For this reason she never assumes the entertaining active personality of her more excitable cousin. Hero's stock character seldom appears in contemporary literature due to a change in sexual mores. In most countries today, a woman would not be sentenced to death or banishment due to sexual activities. However, for Shakespeare's day, Hero's story remained compelling, providing high drama in the midst of comic activity.

See also: Beatrice; Benedick; Claudio; *Much Ado about Nothing*
References: Barton, 1974; de Rougemont, 1983

HEROES

Festus Iyayi's realistic novel *Heroes* (1986) examines the imperialistic approach of those political and social powers in his home of Nigeria that take advantage of the lower-income classes. Various Nigerian tribes have been led to believe that tribal differences supported the Nigerian civil war of the late 1960s, the armed conflict that forms the setting for Iyayi's novel. Iyayi declares through his novel that differences in social class, not tribal affiliation, lay behind the dispute. He establishes his novel's journalist protagonist, Osimi Iyere, as one who at first believes in the propaganda of national unity preached by the Federal troops as they battle the Biafran rebels. But Iyere will observe for himself the crass indifference to humanity of the Federal leaders, who indoctrinate many of their followers with their own hate. This firsthand experience leads him to alter his beliefs regarding the war's true heroes. His epiphany then enables him to form the strong romantic relationship he desires with Ndudi, a member of the Obi tribe, and the daughter of his landlord.

Iyere previously believed that in his position as a member of the petty bourgeoisie and a supporter of the Federals, he would forever remain an ideological world apart from Ndudi. To him, she represented the Biafran rebels, even though she and her family had never engaged in any wartime acts. For this reason, he allows himself to be romantically distracted by Salome, the woman who comes to symbolize the Federal forces when she marries one of its high-ranking officers. Iyere's eventual shift of affection from Salome to Ndudi accompanies his shifting political loyalties. Thus, Iyere solves the conflict in the love triangle when he symbolically chooses the stand represented by Ndudi, that of tribal independence, over the power-hungry Federal leaders who kill and rape for their own material benefit. Ndudi and Iyere, previously separated by their differing opinions regarding the war as well as by their social differences, unite following his realization.

The novel opens with Iyere contemplating his country's state of civil unrest. As the Federals approach his town, he mentally celebrates their arrival, hoping that peace will accompany them. But just as the corn he has so carefully nurtured suffers destruction from one violent rainstorm, so the Nigerian people will suffer from the violence brought by the Federals. This symbolic imagery serves as foreshadowing of the destruction of his political ideology. It will be later reemphasized as Iyere compares Ndudi to the corn, tender and slight but still brave against the onslaught of political turmoil. Iyayi uses italicized words to portray his character's thoughts for the reader as Iyere conducts a mental conversation with his "other self." This allows the reader to understand the great struggle Iyere suffers as he makes one of his biggest life decisions. Even though in the opening pages he cheers aloud at the Federals' arrival, repeating their ultimately empty slogan, "One Nigeria!" his cheers will cause a bitter taste to arise in his mouth before the passing of many days.

The first signs of trouble for Iyere occur at an assemblage of the town's people, who are called by the soldiers to meet in the local stadium. He urges Ndudi's father, Ohiali, to attend, assuring him he has little reason for concern. Ohiali fears that his membership in one of the warring tribes will mark him as a traitor in the eyes of the Federals, even though he has not participated in the war. He decides not to attend, but Iyere does. The journalist comes away having been beaten by the soldiers without cause. In this scene, Iyayi introduces the seductive Salome, and the reader understands that her affair with Iyere had ended

a fledgling romance with Ndudi. Salome rescues Iyere, using the power she possesses due to her recent marriage to a Federal officer to subdue the hostile soldiers.

Following his beating, Iyere reconsiders his advice to Ohiali, warning the old man not to register with the Federals. He has heard grim stories, such as that of his fellow journalist whose landlord was murdered by the soldiers for having harbored rebel tribe members in a cavity in his house above its ceiling. In one of many gruesome scenes that promote among readers the realization of the horror perpetrated by the Federals, Iyere learns that the soldiers fired into the ceiling, causing blood to drip to the floor below, before marching his friend's landlord outside to execute him. This tale acts as chilling foreshadowing of Ohiali's fate. The innocent Ohiali decides to register to demonstrate his willingness to comply with Federal rules. On the following day, in utter horror and complete disbelief, Iyere watches the soldiers summarily and without cause execute Ndudi's father. The scene is all the more pitiable because Ohiali tries to run to freedom and is gunned down from behind.

This incident so personalizes the violence that Iyere can no longer ignore the arbitrary cruelty of the soldiers. He experiences the first of several realizations, or epiphanies, that bring on a change in his views of life, love, and the war. Although the trip will be dangerous, he agrees to drive Ndudi and her family back to their home village to bury Ohiali. Along the road, they must suffer the indignity of strangers repeatedly peering at Ohiali's body in its casket at each Federal checkpoint. Eventually Iyere leaves Ndudi and her family to accompany soldiers to the front at Asaba. When the lovers part, he desires to leave something behind, telling Ndudi that he will return to claim it. She refuses to care for any of his physical possessions, stating that she wants him to return for her love and for nothing else. As Iyere departs, he vows to one day return and marry her.

The remainder of the novel traces Iyere's encounters with the Federal soldiers. One of those soldiers sums up the attitude of war as that of a prostitute: one day war sleeps with the Federals, the next with the Biafran rebels. His words remain a grim foreshadowing of Ndudi's future fate, as she will eventually be raped by members from each side of the war on the same morning. She suffers an attack by two Biafrans as they depart, yielding possession of the town, and also by two Federals as they arrive to take control. Ndudi at that moment becomes highly symbolic of the country of Nigeria itself. The soldiers' actions prove that neither group is inherently honorable.

Iyere realizes at last that there exists little glory or glamour in battle. When he learns that the Biafrans have overtaken Oganza, the town where he left Ndudi, he curses himself for not bringing her with him. In another moment of understanding, he suddenly grasps that his prejudices regarding the Nigerian tribes had caused him to hate Ndudi during the time that he believed the Federals represented the "right" force in the war. Iyayi frames his thoughts in effective imagery, as Iyere envisions love and hate as two sides of a coin, with both rolling on the coin's edge, which represents life. The war dissolves into nothing more than a war of words, falsehoods, and rumors, with little ideology to ennoble its desperate acts.

As he suffers further physical abuse, Iyere observes not only the overwhelming cruelty of the Federal officers but also their arrogance and waste. He comes to understand that if war has any heroes at all, they are not its self-aggrandizing leaders. Rather, the common soldier who must simply follow orders is the hero. Iyere comes to despise the fear of reprisal on which the war is based, determining a third army should be formed to fight the generals, politicians, and businessmen who represent Nigeria's enemies in both peace and war. His thoughts constantly return to Ndudi as he realizes that love cannot be love unless it is shared; only then does it fulfill its purpose.

A final horrendous slaughter of soldiers on both sides of a battle leaves Iyere feeling numb. When the top-ranking Federal officers depart the battle for a celebration of the promotion of Salome's husband, they abandon their troops, leaving them unsupported and vulnerable to certain massacre. In a scene poignant for its supreme irony, many of those Federal soldiers who attempt to escape being shot by the Biafrans are later executed for desertion on the orders of the same officers who left them to die. Iyere cannot help admiring the camaraderie of the common soldier, and he echoes Ernest Hemingway's nihilistic philosophy as he recall's that author's statement that the isolated individual stands no chance of survival.

In Iyere's plea to the soldiers that they learn the truth regarding the greed and power-based insanity of their supposedly ideological leaders, Iyayi also makes a plea to readers to adopt a new approach in their attitudes toward Nigerian unrest. The author employs his art as political statement, concluding the novel with Iyere's thoughts for the future. As Iyere comforts Ndudi following the quadruple rapes, he vows to himself that circumstances will change, if not with this war, then with the next. An emerging movement will at last write the true history of the war, allowing no praise for the generals who take credit at the expense of their troops. It will be a history in which all heroic individuals, both male and female, will receive their due.

See also: Iyayi, Festus; Iyere, Osimi; Ndudi; Nihilism; Violence; War
References: Hoffman and Murphy, 1996; Udumukwu, 1996; Wendt, 1990

HERRERA, MERCEDES

Mercedes Herrera, who eventually becomes the Countess de Morcerf in Alexandre Dumas's historical romance, *The Count of Monte Cristo* (1844), remains an innocent victim of the plotting against her fiancé, Edmond Dantes. Dantes, who later assumes the alias "the Count of Monte Cristo," remains Mercedes's first and lifelong love. But the happily-ever-after relationship usually achieved by young lovers of romance does not develop for Mercedes. Instead, she becomes a pawn in the game to ruin the innocent nineteen-year-old Dantes.

Following Dantes's imprisonment on charges of treason during the period when Napoleon was exiled to Elba, Mercedes struggles to care for herself and for her lover's aged father. Unbeknownst to her, Ferdinand Mondego, a fisherman who claims to be Dantes's friend, actually conspires to put him in prison. Ferdinand's jealousy over Mercedes's love for Dantes had inspired him to commit the early betrayal that forever alters the lives of the two lovers. He pressures Mercedes to marry him instead of waiting for Dantes's return. Although Mercedes considers Ferdinand a friend, she does not love him, and she refuses his offer out of loyalty to Dantes.

Following the elder Dantes's death, Mercedes has no resources; all of Monsieur Dantes's money has been extorted from him by the enemies of his son. Her predicament remains pitiable, for a woman had little choice in the early nineteenth century but to turn to the support of a willing male when left on her own. The threat of destitution forces her to comply with the wicked Ferdinand's demands for her hand in marriage. He rises to power and attains the title of Count de Morcerf, gaining his wealth mostly through yet another betrayal, this time of a Greek official named the Pasha Ali.

Although during her marriage Mercedes gains education and status as well as a son, she remains unhappy and unfulfilled. Her importance to the novel occurs when, years after her marriage to Ferdinand, she alone recognizes the famous Count of Monte Cristo as her first love, Edmond Dantes. Upon discovering that Edmond was the mysterious man who rescued her son, Albert, from kidnapping by bandits in Paris, Mercedes decides to help Dantes by keeping his secret. Her loyalty in not revealing the Count's true identity redeems her as a character, even though she has been forced to consort with Dantes's enemies. She shows her enduring love for Dantes when she convinces Albert not to engage the Count in a duel.

Mercedes's later abandonment of her husband when she learns of his evil actions further redeems her, as does her eventual return to the elder Dantes's house. In this place where she had spent years caring for an old man while yearning for his son, now forever lost to her, Mercedes spends the last part of her life in prayerful isolation.

See also: The Count of Monte Cristo; Dantes, Edmond; Mondego, Ferdinand

References: Campbell, 1974; Campbell, 1988; de Rougemont, 1983; Grierson, 1974; Hulme, 1974; Spurr, 1972

HEYWARD, MAJOR DUNCAN

Like the other characters in James Fenimore Cooper's most popular historical romance novel, *The Last of the Mohicans* (1826), Major Duncan Heyward is a stereotypical character. His presence in the nonstop adventure story that takes place in the American West of the eighteenth century serves as a reminder of the chivalric heroes from the romance tradition upon which Cooper bases his plot. Heyward is clean-cut, dashing, brave, and always ready to defend the honor of his two

female charges, Cora Munro and her sister Alice. Although not the novel's hero, Heyward is an admirable figure in his army uniform as he participates in the French and Indian War (1754–1963) that forms a backdrop for the novel. Termed "manly" by the novel's narrator, the major may always be counted upon to retain a cool head when confronting danger. His skills in manners parallel those in battle, making him a perfect example of the gentlemanly warrior and an excellent contrast to the Indians in the novel, who are portrayed intentionally by Cooper as "uncivilized savages," and even to the rough-edged scout and hero, Hawkeye. It should be stated, however, that Cooper did not necessarily view what he saw as the Indians' natural state as a negative. In many instances his Indians appear less "savage" than the whites who ravished Indian territory. Those Indians shaped as villains by Cooper generally reflected the influence of unsavory white settlers.

His role of escort to the two Munro sisters as they travel between Fort Edward and Fort William Henry proves a bit of an embarrassment when he discovers that their Huron Indian guide, Magua, leads them in a circle in preparation for an Indian ambush of their group. When the novel's true heroes, Hawkeye and the Mohican Indian Chingachgook, come to their rescue, Heyward is intelligent enough to submit to their instructions; a good soldier, he recognizes a qualified leader. Throughout the remainder of the story, Heyward follows the suggestions of the western scout and his Indian friend, to his own and the women's benefit.

In addition to fulfilling the male romantic role in the story, Heyward acts as a mouthpiece for several of Cooper's themes, most notably that of racism. Early in the story, he joins Cora and Alice in assessing the countenance of Uncas, nephew to Chingachgook, who excels in what Heyward terms "natural qualities" that ennoble any man. When the Indian is connected to the beautiful and heroic aspects of nature in a positive manner, Cora reminds Heyward to remember the dark coloring of Uncas's skin as he praises him. The reason behind the embarrassing silence that follows her remarks will later become clear during a conversation between Heyward and Cora's father. Her father misinterprets an innocent remark by Heyward as a derogatory comment on Cora's mixed heritage, at which point the reader learns she is a product of miscegenation. Although Heyward was not privy to this information, he serves as a springboard into the subject of racism through these remarks.

When his romantic intentions toward Alice Munro surface, Heyward's role shifts to that of prime protector of her well-being. In this role, Heyward participates valiantly in various skirmishes with Indians and against environmental elements, representing the many brave individuals who risked their lives to bring civilization to the American West. The perfect amalgam of manly virtues, Heyward attains victory in battle as well as love and remains an important character in Cooper's novel.

See also: The Black Experience in America, 1600–1945; Cooper, James Fenimore; Hawkeye; The Last of the Mohicans; Munro, Alice; Munro, Cora; Violence; War

References: Barker, 1996; Budick, 1996; Campbell, 1949, 1968; "Cooper, James Fenimore," 1986; Frye, 1976; Price, 1983; Wimsatt, 1974

HIGGINS, HENRY

Henry Higgins makes a delightful, if acerbic, protagonist for George Bernard Shaw's play *Pygmalion,* first produced in 1913. His character type, the strong masterful myopic male who considers himself the "creator" of a successful female, appears in various forms throughout romantic fiction. The character of Higgins finds basis in the mythical sculptor-king Pygmalion, who creates a statue of the perfect woman and names it Galatea, represented in Shaw's drama by Eliza Doolittle. When the king falls in love with his statue, Aphrodite breathes life into Galatea, creating a human with whom Pygmalion may share romance and life. Even though the conclusions of the two stories differ greatly, presenting a continuing problem for sentimental readers of Shaw's work, the plots remain similar in many ways.

Shaw called his tale a "romance," meaning it contains the romantic aspect of transformation through Eliza's "betterment." But audiences have long misinterpreted the term, insisting that Eliza and Henry reach a happy-ever-after relationship. Even Shaw's "sequel," a narrative in which Eliza marries Freddy Eynsford Hill, has had little success in convincing audiences that Higgins and Eliza remain worlds apart both philosophically and physically. Readers should pay more close attention to Higgins's statement that the only way

of escaping trouble in life is to kill things. He believes happiness to be related to improvement, whereas Eliza wishes for shared passion.

Higgins, a phonetician or language expert, discovers Eliza, his future "creation," on the streets of London. Although a lower-class working girl relegated to selling flowers on the street, Eliza aspires to one day work as a clerk in a flower shop. Her heavy cockney accent, however, hints at her low origins, preventing the realization of her dream. When the arrogant Higgins brags to fellow phonetician Colonel Pickering that he can transform the "gutter snipe" through proper speech in only three months, Eliza hears him. Mistaking Higgins's intentions, Eliza states repeatedly that she is a "good girl" who will not be used by nefarious males. The two confirmed bachelors depart for Higgins's house, but Eliza appears the following day to take Higgins up on his claim, offering to pay for his services.

Thus begins Higgins's "work" on his "project." He promises that Eliza will pass for a duchess due solely to her vastly improved speech. This belief allows Higgins to act as a mouthpiece for Shaw, who publicly affirmed his belief in the importance of proper English pronunciation. In the play's preface, Shaw states that "it is impossible for an Englishman to open his mouth without making some other Englishman hate or despise him for it." Shaw's "hero" remains the man who can reform England's speech, and Higgins fits that heroic requirement.

It is important for readers to keep in mind the fact that Higgins does represent a deity of sorts. This places him above everyday human concerns, such as that for Eliza's future. Although Higgins hears several other characters express concern over what Eliza will be capable of doing following the conclusion of the "project," he summarily dismisses those concerns. A true scientist, Higgins focuses on success and achievement without considering the possibility that his experimentation might well promote human suffering.

When his success results in Eliza's inability to return to the street or work in a flower shop, he remains totally oblivious to the problem he has caused. Higgins lifts her above the lower class by teaching her proper pronunciation, but correct speech represents only the outward trappings of the upper class. Therefore, he renders Eliza unfit for either class. As a god, he alters a human life and presumes Eliza will be happy with that change, having given no thought to her future. Nor can he see that Eliza desires to share a loving relationship with him. He explains to his mother that Eliza may now "go her own way" due to "all of the advantages" he has bestowed upon her. When Mrs. Higgins attempts to explain that he has given Eliza the manners and habits disqualifying "a fine lady from earning her own living without giving her a fine lady's income," he misses the point altogether, insisting he can find her some "light employment." His inability to reach an understanding of the situation guarantees that Higgins remains a flat character.

The conflict in Higgins's relationship with Eliza represents the age-old dichotomy of rationality versus imagination. For all his professional visionary achievement, Higgins remains peculiarly blind to human emotions. His work consumes all of his passion, and he believes the goal of life is self-improvement and achievement. Eliza wishes only for love and companionship and is insulted by Higgins's invitation to live with him and Pickering like three old happy bachelors. She is dissatisfied by his explanation that the important point about manners is "having the same manner for all human souls" because one is as good as another. Eliza reacts by explaining that she does not want to be equal to everyone else in his eyes but to be someone special.

Higgins will, as he states, go his way and do his work without caring what might happen to either himself or Eliza. But enthusiastic audiences will likely continue their transformation of Shaw's Higgins into a hero who develops a love for Eliza Doolittle.

See also: Doolittle, Eliza; *Pygmalion;* Romance; Shaw, George Bernard

References: Demastes and Kelly, 1996; DiBattista and McDiarmid, 1996; Drabble, 1995; "Shaw, George Bernard," 1993; Shires, 1992

HONEYCHURCH, LUCY

E. M. Forster's humorous romance, *A Room with a View* (1908), offers a lighthearted look at the sexual mores of Victorian Age England, adopting as its heroine the enigmatic Lucy Honeychurch. As her surname indicates, Lucy represents a combination of both the sweet and the staid. She wishes to observe strict Victorian edicts against passionate relationships between men and women, based in part on the rules of organized religion. Simultaneously, she nurses a secret desire

to enjoy the sweet ecstasy of total immersion in those forbidden passions. Unlike many Victorian romance heroines who remain stifled and unfulfilled in loveless marriages, evolving into little more than stick figures established as representatives of the "good" Victorian woman, Lucy achieves her goal of true love.

Forster uses many basic romantic elements as he portrays Lucy's quest for marital bliss. She begins her search with a journey from her native England to Italy. This warm, Mediterranean country offers a fine setting to frame Lucy's newly aroused passions. She travels with a comic guide/helper figure in the character of her cousin Charlotte. In her unfortunate position as an old maid, Charlotte acts as cautionary tale to the lovely Lucy, providing living proof of what might happen to a young woman who passively waits for romance to claim her. Charlotte symbolizes the puritanical attitudes often closely associated with Victorian times. When the two women meet George Emerson and his father, also traveling in Italy, Lucy feels an attraction to George. She denies her attraction, however, because George does not behave as the stereotypical Victorian male should. He is neither fussy nor "correct," acting more on instinct instead of depending on reason. When he kisses Lucy in an Italian field of wildflowers, she secretly enjoys the experience but pretends to be insulted, playing the role of a well-bred woman.

Cousin Charlotte observes the kiss and begins to counteract her own Victorian training when she shares the scene with a female writer of sensationalistic romances. That kiss will come back to haunt Lucy in the form of a scene in the novelist's next book. This would not present much of a problem, except that when Lucy returns to England, she becomes engaged to another man, a prig named Cecil Vyse. In representing the prototypical Victorian idea of a cultured and severe male, Cecil's repressed demeanor allows him to act as a foil to the openly expressive George. A love triangle is formed, and Lucy must choose between the two men. Although she pretends to have forgotten George, she cannot help comparing Cecil's cold, unsatisfying, and formal approach to romance to that of the warm-blooded George. The contrast between the two is emphasized when Cecil procures and reads aloud from the very romance novel that captures for eternity Lucy and George's kiss. Cecil's surname, like

Lucy's, symbolizes a certain aspect of his personality; he possesses a mean streak that causes him to enjoy the discomfort of others, particularly if he is the cause of that discomfort.

George and his father move into the village close to the Honeychurch home, ironically on Cecil's recommendation when he meets the two by chance in an art museum. George professes his love to Lucy, but she rejects him, not from any inherent dislike on her part, but because it is the thing to do, according to her judgmental society. The ever-passionate George exposes his poet's soul when he explains to Lucy that Cecil does not love her; he only desires her as a beautiful object. Still denying to herself that she loves George, Lucy unconsciously repeats his speech to Cecil as she breaks their engagement.

True to comic form, Lucy must stumble over her Victorian morality several times before she at last recognizes and acts upon the love she feels for George. With help issuing from some surprising sources, such as stuffy Cousin Charlotte, Lucy at last admits she loves George.

Forster engages repressed Victorian practices with good humor, preserving the best of the characters' beliefs while emphasizing the folly of the repression they may have caused. Lucy serves his purposes well, becoming a fully realized character as she defeats society in its attempt to dictate her behavior and her emotions.

See also: Forster, E. M.; *A Room with a View;* Victorian Age

References: Albright, 1997; Ellem, 1971; Forster, 1956; Lago, 1995; McDowell, 1977; Price, 1983; Stone, 1966; Trivedi, 1979

THE HORSEMAN ON THE ROOF

Jean Giono's novel *The Horseman on the Roof* stands as a fine example of a medieval romance set in the age of Napoleon. Originally published in 1951 as *Le Hussard sur le toit* and in English in 1954, the book contains all the aspects of classical romance, including a chivalrous knight and a damsel in distress.

Instead of battling mythical beasts, the novel's hero, Angelo Pardi, fights Austrians invading his homeland of Italy and the horrific cholera plague while he is in exile in France. His code of honor, love for battle, devotion to his charge, and sense of humor mark him as a descendent of his medieval brothers in chivalry. The novel's female protagonist, Pauline, the Marquise de Theus, also

reflects medieval romance values. She holds her marriage dear, values courage and honor, and, although she needs Angelo's help, plays a most active part in her journey to reunite with her husband. Angelo greatly admires her skill on horseback and with firearms and considers her not just a woman in need but also a fellow adventurer. He volunteers to escort her to her husband in the south of France on his way to Italy with funds to support the Italian rebel cause. The author contributes an entertaining additional element of suspense by refusing to reveal Pauline's identity and aristocratic standing until the novel's conclusion. For much of the novel, she is referred to simply as "the young woman."

The novel opens with the attempts of Angelo, an Italian political refugee hiding in France, to reunite with his fellow patriot and foster brother. Angelo must remain in hiding due to his having killed the Austrian Baron Swartz in a duel. His own peers, members of the Italian *carboneri* (civilian police), sanction him as irresponsible for participating in a duel rather than simply assassinating the relatively insignificant political figure. Angelo's choice to fight face-to-face remains an important symbol of his honor, and he readily admits his sentimentality for the ancient chivalrous code. This same code causes him to help a Frenchman in treating cholera victims and later a nun in cleansing the dead in preparation for burial, which most others avoid out of fear of everything and everyone associated with the plague.

Before coming to France, Angelo served in the Italian military with the rank of colonel, a rank purchased for him by his mother, the Duchess Ezzia Pardi. Interestingly enough, Angelo seems to have inherited his adventurous approach to life from the duchess who, in one letter, urges him to always be foolhardy, explaining that is the only way of gaining pleasure in life. Her words help develop Angelo's characterization when she encourages him to engage in "crazy" activities to help overcome his three natural passions: melancholy, gravity, and solitude.

Angelo's monologues throughout the novel reveal much about his attitude toward life and provide some of the most entertaining parts of the narrative. Giono places his character in hiding on the rooftops of the French town of Manosque in order to allow his musing upon his new perspective of life. Unhorsed and hiding from an angry mob who seeks to kill him, Angelo peers down at the world and expounds upon the meaning of life and humankind's place in it. Highly romanticized, his ideas are, as the narrator points out, unoriginal and even false but sincere to a fault.

Although his aristocratic social position allowed him the right to be scornful of others, he takes his soldiering duties seriously. He regards the ideals of liberty as the religious regard the Virgin Mary and is described by the narrator as one of those men who will remain at the age of twenty-five for his first fifty years. All of these aspects legitimatize his motivations to behave in a chivalrous manner and so support his eligibility to be a knight. They also act in parallel with Pauline's attitude toward the aristocratic position she inherits when she marries a marquis. Born into a lower social and economic class as the daughter of a country doctor, she effects none of the airs expected of the powerful wealthy.

The novel presents much in the way of adventures, as Angelo escapes death on several occasions. While living on the rooftops of Manosque, he enjoys the company of a cat, a mythic symbol of the many lives with which Angelo seems blessed. Possessing near-magical qualities of survival, Angelo triumphs in multiple armed skirmishes and over his exposure to cholera with no ill effects. And with Pauline, he eludes the French military who would prevent their travel.

In addition to the abundant action of the novel, the characterizations of both Angelo and Pauline enjoy some depth, although neither experiences any change that could act to classify them as dynamic characters. As symbolic romance figures, they share no physical involvement. They exult in other passions, those of faith, honor, and the joy growing from a shared adventure. Giono's tale remains a romance in the traditional sense of the word: a story of adventure, of a knight coming to the aid of a virtuous lady, and of the transformative effect of ideals such as loyalty and honor. When Angelo returns Pauline to her husband's castle, he has never attempted to take advantage of her position as the stereotypically helpless female. Even when he rips her clothes away to massage her freezing limbs in order to promote circulation when Pauline suffers an attack of cholera, Angelo's chaste chivalrous intentions remain intact.

As Angelo says of himself, he is a character who sees things as if through a magnifying glass;

he always does ten times too much. He tries to convince himself to accept the fact that sometimes ordinary things occur; he should not constantly pursue big ideas, describing those ideas with big words, and imagining majestic enterprises when small movements will do. But Angelo exists in a magnified world of romance, no place for a simple man and a perfect environment for the man who describes himself, like Angelo does, as doubled, tripled, centupled. All the better that he should join forces with an adventuress who would sacrifice her own life before that of her horse; these two remain apt soulmates.

See also: Chivalry; de Theus, Pauline; Pardi, Angelo; Quest; Romance
References: Campbell, 1974; Campbell, 1988; Grierson, 1974; Hulme, 1974; Radway, 1991; Raphael, 1996

THE HOUSE OF THE SPIRITS

A romantic epic covering three generations of the South American Trueba family, Isabel Allende's *The House of the Spirits* (1982, trans. 1985) focuses on themes of mysticism, politics, love, war, and family relationships. This novel gained popularity in South America before appearing in translation in 1985 to an enthusiastic reception from English-speaking audiences. Incorporating elements of magic realism while featuring the harsh realities present in a country undergoing revolution, Allende opens her novel at the beginning of the twentieth century. The specific setting of the novel is never identified, emphasizing the fact that the characters could be placed in any nation suffering upheaval. Readers familiar with Allende, however, will want to identify the setting as Chile, the author's own home for many years and the country where her uncle Salvador Allende, while president, was assassinated during political riots.

As the story begins, Clara del Valle, whose first name reflects her clairvoyant talents, predicts a death in the family. What follows acts as foreshadowing for future members of the Trueba family. Clara's father, Severo, a political candidate, receives poisoned alcohol in the guise of a gift. His beautiful eldest daughter, Rosa the Beautiful, drinks the poison meant for her father and dies. In this manner, fate warns the family that political dispute will bring misery to future innocents, members of their own family, as well as to members of the public at large. After Clara hides in

Meryl Streep and Jeremy Irons appeared as Clara del Valle and Esteban Trueba in a 1994 film version of Isabel Allende's The House of the Spirits, *a romantic epic focusing on themes of mysticism, politics, love, war, and family relationships.* (Photofest)

order to witness Rosa's autopsy, which takes place on the family's kitchen table, she stops speaking and remains mute for nine years.

The first person narrator who occasionally intrudes to help lead readers through an otherwise third person narration is Clara's future husband, Esteban Trueba. Allende uses Esteban's voice to allow readers insight into his character. In addition, at the novel's conclusion when Esteban's granddaughter, Alba, assumes his narrative duties, readers understand the close connection between those two characters. The early narration establishes Esteban as a man of tempestuous temperament who experiences an overwhelming rage and lust sparked by the loss of Rosa the Beautiful, the girl he intended to marry. He later marries Clara but never fully accepts the loss of Rosa, who becomes in his mind a monument of perfection. Although Clara eventually becomes his passion, it is a passion that rankles as well as tempts him. His uncontrollable sexual appetite leads him to the beds of many women and eventually separates him emotionally and physically from Clara as well as from their daughter, Blanca.

Blanca will fall into a forbidden love with Pedro Tercera García, the son of Esteban's peasant foreman. Although Esteban engages peasant women in sexual abandon, his harsh double standard will not allow him to accept his daughter's loving relationship with a member of the same group he so abuses. The repercussions of Esteban's sins of passion, both for love and for revenge, will eventually wreak havoc on his family. Esteban's lack of control remains his fatal flaw, and, like other tragic heroes, he will suffer mightily for it. The only positive result of his various affairs is the lifelong friendship he forms with Tránsito Soto, a prostitute who will rescue Esteban and his family in his old age.

Clara and Esteban establish a family in far from normal circumstances. He builds her a beautiful mansion, but she remains incapable of completing the household chores due to her sensitivity and distraction. Her sensuality provokes Esteban, who fears he will never possess her as he wishes; she seems to belong to a world of apparitions. In contrast to Esteban's rough ways, Clara possesses the soul of an artist, and her journals, in which she records the story of her life, allow Allende to emphasize the importance of art and its eternal quality.

Esteban's sister, Férula, joins Esteban and Clara as housekeeper and as nurse to the couple's first child, Blanca. An unmarried woman with a strict religious sensibility, she also develops a terrific passion for Clara, whom she enjoys treating like a child, even bathing her. Férula remains as obsessive about her practice of religion as Esteban is regarding politics, and both obsess over Clara. In time, Esteban's irrational jealousy drives Férula from their home and to an eventual death in isolation. Her spirit later appears before the entire Trueba family.

When Blanca is a young girl, Clara decides to accompany Esteban to his ranch, Tres Marías. The workers fear Clara's powers, but they accept her because she seems to have worked a magical alteration in Esteban, their *patrón*. They all appreciate his kinder demeanor and the fact that he no longer rapes women in the fields. Before long Clara ceases her visionary activities. Instead she deals with more earthly matters, voicing the political interests of her dead mother in an attempt to convince the peasants to live more humane lives. When she urges men not to beat their wives, however, they find this a curious suggestion, and no one takes her political visions as seriously as they had her supernatural.

During this first visit to the ranch by Clara and Blanca, a new aspect of love is introduced when Blanca first encounters Pedro. Their affection remains doomed from the beginning due to their difference in social status. Because Blanca is the daughter of the wealthy *patrón,* marriage to Pedro is impossible. Their relationship resembles that of other famous romantic couples caught up in a love forbidden by their culture, such as Heathcliff and Cathy from Emily Brontë's *Wuthering Heights* (1847).

Eventually the Truebas return to the city because of concern about Clara's second pregnancy. She again descends into silence, and Esteban comes to understand that his wife's silence is her last refuge. This allows Allende's emphasis on and inversion of a traditionally feminist theme. Feminist critics of literature stress the oppressive effect of silence inflicted upon women by men, but Clara voluntarily claims silence as a kind of self-protection, thus drawing power from a traditional male weapon against women. Her

recurrent visions disturb the Trueba family, as do the groups of spiritualists, artists, and charity cases who congregate in the big house.

Like Clara's father, Esteban establishes a political career, becoming an arch-conservative defending the rights of the wealthy against the wrath of political revolutionaries who represent the working class. Clara predicts correctly the birth of twin boys, and Esteban flies into a rage when she tells him she will name the sons Jaime and Nicolás. He protests that the names come from neither his nor Clara's family. When Clara explains that she does not want to continue to reuse names that might cause confusion in the notebooks she keeps that contain her life, Allende brings the act of writing into focus as a historical, as well as creative, act.

Esteban slips back into his old ways by attending the local whorehouse, where he meets his old friend, Tránsito. Because Esteban supplied her with the seed money to establish her own brothel, she feels indebted to him and willingly spends the night with her former *patrón*. Although prostitutes traditionally occupy a position of low social status, Allende elevates Tránsito through her use of imagination and intellect. Her comparison to a bird remains apt, as the caged bird has long been recognized in feminist literary analyses as symbolic of repressed women. But again, Allende inverts a popular theme because Tránsito will be caged by no one; she is the bird who has escaped the cage of economic depression and dependence on the charity of men to achieve freedom.

Clara's clairvoyance intensifies again, and she is described as flying like an airplane, unattached to land, as she consults various religions and spirits in search of God. The twins mature into vastly different people. Jaime proves true to his solitary personality by becoming a doctor who cares for the poor, much to Esteban's dismay, whereas Nicolás adopts the approach of the playboy, mimicking his father. At almost the center of the book, while Blanca, Clara, and Esteban are visiting the ranch, an earthquake occurs that serves as a portent of changes in the Truebas' comfortable lifestyle. Protected by class and status, Esteban is allowed no special privilege by nature, and he suffers disabling injuries, reducing him to an invalid who must be cared for by others. Clara also undergoes a role change, as she takes charge of physical arrangements for the first time ever. Pedro, still a ranch hand, takes advantage of the *patrón*'s convalescence to bring revolutionary pamphlets onto the ranch that urge the peasants to rebel. Blanca learns the art of pottery from Pedro's aging father and so becomes the second artist in the family. She and Pedro meet secretly for many months, but she knows they can never marry.

From this point onward, the plot pushes relentlessly toward a resolution that seems to uphold the old axiom regarding the fall of the mighty. Esteban's physical injuries heal, but he undergoes a series of losses and misfortunes that serve to balance the undeserved good fortune of his youth. His strident anti-Communist political stance acts as a wedge between himself and Jaime, now the confidant of a Socialist leader known as "the Candidate," for whom Jaime remains willing to sacrifice his life. Esteban's public conflict mirrors his private turmoil; in a highly tense scene following his discovery of Blanca's clandestine meetings with a stranger she will not identify, he strikes Clara. Clara vows never to speak to him again, removes her wedding ring, and resumes her maiden name. In her departure with the pregnant Blanca, she forges the bond uniting the three generations of Trueba females that will give Blanca, later forced into a loveless marriage by her father, and eventually Alba, Blanca's daughter, the will to survive life's pain and humiliation. Esteban's fury drives him to discover Pedro's hiding place with the help of a young boy, Esteban García, who is in reality Esteban's grandchild from one of his many youthful sexual encounters. Although he stops short of killing Pedro, Esteban chops off some of the young man's fingers, a grave injury because Pedro is a musician. More important, he abuses the young Esteban, who determines to extract his own future revenge against the Truebas.

With Clara's eventual death, Esteban suffers the torment of an irreplaceable loss. A revolutionary coup leaves no member of the Trueba clan untouched. A severe blow to Esteban occurs when his treasured Alba, a grandchild meaning more to him than any of his own children, is kidnapped by revolutionaries led by the wicked Esteban García. Stripped of his political power and wealth, Esteban must humble himself to seek the help he needs to recover the remnants of his family. While imprisoned, Alba suffers for her grandfather's actions at the vindictive hands of García. She depends for her very life upon Clara's

spirit, which nurtures her through a physical and emotional torture that would otherwise have caused her death.

True to her name, which translates as "white," symbolizing purity, Alba eventually heals the wounds of revenge suffered by her family. Allende offers closure to the novel's drama when Alba takes up her grandmother's journals. The story concludes with the first few words of Clara's tale, symbolizing the fact that lives may end, but their artistic products, particularly the stories they tell, live forever in the telling.

See also: Allende, Isabel; del Valle, Clara; Trueba, Esteban

References: Baldock, 1994; Bridgwood, 1986; "Isabel Allende," 1997; Jenkins, 1994; Tawse, 1997; Zamora and Faris, 1995

HUGO, VICTOR

Victor-Marie Hugo, considered by many to be the most important of the nineteenth-century French romantic novelists, was born on February 26, 1802, in Besancon, France. He was the third son of his beloved mother, Sophie Trebuchet, a woman conservative by nature who had married

Victor-Marie Hugo is considered by many to be the most important of the nineteenth-century French romantic novelists. (Library of Congress)

a soldier, Joseph Leopold Hugo. Sophie told her son stories of his heroic but physically absent father, an accomplished man who attained the rank of general. Victor moved about with his mother as a child, ostensibly following his father, who campaigned in the Napoleonic Wars, but most likely because Sophie wanted to be near General Victor Lahorie, her lover and Victor's godfather. His parents separated when he was sixteen years old.

Hugo first showed his writing talent in a Paris preparatory school, where he won prizes for poetry and helped found a literary magazine to which he contributed. The magazine would fail in 1821, the year in which his mother died. His first recognized writing appeared in the form of verses written on the assassination of a nephew of King Louis XVIII, the Duc de Berri. The king recognized Hugo with a personal gift and would later grant him an annual royal pension of 3,000 francs, relieving the poet's abject poverty. Hugo's future as a writer became secure.

He continued his success with a poem celebrating the coronation of Charles X, earning Hugo the title of Chevalier of the Legion d'Honneur at the young age of twenty-three. Married to Adele Foucher, Hugo enjoyed his family, one that eventually produced four children. In 1827 he wrote what would be known as his manifesto of romanticism, the *Préface de Cromwell*. His early writings reflected his mother's conservative influence, but his later great works he would shape after the interests of his politically outspoken father. Hugo's support of the crown wavered during the period 1828–1830, when a dispute over Napoleonic titles challenged his political beliefs. His play *Hernani* (1830) achieved an important position for him among the Romantics because it shattered the artificial rules of French drama. The play sparked vigorous audience discussion and disputes during its more than one hundred performances. While writing for the theater, Hugo met Juliette Drouet, an actress who served as his mistress for the next fifty years. She would be one of many, but the only one whose attentions remained lifelong.

Hugo's career reached full stride with his novels. A prolific writer, he is said to have written one hundred lines of verse or twenty pages of prose each morning. His work included *Notre-Dame de Paris* (1831) (*The Hunchback of Notre*

Dame), an often-dramatized work that still captures the imagination of reading and theater audiences more than 150 years after its publication. He wrote in 1832 the drama *Le Roi s'amuse* (*The King's Diversion*), a work upon which Giuseppe Verdi later based his opera *Rigoletto*. By age thirty, Hugo claimed the reputation of France's greatest living writer and was created a peer of France in 1845 by Louis-Philippe. Although his daughter's death in 1843 caused a ten-year cessation of writing, Hugo began in 1845 to write the novel *Les Misérables* (*The Unfortunate Ones*), a work featuring the struggle of humanity against its own evil.

Although he served as a supporter of Napoleon II in his office of deputy in the National Assembly, with the fall of Louis-Philippe in 1848, Hugo suffered disillusionment. This time, the challenge to his beliefs shaped him into an outspoken advocate for social political issues. His interest in education for the masses and social injustice made him a premier humanist of his age. In 1852, when Louis-Napoleon declared himself Emperor Napoleon III, Hugo joined those at the barricades, later becoming an exile in Brussels and then Guernsey. His writings reflected his political proclivities, and in 1859, he rejected amnesty, refusing to return to Paris. One story regarding Hugo is that following his submission to his publisher in 1861 of the first volume of *Les Misérables,* a novel showcasing his sympathy for the French masses, he sent a telegram to his publisher bearing only the following message: "?" Supposedly, the publisher replied, "!"

With the fall of Napoleon III to the Prussians in 1870, Hugo returned triumphant to Paris, where he enjoyed election to the National Assembly. In 1871 Hugo was in Brussels following the death of his son, where crowds identified him with the excesses of the short-lived Paris Commune. Although Hugo had never expressed full support for the group, the mob attacked his dwelling, breaking windows and shouting derogatory phrases. Expelled by the Belgian government, Hugo returned to Paris.

Until he suffered a slight stroke in 1871, Hugo continued to write with much vigor. On his eightieth birthday, he enjoyed a celebration staged by all of France that included a procession and cheering crowds encircling his Paris home. Although Hugo requested a simple funeral, when he died in 1885 his body lay in state beneath the

Arc de Triomphe; the funeral procession required six hours to pass by.

See also: The Hunchback of Notre Dame; Les Misérables
References: Brombert, 1986; Charlton, 1984; Hugo, 1984; "Les Misérables: Victor Hugo," 1997; Lovejoy, 1974; Masters-Wicks, 1994

THE HUNCHBACK OF NOTRE DAME

Victor Hugo's Gothic romance, *The Hunchback of Notre Dame* (1831), first printed in France as *Notre-Dame de Paris,* contains every element necessary to an exciting romance tragedy. The dark and foreboding cathedral offers a mysterious Gothic setting; characters include a beautiful heroine, an evil sorcerer, and an ironic monster/hero; themes include magic, love, death, and violence; and love acts to convert the beastly hunchback to a more human figure.

As the leading writer in the French Romantic movement, Hugo gained fame for his realistic shaping of characters so compelling that they have become classics in literature. He supported fellow romantic writers such as Englishmen Sir Walter Scott and George Gordon, Lord Byron, in their fight for a literary freedom that departed from conservative classicist ideals. His highly representative characters symbolize many of those virtues and vices highlighted in allegorical literature, yet remain totally human through their individual faults and strengths. Hugo uses Quasimodo, his ugly, humpbacked, bristling hero, to break with tradition in stressing the value of the "lowly" along with that of the elevated "sublime." Although *The Hunchback of Notre Dame* is not an allegory, its tone remains pleasantly didactic as it appeals to readers to reevaluate their own attitudes toward their fellow humans.

Set in fifteenth-century Paris, the novel examines the lives of several individuals whose destinies become intertwined. Supposedly Hugo received inspiration for the novel during a visit

Lon Chaney played the title character in the 1923 film version of The Hunchback of Notre Dame, *Victor Hugo's 1831 Gothic romance of magic, love, death, and violence. (Photofest)*

to the famed cathedral of Notre Dame, where he discovered in an obscure tower wall the carved Greek word for "fate." He adopts as his major theme the powerlessness of humankind to determine their own fortunes. His figures include Esmeralda, the lovely and innocent young Gypsy girl; Claude Frollo, the evil priest; Phoebus de Chateaupers, the handsome young army captain; Gringoire, a poverty-stricken poet; and Quasimodo, a version of the stock dwarf character of romance. The cathedral is such a strong presence in the tale that it can be considered a character in its own right. On the one hand, Notre Dame represents God's grace and sanctuary offered to society's outcasts, such as Quasimodo, and to those it would victimize, such as Esmeralda. Simultaneously it represents God's judgment, demanding eventual atonement from the conniving, like Claude Frollo's scholar-brother, Jehan, and the wicked, like Claude Frollo himself.

With so many male figures and one prominent female, readers anticipate a tangled web of love triangles, spurned love, and unrequited love, and Hugo does not disappoint. Although Esmeralda marries Gringoire, theirs remains a mock union, designed only to rescue the poet from execution by her fellow Gypsies. The "marriage" represents no feelings of love on her part. Gringoire is too foolish to experience true love, but he would enjoy a carnal relationship with Esmeralda. The fact that she is a Gypsy leads him to mistake her for a wanton, but her innocence motivates rejection of his weak bid for a relationship. Her heart belongs instead to the dashing Phoebus, whom the girl envisions as a godlike hero. Her passion goes unrequited, for Phoebus is engaged to a young woman of high status and wants only to use Esmeralda for a brief physical dalliance. The twisted mind of Claude Frollo, having dismissed any remnant of the sacred part of his priestly office long before, motivates his carnal desire for Esmeralda. The priest remains far more diabolical than the poet and the captain, however, because his mad soul seeks not only to seduce Esmeralda but also to possess and control her. Naturally, his declarations of devotion to Esmeralda are rejected, leaving him to desire and celebrate her execution for his own crime. Finally, Quasimodo loves Esmeralda with the only pure devotion of the group. His innocence in such matters matches her own, but his hideous figure repulses her. A

fiercely loyal being, Quasimodo devotes all his fearsome physical strength to her rescue, first from public mobs and eventually from his former master, Claude Frollo.

As Hugo reveals the background of his hero and heroine, marked similarities between the beauty and the beast become evident. Each is raised by a family other than his or her genetic one. Although the lovely Esmeralda is supposedly kidnapped as a toddler in about 1467 from the woman all of Paris knows only as the recluse of Trou aux Rats, the hideous Quasimodo is left on the doorstep of the cathedral. Esmeralda's environment appears to be a nurturing one, despite the lawless lives led by the Parisian Gypsy group. All of Paris regards Esmeralda as a jewel of sorts, and the citizens seem to prize the familiar figure of the dancing girl and her trained goat Djali. Hugo emphasizes the fickleness of what modern readers would term mob psychology when the populace turns on Esmeralda, accusing her of witchery. Quasimodo also has an unusual upbringing by the priest Claude Frollo, one that was devoid of love. Frollo has an unquenchable desire for knowledge, spending all of his time with books and none enjoying human contact. After mastering legitimate learning, his turn to alchemy and a study of the occult drives him insane. Rather than nurturing Quasimodo, the priest trains him as a servant, and the simple-minded hunchback is willing to perform all that Claude Frollo demands. Certain quarters of Paris also know the hunchback well. They hold him in an ironic esteem, causing his election to the office of Prince of Fools during a joint celebration of Epiphany and the impending marriage of the son of Louis XI to Margaret of Flanders. Both Esmeralda and Quasimodo take part in the pageantry; as the "prince," he gains the seat of honor to view her dance performance, and their lives become eternally linked.

The orphaned states of the two main characters are similar to that of Gringoire. Although not a very sympathetic figure, Gringoire adds to Hugo's portrait of an uncaring aristocracy that deals harshly with its citizens and victimizes even children. His father hanged, his mother murdered, the poet was left to wander the streets throughout his childhood. He presents to Esmeralda a litany of jobs for which he found himself unfit; he undertook the position as poet because he could do nothing worthwhile.

Gringoire's claim that all poets are scoundrels echoes the belief of many people of his age. Hugo seems to enjoy the irony of giving to the dullest character the title indicating the most well-developed imagination.

Claude Frollo commands Quasimodo to kidnap Esmeralda, but their attempt fails when Phoebus intervenes, sweeping the girl onto his horse and carrying her to safety. She falls in love with him following this heroic act, but he uses her later simply as entertainment for his fiancée and her friends. Gringoire observes the attempted kidnapping but does not recognize Quasimodo's hooded accomplice as the once-righteous priest. Following this event, Gringoire loses his way within a Parisian slum and is captured by Gypsies, who demand that a female claim him as a husband to prevent his execution. Esmeralda's volunteering for this position offers evidence of her goodness and compassion.

Another example of Esmeralda's admirable traits emerges when Quasimodo is "tried" for keeping company with a witch (Esmeralda) and a sorcerer (Claude Frollo). His punishment results in his being publicly shamed through a whipping at the pillory, which he bravely undergoes, but during which he suffers a tormenting thirst. The priest deserts Quasimodo in his moment of need, and only Esmeralda steps forward to relieve that thirst by offering the hunchback a drink. This creates the slavish loyalty toward Esmeralda that Quasimodo previously reserved for the priest.

A clandestine meeting between Esmeralda and Phoebus drives the voyeuristic Claude Frollo to distraction. When he leaps from his hiding place to stab Phoebus, Esmeralda's fate is sealed. Accused not only of attacking the captain of the king's archers but also of witchcraft, the girl receives a sentence of death. Although she operates under the impression that Phoebus is dead, Esmeralda later learns of his survival. Quasimodo hides her away in Notre Dame, where the girl's innocent virginity establishes her parallel to Mary, mother of Jesus. But Esmeralda abandons her hiding place in order to reunite with Phoebus, even though he has never stepped forward in her defense.

In what follows all the subplots come together. Gringoire is convinced by Claude Frollo to release Esmeralda from her locked hiding place in the cathedral when the king's guard places the church under siege. The poet leads Esmeralda to the cloaked Frollo; when she discovers the identity of the man she thought would act as her savior, she refuses once again his demand that she become his possession. Fleeing Frollo, the girl seeks refuge in the madwoman's cell. Thus, through the coincidence so popular in nineteenth-century romances, Esmeralda is reunited with her mother. But their joy is brief, as she reveals her hiding place and is recaptured when she calls out to Phoebus, who ironically never hears her. Quasimodo completes his life's mission through the murder of his evil master, the necromancer priest, casting him to the stones below as he stands in a tower of the cathedral laughing at Esmeralda's execution. The hunchback proves the only honorable character, and Hugo allows another symbolic marriage in Quasimodo's union with Esmeralda in death. Their skeletons are later discovered among the remains of the executed, he cradling her in his lap.

Quasimodo is the only character in the novel who changes. The conflict caused by his loyalties to both the priest and the girl eventually forces him to make a choice, and in this decision to choose good over bad, readers may discern an epiphany for the hunchback. His deformity allows Hugo's mirroring of the coexistence of the hideous and the beautiful in literature as they often appear in real life. In his position as bell ringer of the cathedral, Quasimodo may be identified with one of its exterior gargoyles—frighteningly ugly and evincing a terrible physical power. But his internal strength and faith make him more akin to the spirituality of the domineering Parisian fortress, the cathedral of Notre Dame.

See also: Beauty and the Beast; Frollo, Claude; Gothic Romance; Quasimodo; Romance; Violence

References: Brombert, 1986; Charlton, 1984; Ellis, 1989; Lovejoy, 1974

HURSTON, ZORA NEALE

Born Zora Lee Hurston on January 7, 1901, in Alabama, this American writer became a seminal figure in American literature, producing poetry, essays, dramas, short stories, and novels. Inspired by black artists such as poets Georgia Douglas Johnson, Bruce Nugent, Jean Toomer, W. E. B. Du Bois, essayist and fiction writer Marita Bonner, and poet Langston Hughes, Hurston would herself serve as inspiration to a later generation of writers.

The work of folklorist and fiction writer Zora Neale Hurston, pictured in the 1950s, was underrated and forgotten for many years, but she would later inspire a whole new generation of writers. (Library of Congress)

At age three, Hurston moved with her family to Eatonville, Florida, north of Orlando, a town she later described as America's first incorporated all-black community, where her father served as a Baptist minister and three-time mayor. She first attended a school founded by former students of Booker T. Washington and continued her education through high school, touring briefly with a Gilbert and Sullivan troupe while serving as maid to the lead singer. When she worked as a waitress in Baltimore, Hurston attended night high school and later began college courses at Howard University in Washington, D.C. She graduated with an associate's degree, majoring in English.

Her writing career began at Howard in 1922 when she contributed poems to *Negro World,* the newspaper of the Universal Negro Improvement Association, and with a short story that appeared in *Opportunity,* a literary journal sponsored by the Urban League. As the winner in a contest sponsored by *Opportunity,* Hurston met poets Langston Hughes and Countee Cullen at an awards dinner. Pursuing an interest in anthropology, she was admitted as the only black student to Barnard College, where she was sponsored by

one of its founders and for whom she worked as a domestic. Studies with anthropologist Franz Boas led to fieldwork in Harlem, further publishing, and a $1,400 research fellowship from the Association for the Study of Negro Life and History. Later Hurston would by chance meet Langston Hughes in Mobile, Alabama, and invite him to travel through the South with her on the way to New York. Although they agreed to collaborate on a writing project, they later terminated their relationship due to hostility over rights to the collaboration.

Hurston's academic interests led her to Haiti and the Bahamas, where she studied local folklore and dialects resulting in the novel *Mules and Men.* The story features a character based on "Big Sweet," an acquaintance she met while researching at a sawmill camp in the Everglades. During 1929 she worked to organize her 95,000 words of stories, including material on religion and the practice of conjuring, and she transcribed a sermon by the Reverend C. C. Lovelace that eventually became part of her first novel, *Jonah's Gourd Vine* (1934). Her novels contain many such autobiographical elements. Scenes of town life in the all-black community featured in her second novel, *Their Eyes Were Watching God* (1937), were doubtless based on her childhood experience in just such a community. Richard Wright would fault her in a review of that novel for the use of "minstrel technique," an approach that, ironically, would garnish her much later fame.

Hurston traveled to Jamaica on a Guggenheim Fellowship in 1936; a renewal of the award also allowed her to return to Haiti. During that visit, she suffered one of many liver and intestinal ailments, perhaps due to local parasites and bacteria. As her publication credits mounted, Hurston was pressured by reviewers to write "social document fiction," incorporating a liberal attitude toward black-white relations, to which she reacted angrily. She later supervised the Negro unit of the Florida Federal Writers' Project, during which time she published a third novel, *Moses, Man of the Mountain* (1939); received an honorary Doctor of Letters from Morgan State College; recorded songs and stories for the Library of Congress; and for one academic year was on the faculty at the North Carolina College for Negroes in Durham, leaving after a dispute with its founder and president. She would marry and divorce twice and end one engagement.

In 1943, while living on a houseboat, Hurston received the $1,000 Anisfield–Wolf Book Award for the best book on race relations for her autobiography, *Dust Tracks on a Road* (1942); as sponsor of the award, the *Saturday Evening Post* featured Hurston on its cover. When accused by the assistant executive secretary of the National Association for the Advancement of Colored People (NAACP) of making vicious comments in order to promote sales of her works, Hurston claimed she was misquoted. The following year she would contribute to the "My Most Humiliating Jim Crow Experience" series in *Negro Digest,* recounting her examination by a medical specialist in a laundry closet, rather than in his office. After Lippincott's rejection of several writing proposals, Hurston contracted with Charles Scribner's Sons in 1947, receiving an advance of $1,000 for her final novel, *Seraph on the Suwanee,* published in 1948.

Following dismissal in 1949 of child molestation charges that brought on a severe depression, Hurston took a job as a maid in an affluent district of Miami. When her identity was discovered, she stated that she was exhausted, "written out," and that she intended to begin a magazine "for and about domestics." She did begin writing again, and in 1951 moved to Eau Gallie, where her beautiful garden became famous. The next five years she lived contentedly, apart from the controversy and difficulty with relationships she seemed to have experienced since her youth. But she encountered problems selling her work, ill health due to drinking impure water, and obesity. She regained notoriety while covering the trial of a black woman, Ruby McCollum, charged with the murder of her lover, a prominent white doctor. Hurston had to appeal to William Bradford Huie, a journalist and well-known southern anti-segregationist, to aid her in gaining permission to interview McCollum. In 1955 she wrote a widely reprinted letter to the Orlando *Sentinel* condemning the 1954 *Brown v. Board of Education* ruling. Hurston criticized the implication that black children could learn only when in the company of whites. Her action gained her the anger of civil rights leaders.

By 1956 one book proposal had been rejected by Scribner's, and Hurston was evicted from her house when her landlord sold it. After receiving an award for "education and human relations" at the Bethune-Cookman College, she became employed at $1.88 an hour filing technical literature, a job she detested, at the Patrick Air Force Base library in Cocoa Beach. Hurston was fired in 1957 by a supervisor who said she was "too well educated." Later she worked as a substitute teacher in a segregated public school for blacks while writing articles on various subjects and pursuing her interest in voodoo and black magic.

Hurston spent the rest of her life in Fort Pierce, occasionally writing for the *Chronicle* and working on a biography of Herod the Great that had occupied her energies for several years. Following a 1959 stroke that left her weak and mentally distracted, Hurston survived with the help of welfare payments that paid for medicine as her condition deteriorated. She refused to contact any family members or friends, following a pattern of many years. Zora Neale Hurston died on January 28, 1960, in the Saint Lucie County Welfare Home. Following a funeral paid for by a collection from local acquaintances, she was buried at the Garden of Heavenly Rest in Fort Pierce in a segregated cemetery and in an unmarked grave.

Hurston published four novels but never a collection of her short stories. The drama on which she collaborated with Langston Hughes, *Mule Bone: A Comedy of Negro Life,* was not published until 1991.

See also: The Black Experience in America, 1600–1945; *Their Eyes Were Watching God;* Woods, Janie Crawford Killicks Starks
References: Carr, 1987; Gilbert and Gubar, 1996g; Graham et al., 1989; Henderson and McManus, 1985; Radway, 1991; Schleiner, 1994; Travitsky, 1990; Wall, 1995

INITIATION/COMING-OF-AGE STORY

See Bildungsroman

IVANHOE

As Sir Walter Scott's most popular novel set in the Middle Ages, *Ivanhoe* (1819) offers a perfect example of the chivalric romance. Featuring two of the most beloved English adventure characters, Robin Hood and Richard the Lion-Hearted, the story set in 1194 boasts all of the elements one expects to find in a tale of chivalry, including knights, damsels in distress, jousting tournaments, and other tests of knightly skill and honor. Although Scott himself did not approve of chivalry and the bloody contests to which its practice led, he created a plot to satisfy anyone who enjoys tales of the knights of old. A lover of history, the author called on his knowledge of the Middle Ages to present a realistic tale, although, like many writers of historical fiction, he does conflate time. Argument continues over the existence of an actual Robin Hood, with reports of such a man hearkening from the century following the one that frames *Ivanhoe*. An additional historical point ignored by Scott is the fact that by the time of Richard the Lion-Hearted, little distinction between the Normans and the Saxons was made. Such points do not, however, diminish the continuing popularity of his novel.

The book's major villain and a Knight Templar, Brian de Bois-Guilbert, appears in its opening as he journeys to the home of Cedric the Saxon. When he loses the way, a stranger claiming to be on a pilgrimage to the Holy Land guides him to the Saxon stronghold. Because Bois-Guilbert represents the Normans, Cedric reluctantly welcomes him into his home as he adheres to the customary behavior toward travel-ers who request shelter. He also invites an elderly Jew, Isaac of York, to spend the night and rest from his journey. Cedric remains important to the story as the father of Wilfred of Ivanhoe, the novel's hero. He also serves as guardian for the beautiful Lady Rowena, who traces her heritage to ancient Saxon royalty. An arranged marriage between Rowena and Athelstane of Coningsburgh has caused Rowena and Ivanhoe great consternation, as they are deeply in love. Thus, Cedric has banished Ivanhoe from his home.

Overhearing Bois-Guilbert plan an ambush on the wealthy Isaac, the pilgrim warns the latter to depart Cedric's home early the following day. This is the second "good deed" on the part of the unidentified stranger, and it confirms for most readers his identity as Ivanhoe. Isaac does as the stranger advises, and both quietly depart for their destination of Ashby de la Zouche the next morning. Ashby will host a tournament held by Prince John, who serves as England's Regent during the absence of his brother, King Richard. Whoever wins the tournament will choose any woman he wishes to be the Queen of Love and Beauty; she will award the prize of passage of arms. This contest is one of three scenes of combat employed by Scott as the climax to each of the three plot sections.

The mysterious pilgrim enters the contest, adopting the title of "Disinherited" that appears on his shield. He challenges Bois-Guilbert to a chivalric contest in which they charge one another on armored horseback. Both men splinter their lances in the first charge, and on the second, Ivanhoe knocks his opponent to the ground with a blow to the helmet. Five additional knights will be vanquished by Ivanhoe, earning for him the title of the tournament victor. For the Queen of Love and Beauty, Ivanhoe names Rowena, perpetuating the theme of forbidden love between these two characters.

Ivanhoe competes again in the following day's tournament, and with the help of a mysterious black knight called the Black Sluggard, he vanquishes three more opponents. Again, he claims the title of champion, and he must remove his helmet to accept the prize of the chaplet from Rowena. This causes him to be recognized as Ivanhoe just before he faints from loss of blood.

Isaac of York, sitting nearby with his daughter Rebecca, agrees with her to nurse Ivanhoe back to health. As they depart Ashby, they attach themselves to Cedric's entourage; the Saxon remains ignorant of the fact that the tourney champion is his son.

Before Isaac and Rebecca arrive at their home with Ivanhoe, they are attacked by a group of Norman knights, including Bois-Guilbert, Maurice de Bracy, and Reginald Front de Boeuf. Imprisoned in de Boeuf's castle, they discover that de Bracy desires Lady Rowena, whereas Bois-Guilbert wants to gain possession of Rebecca. He asks her to convert from her Jewish faith to Christianity so that he might marry her. Help arrives in the form of the Black Sluggard, revealed to be Richard the Lion-Hearted, who has returned home in disguise in order to check up on his brother's rule. Robin Hood appears in this scene to escort the captives to safety in the forest, and this act of derring-do marks the novel's second climactic battle scene. But the rescue has not been entirely successful, for Bois-Guilbert escapes with Rebecca as his captive.

In the next part of the story, the suggestion of magic is introduced, emphasizing the superstition of that early age. When Rebecca is accused of casting a spell on Bois-Guilbert, the Knights Templar sentence her to be burned at the stake as a witch. This allows Scott to include the ancient rule afforded accused women to choose a champion as a defender against the charges. Bois-Guilbert agrees to defend the Templars against whoever steps forward to fight for Rebecca.

On the day of her execution, Rebecca anxiously awaits the arrival of her champion, who finally appears at the third and last call for her defense. The injured and exhausted Ivanhoe appears, beginning the third and final climactic scene of combat. Bois-Guilbert downs Ivanhoe and his horse with his first blow. But Bois-Guilbert falls to the ground himself, supposedly a victim of his own evil passions. Thus, Ivanhoe retains his champion status and also avoids killing another.

King Richard then appears with a band of knights to arrest Rebecca's accusers as traitors. The royal standard is raised in place of the Templar's flag, and Richard claims his throne with Robin Hood as his follower. Rowena is free to marry Ivanhoe following Athelstane's agreement to drop his claim for the lovely young woman. At last convinced that his son is a worthy knight, Cedric agrees to the marriage. As Isaac and Rebecca depart England for Spain, they hope to find a happier life than was offered them in the land of the Normans and Saxons.

In addition to the romantic plot featuring Ivanhoe and Rowena, a subplot focuses on the two symbols of England's rule—Richard and John. Richard parallels Ivanhoe as a noble, heroic character, and their joining forces in battle reinforces their similarities. John, however, represents the evil of an ego so self-absorbed that he cannot properly rule the country. His character parallel is Bois-Guilbert, whose ideas of love are so perverted that they literally kill him. Although Richard and Ivanhoe both participate in battle, they initiate none of the combat. That is done by John and also by Bois-Guilbert, who sparks a minor war by kidnapping Isaac, Rebecca, and Ivanhoe. The support these negative characters give to empty acts of chivalry, based not upon honor but rather upon deceit and self-aggrandizement, allows Scott to voice his disapproval of the idea of chivalry and the often deadly consequences of its practices.

Still, Sir Walter Scott affords readers a view of a period in history to which he is obviously attracted. The romantic ideals that proved tragic in practice could still support an excellent fantasy tale.

See also: Chivalry; Quest; Rebecca, Daughter of Isaac; Rowena, Lady; Scott, Sir Walter; Violence; Wilfred of Ivanhoe

References: Bayley, 1960; Duncan, 1992; Grierson, 1974; Hulme, 1974; Pater, 1974

IYAYI, FESTUS

Festus Iyayi, a radical Nigerian writer, produces novels highlighting the inequities of a situation in which a small group of privileged, wealthy individuals controls and abuses the poverty-stricken laboring class. When he considers gender relations, his works of social commentary focus more on gender inequity than on romance. Relationships between his male and female characters remain tightly controlled by the outside forces of economics and politics, placing all of his main characters in conflict with culture. When romance does develop, it blooms amid cultural chaos. Iyayi strives to mirror the real political and economic situation of Nigeria, revealing class struggle rather than struggles among differing

Nigerian tribes as the cause of its 1968 civil war and current unrest.

Born in 1947 in Benin in southern Nigeria, Iyayi took his place in a family whose tribal membership dictated their possession of farmland. The mixed tribal makeup of his community allowed his early exposure to the Yorubas and the Ibo who worked at iron smelting, glass making, and sewing. His close extended family participated in an oral tradition of storytelling, the importance of which Iyayi realized when he later began his writing career. In various interviews, he has commented upon the effect of being taught as a child in English, a language he did not know until he began school. It acted not only to separate the native population from their natural dialect but also caused the children to consider their own cultures less than worthy.

From 1969 to 1975 Iyayi attended the Kiev Institute of National Economy in the Russian Ukraine, a period of life important to the development of his political ideology. An early experience that shocked Iyayi was his encountering whites cleaning toilets in the Russian airports, a job he had seen only blacks perform while living in Nigeria. The few blacks in Russia experienced discrimination, causing Iyayi to lead a demonstration by black students against the Ministry of Education at the beginning of the 1970s. He graduated with a master of science degree in economics and also with an increased appreciation for the Russian people and Russian literature. Iyayi later earned a doctorate in economics from the University of Bradford in England and married, eventually fathering four children.

Following a stint from 1974 to 1977 as a journalist, Iyayi took a position as an industrial training officer in Nigeria. He attracted attention as an author with his 1979 novel, *Violence,* termed by some critics as the first social realist Nigerian novel. Motivated to write the novel due to his increasing anger at the economic disparity between his country's social classes, Iyayi vividly portrays characters who represent the conflicting groups. In *Violence,* the disreputable rich are represented by a prostitute and a man who gains his fortune from illegal paybacks in his award of government contracts. As its title indicates, the novel features violence as a theme, stressing that only physical and emotional violence can join the rich and the poor. A year after its publication, in 1980,

Iyayi earned an appointment as economics lecturer at the University of Benin in Nigeria.

His radical stance took a more public turn when Iyayi joined the Academic Staff Union of Universities, a group perceived by law enforcement as radical. He served as president of the union's university branch from 1982 to 1986 and later as the national president from 1986 to 1988. His second novel, *The Contract* (1982), featured the greed of those who broker government contracts. The personal chaos that awaits the novel's young protagonist is foreshadowed by the environmental chaos he discovers upon returning home to Nigeria. He quickly assimilates into an economic system that embraces corruption as an institution. One of the first Nigerian authors to use the art of the novel to highlight a perspective based on class, Iyayi repeatedly emphasizes the sad plight of the common Nigerian, stressing socioeconomic stratification rather than tribal affiliation as the true basis for solidarity.

His 1986 novel, *Heroes,* won the Association of Nigerian Authors award in 1987 and the Commonwealth Writers' Prize in 1988. The title remains ironic, as the novel disproves the theory that military generals are heroes. Once again, Iyayi champions the common person, this time represented in the enlisted soldier, proving that the corruption in the top ranks of the military imitates that in the top ranks of government. In his main character, Osimi Iyere, Iyayi shapes a hero not caught up in an existential isolationist quandary like many modern Western fictional heroes but instead acting as a symbol of Nigeria itself. Iyere is a member of the petty bourgeoisie who changes his initially supportive opinion regarding the actions of the Federal government and finds himself identifying with the working class, or proletariat in Marxist terms, rather than with the group holding political and economic power. One shocking scene, in which Federal troops murder Iyere's landlord, who is also the father of his girlfriend Ndudi, is drawn from Iyayi's real-life experience. In 1968, while he attended Higher School, he observed many atrocities perpetrated by Federal troops, including an execution of three men who were shot in close proximity to his school.

In order to question such unfair practices, Iyayi joined, in addition to the union, the Civil Liberties Organisation, and the Committee for the Defense of Human Rights. The union, supporting the needs of the proletariat, finally suffered banishment in 1988, primarily due to Iyayi's persistent radicalism. Iyayi himself was charged with treasonable felony, suffered an invasion of his home by the secret police and their dogs, and lost many of his family's possessions. Subsequently he lost his university position due to "Decree 17," a statement allowing anyone to be fired if the president and authorities believe that action will serve the public interest. Iyayi later worked in business as a private consultant.

No further writing of note by Iyayi has appeared. The disastrous Nigerian economic plunge during the 1980s may account for his silence. Many intellectuals deserted the country over the decade following the crash, and those who did not depart became caught up in the economic and cultural chaos, much like that depicted in Iyayi's novels. Iyayi himself may have fallen victim to the diminished creative climate that followed Nigeria's upset. In *Heroes,* the author advocates the creation of a "third army," one designed to combat ideological misconceptions and enable differing tribes to recognize their common needs and interests. His attack through his art upon Nigeria's dominant ideology acts as a warning to the Nigerian common person, regardless of tribal affiliation.

See also: Heroes; Iyere, Osimi
References: Chréacháin, 1991; Maduakor, 1997; Udumukwu, 1996; Wendt, 1990

IYERE, OSIMI

Osimi Iyere, the protagonist of Nigerian writer Festus Iyayi's political novel *Heroes* (1986), represents a nontraditional romance hero. As one of Nigeria's political activists, Iyayi offers not the typical self-absorbed, angst-ridden Western romance hero but one more closely identified with Nigeria itself. Iyere acts not in isolation but as a part of a political movement represented at one extreme by the powerful Federal troops and at the other by members of the various indigenous Nigerian tribes. The setting is the 1968 Nigerian civil war.

Iyere begins his quest for the truth by first supporting the political ideology of the Nigerian government. An intellectual committed to identifying and then changing the causes of Nigerian unrest, Iyere represents the emergence of a petty bourgeois conscience. At first prejudiced against the attitudes of members of the various tribes, the

Ibo, the Hausas, and the Yorubas, Iyere discovers that class, rather than tribal, differences support the Nigerian civil war. This allows his eventual epiphany regarding the importance of revolution and also his capacity to better respect his Ibo girlfriend, Ndudi. This remains important to his development of a social conscience, for as a member of the petty bourgeoisie, Iyere enjoys freedoms and advantages that Ndudi's family cannot. His position of superiority causes him to remain skeptical regarding the places of tribes in a modern Nigeria.

As a cynical political editor for the *Daily News,* Iyere observes the war from a safe perspective. When he moves to the front at Asaba, he becomes acquainted with the common soldier as well as with members of the Federal rank and file. His support for the Federals erodes as he observes firsthand their arrogance and waste, and he begins to question mass killings of both soldiers and tribal members inflicted during the Federal invasion. He begins to develop sympathy for the everyday soldiers, members of the proletariat, or working class. Iyere's change in perspective will eventually help him to achieve success in his quest for the truth. In this way, Iyayi attempts to convince readers to undergo the same alteration.

Iyere's maturity occurs partially as a result of his constant internal struggle, a conflict represented by Iyayi in his character's ongoing mental arguments. The reader listens to Iyere's thoughts as he struggles for meaning in what he observes, a struggle that leads him to identify the faith he placed in the Federals as one based upon false security. He finally rejects his initial acceptance of and identification with the Federals' hollow slogan regarding a unified Nigeria when he observes the soldiers shoot Ndudi's father, also his landlord, in the back. Thus, the story may be considered an initiation/coming-of-age tale for Iyere.

His lovemaking with Salome acts to symbolize Iyere's unsettled ideas regarding romance as he yields to sexual temptation. Just as with his political views, his ideas regarding love must undergo challenge, change, and development before he can construct a solid relationship with Ndudi. Salome's name may be symbolic, as it suggests the biblical temptress complicit in the execution of John the Baptist. Like many heroes engaged in a quest, Iyere finds himself the victim of seduction as he becomes temporarily distracted from his search for a goal. His sexual pleasures remain balanced by the pain and degradation Ndudi experiences when she is raped by representatives of each of the warring factors, two Federals as well as two Biafrans.

Iyere's heroic quest finds symbolic completion at the Asaba bridge. Risking his own life to rescue drowning soldiers, Iyere undergoes a baptism, or renewal of sorts, that allows him to begin life anew when he emerges from the water. He pleads with the soldiers to listen to the truth, that the hatred reflected by war remains based on the personal prejudices and ambitions of political figures.

For all his earnest sympathy, Iyere cannot actually become a part of the proletariat. In his honest effort to know the common soldiers, he identifies with their needs, but the solidarity he desires cannot be achieved at that particular moment in time. The alienation of what may be termed "marginalized groups," meaning those

not in political or economic power, remains inherent to the Nigerian way of life, a way of life in which Iyere's role remains that of the intellectual. When Iyere thinks of a leader of his visionary third army, it is an intellectual like himself, not a member of the lower tribal classes.

Thus, although committed to social change and totally disillusioned by the government's approach to order, Iyere remains ambivalent regarding the common person. His love for Ndudi proves a stabilizing influence in his personal life, but his long-ingrained public image as a member of the intellectual petty bourgeoisie is not one from which he can free himself overnight. He may represent Iyayi's hope for change, but closely connected to that hope is the realization that any change will be a long time in coming.

See also: Heroes; Iyayi, Festus; Ndudi; Violence; War
References: Chréacháin, 1991; Udumukwu, 1996

JAMES, HENRY

During a fifty-year writing career, American writer Henry James produced a large collection of fiction, including novels, novellas, and short stories as well as plays, travel portraits, essays, and autobiography. Born in 1843 in New York City to a prosperous family who lived near Washington Square, James enjoyed the company of several siblings. He was the younger brother of William James, later a celebrated psychologist and philosopher, and older brother to a sister, Alice, a writer who would contribute to the personal narrative genre through her work *Diary*. Henry enjoyed repeated exposure to new ideas because his philosopher-father saw to it that all the children changed schools often. They lived from 1855 to 1860 in various European countries and visited points of cultural interest while enjoying educational experiences in foreign schools and with tutors. James would later incorporate his in-depth knowledge of things European in shaping the plots and characters of his fiction.

Although he attended Harvard to study law, he left after one year to settle on a writing career. By 1864 he had published pieces in *The North American Review, The Nation,* and *The Atlantic Monthly;* the *Monthly* also serialized James's first novel in 1870. James become the first famous American expatriate writer when he moved to Europe in 1875, spending a year in Paris, where he met Ivan Turgenev and many French writers such as Gustave Flaubert and Emile Zola. His interaction with these acclaimed artists permanently affected his outlook on life and his writing, encouraging him to focus on psychological aspects of his characters. By 1876 he had settled in London and would buy a residence later in Rye, Sussex. His immigration from America would be followed by other American writers in short order. Edith Wharton later moved to Paris and became James's friend and correspondent and an author he wrote of with much praise.

Critics separate James's extended career into three stages. In the first he penned realistic works contrasting American and European traditions and the manners that they spawned; this stage produced his famous novella, *Daisy Miller* (1879), and later the novel considered one of his finest works, *The Portrait of a Lady* (1881). Many readers feel that the later novel's main character, Isabel Archer, represents a more mature Daisy Miller. Isabel is a woman who need not die for her beliefs but who will suffer for them all the same. James began outlining *The Portrait of a Lady* in 1878, the same year he began an intensive study of works by Nathaniel Hawthorne, an author who, along with George Eliot, Turgenev, and others, has been suggested as an influence on *Portrait*.

First serialized in the British publication *Macmillan's Magazine* (October 1880), *The Portrait of a Lady* also appeared one month later in *The Atlantic Monthly.* When the story appeared in book form in November 1881, it was in two different versions, one American, one European. With this novel, James wanted to reach the challenge set for him by his brother William to write "bigger" stories. *Daisy Miller* and *Portrait* both feature young, idealistic, independent American women searching for self-actualization in Europe. Their themes of innocence and experience help to demonstrate the undesired end met by those who insist on pursuing a romantic dream in an unromantic age.

The settings of James's novels remained very important during this stage, as they often symbolized the characters who inhabit them. Some believe his heroines were in part based on a beloved female cousin, Mary Temple, who died of tuberculosis at the age of twenty-four before ever realizing her potential. Both Daisy and Isabel bring upon themselves disastrous experiences in love and romance.

The chief works produced during a second phase focusing on social issues in a more naturalistic mode included *The Bostonians* (1886), a satire on the feminist movement, and *The*

Princess Casamassima (1886), whose plot is built around the actions of a London anarchist group. Although these and other of his works would gain future popularity, they did not garner the fame James desired. In the 1890s he began writing for the stage without success, but the failure in that area seemed to rejuvenate his fiction writing.

Subsequent third stage works lacked the ethereal narrative intervention of his first writings, instead evidencing tightened characterization and highly scenic settings, but still featuring heroines caught up in the evil turns of life. *What Maisie Knew* (1897) and *The Awkward Age* (1899) were accompanied by *The Turn of the Screw* (1898). This last work is still considered among the best of the horror genre. Still to come were James's *The Wings of the Dove* (1902) and *The Ambassadors* (1903), among other notables.

When James's complete fiction was published by Charles Scribner's Sons in four volumes between 1907 and 1909, he carefully revised his work and composed Prefaces providing the artistic background of, and considerations for, each work. These commentaries were published as *The Art of the Novel* (1934), providing a comprehensive theoretical statement regarding his individual artistic approach and reflecting on writing activity in general. After publishing a travel book expressing negativity toward American society, in 1915 James became a British citizen. He died at his Rye, Sussex, country house on February 28, 1916.

> *See also: Daisy Miller; The Portrait of a Lady*
> *References:* Bamberg, 1975; Beach, 1959;
> Bevilacqua, 1996; Carpenter, 1988; Cowley, 1973;
> Feidelson, 1975; Friedman, 1995; Geist, 1996;
> Pizer, 1995

JANE EYRE

In 1847, Charlotte Brontë published one of the most compelling of the classic Gothic romances in her novel *Jane Eyre*. Among the expected Gothic aspects of the novel are a passionate, explosive Byronic hero in the form of Mr. Rochester; a cavernous house that hides mysterious secrets; a madwoman; death and cruelty; and a heroine put at great risk. The importance of the novel centers on this heroine, the diminutive Jane Eyre of the novel's title. For in Jane's shy yet intelligent and perceptive approach to life lies the heart of Brontë's story.

The novel opens with scenes from Jane's early childhood that will remain crucial to her future. An orphan, she must survive in a relative's family where she is unwanted and unappreciated. Even as a very young child, she discerns the problem to be one of difference; she is unlike the egocentric and cruel members of the Reed family who so mistreat her. The cruelty inflicted on Jane in that house as well as at Lowood, the hateful school she later must attend, breed in her a deep-seated suspicion regarding her chances at happiness in life. Still, she will not be discouraged by the sad lot that seems to be hers, even after the death of her best school friend, Helen Burns.

Brontë gives Jane an inquiring mind that seems never to get enough of books. Like the author herself, Jane matures in the company of strangers made friends by her voracious consumption of the stories they inhabit. Displaying the spirit and zest for life experiences that characterize her into adulthood, Jane triumphs over the disasters at Lowood to move from the station of student to teacher. Eventually prompted by her desire for exposure to things beyond Lowood's walls, she applies for a position as governess.

In this first portion of the novel that sees Jane into adulthood, Brontë supplies much in the way of symbolism that will continue throughout the story to satisfy the alert reader. Names are important, as evidenced by the pomposity suggested in the schoolmaster's name of Brocklehurst; the hint at sanctuary in the name of Jane's favorite teacher, Miss Temple; the later inclusion of St. John Rivers, suggesting the cleansing power of water and his connection to religion; and the hint in Jane's own name at something plain and ordinary. The name Thornfield, for the manor where Jane will act the governess, signals readers that she will endure a struggle there in an unpleasant and "thorny" environment.

Colors and textures are also important in the novel, such as the red, reminiscent of hell and its red-orange flames, of the room where Jane is at first confined in the Reed home and believes she sees the ghost of her Uncle Reed. When Brocklehurst arrives to visit with Aunt Reed regarding Jane's move to Lowood, he appears to the child Jane as a black pillar with a stony countenance. Later, Rochester's attic, literally a living tomb for his first wife Bertha, will be labeled black as a vault.

Jane's reading materials are important symbols in revealing how she educates herself and how her thoughts about the world around her are evolving. Examples include her comparison of her wicked cousin John to the evil Roman emperors about whom she has read in Oliver Goldsmith's eighteenth-century *History of Rome;* her mention of *Pamela* (1740), Samuel Richardson's tale of romance related through letters; her praise of stories containing fairies and mystical elements, such as *Gulliver's Travels* (1726) by Jonathan Swift and the *Arabian Nights;* and her rejection of Helen's copy of Dr. Samuel Johnson's *Rasselas* (1759) due to its serious nature. Brontë offers the reader a multitude of such hints that support the shaping of Jane as a woman of intelligence and creativity, a subject worthy of psychological study as she searches first without and then within herself for the happiness that eludes her.

Jane's second move, from Lowood to Thornfield, exposes her to her fate when she meets Mr. Edward Rochester, her "master." Their first accidental meeting, during which time they do not know one another's identities, provides important foreshadowing. He must lean against Jane, small though she may be, for support after slipping and injuring himself. He will assume this same stance again, both literally and figuratively, as she eventually aids his recovery from the more serious physical and psychological injuries caused by a fatal fire and the pain of his separation from her.

The time Jane spends with Rochester develops beautifully various Gothic images and themes. The house itself is large and rather foreboding, and mysterious noises bounce about its halls at night. Jane experiences a visit from a shape she believes to be real, but one Rochester claims is a product of her imagination. Jane's charge and Rochester's "ward," the little French girl Adele, hints at the master's nefarious past, as does the presence of the ironically named and enigmatic Grace. The dashing of Jane's happiness by a revelation from a dark past forces her acceptance of the warning offered by the presence of the first Mrs. Rochester, literally and figuratively trapped in a patriarchal marriage. Jane's subsequent homelessness on the moors as she herself borders on insanity, her adoption by the kind Rivers family, her attempt to keep her identity a secret, and the tortures she suffers when considering St. John's offer of marriage combine to promote a distinct Gothic flavor. Even the revelation

of her blood relation to the Rivers marks the use of coincidence common in all classic romances.

Of all these elements, the horrible fire that occurs at Thornfield in Jane's absence provides the novel's Gothic hallmark. The fire symbolically cleanses Rochester of his sins, which are embodied in the helplessly insane Bertha Mason Rochester and her plunge to her death. Rochester's injuries from the fire, resulting in the loss of the use of one hand and partial blindness, serve as a sacrifice allowing his return to grace and chance at the second life that Jane offers when she returns. This fire would reappear in Gothic romances over the ages, most notably in Daphne du Maurier's *Rebecca* (1938), in which another Byronic hero atones for past sins through a cleansing fire that, through its destruction, wipes away the haunting presence of a previous wife and offers a clean beginning for the novel's romantic couple.

For all of its satisfying action, *Jane Eyre's* glimpse into its heroine's mind remains its finest gift. At one point, Jane assures readers, "I am merely telling the truth," and her compelling voice makes her statement believable. From the scene in which she looks out over the world from the lofty rooftop of Thornfield Hall, longing for the power supplied through the vision of imagination, to her statements regarding the mistaken stereotypes of women, to her plucky confrontation of her master when she challenges his right to command her and his mistaken idea of superiority, to her confession that she enjoys looking at the object of her love, Jane offers a heroine worthy of reader admiration and identification. This aspect alone makes Charlotte Brontë's story of initiation on the part of her young character a remarkable gift to the tradition of Gothic romance.

See also: Bildungsroman; Brontë, Charlotte and Emily; Gothic Romance; Patriarchal Marriage; Rochester, Edward; Violence
References: Armstrong, 1990; Drabble, 1995; Ellis, 1989; Leavis, 1966

JONES, TOM

As the hero of Henry Fielding's comic epic romance, *Tom Jones* (1749), the title character made his novel an instant best-seller. Fielding uses Tom to highlight the follies of human nature in a manner by which we can all laugh at ourselves. True to Fielding's penchant for the classics, Tom occupies center stage in a classical initiation/coming-of-age story of the good man falsely accused. As indicated by the novel's full title, *The History of Tom Jones, a Foundling,* Tom provides an example of a man of uncertain origins who depends on neither wealth nor title to make his fortune.

From the moment the infant Tom makes an inauspicious entrance into the world by mysteriously appearing on Squire Allworthy's bed, he captures the kind Squire's heart. As indicted by his surname, the Squire remains a fine and respectable landowner who lives with his sister, Miss Bridget, in the English countryside outside of London. In an attempt to do right by the infant, the Squire searches for his mother. His suspicions light upon Jenny Jones, a pretty girl who lived in his household for a time nursing Miss Bridget through an illness. Thus begins an enormous misunderstanding that will have tremendous consequences for all of the novel's main characters.

When Jenny does not deny the kindly Squire's accusations, he sends her away from the neighborhood in order to avoid a scandal. Soon to follow Jenny is the local schoolmaster, Mr. Partridge, suspected of being Tom's father. Both of these individuals stand in the wings, as it were, awaiting their reentrance into the story and Tom's life.

Tom gains a playmate when Miss Bridget marries Captain Blifil and delivers a son. Shortly after the boy's birth, Captain Blifil dies, leaving the Squire a second boy to care for. As the two mature, Blifil becomes Tom's foil and his nemesis. Tom exudes good nature, high spirits, and spontaneity, whereas Blifil remains sullen, accusatory, and seemingly without joy. The boys' two schoolmasters, aptly named Mr. Thwackum and Mr. Square, dote on Blifil, an outward picture of intelligence and good behavior, but they consider Tom a devil. He does indeed suffer frequent "thwacks" from his teacher, who believes in the discipline of the rod. Blifil goes out of his way to ensure Tom will be caught at his various harmless mischiefs as frequently as possible. A reader familiar with classical romance can predict Tom's and Blifil's eventual competition for the attentions of a beautiful young lady. Her name is Sophia Western, daughter of Allworthy's neighbor, Squire Western.

Sophia enters the novel at age eighteen, but a flashback alerts readers to the fact that she and Tom had interacted as children. Tom caught a bird for Sophia, which she confined and trained as a pet, until Blifil one day set it free. In an attempt to recapture the bird, Tom fell into freezing water, to Sophia's great concern, but emerged unharmed. He might have achieved hero status except for Blifil, who upset Sophia by announcing he had seen Tommy, as the bird was named, carried away by a hawk. This scene perfectly expresses the relationship among these three characters, highlighting Tom's generous nature and Blifil's scheming one. When all three mature, Tom gains Sophia's love, but she acts interested in Blifil in order to draw suspicion away from her feelings toward Tom.

When Squire Allworthy becomes ill, his death seems imminent, and he makes known the fact that Tom, along with other members of his family, stands to inherit. Tom appears to be the only one satisfied with his portion of the fortune, for which he cares little. He remains far more concerned with the Squire's health. Although the Squire does not die, Bridget Blifil does, as she travels from London to visit her brother. Tom celebrates the Squire's recovery by going on a drinking binge, an activity that furthers his reputation as the local ne'er-do-well.

Classical romance turns on coincidence and misunderstandings, and Tom suffers for many of these. When Squire Western's sister approaches Sophia to tell her that her father has arranged a match for her with Blifil, she at first misunderstands, believing that Mrs. Western means she will marry Tom. She gives herself away in her excitement, and her aunt forces her to see Blifil, threatening to release the news of her secret love for Tom if the girl does not comply. As Mrs. Western emphasizes, Squire Western will never permit his daughter to marry Tom, a man with no money and no family background. Tom remains ignorant of the forces that work against him, which include Blifil's lying to Squire Allworthy. Blifil informs the Squire that Tom had celebrated his benefactor's impending death by engaging in a drunken brawl. The Squire cannot excuse such action, and hurt and angry with Tom, he banishes the boy from his house.

By this point in the novel, Tom has reached his maturity and is ready for the many adventures the future holds. Although readers may guess that he will eventually be reunited with Sophia, he must first engage in a number of arguments, duels, and confrontations with various men and women as well as acting as the go-between for two star-crossed lovers in London.

Tom eventually proves himself not only heroic in his tendencies and actions but also a truly worthy person by birth. Like other foundlings in classical romances, such as *Daphnis and Chloe,* Tom's heritage will be discovered, his true identity revealed, and his redemption accomplished. He must first learn the dual lessons of prudence (caution) and circumspection (thinking about a situation before plunging headlong into action). As the novel's narrator makes clear, the successful man must balance an innate goodness and open, friendly character with those two elements. His kind treatment of Blifil at the novel's conclusion reflects Tom's more mature character, once he grows out of his mischievous and flirtatious ways.

Tom Jones allows Fielding to bring full circle his message of tolerance and the necessity for a sense of humor. He proves Fielding's belief that a basically good person, despite the occasional surrender to temptation, could achieve redemption.

See also: Longus; Romance; *Tom Jones;* Western, Sophia

References: Hipchen, 1994; Mace, 1996; Richetti, 1996; Smallwood, 1989; Smith, 1993; Thomas, 1992; Tillotson, Fussell, and Waingrow, 1969; Tumbleson, 1995

JORDAN, ROBERT

As the main character of Ernest Hemingway's 1940 novel of love and war, *For Whom the Bell Tolls,* Robert Jordan delivers an unmistakable message to readers. Echoing the sentiment from John Donne's *Meditation XVII,* which contains the line adopted by Hemingway as his title, Jordan stands as a model of one willing to die for his belief. He does not question his death but rather embraces it, knowing it will bring freedom and happiness to others.

As an American instructor of Spanish from Montana, Jordan appears quite out of his element in the mountains of Spain, where he acts as a guerrilla fighter. A highly autobiographical character for Hemingway, Jordan has the same idealism as the author, who also joined the Spanish rebellion against the Fascists prior to World War I. Jordan anticipates the difficulty involved with his assignment to destroy a bridge with explosives. He does not, however, anticipate falling in love with Maria.

For Jordan, Maria symbolizes not only love but also his concern for the Spanish people in general. Having suffered as a kidnapping victim at the hands of the Fascists, Maria symbolizes all of Spain. The two lovers are brought together by Pilar, a brave freedom fighter herself who leads the rebels who will help Jordan accomplish his goal. She has served as a surrogate mother to the frightened Maria, who hovers near madness following her victimization by the enemy. When Jordan rescues Maria, first with his love and then by sacrificing his life, he symbolically also helps to rescue Spain.

Although the lovers of the novel do not end up sharing a life together, their love cannot be labeled unrequited or star-crossed. They do enjoy several episodes of physical lovemaking during their brief four days together, and their eventual separation is brought on by the choice Jordan makes to stay behind and fight the Fascists following the bomb blast. Because he is too badly wounded to proceed, Jordan concludes that he can best serve Maria by improving her chances of survival through his sacrifice.

Hemingway develops Jordan into a fully rounded and intriguing character. His complex emotions and dedication to a cause add to character development, and his first-time love for Maria leads him to realize that his desire for her survival is greater than his own desire for life. Therefore, he changes from his position in the story's beginning as a forceful and determined soldier fighting for an abstract cause, to a man defending another individual who represents his ideals.

See also: *A Farewell to Arms; For Whom the Bell Tolls;* Hemingway, Ernest; Nihilism; *The Sun Also Rises;* Violence; War

References: Cowley, 1973; Defazio, 1996; Donaldson, 1996; Hen, 1996; Hily-Mane, 1995; Hotchner, 1966; Moreland, 1996; White, 1933, 1968

THE JOURNEY

Jiro Osaragi's 1960 romantic novel, *The Journey,* supports its title by narrating details regarding three individual quests for love and emotional fulfillment. In the love triangle composed of a charming man addicted to gambling, Ryosuke Tsugawa; a hopeful young professional woman, Taeko Okamoto; and a poor but honorable scholar, Sutekichi Ata, none of the members experiences true love. Taeko loves Ryosuke, who loves only himself, and Sutekichi loves Taeko, but she does not reciprocate. Although none of the three young people enjoys true romance, each discovers through his or her romantic experience their place between the poles of tradition and change that threaten to bifurcate Japan. As an author who disliked the changes brought to traditional Japanese values by modern American ways, Osaragi employs the dichotomy of modernity versus tradition as a framework for his plot in which various characters represent the two opposite ideas.

The novel opens with a graveyard scene, in which Taeko discovers Ryosuke visiting her dead cousin Akira's grave. She learns the two were classmates at college, and the details Ryosuke shares regarding Akira's treatment by his father, Uncle Soroku, confirm Taeko's attitude toward her uncle, a man so cold and miserly as to charge his own son interest on a loan. Soroku represents the traditional Japanese citizen, but he is so shaken by the loss of his son that he can no longer function in the changing environment. The story later reveals him as a man who loved his son very much and who now regrets never having shown that love.

Following a suicide attempt at sea, Soroku will attempt to know Akira better by retracing a mountain climb the young man had made. His journey reflects an interesting reversal of the traditional quest, in which a son seeks his identity by searching for that essence representing his father. Soroku, although an elderly character, eventually undergoes an epiphany when he realizes that in its outrageous power, war reversed the normal process through which a son lives on after his father. In his case, war imposed upon him, as Akira's father, the duty to live for his son. This brings new value to his life, and he abandons all thoughts of suicide.

Akira's death in war balances Ryosuke's survival, for which he cannot account. One young man's physical death mirrors the other's emotional destruction, as Ryosuke struggles to find anything to care about in the world. Osaragi thus investigates the damages perpetrated by war that extend beyond death of the body. Ryosuke retains his life, yet he never regains his psychological grip on reality, as he plunges headlong into the new society created by western influences.

In this book, American characters represent decadence and immorality, and Ryosuke remains drawn to the glitz and promise of quick riches offered by their lifestyle. He sleeps with a Japanese businesswoman, Kaoruko, who earns a living by catering to the Americans in order to better her own chances of gaining material wealth. Ryosuke sees no contradiction in his actions, even though his actions make him unfaithful to Taeko, who believes in his romantic commitment to her. His total self-absorption prevents his capacity to love anyone other than himself; thus, he remains a flat character.

As the female representative of the younger Japanese generation, Taeko represents the postwar change that brought women into the workplace. An illegitimate child, born to her father's servant, she was raised without indulgence and enjoys the feeling of independence that her life away from her family yields. At one point she visualizes her mother as a pathetic figure who always sacrificed herself for others. This traditional demand made upon Japanese women Taeko refuses to accept. She resists the attempts of her more traditional half-sister to arrange a marriage for her to a promising Japanese man, desiring to discover true love on her own. But concurrently, she longs for a love relationship involving traditional commitment, something Ryosuke cannot provide. For a time, Taeko tolerates his self-centered behavior and in the novel's conclusion even helps him escape his crushing gambling debts. Ironically, she steals the money necessary to free Ryosuke from debt from her wealthy uncle, the man Ryosuke criticizes early in the novel for begrudging his own son a loan. Taeko contrasts greatly with the novel's older female, Kaoruko, who feels any act that others do not witness and criticize remains acceptable; she drops all ideas of "proper behavior" in order to succeed in the world of business. Taeko will instead retain her values, prioritizing human relationships above material gain.

Taeko rejects an offer of marriage from Sutekichi not because of his poverty but because she feels no passion for him. Although Taeko remains single with no romance in her life at the novel's conclusion, her first experience in physical love and her discovery of Ryosuke's true nature help her gather valuable information about her own attitudes and feelings. Thus, she evolves into a dynamic character who develops the strength to continue her journey in search of love.

The third member of the younger generation, Sutekichi, pairs with an elderly professor, Yoshitaka Segi, who acts as the voice of tradition throughout the novel. In contrast to Soroku, Segi retains his traditional beliefs, which remain unshaken by war or the alteration in culture. He complains mightily about the changes but retains his optimism and sense of humor regarding those things he cannot affect. He, along with his protégé Sutekichi, symbolizes education as the salvation of Japan's future generation. He is fond of reciting poetry and thus represents the imaginative powers of art to elevate humans above the mundane. In addition, Segi serves as the guide/counselor often included in romantic quests. He expresses aloud a theme central to the novel, that the journey one makes remains more important than actually reaching the goal. The journey traveled for its own sake results in the development of true humanity.

During his quest for happiness, Sutekichi will embody his teacher's ideals as he might those of a father. Trapped in a teaching job he does not enjoy, Sutekichi longs to follow his original dream of retracing the route of Alexander the Great but is prevented, partly by postwar social unease in which individualism arrived in Japan too late to work to his advantage. Scholarly research remains out of reach due to his poverty, and his dream journey seems to shrink in importance when people of his own time continue to die by the roadsides from starvation. He meets Taeko because he and the professor care for her Uncle Soroku following his suicide attempt. When he later proposes marriage to Taeko and is rejected, he gracefully accepts that rejection, relying on his sense of honor to still wish her well on her life's journey. His willingness to sacrifice for others represents his choice of the value of tradition over the materiality represented by modern culture. When the professor tells Sutekichi late in the novel that only a strong and honorable spirit allows humans freedom, he speaks to a young man who represents that spirit perfectly.

The Journey supplies a satisfying collection of characters who embody, sometimes through inversion, various ideas of the romantic quest. Osaragi makes clear that constant movement toward one's goal remains more important than the attainment of that goal. This theme qualifies his novel as a modern quest, in which the traditional physical journey is represented in several instances by a psychological journey. Some characters mature without necessarily finding a reward beyond an advanced understanding of self.

See also: Ata, Sutekichi; Okamoto, Taeko; Quest; Tsugawa, Ryosuke; War
References: Campbell, 1968

KARENINA, ANNA ARKADYEVNA

The heroine of Leo Tolstoy's 1875–1878 novel, *Anna Karenina,* embodies the tragic consequences of forbidden love in a judgmental society. Married to Alexey Karenin, a Russian government official seemingly incapable of passion, Anna allows her own passion freedom of expression when she falls in love with the dashing aristocrat and soldier, Count Alexey Vronsky. From its inception their love remains doomed by social censure. Anna meets Vronsky when she travels to Moscow in hopes of convincing her sister-in-law, Princess Darya "Dolly" Alexandrovna, not to divorce her brother, Prince Stepan Arkadyevitch "Stiva" Oblonsky. Multiple instances of situational irony and foreshadowing occur at this point in the novel. Later, in a situational reversal, Dolly will attempt to influence Anna's husband not to seek divorce, although, in the end, Anna desires an official dissolution of her marriage. In addition, in this early scene, Anna, Stiva, and Vronsky learn of the accidental death of a railway employee beneath the wheels of a train; later, Anna will cast her own body beneath a train in a desperate suicide resulting from her disenchantment with Vronsky and herself.

Anna is a beautiful woman, a fact constantly reemphasized by Tolstoy, who repeatedly remarks on her lush black hair and small, well-shaped hands. Her physicality remains important to her allure, as does her intelligence and passion. Although Anna seems egocentric at times, she approaches life with an honesty to be admired. She seeks to leave an unsatisfactory and stultifying relationship with her husband and enjoy the love of a passionate and attentive man, but her culture rejects this notion of love or, rather, its inherent honesty. Many members of the aristocracy engage in love affairs, but they choose the more acceptable route of lying about their activities to their spouses.

Tolstoy uses Anna's situation to bolster his theme of inequality among individuals in late-nineteenth-century Russia. As a woman, Anna, although an aristocrat, finds herself at the mercy of a different kind of inequality. She is forced to accept the tenet of the upper social classes that a woman must be properly attached to a man in order to maintain her social status. Her peers rejoice in Anna's predicament during her separation from Karenin, reveling in her difficult position, because many had been so jealous of her perfection of body and soul. Her "sin" supplies much fodder for gossip and social intrigue, even for Vronsky's mother-in-law. She first regards her son's actions toward Anna as a kind of courtly love, acceptable for the certain air of importance it allows a man in good society. But Anna she eventually holds in disregard as a fallen woman, ignoring her son's part in that fall from grace.

Karenin's action, or lack of action, when facing the fact of Anna's affair drives her to hate him even more than she had before. The marriage might have been saved had her husband acted with any passion over his discovery; even a display of fury would have proved he cared for Anna. But his pragmatic approach drives Anna to distraction and pushes her into a physical relationship with Vronsky. Her resultant pregnancy and delivery almost kills her and wins Karenin's heart again, preventing his acting upon his decision to divorce. But eventually he can no longer tolerate Anna's escapades with Vronsky, and Anna moves out to join Vronsky, first in a trip to Italy and later in a return to Moscow. Ironically, Karenin refuses to divorce Anna upon her return, although Vronsky pushes for the legal ruling. He fears that his offspring will remain Karenin's, and any inheritance of his title or property will be disallowed. Such concerns cause a barrier between him and Anna, who does not desire a divorce, purportedly because she at first believes that she should suffer for the evil she inflicts on her family. She has given up her beloved son with Karenin for Vronsky, and she worries that the trade was an unworthy one. When she at last agrees to request a divorce, even though she vows to have no more children with Vronsky, her decision accompanies doubt regarding Vronsky's love.

All this time, Vronsky is able to move about in his normal social circles, but Anna is confined to their home and the care of their daughter, whom she cannot love. Jealousy worms its way into her soul, and the suicide follows a stream-of-consciousness stylistic outpouring of her thoughts and emotions regarding her life and all of those who have betrayed her. Like many classical tragic heroines, Anna brings her misery on herself, but also to blame is the unforgiving and blatantly hypocritical society in which she lives. Although members of her circle should recognize her tragedy as their own, they instead reject Anna's humanity, and she ends her life with a bitter mental barrage against the inequities of life.

See also: Anna Karenina; Chivalry; Forbidden Love; Levin, Konstantin Dmitrievitch

References: Bayley, 1968; Bychkov, 1968; McMillin, 1990

KINCAID, JAMAICA

Born in 1949 on the island of Antigua in the British West Indies, Elaine Potter Richardson, later to assume the pen name Jamaica Kincaid, endured an unhappy childhood with a cruel mother and a basically absent father. She did enjoy a strong reading program in school, where she encountered authors such as Rudyard Kipling and Thomas Carlyle. Although not much fiction was read in her home, her mother did enjoy biographies that included books on Wolfgang Amadeus Mozart and Florence Nightingale. When her mother remarried, she expected Elaine to help in the support of her children. Because she was the eldest, Elaine left home to work as an au pair in New York City at age sixteen. She describes herself as lonely and depressed during this period of servitude. Although she knew nothing of the writing world in her teens, these experiences would later be featured in her first novel, *Lucy* (1990).

In later years, Kincaid freely discussed her move to New York and its objective of escape from her oppressive mother. At first she simply worked at any job available in order to survive, including secretarial and modeling positions and one stint as a backup singer. She dyed her hair blond and gained a reputation for outlandish behavior, once attending a Halloween party wearing nothing but a string of plastic bananas

around her waist. At age twenty four, she decided to become a writer, realizing she wanted to share her strong opinions with others. Her application for a secretarial position at *Mademoiselle* magazine was rejected, something Kincaid could not understand because she had been treated so well in interviews. Kincaid found shocking friends' implications that her rejection was likely based on *Mademoiselle's* unwritten policy of hiring only white girls. Never had she conceived of her identity as simply that of a black woman.

Kincaid began a successful career at *The New Yorker* after one of the founding writers from the popular television show *Saturday Night Live* introduced her to George Trow, a New York writer. She had written for the *Village Voice* and eventually submitted an essay to *The New Yorker.* Publisher William Shawn chose the piece for publication in the magazine's popular "Talk of the Town" column. As a writer for the magazine, she garnered attention not only for her personal essays but also for articles featuring gardening, a hobby that became her passion. Kincaid's distinctive voice developed during her tenure with *The New Yorker,* despite several clashes with Shawn regarding her choices of terminology; he generally bowed to her wishes. She credits Shawn for increasing her confidence in the importance of her stories and herself as a young black female writer among *The New Yorker's* contributors, most of whom were white males, many graduates of Harvard and Yale. In 1984 her collection of short

Jamaica Kincaid has become known as one of the most important contemporary West Indian women writers for her relentless, disturbing prose and varying fiction-writing techniques. (AP/Wide World Photos)

stories, first published by Shawn in *The New Yorker,* appeared in print with the title, *At the Bottom of the River.* Kincaid eventually married Shawn's son, musician William Shawn, in 1979. In 1985, both were offered teaching positions at Bennington College in Vermont, where they settled and had two children. Kincaid's first novel, *Annie John,* saw publication in 1985 and was followed by a nonfiction book, *A Small Place* (1988), featuring her birthplace of Antigua.

Her parting with the famous magazine after almost twenty years of work came following Kincaid's discovery that a Hollywood personality had been hired to edit an issue on women. Remaining true to her reputation for possession of a tempestuous character, the author made no effort to hide her openly hostile reaction toward *The New Yorker's* editor, Tina Brown, or her low opinion of the periodical. She threatened to take the magazine to court should it publish a final article she wrote focusing upon her brother's death.

With the publication of *The Autobiography of My Mother* (1997), Kincaid became known as the most important of the contemporary West Indian women writers. Her works have been described as relentless, containing a disturbing prose that shapes intense, often unpleasant, images. She adopts varying fiction-writing techniques, including social realism, allegory, and symbolism as well as some magic realism. Her mother's presence seems to linger in the background of each of Kincaid's three novels. Kincaid describes her mother as a woman who should never have had children, an attitude projected onto the difficult relationships her female characters have with their mothers. Sex assumes an important role in her fiction, supporting her belief that female sexuality is both a statement of independence and a weapon that can be turned against women. Her main characters tend to be women, causing many to regard her as a feminist spokesperson. Kincaid has said that the freedom to write without self-consciousness, without feeling any shame for her origins, remains crucial.

See also: Lucy; Potter, Lucy Josephine

References: Birbalsingh, 1996; Brady, 1996; Garner, 1997; Kincaid, 1995; Nagel, 1995

KING, TABITHA

Born in 1949, American writer Tabitha King matured as the fourth of eight children at her home north of Bangor, Maine. Raised as a Catholic, she developed her writing ideas by listening in the local general store to stories told by members of her local community. An avid reader and writer from an early age, King worked at various odd jobs as a girl and eventually attended the University of Maine at Orono, where she graduated with a bachelor's degree in history. She would return years later to accept an honorary doctorate from her alma mater.

While in college, she met her future husband, Stephen King. Although her parents felt that King would never amount to much, Tabitha married him anyway in 1971 when both writers were in their twenties. They had three children and settled in Bangor, Maine. She describes their early years as financially difficult. He taught high school, and she worked part-time shifts in a local donut fast food chain. That all changed in 1974 with the publication of his novel *Carrie.* Tabitha spent most of her early married years involved in family activities with the couple's children. As adults, their daughter became a restaurateur in Portland, Maine, and both of their sons became storytellers, like their parents.

King's Maine background has supplied the setting for most of her novels. Except for her first and her most recent novels, all take place in the same town of Nodd's Ridge, a fictitious small northern Maine community. The Nodd's Ridge series includes *Caretakers* (1983), *The Trap* (1985), *One on One* (1993), and *The Book of Reuben* (1995).

More than any other trait, realism inhabits King's novels. She has said that American women too often accept without question a patriarchal bill of goods that begins with the romantic vision of love presented in fairy tales. For this reason, her own female characters are tough, generally survivors of emotional or physical abuse, and remain caught up in the demands of an often unkind human existence. An example of such a character may be seen in *One on One.* That novel allowed King to display her knowledge of sports as she shaped her teenage basketball-playing female protagonist, Deanie Gauthier. Far from a storybook princess, Deanie earns the nickname "the Mutant" for her unconventional tough-guy appearance. She survives social and domestic violence and abuse so realistically portrayed that some readers may take offense at the novel's disturbing scenes. However, such authentic scenes appeal to King's largest audience, that of young adults.

King believes love between two individuals to be all-important, but equally important to a relationship is unshakable trust. Her 1998 novel, *Survivor,* set in the fictitious Maine town of Peltry, features a woman who separates from an unfaithful man but later permits him to reenter her life, an act King labels a big mistake. King describes it as a story about love and marriage, American-style. To King, fidelity within marriage remains crucial, as does mutual support by each member of a couple of the other's pursuits.

The partnership in her own marriage is evident. The story of King's rescue of her husband's first novel from the trash has become the stuff of myth. Likewise, when she complained of having no time to write while her youngest child was an infant, her husband helped her career by buying her a typewriter. He then told her to stop whining and sent her out to rent an office. The result was her first book, *Small World* (1981), a horror story about a woman who has the power to shrink others. Her husband's editor, George Walsh of Macmillan, was surprised by the manuscript's high quality, and he agreed to publish the book. It met with some critical success, and by the time it appeared in print, King had begun to focus on her Nodd's Ridge series. One manuscript in that series was rejected, an occurrence, King says, that most people do not imagine happening to a reputable author. All of her novels address themes drawn from King's own life, such as the pressures of being a young parent and issues of female independence. Her plots, however, are only autobiographical to the extent that those based on one's general experience can be.

In addition to completing duties that came with an appointment to a judicial advisory committee for the Maine Court of Appeals, she also serves on the Board of Trustees of the Maine Public Broadcasting Company. She may be found working as a member of the board of an adolescent shelter and also at the University of Maine Press. In 1996, King served as chairperson of the $8.5-million fund used to remodel Bangor's library. The Kings have donated millions in funds to Maine libraries as well as $4 million to the state's universities. A recent personal donation by the Kings of $10,000 will help build the new Gloucester Public Library, on whose board of trustees Tabitha King serves. Her actions empha-size her belief in a writer's responsibility to actively embrace social issues. According to King, part of a writer's obligation to readers is to transform crucial information regarding important issues into enjoyable reading.

Future projects may include a second novel set in Peltry focusing on assisted suicide, a topic raised in *Survivor,* in addition to a work about King's siblings. She would also like to travel to Eastern Europe, where her books sell well, and collect information for a book about the concentration camps of World War II. Although her works have found a bigger audience in Germany than in America, King remains undaunted, expressing an understanding of the fact that most books do not create the phenomenon enjoyed by her husband's works.

See also: One on One

References: Anstead, 1997; Rice, 1997; Shattuck, 1997

THE KITCHEN GOD'S WIFE

The title of Amy Tan's modern romance novel *The Kitchen God's Wife* (1991) hints at the power struggle between men and women on which its major plot is based. Ostensibly a male, the kitchen god rules what has traditionally been thought of as the woman's domain, a fact that immediately suggests gender tensions. The female presence in the title is labeled "wife," but due to association with a god, her position elevates to that of goddess, with the wife's arena then becoming the center of focus. As this story based on the oral tradition unfolds, the kitchen god reveals himself as a sardonic, cruel spirit who revels in the misfortune of those inhabiting his kingdom, the kitchen. This imagery also applies to the main couple in the novel, Winnie Louie and Wen Fu, joined in a patriarchal marriage in which the man's word rules.

Tan supplies a major and a minor plot, featuring mother-daughter protagonists. The book begins in first person narrative, told from the point of view of Pearl Brandt, a first-generation Chinese American born to Winnie and, supposedly, Jimmy Louie. Involved in a successful marriage with an American, Pearl struggles to accept the values shared by her Chinese mother and her Aunt Helen. All three women keep secrets from one another: Winnie hides her past and an early failed marriage in China from her daughter; Pearl hides her diagnosis of multiple sclerosis from her mother; and Helen hides the false nature of her self-diagnosed brain tumor from both. When Helen threatens to tell Pearl's secret to Winnie and to divulge Winnie's secret past to Pearl, the narrative shifts to first person from Winnie's point of view. Thus, the narrative structure is that of a story within a story. Helen's threat becomes a catalyst allowing all three women to reveal their various secrets. The ensuing narration regarding Winnie's first marriage in China to Wen Fu contains the novel's major plot line.

Winnie's story contains the basic elements of an arranged marriage of a younger woman to an older man that can only end in disaster. As a naïve and protected Chinese girl, Winnie remains unaware of the facts regarding sex. She marries Wen Fu at the urging of her guardian aunts, who consider the union a good material match for Winnie. Her father, from whom she was separated at an early age when her mother mysteriously disappeared, grants permission for her to marry. From the immediate loss of Winnie's generous dowry to her husband's greedy family to the rude awakening regarding sex that she undergoes at her abusive husband's hands, the new bride finds marriage a disappointment. Her disillusionment grows as Wen Fu becomes increasingly physically and psychologically abusive. His manner of foreplay involves forcing Winnie to say and do things she finds repulsive, and he never gives a thought to satisfying her sexually or emotionally. As is common in a patriarchal marriage, Wen Fu as husband finds support within his culture, no matter how criminal or base his actions toward his wife.

Pearl listens in horror as Winnie relates the misadventures she experienced during the late 1930s and 1940s in war-torn China with her serviceman husband. Incidences related by Winnie include the loss of three children; her suffering of Wen Fu's abuse of her babies and his repeated rapes; the degradation of having to grovel before him in the presence of others; the experience of living with her husband's concubine; her suffering the torture of multiple near-escapes from her slavelike existence and the consequent punishments by Wen Fu; her evasion of Japanese bombings; her imprisonment for the attempted "kidnapping" of her own son; and finally the discovery of true love through her second husband, Jimmy Louie. Winnie's life mirrors that of the warring country around her. As China seeks

to escape Japan's tyranny, Winnie's near-death experiences during bombings and her repeated terror-driven flights through the mazelike city in search of a safe exit from the marketplace parallel her own quest for freedom from oppression by her husband.

Aunt Helen, who is not Winnie's sister at all but a friend she first met during the equivalent of basic military training for their husbands, provides an unusual twist on the confidante role often present in the story of failed marriage. She's also an ironic representation of the guide figure inherent to quest literature. Originally called Hulan, Helen both hinders and helps Winnie in her attempts to escape from Wen Fu. Having been raised in the same patriarchal society as Winnie, Hulan supports Wen Fu in his dominant position as husband. She observes his abuse of Winnie, and not only does she not try to prevent it, at times she even plays a part in allowing Wen Fu a freer hand. In one of the most heartrending scenes of the story, Hulan leads Wen Fu to the hiding place of Winnie and her young son, where Winnie overhears Hulan reminding Wen Fu that he has promised to offer his wife better treatment. Returning home with Wen Fu is a doubly bitter experience for Winnie, betrayed by a friend she should have been able to trust. Later, when Winnie has returned to her estranged father's house with Wen Fu and their son, she seeks another guide figure, her cousin Peanut, and discovers a safe house for women hiding from abusive husbands.

Tan's handling of Jimmy's appearance and place in Winnie's drama also varies from the stereotypical "white knight" appearance in Western fairy tales. Jimmy supports Winnie, and his love plays an important part in her final separation from Wen Fu and departure from China, but ultimately Winnie must assume the active role and free herself. She describes herself to Pearl as both strong and weak, but in truth, her androcentric culture is what weakens her position, resulting in the death of three children and causing her to abort several more. Winnie reveals to Pearl that Wen Fu was her biological father, after describing a harrowing final encounter with him involving his last rape of her in revenge for their divorce.

The novel includes fascinating detail regarding World War II China, Chinese customs, especially regarding food, Chinese superstitions, and a nonoccidental vision of hope. In one interesting passage highlighting the difference between American and Chinese ideology, Winnie discusses the definition of the words "fate" and "destiny." Her Chinese background leads her to accept that she has no control over the powers determining her life. Jimmy, however, feels that a kinder controlling force, that of God, unites the two lovers.

The novel contains many elements from the romantic quest: the journey; loss by the main character; a guide figure; mysticism, or magic; ghosts; trials; a descent into darkness, or Hades; a journey over water; an epiphany; and the final winning of the prize represented by Winnie's freedom and also metaphorically as a treasure in Pearl. With the character Winnie Fu Louie, Tan neatly substitutes a female figure for the traditional male hero. The traditional love triangle, represented by Winnie, Wen, and Jimmy, is also emphasized.

See also: Fu, Wen; Louie, Jimmy; Louie, Winnie; Love Triangle; Patriarchal Marriage; Quest; Violence; War

References: Chen, 1995; Davis, 1994; Foster, 1996; de Rougemont, 1983; Radway, 1991

KNIGHTLEY, GEORGE

In Jane Austen's 1815 romantic novel, *Emma*, George Knightley lives up to his surname in acting the white knight to the novel's protagonist, Emma Woodhouse. A perfect example of male decorum and grace, Knightley fits well into this novel of manners, as Austen's books have been labeled. He assumes his position as love interest in a predictable but highly enjoyable plot.

Knightley knows Emma and her wealthy father because his brother John married Emma's sister, Isabella. He often visits the Woodhouses at their estate in Highbury, where he observes Emma's spoiled yet charming and well-meaning demeanor with some amusement. Emma becomes convinced of her talents for matchmaking following the marriage of her governess, Anne Taylor, to the Woodhouses' neighbor, Mr. Weston, thanks to Emma's efforts. She then takes on the project of finding a husband for Harriet Smith, an activity that will cause for Knightley both consternation and the arousal of love toward Emma. True to Austen's style, both characters will suffer through several misunderstandings before they discover each other's feelings and can act on those feelings.

Knightley begins the story feeling brotherly toward Emma, who seems to require some super-

vision. He disapproves of her meddling in Harriet's affairs, particularly when Emma discourages Harriet from accepting the marriage proposal of a fine local farmer, Robert Martin. Emma believes that Harriet should make a "better match," and she sets her sites on the hand of the local vicar, Mr. Elton. As Knightley watches, Emma manages to cause Mr. Elton to fall in love with her, although she has proclaimed that she will never marry. When her plans fall through, causing both Harriet and Mr. Elton some degree of discomfort, Emma agrees with Knightley that she should no longer play games with the lives of others.

Emma continues her mischief, however, this time seeking a match for Harriet in the handsome Frank Churchill, stepson of her former governess. In the meantime, Knightley fulfills the promise of his name by "rescuing" the stranded Harriet when no one will dance with her at a local ball. His actions please Emma, and the two dance together, foreshadowing their eventual union.

Later, when Frank Churchill rescues Emma and Harriet from harassment by Gypsies, Emma believes Harriet to be captivated by Churchill when in truth, the girl has strong feelings for Knightley due to his gentlemanly behavior at the dance. This opens the way for much romantic confusion and amusement, and the couples eventually sort themselves out. Harriet will end up back where she started, with Robert Martin, the man she wanted to marry anyway. Emma will end up marrying Knightley, but not before he guides her to an epiphany that makes her, as all heroines should be, a more mature character.

For a time, Emma finds herself attracted to Frank Churchill, a man whom Knightley dislikes. He feels that Churchill acts as a bad influence on Emma by encouraging her gossip about the beautiful Jane Fairfax. Jane, an orphan raised as the ward of a well-to-do family, must now seek a position in order to support herself. First, she visits her silly and talkative aunt, Miss Bates. Through the array of characters, Austen emphasizes the strictness of the English social class system. Unusual because she is a wealthy single woman and heir to her father's property, Emma should show concern for those not on her own level, setting an example for fair treatment of the common person. Knightley's discomfort over Emma's behavior has to do with the fact that she is not practicing such an attitude. She behaves with some condescension toward Jane Fairfax and especially toward Miss Bates, who had held a higher social position before losing her wealth. Even though Miss Bates remains difficult to tolerate at times with her continual chatter, Emma's good breeding should promote her graciousness. Instead, Emma makes a vindictive and hurtful remark to Miss Bates in front of others.

For this remarkably rude occurrence, Knightley takes Emma to task, scolding her and correcting her behavior. Shocked by how hurtful she finds his lack of approval, Emma realizes two things: first, that he is right; she should act with respect toward others, regardless of their social position; and second and more important, that she values Knightley's approval. From this second realization grows her love.

Knightley presents an admirable figure in what many consider Austen's best written novel. Although not a dynamic character himself, having already achieved his maturity, he provides the guidance through which Emma may achieve her own maturity, developing a graceful and caring attitude toward others. To Emma's gentle initiation/coming-of-age experience, the character of George Knightley remains imperative.

See also: Austen, Jane; Brandon, Colonel; Darcy, Fitzwilliam; *Pride and Prejudice; Sense and Sensibility*
References: Copeland and McMaster, 1997; Gard, 1992; Praz, 1974

KUNDERA, MILAN

Milan Kundera was born in April 1929, in Brno, in what was then Czechoslovakia. His artistic interests emerged early, and he played in a jazz band as a young man. One whose political ideology inhabits much of his early writing, Kundera was twice a member of the Communist party, first from 1948 to 1950 and then from 1956 to 1970. Although he supported some Communist views, he was expelled from the party during both of his memberships for opinions described as "heterodox." His outspoken opinions caused conflict with national political powers that subsequently threatened his position as an employee of the Film Factory at the Academy of Music and Dramatic Arts in Prague. He taught there until his dismissal in 1969, after which his works were denied legal publication in Czechoslovakia. Kundera's response to this treatment culminated in a move to France in 1975. He taught at the University of Rennes from 1975 to 1978 and then took up residence in Paris, where he has lived for years with his wife, Vera Hrabankova.

Due to his political involvement and eventual censorship, Kundera is known to most Czechs only by his works produced during an early period of writing that are not well known by a foreign audience. Works published in Prague from 1953 to 1975 include poetry: *Man: A Broad Garden* (1953) and *The Last May* (1957); drama: *The Owners of the Keys* (1962) and *The Blunder* (1969); and fiction: *Zert* (*The Joke,* 1965), *Laughable Loves* (1968), and *Life Is Elsewhere* (1969). These works remained accessible to the Czech public for a time, but Kundera later established a moratorium on their publication. Presently they can only be located in rare bookshops and libraries. Critics believe Kundera sequesters his past works in order to hide his history as a collaborator with the Communist regime.

Kundera's essay regarding the Czech writer Vladislav Vancura, "The Art of the Novel" (1961), and his novel, *The Book of Laughter and Forgetting* (1978), both written in French, have not yet been translated into Czech. From 1989 to the present, *The Joke, Laughable Loves,* and an additional novel titled *Immortality* (1990) are his only republished works. Thus, his native Czechoslovakia knows the early Kundera, whereas readers outside his native country know the later Kundera.

A prolific writer, Kundera's more recent works include a collection of essays, *Testaments Betrayed* (1995), a novel, *Slowness* (1994), and the popular realistic romance, *The Unbearable Lightness of Being* (1984), which was well received and made into a movie. This novel depicts the relationship of a husband and wife and a love triangle they form with the husband's mistress during the Russian occupation in Czechoslovakia.

The criticism applied to Kundera's work often judges its social value rather than its artistic value, and some critics feel Kundera's accuracy in his descriptions of Czechoslovakian society are lacking. Due to the author's background, his art often becomes a weapon in an ideological war of sorts, and his novel *Life Is Elsewhere* has been described as Kundera's attempt to settle accounts with, or to cleanse, his past. His early works, particularly his popular poetry, include abundant symbols of the political reality of Communist Czechoslovakia during the 1950s.

In some later works Kundera refers to specific philosophers or influences on his thought and works, such as Friedrich Nietzsche, Parmenides, and René Descartes, and seems to sympathize with the approaches of twentieth-century writers such as Franz Kafka and Thomas Mann. But Kundera's work differs from that of those writers in its accessibility to the reading public. His fiction strikes readers as pleasant and easy to read. His repeated theme of the human attempt to transcend barriers presented by societal and individual conventions and convictions appeals to his readers and supports Kundera's continued popularity.

See also: The Unbearable Lightness of Being
References: Catalano, 1995; Lippi, 1984; Misurella, 1993

LAST, BRENDA

As the completely degenerate love interest for Evelyn Waugh's protagonist, Tony Last, in his 1934 satirical novel, *A Handful of Dust,* Brenda Last quickly earns the reader's well-deserved disgust. She plays the part of a bored aristocratic housewife, contemporary to Waugh's own time, who seeks total indulgence apart from her family, which includes one son, John. Readers may sympathize with her loss of patience with her pedantic husband. Tony Last fixates on the upkeep of a centuries-old mansion on his estate of Hetton, which is described in guide books as devoid of interest; the words might describe the boring Tony himself. Even so, Brenda's treatment of Tony and John remains inexcusable. Brenda's egoistic behavior falls a notch below despicable as she abandons any thought of duty toward her family, replacing them with the social-climbing John Beaver, a worthless leech. Although revolting, Beaver, desperate for acceptance by Brenda's social crowd, is no less than what Brenda deserves.

Waugh satirizes the entire London social scene through Brenda's activities in town, where she moves to get away from her country home. All the stock characters surround Brenda, including Tony's best friend, Jock Grant-Menzies, a politician who pretends to protect the rights of the farmer but in actuality promotes the riches of the already rich. The book's most shocking scene well illustrates Waugh's opinion of the shallow quality of his characters and the real-life figures they represent when Jock must bring to Brenda in London the terrible news of her son's death during a hunting accident at Hetton. When Jock informs her that John is dead, Brenda believes for a moment that he means her lover, John Beaver, and does not catch herself before expressing relief that it was only her son who died. Despite Jock's shock at her reaction, he himself remains so shallow and accepting of such behavior in others of his own social status that he later marries Brenda.

Brenda eventually sues Tony for divorce, forcing him to enact a ridiculous charade of adultery so she may have grounds to sue. After having had her way with the gullible Tony, Brenda at last incites his anger when he realizes that she wants to force him to give up Hetton so that she might support Beaver. This is too much even for his amiable and unimaginative self, and Tony ruins Brenda's plans through his failure to comply.

The shrewd Brenda possesses the self-preservation instincts of a fox and remains a survivor. Poor Tony, however, does not share her attributes for survival and ends up losing himself in the jungles of South America. Too busy with Jock, her new husband, to even attend Tony's memorial service at Hetton, now inhabited by Tony's cousins, Brenda disappears from view to take up where she left off, attending an endless cycle of luncheons and social events. A flat, disagreeable character, Brenda Last serves Waugh well in his relentless attack on the aristocratic conventions he so disdained.

See also: A Handful of Dust; Last, Tony; Waugh, Evelyn
References: Gaye, 1996; Read, 1974; Wolk, 1993

LAST, TONY

Tony Last acts as the ironic romantic quest hero in Evelyn Waugh's satirical novel *A Handful of Dust* (1934). Shaped irreverently by Waugh to represent the quintessential landed gentry of England, Tony's surname remains significant, for he will be the last of his illustrious line. He remains obsessed with Hetton, his ancient house and the family estate, much to his wife Brenda Last's irritation. Brenda finds Hetton a competitor for Tony's attention and money. Renovated in 1864 and of a no-longer-interesting Gothic style, Hetton symbolizes Tony and his focus on an outmoded way of life. Tony's reluctance to entertain in the ungainly behemoth mansion irritates Brenda who, although she does not appreciate the estate for its family value, would like to at least have visitors to break the monotony of country life. Her boredom with Tony and his homey, stuffy lifestyle begins an escalating conflict between husband and wife that ends disastrously when she takes for a lover the parasitic John Beaver.

Although Tony's situation remains pitiable, readers will likely agree with Brenda that he is pedantic and pretentious. He attempts to act in a manner befitting the status of his ancestors, enjoying nothing more than chatting with the estate's vicar regarding his sermons and organizing fox hunts for the locals, two activities he considers part of his duties. He focuses so closely on these basically useless activities that he does not recognize Brenda's jaunts to town as a signal of danger for the future of their marriage. Eventually she takes an apartment in London, a luxury they can ill afford due to Hetton's financial demands, ostensibly in order to take classes and educate herself. Tony's provincial myopia blinds him to the fact that Brenda is having an affair. He regrets Brenda's absence mainly because his idea of the perfect country manor remains incomplete without a wife to assume the requisite tranquil pose alongside Tony and their only child, John.

Waugh relentlessly reveals Tony's narrow-minded stupidity as he showcases Brenda's obnoxiously self-centered existence. In a sharply drawn caricature of the divorce process as viewed by the wealthy, Waugh manipulates Tony through an embarrassing escapade with a woman of questionable character. Tony hires her specifically to stage an affair so that Brenda may have grounds for divorce. Tony does briefly exhibit some strength of character when he discovers that Brenda intends to take his money and, worst of all, Hetton, in order to support John Beaver. The shock of her demand brings him to his senses, and he refuses to comply. The tragic loss of their son to a hunting accident means that Tony's distant relatives will inherit Hetton, much to Brenda's dismay.

Tony begins his ironic quest following his marriage's dissolution as he sets out on a sea voyage in pursuit of South American treasure. Waugh includes every aspect expected in a quest, but then subverts the plot. Tony's less-than-astute partner, Dr. Messinger, who acts not as an able guide bearing a message but more as one who creates a mess, leads Tony astray and brings on his own death. Tony's life is saved by a reprobate living in the jungle, a white man named Mr. Todd,

who, because of the fact that he exercises total control over the local natives, somewhat resembles Joseph Conrad's renegade character Kurtz in his African adventure novella, *Heart of Darkness* (1902). To his despair, Tony discovers that Todd saved him in order to enslave him. Unable to find his way out of the dense jungle, Tony must do whatever Todd bids him. When Todd drugs Tony and shows his watch and a freshly dug grave to two explorers who come looking for the young English aristocrat, his fate is sealed. Tony sleeps through his only chance for rescue, and those who would have taken him home instead return to England with the story of his death.

Rather than proving himself a hero who returns home victorious with his treasure, Tony spends his last days deep in a South American jungle with the crazy Todd, who demands that Tony read and reread aloud to him novels by Charles Dickens. The only remembrance of Tony in his much-revered England comes from his lesser cousins who, although hardly gentry material, at least share his appreciation for Hetton, their new home.

See also: A Handful of Dust; Last, Brenda, Quest; Waugh, Evelyn

References: Gaye, 1996; Read, 1974; Wolk, 1993

THE LAST OF THE MOHICANS

As probably the most popular of James Fenimore Cooper's historical romances, *The Last of the Mohicans* (1826) captures the adventure and allure of the westward movement in eighteenth-century America. Although modern readers may stumble over or find amusing Cooper's profuse description and overblown style, his characters and their battles against the elements still offer high entertainment. *The Last of the Mohicans,* a story framed by the French and Indian War (1754–1763), offers its readers ample external conflict, including full-fledged battles between Indians and soldiers and single hand-to-hand combat between the novel's clearly delineated "good" and "bad" characters. These characters include the wildly popular frontier scout, Natty Bumppo (Hawkeye); his companion and friend, Chingachgook; Chingachgook's nephew, Uncas, the last of the Mohicans represented in the novel's title; and the dastardly renegade Huron Indian, Magua. Rounding out the collection of main characters and bringing themes of love and romance to the novel, are two damsels constantly

Daniel Day-Lewis starred as Hawkeye in the 1992 film version of the most popular of James Fenimore Cooper's historical romances, The Last of the Mohicans *(1826), a novel that captured the adventure and allure of the westward movement in eighteenth-century America. (The Kobal Collection)*

in distress, Cora Munro and her sister Alice, and Alice's love interest, Major Duncan Heyward.

The novel's opening scene introduces readers to the Munro sisters, Major Heyward, David Gamut, a singer from Connecticut, and the Huron Indian, Le Renard Subtil, who assumes the name Magua. Although Magua is to lead the small contingent from Fort Edward to Fort William Henry where the Munros' father commands, they learn in midafternoon from travelers that their so-called scout has been leading them in circles. The travelers identify themselves as Hawkeye, Chingachgook, and Uncas and attempt to capture Magua, but he manages to escape. Heyward, ever-mindful of the threat to his female charges, convinces the travelers to guide them to Fort William Henry, but Magua leads a band of Iroquois Indians that surprises the group under cover of night. With little ammunition and no way to defend their position, Hawkeye and his companions leave the Heyward party in an attempt to gather supplies. The hostile Indians capture the travelers, and Heyward attempts to convince Magua to break away from

the party and escort the white people to Fort William Henry.

At this point in the novel, Cooper introduces a new conflict. The presentation thus far emphasizes external conflict between two competing powers. Now romantic conflict enters the story when Magua agrees to follow Heyward's plans only if Cora will agree to live with him as his wife. Naturally Cora refuses, pushing Magua into a rage in which he threatens to kill all of the whites. Readers of Cooper's time might be scandalized by the thought of Cora marrying Magua, but they could remain comfortable knowing that the idea of such forbidden love was not embraced by Cora. However, Cooper creates an even stickier problem later by hinting that Cora, of her own volition, falls in love with Uncas. These suggestions of interracial marriage are complemented further by the fact that Cora apparently has a slave ancestor in her genealogy, making her a product of miscegenation. Many nineteenth-century readers would find such plot aspects revolting.

Hawkeye and his companions return in time to rescue the party, killing several Iroquois in the process. They finally reach Fort William Henry and Colonel Munro after they convince a French sentinel from Major General Louis Joseph Marquis de Montcalm's troops to let them pass. Chingachgook kills the sentinel, claiming his scalp, and the party finds their destination surrounded by the enemy French troops, with Montcalm in command. The French succeed in laying siege to Fort William Henry, and Colonel Munro agrees to surrender when Hawkeye's attempt to bring help from Fort Edward and its commander Webb fails. While at the fort, Heyward perpetuates the theme of romance when he alerts Colonel Munro of his courting intentions toward Alice. This ends the first of three lines of adventure in the novel.

By now, the main characters are well defined. The two women, labeled "females" by Cooper, remain flat stereotypical figures. Cooper establishes them as traditional opposites, in that Cora, with her dark coloring, represents passion and independence and seems aligned with nature, whereas the fair Alice remains frail, helpless, and easily frightened. Neither is capable of much in the way of action, and Cooper keeps them passive and, for the most part, silent regarding the action around them. Heyward also remains stereotyped as the gentlemanly escort, an able man, but not remarkable by comparison to the novel's hero, Hawkeye, and his Indian companions. Even the "good" Indians suffer a reduction through stereotype to silent, dignified, "noble savages."

The second adventure begins as the exiled soldiers and travelers depart their fortress for Fort Edward. Along the way, a slaughter of the white soldiers begins that the wicked Montcalm ignores. Left in the care of the highly ineffectual David Gamut, Alice suffers capture by Magua, and Cora gives chase with David close behind. Cora's torn-away veil serves as a signal to Heyward, Hawkeye, Chingachgook, and Uncas, who trail the captives to Magua's camp. As they near the Huron encampment, following a rapid and exhausting chase, they meet David wandering in the woods. David informs them that he enjoys freedom because the Hurons believe his habit of breaking into song indicates insanity. The Indians respect madness and believe it makes David incapable of escape. He relates the news that Cora may be found with a nearby tribe of Delawares, but Alice remains in the Huron camp.

In the third section of adventure, multiple disguises and guerrilla tactics are employed as Alice is freed, Uncas is captured and freed again, after showing courage in confronting Magua, and the party attempts to free Cora. Magua, however, claims Cora from the Delawares who allow his release, according to their custom, but Uncas, apparently in love with Cora, promises to follow. In a final bloody scene, Uncas is killed by Magua, Magua in turn is shot by Hawkeye, and Cora falls prey to a Huron attack. She returns to the nature with which she is identified when she is allowed to rest beside Uncas in their graves in the nearby woods. Hawkeye grieves for the loss of his way of life to invading settlers, and Chingachgook mourns the loss of his son Uncas, literally the last Mohican.

Although Cora's death may come as a surprise in that the death of a major female love interest remains nontraditional in romance, Cooper's critics believe this happens to free the author from the burden of dealing with an interracial romance between Cora and Uncas. The novel's action-filled plot more than balances weaknesses in characterization and style, however, making *The Last of the Mohicans* a novel of enduring popularity, as evidenced by its continued reading and conversion to film in at least four versions between 1920 and 1992.

See also: The Black Experience in America, 1600–1945; Cooper, James Fenimore; Forbidden Love; Hawkeye; Heyward, Major Duncan; Magua; Munro, Alice; Munro, Cora; Uncas
References: Barker, 1996; Campbell, 1968; Campbell, 1988; "Cooper, James Fenimore," 1986; Ousby, 1988; Wimsatt, 1974

LAWRENCE, D. H.

David Herbert Richards Lawrence was born the fourth child of a coal miner in 1885 near Nottingham, England, in Eastwood. A sickly infant, he contracted bronchitis early and would remain in poor health throughout his life. Although he began school at age four, his mother, Lydia, withdrew him, and he did not return until age seven. This late start influenced his lack of social involvement, and he spent most of his time with his sister Ada. He would eventually develop into a fine student, receiving the only scholarship to Nottingham High School ever awarded a student from his Beauvale Board School. Although it strained his family financially,

Lawrence began attending high school at age thirteen, where he studied hard. The train rides to and from school caused his absence from home for the entire day, and he made few friends in school. One acquaintance who invited Lawrence to visit his home expressed horror upon discovering that Lawrence's father was a coal miner. They had no further contact.

The young Lawrence spent any extra energies helping his overworked, ignored mother. Their relationship and his father's employment in the Brinsley Colliery supplied the autobiographical details that would later appear in Lawrence's third novel, *Sons and Lovers* (1913). At the turn of the century, Lawrence went to work at age fifteen for a surgical appliance manufacturer. The fourteen-hour days spent in dark conditions with little ventilation increased Lawrence's susceptibility to illness, and he contracted pneumonia within six months. Lydia nursed him back to health, and he became what was known as a pupil school teacher, a teacher expected to continue daily lessons with the masters before the students arrived. At last Lawrence made some friends, and he began a secret writing career. The farm family of his companion, Jessie Chambers, provided him a home away from home where he could blossom apart from family tensions. His first story won a £3 prize in a contest, but he entered under Jessie's name, so his own name did not see print.

In 1904, Lawrence passed in the top thirty-seven of two thousand candidates for an examination for the King's Scholarship. His performance guaranteed him a place at Nottingham College, but he could not immediately take advantage of the scholarship due to financial hardship. By 1906 he was able to attend college, but he became disenchanted with the whole experience. His schoolmasters lacked the enthusiasm and intelligence he anticipated. In 1908, as a qualified teacher, he took a position in Croydon at Davidson Road School, where he impressed the schoolboys and his headmaster with his encouragement of his students to use their imaginations. All of his free time he now filled with writing, and in 1911 his first novel, *The White Peacock,* was published. His happiness at this accomplishment was diminished by his mother's death from cancer a month before the publication.

Again Lawrence suffered a bout with pneumonia and suffered lung damage. When a doctor informed him that further teaching might lead to tuberculosis, Lawrence followed an uncle's suggestion to become a Lektor at a German university under easier conditions than those at the public school. His consultation regarding this plan with Ernest Weekley, a Nottingham College professor, led to an affair with Freida Weekley, mother to the professor's three children. She accompanied Lawrence to Germany, where she requested that her children join her. Ernest Weekley would not comply, bombarding the couple with threats and abuse that led to animated arguments between Freida and Lawrence. Lawrence suffered both anger and guilt over his part in Freida's loss of her children, and he again experienced the feelings of helplessness that his mother's suffering and death had engendered.

Although they had little income, the couple traveled about Germany, mainly by foot, and Lawrence was at one point accused of being a spy. They traveled through Switzerland and ended up in Riva, Austria, near Italy, a land that fascinated Lawrence. He continued to write and made revisions to *Sons and Lovers* as they moved about. Lawrence added levity to the relationship by demonstrating his talents in imitation. He "performed" for Freida and their friends, offering parodies of chapel services he had attended as a child and acting out events from his life in a charming and self-deprecating manner. These charades became famous among Lawrence's friends and American acquaintances. Despite their troubles, Freida Lawrence once declared she had not lived until she met her lover.

Sons and Lovers appeared to a mixed acceptance, although it would become Lawrence's most famous work. Its lack of financial success made Lawrence fear he might have to return to teaching, but his succession of short stories, articles, essays, and poetry helped support him and Freida. They returned briefly to England in 1913 in hopes of reuniting Freida with her children, but she was denied that privilege. Following her divorce in 1914, the two married at last in London. Prevented from returning to Italy by the outbreak of war, they remained in England for five years, an interminable period for Lawrence. Freida, originally from Germany, was accused of spying, and Lawrence's next novel, *The Rainbow,* was banned. The former playful attitude that dominated his life seemed lost to the embittered Lawrence.

Able at last to return to Europe, Lawrence continued his writing, and a fictional account of his and Freida's first years together may be found in his unfinished novel, *Mr. Noon*. The Lawrences traveled to Sicily, Ceylon (now Sri Lanka), Australia, and New Mexico in search of fulfillment, returning to Europe for the final time in 1925. His last novel, *Lady Chatterley's Lover*, was banned in 1928 and his paintings confiscated. He eventually took up residence in a tuberculosis sanatorium in Venice called Ad Astra. Following a brief stay, he departed for the villa Robermond, belonging to writer Aldous Huxley. He died the next day in March 1930 at age forty-four. Publications of his work after his death include a novelette, *The Virgin and the Gipsy* (1930), and a collection of poetry, *Last Poems* (1932). Hailed an excellent author by the mid–twentieth century, Lawrence gained posthumously the fine literary reputation that escaped him while alive.

See also: *Sons and Lovers*

References: Becket, 1997; Boulton, 1997; Burns, 1980; Chambers, 1981; Croom, 1997; Dix, 1980; Drabble, 1995; Lawrence, 1964; Niven, 1980

Frances Drake and Frederic March played Fantine and Jean Valjean in the 1935 version of Victor Hugo's 1862 novel Les Misérables, *an adventurous romance as well as a sociological commentary on poverty and life in the slums of Paris. (Photofest)*

LES MISÉRABLES

Victor Hugo's novel *Les Misérables* first saw publication in 1862 after Hugo dedicated fourteen years to its writing. Since that time it has enjoyed constant reissue and has been translated to film and to the stage and inspired plots for television shows as well as movies. His romantic story of the convict, Jean Valjean, set in the early nineteenth century preceding the French revolution of 1830, joins Hugo's other works in focusing on the social inequities that concerned him. Although Valjean's life story acts as the core of the novel's plot, the book introduces a large number of additional male and female characters, including the poor woman, Fantine, her daughter Cosette, Cosette's love, Marius Pontmercy, and the obsessed Monsieur Javert, a police inspector who spends his life persecuting Valjean. In addition to providing an adventurous romance to his readers, in *Les Misérables* Hugo shapes a sociological commentary on poverty and life in the slums of Paris.

The story begins in 1815 when the convict Jean Valjean leaves prison after nineteen years. Originally sentenced to serve five years for stealing a loaf of bread for starving family members, Valjean incurs additional time due to his escape attempts. During his lengthy prison stay, he develops a reputation for his massive size and strength. His first contact with the outside world, about which he bears only terrible memories, comes when the Bishop of Digne offers him shelter and food. Valjean repays his kindness by stealing his silver. When the police capture and return him to the bishop, Valjean expects the worst. Strangely, the bishop not only allows him to keep the silver with his blessings but adds to the booty a pair of silver candlesticks. This good deed encourages Valjean to begin life anew in support of others like himself who need the aid that the French power structure too often witholds.

In one of several digressions occurring throughout the novel, the reader then meets Fantine, a lovely Parisian girl who gives birth to an illegitimate daughter in 1817. Perceptive romance readers understand that the child, named Cosette, will later play an integral part in Valjean's story. As for Fantine, she serves basically as a vehicle to bring Cosette to the story and to illustrate the terrible fate that befalls poverty-stricken women who must take to the streets.

For a time Fantine finds employment in a glass factory owned by Monsieur Madeleine in the town of M—. Madeleine gains a reputation as one who takes extreme measures to aid the poor. Fantine must pay the wicked Thénardiers to care for Cosette while she works, and they demand more and more money for the poor treatment they give to the child. Eventually, they leak the information that Fantine bore a child out of wedlock, causing her fellow factory workers to insist upon her dismissal; unbeknownst to Madeleine, the foreman fires Fantine. Without work, she must become a prostitute to meet the Thénardiers' escalating demand for funds. In a typical romance tactic, that of the use of disguise, Madeleine turns out to be none other than Jean Valjean; he had broken his parole in order to move to M—. He rescues Fantine from the streets, but, stricken with tuberculosis, she cannot be saved.

At this point, the character of Javert assumes importance. The reader learns that Javert was born and raised in prison, a fact that has caused him to fixate on upholding the letter of the law, regardless of the consequences or the fairness of the laws. He recognizes Madeleine as the ex-convict Valjean after witnessing him perform a prodigious act of strength. Javert tricks Valjean into identifying himself, and he appears to arrest Valjean for breaking parole as he speaks with Fantine in the hospital. Having suffered conflict with the police inspector before, Fantine faints from fright when Javert arrives. She dies after having extracted a promise from Valjean to care for Cosette.

These circumstances begin another round of arrest and then escape for Valjean. He succeeds in finding Cosette, then eight years old, and he removes her from the wicked home in which she has been raised. In what amounts to a beauty calming the beast, Cosette wins the huge ex-convict's heart, and the first theme of love emerges in the novel. They will be rescued from Javert by a peasant at a convent whom Valjean had aided in the past; thus, his good works begin to result in tangible benefits for him. This turn allows Hugo to emphasize the redemptive powers of one human's love for another. Valjean and Cosette take shelter at the convent as she matures.

More years pass before the pair departs the convent for Paris. They exist unnoticed there until the inopportune arrival of the Thénardiers, who take up life in a tenement slum, assuming the name Jondrette. Next to the Jondrettes lives Marius Pontmercy, a poor young lawyer who will eventually become Cosette's lover. Not always a bad man, Thénardier had once rescued Marius's father at the battle of Waterloo, and Marius later promised his father to repay Thénardier's brave act. Even though at this moment in the story he does not realize that Thénardier is his neighbor Jondrette, when the Jondrettes suffer eviction, Marius pays their rent. Like other romances before and after it, the novel abounds with the coincidence necessary to intertwine the lives of its many characters.

Hugo's emphasis on social inequality continues as Marius joins a group planning civil revolution. After Marius follows them home one day, Valjean removes Cosette to another location. Thénardier's daughter, Eponine, loves Marius, but Marius loves Cosette. Marius spies on the Jondrettes and discovers Jean Valjean visiting them; he recognizes the old man as Cosette's companion. When he later overhears the Jondrettes plotting against Valjean, he becomes alarmed for Cosette's sake. Still ignorant of any of these various players' true identities or relationships to one another, Marius alerts Javert that some harm may come to the old man.

From this point forward, the plot moves quickly toward its climax, the time at which all identities and connections will be revealed. Again positioned in his hiding place, Marius observes many armed men enter the Jondrette apartment to confront Valjean when he appears to pay the blackmail monies demanded by Thénardier/ Jondrette. The horrified Marius learns Jondrette's true identity and struggles to decide whom to defend. As Marius watches, Valjean tricks the robbers by sending them to a fake address, supposedly to get more money from his daughter. Marius adds another important element to the classic romance when he tries to deliver a secret note of warning to all in the apartment just as Javert arrives. Javert succeeds in arresting everyone except Valjean, who escapes.

When Marius locates Cosette and learns that she and Valjean plan a move to England, he appeals to his estranged grandfather for help. This appeal by a poor young hero to an older, wealthy, obstinate patron remains another romance plot staple, and readers know that Marius's appeal will be denied. Eponine, the figure of the unrequited lover, finds Marius at Valjean's deserted house and informs him that his friends await his participation in the revolt they plan at the barricades. Both young people go to the barricades, where Marius despairs of living without Cosette. But it is Eponine who will die for Marius, her love never appreciated. At the barricades they discover that Javert has been taken captive and tied up as a spy. Before Eponine dies, she makes the supreme sacrifice for her love by handing him a note that reveals Cosette's location.

The note passing continues to be important to plot, as Valjean finds a note from Marius to Cosette and makes his way to the barricade. When he discovers Javert, Valjean continues to act on his vow of kindness as he frees his longtime nemesis. Luckily Valjean also discovers Marius, who has been wounded during the revolution, and Valjean wanders about looking for a way out of the locked area. Thinking he has discovered freedom, Valjean meets a man, the disguised figure of Thénardier, who agrees to help him escape for a payment. Outside, Valjean encounters Javert, who again takes him into custody. The criminal agrees to accompany Javert but asks to be able to deliver Marius safely to his grandfather. Tormented over whether to comply with his duty as dictated by the institution of law and return Valjean to prison or repay his kindness by setting him free, Javert throws himself in the Seine River and drowns.

After recovering from his wounds, Marius marries Cosette, and Valjean reveals that he is an ex-criminal. His revelation brings Cosette to understand that Valjean is not her real father. Gradually Marius prevents Valjean's visits to Cosette until he learns from Thénardier that Valjean saved his life at the barricades. The young couple rushes to locate Valjean, and they discover him on his deathbed. He hands the silver candlesticks, representative of his legacy of an attitude of fair treatment to all, to Cosette as he dies.

Victor Hugo's *Les Misérables* remains important, not only as a major contribution from the nineteenth-century French Romantic movement but also as a novel of universal appeal. Its themes and characters remain timeless, and readers continue to identify with Hugo's passion for individual freedom, including the right to love and serve oneself by serving others.

See also: Cosette; Fantine; Hugo, Victor; *The Hunchback of Notre Dame;* Romance; Valjean, Jean; Violence; War

References: Charlton, 1984; de Rougemont, 1983; Lovejoy, 1974; Masters-Wicks, 1994

LEVIN, KONSTANTIN DMITRIEVITCH

The character of Konstantin Levin not only remains crucial in Leo Tolstoy's monumental novel of romantic tragedy, *Anna Karenina* (1875–1877), but he also most likely serves as an autobiographical character for the author. As a wealthy farmer, living in the period prior to the nineteenth-century emancipation of the serfs (1861), Levin reflects Tolstoy's own political ideology. Tolstoy had to choose whether to remain faithful to his elevated social group, members of which became involved in bureaucratic corruption contributing to the poverty of most of Russia's population, or support the common person's revolution. Levin, from whose point of view much of the novel is told, undergoes a similar personal struggle as he searches out his place in Russia's escalating political and social unrest. Additional conflict arises as he attempts to win the heart of the Princess Catherine Alexandrovna "Kitty" Shtcherbatskaya. Neither of these problems offers a quick or easy solution, but Levin's strength of character, honesty, and overwhelming love for country and Kitty combine to allow his eventual triumph. Although Tolstoy may have intended Levin to act as a minor character in a subplot supporting the action centering on Anna Karenina, the farmer's compelling personality threatens to consume the reader's interest and sympathies. As the only male in the novel who does not act strictly from self-interest, Levin becomes a romantic hero in every sense of that term, making sacrifices for others at various junctures in the lengthy story.

The novel features several intersecting love triangles in which Levin unwillingly participates. In the main plot line, Anna Karenina, trapped in an emotionally stifling marriage to the government official, Alexey Karenin, loves Count Alexey Vronsky. She will, after a time, leave Karenin and their son for the count. Levin loves "Kitty," but she also nurses an infatuation for Count Vronsky. Even though the count never envisions Kitty as a serious contender for his affections, the attention he pays to the naïve and inexperienced young woman kindles her hope that he does bear romantic intentions. Anna's brother, Prince Stepan Arkadyevitch "Stiva" Oblonsky, also an old friend to Levin, is married to Kitty's older sister,

Princess Darya Alexandrovna, called "Dolly." Although friendly and helpful to Levin, Stiva does not cut a sympathetic figure as a so-called public servant engaged in as many questionable financial schemes as he is extramarital affairs. Levin's consultation with Stiva occurs in the early part of the novel, before he discovers the ideological chasm that separates the two men. Stiva and Vronsky act as foils to Levin, who ultimately proves to be the novel's only admirable male.

As a longtime friend of Kitty's aristocratic family, the Shtcherbatskys, and a man of position in his own right, Levin assumes that his plan to request Kitty's hand in marriage will be well received. Unfortunately, although Kitty's father values Levin's position and his reputation as an ethical individual, his daughter has interest only in the dashing Count Vronsky. Kitty's mother favors the handsome socialite count and hopes for a match with her daughter. Kitty views Levin only as an appreciated but unromantic older friend. Levin suffers cruelly when Kitty rejects his proposal, but she remains confident that the count will soon make his own bid for her hand, not knowing of his romantic designs on Anna.

Both Levin and Kitty struggle to handle the rejection of their real and imagined loves. The novel devotes much space to details of Levin's private life as he manages his farm, trying to understand the local peasants and their needs. Levin also remains distracted by the fate of his talented but doomed brother, whose terminal illness compels Levin to examine his own spiritual beliefs. The inner turmoil Levin experiences as he tries to decide whether to support governmental control or the serfs' desire for the emancipation that would occur in 1861 mixes with his search for some kind of peace in regard to religion. Of all the characters, Levin's eventual epiphany regarding the kind of life he must live remains the most notable, leading to his strong development into a dynamic character.

Tolstoy's vivid, detailed characterization and conflict-filled plotting causes readers to feel much frustration over Levin's unrequited love for Kitty. But eventually Kitty overcomes her pride, righting her previous error in rejecting Levin as not romantic enough to satisfy her sensibilities. Because she must act the restrained role expected of a properly trained aristocrat and lady, she cannot simply blurt out the news of her change of heart to Levin. Only when he also places his love

for Kitty before personal pride does he develop the insight to recognize the change in her. Following her realization and subsequent show of warmth and encouragement to Levin, he extends a second request that Kitty become his bride. Their union, based on a respect for one another that the other characters do not bear toward their respective romantic partners, becomes the novel's strongest love.

Levin best personifies Tolstoy's themes of revolution and religion as he endures a personal revolution of his own regarding political ideology and faith. He acts to help readers understand the changes affecting Russia's socioeconomic conditions. Through his male characters, Tolstoy offers various reactions to the unsettling cultural events in nineteenth-century Russia. Vronsky refuses to accept the reality of change in tradition, escaping into the disciplined and intellectually undemanding life of the military following Anna's suicide. Stiva Oblonsky practices avoidance through alcoholism and materialism, whereas Anna's husband, Karenin, loses himself in mysticism, a spiritual route Levin investigates but then rejects, recognizing it as a cause for false reliance.

Konstantin Levin offers readers hope in the midst of a story of great romantic and national tragedy. He continues to search for answers to his many ideological and spiritual questions, discovering a strength of character that supports his mental and emotional investigation without threat to his existence. With Kitty's love to bolster that strength, and the promise of new life through his children, Levin exists as a testimony to the importance of moral fortitude and courage in combating the inescapable challenges brought about by drastic change.

See also: Anna Karenina; Karenina, Anna Arkadyevna; Love Triangle; Tolstoy, Count Leo; Violence; War
References: Bayley, 1968; Bychov, 1977; Frye, 1976

LIKE WATER FOR CHOCOLATE

Although not Mexican writer Laura Esquivel's first effort, her 1989 novel, *Like Water for Chocolate,* first garnered her international attention when published in translation in 1992. The book also appeared in a screen version that same year. A tale of forbidden love that finds a way through the magic of human perseverance to conquer all, the novel received the prestigious ABBY Award, given by the American Booksellers Association to the novel they most enjoy selling,

Marco Leonardi as Pedro Muzquiz and Lumi Cavazos as Tita de la Garza appeared in the 1992 film version of Laura Esquivel's 1989 novel Like Water for Chocolate, *a tale of forbidden love that finds a way through the magic of human perseverance to conquer all. (Photofest)*

in 1994. Although termed "popular fiction" by some critics, the novel reflects many aspects of the classic romance tradition, framed in the magic realist technique of storytelling first made popular by Gabriel García Márquez. Esquivel adds her own personal touch by prefacing each chapter with a traditional Mexican recipe that accents the chapter's subject matter.

The plot focuses on the novel's heroine, Tita de la Garza, and is narrated by Tita's grandniece. Reading very much like a fairy tale, the story opens in the de la Garza kitchen, the setting for much of the plot. The first of many instances of magic realism occurs in the description of Tita's birth. Mama Elena goes into labor while peeling onions, which causes her unborn baby to weep a river of tears. The river gushes forth as birth waters, and the salt left behind after drying is collected in huge bags and used for cooking. This foreshadows Tita's intimate connection to life, passion, and the artistic pursuit of cooking.

As the youngest daughter of the family, Tita must follow tradition and remain unmarried, caring for her mother rather than for a family of her own. When her father dies two days after her birth, there is no hope of another baby assuming Tita's traditional responsibility as a virtual servant to Mama Elena. Mama Elena's milk dries up due to the shock of her husband's death, and the family's cook, Nacha, must nourish Tita in the kitchen with teas and other special formulas. The cook becomes a surrogate mother for Tita, whose own mother treats her harshly. Tita is not even allowed to play with her sisters, Gertrudis and Rosaura, due to Rosaura's being burned on a griddle, an accident blamed on Tita. Through this episode, Esquivel establishes the lifelong conflict the two sisters will experience. Although Tita may not birth children of her own, the kitchen, with its warm nurturing imagery, allows her to mother all those who eat at her table, permitting an outlet for passions that other family members seldom experience.

When Tita becomes a young woman and the handsome young Pedro Muzquiz expresses his love, she responds in kind. Mama Elena dashes Tita's hopes for marriage, reminding her that no woman in her family has ever questioned the tradition in which Tita finds herself trapped. When Pedro and his father visit to request Tita's hand, Mama Elena instead offers her eldest daughter, Rosaura, and Pedro accepts. In a particularly cruel move, Mama Elena orders Tita to be in charge of the wedding feast.

At first crushed by the engagement of her lover to her sister, Tita soon understands that Pedro will marry Rosaura only in order to be close to her. They declare their love as eternal, even though fortune seems determined to separate them. As Tita thinks of not sharing life with Pedro, Esquivel introduces traditional romantic paradox through the imagery of a heated passion that burns like ice. Because Tita cannot seem to warm herself, she continues work on the crocheted bedspread she had hoped would one day cover the bed she shared with Pedro. Due to cultural tradition, theirs becomes a forbidden love.

On the night before the wedding, Tita can hold her tears no longer, and she cries into the wedding cake batter. Nacha observes Tita's grief and, sharing the girl's sorrow, bids her go to bed while Nacha finishes baking the cake. During the feast the following day, all of the guests grow ill, vomiting their food. The wedding cake intoxicates everyone with Tita's sorrow through the ingredient of her tears.

Rosaura becomes so ill that she and Pedro remain unable to consummate their marriage, a condition that works to the reluctant Pedro's advantage. He delays having sexual contact with Rosaura for months until she begs him. Pedro shows that his heart remains loyal to Tita when he prays that what he does is not for lust but in order to produce a child to glorify God. He pays only scant attention to Rosaura, as he suffers in a love triangle that offers no solution. Convinced that Tita purposely ruined her sister's wedding, Mama Elena administers a beating that puts Tita to bed for two weeks. However, Tita's physical pain remains easier to bear than her emotional pain; not only does she long to be with Pedro, but she grieves for Nacha, who dies on the evening of Rosaura's wedding. Chencha, a young maid, becomes Tita's friend and confidante from that point forward.

Tita assumes full duties as the ranch's cook, and other magic occurrences are sparked from her cooking. When she uses the rose petals from flowers given her by Pedro to cook a special sauce, the passion represented by those traditional symbols of love affects the entire family. Gertrudis, the middle sister, receives most of Tita's and Pedro's combined passions, causing a heat that she runs to the shower to relieve. Her heat literally lights the outside bath on fire, and she runs naked through a field where she is swept up by a rebel hero, her equal in passion.

Tita lies to Mama Elena, telling her that Gertrudis has been kidnapped by the hated federal troops, but the local priest later brings the news that Gertrudis now works as a prostitute. Mama Elena at that moment destroys all memory and proof of the existence of her middle daughter, forbidding everyone to speak of Gertrudis. Part of the frustration Mama Elena endures over the fate of Gertrudis and over Tita's forbidden love for Pedro stems from her own past. She also loved a man she could not marry, and he was actually Gertrudis's father. The discovery of this fact had killed her husband soon after Tita's birth. The reappearances of federal troops throughout the novel allows Esquivel to emphasize the themes of oppression against the Mexican people through the Mexican civil war, paralleling Tita's oppression through thwarted love.

Eventually Rosaura delivers a son, but because she is unable to nurse him, he ends up in the kitchen as Tita had when an infant. Tita's love for Pedro and his son allows her breasts to produce milk, so she literally nurtures the baby along with symbolically nurturing the remainder of the family through her cooking. She and Pedro meet on occasion, furtively sharing physical love, but the brief contacts keep their passion high. Mama Elena, ever distrustful of Tita and Pedro, plots for Rosaura, Pedro, and the baby to move north to Texas. The subsequent news of her nephew's death causes Tita finally to revolt against her mother's oppression because she blames Mama Elena.

This episode appears almost exactly halfway through the novel, dividing it into two portions. The first represents Tita's enslavement through her obedience to her mother and to outmoded customs, whereas the second brings liberation to Tita through the discovery of her own identity, a discovery promoted by the love of Dr. John Brown. John stands as part of a love triangle that includes Tita and Pedro. As a man of science, John represents reason, while Pedro represents passion, and Tita must choose between these age-old opposites.

Tita escapes into a world of silence, hiding for days in the pigeon coop, refusing to speak or eat. Long a symbol of oppressed women, the bird cage represented by the coop acts as a fitting setting for Tita's suffering. She is carried away from the ranch by Dr. Brown, called by Mama Elena to take Tita to an insane asylum. Thus, John Brown both literally and symbolically releases Tita from her cage of oppression at the hands of her mother and tradition.

A gentle man totally consumed with love for Tita, John takes her to his house, where she will eventually recover. During this time, John relates a folktale that is crucial to the plot's later climax. In explaining how matches work due to their sulfur content, he tells Tita that all humans have candles inside that provide warmth. Lit through love's passion, one candle provides a desirable light, but if the entire group is ever inflamed, the body will be consumed by passion. The person will see beyond his or her normal vision into a glorious tunnel of light that humans forget with their birth. If the person answers that call to recover his or her divine origins, life will be left behind as the soul departs the body. More accepting of her fate at this point in her life, Tita agrees to marry John, although she still loves the absent Pedro.

When marauding federal troops kill Mama Elena, Tita returns to the ranch she swore she would never again see. Gertrudis comes home for the funeral, as do Rosaura and Pedro. Pedro must be nursed back to health by Tita and John following an accident in which he suffers terrible burns. Tita and Pedro eventually consummate their love again, and Tita believes herself to be pregnant. Mama Elena begins to visit Tita as an evil spirit, accusing her daughter of the worst kind of sin as she curses her. Tita has also communed with Nacha's good spirit as she seeks advice on various matters. With encouragement from Gertrudis, Tita at last accepts herself and all of her emotions, and she furiously dismisses the spirit of Mama Elena by revealing her knowledge regarding her mother's illicit love affair with the father of Gertrudis. The spirit never again appears, the pregnancy turns out to have been hysterical, and life continues on the ranch.

Gertrudis and her rebel husband depart, but Pedro and Rosaura remain. Tita finds ironic Pedro's expression of jealousy over her engagement to John, when he has been married for several years. When delivering a daughter named Esperanza, which means "hope," Rosaura almost dies, and John announces she can have no more children. As she had with her nephew years before, Tita adopts her niece as her own child, nursing it and delighting Pedro. Tita at last confronts Rosaura with the truth that Pedro loves only her. Her sister's response is to take Esperanza from Tita's care with the announcement that Tita, a woman made filthy by Pedro's attentions, cannot care for her daughter. Rosaura declares that Esperanza will never marry and will care for her in her old age, according to family tradition, thereby making especially ironic the baby's name.

Tita enjoys the victorious feeling her declaration of passion supplies. But facing her fiancé is far less pleasant, particularly when John forgives her, even for having had sex with Pedro. Impressed with John's strength and love and his promise of happiness, Tita knows she must choose between the two men.

The final chapter moves ahead twenty years to the wedding of Esperanza to John's son Alex from his early marriage. The reader learns that Tita did not marry John, who has remained a faithful and devoted friend. Tita and Pedro worked out an agreement with Rosaura by which they swore to keep their love a secret and be discreet about meeting, maintaining for Esperanza's sake the appearance of a good relationship between Rosaura and Pedro. Rosaura agreed to share Esperanza with Tita; she would take charge of the child's education, and Tita would feed her. Rosaura's indigestion and resultant bad breath and flatulence cause Pedro to resist her company. Although supplying a touch of humor for the reader, Rosaura's gastric condition has tragic results when it leads to her death twenty years later.

At Esperanza's wedding, all who eat Tita's meal again experience overwhelming passion, this time of a sexual nature. All the attendants, except for the faithful John, depart the ranch, anxious to make love with their partners. Tita and Pedro no longer have reason to observe the ruse of chastity. They enter a beautiful candlelit room to make love, each thinking the other has prepared it. In actuality, Chencha has readied the room. She departs the ranch, as do the ranch animals, as if instinctively fleeing disaster. In her joy and passion, Tita sees the tunnel John had described years before, but she resists following its path. She desires instead to remain on earth and experience continued joy with Pedro. Pedro, however, has not her strength; his soul has made the journey causing his death.

When the chill that had overcome Tita as a young woman upon the realization that she and Pedro would be separated threatens to return, Tita takes hold of a box of candles given her by John, and she consumes the candles. Her passion inflames them, and in turn the candles consume her and ignite the house in a funeral pyre for the two lovers. Stone and ash erupt as if from a volcano, and neighbors miles away think they are viewing celebratory fireworks for Esperanza's wedding. When Esperanza returns from her honeymoon, she finds only a mountain of ash in place of her childhood home, along with Tita's cookbook.

The narrator concludes the story by referring to the Christmas rolls that her mother, Esperanza, had taught her to bake. She notes that as long as someone continues Tita's cooking traditions, Tita will live on.

See also: de la Garza, Tita; Esquivel, Laura; Forbidden Love; Love Triangle; Magic Realism; Muzquiz, Pedro

References: de Rougemont, 1983; Frye, 1976; Zamora and Faris, 1995

LINTON, EDGAR

Edgar Linton serves the important function of acting as foil for Heathcliff, the Byronic protagonist of Emily Brontë's Gothic romance, *Wuthering Heights* (1847). Raised in luxury with wealth and high social position, Edgar is born into a lifestyle that makes him a perfect match for Heathcliff's love and soulmate, Catherine Earnshaw. Because Cathy also occupies a higher social niche than Heathcliff, a foundling raised by her family, the two cannot marry. Edgar becomes an important character in the novel only after Heathcliff and Cathy share a childhood of devotion to one another. In a fateful occurrence of the type so important to Gothic romance, Cathy captures Edgar's attention and his heart when she is forced to remain at his house for a lengthy period of time due to a non-life-threatening injury. A pitiable love triangle forms between Edgar, Cathy, and the unfortunate Heathcliff, who has not a chance of winning Cathy. Edgar, like his luxurious home, Thrushcross Grange, comes to symbolize the material goods to which Heathcliff can make no claim. Members of both the well-to-do Earnshaw and Linton families view Heathcliff's affection for Cathy as a forbidden love, and all discourage it. When Heathcliff comes to believe that Cathy will not marry him but will instead marry Edgar, he departs the British moors for America.

Edgar does love Cathy, but he cannot compete with the spiritual passion she shares with Heathcliff. Although he provides well for Cathy, when Heathcliff returns years later a prosperous man, Edgar emotionally loses Cathy to his brooding, angry rival. Cathy never physically leaves Edgar, but she joins her soul to that of the near-demonic Heathcliff.

Knowing that Cathy will not leave Edgar to share his life, Heathcliff sets out to wreak revenge on the Linton family and on Cathy's drunken brother, who had mistreated Heathcliff as a child. He begins by encouraging the affection of Edgar's sister, Isabella, who admires Heathcliff and views her infatuation with him as a rebellion against her conservative brother. Edgar is appalled when Isabella marries Heathcliff, for whom Edgar feels both fear and revulsion. When the Linton baby, named Catherine for her mother, is born, Cathy dies, much to Edgar's sorrow and Heathcliff's fury. At that point, Heathcliff pinpoints Edgar as a target for destruction.

Brontë uses Edgar to help the reader fully understand the tremendous capacity Heathcliff harbors for hate. A weak man by comparison to Heathcliff, Edgar cannot stand up to his emotional brutality. Edgar hates Heathcliff all the more due to his emotional abuse of Isabella, who eventually leaves Heathcliff, although they have a son named Hindley. Isabella dies an embittered woman, leaving Edgar to face his nemesis alone.

Never fully recovering from the loss of Cathy, Edgar clings to their daughter Catherine as his life's only joy. His attempts to keep Catherine away from Heathcliff and the sickly Hindley fail, allowing her to become a pawn in Heathcliff's vengeful plot. Edgar will die a broken and unhappy man who loses his wife, his daughter, and, ultimately, all of his physical possessions to the wild young foundling raised by the Earnshaws.

See also: Earnshaw, Catherine; Forbidden Love; Gothic Romance; Heathcliff; Love Triangle; Rochester, Edward; Violence
References: Clayton, 1987b; Daiches, 1965; Winnifrith, 1996

LONGUS

Absolutely no information exists regarding the origins and life of the writer called Longus, famous for his authorship of the classic romance *Daphnis and Chloe.* Some even question the accuracy of the author's name itself. On one manuscript it appears not as *Loggus,* a name equivalent to *Longus* in Latin, but rather as *Logos.* Because "logos" translates literally as "word," what early readers took for an author's name could simply be a part of the work's title. If an individual named Longus did write *Daphnis and Chloe,* he was likely an Italian who wrote in Greek. He refers to the island of Lesbos, indicating, but in no way proving, a knowledge of Greek geography. His mention of the lesbian vines, a junglelike allusion, and of the snows of Lesbos may just represent the age-old notion that lovers will suffer the punishments of burning heat or freezing cold in order to realize their love.

Even the date of the work remains uncertain. Based strictly on an analysis of the story's style and content, critics place its origin in the late second or early third century A.D. It falls within a group of Greek stories whose authors were labeled *Erotici Graeci.* Although this title suggests writers of eroticism, this group received that name simply because they wrote stories about love.

Longus applies a standard pattern to *Daphnis and Chloe* of young love, a forced separation of the lovers, adventures incurred by both, and a fidelity that serves eventually to reunite them. However, Longus's approach differs from that of his fellow *Erotici Graeci* in two ways. First, he emphasizes pastoral aspects that would become common conceits in Renaissance poetry. Second, his rendition is more cerebral. He uses less of the sentimentality and coincidence that support works by his fellow writers, instead incorporating humor and irony to comment on the sexual experiences of his characters, whose relationship has a universal quality.

Homeric references abound in the work, and Longus also inserts allusions to myths. In ancient tales, Daphnis was a son of Hermes, and his name suggested "laurel," the name of the sacred tree belonging to Apollo. Chloe developed from a cult name for Demeter, meaning the first plant shoots that appear in the spring. Longus compares Daphnis's beauty to that of Dionysus, and eventually readers learn he is the offspring of one Dionysophanes, a name also suggesting Dionysus. Direct religious references, in addition to Dionysus, include Eros, Pan, and the Nymphs, and all of these mystical characters bear an important role in the story's plot. Not a religious tale by any stretch of the imagination, Longus's *Daphnis and Chloe* most likely incorporates mystical references in order to emphasize the piety connected to the pastoral life of the simple shepherd.

Like many of the ancient authors, Longus's identity remains shrouded in mystery. That mystery does not diminish the importance to the romance tradition of the work bearing his name.

See also: Introduction; *The Sound of Waves*
References: Turner, 1989

THE LOST GENERATION

The lost generation is a phrase coined by American writer Gertrude Stein, referring mainly to a group of rootless, disillusioned, expatriate young writers who resided in Paris in the 1920s and 1930s. Including F. Scott Fitzgerald, Sherwood Anderson, Sinclair Lewis, and, most notably, Ernest Hemingway, the lost generation writers produced novels featuring the effect on the American imagination of the horrors and brutality of World War I, supposedly a war to end all wars. In a backlash against the sentimentality of nineteenth-century romanticism, the realism that emerged in the fiction of the early twentieth century often focused on war as a symbol of the ignoble human condition. Hemingway's war novels, including *The Sun Also Rises* (1926) and *A Farewell to Arms* (1929), shaped cynical characters who had survived the war but lost their innocent view of life. The phrase "lost generation" actually appears in *The Sun Also Rises*.

See also: A Farewell to Arms; Fitzgerald, F. Scott; *For Whom the Bell Tolls; The Great Gatsby;* Hemingway, Ernest; Nihilism; *The Sky Is Red; The Sun Also Rises*
References: Beach, 1959; Carpenter, 1988; Cowley, 1973

LOTUS BLOSSOM

Although a minor character in Pearl Buck's Pulitzer Prize–winning novel, *The Good Earth* (1931), Lotus Blossom remains important to helping readers understand the early-twentieth-century Chinese culture that Buck describes. She serves the novel's protagonist, Wang Lung, as concubine and second wife, usurping the honored position of his first wife, O-lan. Lotus's dainty beauty contrasts greatly with O-lan's clumsy homeliness, as does her fussy personality with O-

lan's willingness to serve. Thus, Lotus Blossom acts as a foil for O-lan. Readers learn more about the patriarchal marriage that Wang Lung shares with O-lan through his bringing Lotus into his household. Even though he suffers some guilt over the automatic reduction of value of O-lan that occurs through his actions, Wang Lung also knows that such action is his right. His status as a successful and wealthy landowner, and as a man, allows him to treat his various women in any manner he chooses. Lotus never plays a great part in Wang Lung's life, neither encouraging nor discouraging him in his everyday activities. As self-centered as she is lovely, she behaves exactly as Wang Lung expects. With O-lan's death comes a feeling of loss for the reader that would not be experienced with Lotus's demise. When her own servant, the young Pear Blossom, eventually usurps Lotus's position in Wang Lung's affections, readers feel some satisfaction. Lotus gets no more or less than she deserves, eventually suffering a similar fate to that she inflicted on the faithful O-lan.

See also: Buck, Pearl Sydenstricker; *The Good Earth;* Lung, Wang; O-lan; Patriarchal Marriage
References: Armstrong, 1990; Lipscomb, Webb, and Conn, 1994

LOUIE, JIMMY

Although a minor character who has already died before the beginning of Amy Tan's *The Kitchen God's Wife,* Jimmy Louie serves as the third part of a love triangle allowing his wife, Winnie, to escape from an oppressive marriage to Wen Fu in post–World War II China. Jimmy's character appears midway through the novel as Winnie Louie relates to her daughter, Pearl Brandt, her secret past. A Chinese by birth, Jimmy serves as a translator for the Americans during the war.

A crucial moment in the novel occurs when Jimmy meets Winnie (then called Wei-Wei), Winnie's friend Hulan, and her husband, Wen Fu. He gives them Americanized names: Winnie, Helen, and Judas, a significant name for the evil Wen Fu. This renaming acts as a symbolical renewal for Winnie, whereas Jimmy's Christianity and belief that a higher power orchestrated his meeting of Winnie makes the act doubly significant. They share a dance during which each feels a mutual attraction, but Jimmy's presence gains importance only later in the novel.

Sparked by a chance reunion in about 1945, romance between Jimmy and Winnie develops, until they share a marriage based on love that contrasts greatly with Winnie's first abusive, patriarchal marriage. Wen Fu causes Winnie to serve a two-year imprisonment in China while Jimmy travels to America, building on his strong religious beliefs to become a preacher. Winnie eventually joins Jimmy, but only after Wen Fu rapes her. The reader learns that Pearl is actually Wen Fu's biological child, raised believing Jimmy to be her father. Pearl's name reflects her position as a jewel, something of great worth, in the eyes of her parents. Jimmy's positive cultural influence helps Pearl overcome any possible negative effects caused by her father's legacy. Although not a dynamic character, Jimmy remains vital to Winnie's success story. He undergoes no change himself, but his love helps Winnie to evolve as a character.

See also: Fu, Wen; *The Kitchen God's Wife;* Louie, Winnie; Love Triangle; Patriarchal Marriage; Tan, Amy; War

References: Armstrong, 1990; Brown, 1996; Chan and Harris, 1991; Chen, 1995; Foster, 1996; Price, 1983

LOUIE, WINNIE

The protagonist of Amy Tan's *The Kitchen God's Wife,* Winnie Louie represents a strong female quest heroine. She participates in the oral tradition of storytelling by relaying to her daughter Pearl Brandt the gruesome details about her secret first marriage to Wen Fu. She married in China as a naïve girl, soon to be horrified by her husband's abuse. Trapped in a patriarchal marriage in which the husband's actions are supported by tradition, Winnie undergoes multiple humiliations and physical and psychological abuse by Wen Fu, who also disposes of her dowry. She dreams of escaping the terror-filled relationship early on and launches into what will prove to be a lengthy and difficult quest to achieve that freedom.

The horror of Winnie's marriage is mirrored in the horrors of the Chinese war with the Japanese, a war that threatens the Chinese traditional way of life and provides a partial framework for the novel's plot. Winnie describes herself to her daughter as both weak and strong. She feels weak due to her lack of power within her first marriage but strong in the fact that she never ceased hoping for a better life. She saves a set of silver chopsticks from her dowry, symbolizing the value of her hope, hidden away but ever-present.

Her constancy in never losing faith that she will escape the torture of Wen Fu is at last rewarded by the devotion of her second husband, Jimmy Louie, a devout Christian who supplies the symbolic Americanized name of Judas for Wen Fu. First she must suffer through much additional pain and anguish, particularly when Wen discovers her feelings for Jimmy. Although Wen does not love Winnie, neither does he desire her to find fulfillment with Jimmy. Theirs becomes a frustrating love triangle in which, for a prolonged period of time, none achieves happiness.

Winnie loses three children to Wen's violence and makes the horrific decision to abort additional pregnancies to prevent the similar abuse of any future children. In this manner, she sacrifices the ultimate in love and pride to her nemesis. Eventually imprisoned for two years on account of Wen, Winnie finds her confinement easier to suffer than the emotional prison in which her husband has entrapped her. At last free to go to America and unite with Jimmy, Winnie suffers a final rape at the hands of Wen, an encounter that at last brings her joy in the form of her daughter, Pearl. Jimmy raises Pearl as his own, and Pearl learns of her real parentage only through Winnie's narrative.

Winnie Louie must be seen as a victorious quest heroine and a dynamic character as she evolves from an innocent girl into a mature and savvy woman and mother. She meets many symbolic monsters in her journey through life as she seeks the reward of love. A descent into the hellish relationship with her husband brings her close to death, and she suffers the personal losses required of all quest heroes and heroines during her quest. She triumphs, however, eventually embarking on a sea journey to America and producing her own greatest treasure in her daughter, the symbolically named Pearl.

See also: Fu, Wen; *The Kitchen God's Wife;* Louie, Jimmy; Patriarchal Marriage; Quest; Tan, Amy; War

References: Armstrong, 1990; Brown, 1996; Chan and Harris, 1991; Chen, 1995; Foster, 1996; Price, 1983

LOVE IN THE TIME OF CHOLERA

In his 1985 magic realist novel, *Love in the Time of Cholera,* Gabriel García Márquez chronicles a fifty-year story of unrequited love. Shaped mostly through flashback, the plot focuses on a love triangle that includes Fermina Daza, her physician-husband Dr. Juvenal Urbino, and the bastard Florentino Ariza. Soon after the novel opens, Juvenal Urbino dies in a freak accident. Fermina Daza experiences much grief over his. Readers learn that Florentino Ariza and Fermina Daza had been young lovers decades before, and Florentino Ariza's feelings for her have never altered, even throughout her lengthy marriage. Florentino Ariza surprises Fermina Daza in her home following the funeral, when he declares his undying love for her. Insulted that he should approach her in such a manner during her time of mourning, Fermina Daza orders him from her house and retreats to her room. However, they begin slowly to communicate in the same manner they had used as young lovers, by writing letters. Thus they begin, in their seventies, to reclaim a love aborted many years before.

The story flashes back to a time when both Fermina Daza and Florentino Ariza were little more than children. Florentino Ariza, a serious penniless poet-musician, becomes enthralled with the wealthy young schoolgirl Fermina Daza. He watches her in the park by day where her maiden aunt closely guards her. Romancing Fermina Daza with nighttime violin serenades and original poetry, Florentino Ariza falls hopelessly in love. They exchange many letters, one of several ways in the novel that García Márquez emphasizes the importance of writing, and eventually Florentino Ariza wins Fermina Daza's devotion as they share a forbidden love. Because Fermina Daza belongs to a distinguished and wealthy South American family, her father will not permit the wedding. He sends his daughter away, and Florentino Ariza also departs, heartbroken and sick from love. He compares the passion he feels to the illness of cholera, a disease that often runs rampant in South America.

Eventually Fermina Daza returns, as does Florentino Ariza, but she accepts the proposal of the soon-to-be-renowned physician, Dr. Urbino. The two marry, and García Márquez establishes the age-old dichotomy of imagination versus logic by setting the poet Florentino Ariza in competition with the scientist Dr. Urbino for Fermina Daza's love. Florentino Ariza's poetry best symbolizes him when one of the novel's figures speaks of the dangerous character of the poet. As for Dr. Urbino, he will eventually make great progress in helping bring the cholera epidemics under control. Florentino Ariza's earlier comparison of love to the illness that Dr. Urbino champions suggests that as a scientist, Dr. Urbino controls his passions too well.

Over the years, Florentino Ariza observes Fermina Daza, although she is hardly aware of his presence. He gradually develops his acute sense of business, at first earning an income by writing love poetry for others. A very passionate man despite his small size and funereal demeanor, Florentino Ariza loves women. Much of the novel's humor derives from his many love affairs and his attitude toward intimate relations with other women, which in no way detract from the more elevated passion he nurtures for Fermina Daza. His feats in bed are edged with aspects of magic realism, as are his ideas regarding the metaphysical powers of love.

At one point, Florentino Ariza wins a poetry contest for which Fermina Daza presents the prize, but she barely acknowledges his existence. Although Florentino Ariza knows Dr. Urbino, the latter knows nothing of Florentino Ariza or his love for his wife for some time. When Florentino Ariza finally meets Dr. Urbino face to face, he decides not to reveal his secret. His discovery that the doctor shares his passion for Fermina Daza comes as somewhat of a shock. By the time Dr. Urbino dies and Florentino Ariza may at last approach Fermina Daza again, both of the lovers have changed drastically. As time passes, however, they discover their feelings have not changed.

García Márquez offers a challenge to the stereotypical image of older couples as no longer interested in a physical relationship. Ever the careful and devoted lover, Florentino Ariza dissolves Fermina Daza's defenses. They at last consummate their love, emotionally as well as physically, aboard a ship emptied of all except its captain. The ship moves up and down a river in a kind of mock quest, flying a flag that signals the presence of cholera to ensure that no one will approach the boat. Florentino Ariza's years-old reference to the similarities of love to cholera takes on a renewed meaning, as does his love.

See also: Ariza, Florentino; Daza, Fermina; Forbidden Love; *The House of the Spirits; Like Water for Chocolate;* Love Triangle; Magic Realism; Quest
References: Stratton, 1987; Zamora and Faris, 1995

LOVE TRIANGLE

The term *love triangle* indicates one of the most common plot ploys in romantic fiction, that of the romantic involvement of three people, two of whom generally love the third. Only one of the two will win the love of the third character, bringing conflict to those plots containing love triangles, many of which involve an already married, engaged, or promised couple and an interloper. The three characters may consist of any combination of genders, and the members may be lovers in an emotional or a physical sense. Although modern romances often feature multiple women competing for the love of one man, the most traditional situation involves two males, often from differing social classes, vying for the love of a female (see *Anna Karenina, Doctor Zhivago, The Great Gatsby, A Handful of Dust, The Journey, Love in the Time of Cholera, Madame Bovary, A Room with a View, Tom Jones, Wuthering Heights*). Differences between the competitors may involve class differences, racial differences (see *The Last of the Mohicans, Of Love and Dust*), and cultural differences (see *The Awakening, Daisy Miller, Gone with the Wind, Sophie's Choice*). In some instances, one member of the triangle may be acquainted with his or her competitor but remains unaware that they share the same object of affection or interest (see *The Scarlet Letter, A Tale of Two Cities, The Thorn Birds*). Another plot twist involves complete ignorance regarding the existence of a third character on the part of the protagonist (see *Jane Eyre*).

When two men are involved, they may compete on a material or physical level for the attentions of the woman. When two women compete for the love of a male, they generally act in a more emotional realm, offering a psychological support missing from the relationship between the man and the other woman (see *The Accidental Tourist, Ethan Frome, The French Lieutenant's Woman, Like Water for Chocolate, The Prince of Tides, The Unbearable Lightness of Being*). Occasionally, multiple love triangles exist between a single character of one gender and multiple characters of the opposite gender (see *Enemies: A Love Story),* or one character may cause conflict for multiple couples (see *The Robber Bride*).

In some cases, a member of a love triangle may already have died, but her or his presence remains strong enough to negatively affect the relationship between the remaining two people who may be caught up in a love affair themselves (see *Rebecca*) or may continue in some type of emotional competition despite the removal of the

love interest (see *Wuthering Heights*). In other instances, the third character may have already died but returns as a ghost (see *Beloved*). In *Beloved,* the ghost is actually the dead child of the female protagonist, but her otherworldly possessiveness interferes with romance for her mother. This situation, of a family member other than a spouse, such as a child or mother, acting as the third member of a triangle, may exist when characters are living as well (See *The Shadow Bride, Sons and Lovers*).

Whatever the exact situation, the love triangle continues to prove invaluable in tales of romance. Reflecting reality, the conflict caused by intertwined, inharmonious love relationships remains an appealing and compelling aspect of romantic plots.

References: Armstrong, 1990; de Rougemont, 1983; Hoffman and Murphy, 1996

LUCY

Jamaica Kincaid's 1990 autobiographical novel, *Lucy,* contains many aspects of the romantic quest and several traditional romantic elements. Kincaid inverts these traditional aspects to fit her nontraditional female quest protagonist, Lucy Potter. In addition to gender-related themes, *Lucy* includes themes of identity, alienation from self and culture, daughter-parent relationships, and expression through the written word. The theme of romance is subverted by Lucy's untrusting attitude toward the opposite sex. Although she enjoys physical encounters with men, she desires no love relationships. She bases her decision on her perception of men as deceitful, a perception that apparently grew from Lucy's observation of the interaction between her parents and her husband's various lovers.

As a quest heroine, Lucy partakes in a journey over water from her home in the West Indies to America, where she encounters various adventures. Kincaid offers guide figures for Lucy, but ultimately they all prove to be false, or ironic, guides. Lucy works as a nanny, caring for the four children of a wealthy married couple, Mariah and Lewis. Even though Mariah at first seeks to provide advice for Lucy, a teenager in a foreign culture, ultimately Lucy can better evaluate Mariah's circumstances than Mariah can her own. Mariah's wisdom proves a false wisdom, inherited from a twentieth-century patriarchal culture that continues to oppress its females. When Mariah's supposedly perfect marriage begins to disintegrate, her cultural training prevents her from recognizing a situation that Lucy easily sees. Similarly, Lucy's friend Peggy seems at first a type of guide figure. Like Mariah, however, Peggy does not know herself, so she cannot provide good advice for Lucy. Peggy warns Lucy against taking her acquaintance Paul as a lover, claiming that she detests Paul and that he is not to be trusted. Yet ultimately Peggy ends up in an affair with Paul. Although the two do not confess their involvement to Lucy, she figures it out through intuition. The only problem Lucy sees is the couple's future disappointment when they discover that she does not care about their involvement. Lucy anticipates these developments and determines to use her perception of human nature to prevent the deception regarding romance that her new culture propagates. She does not, however, develop a clear perception regarding her relationship with her mother, who sends her dozens of letters that the she refuses to read.

Much of Lucy's curiosity focuses on sex. Kincaid continually loops through Lucy's adolescent and pubescent memories as part of her character's search for identity. The clear definition of herself, separate from her mother, becomes the goal, or treasure, that Lucy seeks on her quest. With a discussion of Lucy's name, Kincaid offers a fine example of the theme of both identification with, and separation from, a parent that is inherent to most quest stories. Because one's name acts as the most intimate signifier of identity, Kincaid can appropriate this tool in exploring Lucy's ideas about herself.

Just as Kincaid, born Elaine Potter Richardson, chose a new name for herself when she began her writing career, so Lucy searches for a different name as a child. She hates her name, Lucy Josephine Potter, for various reasons, and at first decides to appropriate the first names of some favorite authors and characters. This action foreshadows Lucy's later choice of writing for a vocation, and it also aligns Kincaid with a strong heritage of women writers. Lucy unwittingly at last chooses, and then announces, a name for herself that makes her mother furious. It is the name of her father's lover, who tried to murder her mother while she was pregnant with Lucy. Perhaps in retaliation for Lucy's innocent mistake or perhaps due to the strain of her pregnancy with a fourth unwanted child, her mother informs Lucy that she was named for Lucifer, or the devil.

Again, Kincaid revels in subversion. Although the expected reaction on Lucy's part to her mother's revelation would be bewilderment or pain, Lucy instead reacts with joy. She finds thrilling her association by name with Lucifer, John Milton's ultimately romantic figure from *Paradise Lost* (1667), a character later evaluated by many as a quest figure. Thus, Kincaid's subversion echoes that of literary critics that have commented on Milton's Satan as a Byronic hero in the centuries following his introduction. Most tellingly, this scene permits emphasis on the all-important identity element found in quest stories. Lucy understands the parallel between herself and Lucifer as that of two devil-children produced by god-figures. Her beliefs regarding her mother's unattainable position and the great emotional gulf separating the two becomes clear in this, the novel's climactic scene.

Ultimately, Kincaid's romance involves mother-daughter relationships rather than relationships between men and women. The consideration of this relationship remains crucial to Lucy's epiphany regarding her own identity. She finds that identity in the novel's concluding words. A release of tears of shame that smear her first written words as a budding author represents a baptismal cleansing of Lucy's past that will free her creative instincts.

See also: Bildungsroman; Kincaid, Jamaica; Paul; Potter, Lucy Josephine; Quest
References: Brady, 1996; Campbell, 1949, 1968; Ferguson, 1996; Garner, 1997; Kincaid, 1995; Nagel, 1995; Simmons, 1994

LUNG, WANG
Pearl Buck's rendering of Wang Lung, the Chinese protagonist of her 1931 novel, *The Good Earth,* results in a character with a strong attachment to the land from which the book takes its name. A farmer by vocation and dedication, Wang Lung retains his lifelong belief in the ultimate value of the land through all his various stages of life. He admires the land, and even though it sometimes treats humans capriciously, from that land Wang Lung draws his strength. Everything else—family, personal desires, life, and even death—remain secondary to the land's importance. This importance offers the focus for Wang Lung's activities.

When he brings his new wife O-lan to his home to live with himself and his father, she becomes a part of the system to gain the most the land has to offer. As partners the two work diligently to ensure the land's production of grains that bring their growing family prosperity and satisfaction. Wang Lung feels pride in his new wife, despite her unattractive features and large feet, mainly because she does serve both him and the land well. Theirs is a patriarchal marriage, and Wang Lung rules his wife as he does the rest of his property. However, when she asks to return to the great house of Hwang to display her son and tout her successful marriage to her former owners, he agrees to allow this. Subsequent to her visit, Wang Lung purchases some of the Hwang land. In this manner, the land takes on a new significance, allowing the farm family to claim a part of what belonged to a family of a much higher social level than their own.

Wang Lung undergoes the test of famine and despair, as the pride he once feels for his wife and two sons dissolves into the pain of not being able to provide for them. The drought that turns the land against him follows the birth of his first girl, and he takes the girl's appearance as a bad portent. As the family's leader, he decides to move everyone south to a city in hopes of finding food. O-lan, starving and weakened, delivers their fourth child but strangles the infant girl, understanding she would cause a further burden to Wang Lung. The two again become a team in the city, subsisting in a shelter built from mats. He pulls a rickshaw, and she and the boys beg in order to feed themselves. Their daughter shows evidence of retardation, and in a strange inconsistency, Wang Lung feels much affection for the child that he labels "the fool." Wang Lung must protect himself from kidnapping by soldiers who "enlist" the poverty-stricken slum inhabitants to go to the war front. A revolution allows Wang Lung's family the opportunity to return home, after they participate along with the other residents of the city's poor quarter in the looting of wealthy households while their inhabitants flee the uproar in terror.

A return home means a return to the land, the source of Wang Lung's strength. His return to wealth, however, brings with it new challenges. No longer required to work the land himself, he becomes bored with his life. His boredom is exacerbated by the sudden rebelliousness of his

sons and also by relatives who take unfair advantage of their blood relationship to Wang Lung's prosperous family by moving in. In an act that causes many readers to judge him harshly, Wang Lung acquires an expensive mistress, Lotus Blossom, whom he settles in a new inner court in his home. The guilt he feels over the subjection of O-lan to such an indignity is not strong enough to alter his behavior. The beautiful Lotus offers him a chance to enjoy the beauty appropriate to his high social status. But with her arrival, O-lan's position in the household and in his eyes diminishes. Even his family, which now includes five children, does not bring Wang Lung much happiness. He feels competition from his oldest son for Lotus's attentions, and she does not like his younger children. When Wang Lung evicts his eldest son, once his pride and joy, from the household and feels guilty over his rejection of his longtime helper, O-lan, the delight he hoped to find with Lotus diminishes. Only with his renewed attention to the earth does he find happiness. He grieves briefly following O-lan's death and that of his father, but that death is followed by the birth of a new grandson, emphasizing the eternal balance of life. Wang Lung's vulnerability shows only occasionally, such as when he learns his daughter-in-law is too weak to nurse her child. Readers suspect that he remembers with longing the strength of O-lan, who gloried in nursing all his children, even as she worked alongside him in the fields.

As Wang Lung's life proceeds and his children mature, he enjoys continued wealth. Conflict occurs in his relationships with his children and also with Lotus Blossom. When her young attendant, Pear Blossom, catches Wang Lung's eye as well as that of his youngest son, Lotus feels jealousy. She remains a part of the household, however, and Wang Lung's only wife until his death. From Wang Lung's youngest son comes the sole romantic spark in the novel. He nurtures his love for Pear Blossom on the western tales of chivalry that he reads as he becomes, like his two older brothers, a scholar rather than a farmer. When he realizes he can never possess Pear Blossom, he runs away, ostensibly to fight at war, an act traditional in romance literature for one who suffers a love that can never be realized.

Buck shapes a hero in Wang Lung whose heroism comes from his acceptance of the life-and-death cycle. He works honestly within his culture to become all a farmer should and cannot really be faulted for any behaviors that appear unseemly in his relationships with women. He does no more or less than he should within his society and triumphs over life's challenges repeatedly due to his devotion to his land. At the book's conclusion, when readers learn that Wang Lung's sons will sell his beloved land at his death, Buck does not promote any feelings of pity for the old man. Rather, she abruptly concludes the tale with the young men lying to Wang Lung, smiling over his head as they share their secret. Wang Lung will die with his land intact, unable to control its destiny. Most important is that he return to the dust that cradles O-lan and his father and that offered him a lifetime of hope and prosperity.

See also: Buck, Pearl Sydenstricker; *The Good Earth;* Lotus Blossom; O-lan; Patriarchal Marriage
References: Armstrong, 1990; Hoffman and Murphy, 1996; Lipscomb, Webb, and Conn, 1994

MADAME BOVARY

Gustave Flaubert's 1857 romance, *Madame Bovary*, has been proclaimed the most influential of the many great nineteenth-century works of fiction. A story of a socially oppressed woman whose passion for life is squelched by her patriarchal environment, the work was the only one of its kind in its day. Considered pornographic by some, merely threatening by others, Flaubert's first and most superior novel was immediately censored in his home country of France. It projected a scorn for society by its author that society reflected back upon him and his family when the French government indicted Flaubert for indecency. However, the public's concern over the novel's moral issues did not long distract readers from its revolutionary focus on social and gender inequities.

Emma Bovary appeared as a new type of woman, independent of the various attributes of the stereotypical female romance character. Many believe that Emma was based on Flaubert's mistress, Louise Colet. Flaubert's ability to realistically reflect the society of his day was demonstrated when multiple women claimed that they felt they *were* Emma Bovary. Readers' high level of identification with a character fueled the fire of an androcentric system's anger against Flaubert. Through Emma's emotional and psychological suffering, Flaubert offered a representation, in his opinion, of the typical woman. His novel acted as a cautionary tale, warning husbands of the consequences of neglecting their wives. This was a message an androcentric nineteenth-century society did not want to hear. Thus, a furor emerged that centered not upon Flaubert's theme of neglect, but rather on Emma's two illicit sexual affairs and their consequences for her family.

Critics praise many aspects of the novel, one being Flaubert's approach to narration. Although the novel begins in first person, apparently related by a friend of Emma's husband, Charles Bovary, it later switches to third person. The change allows readers to see events from Emma's perspective, challenging the reader to empathize with Emma's loneliness and to resist becoming judgmental over her sexual indiscretions. Flaubert also resists the urge to add moral commentary, even though it was common for authors of his day, such as English writer Charles Dickens and Russian authors Leo Tolstoy and Fyodor Dostoyevsky, to insert comments in their narratives. This lack of authorial intervention allows readers to develop ideas on their own.

The novel's abundant symbolism aids in understanding its main character, and its consistent foreshadowing prepares readers for a tragic conclusion. For instance, Charles's intellectual failings prevent his gaining a medical degree, resulting in his clumsy practice of medicine. His lack of degree and skill symbolizes his personal failings as a husband. He lacks ambition and passion, two characteristics that Emma possesses in abundance. In addition, on the day of Emma's wedding to Charles, the celebration is described in great detail, but the reader observes that Emma does not enjoy it. She rejects her lot, that of a peasant, and longs for a more socially elevated life. It also acts as foreshadowing of the day she will borrow huge sums of money in hopes of transcending her middle-class existence, bankrupting herself and Charles. The ball Emma attends at the grand chateau of La Vaubyessard, a nobleman living close to her home village of Tostes, symbolizes the attainment of her dream. But the fantasy is short-lived, ultimately increasing Emma's frustration and foreshadowing her inability to distinguish between reality and fantasy. When the Bovarys' daughter, Berthe, is born, she should symbolize a new life for Emma, who has a chance to be reborn herself. Instead, Berthe comes to symbolize Emma's increasingly burdensome feelings of responsibility toward a way of life she finds repulsive. Where the dashing, rascally Rodolphe seems to symbolize all that Emma desires in life, he misrepresents his intentions of marriage. His indecent behavior and use of Emma as simply a sexual plaything symbolize the false promise of the images of romance that Emma learned to crave from her childhood reading.

The title is important, for it makes clear that, like most women, Emma gains significance due to her relationship to her husband—to her role as "Madame" Bovary—not as Emma Bovary. This reflects society's attitude toward women, who are often evaluated only on the basis of their relationships with men. Flaubert also provides a perfect example of the male gaze, a literary element important to feminist critics. Traditionally, when men stare at a woman, assessing her physical beauty, they overlook intellectual or character traits. By objectifying the female, they treat her like they might an object of art rather than a fellow human being. All of the men in the novel employ the gaze upon first meeting Emma. We learn characteristics of the males not from Emma's description of them, but from the details of their perception of Emma.

Emma Bovary's tragedy established a hallmark that provided both inspiration to, and a basis of comparison for, subsequent romance writers. Authors influenced by the character of Emma and her story or by Flaubert's naturalistic approach included Kate Chopin, Willa Cather, John Dos Passos, Henry James, and many others. The novel's lasting effect may be proven in its wide translation, its three film versions appearing from 1934 to 1991, and in its continued reading more than a century following the initial negative reactions it evoked.

See also: Bovary, Emma; Flaubert, Gustave; Patriarchal Marriage
References: Cowley, 1959; Gourgouris, 1995; Sturrock, 1994; Wood, 1994

MAGIC REALISM

Magic realism refers to a kind of writing in which a blending of the realistic and the fantastic occurs. First made popular by the South American Nobel Prize winner Gabriel García Márquez (see Love in the Time of Cholera), the technique has also been used in romantic novels by Isabel Allende (see The House of the Spirits) and Laura Esquivel (see Like Water for Chocolate). Magic realism differs from realism in that the effects of natural laws governing time and space

may be suspended from time to time throughout an otherwise realistic story. It differs from fantasy in that such natural laws remain in place during much of the story. Fantastic elements in magic realism are accepted by the characters, who deal with them as they would realistic elements. One of many examples in Esquivel's Like Water for Chocolate may be found in a scene in which the main character, Tita, cooks a dish using the rose petals given to her by her secret lover. All who taste the food experience Tita's passion, especially her sister, who is overcome by the heat of love. When she races to the outhouse shower to cool off, the structure catches fire from the heat of her passion, but the cause for that fire is never questioned. Magic realism asks readers to suspend their disbelief only at certain moments in a plot. García Márquez, Allende, and Esquivel all attribute their use of magic realism to the influence of a great storytelling tradition within their families.

See also: Allende, Isabel; Esquivel, Laura; García Márquez, Gabriel
References: "Isabel Allende," 1997; Jenkins, 1994; Smith, 1997; Tawes, 1997; Zamora and Faris, 1995

MAGUA

In James Fenimore Cooper's historical romance, The Last of the Mohicans (1826), the Huron Indian, Magua, serves as the most frightening and threatening of its several villains. An individual who pledges allegiance to no one other than himself, he uses both factions participating in the French and Indian War that acts as background for the novel to his own benefit. A stereotype of the ignoble Indian, Magua serves to create chaos and terror for all of the story's good characters, but especially for the dark beauty, Cora Munro.

Magua's true name is Le Renard Subtil, a name that reveals his supposed loyalty to the French. Present in the novel's early scenes, Magua purports to act as scout for a party composed of four whites, Cora Munro, her sister Alice Munro, Alice's eventual sweetheart, Major Duncan Heyward, and David Gamut, a singer. After several hours of travel, however, the group discovers it seems to be moving in circles, based upon information from some mysterious travelers who intercept the women and their companions in the woods. These travelers become the novel's true heroes. Led by a white woodsman name Hawkeye, the Indian chief Chingachgook, and his nephew, Uncas, the last of the Mohicans to which the novel's title refers, they will take over the duty of guides for Major Heyward and his charges. They attempt to capture the wily Magua, but he executes the first of several escapes. He returns later with a group of Iroquois Indians and ambushes his former charges.

When the Indians successfully capture Heyward, the Munro sisters, and Gamut, Heyward appeals to Magua to leave the Iroquois marauders and instead guide them safely to Fort William Henry, where the Munro sisters' father holds command. At this stage of the story, Cooper introduces conflict and unease when Magua agrees to act on Heyward's plea only if Cora Munro, whom he admires much for her beauty, will become his wife and slave. This proposal elicits a violent reaction from Heyward, who terms Magua a "monster," and Cora goes a step further, associating the Indian with Satan himself when she questions whether he intends to stand between her and God. Even the retiring Alice declares that for Cora to become Magua's wife would be far worse than death. When Cora refuses the plan, the furious Magua threatens to kill the entire group, hurling an ax with such accuracy that it cleaves some of Alice's curls from her head.

Nineteenth-century readers would have found the Indian's proposal to mix races in marriage an outrageous example of forbidden love. Magua's reduction to a villain remains all the more effective for Cooper's earlier reflection, through dialogue between Cora and Major Heyward, on the obvious nobility of Uncas, who acts as Magua's foil.

Magua continues to cause conflict for the novel's heroes throughout their adventures. Although his captives escape once, he will recapture them, as well as Heyward and Uncas. In one memorable scene, Magua displays an effective approach to rhetoric, as his speech whips his comrades into a fury, promoting their desire to kill their captives. This scene allows Uncas and Magua to stand face to face, challenging one another for the prize that Cora represents.

Uncas eventually dies for his love at Magua's hands. Hawkeye, the novel's true hero, will in turn kill Magua, and Cora falls victim to another Huron brave. As a villain, then, Magua succeeds in eliminating the novel's lesser hero and even one of its heroines, even though he loses his own life

in the process. His actions remain important, for they allow Cooper to avoid altogether the sticky social situation represented by a romantic union between a white woman like Cora Munro and even the most noble of Indians, such as Uncas, the last hope of the Mohican tribe.

See also: Cooper, James Fenimore; Forbidden Love; Hawkeye; Heyward, Major Duncan; Munro, Alice; Munro, Cora; Uncas
References: Barker and Sabin, 1996; Budick, 1996; Frye, 1976; Price, 1983

MARIA

In Ernest Hemingway's wartime romance *For Whom the Bell Tolls* (1940), the young Spaniard, Maria, acts as love interest for the novel's protagonist, the American Robert Jordan. In addition, she symbolizes Spain itself and the revolutionary atmosphere of her country just previous to World War I. As a victim of the Fascist forces of Francisco Franco, Maria makes concrete Jordan's abstract dedication to freedom for all humans, regardless of nationality. His love for Maria may be seen as symbolic of his total commitment to the Spanish revolutionary cause of freedom.

When Jordan, a Spanish instructor from Missoula, Montana, arrives in Spain in May 1937, he becomes a bridge blower for the Republicans. When he reaches a guerrilla band in hopes of soliciting their support for a bridge bombing mission, he encounters Maria. Whereas the other band members are soldiers for a public cause, Maria fights to overcome the effects of a private encounter with the enemy. Because she has been physically tortured and abused by Fascist forces, she symbolizes the ravages of war. Her emotional fragility reflects that of her body and mind, as she verges on insanity caused by her harsh treatment. Her shaved head, an unnatural attribute for a beautiful woman, serves to emphasize Hemingway's theme of the loss of order during the chaos of war. In the circumstances of armed conflict, humans must look for different signs of beauty in each other. One such sign is devotion to a cause.

Important to Jordan's character development is the fact that Maria insists upon their relationship. Jordan does not seduce her; her innocence and youth would prevent his ever forcing his attentions on her. That Maria may still symbolize purity, even following her recent experiences, is emphasized by her name, which suggests that of the virgin Mary. Jordan becomes Maria's unlikely protector and lover during their brief relationship, offering the ultimate sacrifice when he trades his own life for hers at the novel's conclusion.

Although Maria and Jordan do not remain together, their relationship is crucial to the story. Jordan rescues Maria from her victim role; through the power of love, she may heal emotionally. Maria enjoys a rebirth of sorts in Jordan's arms, her youth and their experience combining to symbolize hope for a new political order in Spain.

See also: A Farewell to Arms; For Whom the Bell Tolls; Hemingway, Ernest; Jordan, Robert; The Lost Generation; Nihilism; Pilar; The Sun Also Rises; War

References: Cowley, 1973; Defazio, 1996; Donaldson, 1996; Hart, 1995; Hen, 1996; Hily-Mane, 1995; Hotchner, 1966; Moreland, 1996; White, 1933, 1968

MAUGHAM, W. SOMERSET

William Somerset Maugham remains best known for his realistic approach in his fiction to romance and life in general. Born in Paris in 1874, where his English father worked at the British embassy, Maugham would eventually publish twenty novels, dozens of short stories, travel books, and volumes of essay and autobiography during his sixty-year career. Although never touted as a writer deserving of the same critical acclaim as his contemporaries, James Joyce and D. H. Lawrence, Maugham's realistic fiction was immensely popular. The Nobel Prize for literature may have escaped him, but by his eightieth birthday, Maugham's book sales in the United States alone totaled four and a half million.

When he was orphaned at the age of ten, Maugham went to live with his uncle and experienced an upbringing that he would utilize in his later novel, Of Human Bondage (1915). Shy due to a stutter, he received an education at King's School in Canterbury, where he developed a strong sense of aesthetics. He spent a year in Germany at Heidelberg University, attending lectures on philosophy, studying German, and writing the first of twenty-nine plays. Upon returning to England, he continued writing while a medical student at St. Thomas Hospital, publishing his first novel, Liza of Lambeth, in 1897, the same year he received his medical degree. The popular reaction to his realistic novel featuring

the lower classes encouraged him to abandon any ideas about establishing a medical practice in order to write full-time.

Maugham's writing reflected the influence of writers such as Guy de Maupassant, Anton Chekhov, and fellow Britons Joseph Conrad and Oscar Wilde. The skeptical viewpoint his characters evince is credited to Maugham's studies of philosophers Arthur Schopenhauer and Bertrand Russell. His writing has been labeled simple, lucid, and euphonic, using language in an informal yet fluent way and based on traditional narrative techniques. Fraught with a detached irony, Maugham's plots deal with various topics from love to racism.

His works focus on adults interacting with other adults to solve traumatic emotional and psychological conflict. His characters remain imperfect and often "sinful" but are usually redeemed by personality traits such as joie de vivre. According to Maugham, a joy for life could compensate for a multitude of sins like irresponsibility, egotism, or instability. He avoids issuing any kind of editorial judgment on his characters, depicting them through dialogue and action only. His stories avoid melodrama by approaching action realistically; some action occurs away from the reader's eye and is learned about, as in true life, only by its later consequences.

When Of Human Bondage appeared in 1915, it garnered the success that propelled Maugham into his lengthy career. Labeled one of the best English novels of its time, his highly autobiographical work features a young medical student, Philip Carey, who would like to paint but learns that he lacks the talent to do so. Raised by a selfish, grasping uncle and burdened by a club foot that hobbles him both emotionally as well as physically, Carey repeatedly returns to an unsatisfying love affair due to his poor self-image, thus reinforcing the idea of bondage alluded to in Maugham's title. Additional novels included The Moon and Sixpence (1919), a story based on the French painter Paul Gauguin and featuring the theme of conflict between an artist and the conventions of society, and The Razor's Edge (1944), whose protagonist also fights society's preconceptions of his proper place in life. Most of Maugham's fiction appeared between 1915 and 1945, with many of his short stories first published in magazines such as Collier's, Cosmopolitan, Nash's, and The Smart Set before appearing in book collections. Eight of his novels and short stories were translated to film.

Although some biographers have depicted Maugham as strictly a kindly and charitable individual, the more honest accounts present him as a complicated and acerbic man whose bisexuality, unsuccessful marriage, and unhappy later life often influenced his writing. Fortunately, after his death in 1965 Maugham left behind a voluminous correspondence that sheds light on his philosophical, literary, and personal influences.

See also: Of Human Bondage

References: Archer, 1996; Drabble, 1995; Heil, 1996; Sopher, 1994

MCCULLOUGH, COLLEEN

Colleen McCullough, destined to become Australia's best-known author, was born in 1937. Originally from New South Wales, she was very close to her brother, whose later death she found quite painful. Her father worked in the sugarcane fields, but her mother was determined to educate her children to do something else. Colleen eventually graduated from the University of New South Wales with an honors degree in science. Her various vocations include, in addition to professional writer, teacher, journalist, library worker, and bus driver. She enjoyed the study of neurophysiology and later earned a master's degree in London from the Institute of Child Health. She served first as a research associate in neurophysiology at Yale University, where she eventually took the position of head of research laboratories in the Department of Neurology.

Although she loved her work in the sciences, McCullough began writing part-time for extra income. Her first novel, *Tim* (1974), was quietly received. The love story of a middle-aged woman and a handsome younger retarded man, this novel continues to receive positive critical acclaim, although it was not a big hit with the popular reading public. In 1977, McCullough was finishing preparations to travel to England to begin nurse's training when her publisher received her manuscript *The Thorn Birds*. The novel garnered instant fame for McCullough, who received the largest advance ever given for a paperback book, $1.9 million. The highly romantic tale of forbidden love between a New Zealander and a priest, *The Thorn Birds* remains a wildly popular novel and became a television miniseries. McCullough published seven additional novels, but none achieved the popularity of *The Thorn Birds*. The novels include *An Indecent Obsession* (1981); *A Creed for the Third Millennium* (1983), her only science fiction attempt; and *The Ladies of Missalonghi* (1987), which she terms her "fairy tale." Although she was accused of plagiarism by the family of L. M. Montgomery, author of the Anne of Green Gables series, no legal suit was brought against McCullough. Her later Master of Rome series, based on thirteen years of research into the history of Rome, includes *The First Man in Rome* (1990), *The Grass Crown* (1991), *Fortune's Favorites* (1993), *Caesar's Women* (1996), and *Caesar* (1998). Many critics praise her attempts to write about various subjects in her novels. None, however, have achieved the popularity of *The Thorn Birds*, which became the fifth-best-selling novel of its decade.

Her anonymity lost and her fame assured following the success of *The Thorn Birds,* McCullough canceled plans for further schooling and moved to tiny Northfolk Island in the South Pacific. She found privacy and a husband there, marrying Ric Robinson when she was forty-six years old. He raises palm trees while she writes, keeping more than a dozen typewriters on hand. The island's undependable power system makes the use of a computer risky. Her husband participates in the island's governance, and McCullough enjoys volunteer work. She serves as a consultant in clinical neurophysiology to the royal North Shore Hospital at Sydney. In 1993, she received a Doctorate of Letters from Macquarie University in honor of her research into ancient Rome.

Said to be at her best when writing about women characters, Colleen McCullough remains important to the world of fiction for her best-selling second novel. *The Thorn Birds*'s characters, Meggie Cleary and Father Ralph de Bricassart, remain this versatile novelist's best-known creations.

See also: The Thorn Birds

References: Bridgwood, 1986; Faison and Whipple, 1996

MILLER, DAISY

Daisy Miller represents the epitome of the American spirit in her desire for independence. Her female character type would reappear in several of Henry James's books following the publication of his novella, *Daisy Miller,* in 1879. Daisy herself remains essential to James's penchant for

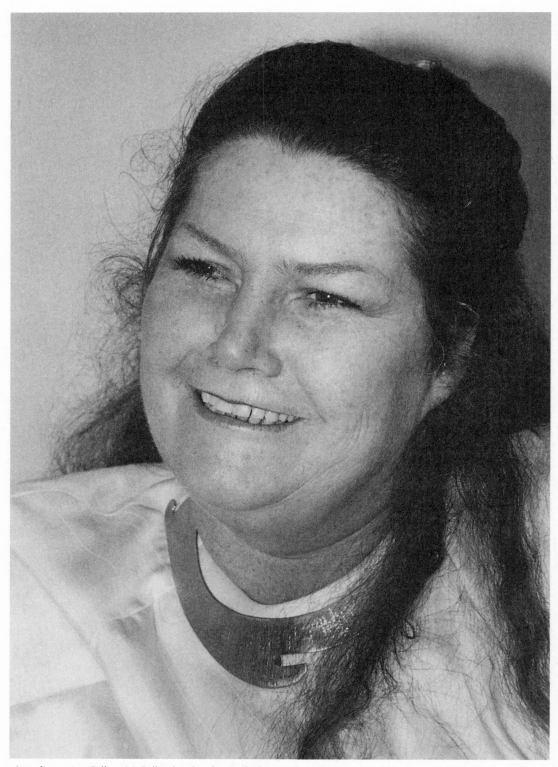

Australian writer Colleen McCullough is best known for her 1977 novel, The Thorn Birds, *the highly romantic tale of forbidden love between a New Zealander and a priest. (UPI/Corbis-Bettmann)*

creating significance from barely noticeable scenes. She is that most unusual of main characters who must be termed "flat" because she undergoes no change, and her point of view is not used to tell the story. Yet she remains omnipresent. From the moment she meets fellow American traveling abroad, Frederick Forsythe Winterbourne, Annie P. "Daisy" Miller dominates the narrative stage.

Although "spoiled" might be an accurate adjective to apply to Daisy, the casual observer of James's character shaping quickly notices that label does not apply. Daisy Miller spoils no one's fun and takes no unfair advantage. Her beauty quickly enthralls all who meet her, but she seems impatient with such shallow topics. If Daisy seems accustomed to getting her way, it is because her way remains so appealing and her honesty so disarming. As made clear by Winterbourne's thoughts, an independent and intelligent young woman must be considered overindulged and single-minded, unlike her male counterpart, who would be called bright and enterprising for expressing the enthusiasm and thirst for experience that Daisy expresses. Thus, James incorporates the theme of gender inequity shaped by faulty cultural attitudes.

James so thoroughly understands his characters' psyches that he must allow them to do what they will, even when the consequences will be tragic. Readers who protest Daisy's eventual death from malaria as an undesirable conclusion to James's story overlook the fact that those who surround her attempt to kill Daisy's spirit from the first page. At age twenty-seven, Winterbourne, whose name represents the frigid climate that will kill a daisy, reflects an oppressive maturity that does not know whether it remains young or has already grown old. As much as he would like to think otherwise, Winterbourne serves only as a mouthpiece for the social harpies who descend upon Daisy to destroy her independence by muzzling her mind. He remains dependent on two of the older women who criticize Daisy, suffering torn loyalties between the social right they represent and Daisy's social wrongs. Caught up in a destructive love triangle, his jealousy over Daisy's relationship with the romantic Italian, Giovanelli, promotes tunnel vision in the young American that disallows his faithful championing of Daisy's approach to life. With Winterbourne's weak favor as her only support, Daisy cannot expect to survive the social gauntlet she will be made to run.

Daisy brings romance as well as tragedy to James's story; her beauty, intelligence, and wealth make her the perfect candidate for the perfect young man. But Daisy Miller neither asks for nor requires perfection. She desires only a true friend, someone with whom she can exchange ideas. The social niceties she finds banal, and logic dictates that only Giovanelli, free from the oppressive attitudes toward ritual that seem to possess Americans, can provide an outlet for Daisy's inquisitive mind.

Poetic justice dictates that her independent spirit will cause Daisy Miller's literal, and literary, death. She meets her end, but not as the typical tragic romantic heroine. Instead Daisy Miller dies, not for the love of a man but for loyalty to her own instincts.

See also: Archer, Isabel; *Daisy Miller;* James, Henry; Love Triangle; *The Portrait of a Lady;* Winterbourne, Frederick Forsythe
References: Caeserio, 1979; Frye, 1976; Hart, 1995; McQuade et al., 1987; Washington, 1995

MISCEGENATION
See The Black Experience in America, 1600–1945

MISHIMA, YUKIO
Born in 1925 in uptown Tokyo as Kimitake Hiraoka, Yukio Mishima would become the leader of Japan's postwar generation of novelists. His mother was well versed in literature, part of a family of educators and Confucian scholars, and his father worked for the Agriculture Ministry as deputy director of its Bureau of Fisheries. Mishima was raised in an upper-class neighborhood, where he enjoyed the space of a two-story house and the service of a houseboy and a half-dozen maids.

The young Mishima spent his first twelve years living in the first-floor sickroom of his grandmother. He said that she believed "bad friends" lurked outside the house and that he should remain in the safety of her room. During the great amount of time he spent with her, he occupied himself in reading many types of stories. *Arabian Nights,* a book titled *Children's Literature of the World, Robinson Crusoe* (1719) by Daniel Defoe, and *Treasure Island* (1883) by Robert Louis Stevenson, along with works by the

Japanese writer Tanizaki Junchiro, sparked his imagination, and Mishima began writing his own children's stories.

As a youngster, Mishima first became impressed by gruesome stories containing imagery of blood and death. At the age of twelve, he wrote his first fiction while a student at the Peers School. The editor of *Bungei-Bunka* (*Art and Culture*) noticed the work and asked Mishima to write a story for his publication. For that story, he adopted the pen name that would soon become famous. He viewed Kabuki, or Japanese theater involving dance, at age thirteen and saw German and French operettas as well as foreign movies, although his grandmother feared the possible negative effects of such activities. Very involved with Kabuki and also puppet shows in his junior high school years, he finally experienced the Japanese theater known as Nō when fifteen. Theater had a great effect on Mishima's life, and he would later comment on missing Nō during his trips outside Japan. Despite Mishima's writing success, his father discouraged his son's creative tendencies, urging him to resist the swelled ego that might be caused by the attention his stories gained.

In 1944, Mishima began attending the Imperial University, where he studied German law. When World War II broke out, he received a draft notice but did not serve in the army. He worked instead in an airplane factory and eventually graduated with a college degree in 1947.

Two years later Mishima achieved literary success when his novel *Confessions of a Mask* (*Kamen no kokuhaku,* 1949) was published. He followed this achievement with other works, including *Thirst for Love* (*Ai no kawake,* 1969), *Forbidden Colors I* (*Kinjiki,* 1968), and *Forbidden Colors II* (*Higyo,* 1968). In 1954 his work based on the classical romance tradition, *Shiosai,* later translated as *The Sound of Waves* (1956), won the Shinchosa Literary Prize and would be twice made into a film. This novel achieved a high popularity with western readers, probably due to his use of many aspects of the western tradition of the romance genre. However, Mishima could not account for his work's wide acceptance, claiming he never wrote with westerners in mind. He explained that a visit to Greece inspired the story, one of his first to consider the surface of human relationships rather than the hidden side. The simplicity of life and sunlight in Greece permanently af-

fected Mishima, causing him to feel revulsion toward the Japanese intellectual and what Mishima described as the haggard look worn by intellectuals that celebrated their suffering. His book *The Temple of the Golden Pavilion* (*Kinkakuji,* 1950, trans. 1959) spawned ten different film versions. Additional works include *Five Modern Nō Plays* (1957) and another novel made into a movie, *The Sailor Who Fell from Grace with the Sea* (1965). Mishima also developed a reputation in a nonliterary arena as an obsessive bodybuilder, which led to a study of karate and the samurai arts known as kendo and Bushido.

In the 1960s Mishima denounced the West's influence on Japan and became an increasingly militant figure. He joined ultranationalist efforts to resist the impact on culture from outside Japan, and his name became associated with militant movements. In 1967 he entered the basic training unit of the Army Self-Defense Force. The following year Mishima created his own army of civilians, called the Shield Society. Others viewed the group as a conservative militaristic endeavor, but Mishima characterized its mission as the promotion of Japan's return to tradition, particularly that of the samurai. Mishima trained new recruits, designed their uniforms, and even wrote a marching song for the Shield Society.

Regardless of his military pursuits, Mishima continued writing, an activity he practiced from late night until dawn. The first two volumes of *The Sea of Fertility,* the work that would be his last, were published in 1969. In that same year, Mishima wrote a ballet and two three-act plays, and he continued serving as a member of the board of directors of the Japan Symposium on Culture. In order to prevent unscheduled interruptions of his writing by his cadets, he organized regular advisory meetings with them in the rented lower floor of a coffeeshop. He purposely distanced the cadets from his literary achievements, believing youth with literary interests to be unsuited to the military life.

To celebrate the one-year anniversary of the Shield Society in 1969, Mishima held a dress parade and invited dozens of foreigners as well as Japanese to a celebration of his militaristic efforts. He never again spoke to those who did not accept the invitation. The anniversary date would later serve as the day of his suicide, for which he planned carefully, enlisting the aid of three cadets. The suicide ceremony was prepared far in advance, and Mishima begin isolating himself from others before the event in order to sever personal ties. In 1970, he submitted the final volume of *The Sea of Fertility,* and on November 25, he and the society cadets entered the headquarters of the Army Self-Defense Force to meet with the commander. Mishima promptly took the commander hostage and delivered a ten-minute speech from a balcony to the crowd gathered below. Following the ideological speech, to which some members of the crowd reacted with jeers, Mishima returned to the commander's office. There he committed ritualistic hara-kiri using the samurai sword. He first plunged a dagger into his abdomen, drawing it across his body in a seventeen-centimeter incision. After this horrific demonstration of physical control, Mishima was beheaded by his cadet assistants. The suicide strongly resembles that described in Mishima's widely anthologized short story, "Patriotism" ("Yukoku"), reprinted from *Death in Midsummer and Other Stories* (1966).

A letter written by Mishima before his death requested his burial in military uniform. He indicated that his loyalty was to the militant movement supporting Japan's ethical traditions rather than to the arts. He requested that the Japanese character for sword, *bu,* rather than that for pen, *bun,* be included in his Buddhist name. Mishima's *Complete Works,* which included his very first story, were published posthumously and contain all his writing, both childhood and adult.

See also: Forbidden Love; Hatsue; Longus; Shinji; Romance; Quest; *The Sound of Waves*
References: Atkinson, 1989; Hutton, 1993; Keene, 1995; Longus, 1989; Wolfe, 1989

MITCHELL, MARGARET

Born in 1900 in Atlanta, American writer Margaret Munnerlyn Mitchell wrote one of the most popular novels of all times in her American Civil War romance, *Gone with the Wind* (1936). Mitchell's mother, Mary Isabelle Stephens, came from Irish-Catholic stock, and her father, Eugene Muse Mitchell, descended from the Scotch-Irish and French Huguenots, and various family members had participated in the Civil War.

Interested from an early age in the tales of the Civil War that she heard from relatives and aged Confederate veterans, Mitchell rode through the Atlanta countryside on her pony gathering stories. An imaginative girl called "Peggy" by family

and friends, Mitchell was known to arise in the middle of the night to write in a manner that some labeled obsessive. She lived with her mother and attorney father in a number of Atlanta homes, including her favorite on Peachtree Street beginning in 1912. Not an exceptional student, Mitchell attended private school until announcing to her mother that she hated mathematics and intended to drop out. As the story goes, her mother took Mitchell to a rural southern area to view plantation homes in ruin. She chastened the young girl by lecturing that such ruin would again visit the South, and the only manner of escape from destitution available was the application of knowledge and physical labor. Not only did this stern lecture motivate the errant Mitchell to return to school, but her mother's topic reappeared as a theme in *Gone with the Wind.*

Mitchell attended Smith College in 1918, following the involvement of the United States in World War I. The death of Clifford Henry, her fiancé, killed while fighting in France, was closely followed by the death of her mother during a flu epidemic in 1919. She returned to Atlanta to care for her father and brother, Stephens.

There Margaret Mitchell gained a reputation as an independent thinker. Although she participated in a debutante "coming out" ball, she disagreed with her high society peers over the distribution of the money they had raised for charity. Like the fictional Scarlett would later do with Rhett Butler, Mitchell supposedly caused a scandal by performing an inappropriate dance at the ball with a Georgia Tech student.

As a 1920s "flapper," Mitchell enjoyed the attentions of two suitors, a football player and bootlegger, and a newspaper man. She chose to marry the bootlegger, Berrien "Red" Upshaw. Their stormy relationship would be a short one, and the two divorced by 1924. This freed Mitchell to return to the newspaper man, John R. Marsh, who had waited for her. Less than a year after her divorce they married, making as their home a ground-floor Atlanta apartment Mitchell termed the "dump."

She worked as a reporter, contributing to the *Atlanta Journal* from 1922 until 1926, when she began work on *Gone with the Wind* while convalescing from several injuries. She spent ten years writing the work that would garner the 1937 Pulitzer Prize after becoming an immediate best seller. The motion picture version of *Gone with the Wind,* released in 1939, remains one of the most popular American films ever made. Although modern and postmodern critics would view the novel as sentimental romanticism that minimized the horrors of slavery and the subordinate position of women in the South, Mitchell's themes were acceptable in her day.

Mitchell herself was later revealed to have taken a progressive attitude toward segregation, involving herself with Atlanta's African-American community during a time when such involvement made her unpopular with her own white community. As a debutante, she had worked in the black clinics of Atlanta, and her concerns for the medical treatment of blacks caused her rejection by Atlanta's Junior League. She also supported early efforts to desegregate Atlanta's police department.

In 1941, Morehouse College President Benjamin Mays approached Mitchell for help in supporting promising black students at his school. She contributed anonymously the sum of $80, enough to sponsor a student through an entire year of school. After receiving a letter from Mays describing the tremendous effect her gift had on the student, Mitchell made regular contributions to a scholarship fund for black students on the condition that Mays would keep secret her participation. He revealed the information only long after her death. Her generosity received publicity when Otis Smith, the first certified black pediatrician for the state of Georgia, released the details. A past president of the Atlanta chapter of the National Association for the Advancement of Colored People (NAACP), Smith had benefited from the Mitchell scholarship funds. When he was a first-year student at Meharry Medical College in Nashville, Tennessee, Smith exhausted his money and told Mays he would have to drop out of school. Mays took care of his tuition and fees, and thirty-five years later revealed that Smith had received one of forty-fifty gifts Mitchell made to African-American medical students.

While crossing the street on August 11, 1949, Mitchell was hit by a speeding taxi. She died from her injuries five days later and was buried in Atlanta's Oakland Cemetery. For decades, *Gone with the Wind* was believed to be her only surviving written work. Later, another piece of fiction, *Lost Laysen,* was discovered. In 1997, a comedy manuscript titled *Oh! Lady Godiva!,* long believed to have been destroyed, surfaced at a University of Southern California library. The drama spoofs Atlanta in the 1920s, its plot involving a search for the perfect woman to portray Lady Godiva. The search remains unsuccessful because all of the suitable candidates sported bobbed hair.

See also: The Black Experience in the America, 1600–1945; Butler, Rhett; Byronic Hero; *Gone with the Wind;* O'Hara, Scarlett; Violence; War; Wilkes, Ashley; Wilkes, Melanie

References: Armstrong, 1990; Flora and Bain, 1987; Hoffman and Murphy, 1996; Joiner, 1996; "Margaret Mitchell House," 1997; "Third Work of Fiction," 1997

MONDEGO, FERDINAND

Ferdinand Mondego acts as one of the antagonists to Alexandre Dumas's hero, Edmond Dantes, in the nineteenth-century historical romance, *The Count of Monte Cristo* (1844). A shipmate aboard the *Pharaon* with Dantes, Mondego sails with him into the Marseilles harbor in 1815. Of all the characters who cause trouble for Dantes, the real name of the Count of Monte Cristo, Mondego is perhaps the most villainous. Not only does he contribute to the plot to imprison the innocent Dantes, but he does it as he pretends to be Dantes's best friend. Later, while Dantes languishes in prison, Mondego steals away Mercedes Herrera, Dantes's fiancée.

A fisherman who supposedly befriends the nineteen-year-old Dantes, Mondego is jealous of his relationship with Mercedes. Along with another villainous fellow shipmate named Danglars, Mondego writes a note to interested authorities, accusing Dantes of smuggling a letter from the exiled Napoleon Bonaparte following the *Pharaon*'s stopover at the island of Elba. After Dantes is arrested on his wedding day and imprisoned on false charges of treason, Mercedes struggles to support herself and Dantes's elderly father. Mondego tries to convince Mercedes to marry him, but her loyalty to Dantes remains steady. However, following the death of Dantes's father, Mercedes at last concedes defeat. The old man leaves her nothing because his son's enemies have also stolen his resources. With her fiancé in prison for life and without income, Mercedes sorrowfully agrees to marry Mondego.

In addition to his betrayal of Dantes and his successful manipulation of Mercedes, Mondego also swindles and betrays the Pasha Ali in the 1823 Greek revolution, stealing most of that official's money. His wealth grows to the point that he gains the undeserved title of the Count de Morcerf. Like all evil men in romance plots, Mondego will answer for his crimes. Eventually, Dantes does leave prison in a daring escape and sets about to ruin the men responsible for his imprisonment.

When Dantes meets Mercedes, she recognizes him but does not reveal his identity to her husband or to anyone else. Dantes uses his contacts to learn of Mondego's deceit against Pasha Ali, who happens to be the father of Dantes's eventual love and traveling companion, Haidee. Dantes then reveals his findings in public. Although Albert de Morcerf, son of Mercedes and Mondego, challenges Dantes to a duel to defend his father's honor, Dantes declines the duel when Mercedes begs for her son's life. When Albert accepts the truth regarding his father, he denounces Mondego publicly, declaring his father deserving of ruin.

In the type of convoluted plot at which Dumas excelled, Dantes gains retribution against all his enemies, including Mondego. Perhaps Mondego's greatest punishment comes in the form of his family's rejection. When Mercedes learns of her husband's many evil acts, she deserts him, as does Albert. Isolated and ruined both financially and politically, Ferdinand Mondego shoots himself. He becomes the second of Dantes's four intended victims, and thus remains crucial to the plot and moral lesson of *The Count of Monte Cristo*.

See also: The Count of Monte Cristo; Dantes, Edmond; Dumas, Alexandre; Herrera, Mercedes; Romance

References: Campbell, 1968; Campbell, 1988; de Rougemont, 1983; Grierson, 1974; Hulme, 1974; Spurr, 1972

MORRISON, TONI

Born Chloe Anthony Wofford in Lorain, Ohio, on February 18, 1931, Toni Morrison unabashedly confesses to a desire to be a force behind the development of a collective body of work by

Novelist Toni Morrison, shown here receiving the 1993 Nobel Prize for Literature, has written many works whose black protagonists face conflict with members of their own race, often resulting in isolation and contempt from their peers. (Reuters/Pressen Bild/Archive Photos)

black writers. This novelist's presence in the literary community has helped promote inquiry into the politics behind the selection of works that constitute the contemporary "canon" of American literature. In asking those who traditionally read works by white European males to embrace multicultural literature, Morrison refuses to accept gender and racial creative oppression by her largely Caucasian androcentric culture.

Morrison believes that her range of perception and emotion is enlarged by her racial and gender experiences and that using her own Midwest as a setting for her novels allows a change from more stereotypical black environments, such as the cotton field or slums. The second of four children born to George and Ramah Wofford, Morrison matured during the Depression and learned from her ship welder father the dangers for blacks in trusting the basically empty promises of the white community, a lesson that became a major theme in her fiction. She also came to understand the alienation of blacks from each other in a subculture that often demands conformity from its own. Morrison's black protagonists generally face conflict with members of their own race, often resulting in isolation and contempt from their peers.

In 1953, Morrison earned a bachelor of arts in English from Howard University, where she minored in classical studies, and she received her master's degree from Cornell University in 1955. Following graduation, Morrison served as an English instructor at Texas Southern University in Houston for two years and at Howard University in Washington, D.C., from 1957 to 1964. During this time she married a Jamaican architect, Harold Morrison, whom she divorced in 1964 after having two children.

Between 1965 and 1985, Morrison served as a senior editor for Random House, where she helped aspiring black writers such as Tony Cade Bambara reach publication. Not until 1969 was her first highly acclaimed novel, *The Bluest Eye,* published. Like her many works to follow, this novel features a community of blacks suffering from internal as well as external abuse and highlights their coping mechanisms.

Morrison assumed a position as associate professor in the English Department of the State University of New York at Purchase between 1971 and 1972 and produced her second novel, *Sula,* in 1973. This book garnered a National

Book Award nomination in 1975 and the Ohioana Book Award of 1975. *Song of Solomon* (1977), which earned both the National Book Critics Circle Award and the American Academy and Institute of Arts and Letters Award, became only the second novel written by an African American to be selected for the Book-of-the-Month Club. It was followed by *Tar Baby* in 1981 and an appointment to the Albert Schweitzer Chair in the Humanities at the State University of New York at Albany from 1984 to 1989. During these years, Morrison wrote a play, *Dreaming Emmett,* and arguably her most well-known and popular novel, *Beloved* (1987). *Beloved* received many awards, including the Robert F. Kennedy Award (1988) and the Pulitzer Prize for fiction in 1988. This novel celebrates spirituality and mysticism in a way not seen before in American fiction, making clear Morrison's belief that science is completely inadequate for explaining certain phenomena in our everyday lives. Her subsequent novel, *Jazz* (1992), appeared to much fanfare, and she became the first black woman and the second American woman to win the Nobel Prize for Literature in 1993.

Morrison feels she shares the concerns of many and speaks to those concerns through her fiction. Thus, a larger sense of humanity as a group is reflected in her characters' struggles to deal successfully with family, community, poverty, and oppression. Morrison attracts and holds her readers by incorporating vivid dialogue and superb narrative devices that evidence her obvious respect for the language. Her mystical imagery, at once religious and superstitious, is such an integral part of the stories and characters that it is immediately believable.

In addition to her many literary awards, Morrison has won the Elizabeth Cady Stanton Award from the National Organization for Women, and her interest in black culture has led her to join several organizations dedicated to human rights. She has been a trustee of the National Humanities Center and has co-chaired the Schomburg Commission for the Preservation of Black Culture.

See also: Beloved; The Black Experience in America, 1600–1945; Violence
References: Blain, Clements, and Grundy, 1990; Davidson, 1995; Dougherty, 1996; Friedman and Siegel, 1995; Middleton, 1997; "Morrison, Toni," 1997

MUCH ADO ABOUT NOTHING

William Shakespeare's drama *Much Ado about Nothing* (1598) features several plot elements that would later be incorporated into much romantic fiction. With a lush Italian villa as its setting, the play's themes of lust and love are suggested by Mediterranean images of bright warm sunshine and the fecundity of a culture that nurtures both crops and romance. The beautiful surroundings are further elevated when Shakespeare introduces exotic and lofty characters, formal festivities such as a costume ball, and music.

The play's major plot involves Hero, the daughter of the governor of Messina, who will be falsely accused of sexual disloyalty to her fiancé, Count Claudio of Florence. Don John, the comedy's villain, lays a trap for Claudio, probably out of jealousy for Claudio's close friendship with Don John's half-brother, the powerful Don Pedro, Prince of Arragon. Bitter over his position as a bastard son, Don John realizes he will not inherit the wealth that goes to his legitimate brother. Apparently a malcontent who enjoys causing trouble for trouble's sake, he focuses his evil intentions on Claudio and Hero. Don John plots for his henchman to woo Hero's serving woman in sight of Claudio and Don Pedro. When the two noblemen hear the henchman call out the name "Hero," they immediately assume that Hero is guilty of a serious indiscretion. At the wedding on the following morning, Claudio questions the innocent Hero's virginity, forcing her to suffer the humiliation of a public rejection.

Mistaken identity and false accusations remain staple plot elements of modern romance writing. Plot details vary, but often the villain is a friend of the male lover, himself in love with the female victim. He sets the scene for a false accusation in order to dissolve the courtship. Normally, the woman slandered is a fiancée, and on occasion she suffers a literal rather than a symbolic death, as Hero does in Shakespeare's drama. Following the revelation of innocence on the young woman's part, many versions take to task the young male lover for his gullibility and lack of faith in his intended mate. Some also include an aspect of conflict between love for one party and friendship for another, reflected in Shakespeare's character, Benedick.

Just as fiction writers have imitated Shakespeare's plots, he imitated those of others. The major plot for this drama was derived from several classical and contemporary sources. Ariosto's tale in *Orlando Furioso* of a romantic encounter in which the Scottish princess Gernevra is mistaken for her maid Dalinda would have been available to Shakespeare in translation by 1591. He also would have known of Edmund Spenser's tale of mistaken identity involving his characters Phedon, Claribell, and the false Philemon, found in the second book of his 1590 work, *The Faerie Queene*. Several French, Latin, and Italian plays had already incorporated such a plot. In 1585, an anonymous English playwright adopted under his title *Fedel and Fortunio* one of the most popular Italian dramatic versions, Pasqualigo's *Il Fedele* (1579). Although each writer adopted the same basic plot, each in turn shaped it according to his narrative needs.

Much Ado about Nothing also contains a subplot introducing a "feuding" couple. They begin the drama at odds but end up admitting that their sparring is an outward sign of romantic feelings. The play's duo of Beatrice, Hero's cousin, and Benedick, a lord of Padua, entertain and delight audiences with a fast exchange of insults and jibes that contrast refreshingly with Hero and Claudio's more sentimental exchanges. Whereas Hero and Claudio represent the naïveté of first love, Beatrice and Benedick symbolize a mature love that does not demand moonlight and roses. They base their relationship on intellect. Shakespeare hints, through Beatrice's initial interchange with Benedick, that she had previously loved him, but that their relationship had not proved successful. Like two chess players who try to anticipate each other's moves, Beatrice and Benedick become perfect partners in a game of love. Although Hero and Claudio's romance exists in the public eye, a necessity due to their aristocratic standing, that of Beatrice and Benedick is observed in various private settings. This encourages audiences to develop a less formal concern for, and attachment to, these tempestuous lovers.

Trickery plays a crucial role in the development of their romance, but this trickery differs from the evil ruse plotted against Hero and Claudio. Friends of Beatrice and Benedick connive to unite the two by planting the suggestion that Beatrice loves Benedick in his mind and that Benedick loves Beatrice in hers. This causes each to recognize the other not as a nemesis but as a partner worthy of love and affection.

Like romance, comedy demands a happy end-ing. As its title suggests, the conflict caused between Hero and Claudio by Don John will be resolved, after much in the way of high drama and comedic display. Although tragedy for a time threatens the happy couple, Shakespeare's plot leaves comedy in firm control, both through the bantering of Beatrice and Benedick and the malapropisms of the local sheriff, Dogberry. The play becomes a celebration of love's victory over the dark forces of jealousy and suspicion. It appeared as a movie in 1993, helping to claim a new generation of devotees to one of Shakes-peare's most widely enjoyed comedies.

See also: Beatrice; Benedick; Claudio; Hero; Romance; Shakespeare, William
References: Barton, 1974; de Rougemont, 1983

MUNRO, ALICE

Like her sister, Cora Munro, and other characters in James Fenimore Cooper's nineteenth-century historical romance *The Last of the Mohicans* (1826), Alice Munro remains little more than a stereotypical romance character. As such, she serves her role well, acting as the fair damsel in distress from the romance tradition that Fenimore used repeatedly in his fiction. Alice plays the love interest for Major Duncan Heyward, a figure rep-resenting the best of the American fighting man in the novel's setting of the French and Indian War. Theirs will be the only romance that sees fruition in the novel, and Heyward and the other male characters will commit multiple acts of der-ring-do in the interest of the Munro sisters.

Described in the opening chapter as the younger and more petite of the two women, Alice boasts golden hair, a blushing complexion that dazzles onlookers, and blue eyes that com-pete with the sky overhead in their brightness. Her description sets her in direct contrast to her darker, more exotic, older sister, Cora. Although devoted to one another, the two differ in other ways as well. Dignified and beautiful, Cora repre-sents the exotic promise of nature in all its fecun-dity and wild allure. She also exhibits a measured amount of strength, actively protecting her younger sister, expressing her opinion on matters social and political, and showing courage when facing dangerous men. In an early scene in which the sisters hear a terrible cry, Cora sets an exam-ple for Alice through her steadiness and obedi-ence of the men in charge of their party. Alice,

however, remains shy and retiring, constantly expressing her shock and surprise by crying out in fear and fainting at opportune moments. At one point her tiny figure must be wrapped in an oversized blanket in order to fool Indian bystanders into thinking that Major Heyward is carrying a mature Indian woman, and her small feet, a mark of the desirable woman of the times, are remarked upon. She literally clings to Heyward on several occasions with a dependence compared in the narration to that of an infant.

Alice is not without her moments of courage, however. When the Huron Indian villain, Magua, demands Cora as his wife in exchange for free-dom for the remainder of the party of white set-tlers, Alice states that compliance to that demand would be a fate worse than death. She agrees to die rather than sacrifice her sister in this manner. Later, when Heyward informs Alice that he has spoken to her father regarding his desire to marry her, she trembles violently, yielding to emotions that Cooper terms "common to her sex" but then straightening up to challenge Magua regarding his next actions.

Alice exists mainly to allow Heyward and his male companions, the scout Hawkeye and the Mohican Indians Chingachgook and Uncas, mul-tiple chances to display their courage. At the end of the novel, she is hidden within a litter that car-ries Cora's body, and her sobs remain the only evidence of her existence. A flat character who experiences no evident epiphany or realization throughout her horrendous adventures, Alice Munro will, the reader assumes, at least live hap-pily ever after in the care of Major Heyward.

See also: The Black Experience in America, 1600–1945; Cooper, James Fenimore; Forbidden Love; Hawkeye; Heyward, Major Duncan; Magua; Munro, Cora; Uncas; Violence; War
References: Barker and Sabin, 1996; Budick, 1996; Campbell, 1968; "Cooper, James Fenimore," 1986; Frye, 1976; Price, 1983; Wimsatt, 1974

MUNRO, CORA

Although a stereotypical character, Cora Munro fulfills a crucial role in James Fenimore Cooper's historical romance *The Last of the Mohicans* (1826). She represents the typical damsel in dis-tress but falls into the subcategory of a somewhat active female, in that she expresses her attitudes openly when allowed. However, in a final evalu-ation, she remains helpless to rescue herself from either physical or emotional threats. Cooper himself reduces Cora and her fairer, more passive sister Alice Munro, to the general category of "female," the label he most often applies to them. Thus, readers who understand nineteenth-century American culture will know the sisters are present mainly for use by the male characters as objects of romance and rescue within a plot framed by the violent French and Indian War. Neither woman is intended to be a dynamic character.

Cooper establishes a familiar dichotomy between the dark Cora and the fair Alice early on, with their initial descriptions appearing at the conclusion of his opening chapter. Cora represents the exotic side of beauty with her dark coloring, produced by a certain richness of blood, according to the author, that threatens to burst its containment. Her raven-black hair immediately allows an identification with nature, an important parallel for Cooper to draw in his nature-centered story. To prevent any confusion between Cora and the American Indians who frequently appear throughout the story, both as heroes and foes, Cooper qualifies his description, staying in step with the attitudes of the time. He assures readers that no measure of coarseness or shadow sits on Cora's brow; she remains in every way the picture of dignity and culture.

Cora does fulfill her exotic promise by adding controversy to the novel's romantic aspect. The story's major villain, the Huron Indian Magua, demands that Cora become his wife in return for the freedom of her sister, their protector Major Duncan Heyward, and another traveling companion. This scene allows Cora to act as any respectable white woman would have been expected to; she categorically refuses the Indian's offer, after first ascertaining that her sister would rather they both die than see such a trade enacted. But Cooper's contemporary readers likely suffered more discomfort later in the story when they discovered that Cora has a slave ancestor and also loves the novel's "good" Indian, the Mohican brave Uncas. This forbidden love guarantees that both Cora and Uncas will suffer death before the novel concludes rather than be allowed to act on a romantic inclination that might leave readers aghast at its challenge to the normal social order.

Cora performs several acts deserving of reader respect. She becomes a voice against prejudice when she suggests that judgment regarding the sincerity of an Indian scout should not be based on the color of his skin. Major Heyward confirms that Cora's father, commander of Fort William Henry, believes Cora to be of noble mind, even a model for his own fighting men. In a time of great personal peril as she is held captive in a camp of Delaware Indians, she meets the gaze of the terrifying Magua with level calm, a reaction that contrasts with the fainting spells of the weaker Alice. Rather than immediately giving in to Magua's threats, Cora makes a sincere and even reverent plea, on her knees, to the Delaware chieftain for mercy for her companions and herself.

Despite her brave acts, Cora is presented to Magua by the Delawares in compliance with their cultural standards. At the moment of her death, she retains her dignity by refusing to comply with Magua's command that she choose her own fate. In a peculiar blend of passive and active behavior, Cora acts as a mouthpiece for nineteenth-century women in general. She expresses aloud the lot that most women shared when she tells Magua that she remains his possession, and he must do with her whatever he will. Uncas will also die for Cora's self-sacrifice, but so will Magua, and thus Cora's actions bring about the story's long-delayed climax.

See also: The Black Experience in America, 1600–1945; Cooper, James Fenimore; Forbidden Love; Hawkeye; Heyward, Major Duncan; Magua; Munro, Alice; Uncas; War

References: Barker and Sabin, 1996; Budick, 1996; Campbell, 1968; "Cooper, James Fenimore," 1986; Frye, 1976; Price, 1983; Wimsatt, 1974

MUZQUIZ, PEDRO

As the young lover devoted to Tita de la Garza but doomed to marry her sister Rosaura, Pedro remains a flat character but is nevertheless vital to Mexican writer Laura Esquivel's magic realist novel *Like Water for Chocolate* (1992). Pedro declares his love for Tita in the first few pages of the novel, but his request for her hand in marriage in denied by Mama Elena, matriarch of the de la Garza family. Tita must follow a family tradition in which the youngest daughter of the family remains single to devote herself to the lifelong care of her mother. When Mama Elena offers Pedro the hand of her eldest daughter, Rosaura, rather than that of Tita, he accepts simply in order to remain close to Tita. This act of sacrifice and attempt to overcome thwarted love places Pedro close to hero status.

Following the birth of Rosaura and Pedro's son Roberto, Rosaura is unable to nurse. To Pedro's delight, Tita's love for Pedro allows her to produce milk and feed the child. When the scheming Mama Elena plots to send Pedro, Rosaura, and their baby to Texas, Pedro and Tita endure a physical separation that threatens to end their relationship. Following the death of baby Roberto, the couple eventually returns to the de la Garza ranch in Mexico for the funeral of Mama Elena. When Pedro discovers that Tita is engaged to Dr. John Brown, a local physician who helped her through the depression and subsequent departure from the ranch that followed the news of Roberto's death, he experiences a jealousy he has not yet known. His passion for Tita remains strong, although circumstances appear to succeed in ending their contact. In a bizarre accident, Pedro suffers terrible burns for which Tita must nurse him, and their relationship is reestablished. Unable to resist their passion after his recovery, Tita and Pedro make love, even though Tita is officially engaged to John. Tita believes she is pregnant with Pedro's child. This reassures Pedro of Tita's devotion and love, but when the pregnancy proves to be false, he again dissolves into jealousy over Tita's relationship with John.

In this love triangle, John Brown's scientific approach to life establishes him as representative of logic, whereas Pedro's physical desires establish him as representative of passion. Even as John tells the fable regarding the flames all people bear inside that may return them to their mythological origins, he also uses logic to explain the scientific theory behind matches and fire.

Tita chooses Pedro as her lover, in spite of John's tremendous support, faith, and love for her. In the novel's conclusion, the reader learns that Tita and Pedro have discreetly enjoyed a lengthy physical relationship after establishing an agreement with Rosaura that their passion will forever be kept secret from the couple's daughter, Esperanza. Twenty years pass, and, following Rosaura's death, Esperanza marries John's son from a previous marriage. Tita's magical cooking fills all who attend the wedding with an uncontrollable sexual passion, so they depart early, leaving Pedro and Tita at last alone. In their final lovemaking scene, which is the first time they have

enjoyed the freedom to cry aloud their joy, the fire within Pedro causes his death. Remembering John's fable, Tita consumes candles, in a suicide scene reminiscent of Shakespeare's *Romeo and Juliet,* to enflame her own internal fires so she may follow Pedro in death.

The concluding scene of the novel includes much platonic imagery in the story of the lovers' return to the perfect world that the Greek philosopher Plato believed all humans occupy before their birth. In addition, the souls of Pedro and Tita unite to form the perfect whole that Plato mentions when he writes of partner souls joined in that unearthly world who suffer division through human birth. According to Plato, humans then spend the remainder of their lives searching for "their other halves."

See also: de la Garza, Tita; Esquivel, Laura; Forbidden Love; *Like Water for Chocolate;* Magic Realism

References: Armstrong, 1990; Zamora and Faris, 1995

MY ÁNTONIA

Willa Cather's romantic novel *My Ántonia* (1918) remains significant to American literature because it was among the first novels to speak about the settlement of the Great Plains. Set in early twentieth-century Nebraska, *My Ántonia* tells the story of a long-lasting friendship between the narrator, Jim Burden, and the heroine and title's namesake, Ántonia Shimerda. In addition to exploring the themes of unrequited and platonic love, the novel also explores the struggle for personal independence, the plight of young pioneer immigrants, and their initiation/coming-of-age in a foreign land. As a student, narrator Jim Burden reads Virgil's lines, "for I shall be the first, if I live, to bring the Muse into my country." He explains that in the original Latin, the word translated as "country" is closer in meaning to region or neighborhood, and asserts that he himself aspires to bring the muse into his country of rural Nebraska. In effect, this is exactly what Willa Cather has done in *My Ántonia.*

The novel opens with a conversation on a train between Jim Burden and a former female classmate. The introductory chapter proceeds from the woman's point of view, explaining that Jim asked her why she had never written about their mutual friend, Ántonia Shimerda, in her career as a writer. She invites Jim to write something about Ántonia and send it to her. The subsequent chapters are Jim Burden's account of his childhood and adolescence with Ántonia, offering a story-within-a-story format.

Significantly, chapter 2 also opens with a train ride, as young Jim is transported as a newly orphaned boy from his Eastern home to his grandparents' ranch on the Nebraska plains. The railroad signifies the expansion of the United States from East to West and the national development, or initiation/coming-of-age, of the United States. It also symbolizes sexuality and sexual energy as it plows through virgin territory. Jim and Ántonia first meet as children on the train, each on their way to a new life in an unknown landscape.

Ántonia's family has recently immigrated from Bohemia, and they designate Ántonia as the family member who will learn English and, in turn, teach the language to the rest of the family. Although only a child and several years younger than Ántonia, Jim will serve as her tutor and translator. The two friends enjoy their lessons together and also their other adventures in the prairie wilderness. These shared activities create a bond of experience paralleling the bond of communication through the spoken language.

Jim and Ántonia quickly develop a fondness for one another, and their two families become close friends. Problems arise when the Shimerdas reach a low point in money and resources. Subsequent charitable advances by the Burden family threaten the Shimerda family pride. Their conflict culminates in the suicide of Ántonia's father who, along with Jim Burden, affectionately addressed his daughter as "my" Ántonia. She mourns her father's loss throughout the novel. Her father's presence, both living and as it exists in Ántonia's memory, signifies the loss of the old Bohemian culture and traditions to the adopted American lifestyle and beliefs.

As they grow older, Jim and Ántonia spend less time together but maintain their dedication to the friendship. Jim struggles with his romantic desire for Ántonia and is disappointed when she does not return his feelings. Nevertheless, until Jim leaves home for college, he and Ántonia feel genuinely proud of one another's victories and compassionate toward one another's losses.

Willfulness is Ántonia's strongest character trait. She insists on performing heavy manual labor when her family needs help on the farm. After Ántonia moves into town she refuses to comply with prudent conventions in order to enjoy herself. This aspect of her character both fascinates and frustrates Jim. He wants to possess her heart and keep her safely within the modest bounds of small-town social conventions.

Ántonia's wild and rugged spirit corresponds to the surrounding landscape. The novel's most beautifully written passages describe the enormity of the sun as it descends to the horizon behind an abandoned plow and the faces and bodies of the people defined by their assiduous agricultural pursuits. Fierce storms, rattlesnakes, drought, and other natural phenomena cause multiple conflicts between man and nature in the novel—the people remain powerless in their struggle to possess and control nature. Likewise, Jim Burden remains powerless in his pursuit of Ántonia. She will not be labeled "my" Ántonia by any man.

The novel concludes with Jim's return to Nebraska to visit Ántonia. His destiny called him to be an attorney for the railroad, thus metaphorically granting him the mobility to trespass between childhood and adulthood, old world and new. Ántonia, however, remained on a farm in Nebraska. She married another Bohemian immigrant with whom she could speak her native language and educate her children bilingually. In the closing scene Jim thrills to see how Ántonia's farm has thrived and how her many children play among the prairie dogs as he did. Ántonia found a way to honor her allegiance to her father's memory and the old Bohemian customs, yet her fondness for Jim, albeit not the romantic love he once hoped for, persisted over the years.

The reader leaves the novel with pronounced images of the wild, often fruitful prairie land. Like Ántonia herself, it could not be tamed or possessed.

See also: Bildungsroman; Burden, Jim; Cather, Willa Siebert; Shimerda, Ántonia
References: Armstrong, 1990; Daiches, 1971; Davidson, 1995; Fetterley, 1993; Hart, 1995; Hoffman and Murphy, 1996; O'Brien, 1996; Rosowski, 1989

NAIPAUL, V. S.

V. S. Naipaul was born in Trinidad in 1932. From his Hindu family, he claims to have inherited a sense of the comedic. He spent his undergraduate days at Oxford, arriving in England in 1953 as a scholarship winner. With great self-confidence, due to his fluency in French and Spanish literature as well as English, Naipaul quickly assimilated to the new culture. The famous author J. R. R. Tolkien once told Naipaul that his language papers were the best he had ever received. His pleasant stay at Oxford was followed by years of desperate poverty, and he worked for the Caribbean service of the BBC, for which he wrote short reviews. He was, however, never interested in doing anything other than writing. At Oxford he produced a lengthy novel, never

Valued by some as a postmodern writer due to his most recent works' abandonment of unification of time and place, V. S. Naipaul stresses a sense of the ironic and absurd in his works. (Hulton-Deutsch Collection/ Corbis)

published and later mistakenly destroyed by a London warehouse workman along with other of his works written prior to 1970.

Naipaul's first three novels and collections of short stories focused on Trinidad. *The Mystic Masseur, The Suffrage of Elvira* (1958), and *Miguel Street* (1959) were all published in London before becoming available in the United States. Although he remained with one publisher, Andre Deutsch, for years, Naipaul eventually switched when his editor protested his change in style. His early treatment in the United States left him bitter. *A House for Mr. Biswas* (1961), now regarded as perhaps his finest achievement, received little attention early on. McGraw-Hill undertook a very small printing of the book, an act Naipaul blames on a mistaken vision of his novel as "native writing."

Naipaul has enjoyed a prolific career, with almost two dozen books to his credit. Much of his writing is autobiographical. In "Passenger: A Figure from the Thirties" from his "novel" titled *A Way in the World* (1995), Naipaul fictionalizes his relationship with an unidentified writer and role model through his character Foster Morris. Autobiographical commentary from that section includes his criticism of Morris's work as writing that suppressed the idea of comedy. This was a problem Naipaul faced early in his own writings after settling in London in 1956. He at first attempted to employ English settings but quickly learned they worked to subdue his comic tendencies. A real-life model for Naipaul may be Charles Dickens; *A House for Mr. Biswas* is said to reflect some of the gravity of Dickens's narration in *Great Expectations.* Naipaul has admitted a debt to Joseph Conrad, one of several writers of the English literature he valued as a young student in Trinidad. In addition to Conrad, he mentions Gustave Flaubert and Honoré de Balzac as favorite writers and has nothing favorable to say about his contemporaries such as Gabriel García Márquez who employ magic realism, something Naipaul refers to as "fluff."

V. S. Naipaul has been called the best of the Caribbean authors writing in English. Critics remark upon his fine style, with which he produces sentences that seem to be colloquial, thanks to his characters and subject matter, but which in fact employ perfect diction. Loose yet skillfully honed fiction by Naipaul has alerted the world to the social and political inequities in his home nation of Trinidad. Although a resident of England for years, Naipaul prefers to write about his homeland. He sharply assesses those forces, religions, and superstitions that oppress the Trinidadian population. He does not reserve his disdain for outsiders; instead, his Third World Trinidadian characters also undergo a negative evaluation by Naipaul. Some of his contemporaries, such as Jamaica Kincaid, do not value Naipaul's approach. Kincaid believes that, although a wonderful writer, Naipaul suffers from self-hatred caused by being a Trinidadian who dwells among the English. Other critics claim that Naipaul remains enthralled with the high civilization that England offers while deploring anything that would pull it down to a lower level. Valued by some as a postmodern writer due to his most recent works' abandonment of unification of time and place, Naipaul stresses a sense of the ironic and absurd.

Naipaul's earliest works appeared in the 1950s. He readily admits that his views have changed over time, causing his latest books to differ in theme and subject matter from his earliest. Most recently, his works have begun to blur the distinction between fiction, universally considered "untrue," and another medium in which he excels, the essay, generally considered to be "true." He refers to other authors who have done the same, such as Marcel Proust and W. Somerset Maugham.

In 1994, Naipaul traveled from Wiltshire, England, to Tulsa, Oklahoma, to present his archives to the University of Tulsa. The McFarlin Library there houses all of his surviving manuscripts as well as his correspondence through 1984. He has also traveled to the United States on occasion to undertake interviews and attend literary gatherings. Of his own work, he has said he only hopes that people will find his books interesting and representative of the postwar era.

See also: The Suffrage of Elvira
References: Baker, 1994; Birbalsingh, 1996; Hussein, 1994

NDUDI

In Festus Iyayi's political novel *Heroes* (1986), Ndudi serves as the story's female love interest for the protagonist, Osimi Iyere, but also as a figure symbolizing the country of Nigeria. In the context of the novel's setting, that of Nigeria's civil war, Ndudi represents the various tribes who at first appear to be at war against one another. As the story progresses, however, Iyayi demonstrates that the power and greed of Nigeria's upper class rather than tribal differences actually motivate the conflict. He uses Ndudi's character to demonstrate the terrible price the indigenous people must pay as pawns in a power struggle over which they have no control. Ndudi's powerlessness, both as a woman and as a tribal member at the mercy of the warring Biafran and Federal troops, is plainly shaped for the reader when, in the novel's final chapter, Ndudi becomes the victim of physical assault. She suffers a rape, first at the hands of two Biafrans as they depart her besieged town, and then immediately after by two Federals who arrive on the scene after assuming the power that the Biafrans surrendered.

Ndudi acts as a voice of maturity and reason for Iyere on several occasions. In one important scene, after Iyere accompanies Ndudi and her family on their trip home with her father's body following his execution, Iyere prepares to leave her to travel to the war front. In his position as a newspaper reporter, Iyere seeks facts regarding the war that will help him expose the false claims of the Federals. He tells Ndudi that he will leave behind some of his equipment as a sign that he will return to her. She rejects this idea, explaining that she wants him to return for the sake of love, not to regain his possessions. This act, along with the strength and fortitude she exercises when forced to cope with her father's murder and her own abuse, inspires in Iyere the courage he must display when caught up in battle. Thoughts of Ndudi motivate him to complete his mission and return home to marry her.

Ndudi remains a flat character, undergoing no particular realization or change herself. She is, however, partly responsible for Iyere's epiphany regarding love and ideology that allows him to mature as a character.

See also: Heroes; Iyere, Osimi; Violence; War
References: Price, 1983; Udumukwu, 1996; Wendt, 1990

NIHILISM

The term *nihilism* represents a body of ideas viewed as radical in its rejection of positive values, such as those embodied in metaphysical notions of God or some other higher good. Nihilism should, by some accounts, not be labeled a philosophy, for it exists as a denial of philosophy. Nihilism acts to negate knowledge, ethics, beauty, reality—basically everything. In true nihilism, nothing has meaning. Those who advocate this belief, or lack of belief, feel that reason, once the touted method to reach truth, can no longer be trusted. Nihilism represents a stage of awareness following naturalism, a view supporting science and open intellectual inquiry as pathways to truth. Nihilists would say that modern science has revealed a closed universe causing individuals to feel confined, bringing with it a sense of the notion of death as extinction. They view the idea that humans occupy the highest position in the universe as either alienation from that universe or, conversely, as a union with the universe. Such a union, far from having a positive effect, results instead in a feeling of extreme unimportance, as the individual human amounts to little more than one grain of sand on a vast beach. Nothing seems to affirm the value of human life.

A term first applied to heretics during the Middle Ages, nihilism in the mid–nineteenth century was applied to those Russian intellectuals influenced by western ideas to judge their own society oppressive, leading them to advocate change through violent revolution. Several fictional Russian novel characters represented this type of thought, the most well known being Ivan Turgenev's Bazarov in his novel *Fathers and Sons* (1862). Modern conservative critics of nihilism claimed that such beliefs, which lacked institutionalized ideology, would undercut order within human society as they worked to destroy the concept of a purposeful human existence.

Intellectuals termed nihilism a necessary phase of thought, proposing that humans must suffer disillusionment with their existence in order to bring about necessary changes for the better. Russian nihilists supported the peasant uprising in the 1870s that led to the assassination of Czar Alexander in 1881. A consideration of nihilistic ideas appears in the romantic Russian novel *Anna Karenina* (1875–1877) by Leo Tolstoy.

One of the earliest and most notable American novelists to incorporate nihilistic thought into his novels was Ernest Hemingway. Horrified and sobered by the mass destruction inflicted by humans upon one another in World War I, Hemingway projects his disillusionment onto the characters in his postwar and war novels, such as *The Sun Also Rises* (1926), *A Farewell to Arms* (1929), *For Whom the Bell Tolls* (1940), and various short stories. A prime example in short story form of Hemingway's nihilistic approach is his widely anthologized story, "A Clean Well Lighted Place." In this story, he repeatedly substitutes in the dialogue of a character repeating the Lord's Prayer the word *nada,* a Spanish term translated as "nothing," for the words of the prayer. Hemingway emphasizes the lack of support for humans given by institutions such as religion and government that are traditionally seen as necessary for survival. His "lost generation" characters discover that in their miserable existence, all that can be counted upon for support is the comfort offered by other human beings.

See also: Anna Karenina; A Farewell to Arms; For Whom the Bell Tolls; Hemingway, Ernest; The Lost Generation; *The Sky Is Red; The Sun Also Rises;* War
References: "Christian Apologetics," 1997; "Nihilism," 1993

OF HUMAN BONDAGE

W. Somerset Maugham's realistic romance *Of Human Bondage* (1915) traces the quest for love of its twentieth-century protagonist, Philip Carey. The significance of the novel's title becomes apparent as Philip all but indentures himself to the needs and desires of the novel's antagonist, Mildred Rogers. The misplaced responsibility he feels toward the dull, demanding, and egocentric Mildred grows not from love but rather from Philip's lack of self-esteem. The deaths of both parents early in his life cause Philip's feelings of abandonment, which in turn lead to an early feeling of diminished self-worth. That feeling is later supported by his heartless guardian, Uncle William, in his emotional abuse of Philip. Philip's club foot also causes him lifelong embarrassment and discomfort. Although certainly not a result of any act, either good or bad, on Philip's part, the physical incapacity makes him feel unworthy of human company and acceptance. It thus symbolizes the emotional and psychological crippling that prevents Philip from establishing a satisfying life or love.

Although Philip shows success in his studies at Oxford, studies insisted upon by the controlling Uncle William, he desires most of all to paint. This conflict allows Maugham to emphasize the age-old classical romantic conflict between science and art, rationality and imagination. Philip's sensitive artistic personality eventually leads him to Paris, a center for artists. Here he meets several important characters, including his lifelong nemesis, Mildred. His initial attraction to Mildred, an unattractive and unpleasant waitress, cannot be explained, nor can his repeated attempts to rescue her from her own weakness. She repeatedly rejects Philip, who repeatedly extends charity and understanding to her when she eventually reappears, always in a needy state.

Worse than Mildred's taking materialistic advantage of Philip is her interruption of his developing relationships with other women. Philip's bondage to Mildred remains closely related to his bondage to his own diminished self-image. He does grow as a human when he accepts the criticism of a talented artist that he will never become a great painter. Unlike a female artist acquaintance who commits suicide, Philip accepts the critical assessment of his shortcomings. He eventually leaves Paris to return to London and take up the study of medicine.

Throughout the novel, Philip exhibits a repeated tendency toward procrastination, based again on his lack of self-confidence. He fails to finish projects as he becomes distracted by poverty and episodes with Mildred. Only with Uncle William's and Mildred's eventual deaths, both symbolic of the breaking of Philip's chains of bondage, can he discover true love and his own destiny.

Of Human Bondage began as a long manuscript first titled *The Artistic Temperament of Stephen Carey.* Maugham notes in the introduction to his novel that he first wrote the story as a twenty-five-year-old aspiring writer. Although he completed a medical degree, he published his first book while still a medical student, and he decided to write additional novels upon graduation rather than practice medicine. The manuscript about Carey was rejected by a number of publishers, causing Maugham to assume that he needed more perspective on his highly autobiographical subject matter before he could do it justice.

The novel includes many autobiographical aspects. Philip's club foot corresponds to Maugham's own stutter, and both the character and the author are orphans. Philip's difficult relationship with his Uncle William corresponds to Maugham's own conflict with his own uncle. Both the author and the character study for medical degrees, and both exercise their artistic temperaments. Thus, reading Maugham's novel about Philip Carey offers some insight into the author.

Like that of many successful artists, Maugham's life contains many aspects of the fictional

Leslie Howard as Philip Carey and Bette Davis as Mildred Rogers appeared in the 1934 film version of W. Somerset Maugham's realistic romance, Of Human Bondage *(1915), which traces the quest for love of its twentieth-century protagonist.*

quest projected through his character. Both author and character leave home in order to mature; both embark on calls to adventure involving their education and the practice of their art; both engage in journeys over water; both have guides in the form of literary and artistic models; both are faced with losses and choices; and both eventually claim the prize available to all quest heroes. The prize may be recognized as Philip's eventual healthy romantic relationship with the daughter of a previous patient and Maugham's development of a tremendously successful literary career. Maugham's use of romantic elements in realistic settings, as is done in *Of Human Bondage,* made him immensely popular. The book was made into a movie several times.

See also: Carey, Philip; Maugham, W. Somerset; Rogers, Mildred

References: Archer, 1996; Heil, 1996; Sopher, 1994

OF LOVE AND DUST

In his tragic novel *Of Love and Dust* (1967), Ernest J. Gaines presents a realistic and frightening portrait of Louisiana in the 1940s. The theme of racism dominates the book and frames the story of a racially mixed romance between a white woman and a black man. Narrated in a compassionate yet sardonic voice by a black plantation employee named Jim Kelly, the story allows a glimpse at ideas regarding oppression and freedom on several different levels.

The most obvious representatives of oppression are the black workers on the plantation of white owner Marshall Hebert. Paid very little for their services, most end up as prisoners on the plantation through the debt they must carry to Hebert's plantation store. The story's protagonist, Marcus Payne, arrives on the plantation as a convict accused of murdering another black. When the plantation's overseer, the Cajun Sidney

Bonbon, places Marcus in Jim's care, Jim eventually learns that Hebert took on Marcus as a favor to his former cook, Miss Julie Rand, who acts as guardian to Marcus. Jim also discovers that Hebert must do as Miss Julie bids due to her knowledge of his past. Thus, Hebert the oppressor is himself oppressed by his own background and by a truth he must conceal.

Bonbon also suffers victimization to some extent. Although he treats the black workers and his young wife, Louise Bonbon, cruelly, he himself is regarded as a member of the lower social strata. As a Cajun, he belongs to a group considered superior to blacks but inferior to moneyed whites. Having performed the "service" for Hebert of killing a man, Bonbon exercises some control over his employer through blackmail. This situation, while beneficial in a way to both men, also makes each suspicious of the other's motives.

An additional prisoner on the plantation is Louise Bonbon. Caught up in an arranged patriarchal marriage to Sidney, she knows no love except for their toddler daughter, Judy, called Tite as a nickname. Married in her early teens, Louise makes several ultimately unsuccessful bids to escape from Bonbon, but he always finds her and brings her back to their small house on the plantation. Her own father directs Sidney to beat Louise should she continue to run away. Louise's hatred for her husband escalates when he openly takes on a black mistress named Pauline Guerine. His regular visits to Pauline are silently accepted by both blacks and whites, although Louise would never be allowed to take a black lover. Through this relationship, Gaines demonstrates not only racial inequity but also gender inequity.

Marcus's rebellious attitude causes trouble from the moment he arrives on the plantation. Willful and recalcitrant, he refuses to dress as other workers do and to stay away from Bonbon's women. When his attempts to seduce Bonbon's mistress fail, he turns to Louise Bonbon, simply as a way to seek revenge against the overseer. When he succeeds in seducing the all-too-willing Louise, all of the plantations' workers fear the price they will have to pay for this exercise of forbidden love. Marcus plots escape from the plantation with Louise, working on the premise that Hebert will help their plan succeed because it will result in the loss of Sidney Bonbon. The scheming Hebert unwillingly agrees to support Marcus's plan in order to rid himself of his thieving overseer. True to character, Hebert plots Marcus's demise as well.

Throughout Marcus's misadventures, Jim seeks to offer advice and guidance, most of which Marcus ignores. Jim is not, however, a detached narrator. He expresses regret over lost love and doubt regarding a once-strong religious feeling that seems to help him little now. In *Of Love and Dust,* Gaines explores one of his favorite questions, that of the importance of faith and organized religion to blacks who desire freedom. Although he does not explore the question in depth in this novel, he does offer it up to the reader through scenes of the plantation blacks regularly attending church and also through Jim's struggles to understand a God who seems basically to ignore the workers' problems. Jim searches for a vision of faith that will satisfy his particular needs, rejecting the organized religion that the blacks inherit from the whites. Marcus also discovers the letdown he experienced from his childhood religious training. Harsh treatment at the hands of others in spite of his prayers caused Marcus early on to believe only in himself. He expects no more from life than what he can accomplish on his own. He remains true to his ideology in planning his escape against insurmountable odds.

Romantic themes in the novel deal with two different interracial love triangles. The one formed by Louise and Sidney Bonbon and the female black worker Pauline remains acceptable to society; that encompassing the Bonbons and the male black worker Marcus does not. This concept Marcus will not accept, and it leads to his death and to Louise's subsequent insanity due to Hebert's treachery.

In the novel's conclusion, Hebert, as the dominant power, claims victory. His actions cause Bonbon to kill Marcus, then depart the plantation with his daughter and plan for his black mistress to join him later. Louise ends up in a mental hospital, substituting for her previous physical prison one of the mind. But there remains some remnant of hope in Jim's at last striking out on his own. He will not remain on the plantation and continue to work for Hebert, who bears the responsibility for Marcus's death. Even though his future remains uncertain, Jim's action in removing himself at last from a near-slave existence establishes the novel's single positive note.

See also: Bonbon, Louise; The Black Experience in America, 1600–1945; Forbidden Love; Gaines, Ernest J.; Guerine, Pauline; Love Triangle; Payne, Marcus; Violence

References: Coombs, 1972; Friedman and Siegel, 1995; "Gaines, Ernest J.," 1994; Hart, 1995; Papa, 1993

O'HARA, SCARLETT

Scarlett O'Hara is perhaps the best-known female character from an American novel. As the protagonist in Margaret Mitchell's 1936 epic Civil War romance, *Gone with the Wind,* Scarlett combines attributes of the traditional romantic female with those of a more modern heroine. She inhabits a traditional central position in a long-enduring love triangle between two men who represent opposite sensibilities, the southern gentleman Ashley Wilkes, and the northern opportunist Rhett Butler. Scarlett also adheres outwardly to the traditional southern code, based on medieval ideas of chivalry, playing the damsel in distress when necessary and praising men who occupy positions of power in her life. But internally, Scarlett remains an opinionated, independent female, attributes that make her attractive to the equally independent and passionate Rhett. The novel's conflict centers on Scarlett's inability to psychologically reconcile her own independent needs with the traditional needs forced upon her by her culture.

Mitchell moves Scarlett from a flirtatious, spoiled, and privileged teenager, daughter of a southern plantation-owner, to a beautiful, shrewd matriarch. Her eventual transition from a soft-mannered girl into a hardened, street-smart woman mirrors that of her society in its attempt to survive the terrors and destruction of war. Scarlett's close association with her beloved home, the plantation Tara, enables her to symbolize both southern geography and its resultant culture. Mitchell, as a child maturing in Atlanta, supposedly received a scolding from her mother regarding the importance of intelligence and strength in personal survival. She personifies this idea in Scarlett, who survives and triumphs over the personal and cultural ravages of the Civil War to reconstruct herself as her culture also regains its footing.

Scarlett first meets her nemesis, Rhett, when she all but proposes marriage to Ashley Wilkes, a move that a well-bred young southern woman trained in the art of subtle manipulation would never have undertaken. When he makes his presence known following Ashley's refusal of Scarlett, Rhett receives the brunt of her fury. When she informs Rhett that he is no gentleman, part of her frustration is grounded in the realization that she also is no lady, at least not in the traditional sense of the term. When Ashley reveals that he loves and will marry his cousin Melanie, this news overwhelms Scarlett. Its effect on her has little to do with passion, for she simply desires Ashley as spoils of the war of love, a very masculine approach to romance. This she will not realize for decades, however, and she vows to center all her attentions on gaining Ashley's love. Part of her ploy involves marrying Melanie Wilkes's brother in a heartless attempt to provoke Ashley's jealousy.

All the men go off to war, except for Rhett Butler, who pledges allegiance to no interests other than his own. Rumors that he runs guns for the highest bidder enhance the mythology that surrounds Rhett. Whatever his true activities may be, he keeps an eye on Scarlett. He remains ever ready to irritate her into revealing the independent spirit that he so values in women, but that the southern code, which Ashley represents and to which Melanie conforms, does not. Scarlett quickly becomes a widow as her boy-husband dies, not in an honorable fashion in battle but from disease. She regretfully dons black widow "weeds" because her culture dictates that she may not, for one year, wear the latest fashions. To raise her spirits, her mother sends her to Atlanta to live with an aunt and, ironically, with Melanie, whom Scarlett detests.

In a memorable scene, Rhett asks Scarlett to dance during festivities intended to raise funds for the southern troops. Having already donated her wedding ring to "the cause," Scarlett further advances her independence by agreeing to dance with Rhett, who "bids" on her for a partner. The two scandalize Atlanta's high society by engaging in an activity forbidden to widows.

As death and destruction overtake Atlanta, Scarlett begins an unwilling maturity. Still languishing in her misplaced affection for Ashley, she agrees to help care for the pregnant Melanie when Ashley requests her help during his leave from combat. More than the earlier birth of her own child, the birth of Melanie's baby, Beau, symbolizes for Scarlett a new beginning. She will emerge, like a phoenix, from the fiery destruction of the war to a rebirth in a new South. The poverty and despair that follow Atlanta's burning temper Scarlett, as fire does a metal. Those weaker than herself, such as Melanie, cannot survive without outside help. Rhett assists the two women and the baby in an escape from the fire, then departs to join the army. Scarlett does not understand his peculiar code of honor in supporting what is now a lost cause. Her self-centeredness and lack of understanding will linger throughout her life, causing her misunderstanding of Rhett, the only man who truly loves her.

As Scarlett experiences emotional loss and starvation back home at Tara, she continues her quest for self-realization. Like the traditional quest character, she loses loved ones, descends into a kind of hell during Reconstruction, but returns stronger than when she began her emotional and physical journey. In her normal egotistical manner, she takes as her second husband her sister's fiancé Frank Kennedy, but as with her first marriage, the union is not for love. Scarlett discovers the value of practicality while other war survivors cannot move past their idyllic view of the South to make a future for themselves. She marries in order to save Tara, her sisters, Melanie, and Ashley, all of whom have come to depend on her.

Even though she bears another child with Frank, Scarlett remains a much more masculine figure, in her strength and support of others, than does either her husband or Ashley. Her hard approach to management of a lumber mill frightens even the males who surround her, all except for Rhett, who still appreciates the actions in Scarlett that others condemn. When her independent streak takes her to an unsavory part of town to conduct business and she encounters trouble with homeless men, the southern code dictates that the attack must be avenged. A group of southern gentlemen go to the camps outside of town to find Scarlett's attacker, and Frank dies as a result. The ever-present figure of Rhett intervenes to rescue the group of southern gentlemen, Ashley included, from the disapproving Yankee law makers who forbid such action.

When Rhett and Scarlett at last unite in marriage, theirs seems a happy union for a time. As long as Rhett can act as a father-replacement for Scarlett, petting and spoiling her like a child, things go well. Their daughter Bonnie represents

for Rhett a love he has never before known, and he agrees to ignore Scarlett's continuing infatuation with Ashley as long as he has the child. At one point, however, his frustration escalates, and in a drunken stupor he rapes the unwilling Scarlett. Although the next morning she awakens genuinely happy about their love making, Scarlett remains unable to express her emotions to Rhett; they have occupied their antagonistic roles too long. Rhett departs for Europe with Bonnie, and upon his return, Scarlett anxiously waits to share the news of her pregnancy, a result of their final night together. But when he casually inquires as to the father's identity, Scarlett's uncontrollable temper flares, and striking out at him, she falls down the stairs, losing the baby.

That loss symbolizes the loss of Scarlett's final chance for happiness. Successful in a material sense, she cannot seem to imitate that success emotionally, mainly because she struggles against admitting her true needs. When she at last identifies that need as Rhett's love, her epiphany comes too late. With Bonnie's accidental death, Rhett sinks into an emotional abyss of loss from which his rekindled affection for Scarlett cannot rescue him. When Scarlett is observed in a suggestive pose with Ashley, Rhett at last gives up on their relationship. His decision seems supported by Melanie's assignment on her deathbed of Ashley's care to Scarlett.

Readers cannot help but hope that Scarlett's identification of Rhett as that "something" for which she searched in a highly symbolic nightmare will at last bring two great lovers together. But Mitchell avoids melodrama by injecting realism in a conclusion in which Rhett and Scarlett remain frustrated lovers. Scarlett's optimism, however, reigns at the novel's conclusion, as she uses her signature phrase regarding the promise of another day's success to cause hope for a reconciliation between American fiction's most famous couple.

See also: The Black Experience in America, 1600–1945; Butler, Rhett; *Gone with the Wind;* Love Triangle; Mitchell, Margaret; Violence; War; Wilkes, Ashley; Wilkes, Melanie
References: Armstrong, 1990; Flora, 1987; Frye, 1976; Hoffman and Murphy, 1996; Joyner, 1996

OKAMOTO, TAEKO

For his novel *The Journey* (1960), Japanese writer Jiro Osaragi creates the perfect modern romantic postwar heroine in Taeko Okamoto. In a story featuring the conflict between tradition and modernity as represented in the patriarchal society of Japan, Taeko, as a female, symbolizes a third related yet separate issue. Through her character, Osaragi considers the place of the newly liberated woman who has no tradition other than one cultivated in the shadow of men. Taeko develops her sense of self-awareness within the Japanese postwar workplace, previously occupied only by males, and within a new order of romance where a woman may cast off old ideas about arranged marriages and search out her own romantic partner. This search represents her private emotional journey as she experiences first the liberating quality of love, then its disappointment. The internal quest is mimicked in the novel by her external movements as she travels back and forth between Tokyo, a city symbolic of the new Japan, and Kamakura, the home of her traditional uncle Soroku. Soroku dwells in the past due to the loss of his son, Akira, during the war in southern China. Taeko's sympathy for Soroku's loss remains an appealing part of her character.

Taeko meets her love interest, Ryosuke Tsugawa, when she visits Akira's grave; Ryosuke explains he was a classmate of Taeko's dead cousin. Osaragi incorporates much symbolism through this meeting that becomes clear upon further reading. One symbolic aspect is that the birth of Taeko's love remains balanced by the death of her cousin. In addition, at the grave begins an ongoing contrast and comparison between the cousin and Ryosuke that helps fully develop Ryosuke's character. Like Akira, he fought in the war. Although he survived the war physically, he remains emotionally dead in many aspects due to that experience. His true personality remains hidden from Taeko, challenging her to reveal its secrets before she may accept Ryosuke for the troubled young man he is.

Taeko herself is balanced by the character of her older traditional sister, Tazuko, who wishes to arrange a marriage for Taeko. These two women, both beautiful and ambitious, could not be more different. Again, the author emphasizes the dichotomy between tradition and modernity by contrasting two characters. Whereas Tazuko believes in subdued public action, Taeko prefers to make her motives clear. For example, rather than acting coy in order to attract a prospective suitor during a date arranged by Tazuko, Taeko

remains honest with the man about her lack of intention to marry for any reason other than love. Tazuko arranges dates for Taeko with men she judges successful due to their prospects for wealth and power, but Taeko holds little interest in such things. As an illegitimate daughter in her family, she never receives the attention afforded Tazuko. Having moved out of a family atmosphere that provided her little warmth, Taeko learns early that the spiritual joys of independence outweigh the trials accompanying any material poverty this freedom causes.

Related to their different opinions on the importance of material wealth are the sisters' quite different attitudes toward their wealthy uncle. Tazuko, needing to borrow money, sees the old man as irascible and illogical; he has a great fortune, yet he refuses to share it with her, even though she offers to pay interest for a loan. Taeko respects her uncle for the emotional pain he experiences in the loss of his only son, although he had treated his son with little affection, and she asks for little in return.

Taeko becomes part of a love triangle for a brief time due to her romantic effect upon a young teacher, Sutekichi Ata, who befriends her uncle and subsequently appears as a guest at his home. From Sutekichi the reader gains one of the better descriptions of Taeko. In considering her unfortunate illegitimate birth to a family servant, he concludes that she possesses an exceptional character, evidenced by her cheerful attitude and complete lack of bitterness toward life. Although Taeko does not return Sutekichi's love, neither does she spurn his right to express that love to her. His words eventually affect her ideas regarding her relationship with the elusive Ryosuke. Sutekichi's expression of an honorable love and the wish that Taeko experience a smooth and happy journey through life stand in great contrast to the self-centeredness of Ryosuke.

As in many novels of romance, in *The Journey* the heroine faces choices. She must choose between the love of two men, but, more important to this story, she must also choose between the long-term security of the unselfish love she desires and the great momentary pleasure awarded by a man whom she cannot trust. Important to Taeko's development into a dynamic character are her recognition and acceptance of Ryosuke's unfaithful behavior in matters of sex and money. By the novel's conclusion, she can acknowledge and reject his traits honestly, acting upon her own high ethical standards to relieve his gambling debts without expecting any return.

Taeko's rejection of Ryosuke as her future husband represents another phase of her independence, as does her awareness that she deserves to receive a love as pure as the one she willingly gives. In this desire for a traditional love based upon trust and respect, Taeko becomes the blend of the traditional and the modern that the author seeks.

> See also: Ata, Sutekichi; Bildungsroman; *The Journey;* Patriarchal Marriage; Tsugawa, Ryosuke; War
> *References:* Bridgwood, 1986; Frye, 1976; Hoffman and Murphy, 1996

O-LAN

O-lan acts as the major female character in Pearl Buck's 1931 novel, *The Good Earth.* Firmly entrenched in the customs of her androcentric Chinese society that regards women as slaves, O-lan accepts her arranged marriage to the farmer, Wang Lung. Wang takes her from her servant position in the great house of Hwang, and she assumes all domestic duties in his household, which also includes his aging father. An ugly, gawky, big-footed woman, O-lan nevertheless engenders pride in Wang Lung, who values her work skills and ethic that seem to match his own. She becomes a partner in every sense of the word in the farming venture that represents everything of importance in life to Wang Lung.

O-lan's multiple childbearing experiences help emphasize the cycle of life and death that Wang Lung values in his relationship to the earth and its bounty. Her physical strength matches that of her uncomplaining character, as O-lan gives birth, then immediately returns to her heavy farm work. Although she and Wang Lung share few endearments, he often silently feels great pride in his wife and in her contributions to his livelihood. He allows her to have a moment of triumph when she returns with her handsome well-dressed infant son to the house of Hwang so all may see the success she has achieved. O-lan supports her husband's decision to purchase additional farmland from the Hwang's, and they enjoy two years of bounty.

Following the birth of two sons, O-lan bears a retarded daughter, a bad sign in Wang Lung's eyes. Drought and famine follow the birth, and when the family must either travel south or starve, O-lan does not protest the move. She delivers a fourth child, another daughter, which she herself kills to relieve the family of the burden of another mouth to feed. Although Wang Lung thinks of his wife as unintelligent and slow, O-lan speaks wisely when she chooses to express herself. With no hesitation, she begs for food and money in the city, teaching her sons to follow suit. During a revolution, O-lan participates in the looting of a rich man's house, stealing handfuls of precious jewels. The family is able to return to their land with the spoils, and Wang Lung begins again.

Throughout this second phase of success and bounty, O-lan again supports her husband. She turns over the jewels to him, asking only to keep two pearls. When she later delivers twins, Wang Lung believes the twin pearls served as a charm promoting the birth, and the couple shares a moment of mirth over this idea. But O-lan's happiness will not last because with Wang Lung's success comes his discontentment. No longer forced to work for himself due to his wealth, he can hire others to go into the field. His boredom with life and unhappiness with troublesome relatives sends him into the town, where he finds a mistress named Lotus Blossom in a whorehouse. One of the novel's most poignant scenes occurs when Wang Lung demands O-lan's pearls in order to present them to Lotus. His wife remains aware of his activities but can only complain. In their patriarchal marriage, she must accept her husband's actions, even when he builds a center court in their home for Lotus to occupy. Her resignation keeps their relationship from qualifying as a traditional love triangle.

O-lan's esteemed position in the family is undermined following Lotus's arrival. Although her children and her father-in-law appreciate her, Wang Lung does not. She seems uglier than ever in comparison to the beautiful and fragile Lotus. The guilt that Wang Lung suffers over the knowledge that he had rejected a woman who has broken her heart for him does not alter his actions. Eventually O-lan dies a long, tortured death. She lives to see her son united with a fine wife and welcomes her death with dignity.

Although O-lan remains a flat character, she greatly enriches the story. Her dedication and devotion to Wang Lung and his vision of life shape her into a strong characterization of a devoted wife and mother. Although she lacks

Lotus's beauty, O-lan is the woman to be remembered long after she returns to the good earth.

> *See also:* Buck, Pearl Sydenstricker; *The Good Earth;* Lotus Blossom; Lung, Wang; Patriarchal Marriage
> *References:* Armstrong, 1990; Davidson, 1995; Lipscomb, Webb, and Conn, 1994; Price, 1983

ONE ON ONE

Tabitha King's contemporary realistic novel *One on One* (1993) incorporates romantic aspects while shaping characters atypical for the classic romance. The novel's female protagonist, high school sophomore Deanie Gauthier, called "the Mutant" by her detractors, is neither beautiful nor helpless. Thus she lacks resemblance to the typical romantic female figure. Deanie's boyfriend, Sam Styles, at first seems a foil to Deanie rather than her love interest. Where Deanie remains insecure and unpopular and a loner, Sam enjoys great popularity and is known for his ability to produce a biblical quote applicable to any occasion. Sam represents the traditional romance champion and protector—he literally saves Deanie's life. His nickname of "Samson," due to his long hair, also suggests his physical strength. In addition, it allows a further contrast to Deanie, who shaves her head and wears outlandish eye makeup and body chains. Finally, the nickname acts as foreshadowing for Sam's eventual loss of his athletic prowess, just as Samson lost his strength.

Both of King's main characters play high school basketball. The basketball court becomes a metaphor for life itself, which may be viewed as a game. Those with well-developed emotional and psychological skills will overcome life's penalties and "win" the game. Despite her rough outward appearance, tattoos, and overdone eye makeup, Deanie is not a "bad" person; she's merely been dealt a bad hand in life's game. She does not deserve her burdens that come in the form of a drug-using mother and her mother's abusive boyfriend. The boyfriend's name, Tony Lord, symbolizes his controlling attitude toward Deanie; he wants to rule her and her mother as the lord of the manor. Off the court, Deanie's life remains totally chaotic, so naturally she has never had to comply with the rules that order the normal teenager's life. Deanie's attack on an abusive fan at the novel's beginning shows that, due to her chaotic lifestyle, she cannot yet accept the idea of order that the rules of basketball enforce. Only with the attention and support she eventually earns from Sam can Deanie accept herself and find her place.

Deanie suffers not only external conflict caused by her tumultuous home environment and the friction with her peers but also internal conflict in struggling with her feelings for Sam. She is a loner, drowning in an emotional isolation, which she outwardly celebrates in her alienating actions. When she is kicked off the team for her attack on the fan, the team loses the game, further distancing her from her peers. Although she may not reveal it, Deanie suffers for the loss, because basketball serves as her only saving grace.

The year following the girls' team's loss, Sam, a 6-foot-7-inch senior center on the boy's basketball team, notices Deanie. His admiration of her hook shot and her dedication to the game motivates Sam to begin helping the girls' team with practice before school. When Deanie falls ill, it is Sam who finds her suffering from pneumonia that has gone unnoticed by her drugged mother. He assumes the role of caretaker, and Deanie warms to the attention that she had never received as a child. Although she remains unsure of her love for Sam, she desires him as a sexual object. Using sex is the only method by which Deanie has ever associated with boys. Despite her sexual experience, Deanie retains a naïveté and innocence that endears her to the reader. Her emotional immaturity and eventual evolution categorize this novel as an initiation, or coming-of-age, story.

King escalates the novel's conflict when a one-time sexual partner for Deanie becomes jealous of her friendship with Sam, convincing Tony Lord that Deanie has been sleeping with the entire boy's basketball team. In the fierce battle that ensues between Deanie and Lord, he smashes one of her waist chains into her face, inflicting a deep cut. When she hides out in an abandoned mill, Sam discovers her and takes her home. This reversal of traditional roles, shaping the male as the nurturer, supports the nontraditional character of King's novel. Sam's father accepts Deanie's presence in the home, assuming Sam could not possibly have a sexual or romantic interest in such a freakish girl.

Deanie dons a protective mask that covers her facial injury so she may play in the state championships. Again, King inverts a common symbol.

Traditionally a character removes a mask to reveal a new identity, but Deanie begins to change her identity when she assumes her mask. Both the boys and girls basketball teams win their championships, allowing Deanie and Sam victories they can share and appreciate. King's abundant description of the basketball games adds much to the novel's realism. Through her relationship with Sam and her growing understanding of the game of life, Deanie becomes a dynamic character.

Unfortunately for both Deanie and Sam, victory on the court does not ensure victory off the court. Leading up to a frightening climax, Tony Lord beats Deanie's mother to death and stalks Deanie to the mill. Sam literally leaps to her rescue when he plunges 30 feet to land on Lord and kill him. Because he breaks both legs at the hips and suffers additional injuries, Sam's basketball career swiftly concludes.

Even after the removal of Lord and the sad demise of Deanie's mother, King's plot does not specifically unite Sam and Deanie. In the concluding scene, however, they appear to be together, as Sam attends a parent-teacher conference the following year for Deanie. His caretaker role intact, Sam apparently remains loyal in his commitment to her.

A very disturbing novel in many ways, *One on One* retains a high popularity with young readers. Its inclusion in catalogues of books for the classroom indicates its acceptance by at least some academics. King's specific subversion of many of the basic elements of romance works to support that genre by calling those elements to the reader's attention. At the same time, she shapes a brutal modern romance with which, for better or worse, young readers seem to identify.

See also: King, Tabitha; Violence
References: Anstead, 1997; Rice, 1997; Shattuck, 1997

O'NEILL, LUKE

In Colleen McCullough's 1977 novel, *The Thorn Birds,* Luke O'Neill represents the character readers love to hate. Not a vicious or mean man, he nevertheless neglects the needs of the book's heroine, Meggie Cleary. As part of a love triangle that also includes Father Ralph de Bricassart, Luke remains a disappointment as a romantic character. His machismo lifestyle rings hollow when compared to the romantic compassion produced by Ralph.

Herein lies much of Luke's problem; he simply falls far short of the ideal set for Meggie by Father Ralph. Within their patriarchal marriage, Luke behaves as he wishes, leaving Meggie without any spending money while he deserts her for months on end. To his credit, his behavior does not reflect laziness; on the contrary, Luke enjoys hard physical labor and the male company it affords. Conflict occurs precisely because he prefers the company of his fellow field workers to that of his wife.

Luke's physical resemblance to Father Ralph first captures Meggie's attention, and he finds holding her interest a simple matter. She remains attracted to the promise of children and a family, if not to true love, and Luke, in turn, wants her money. Had he not been so rough with Meggie in love making and so insensitive to her needs, their marriage might have endured, even with its lack of love. But lack of attention seems to be the one thing Meggie cannot bear.

When Meggie plots to trick Luke into impregnating her before he is ready for a family, his animal desires make this a simple task. Luke does not even visit her following the difficult birth of their daughter, Justine, an act that allows Ralph to take his place at Meggie's bedside. His reason for not coming home, disappointment over Meggie's producing a daughter rather than a son, is to be expected. So blind is Luke to Meggie's lack of feelings for him that he later falls once again for the sex snare she sets for him in order to legitimize her unborn son, fathered by Ralph. His shock over her announcement that she plans to leave him to return home to her Australian ranch, Drogheda, remains evidence of his lack of insight.

For other women trapped in the wilds of Australia, Luke O'Neill might have proven a fine catch. But his rough ways and patriarchal attitude do not measure up to the expectations of the more refined and deserving Meggie Cleary.

See also: Cleary, Meghann (Meggie); de Bricassart, Father Ralph; McCullough, Colleen; Patriarchal Marriage; *The Thorn Birds*
References: Armstrong, 1990; Bridgwood, 1986; Kaplan, 1986; Price, 1983

OSARAGI, JIRO

Jiro Osaragi is a pseudonym for Kiyohiko Nojiri, a Japanese writer famous for dramas and plays reflecting insight into Japanese culture. Born in

1898, Nojiri attended Tokyo Imperial University where he studied political science, French law, and literature. To aid his father, a shipping–company official, in dealing with bureaucratic red tape, Nojiri took a government position in the Treaty Bureau of the Foreign Office. Because government officials could not publish writings under their own names, Nojiri assumed the pseudonym Jiro Osaragi. His name translates as "Near the Great Buddha," significant because the author happened to live in the vicinity of the Great Buddha of Kamakura.

Enthralled by western culture as a young man, Osaragi deals in depth with its influence on Japan following the two world wars. His two most famous novels, *Homecoming* (1955) and *The Journey* (1960), both reflect his familiarity with Japanese history and his interest in art. His works include numerous plays, novels, and travel books, many of which reached best-seller status in Japan. He spent much of his time in two different houses in Kamakura's literary colony that he shared with his "coterie," fans, and several cats. In 1958 he visited the United States, and his postwar romantic novel, *The Journey,* was translated into English in 1960.

Osaragi died in 1973. Following his death, a memorial museum was erected in his honor in Yokohama, where he wrote most of his works while at the Hotel New Grand. The museum houses his personal 30,000-volume collection of books as well as other personal items. Asahi Shimbun, a group that honors significant contributors to Japanese culture and society, established the Jiro Osaragi Prize in memory of the popular novelist.

> *See also: The Journey;* Mishima, Yukio; *The Sound of Waves*
> *References:* "Osaragi, Jiro," 1998; Yap, 1987

OSMOND, GILBERT

Gilbert Osmond is the easy-to-hate villain in Henry James's 1881 Victorian Age novel, *The Portrait of a Lady.* An expatriate American who fancies himself an aesthete, Osmond remains in actuality a dilettante who dabbles not only in collecting beautiful objects but also in collecting beautiful people. The product of a social order in decline, he appears to support social convention while undermining, through the exercise of a perverse power, the very ideals he professes to respect.

Three of his victims occupy the center stage in this novel. The book's heroine, Isabel Archer, finds herself fascinated by what she will later discover is a false front of noblesse oblige on Osmond's part. After rejecting two perfectly acceptable marriage proposals, she falls for Osmond's plot to use her to at last attain notability in society. Others describe Osmond as mean, petty, and odious, but Isabel's enthrallment with what she perceives as Osmond's sensitivity and artistic temperament blinds her to the truth that others recognize. The American pursues a European tradition he can never attain, masquerading as Isabel's soulmate in order to conceal his moral turpitude.

Following their marriage, Isabel realizes that Osmond has placed himself in the midst of the beautiful fecund Italian countryside to camouflage a blackened and withered soul. His serpent-like character fits perfectly in the Edenic landscape he inhabits, and Osmond makes married life a misery for Isabel, controlling her every move when she had once so valued her independence. He knows that Isabel's pride will not allow her to escape even the worst relationship, and he shapes her existence into a private hell.

Madame Serena Merle, a high society woman who gains Isabel's confidence early on, maintains what at first seems to the reader to be a questionable relationship with Osmond. They have some connection, but its basis is not immediately apparent. At Osmond's bidding, Merle guides Isabel, too innocent to recognize the evil that Merle and Osmond represent, into a doomed marriage with him. Only late in the novel does Isabel discover the truth about Osmond and Merle; they were past lovers and the parents of Osmond's daughter and subsequently Isabel's stepdaughter, Pansy Osmond. The misogynist Osmond refused to marry Merle because she did not fit into his well-designed future. He feels no compunction, however, at manipulating Merle into performing his bidding, even when that means the ruination of both the submissive Pansy's and the smoldering Isabel's lives.

Pansy becomes a pawn in Osmond's bid for increased power as he plots to marry his daughter off to the wealthy and socially powerful Lord Warburton, many years Pansy's senior. An added incentive to making sure this marriage takes place is the fact that Warburton earlier had been rejected by Isabel. Without regard to Pansy's feelings, Osmond tries to force Isabel to help him settle the match, even though his daughter loves another man. He hides Pansy away in a convent, exercising his brutish control to literally lock his daughter away.

Osmond acts as the perfect villain to help Isabel, the novel's main character, learn life's cruel lessons. His repugnant acts contribute to her maturation and ultimately help Isabel to grow as a character. Although the reader might like to see Isabel leave Osmond to the lonely fate he deserves, her honor will not permit that. Only by overshadowing his fiendishness with her own honesty and strength of will does Isabel eventually triumph over Gilbert Osmond.

> *See also:* Archer, Isabel; Bildungsroman; James, Henry; Patriarchal Marriage; *The Portrait of a Lady;* Quest; Victorian Age
>
> *References:* Armstrong, 1990; Bullen, 1997; Feidelson, 1975; Hart, 1995; Putt, 1966

OZ, AMOS

Born in Jerusalem in 1939 to parents who had lived for a time in Europe, Amos Oz matured into the most important Israeli author of the mid– to late twentieth century. His parents were Russian Jews who could also speak Polish and read German, English, and French. They were well educated; his father had studied comparative literature. Between the world wars they settled in Jerusalem, where Oz was raised with knowledge only of Hebrew. He believes his parents chose to parochialize him so he would not share the same disappointments in dreams of elsewhere that they had experienced.

Raised during Jerusalem's early era of independence, Oz learned his alphabet as a very young child and decided to become a writer. His plans changed when his mother died in a car crash during his teens. Conflict developed between him and his father, against whose conservatism Oz rebelled. His father's scholastic training seemed, in Oz's eyes, to have crippled him with a dependence on words that resulted in no action. At age fifteen, Oz moved to a kibbutz, a type of commune, where he remained in residence for the next twenty-eight years.

He eventually served as a visiting fellow at Oxford University in England, writer-in-residence at Colorado College, and author-in-residence at Hebrew University. Named in France as Officer of Arts and Letters, he occasionally teaches at Ben Gurion University in the Negev desert but says academics hold little interest. Instead of studying sociology, he would rather be living among the people and telling their stories. The idea of an objective "scientific" study of individuals does not appeal to him. The tempestuous history of Israel supplies much of the subject matter for his prose and essays, and he has written for children as well as adults. Honors earned include the French Prix Femina and the 1992 Frankfurt Peace Prize.

Oz is a well-known supporter of peace between Israel and Palestine. He expresses the opinion that peace without reconciliation may be called for because the Jews and Arabs will never like one another. The most both parties can hope for is an acceptance of their differences. Affection or disaffection should not guide their actions, in his opinion. Polemic writing occupied much of Oz's energies following the Israeli invasion of Lebanon in the Six-Day War. That war caused his great aversion to the extreme and the fanatic, and it led to Oz's support of compromise as a far superior reaction to the conflict in his homeland.

Oz's ideas surface in the themes and characters of his novels as he recognizes the frailty in human nature but simultaneously glories in that nature's variety. He focuses on individuals rather than commenting on the masses, remains passionate regarding the family as the center of human experience, closely examines relationships between men and women, and constructs disturbing stories of animals. The animals in his stories serve as metaphors for human love. Most of his characters remain nostalgic for a simpler past that they may have never experienced except in their imaginations. They always suffer gut-wrenching inner conflict, difficult, if not impossible, to resolve. For Oz, political conflict becomes a metaphor for personal or family conflicts, and he remains fascinated with the capability of the family to survive tremendous duress.

Of his fifteen stories (he rejects the term "novel") and collections of short stories and essays written in Hebrew, thirteen have been translated into several different languages. Works include *Elsewhere, Perhaps* (1966); *My Michael* (1968); *Touch the Water, Touch the Wind* (1973); *The Hill of Evil Counsel* (novella, 1976); *Somuchi* (juvenile, 1978); *Under This Blazing Light* (essays, 1979); *In the Land of Israel* (1983); *Black Box* (1987); and *Fima* (1993). In *To Know a Woman* (1989), his protagonist, an Israeli secret service

Amos Oz, shown in a 1991 photograph, writes tales in which political conflict becomes a metaphor for personal or family conflicts. (AP/Wide World Photos)

man, decides to retire to ponder life following the mysterious death of his wife. Oz purposely removes his spy from the normal adventure novel setting, and rather than probing into others' mysteries, the character explores his own past to determine how it relates to the present.

Oz writes with what he calls an odd blend of compassion and anger. He feels he must understand several viewpoints on an issue in order to inhabit the characters that will represent divergent issues. Working to inhabit his characters while also viewing them objectively, Oz puts himself into the shoes of others, much as a secret agent might do. As a writer, he feels compelled to give voice, through his characters, to conflicting points of view. For Amos Oz the arrangement of words on the page is a moral choice.

See also: To Know a Woman
References: Balaban, 1990; Balaban, 1993; Fuchs, 1984; Grossman, 1986; Oz, 1993; Price, 1995; Wachtel, 1991

PARDI, ANGELO

As the protagonist of Jean Giono's 1951 chivalric romance novel, *Le Hussard sur le Toit,* translated in 1954 as *The Horseman on the Roof,* Angelo Pardi represents the medieval knight reborn into the early nineteenth century. His impeccable manners, his gracious actions, and his humor support his feats of derring-do and identify him as a modern paragon of chivalry. His status as an Italian exile living in France in order to escape persecution by the Austrian empire also aligns Angelo with the loyalty to ideology that characterized the knight's approach to life. When Angelo, acting as the guardian angel his name implies, comes to the aid of a damsel in distress, Giono's medieval characterization is complete.

His whereabouts discovered by Austrian assassins, Angelo must flee the French city of Aix and hopes to warn his fellow countrymen of their betrayal by one of their own. He meets the Marquise Pauline de Theus as she remains, for reasons she will not reveal, within the cholera-plagued city of Manosque. Having taken to the city's rooftops to escape the unfounded persecution of a crowd intent on revenging the massive deaths caused by the plague, Angelo seeks shelter in the mansion Pauline inhabits. When she offers Angelo food and drink, Pauline captures the loyalty dictated by the chivalric code toward anyone who offers aid to a knight.

When not assisting Pauline, Angelo acts upon his knightly instincts in other ways. His aid to a Manosque nun in cleansing the bodies of those dead from the plague helps characterize Angelo as one who, while a member of the Italian aristocracy, identifies with the humanity of all his fellow beings. His loyalty remains evident in his tenacious search for his foster brother and comrade at arms. Most revealing of Angelo's ideology are the various monologues in which he expresses his ideas about honor, fealty, life, and death. His respect for an honorable tradition surfaces, for instance, in his dueling with the man he has been assigned to kill as a political enemy. Angelo finds this approach to vanquishing his foe much more desirable than the simple anonymous assassination that his friends recommend.

Angelo rejoins Pauline when they meet outside Manosque and decide to travel together. Their quests mingle as Angelo transports funds to support his political cause to Turin, Italy, and Pauline insists upon traveling to southern France, despite the military patrols that will attempt to confine both to quarantine. Angelo learns eventually that Pauline's husband is the Marquis Laurent de Theus, a powerful and wealthy Frenchman, and he undertakes her care in the absence of the marquis.

Much of Angelo's behavior qualifies him as keeper of the chivalric code. He always behaves as a gentleman toward his charge; he acts civilly, even with his foes; he uses not only his physical strength but also his mental acuity to outwit those who would halt his journey. He even remains kind to animals, making appreciative remarks about their horses and adopting for a time a cat from a home where cholera has destroyed its inhabitants. Especially noticeable are Angelo's humor and self-deprecatory remarks. He never hesitates to confess that his mother purchased his rank of colonel, proving his honesty, but he also constantly vows to live up to her expectations. His frequent references to his mother and his loyalty to Pauline demonstrate his positive view of women, an outlook that goes beyond the simple proprietary chauvinism expected from a gentleman. An especially enjoyable scene is the one in which Angelo confesses to Pauline his feeling of comradeship with her. Her skills on horseback and with firearms make him want to clap her on the shoulder and indulge in other activities common to fellow soldiers.

Angelo's greatest deed is his rescue of Pauline from the death caused by cholera. Although he must rip her clothes away in order to massage her limbs and increase their temperature, his motivations remain chaste. He delivers her to the castle de Theus, only then discovering his charge's aristocratic identity. The dialogue with the dowager marquise, Pauline's mother-in-law, perpetuates Angelo's characterization as a lover of women for other than sexual reasons. When he rides away to Italy atop a new horse, in the tradition of chivalric romances, he eagerly looks not back toward the damsel but ahead toward battle and the adventures that await.

> *See also:* Chivalry; de Theus, Pauline; *The Horseman on the Roof;* Quest; Romance
> *References:* Campbell, 1968; Campbell,1988; Frye, 1976; Grierson, 1974; Hulme, 1974

PASTERNAK, BORIS

Boris Pasternak's only novel, the war romance *Doctor Zhivago* (completed in 1956), became a worldwide sensation when it underwent translation in 1957. Rejected by Russian publishers due to its critical view of communism, the novel quickly won international acclaim and appeared in a popular film version. A poet by trade, Pasternak wrote his novel partly in reaction to his unpopularity with the Stalinist regime and the suicides of several fellow poets in the face of Soviet oppression. Although the novel gained popularity as a polemic against oppression, it remains primarily an excellent example of the romance form, featuring the elaborate imagery and symbolism to be expected from a poet-novelist.

Pasternak was born in 1890 in Moscow into a cultivated Jewish family that included his father, the prominent artist Leonid Pasternak, and his pianist mother, Rosa Kauffman. Having engaged in a serious early study of music, Pasternak considered a career in the performing arts but later studied philosophy at Moscow University and at Germany's University of Marburg. He escaped military induction into World War I due a physical disqualification, spending the war years as a chemical factory worker in the Ural Mountains. Following the Bolshevik revolution, he found employment in the library of the Soviet commissariat of education.

Pasternak's poetry career began in 1913 when he wrote Futurist poetry under the influence of the major poetic voice for the Bolshevik revolution, Vladimir Mayakovsky. By 1914 Pasternak's first collection of poems, *The Twin in the Clouds,* was published, but he truly came of age in 1917 during Russia's short-lived democratic period,

with his collection *Over the Barriers,* to be followed by *My Sister, Life* (1922). Because poetry occupied a preeminent place in Russian everyday life, Pasternak quickly gained a devoted following. Although his verses remained simple, his themes were supported by an incredible use of imagery and a splendid application of the Russian language that brought him acclaim. His verse revealed the influence not only of the nineteenth-century Symbolist emphasis on mysticism, aesthetics, and Impressionism but also of modernism, the latter evident in his philosophical approach to nature and history. All these stylistic elements would appear in his later prose.

Following the October Revolution and the civil war, Pasternak's poetry turned somber, and he wrote four impressionistic short stories lacking in true plot, including the highly touted "The Childhood of Zhenia Luvers." With this story began his literary and political conflict with censorship by the Soviet regime. A first autobiography, *Safe Conduct* (1931), paid tribute to the German poet Rainer Maria Rilke and other writers Pasternak had found inspirational. His Communist critics noted Pasternak's refusal to follow in his poetry the preferred patterns of social realism. His lengthy autobiographical poem, *Spektorski,* and a collection of basically anti-Stalinist poetry caused his denunciation by Soviet authorities. His position became precarious when Stalin began to purge those Russian elements that he believed hostile to his rule. After 1932, Pasternak published no more poetry for ten years, after which two more collections appeared, *On Early Trains* (1943) and *The Terrestrial Expanse* (1945). During that time, he worked at translations of five Shakespearean tragedies as well as of *Maria Stuart* by Johann Christoph Friedrich von Schiller and *Faust* by Johann Wolfgang von Goethe. The publication of his collections was followed by ten additional years of silence.

In the early 1950s, a rumor had it that Pasternak had been crafting a novel since 1938. His subject matter included the Soviet revolution and World War II. In 1954 Aleksandr Tvardovsky, then editor of a Soviet literary magazine called *Novy mir,* published poetry supposedly written by the protagonist of Pasternak's novel; the poems later appeared as the concluding chapter of *Doctor Zhivago.* The magazine announced that it would publish the entire novel, but that move was stopped by Soviet authorities, who labeled the novel anti-Marxist. The book presented a panorama of Russian culture from the viewpoint of its physician-poet protagonist, Yurii Zhivago. Primarily a moving romance focusing on the love triangle between Yurii, his wife Tonia Zhivago, and his lover, Lara, *Doctor Zhivago* presented in Yurii a character of intellectual sincerity, spiritual independence, and strong religious convictions that represented for Russian censors a reaction against the theories supported by the Communist regime.

Eventually, *Doctor Zhivago* appeared in publication in Italy in 1957, joining other works published out of the country due to Communist censorship. By 1958, Pantheon Publishers in New York had released the novel in translation. Worldwide praise followed, and, as a result, Pasternak was nominated for, and won, the 1958 Nobel Prize for literature. Shaken by threats of political retribution against family and friends, Pasternak rejected the award in order to avoid exile. In the letter in which he announced his decision, he also requested of the Communist leader Nikita Khrushchev that he be granted permission to remain in Russia. The poet and author died two years later in 1960, and "Hamlet," a poem "by" Yurii Zhivago, was read at his funeral. The woman on which the character of Lara was based, Olga Ivinskaya, was later returned to a Siberian labor camp.

Despite Soviet attempts at obliteration and besmirchment, Pasternak's reputation remained a strong one in his home country. By 1972, his *Collected Poems* had sold 170,000 copies in the Soviet Union, and finally in 1987, *Doctor Zhivago* was made available to the Russian people. Due to the openness represented by then-leader Mikhail Gorbachev's policy of glasnost (opening), the poet and his works received official positive sanction by the government.

See also: *Doctor Zhivago*
References: Brunsdale, 1996; Clowes, 1995

PATRIARCHAL MARRIAGE

A *patriarchal marriage* is a relationship in which the husband is deemed the authority in all matters, particularly social and financial concerns. In a traditional patriarchy, women and children assume the father's, or patriarch's, name, and only males, who retain that name after marriage, can inherit property. Closely related in meaning to *patriarchal* is the term *androcentric,* another adjective used to describe a society structured on legal and social systems designed only by males. These two terms are widely used in feminist writings that often attack patriarchal marriage as an instrument of oppression of women.

A brief overview of the historical development of negative attitudes toward women may be helpful in understanding the system of patriarchy and, by extension, the institution of patriarchal marriage. Patriarchy was characteristic of ancient Hebrew societies, and western attitudes allowing males supremacy in the household find basis in biblical edict and stories. The myth of Adam and Eve was used in Jewish and Christian societies to attribute moral turpitude and a weak will to the female. In addition, due to their generally larger size, men have traditionally been seen as physically stronger than women. Thus, men's supposed physical, intellectual, and moral superiority to woman was accepted for centuries. Some of the first Christian writing focusing on women promotes this negative attitude toward women, in addition to expressing an aversion to sex. In the New Testament, St. Paul tells women to remain subservient to men. Women were presented as temptations and snares—traps leading to men's destruction. Until the latter part of the seventeenth century in England, some men believed that women did not have souls. These ideas determined man's relationship to woman in every aspect of society, including marriage, in which the male retained undisputed authority.

In the Greek tradition, the poet Hesiod produced the myth of Pandora, the first woman who later released all the ills known to mankind from their containment in a jar. This promoted the view of women as lacking intelligence and possessing an uncontrollable and destructive curiosity. Another Greek poet, Simonides of Amorgos, produced a long poem that listed feminine faults and compared the nature of women to that of base animals. Although not quite as harsh toward women as Greek literature, Roman literature also contains many complaints regarding women's fickle nature. And Hinduism teaches that a good woman will be allowed to become a man in the next life. Such literature is termed *misogynist* because it reflects a hatred of women.

In the Middle Ages just prior to the Italian Renaissance, love poetry depicted women in idealistic terms. The female subjects of the poems never responded to the poems' speakers, and thus the ideal of women as silent, chaste, and obedient became the norm into Renaissance times. Yet even popular tales of chivalry produced some attacks on women that were part of a debate over their worth. The late-thirteenth-century work *The Romance of the Rose* became important in the *querrelle de femme* (debate about women) that would continue for three hundred years. Christine de Pisan, a fourteenth-century French writer, became famous as the first woman to enter a debate in print over a piece of literature as she vigorously argued against the denigration of women and marriage contained in *The Romance of the Rose.*

In sixteenth- and seventeenth-century England, women's images did not improve much. They could not inherit property, had no recourse through the law if abused by their husbands, and remained on par with children as far as legal rights were concerned. Men could legally divorce women for any stated cause, but women could rarely divorce men. The debates over women's position in society appeared in the "pamphlet wars," in which printed tracts argued in favor of or against women. Some popular derogatory imagery of women included that of monsters or snakes. Lack of education for women contributed to their oppression, according to some of those writers. Negative attitudes extended into the eighteenth century, and with the development of the novel, fiction imitated reality, producing romantic plots containing images supporting a patriarchal society. Although girls could attend school in the 1700s, they were not allowed to advance into higher education. Women writers such as Mary Wollstonecraft, mother of Mary Wollstonecraft Shelley, who wrote *Frankenstein,* argued in favor of the beneficial effects of education on women in her *A Vindication of the Rights of Woman* (1792). By the nineteenth century, Victorian society, with its restrictive social mores, caused women's subservient position to worsen. A double standard punished women's sexual indiscretions with much more severity than those committed by men. In the United States, when women finally gained admittance to institutions of higher education, they often had to sit in the halls to listen to lectures in order not to "distract" male students.

By the twentieth century, such inequalities did not disappear, but they did diminish in many countries, due in large part to the activism of women protesters. For instance, in the United States from 1848 on, women known as suffragists banded together, demanding the right to vote and accepting jail sentences as punishment for voting before passage of suffrage. In 1920 the Nineteenth Amendment at last granted the vote to women in the United States, and in the same year, Great Britain enfranchised its women. Once granted voting power, women slowly gained some voice in the determination of the laws that controlled their lives. Even in the late twentieth century, in few countries has true equality been reached. Some cultures retain social aspects of patriarchal society, such as the automatic adoption by a married woman and her children of her husband's name.

In romantic fiction, individual patriarchal marriages are not always depicted as negative, just as in real life, not all patriarchal marriages cause problems for either partner. In some fictional plots, a responsible loving man cares for his wife and, perhaps, children, with the wife feeling no threat whatsoever from her subordinate position in the household (see *Doctor Zhivago, Rebecca, The Shadow Bride*), even if her husband commits adultery with other women (see *Enemies: A Love Story*). A secondary version of this plot is one in which women recognize the inequality of their cultures but can do nothing to change their inability to inherit or become financially independent. They search for a true love match in which they may enjoy some personal freedoms that will substitute for social and legal equality with their husbands (see *Pride and Prejudice, Sense and Sensibility*). In other cases, the wife may feel oppressed, even if her husband does not abuse her. Culture itself oppresses her, refusing to recognize the wife as an individual separate from her roles as wife and mother (see *The House of the Spirits*). Such refusal causes any desires on the part of the woman, such as the desire to express herself creatively, to remain subordinate to her duties to family. This situation can lead to a feeling of desperation producing emotional or mental suffering and even suicide (see *The Awakening, Madame Bovary*). It may be the husband himself who is unsatisfactory, causing his wife to feel unloved or undervalued. She cannot escape a loveless marriage due to her helplessness to free herself from a legal contract (see *Madame Bovary, The Portrait of a Lady; The Count of Monte Cristo*), but she may accept financial security in place of a loving relationship (see *The Good Earth*). Or she may find herself physically isolated from the world by her husband and powerless to counteract this isolation (see *Jane Eyre*).

Romantic fiction may also depict a patriarchal marriage in which the husband's ultimate control over finances and any children the marriage produces causes misery for his wife. He may withhold financial privileges or the opportunity to share time with her children should she not behave in a manner of which he approves. Her "misbehavior" may involve her engaging in a sexual liaison with another man, an act that marked a woman from traditional societies as pariahs due to a double standard that would condone such actions on the part of her husband (see *Anna Karenina*). If a wife desires divorce, but laws indicate she cannot simply sue, the couple may perform an elaborate ruse, pretending adultery, in order for her to have the proper grounds to separate within a patriarchal society and marriage (see *A Handful of Dust*). In the most terrifying of patriarchal marriages, the wife suffers actual emotional and physical abuse, purposely afflicted upon her by a husband who retains total control over her life (see *Of Love and Dust, Sophie's Choice, The Kitchen God's Wife*).

References: Blain, Clements, and Grundy, 1990; Gilbert and Gubar, 1996g; Graham et al., 1989; Henderson and McManus, 1985; Radway, 1991; Schleiner, 1994; Travitsky, 1990

PAUL

As the male romantic interest in Jamaica Kincaid's novel, *Lucy* (1990), Paul remains important only in his representation of males in general. He becomes a lover for Lucy Potter, the novel's protagonist, but Kincaid does little to develop his character. Like all of the characters in the book except for Lucy, Paul lacks a last name, symbolizing his position as a universal type.

Readers learn two important things about Paul, both of which help to develop Lucy into a dynamic character. She notices his hands when he gestures close to a fish tank, which evokes a memory from her home island in the West Indies that becomes important to the novel. The memory involves a fisherman Lucy had liked who disappears at sea, washed overboard to his death. When she discovers that the fisherman had sexually touched a childhood acquaintance of hers,

Lucy reacts in a way that subverts reader expectation. Rather than being horrified or frightened, she experiences a pang of jealousy. Lucy then recalls that the fisherman always treated her with a respect that identifies her with her mother. This memory allows Kincaid to support the theme of mother-daughter relationships and the identity crises they cause. Additionally, Paul becomes important in legitimizing Lucy's belief about men. When at the novel's conclusion Lucy intuitively figures out that Paul and her roommate are engaged in a secret affair, this information supports her view of men as basically deceitful. She presents this view not in a judgmental manner, but rather as a simple fact that all women should accept before entering into a romantic relationship with a man.

Paul remains a shadowy figure, undeveloped and contributing little on his own to Kincaid's plot. His importance lies in his small but crucial contribution to the shaping of Lucy Potter.

See also: Lucy; Potter, Lucy Josephine
References: Birbalsingh, 1996; Brady, 1996; Garner, 1997; Kincaid, 1995

PAYNE, MARCUS

As his last name suggests, Marcus Payne, the tragic black character in Ernest J. Gaines's novel *Of Love and Dust* (1967), is destined to suffer during his short life. Left without parents and raised by Miss Julie Rand in mid–twentieth century Baton Rouge, Marcus crosses the law as a teen and begins a pattern of social indiscretion that eventually leads to his death.

When Marcus is arrested as a young man for killing another black man, Miss Julie Rand uses her years of service for white plantation owner Marshall Hebert to procure for Marcus a position on the plantation where he may work off any prison sentence. Rebellious and stubborn to the extreme, Marcus will not conform to the life of the plantation worker. Befriended by the plantation tractor driver, Jim Kelly, also the book's narrator, the younger man refuses Kelly's advice regarding the plantation's difficult physical demands. In order to flaunt the fact that he will never accept indenture to Hebert, Marcus dresses for field work in silk shirts and dress slacks rather than in the work clothes the other employees wear. He immediately invites the ire of the plantation overseer, Sidney Bonbon. When Bonbon pushes Marcus to his physical extreme, both in and out of the fields, Marcus develops a hatred for the Cajun overseer that can only be quenched by revenge. Marcus sets out to seduce Bonbon's black lover, Pauline Guerine, although Jim warns him regarding the extreme danger of such action.

As dangerous as his unsuccessful harassment of Pauline is, Marcus's decision to seduce Bonbon's childish wife, Louise Bonbon, is even more dangerous. The thought of the young black man making love to the overseer's white wife terrifies members of the black community, who know that any action taken against Marcus will mean trouble for the entire group of black workers. True to character, Marcus refuses to listen to their pleas, and he succeeds with Louise where he had failed with Pauline. Part of his success is due to the fact that he and Louise, although of different races, are united by servitude to the same man. Caught up in a patriarchal marriage to a man she detests, Louise remains as much a prisoner on the plantation as does Marcus.

Marcus eventually suspects that part of Hebert's reason for bringing him to the plantation is that he needs help in ridding himself of his overseer. Sidney Bonbon is blackmailing Hebert after having killed a man for him. Now Hebert needs a way to rid himself of Bonbon, who regularly steals from the plantation. Unfortunately, Marcus is only half right in his thinking. Hebert's plan to rid himself of Bonbon also includes a plan to get rid of Marcus. Marcus becomes so intent on escaping the plantation that he does not recognize Hebert's offer to aid in his escape as suspicious. The other black workers see through the obvious lie represented by Hebert's offer to help Marcus and Louise leave the plantation and Sidney Bonbon behind.

No amount of argument on Jim Kelly's or any of the other workers' parts can convince Marcus to abandon his escape plan. The forbidden love that he hopes will propel him to freedom in the North and his ambition to beat the white man at his own game blind Marcus to the danger in his plan. Although ostensibly Sidney Bonbon kills Marcus for trying to run away with his wife and daughter, the young man does not die for love. Rather, he dies because of a social system in which justice is due only to the powerful. Bonbon may strike the fatal blow, but southern culture, symbolized by the unrepentant Marshall Hebert, kills Marcus Payne.

See also: The Black Experience in America, 1600–1945; Bonbon, Louise; Forbidden Love; Guerine, Pauline; *Of Love and Dust*
References: Coombs, 1972; "Gaines, Ernest J.," 1994; Magnier, 1995; Summer, 1993; Upchurch, 1995

PILAR

Considered by many critics Ernest Hemingway's "exemplar" character in his war romance *For Whom the Bell Tolls* (1940), Pilar represents the human capacity to fight for one's beliefs. Her ferocious pride in her anti-Fascist ideology and Spanish chauvinism threaten to outshine that of the novel's protagonist, the American Robert Jordan. Hemingway's promotion of a female to a position of leadership remains important, because this variant does not appear often in war stories of that era. Pilar assumes her position from her husband, Pablo, whom she describes to Jordan as a once-brave man who has lost his passion. As her name suggests, Pilar becomes the pillar of strength after Pablo loses his enthusiasm for the guerrilla cause.

Pilar also aids the plot by bringing together Jordan and the Spanish girl, Maria. A victim of Fascist torture and abuse, Maria represents the innocence of Spain's common people, subjected to the chaos created by warring political forces. When Pilar nurses Maria back to health, she symbolically works to heal her country. Pilar trusts Jordan when he appeals to her band of guerrillas for help, and she urges Maria to act on her shy instincts of affection for Jordan. The two become lovers, representing the transcendence allowed the human spirit when individuals indulge in love, hope, patriotism, and the like.

Pilar's intense dedication to the cause of national freedom surfaces when she decides that Pablo, her own husband, may need to be sacrificed in order for the Republican revolutionaries to carry out their mission. Her willingness to dissolve her own romantic relationship balances her act to unite Jordan and Maria. Although Pablo does not have to die, Pilar's decision still remains an important indicator of her level of patriotism. It proves that the public cause must at times supersede the private, as is evidenced by Jordan's decision to sacrifice his own life for that of Maria and Spain in the novel's climax.

Pilar possesses a nontraditional beauty. Her unfeminine strength and physical ugliness contrast with Maria's fragile beauty. To Jordan and other patriots, however, she remains a vision of loveliness; her appeal lies in her dedication and purity. Feminists might criticize Hemingway's conversion of Pilar into a masculine figure before permitting her to hold a position of leadership. However, her relationship with Maria emphasizes her nurturing nature, a characteristic generally associated with females.

Pilar ends the novel every bit as complete a character as when it opens. Passionate, courageous, and honorable, Pilar acts as an ideal representation of the patriotism that runs throughout Hemingway's work.

See also: A Farewell to Arms; For Whom the Bell Tolls; Hemingway, Ernest; Jordan, Robert; The Lost Generation; Maria; Nihilism; *The Sun Also Rises;* War

References: Cowley, 1973; Defazio, 1996; Donaldson, 1996; Hen, 1996; Hily-Mane, 1995; Hotchner, 1966; Moreland, 1996; White, 1933, 1968

PONTELLIER, EDNA

Edna Pontellier, the protagonist of Kate Chopin's novella *The Awakening* (1899), does far more for plot than provide one corner in a nontraditional love triangle. Edna dares to desire the independence that remains the exclusive right of males in her patriarchal society. Her husband, Léonce Pontellier, remains more than willing to support what he sees as Edna's foolish experiments with painting and even her flirtation with a local young dandy, Robert Lebrun. But when Edna increasingly demands more and more emotional as well as physical liberation, Léonce assumes her mental capacities are threatened. In his point of view, only madness could account, in their patriarchal marriage, for Edna's behavior. Even this debilitation would be more socially acceptable than her demands for independence.

Edna begins the novel a naïve young wife to a successful Creole husband and mother to two young boys. Unfamiliar with the local customs in which the even younger Robert Lebrun is encouraged to "romance" her, Edna becomes infatuated with Robert, believing he loves her. She does not realize that the attentions he offers represent a carefully choreographed dance in which he pays her romantic attention yet has no intention of consummating that love. To do that would be to transgress into an area of forbidden love of which Creole culture disapproves.

Robert represents more for Edna than just a dalliance; through the tentative steps she takes as the center of his attention, she begins to gain self-confidence and self-reliance. In a telling early scene, Edna reveals the consternation she feels over her present "safe" situation as a sheltered wife expected to participate in the traditional motherhood role. Léonce returns home late and awakens Edna, who cannot respond to his conversation in the manner he prefers. His belief that she neglects him provides a clue to his attitude that women exist only to reflect the finer aspects of men. After checking on their children, he tells Edna that one of them has a fever. Edna feels certain that the child is in no danger. When Léonce criticizes her attitude, indicating that a mother's place is to care for her children, Edna must escape to the porch, where she weeps while facing the sea. Filled with conflict, she carries on an internal debate, wondering about the reason for her tears while reassuring herself that her husband is wonderfully kind. Yet her whole being fills with a shadowy anguish, an unidentifiable threat that she compares to a mist.

Her inner conflict later escalates, especially after she learns to swim. Having conquered what had for Edna been a lifelong fear of the water, she wonders over her newfound strength and power. Impatient to be free of the role society has thrust upon her, she at one point smashes a vase that represents her domestic sphere and symbolically destroys her marriage as she stomps on her wedding ring. Chopin makes clear that Edna feels acutely the burden of family and the distraction her duties cause. Léonce becomes furious upon discovering that his wife has departed the house rather than remaining to participate in the accepted custom of receiving guests. Edna confronts him openly, without tears or shame, her challenge demonstrating her advanced degree of change.

Robert leaves on vacation, and Edna establishes a painting and sketching studio for herself. Her awakening sexual self-awareness triggers a concurrent awareness of her own creativity. Again, Léonce criticizes her painting as an activity that draws her away from the more acceptable role of homemaker. This acceptable role Edna recognizes early on as embodied in the angelic character of Adèle Ratignolle, a local wife and homemaker. But she rejects this role and Adèle's ideas. Even though Edna had all her life followed the code of silence inflicted upon women by the male-dominated culture, she informs Adèle that she would never sacrifice herself for her children. In the heated argument that follows her statement, Edna notices that the women might as well be speaking different languages, so little do they understand one another. When Adèle protests that, according to the Bible, a woman could do no better than to give her life for her children and that she feels she could do no more than that, Edna laughs and immediately counters that idea.

Edna misses Robert, and as the warmth of summer advances into the coolness of fall, symbolizing the cooling of their romance, she wonders if he will ever return. After hearing some news about Robert and his relationship with other women that she finds upsetting, Edna plunges into the water that had at one time so frightened her. Even in its coolness, she still thrashes about in childlike abandon and emerges as if rebaptized. She visits the irrepressible Mademoiselle Reisz, a local pianist who encourages Edna's painting but, more importantly, allows her to read a letter written by Robert in which he expresses feelings for Edna. Edna reads as the mademoiselle plays, and Chopin again emphasizes the theme of sexuality as linked to creativity. Even though Edna crumples the letter and throws it down, her passion for Robert increases.

In her longing for Robert, Edna allows another, less noble young man, Alcée Arobin, to seduce her. Robert had never meant to threaten her marriage, and when Edna realizes this, she knows she cannot return to her previous suffocating life with Léonce. She returns to the source of her awakening, the sea, and seeks death where she once realized life. As she swims farther away from the darkening land into the "million lights of the sun" reflected from the water's surface, Edna thinks of her family. Although her children and husband were important to her, they would never possess her.

> See also: The Awakening; Chopin, Kate; Forbidden Love; Love Triangle; Patriarchal Marriage; Victorian Age
> References: Budick, 1996; Davidson, 1995; Frye, 1976; Keesey, 1998; Williams, 1974

THE PORTRAIT OF A LADY

Some critics view Henry James's psychological study, The Portrait of a Lady (1881), as a vehicle for the further development of the Daisy Miller character created in his 1879 novella of the same name. In his later protagonist, Isabel Archer, James presents a more fleshed-out version of the naïve Daisy, demonstrating what might have happened to Daisy had she survived to act on her independence and belief in personal honor. Like many Jamesian female characters, Isabel travels from her home of America to Europe, where she will begin her quest for love and partnership in a marriage that will allow her the freedom she desires. What she ultimately discovers is that her romantic sensibilities have no place in real life.

As promised by his title, James spends the entire novel closely examining a single character. His methods transcend romanticism and realism, the two popular novel formats of his day, to present instead a sophisticated psychological study of a complicated figure. His interest lay in the internal human experience rather than in the outward actions of our lives, an interest reflected through Isabel Archer.

James eschews violence and melodrama, depending more on characterization than action or violence to carry his story. Isabel proves equal to this task, developing throughout the novel in a manner that piques reader curiosity as to which of many choices offered she will make and what the consequences of such choices may be. She seems a charmed figure from the outset—intelligent, beautiful, and touting an American independence that sometimes shocks her European companions. The final ingredient to her formula for success comes with her cousin Ralph's generous assignment of half of his own financial inheritance to Isabel. His contribution allows Isabel an independence from the financial realities that controlled most young women's choices in the nineteenth century.

Isabel's self-confidence leads her to turn down two marriage proposals, one that would make her materially wealthy and another that would bring all the passion her life could desire. When she at last chooses as her match Gilbert Osmond, an expatriate American residing in Italy, readers recognize a great error has occurred, so little suspense exists as to the nature of the couple's future relationship. The suspense comes in anticipation of Isabel's reaction when she discovers that her sensibilities have caused a tragic error in judgment. Misled by Madame Merle, a previous Osmond victim, into believing that Osmond's interests and beliefs align with her own, Isabel finds herself also a victim. The only question that remains is, will she react as Madame Merle has, losing all self-respect as she becomes little more than a pawn in Osmond's wicked games?

Isabel's position as Osmond's wife adds emphasis to the theme suggested by James's title. She has become exactly the thing she so despised—an ornamental possession belonging to an egomaniacal male. A portrait exists as a lifeless imitation of the real thing, a description that fits Osmond far more than Isabel. Isabel indeed "poses" for three different portraits throughout the novel at different stages of her life, portraits captured in the eye of the reader and by her various male observers. In each "still life," Isabel appears in black, perhaps as a foreshadowing of the dark forces that threaten her happiness. The first sitting occurs when she arrives in Gardencourt in England. Framed by the Edenic background, supported by its imagery of new life and beginnings, Isabel exudes an excitement and warmth befitting a lovely woman with a glorious future. In a second portrait, Isabel is viewed through the eyes of her stepdaughter's love interest as an apparently poised and confident married woman, a pose that belies her true situation. She poses a final time again at Gardencourt on her return to England upon Ralph's death. Now dressed in funereal black, her mature confidence stems from her firm grasp on reality. The death of Ralph, her onetime spiritual guide, could signal Isabel's own spiritual death.

Isabel chooses to remain with Gilbert Osmond, seeking redemption for her own errors in judgment by helping to rescue Osmond's daughter from a loveless fate. That Isabel elects to remain within a disastrous situation confirms readers' high expectations. The sense of honor she embodies in accepting the situation of her own making alleviates some of the pain of her initial error. Through Isabel and other protagonists, James studies the oppositions between that which is American and that which is European, between works of art and the work of life, between good and evil, and between virtue and moral bankruptcy. Isabel Archer refuses to become an ultimate victim of those conflicts. Her final and best choice lies in her decision to permit an enrichment of her life by those very forces that would destroy an individual of lesser character.

See also: The Age of Innocence; Archer, Isabel; Bildungsroman; *Daisy Miller;* James, Henry; Miller,

Daisy; Osmond, Gilbert; Patriarchal Marriage; Quest
References: Bevilacqua, 1996; Bullen, 1997; Feidelson, 1975; Hart, 1995; Kettle, 1975; Pizer, 1995; Putt, 1966

POTTER, LUCY JOSEPHINE

As the main character in Jamaica Kincaid's 1990 novel, *Lucy,* Lucy Josephine Potter represents a nontraditional romantic quest character. Like classical quest characters, Lucy undertakes a journey across water from her small West Indian island home and engages in various adventures in the new land of America. She also suffers the great loss necessary to the quest when her father dies. Her guides prove untrustworthy, though, and Lucy seems to find only disappointment in the new land as she continues to struggle until the novel's final sentence with questions of identity. These aspects, along with her gender, work together to make Lucy's quest nontraditional. But her quest is not altogether ironic, in that she does profit from her adventures in the book's final scene, when she can shed tears of shame and make the decision to become a writer.

Lucy's narrative never loses the foreign flavor that represents the individual trying to find her place in another culture. The story's minor characters, such as Mariah, Lewis, Peggy, and Paul, remain important in shaping Lucy's persona as she discusses each. In her position as nanny to Mariah and Lewis's four children, Lucy reflects on the false love the couple shares. This allows her to reveal her own attitudes toward love and romance, ones that differ markedly from those of classical romance. Lucy has developed a sophisticated and uncomplimentary view of men and the dangers that they pose to women from her observations of her own parents. More than once, she relates the fact that one of her father's lovers attacked her mother while she was pregnant with Lucy, hoping to kill both the wife and the unborn child. Other incidents involving men reveal them as sexually motivated creatures unable to control their desires and by extension untrustworthy. This view assigns to males the characteristics historically attributed to females.

Lucy's parents' relationship guides her own development of ideas regarding romance. Although she frankly confesses to enjoying sex and engages in physical relationships whenever a male appeals to her, she resists falling in love.

Again, Kincaid inverts traditional gender-related expectations by allowing Lucy to assume an attitude long attributed only to men. Lucy has also kissed and fondled other women, a fact she offers simply in passing, downplaying its importance or shock value.

The climax of the novel occurs when Lucy learns of the death of her father and tells the story of her naming. Issues of identity common to the quest arise when she reveals that she hated her name as a child and once tried to name herself. She first tries on for size names of her favorite authors, such as Emily Brontë, Charlotte Brontë, and Charlotte's most famous character, Jane Eyre. This allows Lucy's association with female authors, foreshadowing her beginning a career as a writer at the novel's conclusion. It also parallels Kincaid's own action in changing her name from Elaine Potter Richardson to Jamaica Kincaid before she began her literary career.

As Lucy continues her story, the reader learns that her mother once told her she was named for Lucifer. Lucy rejoices at the thought of being identified with Lucifer, a child of a god. Lucifer's relationship with God helps Lucy to reflect on her association with her mother, a woman Lucy envisions as a godlike, untouchable creature. Lucy's damaged relationship with her mother becomes clearly delineated in this comparison. In addition, it supplies a final parallel to the classical quest, as many critics consider Satan from John Milton's *Paradise Lost* (1667) a quintessential ironic quest hero.

The book's final scene reveals Lucy at home alone, without the company of her roommate Peggy or her most recent lover, Paul. She suspects the two have deserted her for one another's company. She begins to write for the first time, symbolizing Kincaid's own decision after she ended her position in America as a teenage au pair. When her tears of shame wash away the first words she writes, Lucy undergoes a baptism or renewal of sorts. With the closing words of the novel, Lucy Josephine Potter experiences an epiphany that will allow her to begin her true quest as a writer, one that will take place beyond the pages of *Lucy*.

See also: Kincaid, Jamaica; *Lucy;* Paul
References: Birbalsingh, 1996; Brady, 1996; Garner, 1997; Kincaid, 1995; Nagel, 1995

PRIDE AND PREJUDICE

As perhaps Jane Austen's best-known and most widely read nineteenth-century romantic novel of manners, *Pride and Prejudice* (1813) continues to appeal to readers nearly two centuries after its publication. Austen's first novel features characters who represent the themes suggested by its title. The universal quality of both pride and prejudice may explain the novel's popularity and its transformation into multiple screen and television series versions. Readers can relate to its plot and to the characters who find it necessary to change their minds regarding their social and political stances for the sake of love.

The novel's protagonist, Elizabeth Bennet, also called Eliza and Lizzy, with her unshakable ideas regarding social propriety, symbolizes prejudice. Fitzwilliam Darcy, destined to become Elizabeth's husband following a long series of misunderstandings, suffers from the pride that causes Elizabeth's initial irritation and her later anger. In between the couple's unfortunate first meeting and their final union in marriage exist a number of circumstances that delight and entertain readers as they anxiously await the solution to the conundrum the lovers cause for themselves.

The Bennet family boasts a gaggle of five sisters, but none may inherit their father's property. As in most of Austen's novels, the theme of gender inequity is emphasized. The modest but commendable Bennet estate, like so many in England, is entailed through the male line. This means that a male cousin will inherit the estate belonging to the long-suffering Mr. Bennet. It also accounts for Mrs. Bennet's anxiety over seeing that all of her daughters marry well.

When the wealthy Charles Bingley rents a nearby estate, Mrs. Bennet, a singularly silly woman, badgers her husband until he visits Bingley. Bingley's friend Darcy, also a handsome, eligible bachelor, creates a flutter among the local women until they ascertain his cold formality. When Elizabeth and Darcy's first meeting turns sour due to a remark that Elizabeth overhears Darcy make, her prejudice against him is firmly set. That prejudice strengthens when she discovers that Darcy may be responsible for preventing Bingley from acting on his feelings toward her sister Jane. Emphasizing Austen's theme of class consciousness, the young women and gentlemen seem destined never to unite.

Austen's manner of bringing the two couples together is the creation of a conflict involving Elizabeth and a younger sister that also draws in

Greer Garson, left, played Elizabeth Bennet, while Maureen Sullivan (center) played Jane Bennet and Ann Rutherford played Lydia Bennet in this 1940 film version of Pride and Prejudice *(1813), Jane Austen's best-known and most widely read nineteenth-century romantic novel of manners. (Archive Photos)*

Darcy. Elizabeth meets a soldier named George Wickham and talks with him about Darcy. Wickham fabricates a story regarding Darcy's unfounded cruelty toward him that secures Elizabeth's negative feelings toward Darcy. In reality, Wickham, a onetime protégé of Darcy and Darcy's father, repaid their generosity by attempting to seduce Darcy's younger sister. Elizabeth will not learn this truth until sometime later, and Wickham's lie contributes to her rejection of Darcy's first proposal of marriage.

When the wildest of the Bennet girls, Lydia Bennet, falls in love with Wickham and runs off with him, social ruin threatens the Bennet family. Darcy intercedes to rescue Lydia's good name by ensuring her marriage to Wickham and by providing Wickham with enough money to repay all his debts. He does this out of a generosity of spirit and a love for her that Elizabeth had not previously recognized because her prejudice blinded her to Darcy's true character.

By the novel's conclusion, Elizabeth admits her mistake in not allowing Darcy the opportunity to redeem himself when he first attempts to do so. In like manner, Darcy realizes that his pride in his social position prevented his recognition of the fine characteristics that Elizabeth and Jane embody. These epiphanies, or insights, qualify both Elizabeth and Darcy as dynamic characters. Once Darcy comes to this realization, he may unite with Elizabeth, and Jane and Bingley also find happiness together.

Austen weaves around her major plot several minor plots, developing memorable characters in addition to the romantic couples. Mr. and Mrs. Bennet make an impression as two people of opposite characters and temperaments, an impression echoed in the duo of Wickham and Lydia. Every bit as silly as her mother, Lydia promises to shape herself in that woman's less-than-desirable mold. Wickham, however, deserves that burden, but Mr. Bennet does not. One of

Austen's finest triumphs with a minor character is in her shaping of the Bennets' cousin, Mr. Collins, who stands to inherit their home. A prig and a minion to the wealthy and influential Lady Catherine de Bourgh, Collins's mincing actions and dialogue add comic relief to the sometimes highly dramatic situations. The revulsion both Jane and Elizabeth feel toward Mr. Collins, as he plots to marry one or the other of them, invokes reader sympathy. As for Lady Catherine, her character allows Austen's portrait of the cruelty and arrogance often evidenced by England's aristocratic circle, the type of behavior of which Elizabeth falsely accuses Darcy.

Thus, although it is for the most part a plot sketched with a light touch, *Pride and Prejudice* does contain several serious messages regarding society's unfair elevation of a small group of individuals who gain that elevation merely through birth. Lady Catherine represents a group who believes the father's name alone entitles offspring to the respect of others. Darcy, however, discovers that the earned respect of another can be far more valuable than any inherited wealth or title.

　　See also: Austen, Jane; Bennet, Elizabeth
　　(Eliza/Lizzy); Darcy, Fitzwilliam; *Emma; Sense and*
　　Sensibility
　　References: Armstrong, 1990; Copeland and
　　McMaster, 1997; Drabble, 1995; Gard, 1992;
　　Gilbert and Gubar, 1996c; Price, 1983

THE PRINCE OF TIDES

American writer Pat Conroy's wildly successful 1986 romance, *The Prince of Tides,* incorporates themes that have become favorites with his aficionados, who enjoy his fiction on the page as well as in its many conversions to the screen. Like Conroy's other highly autobiographical novels, this one focuses on themes of religion, family, marriage, social status, sibling relationships, and the importance of geography and resultant culture on every individual's emotional development. Conroy sketches a painful love story between a South Carolinian Catholic coach, Tom Wingo, and a New York Jewish psychiatrist, Susan Lowenstein. Tom's failing marriage and the suicide attempt of his twin sister Savannah provide the foundation for his development of a much-needed relationship with Susan.

Tom obviously suffers from a lack of self-confidence, which is evident in his frequent self-deprecating comments. Although he adores his three daughters and respects his physician-wife, Sallie, his emotional abuse as a child at the hands of his overbearing mother, Lila Wingo, prevents his development of sound, long-lasting relationships. A social climber who found her life with her abusive fisherman-husband unsatisfying, Lila used her three children as emotional props for her own sagging ego. When she finally captures in a second marriage a socialite who will elevate her to her perceived deserved high status, she chooses a man whom Tom detests. Tom reveals these and many additional tales from the Wingo past during therapy sessions with Susan after he journeys to New York to help the therapist understand the cause of his sister's self-destructive tendencies. Before he departs his southern surroundings, Tom learns from Sallie of her affair with a fellow physician. He understands that he can no longer satisfy her emotional needs, just as he cannot meet his own, and he asks only that she not divorce him just yet.

When he first encounters Susan Lowenstein in New York, she exhibits a cool professional demeanor that leads him to believe that she represents all that he hates about what he views as the inhospitable North. During her probing therapy sessions, however, he comes to know her as a fellow human in pain. She deftly guides Tom through his and Savannah's childhood and the many painful experiences that lead to their emotional problems and the death of their older brother, Luke. By discussing Savannah's problems, Tom reveals his own and gives Susan information that will allow her to bring about Tom's healing along with that of his sister.

Not only does Susan provide physical love through an affair that Tom needs, but also she helps him renew his confidence in his abilities as a coach. She does this by introducing him to her son, Bernard Woodruff, who lives under pressure from his father, concert violinist Herbert Woodruff, to become a professional musician like himself. Bernard, however, desires to play football, an action that Herbert categorically forbids. Susan overrides her husband's authority by arranging for Tom to work with Bernard in developing the boy's athletic skills. Having himself grown up with a father who never appreciated him, Tom finds he can easily relate to Bernard's problems. He also discovers that his physical skills mirror highly developed survival skills that allowed him to get past his abusive childhood.

When Herbert Woodruff attempts to humiliate Tom because of his lower social standing at a New York dinner party, Susan leaves their apartment with Tom, and they begin a love affair. At this point, the reader clearly observes that Susan herself has severe marital problems she needs to solve. The love she shares with Tom will allow her a clearer view of what she needs and desires in her personal life so that she can move on after Tom departs.

Conroy's use of imagery and figurative language resembles that of poetry. He includes some of Savannah's poetry and an entire short story within the novel, allowing a direct emphasis on the importance of literature and the art of storytelling. As his narrator, Tom, relates story upon story, Conroy reveals his talent for a weaving of myths that has received much critical praise. He allows the reader to slip from the present into Tom's past and return again. Not only do readers enjoy the conflict between individual adult characters and that produced by the plot's love triangle, but they find themselves immersed in tales of the Wingo childhood with which most readers will identify on some level. Conroy tempers the overwhelming effect of the multiple tales with Tom's early comment regarding the truth of all the extraordinary things that happened to his family. Thus, although framing his modern story with a mythological, mystical approach, Conroy also emphasizes the realism of his markedly twentieth-century tale of complicated psychological personalities. Termed southern Gothic for its proliferation of bizarre characters, suggestions of the mystical, and often dark narration, the novel provides a rich texture to support its tale of redeeming romance. Its abundant imagery caused it to translate well, like most of Conroy's other novels, to movie format.

The Prince of Tides is filled with multiple symbolic objects and occurrences. The pet tiger, Caesar, tamed by Luke, becomes the family protector that Mr. Wingo can never be and symbolizes the ferocious nature that most parents assume in protecting their young. Luke, his own name reminiscent of the biblical physician, also tries to protect his younger siblings, nursing them back to some type of normalcy following each clash between their parents. Their dive together into the nearby water, where they hold hands while immersed, strongly suggests a baptism leading to a new try at life each time they

emerge. Lila's emotionally destructive approach to life turns physical when she decides to sell the family island, itself symbolic of the strength of the Wingo line. As the family protector, Luke, returned from Vietnam, chooses to guard the island from takeover by its purchasers, an act that results in his death and makes Lila his symbolic murderer. Luke's death results in the destruction of the fabric of family in a way that his father's death did not, leading directly to Tom's and Savannah's emotional breakdowns. Within Savannah's children's book exist Satanic visions that symbolize the fictional author's own madness.

Tom and Susan's love affair represents much more than the typical romantic excursion into love and emotion. It literally saves both their lives. Not destined to be a long-term relationship, the love and respect that the two share become integral to an epiphany for Tom. He emerges from his long psychological battle fit to work at the reassembly of his family and his life. But Susan's continuing importance to him is emphasized in the novel's final scene, in which he admits to chanting her name, "Lowenstein," again and again when he returns each night to his southern home in his southern world. Their affair assumes its position in the mythology that supports Tom Wingo's life.

See also: Conroy, Pat; Gothic Romance; Violence; Wingo, Tom

References: Berendt, 1995; Friedman and Siegel, 1995; Frye, 1976; Hoffman and Murphy, 1996; Shone, 1995; Toolan, 1991

PRYNNE, HESTER

Hester Prynne, the Puritan protagonist of Nathaniel Hawthorne's nineteenth-century romance *The Scarlet Letter* (1850), is identified with what is probably the most famous symbol in American fiction. The scarlet "A" adorning Hester's dress symbolizes various things throughout the story, but in every instance it accurately represents Hester herself. At first, its intended meaning, "Adulteress," applies to Hester who, accepting the blame for participating in a forbidden love, never shrinks beneath its weighty indication. But by the novel's conclusion, it may well represent "Angel," for so Hester's Puritan community comes to think of her with the passage of time. Ironically, for all her sin, made material through her daughter Pearl, Hester actually

Lilian Gish appeared as Hester Prynne, the Puritan protagonist of Nathaniel Hawthorne's nineteenth-century romance, The Scarlet Letter *(1850), in this 1926 film version of the novel. (Photofest)*

remains the most innocent of the three main characters. Her sin of emotion at least produces a constructive result in Pearl, a life that could grow and flourish. But the sins of Arthur Dimmesdale, her preacher lover, and Roger Chillingworth, her onetime husband, bring nothing but destruction upon themselves and others.

In a novel abundant with symbolism, the clothing worn by the characters is not the only meaningful signal about their personalities. Hester's surname, like that of the two males with whom she forms a bitter love triangle, remains important as well. Dimmesdale indeed possesses a dim inner vision of self, a myopia regarding his own salvation, and Chillingworth allows his heart to chill and harden into stone. The name Prynne resembles "prim" in appearance and in sound, an adjective representing the proper demeanor for a Puritan woman but one to which Hester does not aspire. For although the prim woman may follow society's rules, she does it only for the sake of appearance, being hypocritical in thought and

emotion. Hester's honesty will not allow such hypocrisy.

Thinking herself abandoned by her husband Chillingworth, who never completed the voyage from Europe to join her in the New World, Hester faces her feelings for Dimmesdale honestly, acting on her love. Her attitude, then, contrasts with that of both men. Dimmesdale never reveals his own adultery to the community, fearful of the reprisal that Hester bravely bears. Chillingworth, finally arriving in Salem just at the time of Hester's trial, never reveals his identity as Hester's husband.

Over the years, Hester's attitude and actions distinguish her from the two weak men who exert the greatest influence on her life. While raising her daughter alone, she completes multiple good works within the very community that damned her. Dimmesdale, however, loses his physical health to the burden of guilt he bears, and Chillingworth's desire for revenge erodes his humanity. Hester uses her needlework talents to convert her "A" from the shameful symbol it was intended to be into a beautiful work of art. In contrast, Dimmesdale sacrifices his talent for preaching to the shame he feels over his adulterous acts, and Chillingworth wastes his art for healing by using it to cause misery in a fellow human being.

As a fallen woman who recovers not only her pride but also her standing in the most judgmental society America has known, Hester Prynne proves little less than a miracle worker. The two men who claim to have loved her in the past would do well to take a lesson from this "weak" female. It is Hester who ultimately triumphs over her sin while teaching those around her about their own.

See also: Chillingworth, Roger; Dimmesdale, Arthur; Forbidden Love; Love Triangle; *The Scarlet Letter*
References: Abel, 1988; Gilbert and Gubar, 1996g

PYGMALION

Although a drama rather than a novel, George Bernard Shaw's romantic play *Pygmalion* (1913) remains important to romantic fiction. In his retelling of the ancient story of Pygmalion, Shaw updates a plot that has a long tradition in romantic fiction. In the original myth, King Pygmalion sculpts a beautiful woman and names the statue Galatea. When he falls in love with his creation, Aphrodite, goddess of love, magically transforms Galatea into a flesh and blood woman. In many romantic plots, a powerful male may take on a female from a lower social class and elevate her through marriage or sponsorship, then claim her achievements as his own.

Shaw's play presents Henry Higgins, a pompous, arrogant, and highly accomplished English phoneticist, in the role of Pygmalion. Eliza Doolittle, a poor but intelligent and ambitious woman who sells flowers on the street, becomes his Galatea. The magic applied by Higgins to enact Doolittle's transformation is that of language. He wagers that a grasp of proper speech will elevate Doolittle to the level of a duchess. The problem with his plan is his lack of consideration for Eliza's future following his "experiment."

When Higgins's plan succeeds, he claims all of the credit, sharing little of his "glory" with Eliza. Although the two do not marry, their relationship reflects many qualities of the patriarchal marriage, with the sole control held by the male. Eliza not only works hard, but she alters her outward identity by assuming a new speech pattern that would normally be indicative of a member of a high social class. She possesses only the trappings, however, of the upper class, making her ineligible to join that group. Simultaneously, her elevated speech has rendered her incapable of returning to her previous life with her peers on the street. By giving the play a less than happy ending, Shaw cautions his audience to focus on the long-term, rather than the immediate, effects of such a transformation.

Shaw could not have predicted the public reaction to his play. Viewers so longed for a happy ending to what Shaw himself termed a "romance" that they co-opted his play, adding a new ending to it. They insisted that Higgins develop some type of permanent romantic relationship with Eliza. The playwright explained that the term "romance" simply indicates a story involving a transformation of some kind, not a love interest developing between its two main characters. Yet in the play's popular musical and movie versions titled *My Fair Lady*, Eliza does indeed return to Higgins. Shaw even wrote, to no avail, a prose "sequel" to his play in which Eliza marries her paramour, Freddy Eynsford Hill. This changed his public's viewpoint not a whit.

Perhaps the most important observation to be made regarding the effect of Shaw's *Pygmalion* is his public's response. He labeled his work a "romance," and a public far removed from the classical definition of the romance genre interpreted that to mean love. As consumers of literature, they simply ignored the poet's intent and projected their own romantic fantasies onto the tale. The effect offers support for the idea that the same work of literature can mean entirely different things to different generations of readers.

See also: Doolittle, Eliza; Higgins, Henry; Patriarchal Marriage; Shaw, George Bernard
References: Brunel, 1992; Campbell, 1988; Frye, 1976

QUASIMODO

Few more memorable characters exist than Quasimodo, the hero of Victor Hugo's nineteenth-century historical romance, *The Hunchback of Notre Dame* (1831). The loyalty and seemingly unshakable love Quasimodo feels for the Gypsy girl, Esmeralda, make him a magnificent romantic figure in a story written by the leader of the French romantic movement. The misshapen body of Quasimodo allowed Hugo to pursue the idea that the ugly as well as the sublime should form the focus of literature and art. Hugo believed that the linking of man's animal and spiritual elements by Christianity allowed writers to present their subjects realistically rather than in the idealized versions seen in ancient writings. Quasimodo's hideous appearance masks a beautiful character, and the contrast allows Hugo to emphasize the Gothic romantic tradition as he incorporates elements from "Beauty and the Beast" fables as well as from the passion of Christ.

With his wicked master, the priest Claude Frollo, and Esmeralda, Quasimodo forms a touching love triangle. His ugly countenance helps magnify the stunning beauty and grace of the Gypsy dancer. His purity of love for Esmeralda contrasts with the wicked intentions of Claude Frollo and also with the purely physical attraction Captain Phoebus de Chateaupers feels for Esmeralda. Naturally the adoration of the girl by both the hunchback and the priest remains unrequited, as does Esmeralda's love for Phoebus. Thus, the basis for tragedy exists, helping promote Hugo's theme of the inevitability of fate.

The novel supplies a personal history for Quasimodo, describing his being left as a foundling for Claude Frollo to raise in the confines of the glorious cathedral of Notre Dame. As the bell ringer, Quasimodo gains a reputation not only for his hideous appearance but also for his important connection to the priest and the church. He at first admires Esmeralda from afar and simply obeys Claude Frollo when he attempts to kidnap her. The attempt fails due to the intervention of Phoebus, an action that promotes Esmeralda's romantic inclinations toward the handsome captain.

Quasimodo's character allows other interesting parallels to be drawn between him and Claude Frollo. Although externally the hunchback possesses a frightening appearance, internally his soul remains pure, free from any dark motivation. Conversely, Claude Frollo, as a priest, should represent virtue, but his tortured and twisted soul conceals dark internal passions that eventually lead him to madness. Whereas Quasimodo's intentions toward Esmeralda remain honorable, the priest's thoughts focus on salacious and immoral acts. Thus, Quasimodo, resembling a cathedral gargoyle, becomes a more proper symbol for the cathedral than does his master.

The love Quasimodo feels for Esmeralda replaces his devotion to Claude Frollo. In the Festival of Fools that coincides with Epiphany and a celebration of the planned marriage of Louis XI's son, Quasimodo is crowned the Prince of Fools. This allows him to observe Esmeralda's performance that serves as entertainment for the occasion. Because the Gypsy comes under suspicion for witchcraft, and much of Paris views the black-robed figure of Claude Frollo as a sorcerer, the hunchback stands "trial" for associating with undesirables. In a move emphasizing the total lack of social justice that forms one theme for the novel, Quasimodo is publicly beaten and humiliated in the pillory. Only Esmeralda responds to his request to quench a burning thirst during his whipping. This scene remains highly reminiscent of Christ's suffering before and during his crucifixion, emphasizing the innocence and purity of both the hunchback as a Christ figure and Esmeralda, whose virginity and innocence sup-

Lon Chaney played Quasimodo in a 1923 film version of The Hunchback of Notre Dame, *in which the loyalty and seemingly unshakable love Quasimodo feels for the Gypsy girl Esmeralda make him a magnificent romantic figure. (Photofest)*

ports her identification with the Virgin Mary. Quasimodo observes the priest turn away and slip from the crowd, and at this point his loyalty transfers from Claude Frollo to Esmeralda.

Because the hunchback possesses the just spirit that most of the other characters lack, he rushes to aid Esmeralda when she later faces execution for false charges of witchcraft and the attempted murder of Phoebus. When he rescues her and carries her away to the sanctuary of the cathedral, he imitates Phoebus's rescue of her from the hunchback's own kidnapping attempt. But Esmeralda does not value Quasimodo's aid as she does that of the captain. No reader can miss the painful irony in the fact that she basically ignores Quasimodo's devotion while continuing to love a man who would not even step forward to provide evidence that might have dismissed charges against her.

The hunchback acts upon his love for Esmeralda when he kills his longtime master for

her benefit. But true love cannot save a young girl willing to sacrifice her life for a man who barely notices her existence. Even Quasimodo will be unable to rescue her a second time from execution. Following her public death, he disappears.

When, about two years following the events described, the vault housing the human remains of those executed is searched for a certain body, two skeletons are discovered in an unusual pose. The skeleton of a crooked-spined man embraces that of a woman to which the remnants of a white dress still cling. Esmeralda's garb strongly suggests a wedding dress, supporting the chapter's title, "The Marriage of Quasimodo." The hunchback's spiritual beauty at last unites with the physical beauty of his love.

See also: Beauty and the Beast; Esmeralda; Frollo, Claude; Gothic Romance; *The Hunchback of Notre Dame;* Violence

References: Brombert, 1986; Charlton, 1984; Dahl, 1947; Ellis, 1989

QUEST

The *quest,* also known as the mythic adventure or the hero's journey, contains many elements found in romance and love stories. Homer's *Odyssey* contains all of these elements and is often considered the prototypical, seminal quest adventure. Aspects of the quest may be found in myths from all cultures. Many contain archetypal characters that correspond to the heroes and heroines of modern fiction. For instance, George Lucas employed the classic quest in shaping his *Star Wars* films. A key to understanding both classic and modern uses of the quest remains the fact that an external journey toward the claiming of a prize usually symbolizes an internal journey resulting in an epiphany, or realization, that changes a character's behavior or outlook on life.

The hero's journey may be considered in various stages, each of which offers the hero both helps and hindrances as he (to simplify matters, the male pronoun will be used hereafter in this entry) moves toward the prize. A first stage could be called "Of the Ordinary World." In this stage, the hero lives a "normal" existence, following his routine. A next stage, often called "Departure," contains substages such as "A Call to Adventure," when something happens to change the hero's life, causing him to leave home. In some myths, the hero may at first refuse the call out of fear or a misunderstanding of what will be required of him. He may meet the important figure of a guide and mentor who directs or prods him to make the required journey so he may fulfill his destiny. The position of guide may be fulfilled by a god or goddess or a simple being such as a shepherd, woodsman, or smithy. Often the journey takes place over water in a vessel, as with Odysseus's voyage. Other quest aspects that may enter in this first leg of the hero's journey include magic or mysticism in the form of some supernatural aid or magical powers offered to the traveler. Athena, goddess of wisdom, served as both guide and supernatural aid for Odysseus. In the Star Wars saga, the figures of Obiwan Kenobi and Yoda fulfill this position for the young hero, Luke. The hero then crosses a threshold, important because it makes his departure definite, and he will not turn back. Occasionally he meets his guide at this stage of the journey, in which powers of every kind appear magnified and safety is left behind.

In the "Initiation" stage, the hero encounters a series of tests. These may include his meeting shapeshifters, tricksters, or monsters. Some may be hideous, such as ogres, but they may also assume the form of a beautiful temptress, to whose deceit the hero temporarily falls victim. In some stories, the hero's guide may be killed by such an evil being, but he leaves behind a magical force that continues to protect, inspire, or guide the hero. This may equate to the loss that the hero generally suffers during the journey; that loss is usually of a loved being. During initiation, the hero must prove his worth by battling multiple enemies. He may feel unequal to his task at any point along the way, as he travels through shadows/darkness. Sometimes this period of "dark before the dawn" is called the "Descent," named for the journey into Hades that classic heroes took. Hades represented a repository for the "shades" or souls of all the dead, and the hero might seek out a dead hero or relative, sometimes a father figure, to get advice. Thus bolstered, the hero moves upward again toward some type of light, wiser and more mature as he turns attention away from the self and toward his assigned task. After victoriously surviving a supreme ordeal, the hero claims a prize. In mythology, that might have been a magical weapon or fortune of some kind, often guarded by a supernatural evil creature, such as a dragon or monster. In the romantic quest of chivalric fiction, the prize could be the love or admiration of a fair maiden or the maiden herself, rescued from a guardian monster, dragon, or snake. In modern quest versions, the journey may be a psychological one in which depression mirrors the descent into darkness, and discovery of one's identity represents the prize.

In the final stage, that of "Return," the hero may actually refuse to go home. Like Odysseus, he may instead wander about, so accustomed is he to his new role in life and so distant seems his old existence. Generally some type of magic helps him turn homeward, and he begins a mystical flight away from the land of his trials. His return may require a rescue by another version of a helper who enters the foreign domain to literally remove the hero. The hero may experience further minor adventures on the road back to his past until he crosses the return threshold and arrives home with his prize. Here he faces yet another challenge; the spreading of the truth the dark gave him in a light-filled world.

Additional elements in some quests include a battle with a monstrous female at some point during the journey, aid in the form of a mother figure, the hero being swallowed and later regurgitated by a huge monster, a lengthy spell-caused sleep or period of drowsiness or disorientation delaying the hero, and shapeshifters that take on the appearance of trusted confidants but who are in reality evil.

References: Brunel, 1992; Campbell, 1968; Frye, 1976

R

RAVID, IVRIA

Ivria Ravid acts as a catalyst for the conflict suffered by her husband, Yoel Ravid, the protagonist in Amos Oz's realistic novel *To Know a Woman* (1989; translated in 1991). Although Ivria has been killed in a freak accident prior to the beginning of the story, she returns throughout the novel by means of flashback. Yoel's attempt to retire from the Israeli secret service to care for his epileptic daughter, Netta, his mother, and his mother-in-law provides a deep psychological study of a man haunted by his past. That past includes Ivria, an enigmatic woman whom, despite the promise in the novel's title, Yoel comes to know no better following her death than he did during her life.

Ivria's relationship to Yoel is paradoxical. At times he considers the closeness they once shared, a bond so intimate that they knew one another's thoughts without speaking. Silence remains an important aspect of their relationship, something in which they both at first took pride. That silence represents a positive when Yoel recalls their first meeting as Ivria worked in her father's fields in Metullah. Yoel lost his way, ironically, during an orienteering exercise in a commander's training course. Although total strangers, the two communicated their attraction to one another, not through the less than ten words spoken, but rather through a sensitivity each had to the other. During this very first meeting, they made passionate love in the fields. Yet their later inability to communicate regarding their daughter's illness is not a sympathetic silence but rather a chasm between the two.

Ivria projects blame for Netta's medical condition onto her husband, who remains absent much of the time, traveling on assignments. She seeks solace in a study of literature that involves her writing of a master's thesis regarding the famed Brontë family. The three Brontë sisters and their brother were a troubled group, yet all of its members loved one another. The title of Ivria's master's thesis, "Shame in the Attic," remains symbolic of her feelings regarding her own dysfunctional, yet basically affectionate, family.

The reader comes to know Ivria only through Yoel's memories, and whether he represents a trustworthy narrator cannot be determined. Such a determination remains unimportant in Oz's plot because Ivria exists as a necessary component of Yoel's life in exactly the form he conceives her. Early in the novel during a flashback, Yoel thinks how essential Ivria remains to his existence. This importance, he realizes, may be in spite of the conflict they suffer or perhaps because of it. Once Ivria is removed from his life, he suffers a disorientation and resultant chaos that he fears he may never conquer.

Yoel's view of Ivria remains the only important one. The fact that her presence haunts him, not in an entirely unpleasant way, attests to her importance. Ivria seems to remind Yoel that not all aspects of life can be controlled, despite Yoel's penchant for control and orderliness exercised through his service to his government. Their earthly relationship began with uncontrollable passion and concludes abruptly in an absurd death. Ivria's existence and demise force Yoel to accept not only the fragility of human existence but also the fact that people never know each other completely.

See also: Oz, Amos; Ravid, Yoel; *To Know a Woman*
References: Balaban, 1990; Balaban, 1993; Fuchs, 1984; Grossman, 1986; Oz, 1993; Price, 1995; Wachtel, 1991

RAVID, YOEL

In Amos Oz's 1989 novel, *To Know a Woman* (translated in 1991), Yoel Ravid searches for an answer to a question he cannot yet formulate, a question that holds the key to his understanding of life. The search qualifies his character as an existential quest hero, caught up in the mundane workings of a life that seems to lack meaning. Following the questionable death of his wife, Ivria Ravid, Yoel mentally interrogates their relationship, using an approach that resembles the one employed in his profession as an Israeli intelligence officer. His memories shape Ivria's character, beginning with their initial meeting as she checked the irrigation on her family's farm where he wandered, a soldier separated from his training group. The two shared their bodies before sharing their thoughts, and that intermingling seemed destined to be eternal. But with the birth of their daughter, Netta, a huge wall of hostility arose between husband and wife.

Yoel searches without success for meaning in his relationship with the remaining members of his family, which includes his daughter Netta, his mother, and his mother-in-law. His relationship with Netta has seemed doomed since Ivria accused Yoel of being responsible for her mild epileptic condition, an accusation that served to separate all three members of the family. Netta seems every bit as determined as her father to find truth in their relationship following her mother's death. Before that truth may be discovered, Yoel must find the three aspects of character that his brother-in-law says he lacks—desire, joy, and pity. These are the goals of Yoel's psychological quest.

As the novel's title hints, Yoel must settle the way he relates with other women before he can come to terms with his conflicts. He seems surrounded by women, from the three that live with him to his sensual neighbor Annemarie, whom he engages in a sexual relationship. Although he willingly meets the basic physical needs of all of these women, acting as a fine provider of material goods for his family and sexual pleasure for Annemarie, he cannot give of himself. He never touches Netta and imagines her an immature girl unable to make decisions on her own, even though she has reached her late teens and become eligible to join the Israeli military service. He even envisions Annemarie as a needy child and finds himself attracted to her emotional fragility. By acting as caretaker for Netta, whom he perceives as ill, for the older women out of a guilty sense of responsibility, and for Annemarie simply because she needs someone, Yoel denies his own needs. He derives only a surface pleasure from his role without enjoying any spiritual growth or joy as a result of his actions.

Annemarie's statement that Yoel has never known what the word *woman* means hearkens back to the problem suggested by the novel's title.

Her assessment of Yoel's desire to treat all women, regardless of their ages or relationships to him, as babies speaks to Yoel's controlling nature. Although Yoel enjoyed an unbridled physical passion with his wife upon their first meeting, he seems to have lost the capacity to give way to emotion without first instituting the checks and controls inherent to his working life.

Yoel reveals this controlling nature in his approach to mundane activities such as housekeeping, yard work, and laundry, and it extends to Netta's relationship with the young man who loves her, Duby Krantz. Although Yoel perceives Duby as little more than a boy, it is Duby who first enlightens Yoel as to his misperception of others. Due to Duby's expertise in engineering, Yoel asks his help in settling a mystery. The house he rents contains a small figurine of a feline predator in full leap, held to earth by one leg attached in a mysterious way to a base. Although Yoel contemplates the figurine from time to time, he cannot determine how the figure remains upright. The leaping cat acts as a symbol of Yoel himself. Duby's revelation that Yoel merely asks the wrong question in wondering why the cat does not fall over begins Yoel's eventual emotional awakening. Duby explains that one should ask not why the figure does not fall, but rather, where the figure's center of gravity exists. It is the very thing Yoel needs to discover about his own life.

Oz's psychological study of a man who pretends to make order out of life's chaos acts as a cautionary tale for all readers. Although in his youth Yoel gave free rein to passion, remaining open to the concerns of those he loved, with age and experience in a professional world demanding detachment, he loses focus. When he finally regains his vision, he learns that the search for truth is of vital importance. Whether that truth comes to light or not, the search will alert him to his center, to the things he must have in order to remain emotionally and psychologically balanced in his life's leap.

See also: Oz, Amos; Ravid, Ivria; *To Know a Woman*
References: Balaban, 1990; Balaban, 1993; Fuchs, 1984; Grossman, 1986; Oz, 1993; Price, 1995; Wachtel, 1991

REBECCA

On its publication, *Rebecca,* Daphne du Maurier's 1938 romantic mystery novel, joined a long tradition of Gothic romance. The novel possesses all of the hallmark elements of a Gothic story. Maxim de Winter acts as the mysterious brooding male with an unexplained past, and his new wife, Mrs. de Winter, finds herself in danger. As the setting, de Winter's huge rambling estate, Manderley, provides ample dark passages and mysterious hallways to double for the traditional Gothic castle. Its influence on the de Winters' lives causes the mansion itself to become a character. The character of Rebecca de Winter, Maxim's first wife, acts as a ghost whose memory haunts multiple lives, including that of her faithful servant, Mrs. Danvers, and her revolting cousin and lover, Jack Favell.

Mrs. de Winter narrates the novel in first person. The story begins following a fire that destroys Manderley. Through flashbacks, the protagonist and first-person narrator gives the reader some background about herself and her thus-far-tumultuous marriage to the wealthy Maxim de Winter. The reader learns of Mrs. de Winter's sensitive nature, her childhood as an orphan, and her companionship with the wealthy American socialite, Mrs. Van Hopper. Mrs. de Winter meets Maxim in Monte Carlo when Mrs. Van Hopper, knowing him to own one of England's most magnificent estates, attempts to force her attentions upon him. The mousy and drab Mrs. de Winter, then unmarried, of course, somehow gains Maxim's attention. He shares with her that he travels in order to escape the pain of the recent death of his wife, Rebecca. When Maxim proposes, Mrs. de Winter does not hesitate to accept, and the two are married.

In the early part of the story, they appear to be deeply in love and enjoy an excursion through France and Italy. The novel presents what appears to be a rather traditional romance, except for the important fact that the narrator lacks a first name; her identity depends solely on her attachment to Maxim as a "Mrs." Thus, when she marries Maxim, she becomes more his possession than his equal. Du Maurier follows the tradition established by Charlotte Brontë in *Jane Eyre* (1847), in which marriage to a strong, wealthy male elevates a poverty-stricken female to a superior social status. However, the surname, literally "of winter," that permits that elevation symbolizes the season of death. It also foreshadows a dark and threatening future that contrasts with the warm fecundity the honeymoon setting suggests.

When the couple return to Manderley, the plot turns mysterious. Mrs. Danvers's obvious resentment toward the new Mrs. de Winter seems to abate only when she discusses her former mistress. At those moments, her eyes assume an unnatural brightness that symbolizes Mrs. Danvers's near-demonic possession by the memory of the dead Rebecca. Through Mrs. Danvers, Rebecca, although physically absent, poses a threat to Mrs. de Winter's life, both mentally and physically. This threat heightens the novel's tension.

Mrs. de Winter devotes much energy to trying to familiarize herself with her new husband, his past, and Manderley. She decides that she literally pales in comparison to the beautiful, dynamic Rebecca who perished in a sailboat accident. Du Maurier carefully delineates the differences between Maxim's two wives in several verbal exchanges between characters, including one between Mrs. de Winter and Maxim's sister, Beatrice. On a first visit to Manderley to meet the new bride, Beatrice tells her it is a shame that she does not ride or shoot, as did Rebecca, and she mutters that she cannot picture Mrs. de Winter in the role of gracious hostess that Rebecca had filled so well. The present Mrs. de Winter receives encouragement regarding her relationship with Maxim only from Frank, the estate manager.

When Mrs. de Winter wanders into Rebecca's rooms one day, she finds them carefully preserved, thanks to Mrs. Danvers's devotion. When the servant suddenly appears, she executes an odd ritual tour of Rebecca's clothing and belongings, forcing Mrs. de Winter to participate. As she physically pulls the new Mrs. de Winter about the quarters, she applies such pressure to her flesh that she bruises her arm. Her voice assumes a strange quality when she suggests that Rebecca returns and walks the halls, watching Maxim with his new bride. The incident sends Mrs. de Winter to bed, and her illness and prone position symbolize her lack of power to combat the spirit of Rebecca and Mrs. Danvers.

Mrs. Danvers is also complicit in suggesting that Mrs. de Winter wear a copy of an ancestral costume to the dress ball Maxim holds at Manderley. Confidant that the dress compliments her best features, the young wife is horrified at its effect on the guests and her husband. She discovers that Rebecca had worn the same design, in white, just like that of the new Mrs. de Winter. The white color becomes highly symbolic in the character development of the two Mrs. de Winters. It represents the purity and innocence of the present Mrs. de Winter, a sacrificial victim to her predecessor's memory. It simultaneously foreshadows the reader's later discovery of the wintry quality of the former Mrs. de Winter, whose beauty had all the warmth of cold white marble. Mrs. Danvers continues to conspire to embarrass and hurt Mrs. de Winter, as if her humiliation of the new mistress helps keeps alive the old. Maxim's new bride comes to believe he still loves Rebecca and thus rejects her.

In the plot's rapidly rising action, Rebecca's sunken sailboat is discovered with a body in it. This casts suspicion on Maxim, who already identified a body pulled from the river as that of Rebecca. When he confesses to Mrs. de Winter that his marriage with Rebecca had been miserable rather than idyllic, she becomes confused. She finds it difficult to accept the arrangement between the two described by Maxim. He tells Mrs. de Winter of the "deal" he made with Rebecca. If she continued to act as Manderley's hostess, Maxim would agree to her sexual flings and interaction with low-class acquaintances. When she began to create a scandal with men connected to Manderley and with her cousin Jack, Maxim confronted Rebecca regarding her inappropriate behavior. He requested a divorce, but she shocked him with the news of a pregnancy. Incensed at the idea of Rebecca's having this hold over him, Maxim shot her, placed her body in her boat, drilled holes in the boat, and opened its seacocks, allowing it to sink. All of this news shocks Mrs. de Winter. However, the revelation that Maxim had not loved Rebecca acts to strengthen her resolve to support him.

In this moment of conflict, the second Mrs. de Winter discovers new inner resources that will help as she walks her husband through his future. This aspect of *Rebecca* distinguishes it from other Gothic romances. The novel's male hero suddenly seems a villain, involved in a murder. But as the plot progresses, Rebecca herself finally becomes the only villain in the novel. Even Jack Favell and Mrs. Danvers have been led by Rebecca herself, and they cannot really be classified as villains.

Jack Favell tries to raise suspicion against Maxim with the discovery of Rebecca's body and the boat. However, an inquest rules the death a suicide, using as its evidence a bolted door on the boat and the holes that caused it to sink. Favell accuses Maxim of murder and threatens to tell the authorities that Maxim killed Rebecca when she told him she wanted to marry Favell. An investigation ensues, culminating in the surprise discovery that Rebecca had cancer. Thus, she tempted Maxim into shooting her as a type of suicide to escape the suffering the cancer would bring.

This ironic reversal allows Rebecca's false promise of new life through her supposed pregnancy to be replaced by the threat of death and destruction through the tumor. The theme of death becomes all the stronger as Mrs. de Winter struggles to retain her composure throughout the legal investigation of her husband's involvement in Rebecca's demise. Du Maurier again heightens the story's tension, this time with a description of death by hanging, the punishment Mrs. de Winter fears Maxim might suffer. Although he is acquitted of all suspicion following the doctor's revelation regarding Rebecca's cancer, Maxim still must pay for his part in Rebecca's death. Mrs. de Winter's dreams as they approach Manderley act as a premonition of the disaster that awaits them.

The destruction of the beloved Manderley that Mrs. de Winter comments on at the novel's beginning also concludes the story, bringing the tale full circle. Manderley burns in a fire so big that it lights the entire western sky around the estate. Much as in the fire near the end of Charlotte Brontë's Gothic romance *Jane Eyre* (1847), du Maurier's fire provides purification. Mrs. de Winter even refers to the "trial by fire" that is said to strengthen humans. It destroys both Rebecca's spiritual presence that had existed through her haunting memory as well as her physical presence that had lived on through Mrs. Danvers. The tremendous loss represented in his home's destruction leaves Maxim weakened and shaken. His physical state allows Mrs. de Winter to exercise her newfound strength to care for her husband and to help establish a new basis for the remainder of their life together. Thus, she becomes a dynamic character, assuming a new role based on an internal strength that she lacked at the time of her marriage.

See also: de Winter, Maxim; de Winter, Mrs.; du Maurier, Daphne; Gothic Romance; *Jane Eyre;* Violence

References: de Rougemont, 1983; Ellis, 1989; Leng, 1995

REBECCA, DAUGHTER OF ISAAC

In Rebecca, daughter of the wealthy aged Jew Isaac, Sir Walter Scott creates one of his most traditionally romantic characters for *Ivanhoe* (1819), a novel set in England during the age of chivalry. Although Rebecca is not of the Saxon clan, she becomes involved with Cedric the Saxon; his lovely ward Rowena, a descendant of Saxon royalty; and Cedric's son Wilfred of Ivanhoe, who loves Rowena. Rebecca never enjoys a love match, as do Rowena and Ivanhoe, but she does become a pawn in a typical romance adventure of strategy and battle.

Rebecca joins Cedric's party in its return from a local jousting tournament, and the entire group becomes captives of three Norman Knights Templar: Brian de Bois-Guilbert, nemesis and challenger of Ivanhoe; Maurice de Bracy; and Reginald Front de Boeuf. Bois-Guilbert desires Rebecca as his own, and Scott uses a scene between the two to reflect on the theme of spirituality. Ivanhoe has been away on the Third Crusade, along with the Saxon king, Richard the Lion-Hearted, so religion has already provided a focus for the novel. When Bois-Guilbert approaches Rebecca, captive in his castle, about becoming his bride, he tells her she must first convert to Catholicism. Although Rebecca's Jewish faith should mark her as the threatening outsider, the Templar comes across as the evil force when he denies the importance of religious practices that he declares are based on fairy tales. When Bois-Guilbert departs her chamber, Rebecca contemplates her own recent action of thanking the God of Jacob, for whose biblical mother she is named, for her safety following the violence of the capture. In adhering to her beliefs, Rebecca achieves heroic status, vowing that no narrow prejudice will ever convince her to renounce her faith.

Although Rowena purportedly remains the novel's heroine, Rebecca becomes its true romantic character. Convicted of witchery for having cast "a spell" over Bois-Guilbert, she faces death by burning at the stake. In her mock "trial," Rebecca again adheres to her traditions, initially refusing to unveil her face in the presence of strangers. In this manner she defends her modesty in the only way available to a female who cannot participate in combat against her foes. Eventually she does unveil her beautiful countenance rather than allowing the lowly guards to touch her, an action that would be, she declares, an affront to female decency. Rebecca then delivers a scathing speech, unusual for women normally held to silence, maintaining her innocence and declaring that God will raise a champion to rescue her. Naturally, Ivanhoe does not disappoint this worthy damsel in distress. But before his appearance, Rebecca speaks out against the deadly foolishness of jousts and the many deaths such games of honor incur. Thus through his character, Scott declares his own feelings. Even though he used as a subject for fiction the one-on-one fatal trials of combat skills that medieval chivalry demanded, he disapproved of the tradition.

After her rescue by Ivanhoe, Rebecca plans to depart from England, hoping to find peace in Spain along with her father, and she again delivers a choice speech. When Rowena bids her stay, as her safety is now assured, Rebecca declines. She reminds the woman of royal lineage of the gulf that separates the two—their differences in breeding and faith. When she presents Rowena with a wedding gift of jewels, she reminds Scott's readers as well as Rowena that great wealth can be the source of either strength or weakness. Scott dismisses Rebecca with an idea that must already have occurred to his readers; Ivanhoe, as Rowena's husband, would likely think of Rebecca more than his wife might have desired. But chivalry rules passion, and Ivanhoe ultimately remains satisfied with his choice of Rowena as his mate.

See also: Chivalry; *Ivanhoe;* Scott, Sir Walter; Violence; Wilfred of Ivanhoe
References: Bayley, 1960; Brunel, 1992; Duncan, 1992; Grierson, 1974; Hulme, 1974; Pater, 1974

THE ROBBER BRIDE

Margaret Atwood's 1993 novel, *The Robber Bride,* updates an old tale. In keeping with Atwood's feminist leanings, this novel replaces the traditional robber bridegroom with a female version. The villainess Zenia acts as a foil to three other female characters, Charis, Roz Andrews, and Tony Fremont. But although Zenia robs the women of the men they love, forming bizarre love triangles for a time with each couple, she unwittingly gives something in return. As they face the conflict of separation from their lovers, the women also experience a surge of strength and self-reliance. Zenia may part them from the male loves of their individual lives, but she simul-

taneously unites Charis, Roz, and Tony as survivors of her seduction. In this community of
women, each individual discovers a personal
identity, as well as an identity as part of a group,
never previously enjoyed.

When the novel opens, the three friends meet
to talk at their favorite rendezvous, an eatery
called the Toxique that overlooks Lake Ontario.
They developed this ritual when they first began
empathizing with one another over their various
losses to Zenia. They believe Zenia dead, having
attended her funeral five years previously, yet
somehow she mysteriously appears on this day at
the Toxique.

Atwood relates each of the women's experiences with the "old" Zenia in flashbacks, moving
in and out of the present and the past. This narrative technique helps emphasize the postmodern
attitude toward history as nonlinear, an attitude
that Tony teaches her students at the college
where she is employed. Because history remains a
social construct, totally dependent for detail and
ideology on its context, a story can begin at any
place, at any time. Zenia's story seems to have
begun with the creation of time itself.

Tony had learned of Zenia's supposed death
and the impending memorial service from a
man identifying himself only as Zenia's attorney.
Zenia, the "mourners" at the service learn, fell
victim to terrorists in Lebanon as an innocent
bystander. Mulling over her memories of that
service following Zenia's reappearance, Tony
remembers thinking that Zenia herself would
have scorned the idea of her assuming the passive part of a bystander. She would also have
rejected the application of the adjective "innocent" to herself. Although Zenia may have upon
occasion projected an air of innocence, that air
proved part of her scam. All three of the naïve
and trusting women had fallen victim to that
particular ruse.

Zenia's ability to portray vulnerability is one
of her finest skills. She also assumes various identities at will. In one of her histories, she is Jewish,
in another, of Romanian Gypsy blood. In some
versions she was prostituted as a child, in others
she romances great and talented men.
Inconsistency proved to be Zenia's single consistent trait. Although Charis, Roz, and Tony had all
known Zenia in college, when she reappears to
each over the following three decades, she
becomes a new person.

Tony was the first to suffer a loss to Zenia.
Their relationship began in the 1960s, when Tony
was nineteen years old and in college. She knew
Charis then as Karen, a somnambulant inhabitant
of her dorm, as she had also known Roz, but not
yet as friends. Neither had she been friends with
Zenia at first. Disdainful of dorm life, Zenia kept
herself apart from the other young women Tony
knew but one day turned up at Tony's room, asking to borrow something. This initial interaction
foreshadows the future, as Zenia will eventually
"borrow" Tony's intellectual ability, then steal her
lover, West, and her money. As with each of her
victims, Zenia locates Tony's weakness, that of
lifelong loneliness, and takes advantage of it. Tony
comes to think of Zenia as the best friend her life
has always lacked. But Zenia's friendship quickly
proves more disturbing than comforting.

As if affected by some magical force, Tony tells
Zenia things she has never shared, such as of her
mother's desertion and her lonely life growing up
with her father. Zenia suggests that Tony must
dispose of her mother's ashes to avoid the lingering negative effects that such a presence surely
causes. Although she does not want to part with
the canister of remains, Tony follows Zenia's suggestion and acts against her will. In a symbolic
scene, fraught with foreshadowing concerning
Zenia's own end, Tony throws the entire canister
of ashes into Lake Ontario, only to watch it resur-
face and bob behind the boat, an unsinkable container, an inescapable force.

Zenia's power also allows her to convince
Tony to write two school papers for her, papers
she can later use to blackmail Tony for money,
and Zenia steals West for a time. However, he
eventually returns, and Tony decides to take him
back. This act forces her to draw on strength of
character to help both of them deal with Zenia's
aftereffects. Tony becomes a history professor,
profoundly affected by her earlier dealings with
Zenia. Her nemesis becomes crucial to Tony's
ideas regarding history and storytelling.

When Zenia appears at Charis's door a decade
later, she supposedly suffers from cancer and
teeters on the verge of death. Charis, who, like
Tony, knew Zenia years before, has become a
mystic who believes in natural healing. She
changed her name from Karen in order to escape
a past identity that carried with it much conflict.
As her new name suggests, Charis possesses a
caretaker personality, which explains the presence

in her modest home of Billy, a conscientious objector to the Vietnam War. The most fragile of the group of women as a victim of child abuse, Charis may suffer the most from Zenia's careless use of others' lives.

Charis welcomes Zenia into her island home, much as she would welcome any stray needy animal that turned up at her door. The island in Lake Ontario symbolizes Charis's separation from the concerns of the larger world, a world she visits only to earn the wages necessary to support herself, Billy, her beloved chickens, and now Zenia. Although Billy and Zenia hate one another when they first meet, they eventually form a degenerate relationship that Zenia perpetuates merely in order to injure Charis. When a pregnant Charis awakens to find Billy and Zenia both missing and the chickens senselessly slaughtered, she searches for the pair. From a distance, she sees a group on the ferry. Some men seem to be taking Billy away, and she believes that Zenia has called American agents to arrest him. Although temporarily abandoned and unable to discover Billy's fate, Charis eventually has her daughter to make her strong, along with the friendship of Tony and Roz.

Roz begins as the more traditional of the bunch, married to a man she adores and with whom she has mothered twin daughters and a son. Zenia's incarnation when she meets Roz is that of a journalist working as a waitress in order to write a story on sexual harassment. This proves important to Roz's relationship with her womanizing attorney husband, Mitch. Roz feels guilty even speaking with Zenia, whom she suspects due to the stories she has heard by this time from Tony and Charis. Again, in a mystical manner, Zenia convinces Roz that she has become a different person since her interaction with Roz's friends. When Zenia casually mentions her past connection to Roz's father, the hook is set and Roz's curiosity aroused. Zenia claims to share Roz's background, one of fear based on her Jewish ethnicity. The two women, however, could hardly be more different. Where Roz is no beauty and remains insecure in her relationship to her handsome husband, Zenia is breathtakingly beautiful.

Zenia cultivates her relationship with Roz, manipulating her way into the production of Roz's magazine. As with her other victims, Zenia seems capable of weaving a type of spell over Roz. Roz suffers even greater conflict than had

Tony and Charis because she knows of the harm Zenia previously caused to both her friends. She must hide her own relationship with this seemingly new Zenia in order not to anger them.

Eventually Zenia attempts to take over not only Roz's magazine but also Mitch. When she fails to get control of the magazine, she forges a check for $50,000, and she ends up casting Mitch off as she has the other men in her life. She exacts a high price from her victims this time, abandoning Mitch, who subsequently drowns in his boat on the lake. Gain results from loss, however, when Roz manages to regain her vision and strength and relinquish the unhealthy need she had always had for her basically worthless husband.

Again threatened by Zenia following her magical reappearance from the grave, the three women pool their now ample resources. A kind of succubus, come to siphon the life from their men and their self-images, Zenia proves her own worst enemy as she empowers the very women she sought to deceive. In their final confrontation with Zenia, each woman evidences a strength that grows from her own identity, discovered apart from the man she loves. Zenia's physical death represents a symbolic death as well of the threat to the women's sense of well-being.

Although Zenia's life is ultimately logically explained, the effect she has on others retains its mystical quality. Even in death, she remains an intimate part of their lives. Tony chooses the date on which to dispose of Zenia's ashes, Charis plans the physical act of disposal, and Roz will say the requisite "few words." But things do not go as planned. The ash urn cracks, leaving Charis to believe that Zenia's spirit is alive and making its presence known. Roz loses control of her own tongue, pronouncing some inane words from her childhood camp experiences. Only the serious Tony seems to retain her composure. Later, in her closing thoughts, Tony wonders what aspects of Zenia mirrored their own, and what parts of Zenia's often ruthless, needy, insistent, hungry personality she shares with her two friends. Of one thing Tony remains confident. Ultimately, the three of them will keep Zenia alive. She will continue to exist as an intimate part of their own private histories.

See also: Andrews, Roz; Atwood, Margaret; Charis; Fremont, Tony; Love Triangle
References: Morey, 1997; Seidman, 1996; Wilson, Friedman, and Hengen, 1996

ROCHESTER, EDWARD

Charlotte Brontë created the character of Mr. Rochester as the male romantic interest for her protagonist in her Gothic romance *Jane Eyre* (1847). Rochester took the literary world by surprise; readers used to mannerly stories were unprepared for this dark Byronic hero. In addition to serving as a love interest for the diminutive character Jane Eyre, Rochester also acts as her foil. He represents wealth and power, whereas she symbolizes the poverty and lack of power of the servant classes. Rochester expresses his passions without restraint, but Jane conforms to societal expectations by holding her own admirable emotions within. When Rochester openly gives his opinion on every matter, Jane withholds judgments, as befits her social station. Rochester has a romantic past, but Jane does not; her past reflects her struggle merely to survive. Such differences due to social class should make theirs a forbidden love. These very differences, however, eventually serve to draw together the unlikely lovers in a

Orson Welles played the dark Byronic hero Edward Rochester in this 1944 film version of Jane Eyre, *Charlotte Brontë's 1847 Gothic romance novel. (The Kobal Collection)*

union that emphasizes all of their combined strengths.

From the first moment Jane sets eyes on Rochester, he confounds her. She observes his fall from a horse before knowing his identity as her employer at the large estate where she serves as governess to Rochester's ward, the French child Adele. Adele symbolizes a part of Rochester's past that both distresses and tantalizes Jane. The reader wonders along with Jane for a time whether Adele is not actually Rochester's own illegitimate child. When Rochester is forced by an injured ankle suffered during his fall to lean against Jane for support, their relationship is set. He will find occasion to utilize Jane's strength again before the novel's end, in roles other than that of the teacher and guide sorely needed by Adele.

Rochester's past remains a mystery for some time, as is typical of a Gothic novel. His present actions also cause a conundrum for Jane, who instinctively understands that he feels positively toward her even as he courts a wealthy woman of his own social status. When unexplained noises are heard throughout Thornfield, the aptly named thicket of secrecy where Rochester resides and Jane is employed, Rochester convinces Jane to blame a servant. Jane does not fully accept Rochester's explanation, however. In Rochester's acceptance of Jane as a confidante despite their differences in social status, he elevates her to the status of intellectual equal. He seems to value this relationship, even though Jane's honest pronouncements often make him smart. Jane literally saves Rochester's life from a fire of mysterious origin that begins in his bedchamber. The fire is extinguished, but it foreshadows another fire from which Rochester will not so easily escape. It also symbolizes the passion building between the two characters and suggests the destructive capacity of such passion.

As the plot progresses, Rochester leads Jane along a tumultuous and dangerous path of deceit before she finally discovers the truth about him on their wedding day. Rochester's past and the frightening sounds in Thornfield are simultaneously explained when a stranger to the estate reveals Rochester's past marriage to his sister, Bertha. Bertha, now insane, resides in Thornfield's attic. She remains responsible for the eerie laughter and howling noises Jane has heard and is identified as the shadowy figure that Jane has, on occasion, observed. Bertha also set Rochester's bed on fire, a symbolic attempt to sacrifice him to love as she herself had been sacrificed through her isolation and his abandonment.

When Jane flees Thornfield, Rochester drops from sight for many pages. He occupies only Jane's thoughts as she contemplates beginning a life apart from her love with a newly discovered family and inherited wealth. But the moody Rochester has become a part of Jane, and she hears him calling to her across the many miles of distance that separate the two. This allows Brontë to emphasize the transcendental belief of romanticism in the permanent metaphysical union of two human souls.

Rochester receives punishment for his past sins in a cleansing baptismal fire that destroys the old and makes possible the new. Thornfield, the material representation of Rochester's past success, burns to the ground, and Bertha, symbolizing Rochester's past failures, leaps to her death. He attempts her rescue at great peril to his own life and suffers the injuries that fate extracts from him as retribution for his sins. He survives as a permanently marked man with the loss of his sight, one eye, and a hand. This use of fire as purification and for punishment will appear repeatedly in the Gothic romances that later imitated those of the Brontë sisters (see *Rebecca*).

Jane returns to her wounded love and nurses him back to health, her devotion working to heal the fire's scars and the emotional scars of a man once unable to love. Both Rochester and Jane become dynamic characters, undergoing epiphanies with the realization of the importance of their attachment to one another.

See also: Brontë, Charlotte and Emily; Gothic Romance; *Jane Eyre;* Violence
References: Allen, 1993; Ellis, 1989; Gilbert and Gubar, 1996a; Leavis, 1966; Pater, 1974

ROGERS, MILDRED

The best way to understand the petty, vulgar opportunist character of Mildred Rogers, from W. Somerset Maugham's *Of Human Bondage* (1915), is purely as an antagonist to the novel's main character, Philip Carey. Whereas Philip remains sensitive and introspective, Mildred is dull and interested only in the external, material business of life. That Philip should be attracted to her, coarse as she is, may be accounted for by his low self-esteem. Perhaps unwittingly at first, but later with the extreme cunning of one familiar with the struggle for basic survival, Mildred repeatedly takes advantage of Philip's subconscious self-loathing. Even though she remains an obvious "user," Philip repeatedly protects and nurtures Mildred to the detriment of his own quality of life. Theirs is a relationship that the modern reader recognizes as abusive to and harmful for both parties.

Mildred is not introduced until the middle of the novel. Described as thin, flat-chested, anemic, with a great deal of hair, Mildred is a sullen waitress at a London café that Philip and his friends frequent. During that initial exposure, Philip says that Mildred's name is odious and pretentious, and he is irritated by her curt unpleasant remarks; he even labels her ill-mannered and a slut. The fact that she is German relates to an earlier remark about a lack of imagination on the part of Germans. But there is an irresistible something about Mildred that brings Philip back to the café again and again. They begin an unhappy and destructive relationship that will continue over the next several years. Mildred's snubbing of Philip in favor of a supposed marriage proposal is only the first of many times that she will use Philip's attention and material goods, only to then desert him.

Mildred represents the best example of the bondage of Philip to which the novel's title refers. No matter how happily Philip's life might be proceeding, any time Mildred reappears, he welcomes her back. After rejection by the man who promised to marry her, she prevails upon Philip to take care of her during her pregnancy and the birth of her illegitimate child. Even though she thanks Philip profusely for his help, Mildred's actions in deserting him once again, this time to run away with Philip's likable but immoral friend, again reveal her self-absorption.

When Mildred returns to Philip a third time, she has become a prostitute. Although one might pity her desperate situation in the face of her treatment by abusive lovers, in a novel about choices, Mildred must bear the consequences of her own. Her hateful response to Philip's refusal to sleep with her, even though she admittedly does not love him, reflects more than ever Mildred's user personality. A supreme moment of situational and verbal irony occurs when Mildred viciously calls Philip a "cripple," referring to his club foot, but her label also applies to his unexplained emotional state regarding his feelings toward her.

Despite her attack on Philip and another subsequent abandonment of him, Mildred is not quite finished with Philip yet. When ill, it is Philip for whom Mildred sends. True to her character, she desires his company not from love but from an instinct for survival; she hopes he can nurse her back to health with his medical skills. But Mildred's syphilis is too far advanced for help, and this time Philip is the one to walk away.

Mildred's vacuous, wasted life stands in stark contrast to Philip's rich quest for understanding. She represents a part of his education, not only about relationships with women but about his own needs and desires. Much like the physical deformity to which he granted too much importance throughout life, allowing it to affect his self-image, Mildred represents an emotional deformity thrust upon Philip. Mildred's death symbolizes an important step forward toward emotional independence for Philip. Oddly enough, his life can only gain completion by the loss of Mildred Rogers.

See also: Carey, Philip; *Of Human Bondage*
References: Frye, 1976; Price, 1983

ROMANCE

The term *romance* originally denoted a composition written in any of the Romance languages. Not until several centuries passed was the term used to mean any tale involving love between two people. During the Middle Ages, *romance* referred to the popular verse or prose genre that focused on legendary subjects and characters, generally involving supernatural occurrences and featuring elements of love. Many romance tales had as a topic the chivalry of knights and courtly love. A related term, *epic,* refers to works of much greater length than romances. Although epics considered topics similar to those found in romance, they did not always feature courtly love. Homer's *Odyssey* is an epic tale and contains many of the conventions that appeared in romance stories.

All romance plots have their roots in Christian or pagan mythology. Myths are narratives that employ supernatural occurrences and characters and that attempt to account for the origin of the earth and to explain human motives for behavior. Because mythology deals with human hopes and anxieties, it naturally focuses on the love relationships that humans form. Early religious romances, such as Italian writer Dante Alighieri's *Inferno* (early fourteenth century) and English writer John Milton's *Paradise Lost* (1667), mix biblical with classical mythological references in explaining humankind's creation, death, and afterlife. Dante's work was labeled a "divine comedy," and Milton's poem has been called both a heroic and a divine epic. Romance, then, remains at the core of all fiction, when that term is understood to mean the story of humans as creatures who participate in classic quests. This vision includes a search for identity, an attempt to conquer evil, and an aspiration for material or spiritual gains as a reward growing from that victory over forces of evil. Metaphors for shipwreck, pirates or looters, magical settings, beings with metaphysical powers, loss of identity, and a regaining of that identity exist in all fiction.

Romances appeared in western Europe as early as the twelfth century, reaching their greatest popularity throughout the thirteenth century and losing favor during the Renaissance. Because they originated as classic ballads and tales presented by troubadours, the stories were eventually recorded at first by court musicians. Later various clerics, scribes, and aristocrats recorded romance tales as entertainment for nobility. Subjects popular at court festivities included the reigns of Alexander the Great, of King Arthur and his knights of the Round Table, and of Charlemagne. The tales often had a moral nature and formed three recognizable groups. Stories such as *Sir Gawain and the Green Knight* featured a test, often administered by a supernatural character, to prove the courage of young knights. A second group reflected on the conflict between duty and passion; *Tristan und Isolde* by Gottfried von Strassburg took this approach. A third group of stories, well represented by Chrétien de Troyes's *Perceval,* focused on a search for the Holy Grail and emphasized the Arthurian legend. In early England, romances became crucial to the fashioning of a national mythology that contributed to the development of England's history.

The romance became more sophisticated over time and invoked strong reactions in readers. A French medieval romance, *Le Roman de la Rose* (*The Romance of the Rose*), provoked one of the first known public written discussions of literature. A lengthy allegorical love poem begun in the early thirteenth century by Guillaume de Lorris, *The Romance of the Rose* influenced readers for generations. A century later, Geoffrey

Chaucer would translate parts of it into English. In the mid-thirteenth century, a poet named Jean de Meun added to the four thousand lines of the *Romance* about twenty-seven thousand additional lines. His additions departed from the original idealism of the work, assuming a didactic character and making women the focus of negative images.

The original work deals with the gradual seduction of a beautiful young lady by a poet. A rose symbolizes the maiden, and the poet undergoes counsel by allegorical figures with names such as Idleness, Pleasure, and Courtesy. Characters working to prevent the poet's triumph include Jealousy, Danger, Shame, and Slander. Guillaume de Lorris's account of simple courtly love concludes with Jealousy building a wall around the rose to protect it from the poet's attentions, and the poem at no time suggests physical contact. When Jean de Meun picked up the story, he departed from the courtly approach to love, emphasizing instead vulgarity. The character of Reason, for example, refers directly to sexual organs, offending the Lover. Women in the new version lack virtue and excel in sensual indulgence. Various representatives from France's educational institutions and its court, including early French poet Christine de Pisan, criticized the negative changes made to the poem. They did not like Jean de Meun's suggestion that men should eschew marriage in favor of sex outside that commitment.

Two centuries later, the topics early readers of romance had found so pertinent to their daily lives greatly diminished in importance. In *Don Quixote* (1605), the Spanish writer Miguel de Cervantes satirizes aspects of the chivalric romance. Through the misadventures of its protagonist knight, Cervantes's story parodies implausible tales of supernatural deeds and valor that had become less applicable to an increasingly sophisticated Renaissance culture. The passage of time had converted once attractive concepts into empty conventions. Examples of ideals no longer honored included the demonstration of love through one person's devoted service to another and the loyalty to concepts of elevated and clearly unrealistic courage. Quixote's ridiculous "medieval" adventures allow Cervantes not only to expose the silliness of romance but to show the consequences one might reap by trying to live by medieval beliefs in a modern age. Cervantes accomplished his goal and produced a fine parody, but *Don Quixote* had an unanticipated effect as well. Cervantes draws on elements both romantic and realistic, imagined and factual, to unite his own era's more concrete values with the ideals of a past age. Rather than destroying and delegitimating romance conventions entirely, Cervantes places them in a different context, thereby redefining and renewing their usefulness in romantic writings.

By the nineteenth century, the early romance genre became absorbed into the tradition surrounding romance writing. Readers brought to the romance an expectation of stories set in exotic locales, either distant or mythological, that stressed adventure and elements of the supernatural while retaining a realistic air. Love between a man and a woman generally formed the focus of such stories. Like other popular fiction genres, popular romance writing reflects the desires of the reading culture that exists at the time of its writing. The romances during this period contained conventions of melodrama and gender-role stereotyping that later romance readers would reject.

By the twentieth century, the romance genre embraced dozens of subgenres, including the Gothic, the contemporary, the Regency, the romantic suspense, the sage, the science fiction, the lesbian, and the young adult. Another category, that of the historical romance, may include aspects of all of the above and is set during a particular time frame that controls its narrative elements.

Romance writing, like other genres, has been ranked by critics as to its presumed quality by the labels "high fiction" versus "low fiction" or "literary fiction" versus "popular fiction." High, or literary, fiction is believed to reflect the truths of a culture, communicating those truths in accomplished rhetorical style that both teaches and delights. Some education or instruction may be required to reach an understanding of such truths. Low/popular fiction is designed only to entertain or amuse and claims no relationship to truth. Little instruction beyond basic reading is required to enjoy popular romance fiction. Both types continue to hold the attention of large reading audiences.

See also: Genre Romance
References: Brunel, 1992; Budick, 1996; Dudley, 1997; Frye, 1976; Hebron, 1997; Looney, 1996; Putter, 1995; Richter, 1996; "Romance," 1995

ROMEO AND JULIET

Probably the best-known romantic tragedy the world over, William Shakespeare's English Renaissance drama *Romeo and Juliet* (1595?) offers a romantic plot imitated multiple times in the drama and fiction of later centuries. The names of the drama's star-crossed lovers, Romeo Montague and Juliet Capulet, remain synonymous with that of an ideal, although also doomed, love. When two feuding families of Verona refuse to reach a peace agreement that would allow Romeo and Juliet to realize their romance and marry, they take their own lives in a double suicide. This tragic conclusion supports the age-old ideal that love is worthy of the ultimate sacrifice.

Ironically, although the drama remains a favorite with viewing and reading audiences, it rates somewhat low in a critical evaluation of Shakespeare's works. Tragedies that would follow during Shakespeare's later creative stages demonstrate more rhetorical control. Critics also note that Shakespeare contradicts his own criteria in writing tragedy when he allows coincidence to direct the destinies of the play's lovers. However, its pathos cannot be denied, and this aspect has retained an overwhelming audience appeal. The completeness with which the two young lovers surrender to one another entices audience sympathy, but the relentless press of violence and revenge that exudes from the dialogue and action leads few to believe that the two will be allowed to experience lasting love.

Just as dramatists who followed Shakespeare would be influenced by his work, Shakespeare himself borrowed from a rich tradition when he wrote *Romeo and Juliet*. The use of a sleeping draught in order to avoid marriage existed as a ploy long before the English Renaissance; the plot appeared as early as the fourth century A.D. in the writings of Greek historian Xenophon. In 1476, Masuccio of Salerno wrote a story featuring star-crossed lovers titled *Il Novellino.* About sixty years later, Luigi da Porto adopted Verona as the scene for his romantic tragedy, giving to his two hostile families the names Montecchi and Cappellati. Other French and Italian adaptations appeared in both poetry and novella form. A translation by William Painter of a 1559 French version by Pierre Boiastuau, titled *Palace of Pleasure* (1567), was a work that Shakespeare likely knew. His version of the Romeo and Juliet story, however, resembles most closely an Arthur

Brooke poem published in 1562, itself based on Boiastuau's work. For a time Shakespeare's version was believed to have been written in 1580. That date was based on the reference by Juliet's Nurse to an earthquake eleven years previous, purportedly Shakespeare's reference to a tremor in London of 1580. More recent critics, however, date the play at about 1595, roughly the same time that Shakespeare wrote *Richard II* and *A Midsummer Night's Dream*.

The drama focuses on the wages of violence by telling the story of two politically powerful and wealthy families whose enmity runs deep, although few who fight for one side or the other can explain how the feud began. When the play opens, the Prince of Verona cautions the families regarding their "pernicious rage," labeling brawlers enemies of the peace that he seeks for his city. The seriousness and potential destruction of the feud is emphasized when the Prince passes an edict that future combatants may suffer the pain of execution.

The younger generation bears the weight of hostility between their elders, a hostility so great it does not allow for a Capulet to fall in love with a Montague. Additional conflict comes from Lord Capulet's plans to marry his daughter, Juliet, to Paris, kinsman to the Prince. Romeo spoils those plans when Juliet becomes enthralled with him at a masquerade ball. The masquerade represents one of traditional romance's more common elements, that of disguise. The two warring factions may mix and mingle with relative ease as long as they remain masked. Romeo and some of his friends use their disguises to attend a Capulet ball, and this is where he first sees Juliet. Before they arrive at the ball, dialogue on the part of Romeo and his friends has represented him as a womanizer, but Juliet becomes his first true love, and they are secretly married by a Franciscan friar.

In the familiar plot, Romeo remains agreeable to trying to bring a peace to the two families, resisting the urge to fight when the enemy challenges. His reluctance dismays his best friend, Mercutio, who dies in a one-on-one fight with Tybalt, Lady Capulet's nephew. For Mercutio's death, Romeo must take revenge, and he is compelled to kill Tybalt, although against his own will. With no chance now for peace between the families, Romeo and Juliet seem doomed to separation. The friar steps in to help the lovers, with a plan for Juliet to drink a sleeping draught, feign death, and meet up with Romeo for escape from their families. Romeo, however, discovers her before she awakens and, thinking her truly dead, drinks poison in a desire to join her in death. When Juliet awakens to discover the dead Romeo, she kills herself with a knife stab to the heart. The grim sacrifice of two of the families' finest young people at last forces both groups to admit their folly, and peace in Verona is secured through tragedy.

This play enhanced the fascination with suicide as the ultimate demonstration of love and dedication, inevitably making the idea of eternal devotion between lovers synonymous with the phrase "Just like Romeo and Juliet." It also adds to the mythic connection between sexual love and death that exists in literature of every era.

Converted to screenplay format multiple times in multiple languages, enacted as a high school drama, and often read aloud in English-speaking classrooms, *Romeo and Juliet* represents the first exposure many have to works by William Shakespeare. Although not critically evaluated as one of his best plays, its enduring popularity testifies to its quality. The fascination with these lovers who willingly gave their lives for one another surfaces as a theme in subsequent drama, fiction, and poetry and in real life. Although unfortunate in some aspects, that effect remains a testimony to the power of art to touch a universal chord in all of humanity.

See also: Longus; Romance; Shakespeare, William; *Sense and Sensibility;* Violence; War
References: Halio, 1995; Kermode, 1974

A ROOM WITH A VIEW

E. M. Forster's *A Room with a View* (1908) presents a delightful Victorian Age romance in which its heroine, Lucy Honeychurch, overcomes her culture's restrictive mores to find satisfying love with the impetuous and innocently improper George Emerson. The novel begins with Lucy enjoying a vacation in Florence, where she meets George while traveling with her spinster cousin, Charlotte Bartlett. In the second part of the story, Lucy returns to her home in England, where she must deal with the attentions of her decidedly proper fiancé, Cecil Vyse. In a love triangle with George and Cecil, Lucy will at last honestly embrace her feelings as she counters her culture's edicts by choosing passion over propriety and

Helena Bonham Carter played Lucy Honeychurch in the popular 1985 film version of E. M. Forster's Victorian Age romance A Room with a View *(1908). (Photofest)*

George over Cecil. A simple story, Forster's tale depends on humor and misunderstandings, most of all Lucy's misunderstanding of herself, to make new timeworn romantic conventions.

As with all of Forster's novels, setting plays a crucial role in *A Room with a View*. The view mentioned in the novel's title could be found nowhere other than Florence, a city exuding mystery and romance. Lucy's gazing from inside her hotel out onto life at the novel's beginning symbolizes her restricted view of relationships with men. She will eventually return to Florence to enjoy the same lodgings, but this time with an extended view of life due to her experiences in romance with George. Forster promotes the theme of romantic passion through the lush fecundity of the hills surrounding Florence. For instance, a field of violets just outside Florence forms the backdrop for Lucy and George's first kiss, as well as the setting for a passionate scene from a romance novel later discussed by the novel's characters. None of the vacationers will leave Florence without being influenced by the passionate Italian atmosphere, to which the city's art and structures also contribute.

The English setting contrasts with the Italian one. England's cooler climate symbolizes a more logical, restrained approach to life, typical of its Victorian Age mores. Here Lucy's newly awakened passions are threatened before they have had a chance to develop. However, Forster imbues his English settings with symbolically hopeful names. For instance, Mr. Beebe, the local clergyman, has a parish named Summer Street, suggesting warm and nurturing surroundings. Lucy's house bears the name Windy Corner, suggesting ever-moving forces and passions that prevent her settling on an incorrect choice in love.

From the novel's opening, Forster offers various pairs of characters who balance one another. Lucy and Charlotte, as younger and older cousins, balance George and Mr. Emerson, as father and son. The two women also act as foils for one another, with Charlotte a fussy old maid and Lucy a vibrant young woman. George is paired with Lucy's younger brother Freddie because both of them are spontaneous, whereas George stands in opposition to Cecil. Other pairs include two delightful elderly ladies, both single, who balance the pair of unmarried males, Mr. Emerson and Mr. Beebe. In addition, Charlotte forms a friendship with a romance novelist bearing the auspicious name of Miss Lavish. Although these two at first glance seem to be foils, Forster surprises the reader by revealing Charlotte's hidden romantic inclination through her relationship with Miss Lavish. Charlotte, as a proper Victorian woman, supposedly eschews the joys of passions in which the also-single Miss Lavish exults. Yet Charlotte seems to adopt Miss Lavish almost as an alter ego, gossiping with the novelist and sharing details of Lucy's first kiss with George in the middle of the field of violets. Those details will later appear in Miss Lavish's romance, *Under a Loggia.* Charlotte's sharing this confidence with Miss Lavish directly contradicts her ongoing instructions to Lucy to remain secretive and discreet. Thus, Charlotte moves beyond her one-dimensional status to prove that, although outwardly she may adhere to a strict moral code, inwardly she rebels against it.

Lucy reacts in shock to the passionate kiss from a young man to whom she has barely even spoken. Yet she obviously enjoys the encounter, despite her verbal protestations. Just as Charlotte claims to have no use for passion and romance when all the while she exults in it, Lucy's claim to outrage conflicts with her true feelings of pleasure. Charlotte makes a fine cautionary tale for Lucy, who eventually refuses to participate in the Victorian ruse that has left her cousin alone and unhappy for many years.

Forster emphasizes throughout the novel the power of art, injecting art and literature references into many scenes. The beautiful piazza at Santa Croce and its magnificent church provide the setting where Mr. Emerson requests that Lucy at least try to understand George, even if she cannot fall in love with him. When she visits the lovely Piazza Signoria, she witnesses a violent stabbing, causing her to swoon and require rescue by George. In this scene George resembles the white knight of tales of chivalry, yet he desires more than just a platonic relationship with his lady. Upon Lucy's return from vacation, Cecil, who has known Lucy for some time, decides that the visit has worked a miracle on the young woman, transforming her into a "da Vinci woman," fleshing her out with both light and shadow. Cecil, the polar opposite of the passionately romantic George, is compared to a Gothic statue. First labeled "medieval," Cecil then is described as well-educated, wealthy, and bearing a sufficient physique, but he proves to be a most unpleasant and manipulative young man. His idea of chivalry, then, contrasts greatly with that of George, a young man who embraces a more modern ideology emphasizing the individual's right to freedom of expression. Cecil views Lucy as an Italian work of art not because his passion for her has been aroused. Rather, as George later explains to Lucy, his desire is only that she become one more beautiful but passive object in his art collection. Forster thus demonstrates that art may either expand or constrict one's horizons.

Following the travelers' return to England, the Emersons end up renting a cottage in the village close to Lucy's home. Ironically, their move to the village comes about through the actions of Cecil. Although Lucy feigns dismay at the idea of the impetuous George reentering her life, she has fallen in love with him. She cannot help contrasting George's passion with Cecil's cold demeanor, particularly when Cecil kisses her. However, Lucy cannot admit her love, even to herself, for some time. Her mother and brother, as well as Mr. Beebe and Charlotte, all become involved in Lucy's drama of romance.

In a warmly humorous rendering of misunderstanding and untruths, Forster guides Lucy toward her eventual union with George. Despite her protests over George's remarks regarding Cecil's inadequacy as a future husband, Lucy eventually realizes the truth in his words. That realization, which a moment she later characterizes as the scales falling from her eyes, offers Lucy an epiphany. She at last confronts Cecil to break their engagement, stating that she refuses his protection, a remark that directly reflects on the description of him as medieval. She also states that she will make her own choices in love and behavior. She repeats almost word-for-word the wisdom that she earlier rejected from George. Her own view of life alters dramatically as she accepts the passion rejected by her society and decides to approach life with a clear vision of her desires.

Although Forster uses his novel to parody Victorian stereotypes regarding proper gender behavior, he never loses sight of his major focus, the development of a prototypical comical romance. When Mr. Emerson urges Lucy to become George's wife because the boy already exists as a part of her, he shatters Victorian proprieties and suggests the romantic vision of two souls joined as one. His pronouncement that more remains at stake for Lucy and for the entire human race than mere love or pleasure gives voice to a crucial point of the novel. Truth itself—the truth of human nature, rather than the false truth of a hypocritical Victorian culture—hangs in the balance, and only Lucy's admission of that truth will secure happiness for herself.

See also: Chivalry; Forster, E. M; Honeychurch, Lucy; Love Triangle; Romance

References: Albright, 1997; Ellem, 1971; Forster, 1956; Lago, 1995; McDowell, 1977; Price, 1983; Stone, 1966; Trivedi, 1979

ROWENA, LADY

Rowena plays an important role in Sir Walter Scott's most popular novel, *Ivanhoe* (1819), as the prototypical medieval lady of noble lineage whose future depends upon the goodwill of her male patron and caretaker. As a ward of Cedric the Saxon in a twelfth-century English setting, Rowena has been promised in marriage to Athelstane of Coningsburgh. Because Athelstane comes from the line of King Alfred, he will be a perfect mate, in Cedric's opinion, for Rowena, who is descended from princes of ancient Saxon lineage. Scott introduces romantic conflict in the person of Cedric's son, Wilfred of Ivanhoe, who desires Rowena for himself. Emphasizing the importance during medieval and early modern times of maintaining a pure aristocratic lineage, Scott has Cedric reject his own son, banishing the young Wilfred from their castle of Rotherwood, in order to make a politically astute match between Rowena and Athelstane. When the antagonist, Knight Templar Brian de Bois-Guilbert, appears, along with a Jewish father-daughter couple, a perfect example of the chivalric romance evolves. Together, the high-bred Rowena and the beautiful young Jewess Rebecca provide several opportunities for Ivanhoe to display his chivalric skills.

Rowena provides motivation for Ivanhoe to return to his father's castle incognito, in order to take part in the tournament at the nearby settlement of Ashby de la Zouche. The young man has been away fighting with England's King Richard the Lion-Hearted in the Third Crusade, and he makes his reappearance before Rowena in disguise. The tournament, organized by the evil John, who challenges his brother's right to the throne, will produce a victor who has the honor of naming the Queen of Love and Beauty. She then will award the winner his prize. Retaining his disguise, Ivanhoe competes in the jousts, besting not only Bois-Guilbert but five additional knights. He must remove his helmet to receive the prize from Rowena, who immediately recognizes her lost love. Rowena presents the prized chaplet to Ivanhoe, but even more prized is the kiss she plants on his hand.

In further adventures, the unscrupulous Norman knights Bois-Guilbert, Maurice de Bracy, and Reginald Front de Boeuf capture the young women and their entourage and take them to de Boeuf's castle. De Bracy aspires to marry Rowena and inherit her fortune. Her captors take pains to treat her well but separate her from Cedric and Athelstane and even her attendants. This allows Cedric and Athelstane to commiserate over her possible future with the Norman enemy. Here Scott inserts a thought prevalent in medieval and Renaissance times, that the noble nature of an aristocratic woman might inspire more noble behavior in any man. Although scholars point out that the division between Saxons and Normans had long been settled by the twelfth century, Scott's use of this conflict adds to plot excitement while bolstering chauvinism. Two powerful groups come to arms for the right to claim a fair damsel.

Rowena will enjoy a rescue through the intervention of none other than the fabled Robin Hood, a further example of the English mythology that Scott uses so liberally. In a typically melodramatic scene, Cedric arrives at her apartment to rescue her. Expecting death at any moment, Rowena stands in a saintly pose, with a crucifix clutched to her bosom. She is carried to safety, and Ivanhoe sufficiently proves himself worthy to his father when he rescues the hapless Rebecca. Athelstane, at first believed killed in battle, resurfaces and agrees to relinquish Rowena, as he is ostensibly now more focused on spiritual and political issues than romantic ones.

Rowena marries her young paragon of chivalry in a ceremony attended by King Richard himself.

Scott draws on and promotes many chivalric traditions in his story. In addition, during an era when a young woman represented little more than barter material, he also reestablishes a plot emphasizing star-crossed lovers kept apart by a disapproving parent. The plot aspects would be used time and again throughout romance literature, later modified to fit more contemporary ideology.

See also: Chivalry; Rebecca, Daughter of Isaac; Romance; Scott, Sir Walter; Violence; Wilfred of Ivanhoe

References: Bayley, 1960; Brunel, 1992; Duncan, 1992; Grierson, 1974; Hulme, 1974; Pater, 1974

SABINA

Sabina is part of a passionate love triangle in Czechoslovakian writer Milan Kundera's 1984 work, *The Unbearable Lightness of Being* (*Nesnesitelná lehkost bytí*). She is the mistress of the novel's male protagonist, Tomas, and also becomes a friend of Tomas's wife, Tereza. Their story is framed by the Russian occupation of Czechoslovakia, and underlying each character is a political, as well as a romantic and an artistic, message.

Although Sabina and Tereza share some characteristics, such as their feelings for Tomas and their artistic talent (Sabina's painting and Tereza's photography), they also serve as foils. Sabina remains self-assured, proud of her body and her work, and independent and places her art above everything else in her life. Tereza, however, becomes totally dependent on Tomas, remains faithful in comparison to Sabina's various romantic involvements, and suffers insecurity regarding her body due to her upbringing. In addition, when the Russian occupation occurs and all three depart Czechoslovakia, Sabina remains in Geneva, later moving on to Paris and finally to various American cities, valuing her artistic and personal freedom above any political ties to her country. Tereza, however, returns to her homeland, where she takes news photographs in hopes of revealing the truth regarding the occupation to the outside world.

Sabina appeals to Tomas's sense of freedom in that she demands no permanent commitment from him. He enjoys her sexual prowess, as they share what Tomas terms an erotic friendship. Sabina even helps find Tereza a job when she moves to Prague to live with Tomas. She remains absolutely free of jealousy where Tomas, or any other of her lovers, is concerned. Her lack of possessiveness does not mean, however, that she will tolerate insensitivity. During one visit to her flat by Tomas, Sabina catches him looking at his watch to check the time during their love making because he does not want to leave Tereza home alone for too long. Although Sabina understands his dedication to Tereza, she regrets the loss of her "libertine," for whom two years of a live-in relationship with Tereza has caused conflict. To get even with him for his glancing at his watch, Sabina hides Tomas's sock, offering him one of her stockings to wear home in the cold. Unable to go outside into the snow with a bare foot, Tomas must yield to her gesture as being no less insensitive than his own.

One scene in particular that explores Sabina's free-thinking personality involves a visit to her flat by Tereza. She comes to take photos of Sabina, knowing full well that she is Tomas's mistress. The two end up playing like children, both nude and photographing one another. Neither holds the other at fault for her usurpation of romantic territory with Tomas. Tereza's pleasure in Sabina's company indicates that she places the blame for the discomfort she feels regarding his many sexual liaisons directly upon her own insecurity rather than upon this "other woman."

A symbol used throughout the novel is Sabina's grandfather's bowler hat. She keeps the hat on a wig stand when she does not wear it. At times it acts as a part of her costume as she performs for others in her flat. After she departs Prague to take up residence in Geneva, the bowler comes to mean multiple things to Sabina. More than just a reminder of her family and of Tomas, with whom she used the bowler as an actress would a prop in her love games, it becomes a sign of her original approach to life. Finally, it turns into a monument to the past. When she makes love again with Tomas in Zurich, they realize they share a past together, represented by the now-occupied Prague and the bowler hat.

Kundera explores Sabina's character apart from Tomas and Tereza as well. While living in Geneva, Sabina engages in a long-time affair with a married man named Franz. Her willingness to attach herself sexually but not romantically to men receives some explanation when Kundera describes Sabina's background. Unlike Tereza, Sabina finds betrayal more alluring than fidelity. She first exercised her own powers of betrayal on her father, described as a puritanical painter of rather mundane works who sparked Sabina's interest in painting. When she fell in love for the first time, he would not allow her to leave home for a year. She rebelled against his attempts to force her compliance through her art when she began to imitate Pablo Picasso and the school of Cubism, efforts at which her father merely laughed. Sabina then left home and cultivated a lifelong appreciation for the unknown and for private revolution.

Yet as an artist to whom vision remains all-important, Sabina feels a revulsion toward all extremes that she comprehends as either light or dark. Too much light and too much darkness blinds, and she views such extremism as a longing for death. This passage goes far to explain why she elects to join neither the political extremism represented by the Communist invaders nor those who resist the invasion. She adopts military terminology, labeling her standard reaction to extremes as "breaking ranks."

As with all of Kundera's characters, the essence of Sabina cannot be reduced to a simple descriptive phrase. She plays a particular role in the novel's plot, but she asks the reader for more than a quick dismissal as the "other woman" or the prototypical "whore with a heart of gold." Framed by war or peace, Sabina represents a personality that lives not only in the here and now but also in her past and her future. This trait allows Kundera to emphasize his particular view of history as nonlinear, a sketch rather than a finished picture. When Sabina hears in America the news of the death of her friends Tomas and Tereza, she suffers enormous regret. The source of her sorrow lies not only in regret over the loss of two remarkable individuals, but because the final link to her past is shattered.

See also: Kundera, Milan; Tereza; Tomas; *The Unbearable Lightness of Being*
References: Catalano, 1995; Misurella, 1993

SAYER, ROSE

Created by novelist C. S. Forester for his 1935 novel *The African Queen,* the Englishwoman Rose Sayer is an excellent example of a character who changes and matures during the course of a novel. As her name suggests, Rose blossoms from a sheltered, virginal, thirty-three-year-old missionary into an independent, forceful, and resourceful female lover by the novel's conclusion. Rose reaches maturity during a physical quest undertaken in 1914, at the beginning of World War I, in order to avenge her brother's death and England's honor. By the novel's conclusion, she gains not only her revenge but also a romantic relationship she had not anticipated.

The unlikely object of her affection is Charlie Allnutt, a mining employee who appears at the African mission founded by Rose and her brother ten years before the novel opens. All the native African workers at Charlie's mine and all of the native inhabitants of the mission have been forced into service with the army of German Central Africa. Rose blames the Germans' forced desertion of the mission for her brother's subsequent death. When Charlie appears at the abandoned mission, Rose wants to bomb a German gunship out of a sense of patriotism to England and loyalty to her brother, whereas Charlie, who feels loyalty only to himself, wants simply to escape war. He regards Rose's idea as patently ridiculous, but when the two are alone on his small steamship, *The African Queen,* Rose manipulates Charlie into pursuing her desires.

Forester uses this early manipulation as one of several methods to introduce what would be considered feminist themes by later readers. Rose fights Charlie with the only tool of protest available to many women, that of silence. She does this while pretending to occupy herself on the boat with the mending of clothing. The narrative voice makes clear that sewing, traditionally an approved female preoccupation, allows a woman the opportunity to observe her male opponent while pretending with a lowered head to keep her eyes on her work. As she sews, Rose symbolically weaves a trap for Charlie, thus emphasizing the theme of weaving found in the earliest of the quest stories, Homer's *Odyssey.* The trap itself, the narrator explains, works only because of the male psyche that demands that the female focus her attention on him. Charlie cannot bear being ignored, so he gives in to Rose.

Rose learned as a child that even though the man's word must be adhered to, the woman often provides guidance essential to their relationship. When Rose takes her place at the rudder of *The African Queen,* she guides not only the boat but Charlie as well. Their early, briefly combative relationship turns into one of mutual admiration. After the couple conquers severe environmental obstacles, their relationship enjoys a final transformation into love.

Rose's clothing also symbolizes her change in personality and her maturation. In the opening scenes of the novel, she struggles with the heat and discomfort caused by impractical restraining undergarments. These undergarments serve little practical purpose, but instead represent cultural edicts to which she feels she must adhere. A later crucial scene follows Rose's steering through a particularly difficult passage along with Charlie, during which they become covered with mud and filth. She bathes in clean water that transforms her physical appearance and symbolizes a baptism or rebirth of her emotional personality as well. When donning clean clothes, she decides to discard the restrictive and impractical undergarments. Rose literally throws away her old skin and emerges transformed, free of gender and class restrictions, as a butterfly emerges from a cocoon.

The fact that Charlie is a small, wiry, and, by conventional standards, unattractive man, matters little to Rose. He helps her bloom as a rose should, offering her the chance to take on responsibility leading to her physical, emotional, and psychological independence. She passionately loves Charlie, not only for the purely physical fulfillment he brings but also for the nurturing role he allows her to fill.

See also: The African Queen; Allnutt, Charlie; Forester, C. S.; Quest; War

References: de Rougemont, 1983; Frye, 1976

THE SCARLET LETTER

Nathaniel Hawthorne's romance *The Scarlet Letter* (1850) introduced the American public to one of its most enduring heroines in the character of Hester Prynne. Hester and the scarlet "A" she must wear as a symbol of her sin against humankind and God have become a part of almost every high school curriculum in the United States.

The novel's appeal comes from its strong characterizations. Hester herself offers a memorable example of integrity, found too seldom in female figures in early American literature. Her strict puritanical community's eventual reacceptance of Hester remains a testimony to the power of honesty and truth. The Puritan minister, Arthur Dimmesdale, his surname symbolizing his restricted vision of self, symbolizes the myopic view of religion that leads an individual to practice the very hypocrisy against which he preaches. He also represents Hawthorne's personal feelings of shame regarding his Puritan ancestors, who indulged in such hypocrisy with tragic results. Some participated in the persecution of Quakers, and Hawthorne's great-great-grandfather, John Hathorne, helped seal the fate of a group accused of witchcraft in early Salem. In order to distance himself from Hathorne, the author inserted a "w" into his legal name. Roger Chillingworth also bears a symbolic surname. He lives a life void of worth, filled only with a cold hatred of those he feels have betrayed him. Although he might like to attribute his emotional torture of Dimmesdale to a love for his wife, Hester, Chillingworth bears affection toward no one. His hate keeps him alive, as evidenced in the novel's conclusion when, after Dimmesdale's death, Chillingworth fades away.

The plot is simple. It opens with Hester's public punishment for having borne a child while living alone. Although she arrived alone at the Puritan community, she was to be joined later by a husband from England, but he never materializes. Her partner in adulterous forbidden love, Dimmesdale, does not confess his complicity, thickening the story's irony when he takes part in Hester's public embarrassment by providing his services as a man of God. Hester's husband, Chillingworth, chooses this day to at last appear in the Puritan community. When he views Hester and her infant, he keeps secret his identity. The explanation for his delayed arrival in the community comes in the form of a kidnapping story. Although Chillingworth arrived in the New World as planned, he was forced to live with Indians for a time. He benefited from this experience by learning the practice of medicine, a practice that will allow him to ingratiate himself with Dimmesdale.

Hester agrees to keep her husband's identity a secret, but she will not confess her own secret as to the identity of baby Pearl's father. Hawthorne takes pains to demonstrate early on that Chillingworth does not possess a naturally evil spirit. He cares gently for the ill infant, quieting Hester's fears by acknowledging Pearl's innocence and separation from her mother's sin. But his jealousy and his desire for revenge combine to transform Chillingworth into a grasping, scheming

human with only one purpose in life. He will discern Hester's partner and inflict upon that man a
slow, torturous death. His transformation into an
instrument of Satan is totally self-determined;
Chillingworth chooses his own fate.

Chillingworth succeeds in his plan, but not
due to his skill in emotional manipulation,
although it may be a highly developed skill.
Rather, Dimmesdale's own feelings of guilt allow
his manipulation by Chillingworth, whose identity he does not know. He thinks of Chillingworth as his personal physician over the ensuing
years, regarding him with an ironic trust.
Chillingworth's blackened soul and somber dress
add to the abundant dark imagery supplied by
Hawthorne. In one scene, he assumes the appearance of a demon during a storm, but Dimmesdale
remains so blind to truth, whether inside or outside him, that the image goes unnoticed.
Dimmesdale's traditional black garb and unclear
view of himself and others also complements the
dark imagery. Only Hester stands out against the
drab, threatening background. Her gold-embroi-
dered scarlet "A" provides the only bit of light, or
enlightenment, in the community.

Hawthorne's story turns on the theme of
redemption and its availability to those who
search it out. The nature of redemption is stressed
by Hester's achievement of grace, sinner that she
may be. Dimmesdale's delayed achievement of
that same state, despite his declared loyalty to the
church and God's teachings, also emphasizes the
all-encompassing nature of redemption. Chillingworth, however, finds no spiritual redemption.
He loses his humanity and thus his soul long
before the story's conclusion.

In the novel's climax, Dimmesdale plans at last
to confess to having fathered Pearl seven years
previously. He plans to follow his confession with
the assumption of responsibility many years after
the fact by taking Pearl and Hester to England to
live as a family. Dimmesdale at last secures
redemption when he publicly confesses from the
same scaffold where Hester suffered her public
humiliation years before. The strain of his own
guilt and Chillingworth's infliction have taken
their toll, and he dies, having achieved salvation
through his confession, an act that allows him to
join Hester in becoming a dynamic character.

In typical Hawthorne fashion, not all details
are made clear. Dimmesdale's dramatic tearing
aside of his garment during his confession reveals,

according to some witnesses, his own scarlet "A,"
like a brand seared upon his skin. Others in the
crowd deny having observed the presence of any
emblem on the minister's body. They also testify
as to the indeterminate meaning of his babbling
in his weakened state, claiming he actually made
no confession. His final act of confession is seen
rather as a type of parable for his audience, a bidding of those members of the community he had
served so well to cleanse themselves of all sin.

There remains no doubt, however, that
Hester's "A" symbolizes a parable to her neighbors. Although Pearl matures apart from the community, secure in the wealth left to her by
Chillingworth at his death, Hester returns to the
location of her sin. When she buries Dimmesdale,
she buries her past, but not its importance to her.
Where she once provided physical sustenance to
the community, she takes on a spiritual ministry
in middle age, welcoming young doubting
women into her home. When Hester dies and is
buried next to Dimmesdale, the letter "A" that
once shamed her becomes instead a monument
to her quality of character.

See also: Chillingworth, Roger; Dimmesdale,
Arthur; Forbidden Love; Hawthorne, Nathaniel;
Prynne, Hester

References: Abel, 1988; Bayley, 1960; Budick, 1996;
Gilbert and Gubar, 1996g; Hart, 1995; Stephenson
and Stephenson, 1993

SCOTT, SIR WALTER

Walter Scott was born in Edinburgh, Scotland, on
August 15, 1771. His creation and popularization
of the historical novel affected dozens of writers
that followed, including American writer James
Fenimore Cooper and English writers Charles
Dickens, William Makepeace Thackeray, and Jane
Austen. One of the first writers to capture in fiction a sense of the effects of political and traditional cultural forces on the individual, Scott's
works helped characterize the movement later
known as romanticism.

As a young man, Scott studied law and eventually became a legal official. This position afforded him time to devote to writing, and he
produced a great deal of poetry in the form of
ballads. His early writings reflect his love of ballads and legends, and although he had translated
some German Gothic romances, his ballads
brought him fame. He published editions of
poetry by the English writer John Dryden (1808)

and also by English satirist Jonathan Swift (1814). Eventually his writing of romantic narrative poetry was overshadowed by that of his contemporary, George Gordon, Lord Byron, and Scott turned to writing novels instead.

He wrote more than twenty novels, all published between 1814 and 1828. The novels feature individuals caught in the conflict caused by different cultures and reflect the influence of that period in the eighteenth century called the Enlightenment. Like many others, Scott valued the individual as a basically ethical person, regardless of social status, religion, political affiliation, or heritage. His series of Waverly novels stress Scott's belief in the necessity of a type of progress built upon past traditions. *Ivanhoe* (1819) features tension between the Norman and Saxon cultures, whereas *The Talisman* (1825) focuses on religious conflict between Christians and Muslims. Many critics believe his Scottish historical novels to represent Scott's best work in their focus on the conflict between a traditional Scottish culture and a more progressive English one. Examples include *Old Mortality* (1816), *The Heart of Midlothian* (1818), *St. Ronan's Well* (1824), *Rob Roy* (1817), *The Legend of Montrose* (1819), and *Quentin Durward* (1823).

Although Scott published his novels anonymously, readers learned his identity. His stories combined with his generosity and modesty to promote his popularity. The tremendous commercial success of his novels allowed Scott to construct a baronial mansion in Scotland, an estate known as Abbotsford. In 1820, he became a baronet. That same amiable nature that made Scott so popular also caused problems in the area of business concerns. He invested in two printing firms that eventually failed, leaving a debt of £130,000 that he spent the rest of his life attempting to repay. He returned to writing, publishing *Chronicles of the Canongate* (1827–1828), *Anne of Geierstein* (1829), and *Count Robert of Paris* and *Castle Dangerous* (1832). After suffering a series of strokes, Sir Walter Scott died on September 21, 1832.

Scott left an immense writing legacy and single-handedly created an interest in Scottish traditions. Although critics often disparage his now outdated writing style, they seldom argue regarding his importance to the development of the historical romance.

See also: Cooper, James Fenimore; *Ivanhoe*

References: Baker and Alexander, 1996; Brunel, 1992; McMaster and Stovel, 1996; Richetti, 1996; Shaw, 1996; Stephenson and Stephenson, 1993

SENSE AND SENSIBILITY

Jane Austen's romantic novel *Sense and Sensibility* (1811) features two sisters as heroines. As the older sister, Elinor Dashwood represents the characteristic of "sense" suggested in the novel's title. A paragon of proper behavior, Elinor's mannerly, controlled, demure behavior allows her to contrast with her younger sister, Marianne Dashwood. As a romantic personality, prone to be guided more by sensibility, or emotions, than by the sense exhibited by her sister, Marianne serves as a foil for Elinor. Very deeply devoted to one another, the sisters also complement each other in their search for happiness through love, even though their methods of finding such love at first greatly contrast. Austen uses these sisters, as she used probably her most popular sister-characters, Elizabeth Bennet and her older sister Jane Bennet in *Pride and Prejudice* (1813), to comment upon her favorite themes of class structure and gender inequity.

The story opens with the death of Mr. Dashwood. His demise throws his widow and daughters into chaos. The girls' stepbrother, John Dashwood, will inherit the Dashwood estate, and Mr. Dashwood requests that John look after his "second family" by providing them with a comfortable yearly income. Unfortunately, John's greedy wife, Fanny, discourages through flattery and manipulation her husband's generosity, and the Dashwood women are granted a very small yearly income. This forces them to search for a small home while suffering eviction from their own estate, which goes to John and Fanny.

Austen's ironic plotting generally allows the villain or villainess to help the heroines unwittingly, and the plot of *Sense and Sensibility* proves no exception. Although Fanny is a negative character, it is her brother, Edward Ferrars, who eventually falls in love with and marries Elinor. Their understanding, however, is delayed by the brand of long-term misunderstanding also common to Austen's plots.

These misunderstandings generally exist due to a lack of communication between her characters, whose culture emphasizes propriety, manners, and custom over honesty. The behavioral code prevents outright declarations of affection between the well-bred young man and woman, and Austen builds humor as well as pathos around this custom, gently satirizing English high society. Because Edward became "engaged" at an early age to a young girl he barely knows, he believes he can never marry Elinor. An honorable man, Edward remains duty-bound to marry his so-called fiancée, even though his heart belongs to Elinor. When Edward tries to explain to Elinor but fails, she is left to learn of his "engagement" from the young woman herself, after which Elinor finds herself engaged in an uncomfortable love triangle. Although she grieves for Edward's love, she respects him for his exemplary behavior in honoring a promise. She never declares her love for Edward, not wanting to increase his emotional and social burden. Further complicating their situation is the fact that Elinor has been reduced to near-poverty, whereas Edward comes from the monied class. Fanny makes clear that a union between the two would be unacceptable. True to her nature, Elinor handles the situation with a quiet but troubled grace.

Although Elinor hesitates to share her feelings with Edward or anyone else, Marianne's actions blatantly declare her enamored state in regard to a wealthy neighbor, John Willoughby. He seems to return her affection as well, but a forced separation from Marianne by Willoughby's wealthy patron sends her into a lovesick depression. The third person in Marianne's love triangle, Colonel Brandon, a powerful and wealthy landowner of the region, must suffer along with Marianne at her rejection by Willoughby. Eventually the sisters discover that Willoughby's rejection of Marianne is based on money. He must marry well because his patroness insists she will cut off his support after she discovers his sexual improprieties with a local girl.

Colonel Brandon has also been scarred by a past love, which was thwarted because of differences in social class. He had loved a working-class girl who disappeared when Brandon was shipped to India in the military. Upon his return, he finds his love dishonored and pregnant. When the young mother dies after giving birth, Brandon agrees to care for her daughter. But the daughter seems fated to repeat her mother's mistake, and she is the girl who becomes pregnant by Willoughby. Brandon keeps all of these details secret until he confirms that Willoughby has rejected Marianne.

In typical Austen fashion, all of the various love affairs work to the best in her masterful resolution of multiple conflicts. When Brandon helps care for Marianne while she has a fever, she learns to love him for his steady, dependable nature. This represents an alteration for the high-spirited girl, who had looked to the dashing Willoughby as the epitome of romance. The epiphany that converts Marianne into a dynamic character occurs with her realization that sense can be every bit as important as sensibility in the formation of a lifelong relationship. Elinor will unite with Edward when his silly, fickle "fiancé" falls in love with his younger brother, Robert. Although Edward has lost his fortune to his brother, Colonel Brandon offers him a living as a pastor in a nearby church, a position that ensures his future comfort. Freed from prior commitments, Edward may propose to Elinor. Both sisters marry for love, as do Brandon and Edward, and even Fanny is happy to see her younger brother married and a part of high society. Only Willoughby suffers from lack of love, for he will have to endure life with a mate chosen only for the income she can provide.

Sense and Sensibility is, as its title promises, a well-balanced novel. Each of the main characters have foils who help clarify the various characters' personality traits. In addition to the main characters mentioned above, Austen provides her readers with her normal assortment of representatives of the various classes. Many add humor to the novel and play necessary roles in uniting the lovers, who remain at odds due to a multitude of misunderstandings. In addition to the affection between male and female, Austen emphasizes the strong bond of love that may unite sisters, adding an autobiographical slant to the novel. Although Elinor and Marianne differ greatly in personality, their love and devotion to one another remain an important focus of the novel. Crucial to the novel's happy ending is the ability of the two sisters to remain in close proximity to one another, and to Mrs. Dashwood, forever. Brandon's generosity makes this possible, and the novel offers a satisfying and happy conclusion.

See also: Brandon, Colonel; Dashwood, Elinor; Dashwood, Marianne; Ferrars, Edward; *Pride and Prejudice*
References: Copeland and McMaster, 1997; de Rougemont, 1983; Drabble, 1995; Gard, 1992; Praz, 1974; Watt, 1963

SETHE

A woman who killed her own daughter rather than allow her to be taken back to the plantation and raised as a slave, Toni Morrison's Sethe from her novel *Beloved* (1987) stands as one of fiction's more compelling protagonists. Lacking a surname and bearing a first name that seems more fitting for a man, Sethe represents a woman searching for her identity when both her gender and her race worked against her advancement within a racist society. Her escape from the inaccurately named Sweet Home farm while pregnant and raising several small children reveals Sethe's courage and her determination to elude slavery, not only for her own sake, but for that of her children. As she sets out on a quest to move from the South to her mother-in-law's Ohio home, Sethe does not even know whether she will ever see her husband Halle again. During her journey, she is aided in delivering her baby, Denver, by one of the few positively characterized white people in the novel. But after only twenty-eight days of freedom and during a celebration of Denver's birth, Sethe is surprised by the appearance of Sweet Home's overseer, who comes to claim her and her children as is her owner's "right" under the Fugitive Slave Law. Hiding in a building behind the house, Sethe cuts the throat of her toddler girl and prepares to kill Denver and herself. Foiled in those attempts but successful in dispatching her toddler beyond slavery's grip, Sethe goes to jail for her crime and later returns to Ohio.

Most of the novel depicts Sethe's struggle to overcome her past and the guilt that threatens to destroy her. When the invisible spirit of the dead child moves into her house, her family fractures as her sons desert her, and Denver lives in fear that she herself may one day be killed by her mother. Only the elements of love and self-acceptance can free Sethe, and their seeds are planted one day with the arrival of Paul D, who had suffered in slavery with Sethe many years before.

The development of love between Sethe and Paul D comes slowly, just as his fingers move slowly over Sethe's scars, easing her pain and his own as well. Paul D has the power to exorcise the dead child's ghost from the house, number 124, and for a time he lives in relative peace with Sethe and Denver. But Sethe lacks the trust necessary to tell Paul D her complete history. She mentions only that she had gone to jail rather than return to Sweet Home. Just as their relationship seems to strengthen, a stranger appears in the form of a young girl, who is the age that Sethe's dead child would have been. When Sethe "adopts" the girl, she becomes the third aspect of a strange love triangle in which Paul D's new affection for Sethe will suffer severe testing.

Although Denver recognizes the girl as the fleshly embodiment of her dead sister, Beloved, Sethe cannot see this for a time. Paul D does not understand the bizarre effect that Beloved has on Sethe, and he eventually leaves the house after Beloved attempts to seduce him. It is Sethe who rescues her lover from her own dead daughter, but she seems unable to rescue herself. Sethe survives one vengeful murder attempt by Beloved but then falls prey to a type of spell woven by the girl. Sethe confines herself to the house and Beloved's presence, as if placing herself under house arrest to pay her debt to her daughter by a type of slavery every bit as insidious as that she had known at Sweet Home. Her inability to eat represents a starving of her soul, as she tries to convince Beloved that she had to kill her but cannot convince herself.

Of the female voices that inhabit the novel, that of Sethe remains the most haunting, more so even than Beloved's. Although Beloved speaks from a kind of Jungian collective unconscious, telling a chilling story of burial and isolation in the ground, Sethe's words are those of a woman who had wished to die but was forced to live in a world that rejects her. Even members of the black portion of her community tend to shy away from 124 due to the ghastly deed that had taken place there. Sethe's husband never achieves his freedom, her mother-in-law dies, her sons desert her, and she is left with one real daughter and one terrible memory child. Paul D's love and devotion serves as a redeeming factor, but ultimately Sethe must find her own grace through self-acceptance and the love of Denver and other women in the community, who at last unite to exorcise Beloved from 124.

Sethe's strength as she suffers such degradations as the stealing of milk from her breasts by young white men, additional physical and emotional cruelties of slavery, separation from family and loved ones, and rejection by her own living daughter stands as a monument to the human spirit. She remains a survivor of a bitter war of the soul and emerges triumphant over her past as she embraces a future with Denver and Paul D.

See also: Beloved; Beloved

References: Atlas, 1996; Dougherty, 1996; McKay, 1997; Morey, 1997; "Morrison, Toni," 1997

THE SHADOW BRIDE

Roy Heath's 1988 romance, *The Shadow Bride,* reflects themes of love, religion, and race as it chronicles a Guyanan physician's struggle for happiness with his willful and possessive mother. As the novel's protagonist, Betta Singh faces constant conflict with his mother, whose own fulfillment seems to rest upon the destruction of her son's independence and sense of self-worth. The conflict begins as Betta returns from his London training as a physician with a desire to battle malaria among poor Guyanan workers on a sugar plantation run by exploitative British expatriates. Betty Singh desires that Betta remain in the Vlissingen Road house in Georgetown, where he was raised, and open a private practice. When Betta later further enrages his mother by marrying, without consulting her, a young Hindu woman named Meena, battle lines are drawn, and any chance for reconciliation seems impossible.

Although definitely the antagonist of the novel, Betty remains an engaging villainess. Separated from her homeland of India as a young woman, she survived multiple miscarriages due to malaria and a harsh patriarchal marriage to nurture Betta, her miracle child. Betta's father, also a physician, dies when his son is just a child, but his influence endures in its effect upon Betty. Following her husband's death, she assumes an active, male-oriented approach to life and yet remains vulnerable to the influence of strong men. This aspect of her character becomes important to Betta due to his exposure to one of the men, the Muslim Mulvi Sahib, who acts as his teacher from childhood until the time he departs for London. The Mulvi Sahib stands in great contrast to another religious figure, that of the Pujaree, a Hindu. These two men symbolize two of the widely varying religious beliefs that contribute to Betta's confusion as he matures. Added to this spiritual confusion is Christianity, symbolized by Betta's adult pharmacist friend, George Merriman.

Heath relates his novel to the romantic quest through various references, most reflecting voyages both literal and figurative, pertaining to Betta and his mother. Both participate in life-altering physical voyages by ship and emotional quests for spiritual awareness and the satisfaction of human love. However, their personal quests differ sharply, mainly due to their different genders. Betty departs her homeland of India against her will as the bride of a husband she barely knows. The reward she should receive, in the form of the love of her husband and a stable family life, she never enjoys. Due to the malaria so rampant in her new home of British Guiana, she is cheated of a large family of children. Intensifying the pain of those losses is the fact that her husband becomes a philanderer, and Betty must raise his illegitimate granddaughter, Lahti. Lahti's presence physically haunts Betty in life and continues its haunting effect even after Lahti's tragic death. The widow eventually marries the Pujaree but discovers him to be just another controlling male who refuses to cooperate with her plan to steal Betta's only son. Ultimately, Betty's life proves little more than painful, and she ends her unsuccessful quest with a tragic and symbolic suicide.

By contrast, Betta's quest proves far more successful. Although he departs his homeland when he travels to London in search of medical training, he returns to achieve his dream of serving the poor on a sugar plantation. But this choice is not without consequence. Not only does his mother try the force of his commitment, but also political problems serve to defeat Betta. However, an important part of this disappointing experience is Betta's successful marriage to Meena. They live a fairly happy life, supportive of one another. Their joint strength enables them to survive the tremendous disappointment of their only son's physical handicaps. A testimony to the strength of Betta's positive influence as well as to the enlightenment of changing cultural values is the fact that both of their daughters travel to America to train as physicians.

Two romantic subplots enlarge and complicate the novel's tale, as they enrich and support its varied themes. In addition to raising Lahti, Betty also raises another ward, Rani, and the two girls become very close. Although secretly in love with Betta, Rani participates in an arranged marriage to the weak-minded Tipu in order to please Betty. She remains symbolic of an ancient system of patriarchal marriage and ritual, in which her loyalty to Betty is expected. Rani achieves a victory of her own, however measured, in gaining independence from the oppressive Betty when she insists that her husband remove their family from the Singh household. Rani also represents a highly moral approach to life, not only through her adherence to custom but in her attempts to influence Lahti. As the two girls mature, they necessarily grow apart, for Lahti engages in wanton sex with another of Betty's hangers-on, the evil and misogynistic Sukrum, necessitating at least two abortions. Lahti eventually marries the worthless Sukrum and is thus forced into a life of misery by her hatred of Betty. In a terrible turn of retribution, Sukrum eventually rapes Betty and causes Lahti's miserable death.

Overall, the novel has a positive tone because of the ironic friendship formed between Rani and Meena, two women both in love with Betta; the healthy and well-adjusted children of their marriages; and Betta's great respect and affection for Meena. Even Betta's eventual realization that an organized scheme of religion offers him little remains positive in that his torment regarding religious practices finds resolution. The novel's deep texture, formed from continuous interweaving threads of engaging thematic emphasis, offers the reader of romance a satisfying experience.

See also: Heath, A. K. Roy; Patriarchal Marriage; Quest; Singh, Betta; Singh, Meena; Violence
References: Nelson, 1995; Radway, 1991

SHAKESPEARE, WILLIAM

Arguably the single greatest influence on English literature, William Shakespeare was born in 1564. No complete and authoritative account of his life exists, but tradition assumes his day of birth to be April 23, 1564. Church records do reflect his baptism on April 24 in Stratford-upon-Avon, Warwickshire, a place that later became synonymous with its famous playwright and poet. The eldest son of John Shakespeare, William had seven siblings. His father was a prominent merchant, and his mother, Mary Arden, came from a landed family of Roman Catholic gentry.

The young Will may have received an education at a local common school and, had he followed the custom of the day, should have served an apprenticeship with his father and eventually taken over the family business. One version of Shakespeare's story posits that he served instead an apprenticeship with a local butcher, possibly due to his father's poor financial situation. Another has him a schoolteacher at a young age. Some evidence regarding his early years may be gathered from his plays. For instance, the fact that

he incorporates into his drama an in-depth knowledge of hunting and hawking suggests that he may have enjoyed some leisure time during maturity. He married a farmer's daughter, Anne Hathaway, in 1582, who was already pregnant, according to some sources. Legend has it that the couple departed Stratford in haste following Will's involvement in a poaching incident at the deer park of a justice of the peace, one Sir Thomas Lucy.

Shakespeare probably arrived in London in 1588, and by 1592, he had already attracted attention because of his acting and playwriting. As was necessary for stage players of the era, Shakespeare secured the patronage of a wealthy aristocrat, Henry Wriothesley, the third Earl of Southampton. He also began writing poetry, and publication of his erotic narrative verse, *Venus and Adonis* (1593), and *The Rape of Lucrece* (1594), along with his *Sonnets,* secured his reputation as a strong Renaissance poetic voice. Important themes arising from his sonnets include his devotion to a mysterious dark lady, never identified to the satisfaction of scholars, as well as to an unknown young man. Shakespeare adopted the Petrarchan, or Italian, sonnet, but transformed it to meet his needs. The Petrarchan sonnet took the format of eight lines of proposal with a six-line rejoinder, written in a set rhyme scheme. Shakespeare formatted his examination of an issue, commonly love, in twelve lines, adding a two-line summary statement and working with a rhyme scheme that differed from that of the Italian sonnet.

Shakespeare's dramas rather than his poetry established his reputation with later generations, although his plays were viewed as rather vulgar by contemporaries. He received credit for thirty-eight plays that he either wrote, modified, or collaborated on with fellow playwrights. He also likely performed in many of his own dramas. As with most writers, Shakespeare's early stage consisted of experiment, producing works containing superficial construction and dull verse by comparison to his later accomplishments. His four early history plays included *Henry VI, Parts I, II, and III* and *Richard III.* All were likely written sometime between 1590 and 1593. As with much of Shakespeare's activity, no precise dates are available for most of his dramas. These plays featured the strife England suffered during historic battles over who would hold the crown. They culminated with a study of evil in the malevolent Richard III, a ruler said to have murdered two children in order to secure the throne. Shakespeare also produced comedies during this early stage, including *The Comedy of Errors* (1592); *The Taming of the Shrew* (1593), with scenes of heated verbal exchanges between lovers that delighted audiences; *The Two Gentlemen of Verona* (1594); and *Love's Labour's Lost* (1594). These comedies depend on well-known romance elements of mistaken identity, forbidden love, and unrequited love that are eventually developed into shared affection, with some having a satirical air. During these years, Shakespeare introduced particular dramatic themes and interests that would reappear in his later plays.

Shakespeare's second period of writing produced his most famous history plays along with comedies and two tragedies. In an evolving individualized style, he wrote *Richard II* (1595), *Henry IV, Parts I and II* (1597), and *Henry V* (1598), plays that examine English history just prior to his previous set of history plays. Incorporating fantasy characters, such as the famous figure of Falstaff, the plays aimed for an emphasis on the truths about human nature rather than for complete historical accuracy. For instance, in *Henry IV, Part II*, the young Prince Harry battles his nemesis, a character named Hotspur. Although both of these men existed historically, they lived in two different eras and never fought hand-to-hand. Thus, Shakespeare collapsed history in order to make his points with audiences. The Henry plays would be adopted during the world wars to promote patriotism in England through film versions, such as Laurence Olivier's highly chauvinistic rendering of *Henry V.* The monarch's famous speech, claiming God's support of England, was used to encourage twentieth-century troops at war with Germany.

One of the most enduring of the Shakespearean comedies, *A Midsummer Night's Dream* (1595), offered viewers a fantastic interweaving of plots regarding various pairs of lovers in a tale that takes place entirely during one twenty-four-hour period. Drawing on its predecessor, *The Taming of the Shrew,* Shakespeare's *Much Ado about Nothing* (1598) would become a beloved romantic comedy around the world, as it introduced another couple who excelled in verbal sparring. Beatrice and Benedick, while purportedly not the play's major love interests, continue to capture the

imagination and joy of viewers centuries after Shakespeare's death with their witty repartee. The drama's plot, in which a woman falsely accused of sexual infidelity eventually is proven innocent, allowed emphasis on the enduring theme of slander, and its effect on women's reputations. Although later viewers found the treatment of Beatrice and her cousin Hero somewhat objectionable, Beatrice carries the day as a frustrated early feminist, repeatedly declaring, "If only I were a man!" *As You Like It* (1599) and *Twelfth Night* (1600) have been labeled Shakespeare's most mature and best developed comedies, presenting a complexity of oppositions representing good and evil, humor and seriousness.

Romeo and Juliet (1595), Shakespeare's most well-known tragedy, established its two young star-crossed lovers, doomed by family enmity, as enduring character types. The playwright concluded his second prolific writing period with the presentation of *Julius Caesar* (1599), also a tragedy featuring political rivalries, but with less intensity than the tragedies to follow.

Shakespeare's third stage includes what critics label his finest tragedies and comedies, those edged by a bitter tone and sometimes labeled his "dark works." *Hamlet* (1601) represents the heights to which his poetic dialogue had developed and remains Shakespeare's most famous and oft-presented play. In the young Danish Prince Hamlet, the playwright shapes a character obsessed not only by revenge but by questions of the validity of his actions. Suicide and death in general exist as strong themes. Shakespeare also uses his drama to comment on the ongoing dispute regarding the place of art in every person's life and the artist's responsibility to the audience. He even incorporates a comment regarding the boy acting troupes of the day who competed with Shakespeare's own dramatic endeavors and calls attention to his dramatic trade with the incorporation of the renowned play-within-a-play. In *King Lear* (1605), tragedy escalates to a more epic scale as Shakespeare draws on an older tale to emphasize age-old themes of greed and power. He constructs a historic plot that would be repeated many times in literature to follow. When Lear decides to "retire" early from his royal duties, relinquishing his royal power and property to his three daughters, he begins a dark journey toward realization that confirms his worst fears. Without his royal title, he finds himself useless to a family that, for the most part, values the material over the spiritual. Only the sacrifice of Lear's "good" daughter, Cordelia, can redeem the evil worked by her two sisters and their spouses. Like other of Shakespeare's dramas regarding royalty, this one acts as a cautionary tale to England's contemporary monarch and to those that follow.

Antony and Cleopatra (1606) examines another type of love, that between a man and a woman who both possess considerable political strengths. Cleopatra, as the ruler of a conquered world, remains dependent on the kindness of her Roman captors. This play contains some of Shakespeare's most erotic poetry and demonstrates love's ability to triumph over politics. Another well-known tragedy and Shakespeare's shortest play, *Macbeth* (1606) also examines political greed and offers some of the most-quoted lines from all of his plays, including Lady Macbeth's insane cry, "Out, damned spot!"

The three tragedies critics identify as tinged by bitterness are *Troilus and Cressida* (1602), *Coriolanus* (1608), and *Timon of Athens* (1608). This group of dramas offers no protagonist worthy of much sympathy or even any admiration; they seem to lack heroes. *Timon* reflects an unbalanced presentation that has caused critics to speculate it may have been a collaboration on Shakespeare's part with another dramatist. In addition, the two comedies written during this stage, *All's Well That Ends Well* (1602) and *Measure for Measure* (1604), in which the morality of Christianity exists as an overwhelming theme, appear much less lighthearted than previous works displaying Shakespeare's humor.

Toward the end of Shakespeare's career, in a fourth stage, he wrote his major tragicomedies. They suggest an air of resignation, an acceptance of the human condition and humankind's inability to influence fate. Although some critics believe this reflects Shakespeare's own late-life resignation, others feel the playwright merely followed the fashion of the day in his writing. All the plays conclude happily, incorporating fantasy elements including distant places in distant times and containing more symbolic elements than previous Shakespearean plays. These works include *Pericles* (1608), a gruesome tale of loss and persecution that concludes with a reunion of the main character and his family. *Cymbeline* (1610) and *The Winter's Tale* (1610) focus on the resolution of domestic problems, basically through the

restoration of family members believed to be lost. Probably the last play written exclusively by Shakespeare, *The Tempest* (1611) concludes with the optimistic suggestion that wisdom and power may be blended to positive effect. This drama, like many of Shakespeare's efforts, focuses on political and familial tensions and romantic love, but within an island world governed by words and magic. In the character Caliban, Shakespeare shapes a creature half-human, half-spirit, whose dramatic interpretation varies with each director.

Shakespeare may have had a hand in writing two additional plays as collaborations in 1613, *Henry VIII* and *The Two Noble Kinsmen. Kinsmen* would not be published until 1634. No additional works have been discovered to account for Shakespeare's activity during his final three years of life. He died in 1616, leaving for succeeding generations a literary inheritance of incomparable value. His dramas enjoy a continued popularity, produced often on stage, adapted for multiple film versions, and read aloud for pleasure as well as education.

For one who contributed such a wealth to English literature, Shakespeare has enjoyed a mixed appreciation. Doubt over the authorship of many of his works causes some to regard the very existence of Shakespeare with skepticism, whereas others believe he may have written only a small portion of the works for which he traditionally receives credit. No one argues, however, against the tremendous artistic value of the dramas themselves. Filled with poetic language unequaled in drama of any age, focusing on matters of interest to all humans in all eras, revealing an insight into human character that continually astounds, the thirty-eight plays credited to William Shakespeare represent a treasure unequaled.

See also: Beatrice; Benedick; Claudio; Hero; *Much Ado about Nothing;* Romance; *Romeo and Juliet*
References: Davis and Salomone, 1993; Drabble, 1995; Grene, 1996; Halio, 1995; Levin, 1974; Levine, 1996; Weitz and Weitz, 1995

SHARP, BECKY

Becky Sharp, the protagonist of William Makepeace Thackeray's social commentary novel *Vanity Fair* (1847–1848), cannot be labeled a heroine. Thackeray makes clear from the novel's subtitle, *A Novel without a Hero,* that the traditionally "good" characters of romance will be missing from his story. Yet Becky's instincts for survival, her wit, and even her knavish personality arouse at least admiration in the reader. The novel revolves around human vanity, and Becky becomes vanity incarnate. For all of her vice, however, Becky Sharp holds no particular ill will toward any one individual. She does not discriminate in her wicked treatment of others, for she engages in such wickedness merely to promote her own fortunes.

As Thackeray makes clear, Becky needs all the good fortune she can create. Life has dealt her a pitiful hand, leaving her orphaned and without funds. She becomes the perfect symbol of the downtrodden who remain the object of the aristocracy's scorn. Becky, however, learns to beat that same aristocracy at its own game. Throughout Becky's highs and lows alike, Thackeray constantly emphasizes the fact that life is made up of one bit of gaming after another, in which the odds may change. His human "fair" provides the perfect setting for Becky to work her charms on those who consider themselves her betters. So egotistical and smug are these individuals that they do not even recognize her manipulation of them.

The early Victorian Age society inhabited by Becky would have sanctioned her aspirations to marry into the aristocracy. Yet the members of the English upper class with whom Becky manages to come into contact all fall victim to her overwhelming charms, especially that of her unremitting flattery. She is shameless in her attentions, first paid to her classmate, but never her friend, Amelia Sedley. Amelia serves as the bottom rung of Becky's ladder to freedom. She also serves as a foil to Becky. Although Becky possesses the survival instincts of an alley cat, Amelia remains sickeningly innocent and naive, never suspecting that Becky merely uses her for social promotion. Amelia even agrees to sacrifice her pompous, overweight brother, Joseph, or Jos, Sedley, to Becky. Believing the two to be in love, Amelia works at playing matchmaker, but she fails. This propels Becky into a new position in the midst of a new group of monied people when she becomes governess to the family of Sir Pitt Crawley.

Eventually Becky wins the heart of the still-married and ultimately foolish Sir Pitt while also ingratiating herself with his spinster sister, the wealthy Miss Crawley. Miss Crawley adds to the evidence provided by Amelia that women may also fall for Becky's charms. When Sir Pitt finds himself free of his wife following her death, he proposes to Becky. Becky shocks everyone by revealing a secret marriage to Sir Pitt's son by a first marriage, Rawdon Crawley.

The two make a perfect couple because Rawdon is a longtime swindler and Becky remains ever-poised to help him in his nefarious dealings. With the marriage, however, he deals himself right out of Miss Crawley's will who, despite her former appreciation for Becky, disinherits Rawdon. In that action, Miss Crawley takes her place with the many other hypocritical figures in the novel. She embraces Becky as long as the young woman remains willing to "keep her place." When Becky agrees to function as little more than a servant, tending the old woman during illness, Miss Crawley finds her most agreeable. The moment, however, that Becky aspires to more than society deems sufficient, Miss Crawley immediately judges her unfit to join her own social rank through marriage.

True to her reputation, Becky finds no obstacle she cannot conquer, including Rawdon's poverty. They manage to live well on practically nothing, constantly eluding creditors as Becky plays on the sympathy of new victims in order to continue the expensive lifestyle to which she aspires. Eventually she betrays Amelia by causing Amelia's husband, George, to fall in love with her. After she conquers George, thereby ruining Amelia's life, she moves on to other notables, such as Rawdon's brother, the recipient of his father's and aunt's wealth. Finally she lights upon the socially well-placed Lord Steyne. Her refusal to aid Rawdon in his attempt to avoid debtor's prison reveals her truly base character. When Rawdon leaves prison through the help of his brother, he discovers Becky at home with Lord Steyne. Even the presence of his much-beloved son cannot keep Rawdon with Becky after he at last sees for himself her true nature.

Thus begins Becky's slide from fortune as she becomes a kept woman for any man who finds himself strong enough for that position. The irrepressible Becky will not be kept down for long, and the reappearance of Jos Sedley offers her the opportunity she needs for a final and permanent escape from poverty, even though that escape costs Jos his life. At last armed with the ultimate weapons of choice in her Victorian Age, wealth and the title that marriage to Jos provides, Becky, or Rebecca, finds her way into the highest eche- lons of British society. This becomes Thackeray's final jab at the society he so beautifully parodies through Becky Sharp and *Vanity Fair.*

See also: *A Handful of Dust;* Thackeray, William Makepeace; *Vanity Fair;* Victorian Age

References: Clarke, 1995; Flint, 1996; Harden, 1996; Hawes, 1993; Reed, 1995; Shillingsburg, 1994

SHAW, GEORGE BERNARD

Born into a cultured Irish Protestant family on July 26, 1856, George Bernard Shaw would become one of the world's best-known drama- tists. In the popular play *Pygmalion* (1913), Shaw updates the ancient Greek myth that a great man can literally shape a great woman from little more than a handful of clay. Shaw's drama demonstrates beautifully a classical theme that exists in various shapes and forms throughout romantic fiction.

Shaw was trained early in music, and he also developed a love of literature when still a small boy. Formally educated in an Anglican school, he began work in 1871 in a land agent's office and remained in that position for five years. In 1876 Shaw traveled with his mother to London, where he studied music and developed an enormous interest in and preoccupation with societal con- ventions. He helped found the Fabian Society, a group dedicated to the gradual promotion of socialism. Shaw registered as a Socialist and defended Socialist ideology, although he admitted to never completing a reading of texts by Friedrich Nietzsche and Karl Marx. He began to write during the early years in London, frequent- ing intellectual and literary circles. Not one of his first five novels was accepted by the various pub- lishers he tried. Having failed to publish fiction, Shaw dedicated himself to work in the media, writing for the London *Star* and *The World,* and in 1895 he became cultural critic for the *Saturday Review.*

Shaw established himself as a musical and lit- erary critic, expressing a special fondness for Richard Wagner and Henrik Ibsen. He wrote *The Quintessence of Ibsenism* in 1891, a study that held up the Norwegian playwright as a realist reformer who introduced what Shaw termed "discussion" into his dialogue. Not surprisingly, Shaw valued most highly works by Ibsen that attacked middle-class hypocrisy. He would later combine his talent for drama with what he envi- sioned as Ibsen's use of theater to move viewers

from attitudes of complacency toward a desire for social reform. The writings of Samuel Butler, a great satirist of Victorian convention, also pro- foundly influenced Shaw.

Shaw gained a reputation for mocking tradi- tional taste and contemporary fashions. His atti- tudes spilled into his creative writing, in which he often attacked English society on moral, aesthetic, political, and religious grounds. His 1892 produc- tion of *Widowers' Houses* focused on the problems of slum housing, laying the blame at the feet of slacker landlords. However, the drama insisted that viewers also comprehend the complex social problems underlying the story's economic prob- lems. Another early play, *Mrs. Warren's Profession,* was written in 1893, but it was long banned from publication due to its theme of prostitution. The play was produced by a private London club five years after its writing, but public performance was still prohibited in London. By 1905, the drama reached the New York stage, but production was immediately censored, the playhouse closed, and the drama's producer and company arrested. Following their eventual release and acquittal, the play returned to the stage in New York, but it would not see performance before a London public audience until 1926.

In 1898 Shaw published a volume titled *Plays Pleasant and Unpleasant,* which included *Arms and the Man, Candida, The Man of Destiny,* and (as part of the "unpleasant"), *Widowers' Houses* and *Mrs. Warren's Profession.* In 1903 he published *A Comedy and a Philosophy,* and in 1906, *The Dilemma of the Doctor.* His criticism of the harsh social rules of post-Victorian English society condemned most of his works to popular failure. But audiences in the United States welcomed his acerbic commentary, and Shaw's works became a hit across the Atlantic.

After North American critics praised *Innocent,* Shaw began at last to be "discovered" in Europe. First Germany and, at last, England responded to the works they had at first rejected. Shaw's pub- lished plays include *Major Barbara* (1905), a play that projects contempt for evangelists who pro- mote their beliefs by feeding the poor instead of attempting to convert the wealthy and influential; *Heartbreak House* (1919), which aligned Shaw with the Russian dramatist Anton Chekhov in its themes of civilization's collapse; and *The Apple Cart* (1929), designed to shock both liberal and conservative thinkers. Termed his most ambitious work, *Back to Methuselah* (1921) is considered Shaw's masterpiece by some critics, although many viewers find its convoluted message regarding man's intellectual capacities boring. Shaw's single tragedy, *Saint Joan* (1923) is considered by many as his finest play. However, some critics envision it as a comedy merely containing one tragic scene, proof of Shaw's lack of imagination in the area of history.

By far his most popular play with the public, *Pygmalion* (1913) caused a bit of a problem when it was converted to movie form. Shaw himself termed the play a romance, not because it contained the theme of love, but because its male protagonist, the great Henry Higgins, was a modernized version of the Greek king Pygmalion, a being elevated above the normal person. Audiences, however, translated the term *romance* into the popular understanding of love between a man and woman. Thus, viewers insisted that the drama's female protagonist, Eliza Doolittle, end up in a long-term relationship with Higgins, a development that Shaw rejected. He even wrote a prose sequel to the drama in which Eliza marries her young admirer, Freddy Eynsford Hill, but the public would have nothing of it.

Pygmalion's Henry Higgins is supposedly based on Arthur Conan Doyle's famous detective character, Sherlock Holmes. Shaw engaged Doyle, his neighbor, in a public argument regarding Shaw's newspaper commentary on the sinking of the Titanic. Doyle argued that Shaw presented the story with an indecent levity and wit, whereas Shaw accused the general press, supported by individuals like Doyle, of overromanticizing the tragedy. By basing Higgins on Sherlock Holmes, Shaw is said to have taken revenge for Doyle's public criticism of him.

The interest in language on which *Pygmalion* focuses mirrors Shaw's own fascination with forms of communication. He believed in the dynamic nature of language and worked to improve traditional spellings, insisting that publishers retain some minor changes introduced into his own spelling. In 1925, Shaw was awarded the Nobel Prize for literature. A crusader until his death in 1950, the playwright assumes a place of importance in the long list of noted Anglo-Irish writers that includes Jonathan Swift, Edmund Burke, and W. B. Yeats.

George Bernard Shaw will be remembered for his cutting wit and his passion for reform.

Although some viewers used his comedic approach to dismiss the seriousness of Shaw's charges against society, his tireless crusading for social causes resulted in his placing before the public disturbing paradoxes that many viewers simply chose to ignore.

See also: Pygmalion
References: Demastes and Kelly, 1996; DiBattista and McDiarmid, 1996; "Shaw, George Bernard," 1993; Shires, 1992

SHELLEY, MARY WOLLSTONECRAFT GODWIN

Born in London in 1797, as a teenager Mary Wollstonecraft Shelley would write one of the world's most popular horror novels, *Frankenstein* (1818). Her infamous love affair with Percy Bysshe Shelley and the circumstances of the writing of *Frankenstein* have become the stuff of myth, tales almost as well-known as the monster story itself. Although Mary Shelley wrote and published additional works, her first novel remains her most beloved.

Mary Shelley's parents greatly affected her development as a writer, an intellectual, and a supporter of social causes. Her father, William Godwin, became famous for the social theories proposed in *Enquiry Concerning Political Justice* (1793), for his support of free love, and as a novelist. Shelley's mother, Mary Wollstonecraft, championed women's rights in *A Vindication of the Rights of Woman* (1792). The Godwins' writings propelled them into the public arena, where they became both celebrated and despised for ideologies that challenged the current social climate. Wollstonecraft died from complications of childbirth when Mary was only two weeks old.

Mary, along with a stepsister, Claire Clairmont, found her father a difficult man to live with, and both fled their strict home life for Europe in 1814 when Mary was sixteen. They accompanied a married poet, the twenty-two-year-old Percy Bysshe Shelley, who had become a close friend of the family, supposedly courting Mary at her mother's grave. The fact that he took both young women gave rise to rumors that Shelley had affairs with both. The group eventually returned to England. Here they continued a nontraditional lifestyle, with Claire becoming Percy's companion while Mary conceived Percy's child and formed a close friendship with a previous acquaintance of Percy named T. J. Hogg.

Within a few months of her escape from her home, Mary prematurely delivered an infant, who died within a few days.

Through Claire, Mary and Percy met George Gordon, Lord Byron, already a famous poet. In an affair she initiated, Claire became pregnant with Byron's child. She convinced Mary and Percy to accompany her to Geneva to be close to Byron. There, during the summer of 1816, Percy and Byron became good friends, and Mary began work on *Frankenstein*.

In October 1816, another of Mary's stepsisters, Fanny Imlay, illegitimate daughter of Gilbert Imlay and Mary Wollstonecraft, committed suicide. In December Percy's pregnant wife Harriett, with whom he had eloped when she was sixteen years old, drowned herself. Mary and Percy married within the month. They chose as their wedding site a church in London's Bread Street, also the birthplace of poet John Milton two centuries earlier. Together Percy and Mary read Milton's *Paradise Lost*. This epic poem's imagery of Satan, as well as Milton's moral and mythological universe, likely influenced *Frankenstein*. The couple faced much future grief and disappointment together. Percy lost all chance of keeping custody of his and Harriett's two children, Ianthe and Charles, due to his "immoral" behavior and self-proclaimed atheism. In March 1818, Mary, Percy, and Claire set sail for Italy with three children and two nurses, where they lived for four years. Here they lost two children, a three-year-old son and a daughter, aged one. Although one child, a son named Percy, did survive, Mary remained grief-stricken. The time spent in Italy proved unusually productive for Percy, who managed to recover from depression and painful kidney infection treatments. However, Mary's relationship to her husband suffered an intense strain, complicated by Claire's presence and Percy's continued flirtations. Percy later drowned, leaving Mary a widow at age twenty-five. She returned to England with their only surviving son, where the immensely popular *Frankenstein* had already undergone adaptation to the stage.

Critics agree the influence of Mary Shelley's various mentors—past writers such as Milton, her own strongly opinionated parents, and her husband-poet—remained mixed. She admired them all, but she also projected in her writing a suspicion of some of their favorite themes, including creativity, the fertile use of the imagination, written expression, and the pursuit of intellectual activity. Although her novel contains some viewpoints found in the writings of her parents, it also contains some correction of and commentary upon their radical ideas. She sought to challenge her mentors and to distance herself from them by producing a story that calls for the strictest judgment to be executed against human capacity for overreaching moral and ethical bounds.

Frankenstein first appeared in three volumes in 1818. Mary's early experiences with pain, death, and tragedy are reflected in the psychologically complex tale of the man-monster created by a Faustian scientist, Victor Frankenstein. Mary herself relates the story that the idea for *Frankenstein* came to her on a June evening during that summer spent in Geneva at Villa Diodati. One of the Shelleys' several visitors, whom many guess to be Byron, proposed that each person present write a ghost story to compete with ones they had been reading. As Mary tells it, Percy had no interest in the project, and Byron's interest also failed. Another guest, John Polidori, Byron's personal physician and companion, suggested a Gothic plot that Mary judged ridiculous, but that he later produced, along with Byron, as a vampire story under the poet's name and the title *The Vampyre* (1819). When *Frankenstein* appeared to an overwhelmingly popular reception, readers guessed the identity of its anonymous author to be Shelley or Byron. Various critics over the decades since the novel's publication have credited Percy with the book's excellent success. They judge its quality far above that of anything else Mary wrote. She did allow her husband to edit and revise her text, leaving critics arguing over exactly what each of the pair contributed. Mary Shelley later wrote four additional novels, travel sketches, tales, and verse, including *The Last Man* (1826), an expression of her liberal social views, and *Lodore* (1835), an autobiographical novel. None of her writing ever matched the popularity of *Frankenstein*.

Contemporary feminist critics have worked to change the notion of Mary Shelley as a one-work writer. Some revisionist critics now see *Frankenstein,* as well as Mary Shelley's other works, as more accomplished and sophisticated than any writings by Percy Shelley. Only long after her death in 1851 did Mary Shelley receive proper credit for her immeasurable contribution, not only to the tradition of horror stories but to the development of the Gothic romance novel as well. Admittedly recognizable in *Frankenstein* are the influences of a multitude of literary works and writers, including the Bible, various Gothic works, the *Arabian Nights,* Milton, Johann Wolfgang von Goethe, Samuel Coleridge, Sir Walter Scott, Ann Radcliffe, Byron, Percy Shelley, Godwin, and Wollstonecraft. The very fact that Mary Shelley called upon so many varied sources proves that she found the literature of her time woefully inadequate to explain her own experiences. Ultimately, Mary identified with her own created monster, a creature who eventually understands himself as a "fallen angel," separated "from joy" through no misdeed of his own.

See also: Beauty and the Beast; *Frankenstein;* Gothic Romance
References: Budick, 1996; Drabble, 1995; Duncan, 1992; Ellis, 1989; Forster, 1956; Gaull, 1988; Hunter, 1996; Praz, 1974; Williams, 1974

SHIMERDA, ÁNTONIA

Ántonia Shimerda is the earthy heroine of Willa Cather's midwestern novel, *My Ántonia* (1918). Both Ántonia's father and her friend, the story's narrator Jim Burden, refer to Ántonia using the possessive "my." Just as the pioneers desired a plot of land to call their own, the male characters wanted to claim Ántonia's heart. In many ways, the novel functions as a love letter from Cather to the Nebraska plains, and Ántonia Shimerda symbolizes a tantalizing land too wild and beautiful to be possessed.

Ántonia displays a devotion for two (often oppositional) cultural forces, and it is through this duality that the major conflicts of the novel are enacted. The Shimerda family emigrated to Nebraska from Bohemia, at about the time the orphaned Jim Burden arrived on the plains to live with his grandparents. Ántonia's familial role is less directly tied to labor because she is the family's only female child. Instead, she assumes the role of both student and teacher, learning the new language of English and passing her knowledge on to her kin. Although at twelve years of age, Jim is three years younger than Ántonia, his intellect and friendly willingness to act as tutor secure his position as Ántonia's translator and companion. Through these translations, the reader becomes familiar with Ántonia's conflict between devotion to the cultural heritage of "the

old country" and her adventures with her new American friend.

Ántonia's love for her father symbolizes a loyalty to and a respect for her Bohemian cultural heritage. The death of Mr. Shimerda acts as a crucial moment in Ántonia's emotional development. Mr. Shimerda's physical presence lingers throughout the text, as does the spirit of Bohemian culture. Both remain recognizable in Ántonia's personality, affecting her attitudes and her speech even as she perfects her translations.

As Ántonia's second love, Jim earns a place in her heart partly because he knew Mr. Shimerda. He actively supports her through the process that includes an acceptance of her father's death, the cultural ritual of his funeral, and her grieving. In this manner, Jim helps Ántonia cope with the literal and symbolic death of her past. However, the theme of "new possibilities" best characterizes their relationship. They spend most of their time outdoors, in love with the power and mystery of the landscape. As they enter adulthood, Ántonia and Jim learn that their platonic love for one another finds its roots in pride. Jim teaches Ántonia to be proud of herself, and she feels a sisterly pride in his accomplishments.

My Ántonia is not a traditional love story. It offers a marked absence of sexual desire—the story does not conclude with a "boy-gets-girl" flourish. Neither can the feelings between Jim and Ántonia be labeled unrequited love. Ántonia will not be possessed by Burden, in part because she needs to keep her father and the old country close to her heart. She eventually marries another Bohemian immigrant with whom she can speak her native language. The novel concludes with Ántonia introducing Jim to her many children and sharing in a feast of reconciliation, at a table spread with homegrown food and friendship.

See also: Burden, Jim; Cather, Willa Siebert; *My Ántonia*
References: Armstrong, 1990; Blain, Clements, and Grundy, 1990; Daiches, 1971; Hart, 1995; Hoffman and Murphy, 1996; O'Brien, 1996

SHINJI

Eighteen-year-old Shinji, Yukio Mishima's protagonist in his 1956 romance novel, *The Sound of Waves,* is a perfect age to symbolize a classical quest figure. He also represents the naïveté and innocence present in prototypical romance characters such as Longus's Daphnis. Although Mishima updates the character of Shinji by allowing him a healthy curiosity about sex, Shinji resists the temptation to act on his curiosity. He remains a rather religious character, often visiting a local shrine and thus conforming to another aspect of *Daphnis and Chloe,* its religious theme. His physical chastity parallels a mental and emotional innocence allowing Shinji to contrast with his more jaded nemesis in the novel, Yasuo Kawamoto. The conflict between these two young men who would otherwise likely be friends fits into the classic romance plot, as they compete for the affection of the chaste young maiden, Hatsue. Although Shinji and Hatsue appear naked before one another, and he resists consummation of their physical love at her request, Yasuo attempts to rape Hatsue. She escapes due to the help of a wasp that stings Yasuo, causing him to lose his grasp on her. Mishima's wasp remains reminiscent of the field creatures such as bees found in Greek romance and quest literature.

Like the shepherds in *Daphnis and Chloe,* Shinji also makes his living with animals, but the sea is his pasture and the fish his herd of sheep. In the novel's beginning, he helps on a local fishing boat, but he eventually expands his horizons by becoming a mate on a large coastal freighter. His journey across water, his successful heroic action during a test of endurance in rescuing the freighter and the men aboard from a destructive hurricane, and his return home to claim Hatsue as his prize all resemble aspects of the romantic quest plot. This novel also acts as a coming-of-age, or initiation, story when Shinji must participate in the voyage and consequent first-time separation from his island home that marks him as an adult. He undergoes an epiphany when he realizes that he will never look at life in the same way after gaining the independence afforded by the journey. His education allows Shinji to regard his island and the world from a much more cosmopolitan point of view. His accomplishments and his change allow him to evolve as a character in contrast with Yasuo, who proves a lazy coward while on board ship.

The topics of class and social strata also receive emphasis as Shinji overcomes his own low status and overshadows Yasuo's status through honorable behavior and heroism. Mishima alters the quest plot a bit by not forcing Shinji to sustain a permanent loss. Instead, Shinji fears the loss of Hatsue, who may be forced to marry Yasuo due to a misunderstanding by Hatsue's father based on local gossip. These events are all typical of a classical romance.

See also: Bildungsroman; Longus; Mishima, Yukio; Quest; Romance; *The Sound of Waves*
References: Atkinson, 1989; Campbell, 1968; Hutton, 1993; Keene, 1995; Longus, 1989; Turner, 1989; Wolfe, 1989

SINGER, ISAAC BASHEVIS

A Polish-born American writer who would eventually garner the Nobel Prize, Isaac Bashevis Singer was born on July 14, 1904. His father's position as a rabbi of the Hasid school of piety and the fact that his mother came from a family of rabbis would have a profound effect on Singer's writing. For Singer, Hasidic Judaism's mystical elements combined strict adherence to Scripture and rites of Talmudic doctrine with an everyday earthiness that related to all human experience. Thus, although the worlds shaped in his fiction remain very much Jewish domains, they include themes of pleasure and suffering to which all readers can relate. Critics appreciate the wide range of characteristics incorporated into the figures in Singer's stories, ranging from saintly elements to the satanic, from quiet contemplation to obsession, from an unwillingness to accept responsibility to a strict adherence to the demands of adult life.

Singer emigrated from his home of Radzymin, Poland, in 1935 and became an American citizen in 1943. Shortly after his arrival, he began to write for the *Jewish Daily Forward,* a Yiddish-language newspaper in New York City. His elder brother, also an author, greatly influenced Singer's outlook on life, contributing to his spiritual liberation and ensuring his contact with contemporary political, social, and cultural ideas of a revolutionary nature. Ever-present themes in Singer's later fiction would be the conflict between tradition and change and the tension inherent in the practice of faith and spirituality in a materialistic world.

Singer began publishing novels in Yiddish in 1935 with his first book, *Satan in Goray* (translated in 1955), a work focusing on the religious hysteria responsible for the seventeenth-century massacre of Jews in Poland by Cossack troops. This book set the tone for his subsequent works,

Nobel Prize winner Isaac Bashevis Singer, shown in a 1978 photograph, incorporates a wide range of characteristics into the figures in his stories, ranging from saintly elements to the satanic, from quiet contemplation to obsession, from an unwillingness to accept responsibility to a strict adherence to the demands of adult life. (AP/Wide World Photos)

all of which featured strong narratives tinged with his characters' passion for life in the midst of despair at the passing of traditions so important to the Jewish faith. Although his works cannot be described as autobiographical, he did draw on his Polish background, along with Jewish fantasy stories and medieval European folklore, in constructing his plots. Singer himself translated most of his works that first appeared in Yiddish.

In 1950 Singer published *The Family Moskat* (translated in 1965), which would be his sole work to incorporate fantasy elements. This novel joined *The Manor* (1967) and *The Estate* (1969; originally published in Yiddish between 1952 and 1955) to form the three works of Singer's family chronicles. The intense characterizations and the description of the disintegration of established families in the face of change resemble that found in works by Leo Tolstoy, one of Singer's favorite authors. The autobiographical *In My Father's Court* (1966) depicts without sentimentality his poverty-stricken childhood in Warsaw. Its tone remains buoyed by a melancholy sense of humor

and lack of illusion. Singer also wrote many short stories, some of which appeared in a 1957 collection, *Gimpel the Fool and Other Stories*. In 1969, he garnered the National Book Award for one of his children's books, *A Day of Pleasure: Stories of a Boy Growing Up in Warsaw.*

Singer's 1972 novel, *Enemies: A Love Story,* later made into a movie, illustrates his characteristic themes of tyrannical passions and their destructive but also creative tendencies. The book's protagonist, Herman Broder, remains typical of Singer's heroes in his craven and lecherous approach to life. Although drawn at times toward religion and orthodoxy, Herman inevitably chooses hedonism over spirituality. Like so many Singer novels, *Enemies* shapes a kind of fallen universe where God remains absent and humans must battle various destructive powers. Although he presents in great detail through memories and dialogue his characters' experiences during the Nazi regime, Singer does not attempt to ennoble them or imbue them with any saintly aspects. They remain survivors, and like survivors of any horror, some use their experiences to enrich their lives, whereas others find in those same experiences an excuse for their weaknesses. Singer's fiction reveals the truth of his statement that, although he never lost sight of the fact that the United States offered displaced Jews the wonderful opportunity of assimilation into its culture, this opportunity also proved destructive to the practice of Jewish traditional rites. He wrote only of Yiddish-speaking immigrants so as to write of what he knew well, including their history, culture, attitudes, and thoughts.

Singer won the Nobel Prize for literature in 1978. Other notable works include *The Spinoza of Market Street* (1961), *A Friend of Kafka* (1970), and *A Crown of Feathers* (1973). He also wrote many additional stories, published as the collection *Stories* (1982) and also *Stories for Children* (1984). A movie version of his play *Yentl the Yeshiva Boy* (1974) was released in 1983. Prior to his death on July 24, 1991, Singer wrote his autobiography, *Love and Exile: A Memoir* (1984).

Best known for his narratives' free movement between the sacred and the profane, Isaac Bashevis Singer left a memorable legacy of fiction containing personified demons, specters, ghosts, and various supernatural powers in which the author said he believed. All of his characters share his imagination if not his moral center, and his stories brilliantly portray the daily ironies of the human condition.

See also: Broder, Herman; *Enemies: A Love Story;* War
References: Bilik, 1981; Farrell, 1994; Forrey, 1981; Friedman and Siegel, 1995; Halio, 1991; *Studies,* 1981

SINGH, BETTA

Betta Singh serves as the protagonist of *The Shadow Bride,* Roy Heath's 1988 romance novel. The novel's setting, British Guiana (present-day Guyana) in the 1920s, embodies the changes brought to his culture through modern technology and western thought. Like a romantic quest figure, he departs his homeland of British Guiana to seek knowledge in London, where he studies to become a physician and eventually returns home. Betta seeks to serve the impoverished peasants who work the sugar fields managed by British expatriates. But like any hero, he must face conflict and loss during his journey. The greatest single cause of both is his mother, Betty Singh.

An unusual figure for her time with her short-cropped hair and men's clothing, Betty commands both fear and respect from her Georgetown community. Betta matures in a house always filled with people, many of whom come to ask favors. For some, such as the girls Lahti and Rani and the boys Bai and Sukrum, Betta's mother provides complete support, and she offers partial support to a number of additional hangers-on. In this atmosphere Betta matures, and he watches all of his mother's favorites adhere to her desires. But when he announces he will not comply with her plan to live in Georgetown and establish a private medical practice, Betta learns the many devious shapes his mother's disapproval can assume. As their conflict escalates, Betta's feelings of loyalty and responsibility toward his mother increasingly conflict with his desire for a public service career and his love for his wife and children.

Although Betty would have liked for Betta to marry Rani, he chooses his wife, Meena, on his own. To his mother, this move is tantamount to betrayal. She spends the remainder of her life focusing on making her son miserable. She accomplishes this in a number of ways, including allowing a Hindu teacher whom Betta never liked to take his father's place in her house as her husband.

Betta endures other conflicts in addition to his relationship with his mother. His spiritual battle culminates in many conversations with his Muslim childhood teacher, the Mulvi Sahib. Each conversation reveals much about Betta's character. This man had first aroused in Betta thoughts of God and the meaning of life. It is the Mulvi Sahib's philosophy regarding the importance of social service that convinces Betta of the need for him to establish a hospital for the poor. As he tries to choose between Christian, Muslim, and Hindu beliefs, Betta faces his greatest intellectual and spiritual challenge.

The novel opens with Betta in old age; the entire story unfolds through the use of flashbacks. Heath marks Betta as a quest hero through the revelation of his memories of trying to come to terms with his dead father as well as with his great teacher. Betta vividly recalls the fear he experienced during his journey home from London at the thought of meeting the Mulvi Sahib again. He anticipates their future struggle, realizing it will equal in ferocity his ongoing struggle to make comprehensible the images he retains of his father. The struggle will challenge his dignity and prove difficult, because, like Betta's father, the Mulvi Sahib has achieved in Betta's mind the status of myth. Like any hero who learns and matures, Betta does eventually separate himself both physically and emotionally from the Mulvi Sahib. That moment of independence brings with it a crucial epiphany for Betta and serves to shape him into a dynamic character. However, Heath complicates the approach to identity by shaping Betta as his mother's namesake, not his father's.

Part of Betta's struggle for dignity involves learning the lesson of acceptance. He must accept his own shortcomings in not being able to save some of his patients and in failing to successfully battle the political machinery that dominates the plantation workers. He must also accept his mother's refusal both to see him as an independent being and to offer his wife and children the affection they deserve. His confusion over spiritual matters threatens to disturb his relationship with his Hindu wife as well as leave him paralyzed with inaction due to too many choices. Finally, he must accept the physical imperfection of his only son with grace and love.

That Betta at least faces his various problems, whether he finds solutions for them or not, marks him as a hero. Although he never understands his mother, he must accept the guilt he feels for her eventual suicide. He learns to balance that emotion with the pride and love for his immediate family and his career that separated him from Betty. Most important to his development as a character, Betta also at last accepts that the unnatural relationship his mother desires with him could and should never be.

See also: The Shadow Bride; Singh, Meena
References: Nelson, 1995; Radway, 1991

SINGH, MEENA

As the female love interest in Roy Heath's *The Shadow Bride* (1988), Meena Singh represents various compromises made by her husband and the novel's protagonist, Betta Singh. Betta is of the monied class, and his mother is a powerful economic figure in the Guyanan community of Georgetown. He chooses, however, not to marry a woman of his own class but instead to marry Meena, a mere shopkeeper's daughter with a very small dowry. The young girl stands for everything that Betta's mother, the possessive Betty Singh,

despises: restricted financial means, the Hindu religion, and a new way of life that includes a marriage in which Betty, as the groom's mother, has no say. Betty's irrational and unnatural jealousy of her son serves to place Meena in a near–love triangle with Betta and his mother.

Meena remains a curious mix of tradition and modernity, a combination that causes her conflict. Although shy and retiring in public, as suits a Guyanan bride, she openly shares her opinions in private with her husband. Although Betta does not demand a patriarchal marriage, in many ways Meena still practices that traditional approach to the life they share. Her shame over producing a girl rather than a boy as Betta's first child hearkens back to her heritage. Meena also experiences feelings of competition with both her mother-in-law and her older daughter for Betta's attention, even though he does little to inspire such feelings.

Meena does evolve into a dynamic character by the novel's conclusion but not as a matter of volition. Caught up in the forces that attempt to separate her from a traditional Hindu approach to life and push her toward more modern, westernized ways, Meena struggles against the change. But as her relationship with Betta grows, so does her self-confidence. She survives threats to the life of her family from the plantation manager where Betta serves as physician. In addition, she overcomes the jealousy fostered by her knowledge of the love for Betta held by Rani, Betty's foster child and Betta's lifelong admirer. Meena will eventually go so far as to befriend Rani, whose traditional arranged marriage causes Rani great unhappiness. Meena also shares with Betta a fierce love for their imperfect third child, the boy they always wanted. She comes to respect the Mulvi Sahib, a character who acts as the novel's symbol of the Muslim religion, where once she feared him. Most importantly, Meena survives both a prolonged emotional attack and a horrifying physical attack by Betty.

Meena ultimately gains wisdom from her ability to see beyond the promise of present happiness to the possibility of future disaster. Her sense of security lies not in the fact that she feels she will never face hardship, but rather that she has successfully become what Betta has made of her. To Meena, life's importance lies in each individual's meeting her predestined fate with dignity. In the end, Meena becomes, as Rani tells her, a rock of strength upon which all of the novel's characters eventually depend.

See also: Forbidden Love; *The Shadow Bride;* Singh, Betta; *The Suffrage of Elvira*
References: Nelson, 1995; Radway, 1991

THE SKY IS RED

Giuseppe Berto's 1948 tragic war novel, *The Sky Is Red,* acts as an antiromance by undercutting traditional romance elements. The tragic air of the novel, although it may evoke sadness in the audience, remains traditional to realistic novels. The novel is untraditional, however, in that teenagers rather than adults are its main characters and victims. Through the circumstances of his four main characters, Daniele, Giulia, Carla, and Tullio, Berto demands that readers take notice of the terrible effects of war on society's most innocent members, its youth.

Romance remains a factor in Berto's story, but it becomes near-perversion through the sexual interaction of individuals little more than children. Tullio, a seventeen-year-old gang leader, loves Carla, a prostitute who is nearly fifteen years old. As hardened products of war, neither teen has much to offer in the way of tenderness. Fifteen-year-old Daniele shares a more idyllic love with the fourteen-year-old Giulia. However, his initiation into what should be the sweet mystery of sex is reduced to a stark confrontation with reality when Carla assumes the role of his teacher. This does not ruin the physical passion that he later shares with Giulia, but the experience does cause feelings of shame and embarrassment.

Although many romance stories present heroic quests involving wartime feats, Daniele's quest counters the traditional elements, as Berto frames his character's activities in failure and defeat. As a product of the upper class, educated and privileged, Daniele does not possess the sensibility or the skills to survive on the street like his friends. Tullio might be viewed as the traditional quest guide figure who imparts knowledge to the hero, but his early death and the cynical attitude toward life that he transmits to Daniele do nothing to help arm the boy against his hostile environment. Berto uses Tullio's belief in communism to promote a bitter message regarding those who would take advantage of the working class and to strike out at religion, an ironic factor in light of the fact that Daniele had, until the bombing of his Italian city and the subsequent deaths of his parents, been enrolled in a Catholic seminary. Another guide figure, an elderly teacher visited occasionally by Tullio and Daniele, offers the opportunity for encouragement and growth. But when Daniele faces the loss of both Tullio and Giulia, the old man can offer no hope. His words have the opposite effect as he explains to Daniele that loneliness remains war's ultimate gift to human beings; one learns not to trust a single person. This idea represents the nihilism so prevalent in novels following the world wars.

Most quest heroes gain some type of reward, either spiritual, in the form of true love, or material, in the form of valuables. But Daniele loses his true love to a debilitating disease, and he leaves behind the only treasures he ever owns—his books, symbolic of an idealistic knowledge rendered useless by war. As a child, Daniele cannot participate in any battles; he only suffers from them.

Although Daniele does begin what seems a return journey home, as do most quest heroes, when he climbs aboard a train, he deems the effort a useless one. His departure from the land where he suffered defeat by the monsters of war, hunger, and loneliness brings no solution. He has lost Tullio, Giulia, and his beloved mother. Even Carla, whose strength, cynicism, and street smarts provide her key to physical survival, remains emotionally dead to the world. Although the old man had at one point urged Daniele to have faith in people, to be patient and wait for the day when humankind rediscovered itself for the greater good, the young boy becomes too exhausted to wait for something that may never occur. Thus the final antiromantic event in the novel is Daniele's suicide. Tullio had died in a type of battle, and Giulia's life was claimed by disease, but Daniele makes a careful choice to end his own life.

Berto's closing narrative describes the town a year after the boy's death, still miserable, its people with no thoughts other than finding food. The Italians have been deserted by institutions they formerly trusted. Crushed beneath the burden of defeat, the already impoverished populace ekes out an existence in a land totally disabled by World War II. The bit of hope offered through the rays of sun and some bright colorful imagery is countered by the approach of winter. Berto's message remains a grim one, a challenge to his readers to prevent for all time the reappearance of such a scene.

See also: Berto, Giuseppe; Carla; Daniele; Giulia;
Nihilism; Quest; Romance; Tullio; War
References: "Christian Apologetics," 1997;
"Nihilism," 1993

SLAVERY

See The Black Experience in America, 1600–
1945

SMITHSON, CHARLES

John Fowles's mock Victorian Age romance, *The
French Lieutenant's Woman* (1969), offers in Charles
Smithson a protagonist-hero who embarks on a
somewhat ironic quest. His quest remains ironic
in that he will discover, at what he believes to be
its conclusion, that his journey toward a full sense
of self has only begun. His confusion reflects the
purpose of a novel that readers find simultaneously predictable and unpredictable. Fowles uses
nineteenth-century Victorian social mores to
construct a plot containing one very twentieth-
century woman, Sarah Woodruff. Like Sarah herself, the story leads readers and Charles astray. Just
as they begin to feel comfortable with what
appears to be a typical late-nineteenth-century
landscape surrounding the village of Lyme Regis
on Dorset's Lyme Bay, Fowles snaps them into
another time frame using narrator intrusion.
Charles acts as Victorian society insists that he
must, but his actions cause repercussions he is not
trained to handle.

Charles first notices Sarah while in the company of his fiancée, Ernestina Freeman. Ernestina
represents all that Charles's androcentric society
admires. She has good breeding accompanied by
ample wealth, the product of new money from
her father's successful business ventures. She listens intently to Charles, regardless of his subject
matter. In Charles she has what would be considered a solid mate. His Darwinian scientific ideas

Jeremy Irons played Charles Smithson, the protagonist-hero of John Fowles's mock Victorian Age romance, The French
Lieutenant's Woman *(1969), with Meryl Streep as Sarah Woodruff in the 1981 film version of the novel. (Archive
Photos)*

mark him as a thinker, and his patronizing attitude toward Ernestina is expected of a man of his era. Charles seems destined to mature into a dull, unchallenged, unruffled Victorian gentleman, married to a woman with no major faults and no imagination.

The situation remains ripe for Smithson's personal revolt, sparked by Sarah. Her reputation as a woman deflowered and then spurned piques Charles's interest and his sexual drive. He becomes a pawn in Sarah's game, for she has created the background information regarding her seduction as a fiction that gossip quickly spreads about the village. That fiction causes Charles's attraction to her. Like other males of the age, he adopts a certain public attitude toward Sarah, one judgmental and tinged with pity. But in private, he lusts after Sarah, finding himself excited by the very characteristics his social mores insist that he ignore. Fowles succeeds in reflecting on Victorian hypocrisy by revealing Charles's true attitude toward Sarah. The reflection carries no censure, however, because such an attraction would be deemed perfectly normal within a few decades following the Victorian era, a time from which the story's narrator seems to come.

When Charles finally consummates his desire for Sarah, he is shocked to discover her a virgin and the entire story of her former love affair untrue. Deeply in love with Sarah, he breaks his engagement to Ernestina, knowing that she may, with support from her culture, publicly embarrass him. She can go so far as to place an ad in the paper and sue for financial damages. None of this is as difficult for Charles to bear as Sarah's mysterious disappearance.

Throughout the novel, Fowles inserts quotations from nineteenth-century writers who had an impact on the Victorian Age, including Matthew Arnold, Lewis Carroll, Thomas Hardy, Karl Marx, and Leslie Stephen. In so doing, he asks readers to reflect on the same rhetoric that filled Charles's world, knowing that readers will apply their own twentieth-century hindsight to the concepts presented. Fowles points out the contradictions inherent even in the writings of great Victorian men who remain possessed of two minds regarding ethics and morality. He also suggests that Charles himself, a fine representative of the Victorian gentleman, is related to his twentieth-century counterpart. This becomes clear as Charles's major positive characteristic, a disdain

for the act of possession, whether that be possession of material goods or of another human being, surfaces.

Charles leaves the trappings of his familiar life behind to meet with Sarah, at last located by a private investigator. Unlike most novel heroes, Charles gets to play out two separate endings in Fowles's novel that demands dual conclusions from a character of dual minds. In the first conclusion, Sarah reveals her most secret of all secrets, that she bore a daughter by Charles. The two seem to renew their passions, and the Victorian novel closes with a tableau of mother, father, and child that promises some type of future relationship, despite Sarah's protestations that she is not good enough for Charles. Then immediately the intrusive narrator, with a warning to the reader, "replays" the scene, absent the melodramatic touch of a child's presence. This time, Charles sees Sarah as something with which he does not wish to be associated. He departs alone, but ready to begin a quest symbolized by the narrator's closing reference to the sea.

In providing two different conclusions to the plot, Fowles does not force Charles to choose the one he prefers. Rather, he proves rhetorically that the same hero can fit into plots suitable to different eras, regardless of alteration of details. Charles Smithson becomes a character in a postmodern plot, one that abandons pat Victorian plot conventions in favor of a mosaic of fiction protocols.

See also: The French Lieutenant's Woman; Love Triangle; Victorian Age; Woodruff, Sarah

References: Baker and Vipond, 1996; Foster, 1994; Friedman and Siegel, 1995; Hart, 1995; Neary, 1992

SONS AND LOVERS

As its title indicates, D. H. Lawrence's novel *Sons and Lovers* (1913), a study in psychological realism, takes as its focus the taboo subject of a son's unnatural love for his mother. Lawrence's best-known novel achieved popularity in the decades following his death, not only in novel form but also as a 1960 movie.

Although Lawrence's protagonist, the sensitive Paul Morel, never acts upon what seems to be a sexual attraction to his mother, Gertrude Morel, the oedipal theme overshadows the story. Paul's attachment to Gertrude is an unhealthy one. Gertrude places the emotionally crippling role of surrogate husband on Paul from a young age. As a pretty, intelligent, middle-class woman, Gertrude should have looked forward to a pleasant and fulfilling life. However, she chooses to follow her heart rather than her intellect in choosing to marry a handsome English miner named Walter Morel. In marrying beneath her social station, Gertrude also marries beneath her spiritual and intellectual level. Although charming, Walter dissolves into alcoholism, offering little physical or emotional support to his wife and their children. Bitterly disappointed in her life, Gertrude turns to her four children, William, Annie, Paul, and Arthur for support. An affectionate and nurturing mother, Gertrude simply oversteps the boundaries of healthy attachment to her children.

At first, William is the focus of Gertrude's affection. When he marries a girl Gertrude does not like and moves away, she has mixed feelings. She views William's actions as both a betrayal and as a hope for the poverty-stricken family's future, because he promises to supply the financial support that Walter has been unable to do. But William dies unexpectedly, throwing Gertrude into an emotional tailspin of remorse. She is pulled up from her despair when Paul falls ill and requires more attention than usual. During this period of nursing Paul, Gertrude also nurses herself back to health and transfers the unnatural attachment that she felt for her eldest son to Paul.

Although their relationship remains admirable in many ways, Paul and Gertrude form an unhealthy codependency. Like all children, Paul outgrows his need for physical care, but when the time arrives for him to form relationships with young women, he finds himself an emotional cripple. The guilt he suffers when he forms an attachment to any woman other than his mother prevents his ever falling in love.

Paul becomes enmeshed in two unhealthy relationships, one with his childhood friend Miriam Leivers, a woman in many ways as controlling as his mother. Because she reminds him of his mother, Paul cannot bear to touch Miriam. The other woman in Paul's life, Clara Dawes, serves as Paul's mistress while he simultaneously romances Miriam. Caught up in an unhappy marriage, Clara meets Paul's physical needs but refuses to shoulder his great emotional burden. When Paul eventually attempts a sexual encounter with Miriam, he becomes physically abusive and grows no closer to finding a solution to his problems in relating to women. A number of love triangles form between Paul and both women and between Paul, each of his lovers, and Gertrude.

Although Lawrence offers scenes that hint at forbidden love between Gertrude and Paul, their relationship never culminates in a sexual encounter. Extensive imagery of touching and closeness with Gertrude, beyond the age for Paul when this would seem healthy, suggests the psychological causes of his problems with romance. Although a young man with some artistic talent, Paul resists leaving home and Gertrude in order to study art. He remains adrift, physically, psychologically, and emotionally.

Only Gertrude's long illness and death from cancer will allow Paul's eventual reconciliation with himself and his father. Gertrude's cancer symbolizes the lingering emotional death she has experienced for years. In its insidious consumption of her strength and will, the cancer mimics the harsh effect of her disappointment over the years on her spiritual well-being. This same emotional cancer threatens to consume Paul.

Paul begins a slow move toward discovering an identity apart from women when he helps enact a reconciliation between Clara and her husband while visiting his mother at the hospital. Although he loses Clara as his sexual outlet through this act, he gains a modicum of self-respect. He at last acknowledges that his and Clara's relationship would benefit neither individual in the long run. She does not try to dominate and control Paul as do Gertrude and Miriam but instead demands that he treat her as an equal. Paul's great emotional needs will not allow this; he does not want the emotional independence that Clara demands.

By involving himself in the Daweses' relationship, Paul chooses at last to acknowledge the complexity represented by the sharing of a mature love between adults. The realization that Clara and her husband share something that Paul has never known acts as an early step toward the recovery of his psychological and emotional health. That recovery does meet an obstacle with Gertrude's death, in which Paul plays a part. His act of administering to his mother the morphine that mercifully ends her suffering comes close to marking the end of Paul's own life. He struggles in an attempt to face life without the support of his mother and considers suicide.

Paul does achieve a reconciliation of sorts with his father, a necessary step in his quest for identity. When both men agree to depart the house that reminds them so much of Gertrude, Paul wanders about without direction for a time. He considers reuniting with Miriam, but when he returns to her he realizes again that she does not fulfill his needs. The freedom he feels following this decision somewhat mitigates his desire for death. Finally, following great internal conflict, Paul experiences an epiphany in which he at last understands that his mother lives on in his love for her. This allows the two to transcend death, and their spiritual union makes unnecessary the physical reunion that his own death would bring.

See also: Lawrence, D. H.; *The Shadow Bride*
References: Chambers, 1981; Drabble, 1995; Lawrence, 1964

SOPHIE'S CHOICE

William Styron's tragic but realistic romance, *Sophie's Choice* (1979), features many of the themes generally associated with all of Styron's fiction. Through this novel's three major characters, who reside in the United States in 1947, Styron focuses on religion and the effects of one's past on the present. In his protagonist, Sophie Zawistowska, Styron offers a study of the effects upon one individual of imprisonment in the Nazi death camps during the Holocaust. Sophie personifies the horrors that most Americans living during the World War II and postwar eras experienced only secondhand through newsreels and journalistic reports. Styron uses his nascent author and narrator, Stingo, to reflect on political and social issues of the American South, particularly slavery, as well as to emphasize the importance of language and writing. Finally, Nathan Landau represents the insanity supporting those cruel acts that humans inflict upon one another, both on and off the battlefield. Clearly the story's antagonist, he symbolizes the monstrous aspect of human nature. This view of Nathan as an ogre is reinforced when, early in the novel, a minor character labels him a *golem*. When Stingo asks the meaning of the term, the character explains it as a monster created by a Jewish rabbi.

The three characters form a love triangle of sorts, with both Nathan and Stingo expressing a sexual and emotional attraction for Sophie. Stingo, however, chooses not to act upon the strong passion he feels for Sophie, whom he sees as an "older woman" and as belonging to Nathan. He chooses instead to share a friendship with both Sophie and Nathan.

When Stingo moves into a cheap Brooklyn apartment, he listens for days to a couple engaging in boisterous sex acts. A young man with raging hormones, Stingo finds himself at first fascinated by the noisy coupling. A neighbor identifies the couple as Sophie and Nathan. Stingo's fascination dissolves into revulsion when he observes the couple for the first time. After viewing a virulent and abusive attack upon Sophie by Nathan, the younger man decides to keep his distance.

This episode becomes one in a long chain of abuse that characterizes the couple's love-hate relationship. Nathan suffers from full-blown paranoid schizophrenia, and throughout the story his mood swings threaten to destroy an already emotionally unstable Sophie. Although Stingo finds Nathan's behavior shocking, like Sophie he falls prey to the abundant charm of which Nathan proves capable in his saner moments. In between his paranoid spells, Nathan engages Stingo in intelligent and lively conversation and shamelessly romances Sophie. Stingo views Nathan's actions with suspicion, but Sophie maintains constant hope for an end to Nathan's "spells." His thoughtful and loving treatment of Sophie during his "up" cycles makes his eventual tirades all the more shocking and terrible. Nathan's irrational actions maintain a constant imbalance for Sophie, who badly needs the steady support that Nathan simply cannot supply.

The abusive aspect of Sophie and Nathan's unhealthy codependency would be regrettable in any form, but it assumes a truly abhorrent nature when Nathan chooses to accuse an innocent Sophie of being unfaithful to him. Even worse, he accuses her of betraying her fellow Nazi prison camp members by surviving the ordeal to which so many succumbed. The first accusation remains patently unjust, for Sophie worships Nathan, viewing him as her literal savior. She would never betray him in either a sexual or emotional manner. The second accusation feeds the guilt from which Sophie already suffers. She remains in constant turmoil over the fact that out of her entire family—parents, husband, and children—only she survived to leave the unspeakably horrid camps to emigrate to America. Although Stingo also suffers verbal abuse at Nathan's hands, he has far less invested in a relationship with Nathan than does Sophie. Stingo exists basically to act as recorder, fulfilling the writer's duty to observe and then reproduce those observations in story form.

Stingo eventually acts as a confessor for Sophie. During her separations from Nathan, she tells Stingo of her history as a non-Jewish Polish citizen, swept up by mistake in the wide net cast by the Nazis. Stingo reveals to his readers that Sophie lied a good bit while relating details of her past. This allows Styron to emphasize a postmodern view of history as nonlinear and subject to change due to individual interpretation. Because Sophie constantly readjusts her story, the reader remains in suspense over the meaning of the book's title, guessing that Sophie's choice will be between Nathan and Stingo. When the appalling truth is revealed, readers learn that Sophie's choice was one the Nazis forced her to make between her two children in the confusion of her arrival at Auschwitz. In a moment of baffled horror, afraid of losing both her children if she did not obey the command to choose, Sophie hands over her daughter to a guard and never again sees the girl. Although she clings to her son for a time, eventually he will also be taken from her. The cause for her emotional and spiritual decay becomes clear, and the reason for the story's abundant foreshadowing of impending death is evident. Both Sophie and Nathan suffer from terminal illnesses—his of the mind and hers of the soul.

The double suicide of Nathan and Sophie has no romantic overtones; theirs is not a *Romeo and Juliet* tragedy of errors. Death offers the only release imaginable to two such tormented souls. Critics cite as a weakness the novel's lack of redemptive qualities. In the view of some, the fact that Stingo will later gain some perspective on events and then record the tragedy for the benefit of others remains an unsatisfying justification for the horror Styron's characters undergo.

The story of Sophie's life remains compelling and worthy of pity. Her death, however, is eased by no promise of a kinder age from a culture that embraced slavery without the excuse of ignorance and for too long turned a blind eye to a mass slaughter of Jews.

See also: Love Triangle; Stingo; Styron, William; Violence; War; Zawistowska, Sophie

References: Bernard and Olesky, 1995; Casciato and West, 1982; Cologne-Brooks, 1995; Friedman and Siegel, 1995; Hart, 1995; Hoffman and Murphy, 1996; Joyner, 1996; Lupack, 1992; Ross, 1995; Weeks, 1995; West, 1995

THE SOUND OF WAVES

The Sound of Waves (1956) has met with both positive and negative evaluation by literary critics. Some insist it remains one of the weakest of Japanese author Yukio Mishima's efforts, written and published simply for its money-making potential. Others find it an important addition to the romance tradition in literature, because the novel reflects many aspects present in seminal romances such as *Daphnis and Chloe*. Notable parallels to that classical romance are obvious in Mishima's plot of love and separation, supported by the theme of the importance of mutual fidelity.

In this work, Mishima tells the story of passionate yet innocent love between the teenagers Shinji and Hatsue. Shinji has grown up in the fishing village on the island of Uta-jima, where he works on a boat. His widowed mother supports Shinji and his brother Hiroshi by diving for abalone. Hatsue, with whom Shinji is unfamiliar, catches Shinji's attention for the first time as she rests on the beach. He discovers that Hatsue is the daughter of a powerful villager, called Uncle Teru. Teru sent Hatsue to live with diving women off the island but calls her back when his only son dies. Shinji hears later from the owner of the fishing ship on which he works that the president of the Young Men's Association, Yasuo Kawamoto, son of a leading village family, plans to marry the beautiful Hatsue. In an early scene that focuses on a meeting of the association, Mishima describes the boys as trying to quote love poetry from Paul Verlaine. In this way, the author further aligns himself with Longus, whose *Daphnis and Chloe* contains several allusions to literature.

Shinji's interest grows into affection as he discovers Hatsue crying, lost at the highest point on their island, a deserted military fort. The elevated location of their first interaction symbolizes the lofty character of the relationship that will follow, even though Mishima supplies sexual imagery focusing on Hatsue's breasts. The female breast supplies important imagery of nurturing, maturation, and sexual allure throughout the novel, themes also found in *Daphnis and Chloe*. Mishima uses his characters' chance meeting to introduce the theme of the dangers of gossip and slander, as the two young people agree they should not be seen leaving the fort together in case someone is watching.

Shinji discovers that he can no longer sleep peacefully because he worries that Hatsue won't find him attractive. The narration that follows explains the naïveté of village boys, who are not exposed to the novels and movies in which city boys find their role models. The teens meet again when Hatsue returns Shinji's wages envelope, having found it on the beach. She laughs when Shinji mentions that he's heard she will marry Yasuo. Mishima again emphasizes the theme of the danger of gossip. Hatsue's reaction to what she obviously considers a ridiculous suggestion allows Shinji to harbor hope for a romance between Hatsue and himself.

Hatsue and Shinji meet again at the island's lighthouse, a location important to the island and to the novel's plot. The lighthouse keeper acts as guide for boats that sustain the village economy, and his wife acts as etiquette teacher for the village's young girls. Shinji has long been friends with this couple, who will play an important role in eventually uniting him with Hatsue. The lighthouse couple's daughter, Chiyoko, who attends university in Tokyo, has a crush on Shinji, something Hatsue discerns from her parents during a visit to the lighthouse. Hatsue refuses to speak to Shinji on the walk to the village, and he later discovers she's been upset by the hints linking him with Chiyoko. When Shinji convinces Hatsue that yet another rumor is false, they kiss for the first time.

When Chiyoko visits from Tokyo, Yasuo accompanies her and helps her from the boat, but it is Shinji's touch for which she longs. Chiyoko knows that she's not an attractive girl, and she's irritated when she realizes that Yasuo believes she likes him. Although Chiyoko's character causes conflict for Shinji and Hatsue and so may be seen as a negative or trickster character, she represents the only liberated female voice in the novel. She wishes just once to hear a man say, "I love you," instead of, "You love me." Mishima again emphasizes the importance of romance literature as Chiyoko thinks of female Victorian Age poets Christina Rossetti, Jean Ingelow, and Augusta Webster.

A later rainstorm drives both Shinji and Hatsue back to the deserted fort, where they strip away their clothes and admire each other's naked bodies yet remain chaste. Hatsue emphasizes that sex outside of marriage is bad, and Shinji's respect for things moral, represented throughout the novel by his frequent trips to the local religious shrine, causes him to agree. Shinji presents Hatsue with a type of informal engagement gift, a beautiful pink shell, symbolizing through its soft color innocence and beauty and through its origination from the sea, life itself. Chiyoko witnesses the lovers' arm-in-arm descent from the fort and out of jealousy starts a rumor that Shinji has stolen Hatsue's virginity. When Uncle Teru hears the rumor regarding his daughter's supposed participation in forbidden love, he orders Hatsue not to see Shinji. Eventually Chiyoko leaves the island. She feels guilty for her lie, especially after Shinji tells her she's pretty.

At first Shinji and Hatsue communicate through secret correspondence, and then they plan a meeting that is foiled by Uncle Teru. During this time, Hatsue and Shinji's mother, through their diving for abalone, become close friends. Hatsue makes a strong political gesture when she presents the prize she receives for gathering the most abalone to Shinji's mother, the second-place winner in the contest. In this way, youth bows to experience, and Hatsue shows her own maturation.

Like classical quest characters, Shinji prepares for a journey across water. He agrees to follow custom and join the crew of a large coastal freighter, although he's puzzled as to why he would be asked when he discovers the freighter is owned by Uncle Teru. His surprise increases when he meets Yasuo, also hired aboard the ship. The crew learns that Yasuo and Shinji offer a stark contrast to one another. Yasuo is lazy and one day brags that he'll soon own the freighter when he marries Hatsue; such boasting causes ill feelings among the crew members. Shinji remains quiet but works hard, impressing the crew as much as Yasuo has angered it. In a climactic adventure scene, Shinji proves himself worthy of the sailors' respect when he must complete a heroic swim to save the ship during an abating hurricane, a swim for which Yasuo declines to volunteer.

During the ship's absence, the lighthouse owner's wife has written a letter to Chiyoko, begging her to visit. Chiyoko writes back, confessing her complicity in the false rumor about Shinji and Hatsue and telling her mother that she'll return home only if her mother will intercede with Uncle Teru on the lovers' behalf. The mother does this along with all the women divers, except for Hatsue herself and Shinji's mother. They're surprised by Uncle Teru, who has already decided to allow Shinji to marry Hatsue after hearing of the actions of Shinji and Yasuo on the ship. Shinji's heroic behavior convinces Uncle Teru to permit his marriage to Hatsue.

The novel's name derives from a line in its concluding chapter in which Shinji listens to the sea. He notices that the sound of the waves remains peaceful and regular, foreshadowing his future life with Hatsue. Mishima incorporates multiple traditional themes and imagery from the romantic quest as well as other aspects of the romance tradition in his novel.

See also: Forbidden Love; Hatsue; Longus; Mishima, Yukio; Quest; Romance; Shinji
References: Atkinson, 1989; Campbell, 1968; Hutton, 1993; Keene, 1995; Longus, 1989; Turner, 1989; Wolfe, 1989

STINGO

In William Styron's realistic novel, *Sophie's Choice* (1979), the character Stingo plays a double role. He narrates the novel in first person as a mature writer looking back on his 1947 experiences with the tragic Sophie Zawistowska and her doomed schizophrenic lover, Nathan Landau. The maturity and perspective of many years allows the older Stingo the ability to analyze events from the past. Concurrently, Stingo exists as a character interacting in the past with Sophie and Nathan. In his twenties and just beginning his writing career, this younger Stingo lacks the maturity to objectively view the events that capture his imagination and emotions during that crucial summer of his youth. Readers come to see that the resolution of the novel's multiple conflicts depend at last on the resolution of conflict between the narrator's present and former selves.

Questions of identity begin for Stingo in the opening pages as he faces a call to adventure for what shapes up as a plot containing many aspects of the classical romantic quest. He invites readers to "Call me Stingo," echoing Ishmael's line from Herman Melville's *Moby Dick* (1851). This reference invokes imagery of a journey across a wide expanse in pursuit of an elusive dream and also allows Styron, in this loosely autobiographical novel, to place himself in the company of great American writers such as Melville. But Stingo is just a nickname; readers are not privy to the true identity behind the speaker's voice.

The opening chapter shapes Stingo as a frustrated author trapped reading awful manuscripts submitted to McGraw-Hill in his position as a junior editor. His sharply barbed criticism of irresponsible writing encourages readers to associate him with a "better" group of writers. When Stingo loses his editor position, a guide figure, who considers himself a failure, advises the young man to go forth and write. Stingo will eventually act on this command. At the first chapter's conclusion, the young Stingo labels his future experiences a "voyage of discovery," further identifying himself as a quest hero seeking his true identity.

An inexpensive Brooklyn apartment represents Stingo's threshold to adventure. Here he will face a monster in the form of Nathan Landau and confront a creature with mystical qualities in the form of Sophie. When first invited to join the couple in an outing, Stingo refuses, having been frightened by Nathan's abuse of Sophie. This refusal represents the quest character's refusal of the call to adventure. Ultimately he does accept the call, forming a relationship of sorts with both Sophie and Nathan. They act to help him face the more important issue of his own identity, an issue advanced and complicated by his southern past and his ongoing interaction with his own father.

Stingo finds himself an unwilling accomplice in slavery due to his inheritance of money gained through the sale of an ancestor's slave. Those ill-gotten gains he accepts as support for his fledgling writing career, but he must bear the guilt that accompanies that support. His emotions balance the guilt felt by Sophie, a non-Jewish survivor of the Nazi invasion of Poland, whose entire family suffered extinction in the Nazi prison camps. Herself a prisoner for a time, Sophie collaborated with her captors, most notably Rudolph Hess, to save her life. Although their situations differ, enough similarities exist between Stingo's and Sophie's pasts for the young writer to be drawn to her. In addition to occupying the roles of victims of another generation's ills, each will become victims of Nathan's pathological evil. Through Stingo and Sophie, Styron emphasizes the wide variety of pain that humans concoct to inflict upon one another.

As an author, Stingo helps support Styron's emphasis on the importance of language and words. That emphasis exists at several different levels. It may be seen in the mature author's narrative; in the fledgling author's attempts to express his emotions and reactions; in Sophie's difficulty with the English language that Stingo finds so charming; in the mixture throughout the novel of traditional English with foreign-language and Yiddish terminology; and in the great contrast between Nathan's logical discussions during his sane periods and his abusive, profane declarations during his bouts with insanity.

The importance of tone in creating a story's mood also becomes clear in the different types of stories that Stingo relates. He acts as a scribe for Sophie's story that remains on every level jarring and deeply disturbing. Simultaneously, he describes his own juvenile sexual desires and pursuits, an act that injects humor into an otherwise bleak narrative. Styron tempers that humor with a wrenching pathos that again emphasizes the disastrous effect on the human psyche inflicted by the dashing of hope and eventual destruction of spirit.

Like all Styron characters, Stingo remains a complicated figure, searching for hope in a seemingly hopeless world. He eventually accomplishes this through his writing, thus earning the quest hero's reward. Such reward comes only following the sacrifice of two people he loves. The written word can have a transfiguring effect on its subject, and Styron does attempt to end the novel on a hopeful note. Many writers have long held the belief that the retelling of tragedies remains essential. Such dark stories may act as cautionary tales to readers or provide readers relief from their own sufferings, which may seem less overwhelming in relation to that of fiction's tragic characters. Many contemporary writers still support the Greek idea of viewers experiencing a catharsis, a healthy release of emotion, when watching and judging the suffering of others. This may be Stingo's and thus Styron's final offering to his readers of Sophie's Choice.

See also: Beloved; The Black Experience in America, 1600–1945; Patriarchal Marriage; Sophie's Choice; Styron, William; Violence; War; Zawistowska, Sophie
References: Bernard and Olesky, 1995; Casciato and West, 1982; Cologne-Brooks, 1995; Hoffman and Murphy, 1996; Joyner, 1996; Lupack, 1992; Ross, 1995; Weeks, 1995; West, 1995

STYRON, WILLIAM

William Styron, destined to become one of the most influential twentieth-century American authors, began his publishing career with the well-received work, Lie Down in Darkness (1951). This novel marked the first of several by Styron to prompt heated debate among its readers. Although some critics praise his realistic use of conflict in stories of human relationships, others attack his approach. Elie Wiesel, winner of the 1986 Nobel Prize for Peace, wrote that he believed the Holocaust an improper subject for fiction as Styron employed it in his highly popular Sophie's Choice (1979). Despite such controversy or perhaps in part because of it, works by William Styron have secured an important position in modern American fiction.

Styron was born in Newport News, Virginia, on June 11, 1925. His father worked as an engineer at the local shipyards, and his mother, a gifted musician, filled the traditional roles of housewife and mother. Styron's lifelong struggle with depression may have roots in his father's having suffered from the same condition. His mother's death from cancer when he was only thirteen years old likely contributed to his feelings of despair. Styron's works reflect these early conflicts and losses in the repeated appearance of themes of depression, desperation, and guilt in his fiction that has been classified as bleak in its depiction of the human condition.

Following a stint in the Marines during World War II, Styron was discharged in 1945 as a second lieutenant. He attended Duke University, where he completed a bachelor of arts degree in 1947 and later studied creative writing in New York with Hiram Haydn at the noted New School for Social Research. Styron's brief experience during this period as an associate editor for McGraw-Hill would surface in his characterization of the writer/narrator of Sophie's Choice. However, unlike that struggling character, Styron found early success at the age of twenty-six with the critically acclaimed Lie Down in Darkness. For this work, he received the Prix de Rome award from the American Academy of Arts and Sciences. Styron was immediately classified as a southern writer, one who seemed a likely candidate to assume the esteemed mantle of William Faulkner. For the next decade, Styron remained a vital figure on the writing scene, often interviewed and quoted.

Following the success of his first novel, Styron relocated to France temporarily to cofound the *Paris Review* with Peter Matthiessen and George Plimpton. In 1952 his novella, *The Long March,* was published, and he returned to the United States the following year. Styron married and settled in Roxbury, Connecticut, where he began work on his second full-length novel.

After seven years of work, *Set This House on Fire* appeared in 1960. But it was Styron's third novel, *The Confessions of Nat Turner* (1967), that assured his critical reputation. The novel focused on themes of slavery and racism, powerful issues during the 1960s in the United States. Selling 200,000 copies in its first year, the novel made its way to the top of the best-seller charts. Although popular reception proved fairly positive, as evidenced by the book's sales, the novel was not received well by all. Some felt Styron made a mistake in choosing for his subject matter the leader of the 1831 Southampton slave revolt. Many protested the characterization of Turner as a tragic figure. Hostile critics claimed that the novel belittled a crucial figure in black American history. Others insisted that a southern white like Styron could not properly write from the point of view of black Americans. The novel became a frequent reference for those arguing that black characters always received poor treatment in literature. In reaction to Styron's work, a group of black writers published *William Styron's Nat Turner: Ten Black Writers Respond* (1968), in which they labeled Styron a racist. A highly controversial work, this novel garnered the Pulitzer Prize, an occurrence that further fanned the flames of racial indignation. Critics in later decades would write that the reaction to Styron's novel was due to hypersensitivity regarding racial issues and was not an accurate reflection of Styron's talent.

Styron's role as a political figure increased in importance with his appearance as a delegate to the 1968 Democratic National Convention. He also appeared as a witness at the infamous 1969 trial for the "Chicago Seven" and as a participant in the 1977 Moscow conference for American and Soviet writers. He continued to publish, releasing *In the Clap Shack,* a 1973 drama. Another inflammatory subject, that of the Holocaust, was the focus of *Sophie's Choice,* a popular novel that became an Academy Award–winning film. Never had Styron's vision been so dark as in this loosely autobiographical

novel. The story, told in first person by a young writer, reflects on the postwar experience in the United States of a non–Jewish Polish woman who had been interned in Auschwitz during the Nazi regime. *Sophie's Choice* helped confirm Styron's reputation as a writer who handles well themes of suffering and evil. Despite the novel's tragic conclusion, some readers insist that the narrator's ability to tell the story reveals the human capacity for hope.

In a confessional article titled "Darkness Visible" that appeared in *Vanity Fair* in 1989, Styron spoke frankly regarding his experiences with clinical depression, for which he had been hospitalized in 1985. This article, along with a 1988 *New York Times* editorial by Styron, renewed discussion regarding the age-old avowed connection between individual creativity and emotional instability.

Styron's collection of essays, *This Quiet Dust and Other Writings,* appeared in 1982 and he republished his *Vanity Fair* essay in 1990, titling it *Darkness Visible: A Memoir of Madness.* For his essay, Styron was honored by the creation of the William Styron Award by the National Mental Health Association. The annual award goes to a prominent American who uses his or her experience with mental illness to help others cope with their own. The author's 1993 fiction, *A Tidewater Morning: Three Tales from Youth,* collects stories previously printed in *Esquire* magazine.

Styron's literary life has been fraught with controversy, but no one could deny his importance to American literature. The proof of his power lies in the fact that in two different decades he managed to stir both the imagination and the indignation of the popular reading public.

See also: The Black Experience in America, 1600–1945; *Sophie's Choice;* Stingo

References: Bernard and Olesky, 1995; Casciato and West, 1982; Coale, 1996; Cologne-Brooks, 1995; Hadeller, 1996; Hart, 1995; Hoffman and Murphy, 1996; Joyner, 1996; Leon, 1978; Weeks, 1995

THE SUFFRAGE OF ELVIRA

V. S. Naipaul's novel *The Suffrage of Elvira* (1958) does not present romantic themes in their traditional sense but rather handles them in a manner that supports his emphasis on political and social concerns. The novel focuses on a political campaign in the small Trinidadian village of Elvira and on the various individuals concerned with the campaign. One of those characters, a young Muslim boy named Foam Baksh, learns the facts regarding political campaigns. Foam also acts, although unwittingly, to help free Nellie Chittaranjan, a local Hindu girl, from the hopeless future represented by an arranged marriage. Religion remains a crucial theme in the novel because the characters' various attitudes toward religion will determine the outcome of Elvira's political election to a great extent.

The wealthy Hindu, Surujpat Harbans, a political candidate, must gain the favor of Elvira's inhabitants in order to win an election. He uses bribes to win the vote of individuals who can influence different parts of the population. Nellie's father, the formal and aloof Chittaranjan the goldsmith, acts as Elvira's Hindu leader. Foam's father, Baksh the tailor, leads the Muslims, even though he himself does not practice his religion formally.

When Harbans approaches Baksh to help with his campaign, Foam agrees to drive a van with a loudspeaker around the area encouraging the populace to vote for Harbans. Foam volunteers not because of any political ideology, but because he has lost a position he wanted announcing movies. The movies are also announced from a van, and Foam's competitor, a writer named Loorkhor, took that position. Thus, working from the campaign van will help ease Foam's disappointment.

Chittaranjan, a dour member of the community, engages in an endless war with his neighbor over the ownership of fruits produced by the neighbor's tree. Chittaranjan desires to curry Harbans's favor as much as Harbans wants his. Chittaranjan hopes that his daughter, Nellie, will marry Harbans's son, and he has informed Nellie that the match has been arranged.

Outside the political intrigue exist several subplots. An Elviran named Dhaniram, also a supporter of Harbans, has a daughter-in-law to whom he refers only by the word that indicates her station, *doolahin*. Dhaniram's son deserted the *doolahin* shortly after their marriage, and she remains little more than a servant to Dhaniram and his crippled wife. Dhaniram defends his son's abdication of family responsibility by claiming he is in Europe studying, a claim that everyone understands is not true. Neither Dhaniram's absent son nor Harbans's son, whom Nellie will ostensibly marry, appears in the novel; they are both merely referred to by others.

Nellie Chittaranjan has no desire to participate in the arranged marriage. She desires instead to attend a technical school in London. Her resistance to a patriarchal marriage balances the negative situation of the *doolahin*, unhappily caught up in just such a patriarchal marriage. The *doolahin* seems to exist as a cautionary tale for Nellie, who desires an education instead of marriage.

As the campaign escalates in intrigue and conflict, a stray black puppy secreted into the household by a younger Baksh son causes trouble for the family. The elder Baksh believes that one night he saw a grown dog who the next day became a puppy, and he interprets this as a bad "sign." Naipaul uses this bit of superstition as well as other suggestions of such to demonstrate the problems that traditional beliefs in religion and signs can cause. Such religion works to depress a culture that wishes to educate itself and become intellectual rather than superstitious. Religion remains a favorite theme in Naipaul's later works, and he employs it to create tension among this early novel's characters. Foam later cleverly uses the local superstition to his and Harbans's benefit to help win the election. He represents a younger generation whose ideas about tradition and custom will change his world.

Nellie, as a young woman resisting marriage in order to seek an education, also represents the future of Trinidad. Having known Foam since she was a child, she confides in him her desire not to marry when he presents her with the puppy, Tiger. Although their meeting remains totally innocent, a passerby observes them alone together and begins a rumor that the Muslim boy and the Hindu girl are involved in forbidden love. Chittaranjan, in true patriarchal style, trusts the rumor before his own daughter, and he restricts her to the house. He feels his plan to marry her off to Harbans's son has been threatened.

Within an entertaining and humorous plot, Naipaul frames in a most engaging voice the story of one town's growing pains. Progress is represented by Elvira's young people, who act outside tradition in order to fulfill their dreams. The *doolahin* runs away with Loorkhor. This allows her personal freedom, Loorkhor the chance at a position as a journalist, and Foam to gain Loorkhor's job announcing movies. By taking matters under her own control, the *doolahin* subverts the normally passive position of the woman in a patriarchal marriage to become an active agent on her own behalf. Because of the untrue rumor about her meeting with a Muslim boy, Nellie is released from the plans for marriage when Harbans rejects her as unsuitable to marry his son. This allows her to travel to London to attend the Polytechnic and become the "new" type of woman her country will need in order to meet the demands of future progress.

Harbans's election to office causes many individuals in Elvira to "win," thus striking a blow for general democracy as well as for individual freedom.

See also: Baksh, Foam; Chittaranjan, Nellie; Forbidden Love; Naipaul, V. S.; Patriarchal Marriage; *The Shadow Bride*
References: Baker, 1994; Birbalsingh, 1996; Hussein, 1994

THE SUN ALSO RISES

Ernest Hemingway's novel *The Sun Also Rises* (1926) takes its place among the many works of fiction written by a group of authors whom Gertrude Stein labeled "the lost generation." Written by American expatriates mostly residing in Paris following World War I, these works reflect the disenchantment of young idealistic novelists horrified by the extent of death and destruction inflicted during World War I. Hemingway focuses on this disenchantment by embodying it in a group of once-promising young people who have become little more than shiftless drifters in their search for grace.

That search takes place in Europe during the 1920s in the midst of reconstruction following World War I. The cultural reconstruction reflects the attempted reconstruction of their lives by Hemingway's various characters. They include Jake Barnes, an American reporter made impotent by a wound suffered in battle; Lady Brett Ashley, Jake's former love; Mike Campbell, Brett's fiancé; and Robert Cohn, a would-be writer and one-time middleweight boxing champion at Princeton. Hemingway emphasizes his trademark idea of grace under pressure as the only possible human response to the trials of a nihilistic world. He accomplishes this through yet another character, a Spanish bullfighter named Pedro Romero. Pedro's courage in the ring serves to balance the cowardice of the novels' main characters. Pedro's character also allows Hemingway to focus on one of his great passions, that of bullfighting, a subject that appeared in several of his stories.

Exposition supplies the background relationships of all the characters, a necessary rhetorical strategy that allows contrast between their prewar interests and aspirations and their subsequent postwar apathy. Jake suffered both physical and emotional emasculation from his injury during service in World War I. His physical wound symbolizes a psychological wound that refuses to heal, thus preventing Jake from enjoying life. It also takes on a greater meaning applicable to the entire group of young people. They all search for fulfillment but remain unable to release the past in order to take advantage of any promise for their futures.

Jake longs only for his lost capacities, both as a lover and a young man possessing aspirations for success. His past romantic involvement with Brett necessarily ended with his injury, and she has supposedly moved on to a new lover in the Englishman Mike Campbell. Another character who cannot accept life's changes, Brett attempts to continue her relationship with Jake, even though this prolongs his mental suffering. Those three characters form a love triangle of sorts, although Mike actually competes with Brett's past for her affections rather than with the impotent Jake. Of the three, Mike remains a more sympathetic character. Brett's characterization as an opportunist who takes advantage of men makes her unsympathetic but simultaneously enables her to achieve some status later, when she finally exerts some self-discipline.

When the novel opens, Brett, Jake, and Robert are enjoying a vacation in Paris, during which Brett pursues Jake. Concurrently Robert, a known womanizer and Jake's acquaintance, focuses his energies on his mistress, Frances Clyne. Jake had originally known Robert as an unhappy man, struggling to write his first novel in Paris. He found relief from his problems through drinking and sports, particularly fishing and the observation of bull fighting. Aspects of Jake and Robert combine to represent Hemingway himself, a troubled young author and veteran of World War I known for his drinking and his devotion to sports. This may be the reason Hemingway begins his novel with an in-depth description of Robert, although that character is not the story's protagonist. Robert touts his position as a "romantic," when in reality his ideas of romance fail him, as had Hemingway's own. Eventually Brett draws Robert away from

Frances. When Robert tells Frances to return to London, she fights back by verbally abusing him before his friends, remarking on his feelings of inferiority and lack of self-confidence.

Mike joins Jake and Jake's old friend, Bill Gorton, on a fishing trip, although Brett's behavior with Jake and her present association with Robert make all members of the group uncomfortable in Mike's presence. Eventually all of the characters reunite in Pamplona, Spain, where they plan to watch the bullfights. Imagery of festivals and pageantry help emphasize the false front of gaiety employed by the group. Everyone indulges in drunken behavior in a ruse of celebration.

The appearance of the bullfighter, Pedro Romero, signals an important turn of events to the novel's plot. Pedro embodies the romantic ideals that Robert so miserably fails to uphold. He also symbolizes the reality of life's challenges, represented by the bull he fights in the ring before hundreds of spectators. When Brett accompanies Pedro to his room, the rejected Robert ferociously attacks and beats the bullfighter. Hemingway thus emphasizes the low levels to which his characters have fallen.

Although injured, Pedro returns to the ring and wins his fight with the bull. Romero's victory, his clear demonstration of grace under pressure, cause Jake's dissatisfaction with himself to deepen. Although Jake verges on an epiphany that promises to change his approach to life, Brett seems to fall even deeper into a quagmire of hopelessness. She again pursues Pedro, and the two leave Pamplona together. As Jake drinks, Mike and Bill depart Pamplona.

Hemingway does at last offer some sign of redemption in his characters when Brett contacts Jake the following day, asking him to meet her at a Madrid hotel. She confesses to having sent Pedro away upon realizing the harmful effect she could have upon him. She contacts Jake because her money has dwindled, and she wants to return to Mike to begin a new future together with him. Thus, Brett changes her approach to life and begins her recovery from the emotional wounds inflicted upon her by disappointment over the past.

The novel's conclusion does not promise happiness for Jake Barnes. As he and Brett ride aimlessly in a taxi through Madrid, their ride acts as a metaphor for Jake's life. Thus far, he has remained aloof from his surroundings, always observing but not interacting. Having lost so much of himself already, he sees no reason to contribute any more to the life around him. This ending helps support Hemingway's nihilistic philosophy, a belief that life lacks meaning. The only meaning available to any human, according to Hemingway, comes through that person's interactions with other human beings and through the acceptance of life's difficulties with a redeeming grace.

See also: Barnes, Jake; *A Farewell to Arms; For Whom the Bell Tolls;* Gatsby, Jay; *The Great Gatsby;* Hemingway, Ernest; The Lost Generation; Love Triangle; *The Sky Is Red;* Violence; War
References: Cowley, 1973; Defazio, 1996; Donaldson, 1996; Hart, 1995; Hen, 1996; Hily-Mane, 1995; Hotchner, 1966; Moreland, 1996; White, 1933, 1968

plot as Darnay's key to freedom on more than one occasion. In a scene that offers strong foreshadowing, charges against Darnay are dismissed due to his strong resemblance to Carton, a resemblance making an exact identification impossible. That resemblance will later save Darnay from execution and death. It also symbolically suggests that the truths employed by justice may not be as clearly delineated as one might think. Justice for one side of an issue may represent ruin for another, especially when both sides believe their agenda to be the only "true" one.

Through the court experience, Darnay and Carton become friends, and both men fall in love with Lucie. The two men serve as foils for one another. Darnay represents an intelligent, educated, sensitive man who employs his life for the good of others. Carton has a history of drunkenness and inactivity, although he possesses a good spirit. Darnay also occupies a position among the landed class, as his French uncle is the Marquis St. Evrémonde. The younger man keeps his position a secret to avoid any conflict it might cause. Although Darnay believes in social equity, his uncle presumes himself above the law due to the power afforded by his money. Darnay visits his uncle in France and begs him, as he has on other occasions, to resolve his differences with the local peasants, but the older man refuses. When his carriage kills a local peasant's child, however, Gaspard, the child's father, cares little for the Marquis's aristocratic status. He murders the unfeeling rich man in bed and later is executed for his crime. Because Darnay inherits his uncle's title, he also inherits the hatred of the local peasantry. His name joins those on the death list constructed by Madame Defarge.

Darnay leaves France and returns to England to claim Lucie's hand. Carton remains a devoted friend, pledging eternal loyalty to the couple, even though technically he forms a love triangle with them. His is not the traditional position, however, because he loves Darnay almost as much as Lucie. In a complicated plot sequence, Darnay ends up a prisoner in the Bastille, ironically his father-in-law's home for eighteen years earlier in life. Assumed guilty under the Napoleonic code, he remains in prison for

A TALE OF TWO CITIES

In *A Tale of Two Cities* (1859), Charles Dickens produced a romance that bequeathed to English literature one of its best-known phrases: "It was the best of times, it was the worst of times." After establishing this opening contradiction, Dickens proceeds to work through the tension caused by such an idea in his consideration of characters trapped within political forces prior to the French Revolution that they can neither control nor affect. The result takes its place among Dickens's other works as a finely crafted tale, brimming with characters all necessary to its complicated plot. Like the scarf knitted by Madame Defarge, a member of France's lower-class revolutionaries, Dickens's plot forms a tightly woven pattern.

The novel opens by employing the age-old romantic element of reunion between personages closely related but long separated. Due to his imprisonment in the dreaded Bastille, Doctor Manette prepares in Paris to meet his eighteen-year-old daughter, Lucie Manette, whom he had not seen since her infancy. He awaits her arrival in hiding above the wine shop of Madame and Monsieur Defarge, where Madame knitted into her long scarf symbols intended to indicate a list of aristocrats doomed to death by the working classes. Then, in a typical Dickensian shift, the novel jumps five years ahead to a courtroom scene in which one Charles Darnay, a language instructor, is charged with treason. Supposedly, Darnay helped ferry secrets back and forth between France and London. The Manettes are present in the courtroom to testify that Darnay indeed shared the boat on which they returned to England from France five years earlier. At this point, Dickens introduces the character of Sydney Carton. Carton remains important to the

Ronald Colman played Sydney Carton and Donald Woods played Charles Darnay, the fateful lookalikes who love the same woman, in the 1935 film version of A Tale of Two Cities, *Charles Dickens's 1859 romantic novel. (Photofest)*

months, causing Lucie and their daughter to despair. The previously laconic Carton decides to at last assume an active role in order to rescue Darnay. Although Carton has not figured as the novel's major love interest, he obviously becomes its hero. Drawing upon the previously established resemblance to Darnay, Carton will assume his friend's position at the guillotine, supplying yet another famous line in his great pronouncement, "'Tis a far better thing I do than I have ever done before." His friends escape back to England, and no one ever identifies Carton.

In addition to supplying excitement in a romance format that includes mistaken identities, unidentified victims and assailants, surprising connections between characters, the passions that rise in love and war, and violence and hope intermingled, the novel asks questions of its readers. How could one and the same era bear both the adjectives "best" and "worst"? How can Carton's death be considered a "better thing" than life? And, most difficult, exactly who are the villains of this novel? Dickens suggests that an era can be "best" on a microscopic level, that is, at the day-to-day level where individual lives evolve, while being the "worst" on a macroscopic scale, where the powers of politics and economy clash. The love depicted in the novel must be judged positive, as love always has been. Yet that very love produces some horrifying results.

Gaspard's love for his child ends in the murder of the Marquis before he can be convinced by Darnay to make amends to the peasants. The murder, although it might be termed "just" in a biblical sense of an eye-for-an-eye, counters civil law and results in Gaspard's death. Darnay, a decent man, takes up the mantle of his ancestor, a wicked man. He will suffer punishment not for his own actions but for those of his family members over which he exerted no control. For this injustice, Carton gives his life, a sacrifice he accepts because a noble death allows him to at last embrace the honor that escaped him in life. Again, justice seems to have been accomplished, but at a terrible cost. Finally, Madame Defarge, responsible ultimately for Darnay's death sentence and Carton's execution, seems the villainous figure. Yet she act out of love for a sister who suffered ruin at the hands of the Marquis, Darnay's ancestor. She also represents a class of people abused by an irresponsible government

that cared more for its own recreation than satisfying its hungry people.

The novel invokes the question of balance, and Dickens offers no solutions to the obvious conflicts that exist between individual approaches to justice and right. Carton departs this world to find justice in another. Likewise, Madame Defarge's life becomes meaningless following her achievement of an ironic justice that leads to her death. Although Darnay and Doctor Manette attempt to uphold human dignity, they are prevented from doing so by the increasingly complex social climate of Dickens's age. The Industrial Revolution threatened individual freedom, and the various prison terms in the Bastille that Dickens presents symbolize that loss. The message of the novel seems to be nihilistic, that no grace remains available to humans during this lifetime. Even imagination, romance's long-term answer to threats to the human spirit, seems unable to bear up under the weight of humans' capacity to inflict evil.

Only in Carton's act does Dickens suggest redemption. He offers no solution to the civil ills he features. Rather, he seems, again, to want to focus on the microcosm, the life of the individual. At that level, the story supports only the possibility of release from sorrow and suffering. Community offers a chance to preserve what the greater world would take from the individual. Carton's love within the community he forms with the Manettes and Darnays offers his sole means of rescue.

See also: Carton, Sydney; Darnay, Charles, Marquis St. Evrémonde; Dickens, Charles John Huffam; Love Triangle; Violence; War
References: Bullen, 1997; Caeserio, 1979; Drabble, 1995; Duncan, 1992; Furbank, 1986; Smith, 1996; Tambling, 1995

TAN, AMY

Amy Tan gained fame as an American author with her fictional presentations of Chinese-American life. Born in Oakland, California, on February 19, 1952, she lived in several California communities before moving to Santa Clara. Tan's Chinese father, a Baptist minister, also worked as an electrical engineer before emigrating to America to escape the war between the Communists and Nationalists in China. Her mother, Daisy, was on the last boat to depart Shanghai in 1949 after the Communist insur-

Amy Tan (1994) has become well known for her fictional presentations of Chinese-American life. (AP/Wide World Photos)

gence began. The situation forced her to leave behind her children, produced in an abusive patriarchal marriage. When she later married John Tan, they had three children, Amy and two sons. At age fourteen, Tan first confronted personal loss when both her father and a brother died from brain tumors within the same year. The remaining family members relocated to Switzerland, where the tension between Tan and her mother escalated.

After graduating from high school, Tan attended the Baptist college her mother had selected. She soon departed, however, to follow her boyfriend, Louis DeMattei, to San Jose where he planned to attend school. This move so angered Tan's mother that the two remained estranged for six months. Further irritating her mother when she left a pre-med program to study English, Tan received both bachelor and master degrees in English and linguistics at San Jose State University. She married Louis in 1974 and later settled in San Francisco, where he practiced tax law and she studied for her doctorate, first at the University of Santa Cruz and later at Berkeley. An interest in the developmentally disabled caused

her to leave the linguistics program in 1976. She became instead a language development consultant to an association for the mentally challenged and would eventually direct training for developmentally disabled children.

When Tan decided to go into business for herself, she found a partner and began a firm specializing in business writing consulting for salespeople and executives. That endeavor led to full-time freelance writing. Tan adopted Anglicized pseudonyms to write several business works, including a booklet designed for IBM. Her success as a business writer allowed her to purchase a house for her mother, and she bolstered her family's comfortable income. The financial success, however, did not satisfy Tan. In hopes of discovering a creative outlet, she first studied jazz piano and then began creative writing. Her first short story, "Endgame," won her admission to a creative writer's workshop. After the story's appearance in a literary magazine, *FM,* it was reprinted in *Seventeen.* Tan's second story, "Waiting Between the Trees," impressed literary agent Sandra Dijkstra, who agreed to represent Tan, encouraging the young author to work on a collection of short stories.

When Tan's mother became ill, she promised herself that, upon her mother's recovery, she would return with her to China to visit one of the three daughters, her own half-sisters, whom her mother had been forced to leave behind forty years previously. The trip gave Tan a new appreciation for her mother and her heritage, and she found the inspiration to complete the book of stories that her agent had encouraged. She received a $50,000 advance from Putnam for what would become *The Joy Luck Club* (1989), a novel featuring the stories of four mother-daughter pairs. The novel achieved best-seller status, won the L.A. Book Award and the National Book Award, and was made into a film in 1993.

Through her various protagonists, all American daughters born to Chinese immigrant mothers, trying to solve the conflicts caused by their Chinese heritage, Tan reflects on a dichotomy representative of the tensions universal to the human experience. She incorporates flashbacks, mysticism, and abundant storytelling to produce material dependent upon the memories of her narrators' ancestors. In *The Joy Luck Club,* Tan inserted a parable at the beginning of each section that connects the forthcoming story with the past. Much of her writing focuses on death and the afterlife, with plot events often drawn from the experience of her own Chinese family. Tan learned that her grandmother had committed suicide, and her mother survived that suicide as well as spousal abuse prior to the wrenching separation from her children born in China. These experiences inspired much of the plot for *The Joy Luck Club* as well as for Tan's second successful novel, *The Kitchen God's Wife* (1991). She followed her second novel with two works for young readers, *The Moon Lady* (1992) and *The Chinese Siamese Cat* (1994).

Tan has admitted to experiencing depression that she initially refused to treat chemically. She feared that drugs would affect her creativity, although she eventually did turn to medication to prevent deep depressive episodes. She associated her experience with that of other writers, who use creativity as a tool to channel personal trauma and angst.

Although unwilling to be categorized as an Asian-American writer, Tan nevertheless has written extensively about the problems inherent in trying to assimilate into one culture while being raised in the ideology of another. She stresses that her fiction may be enjoyed by all readers because all humans experience problems of identity and a certain amount of angst in trying to adjust to their environments. She has warned against the balkanization of her writing, as if she offers a lesson in sociology or politics rather than in fiction. She believes literature should be read as a story, with the reader deriving pleasure from language and the ability of good writing to tap into universal emotions and topics such as love, hope, motherhood, responsibility, family, and societal obligations.

Tan shares many of the frustrations she experienced as a first-generation American woman who finds that her desires conflict with the Chinese traditions practiced by her role models. Some of that tension arises simply from her telling the stories of her heritage. Her use of her grandmother's experiences in shaping the character in *The Kitchen God's Wife,* who suffers rape and humiliation as a concubine and then eventually commits suicide, alienated some of her relatives. Others saw the telling of the story as relief of secret shame too long repressed. Her own mother urged Tan to tell that story and break the silence she had to bear for years.

Tan's third novel, *The Hundred Secret Senses* (1995), features spirituality in a manner that her previous books had not. Although all the works suggest beliefs regarding a spirit world, *Senses* deals directly with Yin people, the spiritual guides who remain unseen but whose effects are very real for the novel's protagonist, Kwan. The reality remains strong enough that Kwan ends up in a mental hospital for seeing "ghosts." Tan conjured Kwan from her imagination, basing her on no particular acquaintance or family member. However, in Kwan's half-sister, Olivia, Tan embedded her own skepticism. Olivia asks existential questions with which Tan identifies, wondering, for instance, about her purpose in life. People have identified Tan with Olivia so strongly that they question whether Olivia's marriage represents that of the author. This Tan denies, but she also understands the assumption and the tendency that readers have to associate authors with their characters.

Although Tan has tried to accept the position of role model thrust upon her by teachers and various Asian-American organizations, she has expressed discomfort over that position. Particularly important to the author is that readers realize the burden writers feel when they are appointed representatives of their cultures. She wishes that all readers would recognize fiction not as a snapshot of any generalized group but rather as a very specific story that should not be compared to others regarding like cultures. Amy Tan has affirmed a desire for readers to recognize that, although her fiction does consider oppositions, it stresses even more strongly similarities and connections among humans, all of whom are caught up in the same life dramas.

See also: Fu, Wen; *The Kitchen God's Wife;* Louie, Jimmy; Louie, Winnie

References: "Amy Tan," 1998; Armstrong, 1990; Brown, 1996; Chan and Harris, 1991; Chen, 1995; Foster, 1996; Price, 1983; "The Salon," 1995; Wong, 1995

TEREZA

In Czechoslovakian writer Milan Kundera's 1984 work, *The Unbearable Lightness of Being* (*Nesnesitelná lehkost bytí*), Tereza figures prominently in the author's investigation of the dichotomies of love and sex and of fidelity and betrayal. In the love triangle formed with herself, her womanizing husband, Tomas, and his mistress and her friend, Sabina,

Tereza symbolizes both love and fidelity. She adores and, with a single exception, remains sexually faithful to Tomas, despite his open affairs with multiple women. In the world Kundera shapes, this makes her neither superior nor inferior to Tomas and Sabina. All are equal in facing life's difficult choices and then dealing with their consequences.

Tereza meets Tomas, a physician, when he visits her home village, and she later shows up on his doorstep in Prague. Following their love making, she becomes ill, requiring Tomas to care for her. This places Tereza in the role of a child, requiring a parent's care. She symbolizes a child in various other ways, as well. Tomas returns throughout the novel to a mental comparison of Tereza with Moses in the bulrushes, a foundling at the mercy of those who take her in. In addition, unlike the self-assured and provocative Sabina, Tereza remains embarrassed by her body and by common bodily functions. Her desire for modesty is a reaction against her upbringing in a household where no privacy was available. Her own mother proved very immodest, walking around naked. Finally, Tereza's devotion to her dog, Karenin, and her love for all animals compliments her childlike image, as do her frequent nightmares regarding abandonment.

Tereza's emotional immaturity does not reflect a lack of intelligence. She reads constantly, a practice she developed as a child, not only for escape but to help in her interrogation of herself and her surroundings. Like the other characters, she constantly questions life and her place in the world. Following such contemplation, she then makes choices, acts that constitute heroism in Kundera's world. For instance, although she at first leaves Prague when the Communists invade, moving to Switzerland with Tomas, she quickly returns in order to participate in antiinvasion activities. She does not join a revolutionary group but instead uses her photographic talents to snap news photos. In smuggling her film out of the country, she hopes that the outside world will understand the truth about the Communist activities in her country. Although her quest proves ironic, in that she discovers the photos may have hurt those she intended to defend, her motivations remain pure. Tereza's act helps Kundera develop a setting filled with restrictions, where characters have little personal freedom but deal with the restrictions as they can.

An important character in her own right, Tereza also acts to elucidate aspects of Tomas and Sabina. As Tomas's eventual wife, she affords him a relationship unlike those he shares with his many sexual conquests. She serves as a foil to Sabina, who does not value fidelity but instead honors betrayal as a positive idea, a sign of breaking tradition and retaining one's independence.

More than Sabina or Tomas, Tereza symbolizes the constant threat of death suffered by those who dwell in military states. She dreams often of death, seeing various images of execution. She also envisions her life after death, not as a positive state but one in which she will suffer endless humiliation. Her naming their dog Karenin, after a character in Leo Tolstoy's tragic novel, *Anna Karenina,* also links her to death. At the point of the animal's death from cancer, Tereza realizes the dog's incredible fidelity to her, an aspect that links her with the animal's innocence and devotion.

Tereza's sensitivity triggers her feelings of guilt toward Tomas. Following Karenin's death on the farm collective where they have moved, she realizes the importance of Tomas having returned to Prague to be with her. Because he would not follow the edicts of the Communist regime, he sacrificed the freedom to practice medicine, becoming a window washer at the command of the authorities. Tereza understands he could still be practicing medicine had she agreed to stay abroad. When she voices this thought with regret, Tomas replies that he does not miss practicing medicine; he at last feels free.

Tereza then experiences another of Kundera's dichotomies, the coexistence of both sadness and happiness. True to her connection to death, she understands the sadness to mean that she and Tomas are nearing the end of their journey together. Even so, the happiness exists due to their union. Because that union remained of utmost importance to Tereza, she finds at last the contentment that had previously eluded her.

See also: Kundera, Milan; Sabina; Tomas; *The Unbearable Lightness of Being*
References: Catalano, 1995; Lippi, 1984; Misurella, 1993

TESS OF THE D'URBERVILLES

Thomas Hardy's philosophical realism novel, *Tess of the d'Urbervilles* (1891), was one of several works that caused critics to deem Hardy's fiction too realistic in its confrontation with sexuality and the conflicts caused by faith. His Victorian Age culture did not embrace the novel's accusations against its practice of legal and social injustice. The book's protagonist, Tess Durbeyfield, symbolizes the English working class and the vulnerability of that group to mistreatment by members of the monied classes. Although Tess falls victim to the temptations of sex outside marriage, Hardy makes clear that she should not bear the blame for her sins. That blame should fall squarely on the shoulders of the two men in her life: Alec d'Urberville, her betrayer, and Angel Clare, her unsupportive husband.

Tess first sees Angel from afar as she participates as a young girl in a peasant celebration. His name becomes an ironic symbol, because Tess believes him to be superior to other young men, but he eventually proves himself no guardian angel. When Tess's father discovers that the Durbeyfield family may be descendants of the wealthy aristocratic family bearing the name d'Urberville, he foolishly decides that work is beneath him. He sends Tess away to earn the Durbeyfields' living, attaching her to a family of Stoke-d'Urbervilles at a nearby village in the hopes that they will embrace her as a fellow aristocrat. Mrs. Durbeyfield does nothing to protect her daughter. She only hopes that Tess will marry a wealthy "relative," thereby securing the family's financial future.

Ironically, the Stoke-d'Urbervilles retain no traceable connection to the aristocracy to which Tess's father aspires; they merely assume the title because no one else in the area wants it. This act foreshadows the common vulgarity of Alec d'Urberville, the family's son, who will act in a reprehensible manner by seducing the innocent Tess. He keeps secret Tess's identity as a "blood relation" from his blind mother, who believes her to be simply another working girl. Mrs. d'Urberville assigns Tess to tend the chickens, hardly the elevated position Mr. Durbeyfield had in mind for his daughter. Although Tess resists Alec's early efforts at eliciting sex from her, eventually she gives in to him. Alec seduces Tess with no intention of marrying her.

When Tess returns home pregnant, her father's only concern is for the support of his family, a responsibility with which he again burdens his daughter. Although Tess's mother worries that Alec will not marry Tess, she shows no real concern for her daughter's state of mind. Tess must travel about working in order to prevent Alec's finding her and using her for continued sexual release. Eventually Tess gives birth to Alec's child, who dies.

Determined to begin a new life and never to marry due to her past disgrace, Tess leaves home again to work at a dairy farm. She finds happiness and contentment there until the young pastor's son, Angel Clare, who caught her attention so many months before, takes an interest in her. Farming is the field Angel chooses for his vocation, having rejected the life of a pastor along with his father's strong religious faith. This explains his frequent presence at the farm, where he studies dairy production. His attraction for Tess grows, and he wishes to begin a romance. Knowing that she should not marry due to her culture's viewpoint regarding her scandalous past, Tess resists Angel's intentions despite her love and admiration for him. She admires his intellectual approach to life, which allows Hardy to stress his theme of the importance of logic over religious faith. Although custom prohibited a minister's son from marrying a dairy maid, Angel pursues what most people in the Victorian Age would consider a forbidden love. He eventually asks Tess to marry him.

Tess at first resists, urging Angel to ask any one of the other dairy maids, all of whom love him. But Angel remains most strongly attracted to Tess's intense beauty and heightened sexuality. He believes Tess to be completely innocent, due to her demure manner. She at last gives in to Angel's intense pressure to marry but decides she must tell him of her past. On the eve of the wedding, she slips a note under his door explaining her encounter with Alec and the baby that resulted. Angel's affection toward her on the following day convinces Tess of his loving nature; he does indeed seem an angel, willing to accept any conflict in order to marry Tess. However, Tess quickly figures out that Angel never read the letter. When she again tries to confess her past, Angel prevents it. Her repeated attempts to divulge her past parallel his repeated attempts to win her heart. Whereas Tess complies with Angel's wishes, submitting to his desire, he silences her and prevents her confession.

When Angel at last understands Tess's past sins, he destroys her emotionally. He proclaims her a sinner and unfit to be his wife. This action establishes Angel as a hypocrite. He has constantly criticized the tendency of individuals to judge one another, proclaiming the idea of religion and its ideology regarding sin to be harmful and incorrect. Thus, Angel Clare, who supposedly separates himself from the idea of sin, ironically denounces Tess, a loving woman of purity and goodness, for past acts over which she had little control.

Angel's actions cause a predictable reaction in Tess. She eventually ends up in the treacherous arms of Alec d'Urberville, after repeatedly trying to reach her husband and convince him of her love. She has no way of knowing that Angel has left the country, thus deserting Tess at her most vulnerable moment. When Angel departs England to pursue his agricultural studies, Tess again falls under Alec's spell, particularly when Alec claims to have converted to Christianity. He actually blames Tess for his most recent obsession with her physical charms. Overburdened with guilt, Tess submits to Alec's request to renew their sexual relationship.

When Angel at last reads a letter from Tess, the time for her rescue has passed. After deciding he still loves his wife, Angel seeks Tess out, only to discover her with Alec. Just as before, Angel leaves Tess in the arms of her oppressor. She can no longer tolerate this position, and she stabs Alec.

The novel's tragic ending supplies an ironic statement regarding justice. English written law requires the death penalty for Tess, yet its moral law forgives the sins of a despicable aristocrat and a false aristocrat at that, merely because of his social station. Not only does Alec cause Tess's early spiritual death, but he also causes her literal death. In the distressing conclusion, Tess welcomes her execution as the only route to freedom. She and Angel do succeed in sharing a few loving days prior to her capture, as he at last seeks grace in his own forgiveness of Tess.

In this novel Hardy takes to task the hypocritical Victorian society in which he lived, a culture that attempted and failed to legislate morality. His age did not kindly receive the novelist's suggestion that certain human instincts can never be overcome.

See also: The Age of Innocence; Clare, Angel; d'Urberville, Alec; Durbeyfield, Tess; *Ethan Frome;* Forbidden Love; Hardy, Thomas; Victorian Age; Violence

References: Bullen, 1997; Pettit, 1994; Sutherland, 1989; Widdowson, 1993

THACKERAY, WILLIAM MAKEPEACE

William Makepeace Thackeray, born in Calcutta to Anglo-Indian parents, moved to England in 1817, where he would later become a critical figure in the development of the novel. Educated as a child at private schools, he attended Charterhouse from 1822 to 1828. He later based the fictional "Slaughterhouse" and "Grey Friars" of his novels on that institution. An advocate of energetic living during his two years at Trinity College, Cambridge, Thackeray lost a good deal of money gambling at cards and departed in 1830 with no degree. During an 1829 visit to Paris, Thackeray became enthralled with that city, and travel in Germany the following year allowed him to meet the great Johann Wolfgang von Goethe. He later studied law in London and worked as Paris correspondent for the *National Standard,* a publication that closed in 1834. The 1833 Indian bank failures claimed most of Thackeray's inheritance, prompting him to plan his career as a painter.

Thackeray studied art in both London and Paris and in 1836 published a book of lithographic caricatures of a ballet. He served briefly as Paris correspondent for *The Constitutional,* a publication established by his stepfather. Although the publication quickly closed, his employment allowed him to marry Isabella Shawe. The daughter of an expatriate Anglo-Irish family, Isabella developed mental problems that would eventually doom her to institutionalization.

Thackeray and Isabella had three daughters following their return to London. Anne, their firstborn, would later become known as the novelist Anne Thackeray Ritchie. Although the second daughter, born in 1838, died, a third daughter, Harriet Marian, arrived in 1840. Called "Minny," this daughter later married Sir Leslie Stephen, father with his second wife of English writer Virginia Woolf. Isabella's insanity led to her confinement in 1840, and Thackeray had to write reviews, comic sketches, parodies, and satires for various periodicals, including *Fraser's Magazine* and *Punch,* in order to support his family. His pieces gained him much fame, and *Barry Lyndon,* his first real novel, appeared as a serial in *Fraser's* in 1844. Thackeray followed this success with three travel books and began to enjoy a growing reputation as a writer.

The successful *Book of Snobs* (1846–1847) parodied the early Victorian Age class consciousness with which he dealt daily; this topic remained a strong component of much of Thackeray's writing. As his first major novel, *Vanity Fair* (1847–1848) appeared in monthly installments, a form that had been repopularized by Charles Dickens. Thackeray subtitled his book *A Novel without a Hero* and, remaining true to his word, developed characterizations of a group including fools and knaves, producing perhaps the most famous fictional female scoundrel in his protagonist, Becky Sharp. His *The History of Pendennis* (1848–1850), a semiautobiographical initiation/coming-of-age story, followed his first novel's success. His unhappiness following the end of a platonic relationship with Jane Brookfield, the wife of a friend, which she dissolved in 1851, is reflected in the melancholy tone of *The History of Henry Esmond* (1852). Critics judge this the most well-planned of his novels, although *Vanity Fair* remains his most popular.

Thackeray toured the United States from 1852 to 1853, presenting a series of lectures based on his book *The English Humorists of the Eighteenth Century* (1853). He produced several other works, including *The Rose and the Ring* (1855), the last and, according to critics, the best of a series of six Christmas books; *The Four Georges,* which provided the basis for lectures during a second tour of the States in 1855–1856 and was published in 1860; and *The Virginians* (1857–1859), a historical novel that followed the eighteenth-century Esmond family, first introduced in *The History of Henry Esmond*. In 1859, Thackeray became the first editor of a monthly literary journal entitled *The Cornhill Magazine.* He resigned the post in 1862 due to chronic ill health.

Thackeray would publish a few additional works in *The Cornhill Magazine,* including a short novel, *Lovel the Widower* (1860); a collection of essays, *The Roundabout Papers* (1860–1863); and his final complete novel, *The Adventures of Philip* (1861–1862). His death in 1863 on Christmas Eve left a final novel, *Denis Duval,* unfinished, but most critics feel that, like other of Thackeray's late works, it would have added little to his literary legacy.

William Makepeace Thackeray's reputation is based on *Vanity Fair,* an enduringly popular work for decades following his death. His witty development of stereotypes, his jovially acerbic view of Victorian society, and his invitation to readers to spot themselves among the crowd at the carnival of vanity continue to attract new devotees.

See also: A Handful of Dust; Vanity Fair
References: Budick, 1996; Bullen, 1997; Clarke, 1995; Flint, 1996; Harden, 1996; Hawes, 1993; Ousby, 1988; Reed, 1995; Shillingsburg, 1994

THEIR EYES WERE WATCHING GOD

Zora Neale Hurston's 1937 novel, *Their Eyes Were Watching God,* features a half-white, half-black female protagonist, Janie Crawford Killicks Starks Woods. Through Janie, Hurston creates a story of abuse, survival, and final fulfillment of her character's romantic expectations. The author's characters and setting reflect on Hurston's upbringing in an all-black town in Florida, where her father served as mayor. Hurston's use of dialect and frequent images of racial and societal discrimination contribute to layered images of societal and cultural abuse and violence appropriate to the various social strata that are part of Janie's individual situation. Her poetic rendering of Janie's thoughts about life offers the reader an enriched reading experience. Natural imagery abounds, from repetitive references to trees representing knowledge, life, sexual reproduction, and security to the use of seasons in describing characters' personalities. Time references remain prominent as Janie's life moves forward yet continually circles back on itself as she repeatedly seeks love.

The story begins as Janie returns to the town that her deceased second husband had helped build. Her neighbors believe her to have been betrayed by the younger man, Tea Cake, who had openly courted Janie and with whom she had disappeared. Janie relates her story to a friend, Pheoby. The product of the rape of her black mother by a white man, Janie's beauty and long black hair draw much attention. As a teenager, she begins an exciting emotional probe of her desires and dreams, only to be squelched by her practical grandmother, who arranges a patriarchal marriage for her to an older man. Logan Killicks wants literally to harness Janie to a plow, using her much as he would a beast of burden. This attitude thoroughly destroys Janie's hopes for the love she believed would accompany marriage.

When the intriguing young Joe Starks appears and offers to carry her away to a better life, Janie agrees. Although her relationship with Joe seems an improvement over that with Logan, he eventually physically and emotionally abuses Janie, working to destroy her sense of independence. His accusations against her are supported by members of their community. Joe misinterprets Janie's attempts to express herself as betrayal, and he comes to believe that she wants to poison him. Hurston's ample use of the donning and shedding of garments to symbolize role changes appears in Joe's jealous demand that Janie wear a scarf to cover the beauty of which she is so proud. When he dies, her removal of the scarf symbolizes her independent state, achievable only outside marriage.

Janie still hopes for love, and she cannot resist the romance offered by Vergible "Tea Cake" Woods. His youth and society's attitude toward what it views as a mismatch don't deter Janie in her quest for a satisfying relationship. Following their marriage, Janie and Tea Cake work side by side while harvesting, a symbol of equity between the genders that Janie has never experienced. However, even Tea Cake becomes abusive, once whipping Janie in order to relieve his own jealousy and fear of desertion by his wife. The positives outweigh the negatives in this relationship, and Tea Cake eventually saves Janie from a rabid dog during a hurricane and flood. He contracts rabies from the dog, and in a heartrending conclusion to their relationship, Janie must shoot Tea Cake in self-defense as he attacks her in his irrational, diseased state. That moment seems the "meanest" of all eternity to the woman so quickly separated from the man who had given her a chance at "loving service."

Janie is put on trial and acquitted. She returns home a triumphant survivor of spousal abuse, societal rejection, and racial discrimination.

See also: The Black Experience in America, 1600–1945; *The Good Earth;* Hurston, Zora Neale; Patriarchal Marriage; Quest; Violence; Woods, Janie Crawford Killicks Starks

References: Carr, 1987; Davidson, 1995; Gilbert and Gubar, 1996g; Graham et al., 1989; Hart, 1995; Henderson and McManus, 1985; Labovitz, 1986; LeSeur, 1995; Radway, 1991; Schleiner, 1994; Travitsky, 1990

THE THORN BIRDS

In *The Thorn Birds* (1977), Colleen McCullough fashions her novel around a forbidden love. The love of Father Ralph de Bricassart for Meghann (Meggie) Cleary begins when the ten-year-old girl arrives in Australia. Father Ralph is twenty-eight. But neither the differences in their ages nor his vow of celibacy and devotion to the Catholic Church defeat a love that lasts for the remainder of both their lives. By focusing on the conflict caused by Ralph's devotion to the church, McCullough emphasizes love's ability to meet and overcome even the most difficult of obstacles.

Long before readers meet Ralph, they come to know Meggie Cleary in her New Zealand surroundings as a spirited, intelligent, vulnerable girl who is easily injured by the harsh nature of her environment. She suffers from the taunts of her own brothers as well as from the pain and shame caused by her beatings at the hands of the local nuns, who serve as her instructors. But she also shows a strength in facing such physical and emotional challenges that will enable her to embrace the difficulties she encounters later in life. Those difficulties include not only her impossible love for Ralph but also her relationship with her mother, Fiona (Fee) Cleary. Although Meggie seems destined to repeat many of her mother's errors, she works to break free from that pattern of self-destruction suffered by a number of women prior to World War I. In searching for her place within a patriarchal culture, Meggie finds she must battle negative attitudes toward women as weak, passive creatures. One reason she so adores Father Ralph is for his feminine virtues; he nurtures when other authority figures in her life scold and ridicule.

As Meggie says at one point in the novel, all the men she loves leave her in the end. This leaving begins with her beloved brother Frank's departure from the largely male family. Meggie faces her first great unsolvable conflict in having to deal with Frank's hatred for their father, Paddy, whom Meggie dearly loves. The cause for this conflict foreshadows events in Meggie's future that eventually help her to reach an emotional equilibrium with her mother. Both of these women must forgo a relationship with the men they love to form basically loveless relationships with others. Meggie discovers that her mother first loved a man she could never marry; with him, she conceived Frank. Even though she belonged to an elevated social class, Fee was forced by her father to marry Paddy, a man of lower social standing, who adopts young Frank. This creates an unresolved tension between Frank and Paddy that affects the entire Cleary family. McCullough uses this plot line to reflect on the position of women at the turn of the century.

They had to find a male to care for them, and they had to pledge allegiance to that male, like it or not. This emphasis on everything male causes Fee's disdainful attitude toward her own daughter, Meggie, whom she snubs in favor of her many sons. Fee realizes through experience Meggie's unimportance in a patriarchal world.

The Clearys move to Australia at the invitation of Paddy's sister, Mary Carson, to run her ranch, Drogheda. Over the next ten years, Meggie falls deeply in love with Father Ralph, causing jealousy in her aged aunt, who remains obsessed with the handsome young priest. Mary realizes that Ralph's ambition and destiny lie within the high offices of the Catholic Church. She knows, as Meggie later learns, that Ralph will never sacrifice those ambitions for fleshly love. She wills the ranch to the church, with Ralph as executor, even though the large Cleary clan should by right inherit it. Leaving a large amount of money in trust for the Clearys, the vengeful Mary cements Ralph's lifelong relationship with Meggie, who represents the love he cannot have. But Mary's financial gift to the church, contingent upon Ralph's management, secures his position as a rising star within its hierarchy.

While Ralph leaves Australia and remains busily engaged in securing first the title of bishop and later that of cardinal, Meggie eventually marries Luke O'Neill. She does so mainly because of his physical resemblance to Ralph, as well as because marriage is the main option for women of her era. She finds herself caught up in a patriarchal marriage, without a penny from her generous allowance or a bit of love and affection granted her by Luke. Her only chance for emotional survival is children, but her daughter Justine brings her little joy. Meggie begins a journey with Justine down the same emotional track traced by Fiona so many years before with Meggie. Mother and daughter do not get along, each taking the other for granted.

When Ralph and Meggie at last consummate the love they have long admitted for one another, Meggie conceives a son. She also learns that, unlike her rough, near-violent experiences with Luke, sex with Ralph leaves her feeling positively about herself; she is no longer simply a sexual object. Her subsequent manipulation of Luke into sleeping with her one last time allows her baby legitimacy and also at last allows Meggie an active role in the life that others continually shape

for her. When Fee later guesses that Meggie's son, Dane, belongs to Father Ralph, the two women at last can reach an understanding through their shared experiences.

Meggie confesses to Fee that Ralph at last found her, but because she realized he would never leave the church, she decided to have Ralph's baby. Through Dane, she could possess at least a part of his father. At this point Fee divulges her secret past with Frank's father, a man much older than she was and an important politician. Like the love shared by Meggie and Ralph, that shared by Fee and her lover could never be realized through marriage, but Fee was left a baby to love and cherish. That Frank subsequently left the family, disappeared for years, served a prison sentence, and returned home a totally broken man should act as a cautionary tale for Meggie. But with the peculiar blindness love brings, she does not anticipate the tragedy in Dane's future.

This scene of shared "confessions" by the two women further perpetuates McCullough's theme of gender inequity. For women, the family remained their only "approved" activity. The forbidden love in which both of these women engaged marked them as undesirables; thus, Fee had to be "married off" to a man she did not love. But by gaining babies from their loves, the women were able to use their inherent reproductive powers to retain a bit of the love the world denied them.

Fee's loss of Paddy just when she realized her love for him makes her more compassionate, allowing her to interact with Meggie at a time when Meggie needs attention. Fee intercedes with Justine, who does all in her power to aggravate her mother. Ironically, Fee helps resolve the conflicts between Meggie and her daughter, even though she could not do the same with her own daughter at that age. McCullough stresses the redemptive power of love that, although disappointed in some areas, may flourish in others.

Meggie vows never to reveal to Ralph that Dane is his son. The irony of Ralph's blindness to this fact that Fee guessed immediately grows as Dane chooses to become a priest. He assumes both the literal and figurative mantle of his father. Ralph loves Dane dearly and helps the handsome young man complete his training for the priesthood, doting on him as if he was his own. When Dane drowns while attempting to rescue some women, Ralph breaks down beneath the burden of his love for the young man. His sorrow increases severalfold when Meggie reveals at last to Ralph that Dane was his genetic son as well as his spiritual one.

When Dane loses his life to the ocean, an ironic symbolism may be seen in water's traditional religious association with baptism, cleansing, and rebirth. His death evokes the age-old edict that sons will pay for the sins of their fathers.

In the novel's conclusion, McCullough again emphasizes the redemptive power of love. After the loss of Dane, Meggie realizes how she abuses Justine. The two are able, in this third generation of women, to at last come to terms with problems that have long haunted the family. With Ralph's death, Meggie's desertion by the men she has loved is complete. But with his death comes an epiphany that helps Meggie become a dynamic character. She identifies with the thorn bird mentioned in the novel's title, who commits suicide by impaling itself on a thorn. Such imagery remains grim, but in the bird's beautiful death song, which even God smiles upon, rests its redemption. Meggie knows that she has searched out this thorn of love herself and that her impalement was a volitional act. In this realization, she achieves a sense of self-awareness that causes her attitude toward Justine and the future to change.

See also: Cleary, Meghann (Meggie); de Bricassart, Father Ralph; Forbidden Love; Violence
References: Bridgwood, 1986; Kaplan, 1986

TO KNOW A WOMAN

To Know a Woman (1989, translated in 1991) is typical of Amos Oz novels in its close study of an individual, the protagonist Yoel Ravid, rather than of a group. Yoel personifies the weakness and fragility of human nature that Oz's fiction emphasizes. The author's passion for the family unit as the center of his characters' experiences is evidenced in a plot encompassing Yoel; his dead wife, Ivria Ravid; their daughter Netta; his mother, Lisa; and his mother-in-law Avigail. The story also includes Yoel's brother-in-law, Nakdimon, and two couples, one a man and wife and one a sister and brother who live next door to Yoel. In addition, Yoel gained a professional "family," made up of two men nicknamed the Acrobat and Le Patron, through his work as an Israeli intelligence officer; Yoel refers to Le Patron occasionally as his brother. All these characters suffer from certain frailties, but from their varieties of weakness and conflict Oz weaves a rich and satis-

fying interrogation of ideas regarding dependence, love, and devotion.

Yoel Ravid negotiates enormous inner conflict, searching for impossible solutions to issues so complex and questions so difficult that he cannot even formulate them. Much of the details of Yoel's life are revealed through flashbacks to times preceding Ivria's death. The reader learns that the two met by accident as she went into her father's fruit fields in Metullah to turn off the irrigation. Involved in an orienteering exercise during a training course for Israeli service section commanders, Yoel lost his way and hid in the field. When Ivria literally tripped over him in the dark, she asked him not to rape her, and he asked her not to alert others to his presence. Then on impulse, the two tangled in a wild love making that they repeated during subsequent clandestine meetings in the field, until Yoel asked Ivria to marry him. Her presence in the fields, sustained by water imported to transform the dry climate of Israel, symbolizes Ivria's ability to nurture Yoel's potential emotional growth. The fact that Yoel was lost in the field and discovers himself again with Ivria, foreshadows his future dependency on her as his life's central force. Where his profession offers a false idea of artificial order, Ivria represents the better course about life, in which order should not be so highly prioritized. Yoel can lose control in a positive way early in his relationship with Ivria in a manner he remains unable to duplicate later in life.

In the first few paragraphs, Oz introduces a symbol of Yoel's situation in a figurine that Yoel discovers when he investigates the possibility of renting a house. The owner has left behind the figure of a predatory feline leaping into the air, three of its paws poised in flight above its base. The figurine represents the mystery involved with Yoel's own attempts to "balance" and reorient himself following Ivria's death. He constantly returns to his contemplation of the figure that displays no apparent point of attachment. At times he feels driven to distraction by his lack of understanding of the figure and, by extension, of his own support system. He also constantly complains of his tired eyes, symbolizing his lack of internal vision. When he longs for the focus he seems to have lost, he actually longs for the knowledge that self-awareness would bring.

Much of Yoel's energy is expended in his attempt to develop a sound relationship with

Netta, a mild epileptic. Her illness represented the main conflict between Yoel and Ivria. Ivria irrationally placed the blame for Netta's illness on Yoel's long absences and what she perceived to be his withdrawal of emotional support for the family. At other times, she would not even admit to Netta's illness, disposing during Yoel's absence of the drugs necessary for their daughter's medical treatment. Although Yoel had been close to Netta during her childhood, Ivria drove an emotional wedge between the two. As a result, when Netta begins to mature, Yoel never touches or confides in her. With his caretaker mentality, Yoel cannot bring himself to share his own hopes and desires with his daughter. He continues to see her as a dependent child despite a maturity made apparent when she receives a summons to report for national service.

Oz also emphasizes the importance of literature throughout the novel, allowing the three Ravids' various reading preference to represent their characters. Shortly before her death, Ivria had begun a master's thesis on the Brontë sisters and their brother. Titling her work "Shame in the Attic," she researched facts regarding the questionable nature of the Brontë siblings' relationships. Her choice of subject matter acts as a metaphor for her own dysfunctional family. Emily Brontë's work, *Wuthering Heights* (1847), also allows Oz to better illuminate Yoel's personality. For Yoel, the ineffectual Edgar Linton, rather than the dynamic Heathcliff, holds his interest. Edgar even appears to Yoel in a dream, wearing glasses that resemble Ivria's. Netta, of the younger generation, reads Israeli poets, whereas Yoel reads Virginia Woolf's *Mrs. Dalloway* (1925). As an object that he believes he left behind during a job in Helsinki, that book represents his past. He had to depart Helsinki hurriedly when he was recalled to Jerusalem to learn of Ivria's accidental death by electrocution. Eventually Yoel finds the book carefully packed away where he had left it with his belongings, hinting that his longing for things past might be satisfied by a closer examination of the present.

Yoel's compulsive personality and desire for order is revealed through his exaggerated house-cleaning and care of his yard. Following his retirement from the service to care for his family of women, he focuses on keeping material things in order, although his life remains in chaos. Slowly his attitude toward women as children who need the care of an authority figure rather than the love of a husband, father, or lover becomes clear. His neighbor and carnal partner, Annemarie, points this out to Yoel, saying he has never understood the meaning of the word *woman*.

Paralleling Yoel's conflict at home is the conflict he feels when Le Patron asks him to return to the service for one final mission. The source he had previously contacted in Helsinki will speak only with him. When Yoel refuses to return from retirement, mainly because he feels a duty to care for Netta and the two grandmothers, the Acrobat substitutes for him in the mission. Yoel reads of the Acrobat's death in the papers, and he suffers from a new guilt for having left his former comrade to be killed in his stead.

When Netta forms a friendship with Duby Krantz, Yoel feels ambivalent toward the young man. Although he had always hoped for a romantic relationship for Netta, Duby is not what Yoel had imagined. It is through Duby, however, that Yoel receives some insight into his problem through their discussion of the mysteriously balanced cat figurine. Duby's expertise in engineering prompts Yoel to ask his opinion as to why the leaping cat does not fall forward. Duby speaks to the matter of questions, such as those Yoel has been asking, when he remarks that Yoel's question is incorrect. He should ask instead, where is the figure's center of gravity? This question represents that unformulated question Yoel had sought in vain to ask about himself. When he examines himself to locate his own center of gravity, he understands that Ivria had played that role. With her demise, he must redefine himself, accept the chaos that surrounds him, and simply perform in the best way possible.

He finds that best way in volunteer work at a local hospital, where patients and medical professionals alike believe in the healing powers of Yoel's hands. It is in this truth of his usefulness to others that Yoel finds a meaning for life. Netta moves in with her boyfriend, Annemarie moves away, and Yoel restructures his existence in order to survive in his society.

See also: Oz, Amos; Ravid, Ivria; Ravid, Yoel
References: Balaban, 1990; Balaban, 1993; Fuchs, 1984; Grossman, 1986; Oz, 1993; Price, 1995; Wachtel, 1991

TO SIR, WITH LOVE

As in most novels incorporating the themes of love and romance, the lovers in Edward R.

Sidney Poitier played protagonist Rick Braithwaite in the 1967 film version of Edward R. Braithwaite's 1959 novel of race and redemption, To Sir, with Love. *(Photofest)*

Braithwaite's *To Sir, with Love* (1959) must overcome conflict, both internal and external. In this autobiographical story, the male protagonist, Rick Braithwaite, and his love, Gillian Blanchard, form a biracial couple. Both are British; Gillian is a native of England, whereas Rick comes from British Guiana. Together they face the prejudice inflicted on them due to Rick's black skin.

Although other themes exist in the novel, such as the problems inherent in teaching children born into the poverty of London's East End, racism permeates almost every scene. Rick's frustration over not being able to find a job in his chosen profession as an engineer is made quite clear. The only reason he accepts a teaching position is because his race prevents his finding other employment. He recalls one interview in which he was told that, although eminently qualified, he would not be hired for the position because it involved supervision of whites. As he takes over the class at Greenslade Secondary School, he must deal with racist remarks from his peers as well as from students. Not only does the low level of student discipline and learning present a chal-

lenge, but his students' ignorance about blacks must be overcome.

The overall tone of the novel remains optimistic, however. Written at a time when education was still believed to be the solution to all ills, *To Sir, with Love* evinces a confidence that all of the students will achieve better lives through the understanding their school experience allows. Innocence and naïveté still have a place in the public arena, and Rick is shocked when the students use profanity or make sexual innuendoes. He views these teenagers preparing to graduate, referred to by all of the novel's adults as "children," as possessing still innocent minds that he might help to shape.

Braithwaite presents an interesting passage early on in which he compares American racism to that of the English. Although he abhors racism in any degree, he feels that the American open acknowledgment of racism is preferable to English attitudes. In America the situation occasionally spurs acts of violence or protest, but those acts seem to lead to incremental changes that gradually improve the situation for blacks. In

England, however, racism is not openly admitted. Instead, it remains insidious, ever present but not acknowledged. This makes its confrontation more difficult. However, similarities exist between the English attitude toward blacks and that found in the southern United States. In both places, a black individual might be embraced by a white family, but as a group, blacks are much hated and seen as a threat to society. Thus, although Rick is eventually accepted, warily, by the "family" of students in his classroom, he constantly faces challenges regarding his race by the community. Rick's problems escalate when he becomes the focus of a schoolgirl crush on the part of one white student, Pamela Dare. Eventually this problem is solved, and with a maturity reflecting the benefit of her education, Pamela becomes the success story of Rick's short teaching career.

Gradually, Rick wins the confidence of his students, beginning in earnest their education in life skills. He takes them to museums and to watch the Harlem Globe Trotters. Viewing the black American basketball players allows a more open discussion of race in class, and Rick feels hopeful that education will overcome prejudice.

In an ironic turn, Gillian, supposedly educated and a teacher herself, also becomes a victim of racism due to her own ignorance. Furious over the disrespectful treatment of herself and Rick at a restaurant, she leaves the place and vents her anger on Rick for not having responded in some manner to the obviously racist treatment. Gillian experiences a sad epiphany, informing Rick that although she has heard of experiences like the one in the restaurant, she had never thought of it happening to her. The strength of her love for Rick allows her to persevere in the face of attitudes that mark their relationship as one of forbidden love. Even her parents protest the idea of her marrying Rick, urging both of them to consider the difficulties that will exist for their children.

Rick's reply to Gillian's father that they will be able to handle the negative attitudes toward their marriage and children seems highly ironic in the face of the next incident at school. When a racially mixed student in Rick's class loses a family member, the students' prejudice becomes chillingly real. This student is popular with his peers, who immediately agree, in spite of their poverty, to collect money for funeral flowers. Yet they refuse to go to deliver the flowers to their friend's

home on the occasion of his mother's death, stating that they simply cannot be seen approaching the house of a racially mixed couple. When Pamela finally volunteers to take the flowers after no one else will, Rick loses the joy he has felt over all the progress he has made with his students. However, in the novel's climactic scene, the class members redeem themselves by appearing en masse at the student's home after all.

The autobiographical aspects of the novel add a realistic bent to the story that convinces readers to accept racism's threat to romance that Braithwaite emphasizes. Even in an era when innocence has abandoned the classroom and fewer voices than ever support the idea that education liberates a closed mind, *To Sir, with Love* remains a popular novel.

See also: Blanchard, Gillian; Braithwaite, Edward R. (Ted); Braithwaite, Rick; Dare, Pamela; Forbidden Love

References: Fraiman, 1993; Herdeck, 1979; Ousby, 1988

TOLSTOY, COUNT LEO

Leo Tolstoy, destined to become one of the greatest fiction writers of all time, was born the son of a nobleman on September 9, 1828. The family estate, Yasnaya Polyana, was located south of Moscow. Orphaned by the time he was nine, Tolstoy gained an education through French and German tutors. He enrolled at Kazan University at the age of sixteen, where he studied Oriental languages and law. His own study of the writings of French philosopher Jean-Jacques Rousseau made him dissatisfied with his formal studies and caused him to leave university in 1847. Tolstoy's great interest in the plight of Russia's poor led him to make a futile attempt to improve the condition of the serfs on his own estate. Following his lack of success, he dabbled in the lifestyle of Moscow's high society, noting the squandering of resources and energy that seemed an accepted aspect of the wealthy, privileged life. He recorded his observations in a diary in which he swore to execute social reform.

Tolstoy came into contact with Cossacks after joining his brother's military regiment in 1852. His experiences surfaced in his short novel, *The Cossacks* (1863), in which he offered a realistic comparison of the sophisticated Moscow socialite to the more natural and, in his view, admirable, Cossack. While continuing his army service in the

Leo Tolstoy, shown in a ca. 1897 photograph, became one of the greatest fiction writers of all time. (Library of Congress)

artillery, Tolstoy wrote *Childhood* (1852), a novel based on his own life. Two additional novels, *Boyhood* (1854) and *Youth* (1856), both drawing on his memories, extended his story and without sentimentality sketched universal incidents important to all young men. Along with *Sevastopol Stories* (1855–1856), a book based on Tolstoy's experience fighting in the Crimean War, these early works gained fame for Tolstoy. In each novel, he emphasizes the natural nobility of the common person as worth more than the so-called aristocracy of birth that he himself enjoyed.

Tolstoy's interest in the peasant class continued when he returned to Saint Petersburg. Always interested in social reform, he traveled abroad and visited elementary schools in France and Germany. Using what he learned from those visits, he established a village school on his own estate that adopted instructional methods foreshadowing those to be developed in twentieth-century progressive education. He married eighteen-year-old Sofya Anderyevna Bers, a member of the Moscow elite, in 1862. The two raised an enormous family consisting of nineteen children. In addition to participating in family life as a devoted father and managing his estate, Tolstoy produced his two greatest works, *War and Peace*

(1865–1869) and *Anna Karenina* (1875–1877). Considered the greatest epic ever of Russian life, *War and Peace* focuses on the period between 1805 and 1815, during the Napoleonic invasion. A tremendous work, the novel contains more than five hundred characters and portrays historical battles and personalities. The political and social movements of the day frame a tale of five different families, all members of the aristocracy. An example of mastery in characterization, the novel renders realistically both the public and private lives of its many subjects, offering psychological insight into each based on Tolstoy's keen observation of the details of human existence. In *Anna Karenina,* Tolstoy emphasizes many of his own major concerns through its main character, Konstantin Levin, a landed aristocrat and social reformer like Tolstoy. Judged to have more artistic unity than the lengthier *War and Peace, Anna Karenina* has been labeled one of the finest psychological novels ever written. Tolstoy investigates Saint Petersburg high society in the 1860s, revealing the degradation it causes for the adulterous Anna Karenina. The rendering of the novel's male characters remains harsh, with depictions of all except Levin as womanizers, thieves, simpletons, religious zealots, and opportunists representing the politically powerful. Levin suffers the same torments over social inequities as did Tolstoy. Like the author, Levin investigates questions regarding spirituality and the meaning of life but never finds satisfying answers to those questions.

Tolstoy's harsh self-judgment grew in later life as he investigated his growing spiritual conflict in *Confession* (1882). He could not excuse himself for his membership in a class that led a basically selfish and unsatisfying existence at the expense of the poorer class. His quest for morality led him to write essays that blasted Russia's social inequity and power-hungry autocrats, along with its coercive government and church authorities. His 1898 work *What Is Art?* indicted almost all contemporary art, including his own writings. The fact that his works remained inaccessible to the masses infuriated him and rendered them useless in his mind. His translated works brought pilgrims from all over the world to Yasnaya Polyana in hopes of receiving advice from a great author who denigrated his own works.

Tolstoy again produced fiction in a collection of brief tales with peasant settings titled *Stories for the People* (1884–1885). Later widely anthologized, selections focusing on spiritual conversion before death included *The Death of Ivan Ilyich* (1886) and *Master and Man* (1895). He chose the topic of loveless marriage for the novel *The Kreutzer Sonata* (1889) and produced in his drama *The Power of Darkness* (1889) a peasant tragedy of lust and violence. His final novel, *Resurrection* (1899–1900), tells the story of a conscience-stricken nobleman. In this novel, Tolstoy predicted his own end, for he became increasingly tormented by the obvious conflict between his ideals and the reality of his life. He attempted to give up his material possessions, a move his wife did not support, and they quarreled often over his ideology. Story has it that she rescued many of his works that Tolstoy tried to destroy, although he succeeded in destroying others. At the age of eighty-two, Tolstoy left home in an attempt to travel by rail car toward Siberia. He died from illness three days later on November 20, 1910, at a railway station.

In his many fictional studies, Leo Tolstoy left a rich legacy of social discontent and considerations of the powerful moral forces present in all human lives. Although he died dissatisfied and disillusioned with his own efforts to improve the world, reading audiences everywhere continue to benefit from those same efforts.

See also: *Anna Karenina; Doctor Zhivago;* Levin, Konstantin Dmitrievitch; Pasternak, Boris; War
References: Bayley, 1968; Bychkov, 1970; Christian, 1978; McMillin, 1990; Tolstoy, 1953

TOM JONES

Henry Fielding's classic romance of human nature, *The History of Tom Jones, a Foundling* (1749), has become a hallmark of English literature. Its indomitable title character, Tom Jones, represents the irrepressible nature of the human spirit as envisioned in Fielding's eighteenth-century culture. Although at times a knave, a womanizer, and a ne'er-do-well, Tom proved the eighteenth-century belief in the natural good and in the fact that, if they are encouraged, positive characteristics may be found in every individual. A figure almost as old as literature itself, Tom assumes his position in a long line of romance tales regarding foundlings, such as Longus's *Daphnis*, whose identities will only be revealed in the final stages of the plot. Like Longus, Fielding adopted a standard pattern for romance that included love, separation, and mutual fidelity amid the usual heroic adventures. In addition to positioning itself on a continuum with its romance predecessors, *Tom Jones* also offered a hero who served as the foundation for the heart-of-gold-playboy figure who would often appear in later fiction.

Fielding's background as a dramatist emerges in the novel's quick dialogue, swift action, and grouping of characters in pairs to act as dramatic foils. For each of the novel's three positive characters, a nemesis exists. Blifil represents Tom's greatest challenge, whereas Tom's kindly ward and uncle, Squire Allworthy, counters the selfish Squire Western's treatment of Tom's love interest, Sophia Western. Sophia herself shines by comparison to Molly Seagram.

Like the comic dramas of Fielding's era, the novel depends on mistaken identity and coincidence to eventually unite Sophia and Tom. There is no hint of tragedy's hallmark, the conquering of deep inner conflict that results in moral epiphany on the part of the protagonist. Although Tom by turns enjoys and suffers a series of adventures, the reader remains confident throughout that virtue, outwardly embodied in Sophia and suggested in Tom, will triumph over evil. Evils do abound, particularly in the figure of Blifil who, from Tom's childhood, does all in his large powers to make Tom's life a misery. Originally considered the "good seed" as compared to Tom's "bad," Blifil will suffer the eventual turn that comes to all villains. However, the novel's emphasis on justice and kindness allows his kind treatment at the story's end by the very individuals whose lives he has nearly ruined. This aspect of the story obviously differs a great deal from tragic tales involving violence and revenge. Tragedy does threaten from time to time, but comedy prevails.

Even when misbehaving, Tom's good nature and well-developed sense of ribald humor leaves readers smiling. Fielding's assurance of Tom's naturally noble character, a fact voiced by Sophia early in the story, allows him much license in allowing Tom to temporarily give in to his high spirits. The settling upon Sophia of the burden of justice and morality complies with the ideology of Fielding's age. Women were paradoxically viewed as both the embodiment of moral standards for society and the cause of the moral downfall of men. Through Sophia's mistreatment by all the men who control her fate, Fielding comments on the plight of women. His shaping of the injustices done her, however, are not intended as moral commentary or a judgment against his society. Rather, Sophia's struggle against and eventual triumph over these forces presents itself not as severe social commentary but rather as a view through a rosy window into a world the narrator shares with his readers like he might an inside joke.

The novel's conflict remains external and its theme evident—an individual's virtue may be easily misunderstood and even go unrecognized by others. However, people's failure to recognize nobility in fellow humans does not negate its presence. Although emphasizing this truth, Fielding offers no criticism of the societal hypocrisy evident in the change in attitude by several characters toward Tom when the so-called foundling's upper-class background is revealed. Rather, Fielding seeks to emphasize the age-old truth that noble character will surface, despite environment's attempts to conceal it. This remains the true message of *Tom Jones,* delivered in an entertaining manner that continues to enthrall readers centuries after its creation.

Tom's enduring appeal for modern audiences, as critics point out, probably lies in his rebellion against society. Fielding himself, however, cautioned that ultimately people must comply with behavioral demands. Regardless of the quality of one's inner being, without actions that support one's good intentions, high character counts for little.

See also: Fielding, Henry; Jones, Tom; Longus; Western, Sophia

References: Drabble, 1995; Hipchen, 1994; Longus, 1989; Mace, 1996; Richetti, 1996; Smallwood, 1989; Smith, 1993; Tillotson, Fussell, and Waingrow, 1969; Thomas, 1992; Tumbleson, 1995

TOMAS

Czechoslovakian writer Milan Kundera uses Tomas, protagonist of his 1984 work, *The Unbearable Lightness of Being* (*Nesnesitelná lehkost bytí*), to illustrate his point regarding the nature of choice. Because humans have only a single chance at life, they will never know whether they make "correct" choices. When Tomas asks himself whether staying with Tereza, his new love and future wife, is better than being alone, Kundera does not attempt to answer that question. It rep-

resents only one of a myriad of unanswerable questions asked by all humans. The importance lies not in seeking an answer but rather in asking and in the action defined by the choice that follows the question. In his mental contemplation of the German saying, *Einmal ist keinmal,* Tomas examines the idea that "what happens only once may as well not have happened at all." Tomas further translates the German to mean that, because we have only one life, we may as well not even live. The novel, however, questions the finality of that pronouncement.

From the story's first pages, readers understand that Tomas is a womanizer, and he at first seems amoral. To him, sex remains an interesting pursuit, unburdened by moral dictates like betrayal and fidelity. He carries on many relationships that he classifies as erotic friendships, particularly with Sabina, the third member of the book's love triangle. Then he meets Tereza, for whom he develops a fearsome attachment and love, but she suffers feelings of betrayal due to his affairs with other women. He does not, however, decide to give up those encounters but rather decides to conceal them from Tereza. True love always detects betrayal, and Tereza knows of his continued trysts. In one poignant scene, she even asks Tomas to take her with him, to include her in the love making, simply so she will not be separated from him. Although Tomas becomes Tereza's caretaker, thinking of her as a child, like Moses, abandoned for him to raise, he cannot at first sympathize with her feelings about betrayal.

Like Sabina, Tomas holds sophisticated views of adult relationships. Sabina views betrayal as a positive, connecting it with independence, whereas Tomas simply does not ever think of his actions as betrayal. Following divorce from his first wife, he abandons his son, preferring never to know him. Yet he remains loyal to Tereza in every way other than sexually. When the Communists invade Prague, he, Tereza, and Sabina all depart for Switzerland. Tereza feels pulled back to Prague by a desire to photograph the occupation in order to enlighten the outside world as to the harshness of the Communist regime. Although Tomas feels no particular patriotic pull to Czechoslovakia, he returns to be with Tereza. He discovers that he loves her fiercely, and in his mind, that love may be separated from sex.

Tomas unwittingly makes a political move of his own when he writes an essay comparing the

Soviet regime to the tragedy *Oedipus Rex,* in which the king, the drama's authority figure, blinds himself on account of all he has inflicted on his family and countrymen. He sends the piece to a paper published by Czech writers as an arm of the country's intelligentsia. That paper had raised the issue of the responsibility for the judicial murders resulting from so-called trials since the Communists had come to power. In swift reaction to the piece, Communists officials asked Tomas to retract his article because many Communists stated they thought Tomas wanted them to gouge out their eyes. Although he meant not to insult only the Communists but rather all dictatorships, Tomas becomes an unintentional political figure, and he refuses to sign a retraction. His refusal marks the end of his medical career, and he follows government orders to become a window washer. Again, Tomas deals with the results of his decision in the best way possible. He enjoys the celebrity that his demotion brings and also cultivates the window washing as a means to increase his number of sexual encounters. As a married man, he rationalizes these acts by thinking of the act of love as involving the soul and the act of sex as involving only the body.

Although the reader may find Tomas's rationalization of the nature of love versus that of sex simply an excuse to copulate with abandon, his character does possess redeeming qualities. He never entertains the idea of abandoning Tereza, feeling cut to the quick by her sufferings. He provides the comfort that she, as an emotionally insecure individual, requires. One symptom of Tereza's insecurity and fear is her constant nightmares, most of which concern death. In a scene that demonstrates Tomas's goodness, Tereza rouses from sleep to discover him staring down at her as he considers the strength of his love. When she asks what he looks at, he realizes that, rather than bringing her fully awake, he should plant the suggestion of a pleasant dream in her mind. He answers that he's looking at the stars, and when Tereza calls him a liar because he's looking down rather than up, he explains they are in an airplane together flying above the stars. With this symbolic vision in mind of independence and escape from the repressive society that so limits their options, Tereza falls asleep again.

Tomas serves several purposes for Kundera, including a reflection on the options available to any one individual during politically difficult times. Kundera himself underwent a challenge to his own creativity during the Russian occupation of his home country, and he presents an amalgam of various members of the Czechoslovakian artistic and scholarly community in the character of Tomas. When the chief surgeon attempts to convince Tomas following the printing of the infamous Oedipus editorial that he is not a writer, journalist, or savior of his nation but a doctor and a scientist, Kundera demonstrates the ease with which individuals may slip in and out of particular roles, especially when someone else applies the labels. By refusing not to bear any one particular label related either to his profession or his political beliefs, Tomas sustains an individual independence not allowed in the broader political scene. That independence, like his many sexual dalliances, comes following careful consideration of various alternatives. This fact of consideration followed by choice allows Tomas to triumph over his circumstances, even as he lives in virtual exile with Tereza awaiting his unpredictable moment of death.

See also: Kundera, Milan; Tereza; Sabina; *The Unbearable Lightness of Being*
References: Catalano, 1995; Lippi, 1984; Misurella, 1993

TRUEBA, ESTEBAN

Esteban Trueba, a willful, perpetually impassioned, and patriarchal figure, serves as one narrator of Isabel Allende's romantic sociopolitical novel, *The House of the Spirits* (1982, trans. 1985). Esteban builds from his own dreams the house referred to in the novel's title, and his wife, Clara del Valle, "the clairvoyant one," summons its spirits. This couple is the first of three generations of Truebas who live and die amid great political and social upheaval during the close of the nineteenth and the beginning of the twentieth centuries in a South American country that Allende never names. Esteban symbolizes the choleric passion representing the "warm humors" attributed to males in medieval times, whereas Clara's cool distraction symbolizes those "cold humors" attributed to females. Just as males were long considered superior to females, so were warm humors more desirable than cold. But it is in his heated passions that Esteban commits those "sins of the fathers" that medieval attitudes believed would be visited upon that father's children. Esteban's actions and his effect on future generations of his family prove that philosophy.

At first in love with Clara's older sister, Rosa the Beautiful, Esteban sees his hopes to marry Rosa destroyed when she dies after ingesting poison. The poison had been placed in a container of liquor intended for her politically active father and serves as foreshadowing of the tragedy political affiliation will eventually bring. The clairvoyant Clara had predicted her lovely older sister's death.

Esteban departs his home, leaving behind his sister, Férula, to care for his invalid mother, and travels to the family ranch, Tres Marías. With the help of his foreman, he manages to restore order to the all-but-destroyed ranch, but he cannot seem to order his own life. He exercises his great waves of passion on local peasant women, conceiving a multitude of illegitimate children. One product of Esteban's multiple rapes, a grandson, eventually inflicts considerable terror and pain upon the Esteban family. A shortsighted man in such matters, Esteban never thinks of such possible consequences growing from his lusty actions. His myopia with regard to morality allows Allende's promotion of the theme of vision. In contrast to his wife, a mystic visionary, Esteban remains blind to the effects of his actions on others. He sees the peasants as little more than animals, fortunate to be able to work for him regardless of the pitiful wages they receive. This aspect of Esteban's character intensifies throughout the story. He protests all discussion of social equality, even though his own wife and offspring participate in political movements to relieve social and gender discrimination. Esteban remains a "man's man," intent upon acting the role of the all-knowing patron, not only with his peasants but with members of his family, especially Clara.

When Esteban returns to ask for Clara's hand in marriage nine years later, she has predicted his arrival following her own nine years of self-invoked silence following Rosa's death. Yet Esteban ignores Clara's various talents for prediction, conversation with spirits from another realm, and physical elevation.

The couple marries, beginning a relationship on which Esteban focuses all of his passion for the remainder of his ninety years of life. He remains fascinated by his wife and devoted to her even when her actions or attitudes provoke him to the heights of anger. Never has he suffered such jealousy and rage as that he feels against his spinster sister when she moves in with the Truebas fol-

lowing her mother's death. Férula's emotional attachment to Clara becomes as much an obsession as Esteban's, and the three briefly form a bizarre love triangle. Férula is the only woman Esteban manages to remove permanently from his life, but she plants a curse of loneliness on her brother's head that he never escapes. Only when he begins to feel himself "shrinking" in physical stature, an effect of Férula's curse, does Esteban begin to question his seemingly charmed role among the privileged in his community.

Esteban takes his place among other male characters in the romance tradition who have represented the objective, scientific approach to life in contrast to their lover's more intuitive, subjective approach. That contrast this novel particularly accentuates through its use of magic realism, centered on Clara and her family. The Truebas' daughter, Blanca, and her daughter, Alba, will also possess unusual intuition, although not as acute as Clara's.

When Esteban expresses his conservative views toward politics and eventually becomes a Republican senator, he places all of his faith in the patriarchal government that will later ruin his personal relationships and cause him public disgrace. Unwilling to change his views toward social and gender inequities, he ignores the warnings of his own son. He suffers through his daughter falling in love with and producing a granddaughter by the son of the foreman of Tres Marías. Apoplectic with rage over this union, Esteban delivers what he feels is justice against the young man and lives to suffer for his rash actions for the remainder of his life. This represents only one in a series of incidents when he allows irrational behavior to separate him from the only truly important element in life, his family.

As the forces of his environment close in, threatening his "big house on the corner" with destruction and despair, Esteban must at last admit that he has operated under the illusion of his own importance and strength for too long. When the false order of his culture collapses, he at last learns that his family offers his only solace. This epiphany grants Esteban the status of a dynamic character, as he undergoes the change necessary for him to at last achieve some type of internal peace.

See also: del Valle, Clara; *The House of the Spirits; Love in the Time of Cholera;* Magic Realism; Violence; War

References: de Rougemont, 1983; Radway, 1991; Zamora and Faris, 1995

TSUGAWA, RYOSUKE

Although not a romantic hero, Ryosuke Tsugawa captures much of the page space in Jiro Osaragi's *The Journey* (1960). As a member of postwar Japan's young adult population, Ryosuke struggles to establish himself in Japanese business society as a disillusioned war veteran. Emotionally crippled by his experiences as a Japanese soldier fighting in southern China, Ryosuke cannot marshal his own psychological forces to overcome the inherent weaknesses in his nature. Because he lacks respect for himself, he cannot respect a lover and thus will fail in attempts to secure a romantic relationship.

When Ryosuke first meets the novel's heroine, Taeko Okamoto, he returns her romantic interest. But these two young people differ greatly in their approaches to love, which also represents their varying approaches to life in general. They first meet accidentally at the grave of Taeko's cousin, Akira, also Ryosuke's college classmate, who died in the same war that Ryosuke survived. Through this early scene, Osaragi asks the reader to compare and contrast Ryosuke's emotional death with Akira's physical one, evaluating who has suffered the greater loss. Although Ryosuke survives physically, the part of his psychological makeup that would permit his enjoying life has been destroyed.

Ryosuke tries to adapt to the western changes in his culture brought about by war. In his business and love affairs, he fancies himself a success in his modern environment. Unfortunately, others do not share this opinion, knowing full well how risky dealings with him can be. Ryosuke takes advantage of everyone he meets, using the war as an excuse for what amount to amoral actions with Taeko. As he explains things to her, he simply does not care about much. Thus, he can tout a love affair with an older woman without compunction. This causes a conflict with Taeko who, although she represents Japan's new woman, retains some traditional ideas about love as a partnership based upon mutual faith. She revolts against the tradition of arranged marriage yet rejects Ryosuke's "modern" suggestion for them to marry but then live apart for financial convenience. This idea represents Ryosuke's general attitude toward his relationship with Taeko; he always chooses the most easy and convenient solution. He will take whatever action may be necessary to gain the financial support he needs, and his large gambling debts and shady business deals require much support. Because of such character flaws, Ryosuke basically moves in a circle, and he makes no emotional or psychological progress throughout the story.

In this way, Ryosuke also contrasts with the third member of the novel's love triangle, Sutekichi Ata. With his self-sacrificial and valorous nature, Sutekichi remains the more heroic of the two men. Also a modern college graduate, Sutekichi struggles with his own ideas of the usefulness of tradition, represented by his relationship with an elderly professor. At the novel's beginning, although attracted by the traditional ethical ideas regarding honor and morality, Sutekichi has not yet clearly established his viewpoint on these matters. His emotional journey, like that of Taeko's, will allow him to change into a dynamic character. Thus he contrasts with Ryosuke, who seems to have insight into his own weaknesses but remains unwilling to change.

Through Ryosuke, Osaragi shows the disillusionment many Japanese inherited from war and the disorientation that resulted from a quick turn to western ways. Although somewhat endearing in his openness in discussing his core problems with Taeko at the novel's conclusion, overall Ryosuke proves himself a failure, both as a lover and an entrepreneur.

See also: Ata, Sutekichi; *The Journey;* Okamoto, Taeko
References: Frye, 1976; Hoffman and Murphy, 1996

TULLIO

Had the character Tullio appeared in a traditional romance novel, rather than in Giuseppe Berto's antiromance *The Sky Is Red* (1948), he would be recognizable as the sidekick to the romance's hero. As such, he would probably be destined to experience love himself, perhaps with some comic complications. But because Tullio, like Berto's other teenage characters, acts to undermine traditional romantic ideas, he instead becomes a tragic figure in an uncaring world. His death offers no meaning for the readers outside Berto's nihilistic framework.

Tullio remains an angry figure, interested in revolution even at his young age of seventeen. His anger and discontent serve as responses to the economic inequities suffered by the working class in postwar Italy. His character contrasts with that of Daniele, a member of the upper class who embodies the bourgeois ideals that Tullio detests. This does not necessitate Tullio's developing hatred for Daniele, however. Instead, Tullio invites the younger boy to join the gang of orphans who band together following the bombing of their town. In his position as leader of the gang, Tullio must acclimate Daniele to a street life for which his pampered life never prepared him. He helps educate the young man in matters other than those he discovered in books during his former life as a seminary student. Tullio takes part in Daniele's initiation into the realities that force all of the children to assume the burdens of adulthood at far too young an age.

Berto compares Tullio's romantic involvement with the almost-fifteen-year-old prostitute Carla to Daniele's love for the innocent young Giulia, Carla's cousin. The four individuals possess ideologies similar to those of their mates. Tullio's Communist beliefs mark him as a highly political figure, campaigning for better conditions for the working person. He suffers no compunction against stealing, envisioning such action as the only choice left to him for survival by the greedy upper classes. This attitude balances that of the cynical, pragmatic Carla, who engages in prostitution without questioning its moral basis; it allows survival. That Tullio suffers no jealousy over her performing sexual acts for money further emphasizes this pair's realistic approach to life. That approach varies widely from the highly moral and naïve view shared by Daniele and Giulia, a view that, in the end, does not aid in the survival of either.

Tullio acts as the author's voice, crying out against the inequities of a system created to enslave some humans while allowing others to profit from their misery. Readers would all agree that at such a young age, Tullio should never have had to make the choices forced upon him. Berto asks readers to take that idea one step further in deciding that no human should ever be faced with the economic and social inequities of his characters, regardless of age.

See also: Carla; Daniele; Giulia; Hemingway, Ernest; The Lost Generation; Nihilism; *The Sky Is Red;* War

References: "Biografia," 1997; Frye, 1976; Striuli, 1986–1989

TYLER, ANNE

Although a northerner by birth, Anne Tyler has written more than a dozen novels and some fifty short stories establishing her as one of the premiere U.S. "southern" writers of the late twentieth century. With such famous southern authors as Eudora Welty and Duke University instructor Reynolds Price acting as major influences, Tyler developed an outlook on her characters and their lives dubbed southern by critics and fans alike. Tyler has produced some of the genre's most enduringly quirky characters, both male and female, all with firm attachments to geography and family. Although confronting challenging themes in her fiction such as infidelity, murder, child abuse, and lifelong enmity between individuals, Tyler avoids the rage and deep passions that often characterize those consumed by such situations. Instead, she offers ordinary people who work within the confines of culture to achieve a quiet grace that propels them to hero and heroine status in the romantic tradition.

Born in Minneapolis, Minnesota, in 1941, Tyler moved with her family to several locations as a child. She matured in the Celo Community, a cooperative farm in North Carolina, settling there at age seven. In the farming venture, her parents, Lloyd Parry Tyler and Phyllis Mahon Tyler, hoped to practice their Quaker faith and conduct a lifestyle centered on ethics and morality for the benefit of their four children. Tyler and her three brothers were homeschooled for several years, an experience that resulted in their receiving a superior education; the three brothers eventually obtained doctoral degrees, and one also became a medical doctor. The family later moved to Raleigh, North Carolina, and Tyler entered Duke University at age sixteen. Having known since age three that she would become a writer, she published two pieces, "The Lights on the River" and "Laura" in *Archive,* Duke's literary magazine. Majoring in Russian and completing her studies in only three years, Tyler graduated Phi Beta Kappa, having twice won the Anne Flexner Award for her creative writing. She credits much of her writing success to Duke instructor Reynolds Price, a man she claims is the only person she ever met who could really teach writing.

In 1961 Tyler began graduate work at Columbia University, intending to take a master's degree in Russian. Although she completed all the required coursework, she chose not to complete her thesis. The following summer in 1962, she worked in Maine swabbing the decks of a ship and acting as proofreader for a local newspaper. She returned to Duke for a year, where she worked in the library and in 1963 married Iranian-born psychiatrist Taghi Mohammed Modarressi. That year also saw her first story, "The Baltimore Birth Certificate," appear in a national publication, *The Critic: A Catholic Review of Books and the Arts.*

While her husband finished his medical residency in Montreal, Tyler continued writing, publishing her first novel, *If Morning Ever Comes,* in 1964. Her daughter Tezh was born in 1965, the same year she published *The Tin Can Tree.* In 1966 *Mademoiselle* recognized Tyler as one of the country's most promising career women. Following the birth of daughter Mitra in 1967, the family moved to Baltimore. Here Tyler enjoyed the luxury of writing while married to a working husband, a condition allowing her the freedom to choose her projects carefully and to reject publishers' suggestions and offers if she pleased. Her family has always remained a major focus, and she declines to make public appearances or give college lectures. She instead reserves her energy for work and the nurturing of her children.

The 1970s were a productive decade for Tyler, who published *A Slipping-Down Life* (1970), *The Clock Winder* (1972), *Celestial Navigation* (1974), and *Searching for Caleb* (1976). She also began work in 1975 as a reviewer for the *National Observer* and contributed until it folded in 1977. The American Academy and Institute of Arts and Letters awarded Tyler $3,000 for her literary excellence and promise in 1977, and a condensed version of *Earthly Possessions* appeared in *Redbook.* Knopf published that novel later in the year, and Tyler became a regular reviewer for several publications, including the *New York Times.*

Her 1980 novel, *Morgan's Passing,* received a nomination for an American Book Award, and Tyler won the Janet Heidinger Kafka Prize for fiction by an American woman. By 1982, she enjoyed great public success, garnering a nomination for the Pulitzer Prize for *Dinner at the Homesick Restaurant.* She received a PEN/Faulkner Award for Fiction, and in 1985, *The Accidental Tourist* earned the National Book Critics Circle Award as that year's most distinguished work of American fiction. This novel, made into a popular movie, presents Tyler's trademark protagonist, who must adjust to the disaster of a senseless killing of his son in a restaurant shootout. Tyler did claim the Pulitzer Prize in 1989 for *Breathing Lessons* (1988) and continued her distinguished career with *Saint Maybe* in 1991. *Ladder of Years* (1995) was followed by *A Patchwork Planet* (1998).

Although Tyler's novels do not include the gloom attributed to southern Gothic, their plots form around a moment of trauma, loss, or challenge faced by their protagonists. Like most normal people, Tyler's characters experience casualties and catastrophes with which they must learn to cope while operating within their everyday cultures. Critics have referred to the losses from death, destruction, or betrayal that Tyler's characters experience as an "intimate violence" that disrupts everyday life and propels the plot into a relentless movement toward resolution. The loss of a loved one may be balanced by the gain of a new love interest, as Tyler creates a tension between the alienation caused by loss and the need each individual has to reconnect to fellow humans. Feminist critics have characterized Tyler's female figures as passive and dominated by men, a charge that may be tied to the characters' deference to cultural, social and regional mores.

Although some of the novels' occurrences and coincidences have been labeled melodramatic or even perverse by critics, they work well within the fabric of the stories. Tyler's couples may be oddly, even painfully matched, but their unusual pairings give them a strength to deal with issues they could never face alone. For example, the excruciatingly introverted Macon and the outspoken, friendly Muriel in *The Accidental Tourist* meet after Macon breaks his leg tripping over Edward, the dog that belonged to his dead son Ethan. Muriel agrees to train Edward who, like Macon, struggles to adjust to Ethan's death. The unlikely couple discover that they deal with similar conflicts in their very different worlds. These include the lack of friendship, the lack of romance, and their difficult positions in relation to their sons. Macon's world is that of a married-but-separated hermit writer, and Muriel's is one of a single mother who, among other things, trains dogs for a living, yet the two offer one another support that persons more familiar, such as family members and friends, cannot provide.

Tyler's formula for plot satisfies her many readers, who know they can expect the out-of-the-ordinary from her characters and their actions. The praise she heaps in her various reviews on other writers for the sharp depiction of concrete detail may also be applied to her own works. Her humor and emphasis on the family and domestic relations continues to capture the imagination of many devoted fans.

See also: The Accidental Tourist
References: Croft, 1995; Davidson, 1995; Evans, 1993; Flora and Bain, 1987; Friedman and Siegel, 1995; Hart, 1995; Kelly, 1996; Kissel, 1996; Salwak, 1994; Sweeney, 1996

THE UNBEARABLE LIGHTNESS OF BEING

Czechoslovakian writer Milan Kundera begins his 1984 novel, *The Unbearable Lightness of Being* (*Nesnesitelná lehkost bytí*), with a consideration of Friedrich Nietzsche's idea of "eternal return." Without an understanding of this concept, the reader cannot easily relate to the events in the lives of the characters that shape Kundera's book. He makes clear from the first page that precise choices and even the consequences of those choices matter little in any eternal scheme, for no experience can recur. Therefore, events that appeared either glorious or terrifying, individuals who appeared courageous or cowardly, a period in time judged either sublime or horrible, will all weigh equally in a final analysis. Human nature makes impossible the retention of original events. Once those events or individuals disappear, they are gone forever, as are their effects. He elaborates on this idea while following the romantic and political involvements of several characters who experience the Russian occupation of Czechoslovakia, as did Kundera himself. In the male protagonist, Tomas, his wife Tereza, his lover Sabina, and, to a lesser extent, Sabina's French lover, Franz, Kundera sketches several different reactions to the conversion of social order into political chaos. He makes clear that the characters' choices themselves are unimportant. Rather, the fact that they make a choice, any choice at all, remains critical.

The character of Tomas offers a study in the carnal man. He practices free sex with any woman he finds appealing and willing. In some circumstances, this one fact would make Tomas an unsympathetic character, because readers would tend to disagree with such a practice. However, by demonstrating that human repugnance toward the idea of multiple sex partners outside marriage remains based on an arbitrary morality, Kundera overcomes reader resistance to seeing Tomas as a positive character. Tomas believes that sex is merely one more gratifying activity of the body, such as eating or relaxation. Love, however, is a spiritual state of being, directly connected to the soul. Because matters of the soul outweigh those of the body, love is not only more important than sex, but the two may even be unrelated. This justifies his rampant sexual indulgence with willing individuals who expect no long-term relationship in spite of the fact that he marries Tereza. She remains his only love, an object for him of tremendous devotion, because of all women, only Tereza evokes his feelings of pity and concern. Tomas compares Tereza to the helpless infant Moses, set afloat to be discovered in the bulrushes by individuals willing to care for him. With Tereza, Tomas has an affair of the soul, while he simultaneously indulges in a purely physical affair with Sabina. Sabina represents a kindred spirit who also prefers what Tomas terms erotic friendships to marriage.

Tereza lacks the self-assurance and emotional independence that Tomas and Sabina enjoy. She loves her husband and even feels friendship toward Sabina, but the guilt regarding her own body, bred into her by her mother, prevents her from equating sex with freedom. She sees free love relationships as betrayals, in every negative connotation of that term. Tereza's choice to practice fidelity causes her great internal conflict in her relationship with Tomas.

Although emotionally weak, Tereza does evidence strength by practicing the courage of her convictions. She at first departs occupied Prague with Tomas and her beloved dog, Karenin, as they emigrate to Switzerland. A photographer, Tereza returns to Prague, hoping to capture with her camera evidence of the cruelty of the occupation that will convince the outside world of Czechoslovakia's suffering. Eventually her efforts disappoint her, and she discovers that her work may even have been used to the detriment of those she sought to aid. When she stores the camera away, she retires an extension of herself.

Because Tomas loves Tereza, he follows her to Prague, although she had not asked him to do so. Kundera does not lavish praise on either character as he moves in and out of the novel to add personal comment and explanation. Instead, he makes a point of discussing the fact that political action and political passivity can both have the same result, reemphasizing his hypothesis that the nature of our choices remains insignificant.

Tomas's action in following Tereza for love causes his eventual loss of the right to practice medicine, although he had been a talented surgeon. When he refuses to retract an essay-turned-editorial written for a Czechoslovakian writer's newspaper and seen as inflammatory by some Communist officials, he is forced to wash windows for a living. This would be classified as a negative result of his choice to write. However, Tomas transforms his "demotion" into a positive by using his multiple contacts with clients to locate additional sex partners.

Sabina's choices differ from those of Tomas and Tereza. Whereas Tomas recognizes no betrayal in his sexual liaisons, and Tereza highly values fidelity, Sabina actually values betrayal. She believes that it represents a breaking of ranks with convention and an ultimate independence. She does not choose to return to Prague but remains for a time in Switzerland and then moves on to Paris and eventually the United States. As an artist and a free spirit, she tolerates neither government nor individual attempts at directives or control. When her married lover Franz attempts to control her, she leaves him. Sabina represents a paradox of sorts, as she seems to value her past, evidenced by her special affection for the symbolic bowler hat that once belonged to her grandfather, yet she constantly moves on, breaking ties with that past.

For Franz, Kundera seems to reserve the most pity. Franz finds himself controlled, first by a manipulative wife and then by Sabina whose control exists, not in any overt manipulation, but rather in the terrific emotion she produces in Franz. He eventually makes the most overt political statement of the group, joining an ironic march of intellectuals and artists who protest the refusal of Cambodia to allow doctors into their country to treat the ill and dying. His motive for his action, however, remains flawed, in that he joins the march for the sake of Sabina, an ex-lover who will never even be aware of that activity. He

thinks of her as an ever-present spirit who views his actions. When he dies following a mugging, the terrible irony of that inconsequential death is lost to everyone except himself. His wife continues her manipulation after Franz's death, using his demise as her own badge of honor.

When Tomas and Tereza move to the country, they seem to at last escape the Communist threat. Kundera employs the archetypal image of nature as pure and removed from human domination. Tragedy invades the Edenic setting, however, when Karenin, Tereza's best friend and constant companion, contracts cancer and dies. The dog's name, derived from *Anna Karenina,* Leo Tolstoy's novel examining human reactions to another military revolution, foreshadows a tragic end for Karenin. When an accident shortly after the dog's burial causes the deaths of Tomas and Tereza, Kundera seems to hint that the animal acted as the final tie between Tomas and Tereza. With his parting, they die, having just found peace with themselves and one another.

In this novel, Kundera's characters face conflict caused by choices of the body and of the soul as well as by strength and weakness, both in a physical and an emotional sense. The various conflicts arise from a cultural and political world where freedom remains restricted. Through his characters, Kundera questions whether the terrible weight of eternal return, such as that experienced by Christ, can be more positive than the unbearable lightness of humans, who exist only for a brief moment that immediately fades when they withdraw. He shapes many unanswerable questions and poses paradoxes, such as the fact that love seeks to possess that which cannot be possessed. Through his examination of binary oppositions, he urges his readers to accept the fact that such dilemmas are not meant to be solved but rather simply investigated.

See also: Anna Karenina; Kundera, Milan; Sabina; Tereza; Tolstoy, Count Leo; Tomas; *The Unbearable Lightness of Being*
References: Catalano, 1995; Lippi, 1984; Misurella, 1993

UNCAS

Uncas is the name given to the Indian character mentioned in the title of James Fenimore Cooper's historical romance, *The Last of the Mohicans* (1826). Although not the novel's main character, he serves an important role in representing all that white people of his period valued in the idea of the "noble savage." His eventual love interest in the novel, the white woman Cora Munro, early on admires the honorable stance of Uncas. A man of few words, Uncas communicates his intentions and ideals through actions. Because Cooper shared his readers' sensibilities, he characterizes Uncas in a heroic manner that assumed a secondary position to the heroism of the white scout, Hawkeye. Even in narration describing in admirable terms Uncas's communication with his uncle, Chingachgook, Cooper assumes what modern readers recognize as a condescending tone toward the Indians.

Uncas performs various feats of heroism throughout the novel in support of the white men who are caught up in the French and Indian War (1754–1763). His nemesis, the Huron named Magua, represents all that Cooper's readers would consider evil in the Indians that inhabited the unsettled portions of America. The two become foils, competing for the devotion of Cora. Magua demands her servitude as a wife in exchange for the freedom of her fellow travelers. Following their escape, a move facilitated through the bravery of Uncas, he continues to pursue her, eventually kidnapping her sister, Alice Munro, knowing that Cora will follow. Uncas naturally pursues them as well and enjoys several scenes in Indian encampments that emphasize his strength of character as well as his physical strength. He stands without flinching during Magua's abuse and pursues his enemy to both their deaths in defense of Cora.

Cooper kills off both the characters of Uncas and Cora rather than face a disapproving reading public by allowing the two to unite in a forbidden love. More important than his role as a love interest for Cora Munro, however, is Uncas's representation of his tribe. With his death, Chingachgook mourns the passing of an entire race of people. In addition, Hawkeye may be verbalizing Cooper's own regret over the loss of freedom represented by the Indian's way of life in the face of the advancing civilization of the white settlers.

See also: The Black Experience in America, 1600–1945; Cooper, James Fenimore; Forbidden Love; Hawkeye; Heyward, Major Duncan; *The Last of the Mohicans;* Munro, Alice; Munro, Cora; Violence; War

References: Barker and Sabin, 1996; Budick, 1996; Campbell, 1968; "Cooper, James Fenimore," 1986; Frye, 1976; Price, 1983; Wimsatt, 1974

VALJEAN, JEAN

Victor Hugo's *Les Misérables* (1862), a novel fourteen years in the writing, features Jean Valjean as its protagonist and romantic hero. Hugo uses the events of Valjean's life, beginning in 1815, to emphasize some of his favorite and recurring themes. In nineteenth-century prerevolutionary France, Valjean encounters the social inequities that Hugo despised. A man of the poor classes sentenced to a lengthy prison term for the theft of a loaf of bread, Valjean embodies the plight of the poor during his era. Without recourse to the power of political connections or wealth, he has no choice but imprisonment. His sentence grows due to two escape attempts, and by the time he finally departs the prison, nineteen years have passed. Although Valjean leaves his cell, his spirit will not enjoy true liberation until he learns the lesson of self-sacrifice for the sake of others.

His first experience with generosity occurs immediately upon his release. Offered a place of refuge by the Bishop of Digne, Valjean sneaks away in the middle of the night with the bishop's silver. When the authorities catch Valjean and return him to the bishop's residence, the clergyman states that the silver does indeed belong to the ex-convict; he even adds two silver candlesticks to the booty. Greatly impressed by this kindness, Valjean departs intending to perform good works for others. This allows Hugo to emphasize his theme of atonement for past errors through good works, an ideology of the Catholic Church. Hugo strengthens his religious theme by inverting the common Christian association of silver with betrayal. Although Christ found himself betrayed on account of silver, the bishop does not betray Valjean.

Valjean departs the area, breaking his parole by so doing, to take up residence in the town of M—, where, to protect his identity, he assumes the name Monsieur Madeleine. Having invested the moneys gained by the sale of his silver in a glass factory, Valjean becomes a wealthy and influential man, and the townspeople elect him mayor. One of the factory's workers, Fantine, must care alone for her illegitimate daughter, Cosette. Fantine becomes another symbolic victim of an uncaring society, driven from the factory by her own peers when they discover her sin of motherhood out of wedlock. Without Madeleine's knowledge, the factory overseer dismisses Fantine. Her dismissal forces her to take up prostitution to finance Cosette's care at the exorbitant prices charged Fantine by Cosette's caretakers. Hugo introduces a recognizable character type in the opportunist, Monsieur Thénardier, head of the household where Cosette lives. The Thénardiers have more money than Fantine because they run an inn of sorts. They mistreat Cosette terribly, a plot element that allows Hugo to emphasize the absurdity of children being punished for the perceived sins of their fathers or, in this case, mothers. In addition, the fact that the Thénardiers can ignore their practice of child abuse while simultaneously scorning Fantine for her prostitution emphasizes the hypocrisy bred by class distinction. When Valjean discovers that Fantine was cast into the streets, he locates her. By now stricken with tuberculosis, Fantine dies in the hospital, having first extracted a promise from the man she knows as Monsieur Madeleine to care for her daughter.

The character of Javert introduces another figure that would become well-known in fiction of later decades, that of the police inspector who fixates on a particular fugitive, dedicating his life to pursuit of the criminal. Himself born in prison, Javert seems to suffer from a perverse type of guilt, again emphasizing Hugo's message against the necessity of offspring suffering for the behavior of their parents. Javert's shame drives him to commit inordinate energy to Valjean's capture. Because Javert became familiar with Valjean's fabled strength as he grew up in the prison where the convict had spent so many years, he recognizes Monsieur Madeleine as Valjean. Ironically, the identification occurs due

Frederic March played protagonist and romantic hero Jean Valjean, with Rochelle Hudson as Cosette, in this 1935 film version of Victor Hugo's Les Misérables *(1862). (Photofest)*

to Valjean's attempts to help another by employing his legendary might.

After Valjean rescues Cosette, the man he aided with his prodigious strength rescues him from another arrest threat by Javert. Through such incidents, Valjean begins to benefit from some of the kindness he has invested in others since his prison release. He lives with Cosette in a convent for a time as the two learn to love each other. Following their move to Paris, the novel's plot grows complicated through the introduction of Hugo's trademark large number of characters and subplots. Cosette believes Valjean to be her father, and he treats her as his own. The onetime thief and convict earns his forgiveness for past indiscretions through his devotion to Cosette.

As Cosette matures and falls in love with the young Marius Pontmercy, the plot emphasizes France's mounting civil unrest. Hugo also focuses on the traditional romantic idea that some passions or causes are worth the sacrifice of human life. He does this not only through the group of revolutionaries who pledge to fight to the death for their beliefs but also through Pontmercy. When he learns that Valjean plans to remove Cosette from Paris, Pontmercy determines to die over the loss of his love while fighting for freedom from social oppression. The conflict Valjean has always encountered with his environment escalates along with the tempers of Paris's poor. Starving and mistreated, a group of Parisians, Pontmercy among them, stages a revolt at some barricades. Valjean again proves himself a hero by rescuing not only the unconscious and wounded Pontmercy but also Javert, whom the crowd has bound as a prisoner.

Overcome with internal conflict over his desire to allow Valjean liberty and his duty as an enforcer of the law to arrest the convict, Javert chooses suicide by drowning. When Pontmercy's wealthy estranged grandfather welcomes him back into the family, Cosette eventually joins

Pontmercy. They plan a life together, all the while never realizing that Valjean had saved the young man from certain death. When Valjean admits to being an ex-criminal and not Cosette's true father, the young couple gradually exclude him from their lives. Although they will find Valjean later after learning the truth regarding his valor, he dies after having again lived alone in poverty. His greatest wish, that Cosette find happiness, has been fulfilled, and he passes to her the silver candlesticks as a dowry of sorts. They symbolize the lesson he had learned earlier regarding forgiveness and acceptance of others. Valjean thus breaks the wicked cycle of abuse of the young by offering Cosette not only a material but also a spiritual legacy.

Jean Valjean's character should not be reduced to a mere moral lesson or Hugo's novel to the status of a cautionary tale regarding the mistreatment of the common person by powerful political forces. Rather, Valjean represents the possibilities afforded all humans, regardless of social class, through spiritual liberation. He had been complicit in shaping his own bitter situation through his repeated futile attempts first to escape physical imprisonment and later to avoid the emotional imprisonment that could result from his trusting others. Valjean overcame his basic mistrust of others and of his own capacity to love, a mistrust ingrained in him at an early age by an uncaring culture. His rejection of those early teachings and his ultimate discovery of the human capacity for forgiveness and love constitute his victory.

See also: Cosette; Fantine; Hugo, Victor; *Les Misérables;* Romance; Violence; War

References: Charlton, 1984; de Rougemont, 1983; Lovejoy, 1974; Masters-Wicks, 1994

VANITY FAIR

As William Makepeace Thackeray's most well-known work, *Vanity Fair* (1847–1848) has assumed a place among the greatest works written in English. Thackeray achieves a rich presentation of characters never intended either to fill the qualifications of traditionally "good" individuals or to be wholly bad. Thackeray prepares readers for this characterization through the subtitle of his novel, which reads, *A Novel without a Hero.* Instead, the characters are believable individuals who make their way through each day, sometimes succeeding in reaching their goals but more often committing foolish or naïve acts in the name of goodness. The narrative voice often editorializes regarding the characters, offering insights into their motivations.

Thackeray's cynical tone helps shape one of fiction's most likable female knaves in the novel's protagonist, the infamous trickster, Becky Sharp. Becky's surname becomes particularly symbolic of her shrewd approach to life. Often she stands apart from the other characters as a keenly honed wit in a sea of dullards. A young woman who believes in creating her own fortune, Becky will sacrifice anyone to her ambition of upward social movement. Although each of the characters reveals flaws, readers have some admiration for the novel's "rascals" as each struggles to overcome the conflicts life hands out. Conversely, those characters meant to be "good" incite some reader dislike because of their practice of an illogical morality.

Becky's first victim is her school friend, Amelia Sedley, who overlooks the selfish nature that earns Becky the animosity of her other schoolmates. When Amelia takes Becky to visit her home, she plays matchmaker between Becky and her brother Joseph, or Jos, Sedley. Home on military leave, the bumbling Jos becomes smitten with Becky, who is happy to promote their relationship, although for practical rather than romantic reasons. Despite his many personal faults, including obesity and buffoonery, Jos would represent quite a social coup for Becky.

Amelia arranges a party for the couple that is also attended by her acknowledged admirer, George Osborne, and a secret admirer, Captain Dobbin. Dobbin withholds declaration of his affection for Amelia, believing Osborne to be a better match for her. Although Amelia's naïveté and goodness may irritate the reader, Dobbin's attempt at gallantry makes him endearing.

Despite her best manipulative strategies, Becky fails to force Jos to commit to a future with her. When the Sedleys learn of Jos's "illness" on the following day and of his imminent departure with his troops, Becky admits defeat. While Amelia suffers over what she believes to be her friend's broken heart, Becky simply makes plans for another foray into high society in search of a man to raise her above working-class status through marriage. Even though she possesses a conniving nature, Becky still remains more appealing than Amelia. Her survival instincts must be admired, whereas Amelia's simpering approach to relationships reflects a weakness of character.

Becky scores a triumph with the husband of her next employer. Hired by Lady Crawley to act as governess to her two children, Becky fixes most of her attention on Sir Pitt Crawley. A self-absorbed man, Sir Pitt returns Becky's interest, never wondering why a young, attractive female would find him appealing. Not one to exert all of her energies on a single individual, Becky also lavishes attention on a wealthy family member and sister of Sir Pitt, Miss Crawley. This elderly spinster cares little for Pitt's present family but possesses a great fondness for Sir Pitt's son by a former marriage, Rawdon Crawley. She uses her wealth to promote Rawdon's social position, even paying the debts of her handsome and dashing nephew. Becky succeeds in also attracting Rawdon's affections.

Eventually Becky moves in with Miss Crawley, who falls ill and will allow no one else to care for her. The situation proves perfect for Becky, who can enjoy Miss Rawdon's luxurious home as well as the open attentions of Rawdon. Lady Crawley's death seems to further increase Becky's chance at a good marriage when it frees Sir Pitt. However, when Pitt throws himself at Becky's feet in a marriage proposal, she reveals her secret marriage to Rawdon. Not only does this startling announcement invoke Sir Pitt's fury, it incites Miss Crawley to rewrite her will and eliminate Rawdon as a beneficiary.

Amelia's love life has also had its problems. Upon the discovery of an embarrassing amount of debt on the part of Amelia's father, George's father demands that George stop seeing Amelia. Thus, the hypocrisy of a society that judges its youth for the sins of their fathers becomes one focus of many in the novel. Due to George's low level of integrity, he at first thinks he will comply with his father's wishes, but Dobbin steps in to bolster George's moral fiber. He insists that George fulfill his obligations to Amelia, knowing of Amelia's love for George. The two marry and move to Brighton, where they discover Becky and Rawdon living an extravagant life without income. Rawdon's debts again escalate. Thackeray again challenges the reader on how to evaluate the characters. Rawdon may appear sympathetic as Becky's victim, yet he must also accept responsibility for his gambling as well as for the myopia that prevents his seeing the true nature of his wife. By this point in the story, the reader has discovered it to be a parody of individual lives lost in a scramble for wealth, status, and valueless possessions. Thackeray drives home his criticism of lofty ideas perpetuated by individuals believing themselves bettered through birth into a particular family. In the end, however, they are no better than those of a lower status, whether that status be material or ethical.

Meanwhile, Dobbin attempts to act as a peacemaker between George and his father. His actions prove unsuccessful, and George is also cut from his parent's will. Captain Dobbin next reports to the characters Napoleon's return from Elba. The Hundred Days campaign begins, and Dobbin and his troops move to Brussels and are stationed in the city along with Jos, who is freshly returned from India. The two couples meet again in Brussels, and George becomes one more infatuated victim of Becky's charms. She definitely fills the role of helpmate to Rawdon, but not in the traditional sense. Actually the stronger of the two, Becky calls upon her expertise in fraud to aid her husband in his swindling. She also helps him evade creditors.

Now begins the real "fair" mentioned in the novel's title, as all the characters come together in a dizzying and colorful performance of betrayal on various levels. The Osbornes and Crawleys attend numerous balls where Becky makes quite an impression on military high society, sharing her affections and attentions with various members of the army's ranks. She does not distinguish between generals and privates. At one particular ball given by the Duchess of Richmond in June 1815, Amelia departs with a broken heart when she finally realizes she has lost her husband to her supposed friend. Napoleon enters Belgium, and the ensuing public battles mirror the private conflicts among the characters.

Unperturbed by the military developments, Becky chooses to remain in Belgium, as does Amelia, who will not leave George despite his scurrilous behavior. Then George dies at Waterloo, whereas Rawdon safely returns to celebrate a happy season in Paris with his beautiful wife. Becky's wit again earns her much attention, but Rawdon ignores her romantic activities, particularly when she gives birth to their son. The baby totally captivates his father. Amelia, having also given birth after her return to London, finds comfort in her child as well. Love for the baby releases her from the nearly insane grief over her loss of George, despite his betrayal of her in turning his affections to Becky.

As might be predicted, Becky becomes bored with Paris and returns with Rawdon to London. Once again they seem to live well on very little, thanks to Becky's talents at manipulation of her acquaintances, particularly the wealthy and elderly Lord Steyne. Although all of London society gossips regarding Becky's relationship with the older aristocrat, Rawdon remains innocent of that development. Becky achieves her life's greatest desire when Lord Steyne arranges her appearance at Court. She and Rawdon meet his brother, now the young Sir Pitt, and his wife. This younger brother, heir to Sir Pitt's fortune, has also fallen in love with Becky, a fact to which Rawdon remains blind. Rawdon does begin to feel isolated from his wife, who spends more and more time advancing her social status at the expense of her own child. As a devoted father, Rawdon attempts to make up for that neglect and even takes the boy to visit Amelia's son. Rawdon becomes Becky's greatest victim, and even his love for his son, an admirable virtue, cannot rescue him from his lack of judgment where Becky is concerned.

Becky refuses to give Rawdon money to settle his gambling debts, in spite of the fact that she wears jewels of mysterious origin. Rawdon goes to debtor's prison and, when he is released later through the help of his brother, returns home to discover Becky with Lord Steyne. This breach of ethics and morality at last drives Rawdon from Becky. He accepts a foreign post and remains forever separated from his beloved son, the price he pays for his own foolishness.

Amelia's poor prospects improve with Jos's return home. He moves his sister and father to a nicer home and does all he can to make his father happy. Captain Dobbin again appears, at last confessing his love to Amelia. Her friendly feelings toward him do not equate to love, however. Possessing a higher moral code than Becky, she will not marry simply for financial convenience. Dobbin continues to work on Amelia's behalf to orchestrate a reconciliation with Mr. Osborne. This time he proves successful, and Amelia and her son receive an inheritance on the old man's death. Amelia at last knows true happiness when she travels to the Continent with her brother, Dobbin, and her son.

Becky appears for a final time when the traveling party encounter her at a German resort. Unable to live down the scandal of Rawdon's departure, Becky had to place her son with the young Sir Pitt, and she took up residence in Europe. She lives with various gentlemen as needed and hopes that upon this latest meeting of Jos, she can win his affection. Only Dobbin regards Becky with distrust, and Jos indeed falls prey to her infamous charm. Ironically, Amelia sees the couple joined years after her attempts to make them a couple and in most undesirable circumstances. Unable to gain a divorce from Rawdon, Becky must remain content simply to travel with Jos, who treats her as his wife. He foolishly takes out a large amount of life insurance, after which his family learns of his death. Becky naturally inherits a great deal of wealth, and the circumstances of Jos's death are never explained, although the details are hardly necessary for the reader. Ever the survivor, Becky remains on the Continent and gains a reputation for benevolence and grace.

In considering Thackeray's characters the ultimate in "lifelike" sketches, critics do not imply that the characters are psychologically complex or even fully drawn. Rather, they represent certain character types found in real life that fall into distinct categories. Thackeray guides his characters as a puppeteer would, using cynicism and sarcasm to tell their stories. He suggests that all his contemporaries had become puppets of the domineering early Victorian culture, one he envisions as both overly sentimental and hypocritical. Thackeray extends to Amelia the uncomplimentary label of "parasite" and sketches with palpable delight society's willingness to accept the newly moneyed incarnation of Becky as legitimate.

By refusing to dwell on the pathos of his characters, Thackeray forces readers to admit to the general darkness of ungoverned human nature. His purpose is not to allow readers a catharsis through an emotional identification with the hard luck of his various characters. Rather, Thackeray asks his readers to assess their own ideology in light of that presented in a novel judged vastly entertaining by decades of readers.

See also: Sharp, Becky; Thackeray, William Makepeace
References: Bullen, 1997; Clarke, 1995; Drabble, 1995; Flint, 1996; Harden, 1996; Hawes, 1993; Reed, 1995; Shillingsburg, 1994

VICTORIAN AGE

The term *Victorian Age* refers to the period from 1837 to 1901 when Queen Victoria ruled the United Kingdom of Great Britain and Ireland. This sixty-four-year period marked the longest reign by any British monarch. Victoria's lengthy reign encompassed vast social and institutional changes that produced clashes between various social and political powers, all of which would affect Victorian fiction. English subjects looked to Queen Victoria as an example of patriotism, honesty, and positive family values. The same subjects, however, also questioned the usefulness of traditional values in a modern age. Victoria's reign exemplified conservative politics and an intense nationalism, as it saw the rise of the middle class to claim a more prominent place in issues of political and social importance. Political movements included Marxism, feminism, socialism, and a resultant unionization of workers, and theories proposed by Charles Darwin and Sigmund Freud offered much for Victorians to consider.

Although nineteenth-century England confronted multiple problems, it also attempted to find modern solutions to those conflicts. A great excitement existed over the idea of invention and the concept that solutions to problems could simply be created, promising betterment for the human condition. Mechanical inventions, such as factory equipment, supported an Industrial Revolution increasing the production of material goods beyond imagination. Yet, despite an acknowledgment of the need for solutions to manufacturing problems, few sweeping social reforms were enacted and upheld. In reality, greater deprivation among lower classes existed than ever before. Like the United States, England adhered to the policy of *laissez faire* (let it be). This phrase supports the idea that socioeconomic factors could be expected to adjust themselves, with no outside interference from governments, to the benefit of all involved. In the midst of such national policy, slums grew, hunger increased, women and children labored as beasts of burden in dragging coal from mines, London seamstresses worked eighteen-hour days during the four-month "social" period and starved for the remaining eight months, pollution increased, and deaths from tuberculosis skyrocketed.

In many ways, the Victorian Age resembles late-twentieth-century American culture, with its worship of independence and material goods and its simultaneous acceptance and questioning of the modern beliefs in institutions of religion, democracy, patriotism, the family, progress, and sexual morality. Much serious Victorian literature reflects a guilt over the contradiction between the morality preached by cultural leaders and the resultant social system under which only the wealthy and powerful benefited. That guilt manifested itself in an often blatant critique of what many authors characterized as social hypocrisy. Many writers became representatives of the masses by combining the Romantic emphases on self, emotion, and imagination with the revived classical ideas of art's public role and the artist's responsibility to his or her audience.

The Victorian Age is known for prudishness, a fact that caused its writers and those in subsequent decades to feel a need for escape from their repressed, overconfident, bourgeois Victorian predecessors. Prudish aspects of the Victorian Age, however, have been overemphasized, and any single characteristic remains inadequate to indicate the nature of a complex age that resembled a second Renaissance in England. Although Victorians were not encouraged to speak of sexual issues, the lengthy novels of the era often focused on them. Restrictions upon vocal expression afforded Victorian writers the opportunity to develop a rich discourse of ambiguous and coded expression, suggesting much but saying little. Sex scandal formed a focus of much Victorian literature, both drama and prose, and it purportedly served to instruct audiences in the type of behavior they should avoid.

As melodrama grew in popularity on the nineteenth-century stage, its elements appeared in romantic fiction as well. Some critics feel the highly charged emotional expression of melodrama, in its description of physical suffering and criminal activity, served as a response to the invasive effects of a culture increasingly driven by commercial markets and capitalist tendencies. The nostalgic fiction of melodrama sought, although it did not succeed, to abolish the social classification and control so prevalent in the nineteenth century. Novels by writers such as Charles Dickens constructed emotionally exaggerated scenes of social and moral scandal. Such scenes frame the development of a young protagonist who moves from a state of innocence to one of experience in the novel plot known as a bildungsroman, or initiation/coming-of-age story.

Romantic, Victorian, and modern fiction all feature moments of recognition and self-revelation that serve to provide centers for human existence. Twentieth-century Irish writer James Joyce would refer to such a moment of spiritual manifestation as an *epiphany,* adopting a religious term from Catholicism that later writers and critics would continue to use. Victorian writers, such as Dickens, although without a label for the moment itself, carried this idea of self-revelation to its furthest extent. They filled their novels with anguished investigations of self on the part of their protagonists and the proper place of that self in its strict and demanding culture. In the work of novelists such as Thomas Hardy, those individuals fail to adjust to society's often unrealistic and inequitably applied demands, a failure that leads to tragedy.

The one aspect distinguishing those inhabiting the Victorian Age from those who came before might be a sense of social responsibility, however inadequate that sense among England's monied classes may have been in the face of rampant working-class poverty and disease. This awareness of responsibility separates the Victorians from the previous age of the Romantics when a focus on the importance of the self as an individual, whole and perfect, was emphasized over a concern for others. John Henry Cardinal Newman reflects this concern for social responsibility in his treatise on education, *Idea of a University* (1873). Newman includes a description of the Victorian gentleman as one who, above all, never inflicts pain on another. A believer in independence, the gentleman works to remove any encumbrances preventing the independence of his acquaintances. He also avoids inflicting discomfort through the discussion of matters that might cause a clash of opinions or in any way cause discontent in others. Newman's gentleman never takes advantage, practices modesty, never confuses issues with personalities, and observes the classic rule to act toward his enemies as if they will become future friends.

Representing a sociopolitical ideal seemingly related to class interest, Newman's description remains indicative of the dissonance that existed between Victorian ideology and the reality of the day. Such paradox is suggested by much Victorian fiction, either in its grim reflection of reality versus ideology or in its ironic assessment of Victorian hypocrisy through parody or humor.

See also: The Age of Innocence; Bildungsroman; *Daisy Miller;* Dickens, Charles John Huffam; Fowles, John; *The French Lieutenant's Woman;* Hardy, Thomas; James, Henry; *The Portrait of a Lady; A Room with a View; Tess of the d'Urbervilles;* Thackeray, William Makepeace; *Vanity Fair;* Wharton, Edith
References: Bullen, 1997; David, 1995; Horsman, 1990

VIOLENCE

Any act in which one person inflicts physical, emotional, or psychological harm upon another may be considered *violence.* Violence may occur in the private domestic sphere, the localized community sphere, the broader state sphere, or the global sphere. Because violence surfaces as a product of adult human relationships in a myriad of ways, it often serves as a focus of fiction dealing with love and romance.

One type of violence incorporated into fiction is that found in the domestic sphere. Violent actions within a circle of relationships may involve the use of fists, weapons, or injurious verbal attacks. Verbal violence generally carries the label "abuse" and may inflict a permanent state of emotional or psychological crippling or harm on its victim. In real life, domestic abuse most often involves violence against women and children by men. Because fiction imitates life, story plots may revolve around themes of domestic abuse in which a man commits the violent act. Such abuse may be seen most often in relationships termed *patriarchal marriages,* in which the male retains control over all aspects of the domestic scene.

Even when not physically harmed, wives, lovers, and children may be emotionally oppressed and violated by domineering males whose actions are approved of by their androcentric societies (see *The Portrait of a Lady*). The addition to verbal abuse of physical abuse may involve beatings with the fists or through the use of various objects or instruments (see *The Good Earth, The House of the Spirits, The Kitchen God's Wife, One on One, Sophie's Choice, Their Eyes Were Watching God*). A sexual aspect may also be incorporated in physical abuse, involving a man's rape of a woman or his forcing of a woman to perform sexually in a way she does not desire (see *Gone with the Wind; Of Love and Dust; The Shadow Bride; Tess of the d'Urbervilles*). The material control men exert over women, along with the fear they arouse in them, often works to make the situation a permanent one from which the women can envision no escape.

Occasionally, the infliction of domestic violence issues from a woman upon a man. This exchange generally incorporates verbal abuse but may also involve the infliction of physical pain, resulting in an unhealthy emotional relationship. Both partners continue this negative relationship due to its addictive quality (see *Ethan Frome* and *Of Human Bondage*).

An additional type of violence is that promoted by racial or ethnic inequality, such as the American system of slavery. One form of violence within slavery was the forced separation of black lovers and spouses from each other and their children, causing tremendous emotional and psychological conflict. Slaveowners and overseers also inflicted physical harm on slaves through beatings, dismemberment, and sexual abuse and rape (see *Beloved* and The Black Experience in America, 1600–1945). The effects of slavery influenced relationships between whites and blacks for decades, resulting in both social and civil laws and taboos against interracial romance and marriage (see *Lucy* and *Of Love and Dust*). Laws barring interracial romance and marriage have been responsible for violence between races other than just blacks and whites, such as American Indians and whites (see *The Last of the Mohicans*).

Romance tales may also shape characters who are in some way "monstrous." Such a character, sometimes through no fault of his or her own, may suffer violence at the hand of others (see *Frankenstein* and *The Hunchback of Notre Dame*). Such violence may be emotional, in the form of taunts and public humiliation, or physical, resulting in execution or another death by other means. Such abuse or death may result from crowd hysteria. In addition, romance plots may focus on violence and resultant death in the form of suicide or murder as a result of a love affair gone wrong. Characters may choose to end their own lives due to disappointment or frustration in love (see *An American Tragedy; Anna Karenina; The Awakening; The Hunchback of Notre Dame; Madame Bovary; Rebecca; The Robber Bride; Romeo and Juliet; Tess of the d'Urbervilles*).

Romantic novels often focus on widespread violence, such as that represented by armed combat between large groups. Politically based and ideologically based conflict and turmoil produced on the battlefield are generally mirrored in conflicts on the domestic scene. Armed conflict may include revolutionary activity, in which insurgents, or belligerents, challenge an established government. It may also involve full-fledged war between governments. Multiple romance plots focus on the effect upon love relationships of such armed combat (see the entry on *War* for examples of such novels).

References: Adams, 1995; Annesley, 1996; Booth, 1996; Cooke, 1996; Cuomo, 1996; Foster, Siegel, and Berry, 1996; Grimm, 1994; Halio, 1995; Koppelman, 1996; Plain, 1996; Price, 1996; Ross, 1995; Tambling, 1995

W

WAR

War may be defined as armed conflict between two or more sovereign governments or states. Civil wars occur between factions within the same government. In a rebellion or revolution, armed insurgents, or belligerents, challenge an established government. This challenge cannot be labeled war because the belligerents do not serve a formal government equipped to fight a large-scale combat on land, on sea, and in the air. In some incidents of one nation fighting another, the governments choose not to label the encounter a war. It might instead be termed a conflict or military action, such as the Korean conflict, an action in which the United States joined South Korea to fight against North Korea. The customs and behaviors of individual cultures govern laws of war. Civil wars generally end by the proclamation of peace, whereas international wars require formally derived peace treaties.

War is a type of violence often seen as an integral element of romantic novels. Multiple romance plots focus on its effects upon love relationships. Those effects include, at the least, the temporary separation of men and women and, at the worst, a permanent separation through death. Other devastating effects of war include the infliction of physical wounds and dismemberment on the battlefield. This may happen to men and women involved in active combat or in ancillary activities, such as providing medical care to the wounded. Men, women, and children, regardless of their social position, may suffer temporary or permanent emotional and psychological scarring as a result of organized armed conflicts. Traditionally, men departed to fight, while women remained on the domestic scene to raise children and maintain national production of food and goods. Some women also accompanied men to war, serving in a medical capacity or as a part of administrative forces. In modern times, women have joined men on the battlefield to engage in armed combat (see *The African Queen; Enemies: A Love Story; The Great Gatsby; The Journey; The Kitchen God's Wife; The Sky Is Red; Sophie's Choice; The Sun Also Rises*).

Examples of revolutionary actions featured in romantic novels include medieval fighting between English factions (see *Ivanhoe*), the American Revolution, the Napoleonic wars (see *The Count of Monte Cristo* and *Vanity Fair*), the French Revolution (see *A Tale of Two Cities* and *Les Misérables*), the American Civil War (see *Gone with the Wind*), the Spanish civil war (see *For Whom the Bell Tolls*), the Italian revolutions (see *The Horseman on the Roof* and *A Farewell to Arms*), the Russian revolution (see *Doctor Zhivago*), and Central and Latin American revolutions (see *Like Water for Chocolate* and *The House of the Spirits*). Circumstances of war or conflict may lead to ideological disagreements among members of the same family or among friends (see *Heroes*), causing domestic chaos on the home scene between lovers and spouses.

References: Booth, 1996; Cooke, 1996; Cuomo, 1996; Forbes and Kelly, 1995; Garcia and Pfeiffer, 1996; Gillingham, 1994; Koppelman, 1996; Plain, 1996; Price, 1996

WAUGH, EVELYN

One of England's more cynical writers of works concerning human relationships, Evelyn Arthur St. John Waugh was born in Hampstead in 1903. At the age of fourteen, Waugh wrote *The World to Come: A Poem in Three Cantos* (1916), a work that was printed privately. Educated at Lancing and Hertford College in Oxford, Waugh went on to teach at a few different private schools. Following this experience, which he found decidedly unrewarding, he took a position writing for *The Daily Express*. He produced another privately printed piece in 1926, *An Essay on the Pre-Raphaelite Brotherhood 1847–1854*.

In his first novel, *Decline and Fall* (1928), a book based on his frustrating experience as a teacher, Waugh found success. That same year, his biography of Dante Rossetti, *Rossetti: His Life and Works*, appeared. He also married Evelyn Gardner and became a member of the Catholic faith, although he would divorce Evelyn in 1930.

Waugh gained a reputation as his country's leading satirical novelist during the next decade, based upon his publication of *Vile Bodies* (1930), *Black Mischief* (1932), *A Handful of Dust* (1934), and *Scoop* (1938). Like his other works, *A Handful of Dust* parodied the irresponsible actions of the English aristocracy. Waugh's methods included not only the witty staging of demeaning incidents based on the greed and foolishness of his characters but also the framing of low subjects, such as the degrading relationship between the aptly named aristocrats Tony Last and Brenda Last, using plot elements from the highly idealized romantic quest.

Additional works during the middle portion of Waugh's life included *Put Out More Flags* (1942) and several travel books featuring his extensive travels in the Mediterranean, South America, and Mexico. *Waugh in Abyssinia* (1936) featured his coverage of Benito Mussolini's invasion of Ethiopia. His final travel book, *A Tourist in Africa* (1960), was published a few years before his death.

In 1937 Waugh married Laura Herbert, and the two settled in the West Country. In 1942, he published two chapters of an incomplete novel under the title *Work Suspended*. After serving in the royal Marines during World War II and becoming a member of the 1944 British military mission to Yugoslavia, Waugh wrote *Brideshead Revisited* (1945). For this popular novel, he drew on his experience as part of the military to construct this story of a group of men reunited following the war. In 1965, Waugh published a trilogy entitled *Sword of Honour* that consisted of the previously published *Men at Arms* (1952), *Officers and Gentlemen* (1955), and *Unconditional Surrender* (1961). His satire based on experiences in Hollywood, *The Loved One: An Anglo-American Tragedy*, appeared in 1948. Waugh's personal favorite from his many works, *Helena* (1950), was a historical novel that used ancient Rome as a setting, but it did not find the success of some of his other works.

Waugh's autobiographical tale of a middle-aged writer in crisis who eventually discovers redemption appeared in 1957 under the title *The Ordeal of Gilbert Pinfold*. A biography, *The Life of Ronald Knox*, was published in 1959, and a single chapter of Waugh's incomplete autobiography, *A Little Learning*, appeared in 1964. He died in 1966. Edited works published posthumously included Waugh's *Diaries* (1972) and *Letters* (1980), both frank revelations concerning the author's often troubled life.

See also: A Handful of Dust
References: Drabble, 1995; Gaye, 1996; Massa and Stead, 1994; Ousby, 1988; Wolk, 1993

WESTERN, SOPHIA

In Henry Fielding's classic bildungsroman, or initiation story, *The History of Tom Jones, a Foundling* (1749), Sophia Western acts as the protagonist's ultimate love interest. Tom enjoys fixations on many women, both of a physical and an emotional nature, but Sophia alone succeeds in permanently capturing his heart. Placed from an early age in a love triangle with Tom and the revolting Blifil, Sophia retains a sense of loyalty to Tom even when others dismiss him as worthless.

In an early illustrative scene, Sophia treasures a pet bird that the sneaky Blifil liberates. Although Tom believes liberty superior to confinement, a belief that reflects on his own personality, he attempts to recapture the bird for Sophia. This act is crucial, for Tom counters his own impulses in order to satisfy the desires of another. Ultimately, this effect that Sophia exerts upon Tom will cause him to choose the philosophical good over the bad.

The incident of the bird allows Fielding, through his various characters, to expound on the idea of human nature and the natural laws it must obey, the main law being the privileging of good over evil. Squire Western, Sophia's father, declares his enduring love for Tom, who placed himself in physical jeopardy for the sake of his daughter. This idea of self-sacrifice for the sake of another relates directly to biblical teaching from both the Old and New Testaments. Thus, Tom's nature as positive is early revealed. Squire Western's claim, however, later turns ironic when he comes to hate Tom on the basis of misinformation. He forbids his daughter's relationship with the only man who can make her happy, causing much conflict for Sophia and Tom.

As a child, Sophia remarks that Tom should not be punished by his schoolmaster for "the effect of his nature," asking then of her companion whether she does not believe Tom Jones "a boy of a noble spirit." This question foreshadows the eventual discover of Tom's identity. Originally a foundling, Tom will be identified as a member of the upper class, the nephew, in fact, of his "ward," Squire Allworthy. This detail allows Fielding to comply with classic foundling tales, such as Longus's *Daphnis and Chloe*. The revelation of Tom's heritage also serves to unite him with Sophia, transforming their forbidden love between individuals of differing social classes into a culturally approved love shared by social equals.

In addition, Fielding uses Sophia to comment on the vulnerability of women to the whims of men during his age. Sophia's father, the very one who proclaims her the love of his life, attempts to force her into marriage with Blifil, knowing that his daughter finds the young man loathsome. In a passionate scene late in the novel, Sophia promises to devote her life to the Squire's happiness, to never marry at all if only he will consider her desires in the matter of marriage to Blifil. The Squire persists in his demands, however, having as little pity on his daughter, the narrator tells the reader, as a jailer does when viewing a weeping wife visiting her prisoner husband or as a man would upon observing a young woman tricked into prostitution.

The reader's sympathy falls squarely upon the long-suffering Sophia and the recalcitrant Tom at the novel's end. Sophia Western's presence remains necessary to Tom's achievement of true love and to the emphasis on the ideal of justice. Of all the novel's characters, only Sophia remains dedicated to the higher moral good throughout the story, even at the expense of her love for Tom. As the narrator adds at the lengthy novel's conclusion, following the multiple true revelations that right all past wrongs, it is his relationship with the virtuous Sophia that helps to correct Tom's admitted vices. Through her efforts, Tom becomes a dynamic, well-rounded character, one who pays for past sins and anticipates a happy future.

See also: Jones, Tom; Longus; *Tom Jones*
References: Hipchen, 1994; Longus, 1989; Mace, 1996; Smallwood, 1989; Smith 1993; Thomas, 1992; Tillotson, Fussell, and Waingrow, 1969; Tumbleson, 1995

WHARTON, EDITH

Born in 1862 to a wealthy, aristocratic New York family, Edith Newbold Jones would later, as Edith

Wharton, write of her own life in novels that reflected on the peculiar responsibilities of the rich. Like all well-brought-up young women, Wharton developed the social graces expected in one of her class. Although she later rebelled against those customs and manners that she found personally stifling, Wharton benefited greatly from the advantages of wealth in receiving home schooling and in being allowed free use of her father's extensive library. Her imagination produced stories that she acted out as a child, and when she was sixteen, her verses were privately published. Wharton never again depended on private publishing, however, to publish her thirty-one major works and other lesser writings.

Following Wharton's social debut in 1879, the family traveled in France and Italy, hoping to boost the declining health of her father. They returned to the United States following his death three years later, and Wharton's engagement to Harry Stevens was announced and then broken off in 1882 due to his mother's opposition. She married Edward "Teddy" Wharton, thirteen years

Edith Wharton drew on her own life to create novels that reflected on the peculiar responsibilities of the rich. (Library of Congress)

her senior, in 1885 and returned to Europe for extensive travel. Her husband felt no interest in Wharton's creativity. Although they preserved the outward appearance of congeniality, their childless marriage remained an unhappy one.

After the couple settled in the United States, Wharton experienced several bouts of depression and two breakdowns between 1894 and 1902. During these times, she suffered from nausea, a melancholy that paralyzed her into inactivity, and exhaustion that caused her to lose her capacity for decisionmaking. Nevertheless, her first published short stories, a collection called *Greater Inclination,* appeared in 1899 and was followed by her first novel, *The Valley of Decision,* in 1902. After 1899, she averaged almost one book yearly for the remainder of her life. Teddy's health suffered a decline during this decade that would produce some of the author's greatest writing, including her 1911 novella, *Ethan Frome.*

Her 1905 book, *The House of Mirth,* showcased her favorite theme of the conflict between duty and love. Her heroine, Lily, whose aristocratic background resembled that of Wharton herself, refuses to marry for wealth and suffers dire poverty and rejection by her peers. Lily symbolizes the woman valued in the most crass social, almost economic way for her beauty only. Numerous additional Wharton novels attacked the pretensions accompanying "old money" by focusing on personal disasters caused by arrogant social rules governing behavior. Like her contemporary Henry James, who much admired Wharton, she explored not only social themes but also the psychological landscape of high society participants.

The Whartons relocated their winter home to Paris in 1907, the same year Edith was to meet Morton Fullerton, a protégé of Henry James. The Wharton marriage had begun to disintegrate when Edith discovered that Teddy had taken her money to support a mistress in Boston, and she began a long-lived affair with Fullerton. At the age of forty-six, she experienced a self-awakening and finally divorced Teddy in 1913. Following the divorce, she established herself as an independent-minded woman of intellect, forming friendships with men of letters and receiving the Pulitzer Prize, the first woman to receive this honor, for her 1920 novel, *The Age of Innocence.*

During World War I, Wharton worked with boundless energy to found shelters for refugees and to perform charitable acts, a preoccupation some critics felt to be responsible for a decline in the quality of her writing in the 1920s. She received the first honorary doctorate granted by Yale to a woman in 1923. Following the war, Wharton experienced a resurgence in creativity and popularity and was elected in 1930 to the National Institute of Arts and Letters. Four years later she received a membership in the American Academy of Arts and Letters. She died from a stroke in 1937 at age seventy-five. Wharton left behind a collection of works that stand as a monument to her intensive scrutiny of the fate reaped by an individual, especially a female, who desires to depart from the edicts of social convention.

See also: The Age of Innocence; Archer, Newland; Victorian Age

References: Bell, 1995; Blain, Clements, and Grundy, 1990; Davidson, 1995; Geist, 1996; Gilbert and Gubar, 1996b; Hart, 1995; Pizer, 1995; Price, 1996; Robillard, 1996; Wegener, 1996

WILFRED OF IVANHOE

Wilfred of Ivanhoe exemplifies the characteristics of a knight of chivalry. As the protagonist of Sir Walter Scott's 1819 medieval novel *Ivanhoe,* the young Ivanhoe meets all the requirements for his role. Possessed of courage, a highly moral sensibility, a desire for ethical behavior in himself as well as others, spirituality, and a loyalty-to-the-death attitude, Ivanhoe makes his mark on his Saxon surroundings. Although he acts as half of the novel's romantic duo through his love for the royal Rowena, Ivanhoe also draws attention to his skills in battle. He personally serves King Richard I, also known as Richard the Lion-Hearted, by following his monarch to the Third Crusades to defend ruler and religion, which were, readers should recall, one and the same in the medieval mind. In addition, Ivanhoe qualifies as a quest character who enjoys adventure in a foreign land, seeks his own identity apart from his estranged father, and returns home to claim his love.

Although Scott personally did not approve of the barbaric tests of skill practiced among knights in the twelfth century, he devotes much attention to scenes of one-on-one combat. They serve as testimony to Ivanhoe's devotion to Rowena, to his courage in his chosen profession, and, equally important, to his willingness to die as champion for a fair lady for whom he feels no romantic connection. The lady in this case is the wealthy and beautiful Jewess Rebecca who, while visiting the Saxon territory with her father, suffers through a kidnapping and a subsequent threat to her life.

Scott incorporates multiple aspects of the traditional romance, including use of disguise. When Ivanhoe initially appears in the novel, it is as a mysterious pilgrim who acts as a guide to his eventual nemesis, Brian de Bois-Guilbert. Bois-Guilbert, a Knight Templar, represents the Norman faction that, according to Ivanhoe's father Cedric, ruined the Saxon culture. Also inherent to the story is the theme of the triumph of good over evil. Ivanhoe clearly represents all that is good. He supports King Richard against his evil brother John; joins forces with the legendary Robin Hood, who battled the evil of oppression; and does battle with the ostensibly evil Bois-Guilbert, first in order to represent the honor of Rowena and second in order to rescue Rebecca from the clutches of the evil Normans. All his enemies fall as Ivanhoe and the other heroic characters band together against them.

Ivanhoe has a foil in Bois-Guilbert, also a knight but a representative of the novel's evil contingent. Scott does allow Bois-Guilbert to repent when he undergoes an epiphany, realizing his folly in helping to orchestrate the trial that could have led to Rebecca's execution. But, true to the code of honor sworn by the knight, Bois-Guilbert must hold to his vow to battle Rebecca's champion in order not to besmirch the reputation of Lucas de Beaumanoir, grand master of the Templars. His convenient death from an attack of spiritual realization before he can kill Ivanhoe, who has been weakened by battle, also stands as a prototypical romantic element.

In the novel's conclusion, Ivanhoe settles his differences with his father, who blesses the marriage between Ivanhoe and Rowena. He achieves an admirable woman as a prize for his battle skills and devotion and the lifelong gratitude of his liege, King Richard I, in addition to earning an identity for himself separate from that of his father Cedric. Thus, the novel ends with an all-around victory of good over evil and with Wilfred of Ivanhoe proving himself the perfect chivalric knight.

See also: Chivalry; *Ivanhoe;* Rebecca, Daughter of Isaac; Romance; Rowena, Lady; Scott, Sir Walter; Violence
References: Bayley, 1960; Duncan, 1992; Grierson, 1974; Hulme, 1974; Pater, 1974

WILKES, ASHLEY

Readers remember Ashley Wilkes as the man who for years received Scarlett O'Hara's misplaced affection in Margaret Mitchell's American Civil War novel, *Gone with the Wind* (1936). His character serves the novel in two vital capacities. First, he acts as foil to the Byronic figure of Rhett Butler, the charming but scandalous soldier-of-fortune who passionately loves Scarlett. Second, Ashley symbolizes the prewar South and its strange combination of an ideology based on chivalric or courtly values with an acceptance of the enslavement of human beings.

With Scarlett and Rhett, Ashley reluctantly forms a love triangle. Although Scarlett pursues Ashley's affection in her youth, he firmly settles his love on his cousin and wife, Melanie Wilkes. Thus, a second love triangle forms between Ashley and the two women, again a reluctant involvement on his part. Ashley finds Scarlett attractive, but he realizes what she cannot—the two are opposites in temperament and beliefs. Scarlett is willful and demanding, demonstrating a strength and independence of spirit that greatly contrasts with the weakness and resultant emotional surrender she observes in those around her. She remains practical to the extreme, ready to put into action any plan that will achieve her desire to remain free from hunger and poverty. Ashley, however, represents the Confederate soldier forced to surrender, who gives up not only his past but also a future to which he can never adjust. Ashley suffers an emotional and psychological, as well as a physical defeat, during the war.

Although Ashley differs markedly from Scarlett in temperament, they share one essential trait. Both cling to the past. Ashley longs for the courtly approach to life on stately plantations; progress holds no attraction for him. Scarlett's fixation on the myth of Ashley's love for her represents her chain to the past. Practical to a fault in every other way, Scarlett clings foolishly to a fantasy that will cause the ruin of her one chance for happiness, her marriage to Rhett Butler.

Ashley's devotion to Melanie, a woman viewed as weak and "mealy-mouthed" by Scarlett, grows over the years. Scarlett refuses to accept his choice, however, desiring Ashley simply because she cannot have him. When Ashley thinks of leaving Georgia following his return from the war, Scarlett's childish tantrum moves Melanie to remind Ashley that Scarlett saved her life and that of their infant son during Ashley's absence. Melanie believes Scarlett's claim that she needs Ashley to help her regain solvency, and she, like her husband, adheres to the chivalric code of meeting one's obligations to another. Because he cannot fight both women, Ashley, again defeated, agrees to stay and help Scarlett with her new business ventures.

Not until Melanie's death does Ashley convince Scarlett that he loves only his wife. His character remains absolutely unchanged from the novel's beginning to its end. Still in possession of the gentleman's code that serves him no longer, Ashley ends the story never learning to accept the changes in his culture. Unlike Rhett and Scarlett, both survivors who triumph over the new system, Ashley simply marks time, yearning for days past.

See also: The Black Experience in America, 1600–1945; Butler, Rhett; *Gone with the Wind;* Mitchell, Margaret; O'Hara, Scarlett; War; Wilkes, Melanie
References: Armstrong, 1990; Flora and Bain, 1987; Frye, 1976; Hoffman and Murphy, 1996; Joyner, 1996

WILKES, MELANIE

Melanie Wilkes represents the prototypical southern lady in Margaret Mitchell's American Civil War novel, *Gone with the Wind* (1936). As such, she acts as a foil to the novel's headstrong, opinionated, and independent protagonist, Scarlett O'Hara. Scarlett uses her feminine wiles to their most charming advantage, but nurturing others is not her strong suit. Whereas Melanie always chooses the self-sacrificial route, obeys her husband, and stays at home in the woman's sphere, Scarlett sacrifices herself for no one, orders her first two husbands around, and runs her own postwar business outside the home. Melanie remains important to plot as part of a love triangle uniting herself, her cousin and husband, Ashley Wilkes, and Scarlett. Scarlett could have her pick of the southern men, but she stubbornly pursues Ashley simply because he loves another.

Melanie symbolizes a generosity of spirit that Scarlett views as an emotional weakness matching Melanie's physically weak state. Yet whatever else Scarlett may think of Melanie, she cannot deny Melanie's faith and trust. Even when Scarlett's designs upon Ashley become public knowledge, Melanie supports her. She owes Scarlett a debt of gratitude for saving her own life and that of her infant son during the bombing of Atlanta. Adhering strictly to the courtly southern code, Melanie shows no outward acknowledgment of the gossip linking Scarlett to her husband. Her purity and lack of guile remain her most consistent personality traits.

Melanie does occasionally demonstrate a surprising strength of character. When a group of men raid a postwar shanty town outside Atlanta to avenge an attack on Scarlett, Melanie keeps everyone's emotions in check. She finds the courage to speak to a local law official, supporting the alibi Rhett Butler concocts for Ashley and the other men. When Rhett shocks everyone by stating before the women and the Yankee lawman that the men have been carousing at a local house of prostitution, Melanie plays along with the ruse perfectly. Her quick thinking and courage in this compromising situation reveal that she also possesses an instinct for survival, particularly when her actions help rescue Ashley, her lifelong love.

Scarlett does not deserve the devotion and friendship of Melanie Wilkes, and that is perhaps the most important aspect of their relationship. Melanie remains a flat character in the story, her personality unwavering. Even on her deathbed, Melanie considers the welfare of those she loves. She asks Scarlett to care for Ashley and for their son and then assures her of Rhett's love. Melanie's words and Ashley's abject grief over the news of Melanie's death force Scarlett to at last realize that her future happiness rests in her relationship with Rhett. Unfortunately for Scarlett, by the time she learns the value of love from the example set by the Wilkes' unshakable devotion to one another, she cannot save her own marriage.

See also: The Black Experience in America, 1600–1945; Butler, Rhett; *Gone with the Wind;* Mitchell, Margaret; O'Hara, Scarlett; War; Wilkes, Ashley
References: Armstrong, 1990; Flora and Bain, 1987; Frye, 1976; Hoffman and Murphy, 1996; Joyner, 1996

WINGO, TOM

Like Pat Conroy's other male characters, Tom Wingo, from *The Prince of Tides* (1986), is autobiographical. Conroy imbues all his male protagonists with certain characteristics that reflect his own personality. These include low self-esteem, a troubled southern family background, and the ongoing questioning of religion and faith. Present conflicts for Tom include his loss of self-confidence as a school coach; his crumbling marriage to his physician-wife, Sally Wingo; the ongoing emotional abuse from his overbearing mother, Lila; the suicide attempt of his sister, Savannah; the death of the eldest Wingo sibling, the Vietnam veteran, Luke; and an affair with Savannah's therapist, Susan Lowenstein. Tom must deal with these multiple conflicts in the present, while also coping with a past family mythology that includes a drunken, abusive father; a pet tiger, Caesar; a childhood rape; his mother's sacrifice of Luke to her social and material aspirations; and his mother's remarriage to a man Tom always hated. Conroy weaves his strong characterization of Tom using these many challenges to strengthen Tom's resolve for a better future.

As readers expect from a Conroy novel, *The Prince of Tides* provides abundant imagery and symbolism filtered through Tom's storytelling. The southern setting remains important, causing some critics to label the novel southern Gothic because of its themes of religion, insanity, and mysterious, mystical occurrences. Also important is the fact that the Tom's father earns his living as a fisherman, necessitating the family's close proximity to the ocean. The sea and water in general play a major part in Tom's past. One scene from Tom's past in particular features the water as the three Wingo children's chosen point of escape from their parents' fighting. During an altercation, they flee their house, jump into the water, submerge themselves, and hold hands. This formation symbolizes their strong relationship as a circle with no beginning and no end. Their eventual surfacing symbolizes a baptism, a renewal of sorts, as the children emerge in hopes of beginning a new life. Although their hopes are never fulfilled, while young, they continue to believe that life could improve.

The stories Tom shares with Lowenstein, the New York City therapist who attempts to help rescue Tom's poet-sister from her depression, form the framework of the novel. At first Tom, the small-town southern boy, and Lowenstein, the big-city professional, appear to be opposites in many ways. However, they eventually share a strong attraction for one another and fall in love, forming love triangles with Sally Wingo and with Lowenstein's concert-violinist husband, Herbert Woodruff.

Lowenstein serves as a guide to Tom's quest-hero-figure, helping him adjust as he takes up temporary residence in foreign surroundings following his journey northward. Tom seeks as his prize the answers to the questions that will allow him to return home and reconstruct his life. Like all quest characters, Tom must face various monsters and challenges. His memories provide all of the monstrous imagery necessary, culminating in his relation of his terrifying and bizarre rape as a child by intruders in his home. The mystical characters within the story include the tiger, Caesar, who rescues the family from its attackers and literally destroys them. The biggest monster Tom must overcome is the detrimental effect on his life of his own mother, the beautiful Lila Wingo. She worked hard to make all of her children dependent upon her and then emotionally deserted each at their most vulnerable moments. A social climber who will sacrifice anything and anyone to her dreams of boosting her class status, Lila inflicts deep pain on each of her offspring.

A crucial aspect of Tom's own success through Lowenstein's friendship is his regaining of his self-confidence as a teacher and coach. Lowenstein administers symbolic therapy to Tom when she introduces him to her son, Bernard, an aspiring football player. As the two form a close friendship, their bond in turn helps to liberate Lowenstein from her controlling and oppressive relationship with her violinist husband. Thus, when Tom and Lowenstein at last separate, a feeling of equanimity remains, each having aided the other and themselves.

Tom discovers a new identity when he learns to accept and deal with the incidents from his past over which he had no control. He and Sally may begin the reconstruction of their family, thanks to Tom's recovery of self-confidence and hope for the future. Although no longer physically present in Tom's life, Lowenstein continues to have a metaphysical affect on Tom. She remains his guide during his newest quest for happiness, as evidenced by the fact that he sometimes repeats her name again and again, like a spiritual chant or mantra.

See also: Conroy, Pat; Gothic Romance; Love Triangle; *The Prince of Tides;* Violence
References: Berendt, 1995; Flora and Bain, 1987; Frye, 1976; Hoffman and Murphy, 1996; Shone, 1995; Toolan, 1991

WINTERBOURNE, FREDERICK FORSYTHE

Henry James establishes Winterbourne as the voice of reluctant reason in his novella *Daisy Miller* (1879). Although strongly attracted to Daisy and her carpe diem attitude, Winterbourne cannot embrace the same approach to life. When he attempts to educate Daisy as to the importance of manners and ritual, he only alienates her, causing her to accuse him of preaching. His cool nature symbolized by his name remains unfit for nurture of the wild and natural spirit that Daisy represents. Winterbourne well represents the Swiss landscape in which the characters are first introduced as well as the passionless upper class to which he belongs.

In the second portion of the story, it is Winterbourne who is out of place beneath Italy's Mediterranean sun. In Rome, he meets his foil in Giovanelli, an Italian gentleman whose passionate and open nature Daisy finds irresistible. Winterbourne establishes himself more as a father figure to the girl, handing out unwanted advice that serves only to align him with the older Victorian women who insist on instructing Daisy in "proper" behavior. He joins the corrective chorus that Daisy finds so offensive.

Winterbourne never understands that in mistrusting Giovanelli, he mistrusts Daisy. He remains hostile toward Daisy's desire for spiritual experience that she gains through exercise of her independence. Even when he at last tries to champion Daisy's cause, defending her honor to the older women who attack her, Winterbourne sounds complacent rather than passionate. When Daisy asks him on one occasion the reason for his solemn demeanor, he tells her in all sincerity that he thought he was "grinning." This episode clearly illustrates their mismatched natures. When Daisy tells Winterbourne that he looks as if he were taking her to a funeral, her remark acts as grim foreshadowing.

In the end, Winterbourne proves only to be Daisy's casual escort. Daisy Miller's looks alone could garner her scores of such men. She desires instead a soulmate, a partner with a sense of adventure, and Winterbourne cannot be that person. On their first excursion together, when Daisy attempts to light a spirit of adventure in her companion through her remarks regarding the ruins they tour, Winterbourne assesses her many observations as lacking in "logical consistency."

James uses this occasion to contrast Winterbourne's rational and dull approach to life to Daisy's use of imagination.

Winterbourne's approach to Daisy is one of curiosity, as if he were a scientist studying a rare species of butterfly. He does not understand that the moment the creature undergoes dissection for examination, its animating spirit released, the vibrant colors that so attract him will immediately fade. When the narrator closes the tragic tale of Daisy Miller by announcing that Winterbourne has returned to Geneva, where his interest has been captured by a "clever foreign lady," the reader is hardly surprised.

See also: Daisy Miller; Miller, Daisy; *The Portrait of a Lady*

References: Caeserio, 1979; Frye, 1976; McQuade et al., 1987; Washington, 1995

WOODRUFF, SARAH

Sarah Woodruff plays the heroine in John Fowles's mock Victorian Age romance, *The French Lieutenant's Woman* (1969). Like the Victorian plot conventions that Fowles employs, Sarah's character is not what she seems. As Fowles adopts the approach of Victorian fiction specifically so that he may then undermine its conventions, he also

Meryl Streep played Sarah Woodruff, the heroine of The French Lieutenant's Woman, *in the 1981 film version. (Photofest)*

develops Sarah as a twentieth-century woman whose actions undermine her development as a Victorian heroine. Although at first shaped with the desirable Victorian characteristics of a woman who suffers for her sexual indiscretions, Sarah will reveal that the stories regarding her love life exist only in her imagination and that of others. She shapes through fiction one Sarah Woodruff for the world to view, but she exists in actuality as something entirely different.

In the novel's opening moments, Sarah's lonely figure appears at the end of a pier in the village of Lyme Regis on Dorset's Lyme Bay. Narrative details suggest a time frame in the 1860s or 1870s, and the couple who observe Sarah represent that era well. Sarah will soon form a love triangle with Charles Smithson and Ernestina Freeman, the two young lovers who gaze at her from afar. Charles and Ernestina represent a fine Victorian couple, with Ernestina eager to please Charles and Charles more than happy to take advantage of his society's patriarchal view of marriageable women such as his fiancée. Smug, self-content, and ripe for a passionate encounter, Charles fancies himself a scientist, spouting the conventions of newly proposed Darwinism. While claiming to be a scientist, however, he scolds Ernestina for removing all sense of romanticism by revealing the details regarding Sarah Woodruff.

Sarah teases the entire village with just enough details regarding her past to allow them all to exert their Victorian hypocrisy as they simultaneously pass judgment on and attempt to "care" for her. Her sins enable the character development of Mrs. Poulteney, an elderly busybody who represents the strict religious code of the times. Urged by a local preacher to exert her Victorian sense of social responsibility, Mrs. Poulteney takes Sarah into her home in order to control the young woman's future behavior. Sarah's sensuality also teases Charles into a proprietary sense of shock when he first comes into contact with her physical allure. His attempts to examine her as a scientific specimen fail, as he envisions himself a hero come to rescue a discontented Madame Bovary.

Fowles uses Sarah's untruths to convert what purports to be a Victorian novel into a very twentieth-century story. For this inversion, he depends primarily on Sarah's actions and, secondarily, the reactions they cause in Charles. Sarah succeeds in drawing Charles's attention away from Ernestina. In a lusty sexual encounter reminiscent of those only suggested in a Victorian melodrama, Sarah seduces Charles. The scene, however, brims with the physical detail that Victorian tales forbade. Although Charles terms Sarah an angel, she plays the role of temptress, requiring a mere ninety seconds to bring her lover to climax. Charles breaks his engagement to Ernestina, not due to any concrete promises on Sarah's part but rather because of assumptions he makes regarding her purportedly loose character.

Sarah's enigmatic character conforms to the demands of Fowles's unique dual ending. In one conclusion, she appears to Charles, who has spent much time searching for her, accompanied by their love child, of whose existence Charles remained unaware. Then, in melodramatic Victorian fashion, she declares herself unfit to wed him, sending him away. However, the narrator steps in at this point and performs a "replay" that allows Charles to refuse Sarah's manipulative behavior. He chooses to leave her behind, a choice that breaks the Victorian codes seemingly guiding the plot.

The narrator closes by referring to Sarah Woodruff as a sphinx but then makes clear that life does not consist of a simple single riddle requiring a simple single answer. She represents only one possible answer to the life Charles has yet to figure out. She may at first appear to be the prize Charles seeks in his quest for happiness and identity. In the end, however, she must be accepted on her own terms and as more important to her own present than to another's future.

See also: The French Lieutenant's Woman; Love Triangle; Smithson, Charles; Victorian Age
References: Baker and Vipond, 1996; Foster, 1994; Friedman and Siegel, 1995; Hart, 1995; Neary, 1992

WOODS, JANIE CRAWFORD KILLICKS STARKS

Janie Crawford Killicks Starks Woods serves as the protagonist and narrator of Zora Neale Hurston's novel *Their Eyes Were Watching God* (1937). The story unfolds from the point of view of the young half-white, half-black Janie, famous for her long black hair. Early in the novel Janie experiences the first stirrings of love when she exchanges an innocent kiss with a boy. Her grandmother swears that Janie will not, like her dead mother, foolishly throw her life away for romance, and she forces Janie to marry Logan Killicks, a much older man. After a few months in a loveless patriarchal marriage, Janie realizes that marriage does not equal love. She matures to womanhood, leaving innocence and naïveté behind, as her dreams of romance die.

When Janie meets Joe Starks, he elicits from her the reaction that Logan never could, and she leaves Logan and her position behind his plow. She carries much hope for the relationship with a man about whom she had fantasized. She envisions the road down which their wagon traces as a new dress, symbolic of her assumption of a new role.

Joe becomes mayor and prosperous store owner in an all-black Florida town, where he sets Janie up as an object for others to admire. His jealousy and possessiveness begin to smother Janie's independent spirit. Once again clothes assume an important symbolic meaning as Joe forces Janie to cover with a scarf the long black hair that had captured his attention. When Janie speaks her mind in public and Joe slaps her, she knows their relationship has ended. Reacting as a typical husband in a patriarchal marriage, Joe rejects Janie and her desire to be independent.

Following Joe's death from cancer, Janie next meets and eventually runs away with Vergible "Tea Cake" Woods. The novel actually opens with Janie's return from her time spent with Tea Cake to the curious questions of her neighbors. They assume her story will be one of rejection by a younger man who has, perhaps, stolen her ample wealth. Janie relays the truth to a friend, Pheoby. In Tea Cake, she at last found romance. Janie's relation of her adventures with Tea Cake help convince the reader that she has been deeply satisfied in love.

Following a destructive hurricane in which Tea Cake sustains the rabid dog bite meant for Janie, she realizes that he has sacrificed his life for her. She wishes she had drowned in the flood with the dog, rather than suffering this emotional death, through Tea Cake, at a later time. Janie grants Pheoby permission to share her story with others but cautions that everyone must discover two things for themselves: God and the truth about life. At the novel's conclusion, garments again become symbolic as Janie imagines draping about her shoulders the light and love that is her history with Tea Cake.

See also: The Black Experience in America, 1600–1945; Hurston, Zora Neale; Patriarchal Marriage; *Their Eyes Were Watching God;* Violence
References: Carr, 1987; Gilbert and Gubar, 1996g; Graham et al., 1989; Henderson and McManus, 1985; Radway, 1991; Schleiner, 1994; Travitsky, 1990

WUTHERING HEIGHTS

Emily Brontë's novel, *Wuthering Heights* (1847), quickly became a hallmark of Gothic romance and one of the most popular novels of its age. Its presentation of a brooding Byronic hero in Heathcliff and its use of the Platonic idea of commingled souls, suggested through Heathcliff and Catherine Earnshaw Linton, both shocked and delighted readers. In a preface to the 1850 edition, Emily's sister, Charlotte Brontë, expressed an understanding of the fact that readers most likely did not share her sibling's interest in events on the moors, nor in the area's language or manners. She adds that the casual observer might even find the moors' inhabitants repulsive. Then Charlotte points out redeeming factors in some of the novel's characterizations that she hopes will overcome the more foreign fictional aspects. Admitting to the novel's horror and darkness, its storm-heated and electrified atmosphere, she asks readers to balance this hyperbole with the obviously tender character of the nurse, Nelly Dean, and the admirable constancy of Catherine's husband, Edgar Linton. Despite her diplomatic presentation, Charlotte fails to distract readers from her sister's sketch of an unearthly and deeply satisfying passion shared by Catherine and Heathcliff. The sedate personalities of some of the lesser characters fade in the brilliance of those two lovers. With a plot containing passion, ghosts, revenge, the conflict of multiple love triangles, and the questioning of metaphysical possibilities, *Wuthering Heights* remains a classic 150 years after its author's death.

As the story unfolds through the first-person narrative of a stranger to the moors, Wuthering Heights is described as belonging to Mr. Heathcliff. Soon the narration switches to third person through the figure of the onetime Earnshaw household servant, Nelly. The remainder of the narrative for the most part uses flashbacks to relate the tragic and enthralling tale of passion on the moors. In addition to presenting the Gothic elements of a heroine in distress, graveyard scenes, death, love, betrayal, and mysterious residences, *Wuthering Heights* offers readers the chance to question the permanence of separation by death. So strong remains Heathcliff's passion for Catherine that he wills her spirit to live even after her flesh succumbs to death.

Heathcliff had been brought to Wuthering Heights by Mr. Earnshaw, father to Cathy and her brother Hindley, to live with the family as a foundling. His social position remained a low one, and Hindley, an ill-mannered young man who inherited none of his station's supposed gentle breeding, tortured Heathcliff in every possible manner, insulting and bullying him. Cathy, however, loved Heathcliff fiercely, and he returned her frighteningly determined devotion throughout their childhood. A slight accident on Cathy's part, however, would alter their relationship forever.

Cathy becomes acquainted with her wealthy neighbors at Thrushcross Grange, finding herself particularly attracted to Edgar Linton and his sister Isabella. When she injures her ankle while visiting the Grange in Heathcliff's company, the Lintons decide she must remain with them during an extended convalescence. Heathcliff's violent reaction at the possibility of a separation and Mrs. Linton's remarks regarding his crude and unacceptable manners foreshadow the approaching conflict. During Cathy's five-week absence from her home, she forms an attachment to the Lintons that threatens her relationship with the jealous Heathcliff. When she decides to marry Edgar, Heathcliff disappears, having overheard Cathy proclaim Edgar to be her future husband. Unfortunately, he departs before hearing her declare to Nelly that no mortal creature could ever part her from Heathcliff. As one would expect from the romance tradition, her statement misses Heathcliff's ears by moments. The very situation Cathy declares an impossibility becomes reality.

Edgar becomes a foil for Heathcliff in the love triangle the two form with Cathy. He remains light, frail, and emotional, easily moved to tears, his gentlemanly actions suggesting a weakness of character. Heathcliff's strong Byronic qualities contrast greatly with Edgar's pampered fragility. Those traits become important in the future battle that Heathcliff stages, not only for Cathy's love but against those who mistreated him in his youth. When he returns years later a wealthy

property owner, having made a fortune in America, he puts into motion a scheme supported by the power his newfound wealth affords.

As Mrs. Edgar Linton, Cathy attempts to appear happy and satisfied. She fails to recover, however, from her separation from Heathcliff, having shared a passion with him that she cannot duplicate with any other individual. Ironically, their attraction becomes destructive, contrasting with the supportive relationship that Edgar willingly offers to Cathy. Heathcliff succeeds in making Cathy miserable by his mere presence, cursing her to unhappiness as a being separate from himself. His ruthless character becomes clear when he responds to Isabella Linton's attentions, not out of any love for her but simply to use her in his fiendish game against the Lintons and the Earnshaws. Edgar protests their marriage to no avail. Unable to admit before marriage that she played only an insignificant part in the love triangle involving Heathcliff and Cathy, as his wife, Isabella at last realizes her husband's emotionally abusive treatment will not change. Like all of the other characters except for Cathy, Isabella comes to loathe her husband. When Cathy dies in childbirth, Heathcliff curses her to a death without peace, demanding that her spirit remain earthbound until he can die and join her.

The rest of the novel engages in an explanation of how Heathcliff achieves his goal of total revenge over the next several years. Isabella deserts him and bears a weakling son, Linton. Following her death, Linton moves in with Heathcliff. Father and son share nothing in common, and Heathcliff decides to use his own son in his diabolical plan. Like his uncle Edgar Linton, Linton remains a weak being, often sick and bedridden. Edgar himself becomes little more than an emotional cripple following the loss of his beloved Cathy, his one delight being their daughter, also named Catherine. In their relationships with their children, Edgar and Heathcliff differ greatly.

Cathy's brother Hindley drinks himself into an early grave, having unknowingly mortgaged Wuthering Heights to Heathcliff. Heathcliff claims victory over his childhood enemy, coming into possession of the house where he had been raised as little more than a servant. His revenge becomes all the sweeter as he takes on the care of Hindley's son, Hareton. Hareton seems a reproduction of the young Heathcliff, rough and dark but possessed of an independent spirit that constantly rejects Heathcliff's cruel treatment. This causes Heathcliff to unwillingly form an attachment to Hareton, although he often abuses the boy.

Into this situation wanders the young Catherine, captivated by the idea that she has a cousin living at Wuthering Heights. Although forbidden by the grieving Edgar to visit what is now Heathcliff's domain, Catherine's headstrong will takes precedence over her father's command. When Catherine and Nelly arrive at Wuthering Heights, Heathcliff reveals to Nelly his intention to force Catherine to marry Linton. This move remains crucial to the revenge he desires against Edgar. When Nelly observes Linton's sickly frame, she states that Catherine will inherit all at Linton's death. Heathcliff has, however, already counteracted this possibility. If the two marry, Linton's possessions remain his own and so do those of his future daughter-in-law. Should his plan succeed, then, he will assume ownership of Thrushcross Grange upon Edgar Linton's death.

All that Heathcliff plans eventually takes place, but following his many dark victories, life holds little attraction for him. He finds he has nothing to love except for the dead Cathy, and he continually visits her grave. Always perceived of by others as mad, Heathcliff descends further into a type of insanity, but he at last knows peace in the anticipation of his end. Cathy Linton Heathcliff, by now a widow following Linton's predicted death, remains with Heathcliff and Hareton when her own father dies. These two cousins form an attachment unanticipated by Heathcliff, but he seems at last to reach a stage in which happiness of the offspring of the two men he had most hated becomes acceptable.

The novel concludes with a suggestion of peace to be found in the death Heathcliff shares with Cathy, as well as in the love and eventual marriage of Catherine and Hareton. In their devotion to one another, the young lovers balance the hate and disappointment experienced by their parents. The passing of one generation will not threaten that to follow, for as the first-person narrator again takes up the story, he comments that the young lovers fear nothing. Together, he suspects, they could confront Satan and all his devilish legions. Not so for Heathcliff, who for a time seemed to become satanic himself, consumed by passion for a woman he could never physically possess. Spiritually, however, Heathcliff and Catherine Earnshaw Linton belonged to one another for eternity.

See also: Brontë, Charlotte and Emily; Earnshaw, Catherine; Forbidden Love; Gothic Romance; Heathcliff; Linton, Edgar; Love Triangle; Violence
References: Allen, 1993; Ellis, 1989; Gilbert and Gubar, 1996a; Leavis, 1966; Pater, 1974; Winnifrith, 1996

ZAWISTOWSKA, SOPHIE

As the protagonist in William Styron's tragic, realistic romance *Sophie's Choice* (1979), Sophie Zawistowska stands as one of the most tragic of modern heroines. She represents various oppressed groups and individuals, most obviously members of the Jewish race persecuted by Hitler. Although not a Jew herself, she suffers internment in Nazi concentration camps in her homeland of Poland during the war. Sophie, actually Zofia Maria Bieganska Zawistowska, suffered not only the general indignities heaped upon the camps' prisoners but also the horrendous loss of both her children, her parents, and her husband. Styron often focuses on American slavery; thus Sophie may also symbolize the enslavement and oppression of American blacks and, more specifically, black mothers whose children were taken from them by force. Sophie also represents all American women of her era in her suffering the indignities and abuse enforced by America's gender inequities. She represents all abused wives and lovers who through desperation attach themselves to violent males. Like too many other females, Sophie relies on fantasy images of white knights and chivalry in an all-too-real world populated by animalistic individuals such as her lover, Nathan Landau. A paranoid schizophrenic, Nathan swings from exalting Sophie to degrading her, practicing a verbal and physical degradation more foul on its intimate level than that inflicted upon her impersonally by her Nazi captors. Finally, she represents a childhood love of the novel's young writer–narrator, Stingo. He learns of Maria Hunt's death from his father early in the novel, and both Maria and Sophie become subjects of Stingo's abundant sexual fantasy life.

Many aspects of Sophie's life attach her to Stingo. Stingo's southern background leaves him with an inherited guilt regarding slavery and the violence caused by segregation, although he himself never participates in the physical abuse of blacks. Sophie's inherited guilt comes from her father, a man she believed to be a liberal-thinking academic who, to her horror, in reality believed in control of the Jews. Whereas Stingo's personal guilt derives from his past neglect of a terminally ill mother, Sophie suffers untold horrors over the "choice" she was forced to make when she entered Auschwitz, a choice that was no choice at all. She does not reveal this nightmarish detail of her past until well into the novel, delaying Stingo's and, by extension, the reader's, understanding of her. Sophie had to offer up one of her two children to certain execution upon entering the camp. Had she not "chosen," both children would likely have died on the spot. As events develop, she never sees either child past a certain point during her stay in the camp, but her offering up of her daughter as sacrifice drives her later to a private insanity that parallels and supports Nathan's public insanity.

Sophie remains a complicated character, seemingly easily analyzed but not easily understood. She reveals her past bit by bit, supplying one painful piece at a time to the puzzle that represents her life as she shares the summer of 1947 with Stingo. Although at first Stingo does not understand her attachment to the abusive Nathan, he gains more understanding later through the revelation of Sophie's story. She confesses to one horror after another, from an attempted seduction of Rudolph Hess, the only strategy that seemed available to her for survival, to what she views as the sacrifice of her daughter, to her rape by other women and later by a stranger's finger in the dark of a crowded subway train.

Unwittingly, Sophie seems to feed Nathan's recently discovered fascination with the Holocaust. Like other Americans, Nathan's first awareness of the Nazi atrocities arrived with American newsreel presentations in about 1945. But only with the Nuremberg tribunal did a full acknowledgment of the horror begin. As vehemently as Sophie would like to forget the tortures, Nathan wants to embrace them as a topic to feed his sick interpretation of reality. In an inversion that could only be attributed to insanity, Nathan physically and emotionally tortures Sophie for her part in and survival of the death camps. He punishes the victim, causing her to further punish herself with survivor's guilt.

Sophie's tragic end remains predictable, yet Stingo's hopeful voice partially counters the inevitability of the suicide pact that ends the suffering of both Nathan and Sophie. As a youthful, postwar, postslavery voice, Stingo remains behind to offer his audience hope for a new beginning in the treatment of humans by other humans. This offering hardly mitigates the horror experienced by Sophie before her death. Even her brief contact with Stingo, an outsider drawn to her fragile beauty, cannot lessen the reader's painful realization that Sophie dies a lonely figure whose capacity for love will never be realized.

See also: Sophie's Choice; Stingo; Styron, William; Violence; War

References: Bernard and Olesky, 1995; Casciato and West, 1982; Cologne-Brooks, 1995; Hoffman and Murphy, 1996; Joyner, 1996; Lupack, 1992; Ross, 1995; Weeks, 1995; West, 1995

ZENIA

In Canadian writer Margaret Atwood's 1993 novel, *The Robber Bride,* Zenia represents a gender subversion of a well-known character type, the robber bridegroom. As indicated by the title, the story involves a female villain who on three occasions steals men from marital or live-in relationships with other women. Her importance as a character lies in her ability to unite the three main female characters against her—Charis, Roz Andrews, and Tony Fremont. Although the three women meet during college in the 1960s, they do not become friends until years later. Over the thirty years that follow their departure from school, Zenia moves into their individual relationships and poisons their lives. Atwood shapes in Charis, Roz, and Tony three women with untested and, in some instances, hidden strengths. Zenia's attacks on their privacy, dignity, and loves force those strengths to surface.

Zenia remains an enigma. In addition to the robber bridegroom of various tales, she may be equated with mythological temptress archetypes and, most notably, with the legendary trickster character. Traditionally, the trickster assumes various forms, including that of a human, animal, and, in some instances, plant or mineral. In these guises, the trickster takes advantage of an unsuspecting victim who does not know her or his true identity. Although Zenia does indeed change her own alluring physical appearance through plastic surgery, she remains most adept at altering her history and personality in order to fool all the other characters in the book. Zenia's customizing of her past supports Tony's idea of history as nonlinear, a social construct that each individual may repeatedly revise. Zenia even appears to overcome death, transforming herself from the corpse at the funeral attended by her three female victims back into her old sensuous self.

Each character, including the three men featured in the story, comes to know a different Zenia. In one history, she is Greek Orthodox, and her sexual abuse as a child leaves her frigid. In another, she was a Jewish war baby from a home destroyed by the Nazis. In yet another, she is Russian and served as a child prostitute in Paris, and an additional version has her the daughter of a Gypsy who was stoned to death by Romanians. In dreams, Zenia appears as a woman in a silk scarf with her throat cut, a jack-o-lantern man, and a demon. In the "real-time" portions of the story, Zenia enters Tony's life in the guise of a student, invades Charis's home as a cancer victim, and attempts a takeover of Roz's position as magazine publisher and wife by posing as a journalist. Each woman loses her man to Zenia, and only Tony regains that love, although in a damaged form. Most important, the three women turn their victimization into triumph when they at last overcome the destructive effect that Zenia inflicts on their self-images. In a plot that sketches a journey through time for its main characters, each woman overcomes her doubts and fears to gain her own identity, apart from the past reality or history in which Zenia played a crucial role.

Ultimately Zenia's identity remains a mystery. Atwood seems to invite readers to choose the history they prefer. In the novel's closing actions, the three women, at last confident of Zenia's demise, take a container with her ashes to scatter them over a lake that has proved very meaningful to each, including Zenia. The container cracks just as Charis prepares to scatter the ashes. True to her belief in mystical occurrences, Charis feels that Zenia's spirit causes the crack; it is a way for Zenia to make herself known, to remain behind in a new form. Perhaps a more plausible explanation exists in Tony's final thoughts of the importance to herself and her two friends of storytelling and of the fact that Zenia will become the focus of many of their stories for years to come. This may be the key to Zenia's spiritual existence; she lives on in the multitude of tales that began centuries ago with the myths and stories of other tricksters like herself.

See also: Andrews, Roz; Charis; Fremont, Tony; *The Robber Bride*

References: Morey, 1997; Seidman, 1996; Wilson, Friedman, and Hengen, 1996

ZHIVAGO, YURII ANDREIEVICH

Russian writer Boris Pasternak's romance, *Doctor Zhivago* (1957), enjoyed huge popularity immediately upon its translation and subsequent publication, partly due to the great personal appeal of its protagonist, Yurii Zhivago. As both a scientist and a poet, Yurii represents the perfect blend of logic and imagination. One of several young Russians introduced in the novel's setting of pre–World War I Russia, Yurii becomes an orphan following desertion and then suicide on the part of his father and the death of his mother. Yurii's isolation is emphasized by the cold, snowy landscape that surrounds his small figure at his mother's funeral. Pasternak repeatedly calls upon such imagery to frame a story in which Yurii will simultaneously enjoy great love and experience great loss.

Yurii and his childhood friend Misha Gordon mature in the household of Alexander Gromeko, a chemistry professor, becoming part of the family that includes a daughter, Antonina Alexandrovna Gromeka, or Tonia. Eventually Yurii will marry Tonia and then involve her in a love triangle with a member of the working class, Larisa Fedorovna Guishar, called Lara. Because their relationship dares to transcend boundaries of class and the institution of marriage, it may be classified as a forbidden love. Yurii first meets Lara when he accompanies a doctor to the attempted suicide of Lara's mother. He observes the young girl's interactions with the lawyer, Victor Komarovsky. Komarovsky first establishes himself as friend and patron to Lara and her seamstress mother, but then seduces Lara while she is yet a teenager. Although Lara does not love Komarovsky, she would remain his mistress if allowed, as that arrangement would guarantee food for herself and her mother. Angered by Komarovsky's later rejection, Lara attempts to kill him, wounding him in a public attack. She eventually becomes a governess and falls in love with Pasha Antipov, son of revolutionaries and himself a revolutionary. By age twenty-three, Yurii discovers a love of poetry but decides that becoming a writer is a capricious notion. He chooses instead to become a doctor, having been influenced by his scientist-guardian. His medical skills and ethics are challenged by the bloodshed and violence that takes place literally in his own neighborhood. Yurii will suffer from the continued political upheaval because the fighting removes him from his family when he is forced to serve as a doctor in the Russian military and, later, as a kidnap victim with the revolutionaries. His nature remains hopeful, however, as Yurii continues to believe that a peaceful solution to the political unrest will be found.

Because the novel became available to the western world during the Cold War, many readers misinterpreted its politically charged plot framework as the main plot emphasis. According to most literary critics, however, Pasternak intended to write a romance, not a political novel. A poet himself, involved in the real-life unrest of Communist Russia, Pasternak produces a protagonist in Yurii who speaks to his own concerns. In his novel, he uses the abuse inflicted by the Russian powers on their own people to emphasize his theme of the universal human right to dignity and ethical treatment. Pasternak did not intend to indict Russia in particular. Instead, he uses his homeland as an example to criticize any and all political systems that seek to take advantage of the common citizen in order to promote a political agenda that gives a very few individuals wealth and power.

Following the marriage of Lara and Pasha, they depart Moscow to move to the Ural Mountains, a setting that will later provide the backdrop to Lara and Yurii's love. The elevation of the mountains and Lara's presence there emphasizes her identification with the passions of nature in a position above the concerns of the city. Emotions and intuition, elements that become important in the mountains, in Lara and Yurii's more natural relationship are closely related to creativity, imagination, and the needs of the poet. Conversely, the city of Moscow stands as a monument not to nature, but to the nature of humans, to their rationality and dependence upon logic.

Omar Sharif played Yurii Andreievich Zhivago, the protagonist who represents the perfect blend of logic and imagination, in the 1965 film version of Boris Pasternak's 1957 novel, Doctor Zhivago, *with Julie Christie as Lara. (Photofest)*

Ironically, its facade remains "colder," through its indifference to human suffering, than that of the mountains, despite their crowns of snow and ice. The city represents the human need for man-made laws supplied by formal institutions, such as religion and science, institutions shown by the world wars to have failed. Because Tonia is closely identified with the city, she symbolizes this sterile, man-made system. Thus, although Yurii attempts to establish an intellectual relationship with Tonia, his poet's soul is drawn to Lara.

Yurii's love for Lara becomes an all-important aspect of his life after he encounters her serving as a nurse on the front, where he treats wounded soldiers. His continuing simultaneous loves for Tonia and Lara balance his dual inclinations toward science and art. Both sets of conflicting desires cause him great consternation throughout the novel. Yurii suffers from this internal conflict as much, if not more, than from the external conflict caused by his environment.

Yurii leaves the Urals for Moscow, only to immediately return to the mountains with his family in an attempt to escape a plague and the October Revolution. He meets again with Lara before he is captured by a contingent of the Red army that forces him to offer its soldiers medical treatment. When he does not return, Tonia departs the Urals without him. Yurii eventually escapes his captors and enjoys the only bit of truly passionate romance ever allowed him during a respite with Lara. Threatened with arrest, the two lovers must part, and in an ironic move, Yurii sends Lara to join her former lover, Komarovsky, for protection. Pasha commits suicide.

When Yurii returns to Moscow, he finds that Tonia has departed with the family. He eventually marries a younger woman who cares for him, but they never share the passion he knew during the brief interlude in the Urals with Lara. Following his death, Yurii's half-brother, Evgraf, locates Tania, a daughter Yurii had fathered unawares with Lara. In caring for Tania and by making public Yurii's poetry, Evgraf promotes his brother's legacy.

The poems, supposedly written by Yurii, that Pasternak supplies at the novel's conclusion symbolize his main character's eventual acceptance of his life. Although Yurii never settles the conflict he feels between rationality and the imagination, he does reach an epiphany of sorts. He comes to believe that the beauty of life's forces will always conquer the human will to control their fellow humans.

See also: Anna Karenina; Guishar, Larisa (Lara) Fedorovna; Forbidden Love; Love Triangle; Violence; War

References: Brunsdale, 1996; Clowes, 1995; Frye, 1974; McMillin, 1990; Williams, 1974

REFERENCES AND FURTHER READING

PRIMARY SOURCES

Allende, Isabel. *The House of the Spirits.* Trans. Magda Bogin. New York: Knopf, 1985.

Atwood, Margaret. *The Robber Bride.* New York: Bantam, 1995.

Austen, Jane. *Emma.* 1816. Boston: Houghton Mifflin, 1957.

————. *Pride and Prejudice.* 1813. New York: Viking Penguin, 1997.

————. *Sense and Sensibility.* 1811. Ed. Ros Ballaster. New York: Viking Penguin, 1996.

Berto, Giuseppe. *The Sky Is Red.* Trans. Angus Davidson. New York: New Directions, 1948.

Braithwaite, Edward R. *To Sir, with Love.* Englewood Cliffs, NJ: Prentice-Hall, 1959.

Brontë, Charlotte. *Jane Eyre.* 1847. New York: Viking Penguin, 1966.

Brontë, Emily. *Wuthering Heights.* 1847. New York: Penguin Classics, 1985.

Buck, Pearl. *The Good Earth.* 1931. New York: Pocket Books, 1938.

Byron, Lord George. *Don Juan. Byron: The Oxford Authors.* Ed. Jerome J. McGann. New York: Oxford University Press, 1986.

Cather, Willa. *My Ántonia.* Lincoln: University of Nebraska Press, 1995.

Chopin, Kate. *The Awakening.* In *The Norton Anthology of Literature by Women: The Tradition in English.* 2nd ed. Ed. Sandra M. Gilbert and Susan Gubar. New York: W. W. Norton, 1996, 1013–1101.

Conroy, Pat. *The Prince of Tides.* Boston: Houghton Mifflin, 1986.

Cooper, James Fenimore. *The Last of the Mohicans.* 1826. New York: Viking Penguin, 1986.

Dickens, Charles. *A Tale of Two Cities.* 1859. London: Oxford University Press, 1998.

Donne, John. "Meditation XVII." In *The Oxford Anthology of English Literature.* Ed. Frank Kermode. London: Oxford University Press, 1973, 1056–1057.

Dreiser, Theodore. *An American Tragedy.* Cleveland: World, 1926.

Du Maurier, Daphne. *Rebecca.* 1938. New York: St. Martin's, 1993.

Dumas, Alexandre. *The Count of Monte Cristo.* 1894. Trans. Adolphe Cohn. New York: Thomas Y. Crowell, 1901.

Esquivel, Laura. *Like Water for Chocolate.* Trans. Carol Christensen and Thomas Christenen. New York: Doubleday Dell, 1992.

Fielding, Henry. *Tom Jones.* 1749. New York: Airmont, 1967.

Fitzgerald, F. Scott. *The Great Gatsby.* 1925. New York: Scribner's, 1953.

Flaubert, Gustave. *Madame Bovary.* 1857. Trans. Lowell Bair. New York: Bantam, 1959.

Forester, C. S. *The African Queen.* 1935. New York: Random House, 1940.

Forster, E. M. *A Room with a View.* 1908. New York: Random House, 1989.

Fowles, John. *The French Lieutenant's Woman.* Boston: Little, Brown, 1969.

Gaines, Ernest J. *Of Love and Dust.* 1967. New York: Random House, 1994.

García Márquez, Gabriel. *Love in the Time of Cholera.* Trans. Edith Grossman. New York: Knopf, 1988.

Giono, Jean. *The Horseman on the Roof.* Trans. Jonathan Griffin. New York: Knopf, 1954.

Hardy, Thomas. *Tess of the d'Urbervilles: A Pure Woman.* 1891. New York: Random House, 1951.

Hawthorne, Nathaniel. *The Scarlet Letter and Selected Writings.* 1850. New York: Random House, 1984.

Heath, Roy. *The Shadow Bride.* 1988. New York: Persea Books, 1996.

Hemingway, Ernest. *A Farewell to Arms.* New York: Scribner's, 1929.

———. *For Whom the Bell Tolls.* New York: Scribner's, 1940.

———. *The Sun Also Rises.* New York: Scribner's, 1926.

Hugo, Victor. *The Hunchback of Notre Dame.* 1831. Cornwall, NY: Cornwall Press, 1947.

———. *Les Misérables.* 1862. New York: Viking Penguin, 1997.

Hurston, Zora Neale. *Their Eyes Were Watching God* (1937). In *Zora Neale Hurston: Novels and Stories.* Ed. Cheryl A. Wall. New York: Penguin, 1995.

Iyayi, Festus. *Heroes.* Harlow, Essex: Longman, 1986.

James, Henry. "Daisy Miller." In *James's Daisy Miller: The Story, the Play, the Critics.* Ed. William T. Stafford. New York: Scribner's, 1963.

———. *The Portrait of a Lady.* 1881. New York: W. W. Norton, 1975.

Kincaid, Jamaica. *Lucy.* New York: Farrar Straus Giroux, 1990.

King, Tabitha. *One on One.* New York: NAL-Dutton, 1994.

Kundera, Milan. *The Unbearable Lightness of Being.* Trans. Michael Henry Heim. New York: Harper and Row, 1984.

Lawrence, D. H. *Sons and Lovers.* 1913. New York: Penguin, 1983.

Longus. *Daphnis and Chloe.* New York: Viking Penguin, 1989.

Maugham, W. Somerset. *Of Human Bondage.* 1915. New York: Doubleday, 1936.

McCullough, Colleen. *The Thorn Birds.* New York: Harper and Row, 1977.

Mishima, Yukio. *The Sound of Waves.* New York: Knopf, 1956.

Mitchell, Margaret. *Gone with the Wind.* 1936. New York: Macmillan, 1964.

Morrison, Toni. *Beloved.* New York: Random House, 1987.

Naipaul, V. S. *The Suffrage of Elvira.* 1958. New York: Penguin, 1969.

Osaragi, Jiro. *The Journey.* Trans. Ivan Morris. New York: Knopf, 1960.

Oz, Amos. *To Know a Woman.* 1989. Trans. Nicholas de Lange. New York: Harcourt Brace Jovanovich, 1991.

Pasternak, Boris. *Doctor Zhivago.* Trans. Max Hayward and Manya Harari. New York: Pantheon, 1958.

Scott, Sir Walter. *Ivanhoe.* New York: E. P. Dutton, 1906.

Shakespeare, William. *Much Ado about Nothing.* In *The Riverside Shakespeare.* Ed. G. Blakemore Evans. Boston: Houghton Mifflin, 1974, 332–364.

———. *Romeo and Juliet.* In *The Riverside Shakespeare.* Ed. G. Blakemore Evans. Boston: Houghton Mifflin, 1974, 1058–1099.

Shaw, George Bernard. *Pygmalion.* 1912. *Androcles and the Lion, Overruled, Pygmalion by Bernard Shaw.* New York: Dodd, Mead, 1930.

Shelley, Mary. *Frankenstein.* 1818. Ed. Paul Hunter. New York: Norton, 1996.

Singer, Isaac Bashevis. *Enemies: A Love Story.* New York: New American Library, 1972.

Spenser, Sir Edmund. *The Faerie Queene.* 1590. New York: Viking Penguin, 1987.

Styron, William. *Sophie's Choice.* New York: Random House, 1979.

Tan, Amy. *The Kitchen God's Wife.* New York: Ivy Books, 1992.

Thackeray, William Makepeace. *Vanity Fair.* 1847–1848. New York: Dodd, Mead, 1943.

Tolstoy, Leo. *Anna Karenina.* 1878. New York: W. W. Norton, 1970.

Tyler, Anne. *The Accidental Tourist.* New York: Knopf, 1985.

Waugh, Evelyn. *A Handful of Dust.* 1934. Boston: Little, Brown, 1962.

Wharton, Edith. *The Age of Innocence.* 1920. New York: Scribner's, 1968.

———. *Ethan Frome.* 1911. New York: Scribner's, 1970.

SECONDARY SOURCES

Abel, Darrel. *The Moral Picturesque: Studies in Hawthorne's Fiction.* Purdue: Purdue University Press, 1988.

"About the Author: Ernest Gaines" by Vintage Books. Internet. Available <http://www.randomhouse.com/jnopf/read/lesson/gaines.html> (9 July 1997).

Adams, Carol J. "Woman-Battering and Harm to Animals." *Animals and Women: Feminist Theoretical Explanations.* Ed. Carol J. Adams and Josephine Donovan. Durham: Duke University Press, 1995, 55–84.

Albright, R. H. "A View of E. M. Forster." Internet. Available <http://world.std.com/~albright/For.html> (28 January 1997).

Allen, Walter. "Brontë." Microsoft (R) Encarta. Copyright © 1993 Microsoft. Copyright © 1993 Funk and Wagnall's.

"Amy Tan: Best-Selling Novelist." *The Hall of Arts.* Internet. Available <http://www.achievement.org/autodoc/page/tan0bio–1> (7 May 1998).

Annesley, James. "Commodification, Violence and the Body: A Reading of Some Recent American Fictions." *American Bodies: Cultural Histories of the Physique.* Ed. Tim Armstrong. New York: New York University Press, 1996, 142–151.

Anstead, Alicia. "Tabitha." *Bangor Daily News: MaineStyle,* 4 March 1997, C1.

Archer, Stanley. "W. Somerset Maugham." In *Beacham's Encyclopedia of Popular Fiction.* Ed. Kirk H. Beetz. Osprey, FL: Beacham, 1996, bio., vol. 1:1222–1225.

Armstrong, Nancy. *Desire and Domestic Fiction: A Political History of the Novel.* Oxford: Oxford University Press, 1990.

Atkinson, David W. "Alienation in the Novels of Yukio Mishima." *International Fiction Review* 16, 1 (Winter 1989): 56–64.

Atlas, Marilyn J., ed. "Being a Variety of Essays on the Works of Toni Morrison: A Special Issue." *Midwestern Miscellany* 24 (1996).

Backsheider, Paula R., and John J. Richetti, eds. *Popular Fiction by Women 1660–1730.* Oxford: Clarendon Press, 1996.

Baker, James, and Dianne Vipond, eds. *John Fowles Issue of Twentieth Century Literature: A Scholarly and Critical Journal* 42, 1 (Spring 1996).

Baker, John F. "V. S. Naipaul." *Publisher's Weekly* 241, 23 (6 June 1994): 44–45.

Baker, William, and J. H. Alexander, eds. *Sir Walter Scott/Tales of a Grandfather: The History of France.* Dekalb: Northern Illinois University Press, 1996.

Balaban, Avraham. *Between God and Beast: An Examination of Amos Oz's Prose.* University Park: Pennsylvania State University Press, 1993.

———. "Language and Reality in the Prose of Amos Oz." *Modern Language Studies* 20, 2 (Spring 1990): 79–97.

Baldock, Bob, and Dennis Bernstein. "Isabel Allende." *Mother Jones* 19, 5 (September–October 1994): 21–24.

Bamberg, Robert D. "Preface." *The Portrait of a Lady.* 1881. New York: Norton, 1975, vii–ix.

Barker, Martin, and Roger Sabin. *The Lasting of the Mohicans: History of an American Myth.* Jackson: University Press of Mississippi, 1996.

Barton, Anne. "Introduction." *Much Ado about Nothing.* In *The Riverside Shakespeare.* Ed. G. Blakemore Evans. Boston: Houghton Mifflin, 1974, 327–331.

Barzilai, Shuli. "Amos Oz in Arad: A Profile." *Southern Humanities Review* 21, 1 (Winter 1987): 19–35.

Bayley, John. *The Characters of Love.* London: Constable, 1960.

———. *Tolstoy and the Novel.* New York: Viking, 1968.

Beach, Sylvia. *Shakespeare and Company.* New York: Harcourt, 1959.

Becket, Fiona. *D. H. Lawrence: The Thinker as Poet.* New York: St. Martin's, 1997.

Beetz, Kirk H., ed. *Beacham's Encyclopedia of Popular Fiction.* 15 vols. (12 of analysis; 3 of biography). Osprey, Florida: Beacham, 1996.

Bell, Millicent, ed. *The Cambridge Companion to Edith Wharton.* New York: Cambridge University Press, 1995.

Berendt, John. "The Conroy Saga." *Vanity Fair* (July 1995): 108–113, 138–141.

Bernard, Andrea, and Elzbieta H. Olesky. "Sophie's Choice: The Depiction of Poles in the American Popular Imagination." In *Images of Central Europe in Travelogues and Fiction by North American Writers.* Ed. Waldemar Zacharasiewicz. Tubingen: Stauffenburg, 1995.

Bevilacqua, Winifred Farrant. "The Portrait of a Lady." In *Beacham's Encyclopedia of Popular Fiction.* Ed. Kirk H. Beetz. Osprey, FL: Beacham, 1996, analyses, vol. 6: 3299–3308.

Bilik, Dorothy. "Singer's Diasporan Novel: *Enemies, A Love Story.*" *Studies in Jewish Literature.* Albany: State University of New York Press, 1981.

"Biografia di Giuseppe Berto." Internet. Available <http://www.mpbnet.it/edu/scuole/berto/biografia/giografi.htm> (21 July 1997).

Birbalsingh, Frank, ed. *Frontiers of Caribbean Literature in English.* New York: St. Martin's, 1996.

Blain, Virginia, Patricia Clements, and Isobel Grundy, eds. *The Feminist Companion to Literature in English: Women Writers from the Middle Ages to the Present.* New Haven: Yale University Press, 1990.

Booth, Allyson. *Postcards from the Trenches: Negotiating the Space between Modernism and the First World War.* New York: St. Martin's, 1996.

Boulton, James T., ed. *The Selected Letters of D. H. Lawrence.* Cambridge: Cambridge University Press, 1997.

Brady, James. "Ross, Kincaid Cross Sabers." *Advertising Age* 67, 7 (12 February 1996): 19.

Bridgwood, Christine. *Family Romances: The Contemporary Popular Family Saga.* London: Routledge, 1986.

Britannica on Line. "Jane Austen." Internet. Available <http://www.eb.com/public/austen.htm> (19 January 1997).

Brombert, Victor. *Victor Hugo and the Visionary Novel.* Cambridge: Harvard University Press, 1986.

Brown, Guilliory Elizabeth, ed. *Women of Color: Mother-Daughter Relationships in 20th Century Literature.* Austin: University of Texas Press, 1996.

Bruccoli, Matthew J., and Margaret M. Duggan, eds. *Correspondence of F. Scott Fitzgerald.* New York: Random House, 1980.

Brunel, Pierre, ed. *Companion to Literary Myths: Heroes and Archetypes.* New York: Routledge, 1992.

Brunsdale, Mitzi M. "Boris Pasternak." In *Beacham's Encyclopedia of Popular Fiction.* Ed. Kirk H. Beetz. Osprey, FL: Beacham, 1996, bio., vol. 3: 1412–1415.

Budick, E. Miller. *Nineteenth-Century American Romance: Genre and the Construction of Democratic Culture.* New York: Twayne, 1996.

Bullen, J. B. *Writing and Victorianism.* New York: Longman, 1997.

Burns, Aidan. *Nature and Culture in D. H. Lawrence.* Totowa: Barnes and Noble, 1980.

Bychkov, S. P. "The Social Bases of Anna Karenina." *Anna Karenina: The Norton Critical Edition.* New York: Norton, 1970, 822–835.

Caeserio, Robert Lyotard. *Plot, Story and the Novel: From Dickens and Poe to the Modern Period.* Ann Arbor: Books on Demand, 1979.

Campbell, Joseph. *The Hero with a Thousand Faces.* 1949. Princeton: Princeton University Press, 1968.

———. *The Power of Myth.* Ed. Betty Sue Flowers. New York: Doubleday, 1988.

Carpenter, Humphrey. *Geniuses Together: American Writers in Paris in the 1920s.* Boston: Houghton Mifflin, 1988.

Carr, Glynis. "Storytelling as Bildung in Zora Neale Hurston's *Their Eyes Were Watching God.*" *College Language Association Journal* 31, 2 (December 1987): 189–200.

Casciato, Arthur D., and James L. W. West III, eds. *Critical Essays on William Styron.* Boston: G. K. Hall, 1982.

Catalano, Alessandro. "Milan Kundera: The Author or His Books?" *The Prague Review* 1 (Summer 1995). Internet. Available <http://194.196.42.99/revue/SEAMER/art.htm> (19 February 1998).

Chambers, David. *Interviews and Recollections.* Vol. 1. London: Macmillan Press, 1981.

Chan, Mimi, and Roy Harris, eds. *Asian Voices in English.* Hong Kong: Hong Kong University Press, 1991.

Charlton, D. G., ed. *The French Romantics.* Cambridge: Cambridge University Press, 1984.

Chen, Victoria. "Chinese American Women, Language, and Moving Subjectively." *Women and Language* 18, 1 (Spring 1995): 3–7.

Chréacháin, Fírinne Ní. "Festus Iyayi's Heroes: Two Novels in One?" *Research in African Literatures* 1, 22 (Spring 1991): 43–53.

"Christian Apologetics: Excerpt from *The Universe Next Door* by James W. Sire." Internet. Available <http://www.apologetics.org/books/zeropoint.html> (22 December 1997).

Christian, R. F., ed. *Tolstoy's Letters.* 2 vols. New York: Scribner's, 1978.

Clarke, Michael M. *Thackeray and Women.* De Kalb: Northern Illinois University Press, 1995.

Clayton, Jay. "Mansfield Park." *Romantic Vision and the Novel.* Cambridge University Press, 1987a, 59–80.

———. "Wuthering Heights." *Romantic Vision and the Novel.* Cambridge University Press, 1987b, 81–102.

Clowes, Edith W., ed. *Doctor Zhivago: A Critical Companion.* Evanston: Northwestern University Press, 1995.

Coale, Samuel. "William Styron." In *Beacham's Encyclopedia of Popular Fiction.* Ed. Kirk H. Beetz. Osprey, FL: Beacham, 1996, bio., vol. 3: 1750–1760.

Cologne-Brookes, Gavin. *The Novels of William Styron: From Harmony to History.* Baton Rouge: Louisiana State University Press, 1995.

Comfort, Alex. "The Ideology of Romanticism." In *Romanticism: Points of View.* 2nd ed. Ed.

Robert F. Gleckner and Gerald E. Enscoe. Detroit: Wayne State University Press, 1974, 165–180.

Conn, Peter. "Pearl S. Buck." Internet. Available <http://dept.english.upenn.edu/Projects/Buck/biography.html> (18 April 1996).

Cooke, Miriam. *Women and the War Story*. Berkeley: University of California Press, 1996.

Coombs, Norman. *The Black Experience in America: The Immigrant Heritage of America*. New York: Twayne, 1972.

"Cooper, James Fenimore." *The Norton Anthology of American Literature*. 2nd shorter ed. Ed. Nina Baym, Ronald Gottesman, Laurence B. Holland, Francis Murphy, Hershel Parker, William H. Pritchard, and David Kalstone. New York: Norton, 1986, 288–290.

Copeland, Edward, and Juliet McMaster, eds. *The Cambridge Companion to Jane Austen*. Cambridge: Cambridge University Press, 1997.

Cowley, Malcolm. *A Second Flowering: Works and Days of the Lost Generation*. New York: Viking, 1973.

———. Introduction. *Madame Bovary*. New York: Bantam Books, 1959.

———. Introduction. *The Portable Hawthorne*. New York: Viking Press, 1948.

Croft, Robert W. *Anne Tyler: A Bio-Bibliography*. Westport, CT: Greenwood, 1995.

Croom, Helen. "D. H. Lawrence: The Young Lawrence." Internet. Available http://cool.virtual-pc.com/ranaim/lawrence/early.html (29 January 1997).

Cuomo, Chris J. "War Is Not Just an Event: Reflections on the Significance of Everyday Violence." *Hypatia: A Journal of Feminist Philosophy* 11, 4 (Fall 1996): 30–45.

Dahl, Curtis. Introduction. *The Hunchback of Notre Dame*. Cornwall, NY: Cornwall Press, 1947.

Daiches, David. Introduction. *Wuthering Heights*. New York: Penguin Classics, 1965, 7–29.

———. *Willa Cather: A Critical Introduction*. Westport, CT: Greenwood Press, 1971.

Das, G. K., and John Beer, eds. *E. M. Forster: A Human Exploration: Centenary Essays*. New York: New York University Press, 1979.

David, Deidre. *Rule Britannia: Women, Empire, and Victorian Writing*. Ithaca: Cornell University Press, 1995.

Davidson, Cathy N., Linda Wagner Martin, Elizabeth Ammons, Trudier Harris, Ann

Kibbey, Amy Ling, and Janice Radway, eds. *The Oxford Companion to Women's Writing in the United States*. New York: Oxford University Press, 1995.

Davis, James E., and Ronald E. Salomone, eds. *Teaching Shakespeare Today*. Urbana: National Council of Teachers of English, 1993.

Davis, Rocio G. "Amy Tan's *The Kitchen God's Wife*: An American Dream Come True—in China." *Notes on Contemporary Literature* 24, 5 (November 1994): 3–5.

de Rougemont, Denis. *Love in the Western World*. New Jersey: Princeton University Press, 1983.

Defazio, Albert J., III. "Current Bibliography: Annotated." *The Hemingway Review* 15 (Spring 1996): 119–128; 16 (Fall 1996): 124–137.

Demastes, William, and Katherine E. Kelly, eds. *British Playwrights, 1860–1956: A Research and Production Sourcebook*. Westport, CT: Greenwood, 1996.

DiBattista, Marian, and Lucy McDiarmid, eds. *High and Low Moderns: Literature and Culture 1889–1939*. New York: Oxford University Press, 1996.

Dix, Carol. *D. H. Lawrence and Women*. Totowa: Rowman and Littlefield, 1980.

Donaldson, Scott, ed. *The Cambridge Companion to Hemingway*. Boston: Cambridge University Press, 1996.

Dougherty, David. "Toni Morrison." In *Beacham's Encyclopedia of Popular Fiction*. Ed. Kirk H. Beetz. Osprey, FL: Beacham, 1996, bio., vol. 2: 1308–1316.

Drabble, Margaret, ed. *The Oxford Companion to English Literature*. Oxford: Oxford University Press, 1995.

Dudley, Edward J. *The Endless Text: Don Quixote and the Hermeneutics of Romance*. Albany: State University of New York Press, 1997.

Duncan, Ian. *Modern Romance and Transformations of the Novel: The Gothic, Scott and Dickens*. Boston: Cambridge University Press, 1992.

Eiss, Harry, ed. *Images of the Child*. Bowling Green, OH: Popular, 1994.

Ellem, Elizabeth. "E. M. Forster: The Lucy and New Lucy Novels. Fragments of Early Versions of *A Room with a View*." *Times Literary Supplement*, May 1971, London ed.: 623–625.

Ellis, Havelock. *The Psychology of Sex*. New York: Mentor Books, 1964.

Ellis, Kate F. *The Contested Castle: Gothic Novels and the Subversion of Domestic Ideology.* University of Illinois Press, 1989.

Evans, Elizabeth. *Anne Tyler.* New York: Twayne Publishers, 1993.

Evans, G. Blakemore, ed. *The Riverside Shakespeare.* Boston: Houghton Mifflin, 1974.

Faison, Linda G., and Robert Whipple. "Colleen McCullough." In *Beacham's Encyclopedia of Popular Fiction.* Ed. Kirk H. Beetz. Osprey, FL: Beacham, 1996, bio., vol. 2: 1245–1249.

Farrell, Grace. "Suspending Disbelief: Faith and Fiction in I. B. Singer." *Boulevard* 9, 3 (Fall 1994): 111–117.

Feidelson, Charles. "The Moment of *The Portrait of a Lady.*" *The Portrait of a Lady.* 1881. New York: Norton, 1975, 741–751.

Ferguson, Moira. "A Lot of Memory." *The Kenyon Review* 16, 1 (Winter 1996): 163–189.

Fetterley, Judith. "Willa Cather and the Fiction of Female Development." *Anxious Power: Reading, Writing, and Ambivalence in Narrative by Women.* Ed. Carol J. Singley and Susan Elizabeth Sweeney. Albany: State University of New York Press, 1993, 221–234.

Flint, Kate. "Women, Men, and the Reading of *Vanity Fair.*" In *The Practice and Representation of Reading in England.* Ed. James Raven, Helen Small, and Naomi Tadmor. Cambridge: Cambridge University Press, 1996.

Flora, Joseph M., and Robert Bain, eds. *Fifty Southern Writers after 1900: A Biobibliographic Sourcebook.* Westport, CT: Greenhaven, 1987.

Foote-Greenwell, Victoria. "The Life and Resurrection of Alexandre Dumas." *Smithsonian* (July 1996):111–122.

Forbes, Jill, and Michael Kelly, eds. *French Cultural Studies: An Introduction.* New York: Oxford University Press, 1995.

Forester, John. "A Very Short Biography of C. S. Forester." *C. S. Forester Society Web Page.* Internet. Available <http://www.teleport.com/~vamberry/csfbio.html> (28 January 1997).

Forrey, Robert. "The Sorrows of Herman Broder: Singer's *Enemies: A Love Story.*" *Studies in Jewish Literature.* Albany: State University of New York Press, 1981.

Forster, E. M. *Aspects of the Novel.* New York: Harcourt Brace, 1956.

Foster, M. Marie Booth. "Voice, Mind, Self: Mother-Daughter Relationships in Amy Tan's *The Joy Luck Club* and *The Kitchen God's Wife.*" In *Women of Color: Mother-Daughter Relationships in 20th Century Literature.* Ed. Elizabeth Brown. Austin: University of Texas Press, 1996.

Foster, Thomas C. *Understanding John Fowles.* Columbia: University of South Carolina Press, 1994.

Foster, Thomas, Carol Siegel, and Ellen E. Berry, eds. *Bodies of Writing, Bodies in Performance.* New York: New York University Press, 1996.

Fraiman, Susan. *Unbecoming Women: British Women Writers and the Novel of Development.* New York: Columbia University Press, 1993.

Friedman, Melvin J., and Ben Siegel, eds. *Traditions, Voices, and Dreams: The American Novel since the 1960s.* Newark: University of Delaware Press, 1995.

Frye, Northrup. "The Drunken Boat: The Revolutionary Element in Romanticism." In *Romanticism: Points of View.* 2nd ed. Ed. Robert F. Gleckner and Gerald E. Enscoe. Detroit: Wayne State University Press, 1974, 299–313.

———. *The Secular Scripture: A Study of the Structure of Romance.* Cambridge: Harvard University Press, 1976.

Fuchs, Esther. "The Beast Within: Women in Amos Oz's Early Fiction." *Modern Judaism* 4, 3 (October 1984): 311–321.

Fuderer, Laura Sue. *The Female Bildungsroman in English: An Annotated Bibliography of Criticism.* New York: MLA, 1990.

Furbank, P. N. Introduction. *Martin Chuzzlewhit.* New York: Penguin, 1986.

"Gaines, Ernest J." *Current Biography* 55, 3 (March 1994): 8–12.

Garcia, Moreno Laura, and Peter C. Pfeiffer, eds. *Text and Nation: Cross-Disciplinary Essays on Cultural and National Identities.* Columbia, SC: Camden, 1996.

Gard, Roger. *Jane Austen's Novels: The Art of Clarity.* New Haven: Yale University Press, 1992.

Garner, Dwight. "Jamaica Kincaid: The Salon Interview." Internet. Available <http://www.salon1999.com/05/features/kincaid.html. (20 August 1997).

Gaull, Marilyn. *English Romanticism: The Human Context.* W. W. Norton, 1988, 197–201.

Gaye, Mamadou. "Evelyn Waugh's 'Heart of Darkness' in *A Handful of Dust.*" *Bridges: An African Journal of English Studies Revue* (7 March 1996): 93–105.

Geist, Edward V. "The Age of Innocence." In *Beacham's Encyclopedia of Popular Fiction.* Ed. Kirk H. Beetz. Osprey, FL: Beacham, 1996, analyses, vol. 1: 48–51.

Gerber, Philip Lyotard. *Plots and Characters in the Fiction of Theodore Dreiser.* Hamden, CT: Shoe String, 1977.

Gilbert, Sandra M. and Susan Gubar, eds. *The Norton Anthology of Literature by Women: The Tradition in English.* 2nd ed. New York: Norton, 1996.

———. Biography of Charlotte Brontë. Gilbert and Gubar. 1996a, 468–472.

———. Biography of Edith Wharton. Gilbert and Gubar. 1996b, 1149–1151.

———. Biography of Jane Austen. Gilbert and Gubar. 1996c, 328–330.

———. Biography of Kate Chopin. Gilbert and Gubar. 1996d, 1011–1013.

———. Biography of Margaret Atwood. Gilbert and Gubar. 1996e, 2215–2216.

———. Biography of Willa Cather. Gilbert and Gubar. 1996f, 1227–1229.

———. Biography of Zora Neale Hurston. Gilbert and Gubar. 1996g, 1488–1490.

——— "Puritanism." Gilbert and Gubar. 1996h, 66–68.

Gillingham, John. *Richard Coeur de Lion: Kingship, Chivalry and War in the Twelfth Century.* London: Hambledon, 1994.

Gleckner, Robert F., and Gerald E. Enscoe, eds. *Romanticism: Points of View.* 2nd ed. Detroit: Wayne State University Press, 1974.

Goode, John. "The Offensive Truth: Tess of the d'Urbervilles." *Tess of the d'Urbervilles / Thomas Hardy.* Ed. Peter Widdowson. New York: St. Martin's, 1993, 184–200.

Gourgouris, Stathis. "Research, Essay, Failure (Flaubert's Itinerary)." *New Literary History* 26, 2 (Spring 1995): 343–357.

Graham, Elspeth, Hilary Hinds, Elaine Hobby, and Helen Wilcox, eds. *Her Own Life.* New York: Routledge, 1989.

Graham, Margaret Baker. "Daphne du Maurier." In *Beacham's Encyclopedia of Popular Fiction.* Ed. Kirk H. Beetz, ed. Osprey, FL: Beacham, 1996, bio., vol. 1: 561–563.

Grene, Nicholas. *Shakespeare's Tragic Imagination.* New York: St. Martin's, 1996.

Grierson, H. J. C. "Classical and Romantic: A Point of View." In *Romanticism: Points of View.* 2nd ed. Ed. Robert F. Gleckner and Gerald E. Enscoe. Detroit: Wayne State University Press, 1974, 41–54.

Grimm, Michael A. "Unfortunate Reality: Fictional Portrayals of Children and Violence." *Images of the Child.* Ed. Harry Eiss. Bowling Green: Popular Press, 1994, 115–141.

Grossman, Anita Susan. "An Interview with Amos Oz." *Partisan Review* 53, 3 (1986): 427–438.

Grossman, Kathryn M. *Figuring Transcendence in Les Misérables: Hugo's Romantic Sublime.* Southern Illinois University Press, 1994.

Hadeller, David. *Gynecide: Women in the Novels of William Styron.* Madison, NJ: Fairleigh Dickson University Press, 1996.

Halio, Jay Lyotard. "The Individual Struggle for Faith in the Novels of I. B. Singer." *Studies in American Jewish Literature* 10, 1 (Spring 1991): 35–43.

———, ed. *Shakespeare's Romeo and Juliet: Texts, Contexts, and Interpretation.* Newark: University of Delaware Press, 1995.

Harden, Edgar F., ed. *Selected Letters of William Makepeace Thackeray.* New York: New York University Press, 1996.

Hardin, James, ed. *Reflection and Action: Essays on the Bildungsroman.* Columbia: University of South Carolina Press, 1991.

Hart, James D. *The Oxford Companion to American Literature.* 6th ed. New York: Oxford University Press, 1995.

Hawes, Donald. "Amelia Sedley: Thackeray's Debt to Fielding?" *Thackeray Newsletter* 37 (May 1993): 1–2.

———. "Thackeray and du Maurier." *Thackeray Newsletter* 39 (May 1994): 4–6.

Hebron, Malcolm. *The Medieval Siege: Theme and Image in Middle English Romance.* Oxford: Clarendon University Press, 1997.

Heil, Douglas. "The Construction of Racism Through Narrative and Cinematography in *The Letter.*" *Literature / Film Quarterly* 24, 1 (January 1996): 17–25.

Hen, Judy. "'Working on the Farm': Hemingway's Work Ethic in *The Sun Also Rises.*" *Ernest Hemingway: The Oak Park Legacy.* Ed. James Nagel. Tuscaloosa: University of Alabama Press, 1996, 165–178.

Henderson, Katherine Usher, and Barbara F. McManus. *Half Humankind: Contexts and Texts of the Controversy about Women in England, 1540–1640.* Chicago: University of Illinois Press, 1985.

Herdeck, Donald, Maurice A. Lobin, John Figueroa, Dorothy Alexander Figueroa, and José Alcántara Almánzar, eds. *Caribbean Writers: A Bio-Bibliographical-Critical Encyclopedia*. Washington, D.C.: Three Continents, 1979.

Hily-Mane, Genevieve. *Ernest Hemingway in France: 1926–1994: A Comprehensive Bibliography*. University de Reims: CIRLE-Press, 1995.

Hipchen, Emily A. "Fielding's *Tom Jones*." *Explicator* 53, 1 (Fall 1994): 16–18.

Hoffman, Michael J., and Patrick D. Murphy, eds. *Essentials of the Theory of Fiction*. 2nd ed. Durham: Duke University Press, 1996.

Horsman, Alan. *The Victorian Novel*. Oxford: Clarendon Press, 1990.

Hotchner, A. E. *Papa Hemingway*. 1955. New York: Random House, 1966.

Howe, Irving. Afterword. *An American Tragedy*. Cleveland: World, 1964, 815–828.

Hugo, Victor. *Compton's Encyclopedia*. Vol. 10. Chicago: University of Chicago Press, 1984, 267–268.

Hulme, T. E. "Romanticism and Classicism." In *Romanticism: Points of View*. 2nd ed. Ed. Robert F. Gleckner and Gerald E. Enscoe. Detroit: Wayne State University Press, 1974, 55–65.

Hunter, Paul. Introduction. *Frankenstein*. New York: Norton, 1996.

Hussein, Aamer. "Delivering the Truth: An Interview with V. S. Naipaul." *Times Literary Supplement*, September 2, 1994, 3–4.

Hutton, Alice H. "Decay of Mishima's Japan: His Final Word." *International Fiction Review* 20, 2 (1993): 99–102.

"Isabel Allende in Conversation with Marina Warner." *Writers Talk Series: The Guardian Newspaper*. Internet. Available <http:\\filament.illumin.co.uk/ica/Bookshop/video/writerstalk/allende.html> (1 January 1997).

"Jean Giono: 1895–1970." *World Authors: Wilson Authors Series*. New York: H. W. Wilson, 1996, 983–985.

Jenkins, Ruth Y. "Authorizing Female Voice and Experience: Ghosts and Spirits in Kingston's *The Woman Warrior* and Allende's *The House of the Spirits*." *Melus* 19, 3 (Fall 1994): 61–74.

Joyner, Charles. "Styron's Choice: A Meditation on History, Literature, and Moral Imperatives." *Southern Writers and Their Worlds*. Eds. Christopher Morris and Steven G. Reinhardt.

College Station: Texas A&M University Press, 1996.

Kaplan, Cora. "*The Thorn Birds:* Fiction, Fantasy, Femininity." In *Formations of Fantasy*. Ed. Victor Burgin, James Donald, and Cora Kaplan. London: Metheun, 1986.

Keene, Donald. "Mushima in 1958." *The Paris Review* 35, 134 (Spring) 1995: 141–160.

Keesey, Donald, ed. *Contexts for Criticism*. 3rd ed. Mountain View: Mayfield, 1998.

Kelly, Rebecca. "The Accidental Tourist." In *Beacham's Encyclopedia of Popular Fiction*. Ed. Kirk H. Beetz, ed. Osprey, FL: Beacham, 1996, analyses, vol. 1: 1–4.

Kermode, Frank. Introduction. *Romeo and Juliet*. In *The Riverside Shakespeare*. Ed. G. Blakemore Evans. Boston: Houghton Mifflin, 1974, 1055–1057.

Kettle, Arnold. "Henry James: *The Portrait of a Lady*." *The Portrait of a Lady*. 1881. New York: Norton, 1975, 671–689.

Kincaid, Jamaica. "Putting Myself Together." *The New Yorker* (February 20 and 27, 1995): 93–94, 98–100.

Kinney, James. *Amalgamation! Race, Sex, and Rhetoric in the Nineteenth-Century American Novel*. Westport, CT: Greenwood Press, 1985.

Kissel, Susan S. *Moving On: The Heroines of Shirley Ann Grau, Anne Tyler, Gail Godwin*. Bowling Green: Popular, 1996.

Kontje, Todd. *Private Lives in the Public Sphere: The German Bildungsroman as Metafiction*. University Park: Pennsylvania State University Press, 1992.

———. *The German Bildungsroman: History of a National Genre*. Columbia, S.C.: Camden House, 1993.

Koppelman, Susan, ed. *Women in the Trees: U.S. Women's Short Stories about Battering and Resistance, 1839–1994*. Boston: Beacon, 1996.

Labovitz, Esther Kleinbord. *The Myth of the Heroine: The Female Bildungsroman in the Twentieth Century*. New York: Peter Lang, 1986.

Lago, Mary. *E. M. Forster: A Literary Life*. New York: St. Martin's, 1995.

Lawrence, D. H. *The Complete Poems of D. H. Lawrence*. Ed. Vivian de Sola Pinto and Warren Roberts. New York: Viking Penguin, 1964.

Leavis, Q. D. Introduction. *Jane Eyre*. New York: Viking Penguin, 1966, 7–29.

Leng, Flavia. *Daphne Du Maurier: A Daughter's Memoir*. North Pomfret, VT: Trafalgar, 1995.

Leon, Philip W. *William Styron: An Annotated Bibliography of Criticism*. Westport, CT: Greenwood, 1978.

"Les Miserables: Victor Hugo—France's Favourite Son." Internet. Available <http://www.ot.com/lesmis/hugo.html> (28 May 1997).

LeSeur, Geta. *Ten Is the Age of Darkness: The Black Bildungsroman*. Columbia: University of Missouri Press, 1995.

Levin, Harry. Introduction. *The Riverside Shakespeare*. Ed. G. Blakemore Evans. Boston: Houghton Mifflin, 1974, 1–25.

Levine, Laura. "Rape, Repetition, and the Politics of Closure in a Midsummer Night's Dream." In *Feminist Readings of Early Modern Culture: Emerging Subjects*. Ed. Valerie Traub, Lindsay M. Kaplan, and Dympna Callaghan. Cambridge: Cambridge University Press, 1996.

Lippi, Tom. "The Tragic Paradox of Modern Life." *Pacific Sun,* 11 May 1984, 24.

Lipscomb, Elizabeth, Francis E. Webb, and Peter Conn, eds. *The Several Worlds of Pearl Buck: Essays Presented at a Centennial Symposium, Randolph-Macon Women's College, March 26–28, 1982*. Westport, CT: Greenwood, 1994.

Looney, Denis. *Comprising the Classics: Romance Epic Narrative in the Italian Renaissance*. Wayne State University Press, 1996.

Lovejoy, Arthur O. "On the Discrimination of Romanticisms." In *Romanticism: Points of View.* 2nd ed. Ed. Robert F. Gleckner and Gerald E. Enscoe. Detroit: Wayne State University Press, 1974, 66–81.

Lupack, Barbara T. "The Politics of Gender: William Styron's *Sophie's Choice*." *Connecticut Review* 14, 2 (Fall 1992): 1–8.

Mace, Nancy A. *Henry Fielding's Novels and the Classical Tradition*. Cranbury: University of Delaware Press, 1996.

Maduakor, Obi. "Iyayi, Festus." *African Writers*. New York: Scribner's, 1997.

Magnier, Bernard. "Ernest J. Gaines." *UNESCO Courier* (April 1995): 5–7.

Massa, Ann, and Alistair Stead, eds. *Forked Tongues? Comparing Twentieth-Century British and American Literature*. London: Longman, 1994.

Masters-Wicks, Karen. *Victor Hugo's Les Misérables and the Novels of the Grotesque*. New York: Peter Lang, 1994.

McDermott, Emily A. "Classical Allusion in *The Count of Monte Cristo*." *Classical and Modern Literature* 8, 2 (Winter 1988): 93–103.

McDowell, Frederick P. W. *E. M. Forster: An Annotated Bibliography of Writings about Him*. Dekalb: Northern Illinois University Press, 1977.

McGann, Jerome J., ed. *Byron: The Oxford Authors*. New York: Oxford University Press, 1986.

McKay, Nellie Y., ed. *Approaches to Teaching the Novels of Toni Morrison*. New York: MLA, 1997.

McMaster, Juliet, and Bruce Stovel, eds. *Jane Austen's Business: Her World and Her Profession*. New York: St. Martin's, 1996.

McMillin, Arnold, ed. *From Pushkin to Palisandria: Essays on the Russian Novel in Honor of Richard Freeborn*. New York: St. Martin's, 1990.

McQuade, Donald, Robert Atwan, Martha Banta, Justin Kaplan, David Minter, Cecilia Tichi, and Helen Vendler, eds. *The Harper American Literature*. Vol. 2. New York: Harper and Row, 1987, 485–489.

Middleton, David Lyotard., ed. *Toni Morrison's Fiction: Contemporary Criticism*. New York: Garland, 1997.

Misurella, Fred. *Understanding Milan Kundera: Public Events, Private Affairs*. Columbia: University of South Carolina Press, 1993.

Moreland, Kim. *The Medievalist Impulse in American Literature: Twain, Adams, Fitzgerald, and Hemingway*. Charlottesville: University Press of Virginia, 1996.

Morey, Ann-Janine. "Margaret Atwood and Toni Morrison: Reflections on Postmodernism and the Study of Religion." *Toni Morrison's Fiction: Contemporary Criticism*. Ed. David Lyotard. Middleton. New York: Garland, 1997.

"Morrison, Toni." *Contemporary Authors, Gale Research, 1993*. Internet. Available <http://www.en.utexas.edu/~mmaynard/Morrison/biograph.html> (17 February 1997).

Munro, Ian H. "Roy A. K. Heath." *Twentieth-Century Caribbean and Black African Writers*. Ed. Bernth Lindfors and Reinhard Sander. Detroit: Gale Research, 1992.

Nagel, James. "Desperate Hopes, Desperate Lives: Depression and Self-Realization in Jamaica Kincaid's *Annie John* and *Lucy*." *Traditions, Voices, and Dreams: The American Novel since the 1960s*. Newark: University of Delaware Press, 1995.

Neary, John. *Something and Nothingness: The Fiction of John Updike and John Fowles.* Carbondale: Southern Illinois, 1992.

Nelson, Connie. "The Shadow Bride." *Library Journal* 120, 18 (1 November 1995): 106.

"Nihilism." Microsoft (R) Encarta. Copyright © 1993 Microsoft. Copyright © 1993 Funk and Wagnall's.

Nissenbaum, Stephen. Introduction. *The Scarlet Letter and Selected Writings.* New York: Random House, 1984, xxvii–xlii.

Niven, Alistair. *D. H. Lawrence: The Writer and His Work.* New York: Scribner's, 1980.

O'Brien, Sharon. *Willa Cather: The Emerging Voice.* Cambridge: Harvard University Press, 1996.

Ousby, Ian, ed. *Cambridge Guide to Literature in English.* Cambridge: Cambridge University Press, 1988.

Oz, Amos. "Writing Toward Imperfect Peace." *Harper's* 286, 1713 (February 1993): 16–18.

Papa, Lee. "'His Feet on Your Neck': The New Religions in the Works of Ernest J. Gaines." *African American Review* 27, 2 (Summer 1993): 187–193.

Pater, Walter. "On Classical and Romantic." In *Romanticism: Points of View.* 2nd ed. Ed. Robert F. Gleckner and Gerald E. Enscoe. Detroit: Wayne State University Press, 1974, 19–25.

Pettit, Charles P. C., ed. *New Perspectives on Thomas Hardy.* New York: St. Martin's, 1994.

Piper, Henry D. *Fitzgerald's* The Great Gatsby: *The Novel, the Critics, the Background.* New York: Macmillan, 1970.

Pizer, Donald, ed. *The Cambridge Companion to American Realism and Naturalism.* Cambridge: Cambridge University Press, 1995.

Plain, Gill. *Women's Fiction of the Second World War: Gender, Power and Resistance.* New York: St. Martin's, 1996.

Praz, Mario. "Romantic Sensibility." In *Romanticism: Points of View.* 2nd ed. Ed. Robert F. Gleckner and Gerald E. Enscoe. Detroit: Wayne State University Press, 1974, 82–95.

Price, Alan. *The End of the Age of Innocence: Edith Wharton and the First World War.* New York: St. Martin's, 1996.

Price, Christopher. "Mightier than the Sword . . ." *New Statesman and Society* (20 October 1995): 20–21.

Price, Martin. *Forms of Life: Character and Moral Imagination in the Novel.* Cambridge: Yale University Press, 1983.

Putt, S. Gorley. *Henry James: A Reader's Guide.* "Organizing an Ado: *Portrait of a Lady.*" New York: Cornell University Press, 1966, 135–160.

Putter, Ad. *Sir Gawain and the Green Knight and French Arthurian Romance.* New York: Oxford University Press, 1995.

Radway, Janice. *Reading the Romance: Women, Patriarchy, and Popular Literature.* Chapel Hill: University of North Carolina Press, 1991.

Raphael, Frederic. "Provincial Passions." *Times Literary Supplement,* 19 January 1996, 26.

Read, Herbert. "Surrealism and the Romantic Principle." In *Romanticism: Points of View.* 2nd ed. Ed. Robert F. Gleckner and Gerald E. Enscoe. Detroit: Wayne State University Press, 1974, 96–107.

Redfern, Walter. "Wild Boars on the Metro." *Times Literary Supplement,* 6 October 1995, 12.

Reed, John Rorty. *Dickens and Thackeray: Punishment and Forgiveness.* Athens: Ohio University Press, 1995.

Rice, Gregory. "The Other King Promotes Love, Marriage in Lewiston." *Sun-Journal* (Maine), 19 March 1997, A1.

Richardson, Mike. "Thomas Hardy." Internet. Available <http://www.prestigeweb.com/hardy/note.html> (8 August 1997).

Richetti, John, ed. *The Cambridge Companion to the Eighteenth Century Novel.* Cambridge: Cambridge University Press, 1996.

Richter, David H. *The Progress of Romance: Literary Historiography and the Gothic Novel.* Columbus: Ohio State University Press, 1996.

Robillard, Douglas, ed. *American Supernatural Fiction: From Edith Wharton to the Weird Tales Writers.* New York: Garland, 1996.

Robinson, Phyllis C. *Willa: The Life of Willa Cather.* Garden City, New York: Doubleday, 1983.

"Romance." *Microsoft 1994 Encarta: The Complete Multimedia Encyclopedia.* CD-ROM. Microsoft Corp., 1994.

Rosowski, Susan J., ed. *Approaches to Teaching Cather's* My Ántonia. New York: MLA, 1989.

Ross, Daniel, ed. *The Critical Response to William Styron.* Westport, CT: Greenwood, 1995.

Rothlein, Liz, and Anita Meyer Meinbach. *The Literature Connection: Using Children's Books in the Classroom.* Glenview, Illinois: Scott, Foresman, 1991.

Russell, David L. *Literature for Children: A Short Introduction.* New York: Longman, 1991, 57.

Salwak, Dale, ed. *Anne Tyler as Novelist.* Iowa City: University of Iowa Press, 1994.

Schleiner, Louise. "Popery and Politics." In *Tudor and Stuart Women Writers.* Indianapolis: Indiana University Press, 1994, 175–191.

Seidman, Barbara Kitt. "Margaret Eleanor Atwood." In *Beacham's Encyclopedia of Popular Fiction.* Ed. Kirk H. Beetz, ed. Osprey, FL: Beacham, 1996, bio., vol. 1: 74–82.

Serafin, Steven. "Gabriel García Márquez." In *Beacham's Encyclopedia of Popular Fiction.* Ed. Kirk H. Beetz. Osprey, Fla.: Beacham, 1996, 694–699.

Shattuck, Kathryn. "Tabitha King: An Oeuvre of Her Own." *Publishers Weekly,* 10 February 1997, 61–62.

"Shaw, George Bernard." *The Norton Anthology of English Literature.* 6th ed. 2 vols. Ed. George H. Ford and Carol T. Christ. New York: W. W. Norton, 1993, vol. 2: 1711–1714.

Shaw, Harry E. *Critical Essays on Sir Walter Scott: The Waverley Novels.* New York: Hall, 1996.

Shillingsburg, Peter. L., ed. *Vanity Fair/ W. M. Thackeray.* New York: Norton, 1994.

Shires, Linda M., ed. *Rewriting the Victorians: Theory History and the Politics of Gender.* New York: Routledge, 1992.

Shone, Tom. *Prince of Tides. The New York Times Book Review,* 2 July 1995, 7.

Simmons, Diane. "The Rhythm of Reality in the Works of Jamaica Kincaid." *World Literature Today* 68, 3 (Summer 1994): 466–453.

Smallwood, Angel J. *Fielding and the Woman Question: Henry Fielding's Novels and Feminist Debate 1700–1750.* New York: St. Martin's, 1989.

Smith, Grahame. *Charles Dickens: A Literary Life.* New York: St. Martin's, 1996.

Smith, J. F. *An Inquiry into Narrative Deception and Its Uses in Fielding's* Tom Jones. New York: Peter Lang, 1993.

Smith, Joan. *Laura Esquivel on* "Like Water for Chocolate, *Destiny and the Thoughts of Inanimate Objects."* Internet. Available <http://www.salon1999.com/oct96/interview961104.html> (2 February 1997).

Snodgrass, Mary Ellen. *Encyclopedia of Utopian Literature.* Denver: ABC-CLIO, 1995, 39–41.

Sopher, H. "Somerset Maugham's 'The Ant and the Grasshopper'—The Literary Implications of Its Multilayered Structure." *Studies in Short Fiction* 31 (1994):109–114.

Spurr, H. A. *Life and Writings of Alexandre Dumas.* Brooklyn: Haskell House, 1972.

Stephenson, Will, and Mimosa Stephenson. "Scott's Influence on Hawthorne." *Studies in Scottish Literature* 28 (1993): 123–132.

Stern, Milton R. Introduction. *The House of the Seven Gables.* New York: Penguin Books, 1986.

Sternlicht, Sanford. *C. S. Forester.* Boston: Twayne, 1981.

Stone, Wilfred. *The Cave and the Mountain. A Study of E. M. Forster.* Stanford: Stanford University Press, 1966.

Stoneback, H. R. "For Whom the Bell Tolls." In *Beacham's Encyclopedia of Popular Fiction.* Ed. Kirk H. Beetz, ed. Osprey, FL: Beacham, 1996, analyses, vol. 3: 1490–1493.

Stratton, John. *The Virgin Text: Fiction, Sexuality, and Ideology.* University of Oklahoma Press, 1987.

Striuli, Giacomo. "Agony of Laughter." *Italian Culture* 7 (1986–1989): 81–94.

Studies in American Jewish Literature: Special Edition on I. B. Singer 1 (1981).

Sturrock, John. "Flaubert and His Disheveled Disciple." *Times Literary Supplement,* 28 January 1994, 5.

Summer, Bob. "Ernest Gaines: The Novelist Describes His Arduous Efforts to Educate Himself as a Writer." *Publishers Weekly* 240, 21 (24 May 1993): 62–64.

Sutherland, John. *The Stanford Companion to Victorian Fiction.* Stanford: Stanford University Press, 1989.

Sutherland, Zena, and May Hill Arbuthnot. *Children and Books.* 8th ed. New York: HarperCollins, 1991, 60, 249.

Sweeney, Susan Elizabeth. "Intimate Violence in Anne Tyler's Fiction: *The Clock Winder* and *Dinner at the Homesick Restaurant."* *The Southern Literary Journal* 28, 2 (Spring 1996): 79–94.

Tambling, Jeremy. *Dickens, Violence and the Modern State: Dreams of the Scaffold.* New York: St. Martin's, 1995.

Tawse, Bonnie. *"Isabel Allende: An Interview."* Internet. Available <http//www.3rdword.com/arhive/Vol2Iss5/Allende.html> (1 January 1997).

"The Salon Interview: Amy Tan." Internet. Available <http://www.salonwanderlust.com/12nov1995/feature/tan.html> (10 February 1998).

"Theodore Dreiser." *The Harper American Literature.* Vol. 2. Ed. Donald McQuade, Robert Atwan, Martha Banta, Justin Kaplan, David Minter, Cecilia Tichi, and Helen Vendler. New York: Harper and Row, 1987, 996–999.

Thomas, Donald. Introduction. *Tom Jones.* London: Rutland, 1992.

Tillotson, Geoffrey, Paul Fussell, Jr., and Marshall Waingrow, eds. *Eighteenth-Century English Literature.* New York: Harcourt Brace Jovanovich, 1969, 726–728.

Tolstoy, Aleksandra. *Tolstoy: A Life of My Father.* New York: Harper, 1953.

Toolan, David. "The Unfinished Boy and His Pain." *Commonweal* 118 (22 February 1991): 121–129.

Travitsky, Betty S. "Husband-Murder and Petty Treason in English Renaissance Tragedy." *Renaissance Drama: Disorder and the Drama.* Ed. Mary Beth Rose. Evanston: North Western University Press, 1990, 171–198.

Trilling, Lionel. Introduction. *Emma.* Boston: Houghton Mifflin, 1957.

Tumbleson, Raymond D. "The Novel's Progress: Faction, Fiction, and Fielding." *Studies in the Novel* 27, 1 (Spring 1995): 12–25.

Turnbull, Andrew, ed. *The Letters of F. Scott Fitzgerald.* New York: Scribner's, 1971.

Turner, Paul. Introduction. *Daphnis and Chloe.* New York: Viking Penguin, 1989, 5–16.

Udumukwu, Onyemaechi. "Ideology and the Dialectics of Action: Achebe and Iyayi." *Research in African Literatures* 27, 3 (Fall 1996): 35–49.

Upchurch, Michael. "An Interview with Ernest Gaines." *Glimmer Train Stories.* Portland: Glimmer Train Press, 1995, 26–45.

Wachtel, Eleanor. "Amos Oz." *Queen's Quarterly* 98, 2 (Summer 1991): 424–431.

Wall, Cheryl A. Chronology. *Zora Neale Hurston: Novels and Stories.* New York: Penguin, 1995.

Washington, Bryan R. *The Politics of Exile: Ideology of Henry James, F. Scott Fitzgerald and James Baldwin.* Boston: North Eastern University Publishing, 1995.

Watt, Ian. Introduction. *Jane Austen: A Collection of Critical Essays.* Englewood Cliffs, NJ: Prentice-Hall, 1963.

Weber, Carl J. Introduction. *Tess of the d'Urbervilles: A Pure Woman.* 1891. New York: Random House, 1951.

Weeks, Mary Louise. "William Styron and the Encapsulated Self." *The Southern Literary Journal* 28, 1 (Fall 1995): 94–97.

Wegener, Frederick. *Edith Wharton: The Uncollected Critical Writings.* Princeton: Princeton University Press, 1996.

Weitz, Morris, and Margaret Collins Weitz, eds. *Shakespeare, Philosophy, and Literature: Essays.* New York: Peter Lang, 1995.

Wendt, Albert. "Interview with Festus Iyai." *Landfall* 44, 4 (December 1990): 412–422.

West, James L. "Voices Interior and Exterior: William Styron's Narrative Personae." *Traditions, Voices, and Dreams: The American Novel since the 1960s.* Ed. Melvin J. Friedman and Ben Siegel. Newark: University of Delaware Press, 1995.

White, William, ed. *By-Line: Ernest Hemingway.* 1933. New York: Bantam Books, 1968.

Widdowson, Peter, ed. *Tess of the d'Urbervilles / Thomas Hardy.* New York: St. Martin's, 1993.

Williams, Raymond. "The Romantic Artist." In *Romanticism: Points of View.* 2nd ed. Ed. Robert F. Gleckner and Gerald E. Enscoe. Detroit: Wayne State University Press, 1974, 269–286.

Wilson, Sharon R., Thomas B. Friedman, and Shannon Hengen, eds. *Approaches to Teaching Atwood's The Handmaid's Tale and Other Works.* New York: MLA, 1996.

Wimsatt, W. K. "The Structure of Romantic Nature Imagery." In *Romanticism: Points of View.* 2nd ed. Ed. Robert F. Gleckner and Gerald E. Enscoe. Detroit: Wayne State University Press, 1974, 219–230.

Winnifrith, Tom. "Charlotte and Emily Brönte: A Study in the Rise and Fall of Literary Reputations." *Yearbook of English Studies* 26 (1996): 14–24.

Wolfe, Peter. *Yukio Mishima.* New York: Continuum, 1989.

Wolk, Gerhard. "Evelyn Waugh: A Supplementary Checklist of Criticism." *Evelyn Waugh Newsletter and Studies* 27, 2 (Fall 1993): 6–7.

Wong, Sau-ling Cynthia. "'Sugar Sisterhood': Situating the Amy Tan Phenomenon." *The Ethnic Canon: Histories, Institutions, and Interventions.* Ed. David Palumbo-Liu. Minneapolis: University of Minnesota Press, 1995, 174–210.

Wood, John. "Flaubert, Love, and Photography." *The Southern Review* 30, 2 (April 1994): 351–357.

Yap, Arthur. "Three Novels on Singapore's Past: Description as a Narrative Form." In *The Writer's Sense of the Past: Essays on Southeast Asian and Australian Literature*. Ed. Kirpal Singh. Singapore: Singapore University Press, 1987.

Zamora, Lois P., and Wendy B. Faris, eds. *Magical Realism: Theory, History, Community*. Duke University Press, 1995.

FURTHER READING

Brinkler, Galer Gisela, ed. *Encountering the Other(s): Studies in Literature, History, and Culture*. Albany: State University of New York Press, 1995.

Caesar, Judith. "Patriarchy, Imperialism, and Knowledge in *The Kitchen God's Wife*." *North Dakota Quarterly* 62, 4 (Fall 1994–1995): 164–174.

Davis, Arthur P. *From the Dark Tower: Afro-American Writers 1900 to 1960*. Davis: Howard University Press, 1981.

Ferraro, Kathleen J. "The Dance of Dependency: A Genealogy of Domestic Violence Discourse." *Hypatia: A Journal of Feminist Philosophy* 11, 4 (Fall 1996): 77–91.

Hall, Donald. Afterword. *Tess of the d'Urbervilles: A Pure Woman*. 1891. New York: Signet Classics, 1964.

Marcuse, Michael. *A Reference Guide for English Studies*. Berkeley: University of California Press, 1990.

"Margaret Mitchell House, The." Internet. Available <http://www.gwtw.org/gwtw-amm.htm> (22 December 97).

Meyer, Susan. *Imperialism at Home: Race and Victorian Women's Fiction*. Ithaca: Cornell University Press, 1996.

Nagel, James, ed. *Ernest Hemingway: The Oak Park Legacy*. Tuscaloosa: University of Alabama Press, 1996.

"Osaragi Jiro Memorial Museum." Internet. Available <http://www.city.yokohama.jp/bconv/ycb/EnglishHP/Photo-bk/Photo9.html> (17 February 1998).

Siepmann, Katherine Baker, ed. *Benet's Reader's Encyclopedia*. 3rd ed. New York: Harper-Collins, 1987.

Stacey, Jackie, and Lynne Pearce, eds. *Romance Revisited*. New York: New York University Press, 1995.

"Third Work of Fiction by Margaret Mitchell is Found." Internet. Available <http://wsf1.usatoday.com/life/enter/books/leb517.htm> (22 December 1997).

Wellek, René. "The Concept of Romanticism in Literary History." In *Romanticism: Points of View*. 2nd ed. Ed. Robert F. Gleckner and Gerald E. Enscoe. Detroit: Wayne State University Press, 1974, 181–205.

Woolf, Virginia. *A Room of One's Own*. New York: Harcourt Brace Jovanovich, 1928.

ABOUT THE AUTHOR

Virginia Brackett, Ph.D., is an assistant professor at East Central University, in Ada, Oklahoma, and is past instructor for the Institute of Children's Literature in West Redding, Connecticut. She has published one hundred articles and stories for adults and young adults in popular magazines such as *Turtle, Children's Digest, Single Parent,* and *Writer's Journal,* as well as in academic journals, such as *Women and Language* and *Notes and Queries.* Her young adult biography, *Elizabeth Cary: Writer of Conscience* (1996), was included in New York Public Library's 1997 catalog of recommended reading for teens.

INDEX